Present Tense

The United States from 1945 to 1968

Third Edition

Michael Schaller
University of Arizona

Robert D. Schulzinger
University of Colorado, Boulder

Karen Anderson
University of Arizona

Houghton Mifflin Company Boston New York

Editor in Chief: Jean L. Woy
Senior Development Editor: Frances Gay
Senior Project Editor: Christina M. Horn
Senior Production/Design Coordinator: Jennifer Meyer Dare
Senior Designer: Henry Rachlin
Senior Manufacturing Coordinator: Marie Barnes
Senior Marketing Manager: Sandra McGuire

Custom Publishing Editor: Todd Corbin
Custom Publishing Production Manager: Kathleen McCourt
Project Coordinator: Christina Battista

Cover Design: Ryan Duda
Cover Art: PhotoDisc Inc.

This book contains select works from existing Houghton Mifflin Company resources and was produced by Houghton Mifflin Custom Publishing for collegiate use. As such, those adopting and/or contributing to this work are responsible for editorial content, accuracy, continuity and completeness.

Printed in the United States of America.

ISBN-13: 978-0-618-50445-9
ISBN-10: 0-618-50445-1
N03438

3 4 5 6 7 8 9 - CM - 09 08 07

 Houghton Mifflin
Custom Publishing

222 Berkeley Street • Boston, MA 02116

Address all correspondence and order information to the above address.

Contents

MAPS AND CHARTS vi

PREFACE vii

1 New Deal and World War: Into the Modern Era   1

Economic Crisis   3

The Roosevelt Revolution   6

America and the World Crisis   17

War on the Home Front   26

Wartime Politics   39

CONCLUSION 40   FURTHER READING 41

★ AMERICAN TRENDS AND ISSUES The Rise (and Fall) of Broadcast Journalism   19

2 From Atomic War to Cold War: Victory and Containment at Home and Abroad, 1945–1952   42

Truman Takes Charge and Prepares for the First Atomic War   43

Demobilization and Building Peace: The GI Bill
  and New Deal Legacy   50

Popular Culture and the Age of Television   53

The Origins of the Cold War and the Birth of Containment   55

National Politics in the Early Cold War and the Origins of the
  Red Scare   67

The Expanding Dimensions of the Cold War   78

CONCLUSION 81   FURTHER READING 81

★ AMERICAN TRENDS AND ISSUES The Rise of the Gunbelt   57

3 America at Home, 1953–1960   83

The Affluent Society   85

The Politics of Moderation   93

Cracks in the Picture Window   94

Sexual Anxieties, Popular Culture, and Social Change   104

Education and Mass Society   108

Continuing Struggles: Civil Rights and Civil Liberties   111

Eisenhower's Second-Term Blues   123

CONCLUSION 124   FURTHER READING 125

☆ AMERICAN TRENDS AND ISSUES High-Tech Medicine   97

4 Generals and Presidents: U.S. Foreign Policy in the 1950s   127

McCarthyism and the Korean War   128

Political and Economic Consequences of the Korean War   134

Eisenhower Takes Command   135

The Ebbing of McCarthyism   139

America and the Challenges of the Third World   141

The Hungarian Uprising and Refugee Politics   156

The Space Race   157

Stirrings of Détente   159

CONCLUSION 165   FURTHER READING 166

☆ AMERICAN TRENDS AND ISSUES Oil   148

5 The New Frontier at Home and Abroad, 1960–1963   168

American Society and Politics in 1960   170

The Kennedy Presidency   175

Kennedy's Foreign Policy   177

New Frontiers at Home   192

The Push for Civil Rights   193

Scientific, Technological, and Cultural Changes in the Early 1960s   199

Assassination   202

CONCLUSION 205   FURTHER READING 206

☆ AMERICAN TRENDS AND ISSUES Nuclear Fallout Shelters—A Blast from the Past   185

6 The Dream of a Great Society   207

Lyndon Johnson: The Man and the President   209
The Great Society: Success and Disappointment   215
Changes in the National Economy   224
The Supreme Court and Civil Liberties   230
Decline of the Great Society   234
Foreign Affairs in the Shadow of Vietnam   237
CONCLUSION 241   FURTHER READING 242
★ AMERICAN TRENDS AND ISSUES Big Dreams, Big Buildings   226

7 The Vietnam Nightmare   243

The Growth of America's Commitment to Vietnam,
   1945–1964   245
The Americanization of the War, 1965   252
Fighting the War, 1966–1967   255
Working-Class War and the Draft   260
Rising Dissent and the Collapse of the Cold War Consensus   264
The Election of 1968   274
CONCLUSION 278   FURTHER READING 279
★ AMERICAN TRENDS AND ISSUES Wagging the Dog: "The Media-Spindustrial Complex"
   and American Foreign Relations   267

8 The Politics and Culture of Protest   280

From Civil Rights to Black Power   282
The SDS and the Rise of the New Left   287
The Counterculture and Mainstream Culture   292
Mass Culture and Social Critique   296
1968: A Year of Cataclysm   300
The Rise of the New Feminism   304
The Legacy of the Sixties   313
CONCLUSION 315   FURTHER READING 316
★ AMERICAN TRENDS AND ISSUES "A Veritable Obsession": Women, Work,
   and Motherhood   307

INDEX I-1

CREDITS I-28

Maps and Charts

Allies on the Offensive in Europe   24
The Pacific War   26
Americans on the Move During the 1940s   30
Divided Europe   66
Birth Rate, 1940–1970   88
Gross National Product, 1946–1970   95
Average Annual Regional Migration, 1947–1960   112
The Korean War   131
Nations Achieving Independence, 1943–1980   142
The United States in the Caribbean and Central America   178
Presidential Election of 1964   215
Voting Rights for African Americans, 1964–1980   221
Growth of Government, 1955–1985   217
Southeast Asia and the Vietnam War   251
Levels of U.S. Troops in Vietnam (at year's end)   255
Presidential Election of 1968   277

Preface

In the 1990s, many Americans displayed what some admirers and a few critics called "triumphalism." The end of the Cold War, the collapse of the Soviet Union, and the strong performance of the U.S. economy seemed proof that the nation's values and institutions had met the test of the post–World War II decades. Many Americans expected that as the world's one remaining superpower, the United States could refocus its attention away from international concerns and toward meeting domestic challenges. But the catastrophic terrorist attacks of September 11, 2001, revived the centrality of international issues. Fear of terrorism, combined with renewed ethnic violence around the world, growing discontent with economic globalization, climate change, and rising energy prices demonstrated that the world remains a dangerous and complicated place. The beginning of the new millennium provoked fresh anxieties and undermined the boast that American prosperity, security, and world dominance were assured.

The third edition of *Present Tense* builds on the balanced account of domestic politics, social and cultural change, economic trends, and foreign affairs of the earlier editions but focuses on the many challenges faced by the United States to its institutions, ideals, and physical security during the past few decades. A new last chapter covers events through spring 2003, including the election of 2000, events since September 11, and the war in Iraq. Several chapters highlight the changing face of American immigration; capital movements and labor politics; the debate over globalization; clashing notions of the role of government in managing people's lives; the ways in which race, class, and gender divide Americans; and the evolving role of the United States in the post–Cold War world.

Each chapter contains a new extended essay called "American Trends and Issues" that traces a theme of special importance over several decades. Among the trends and issues discussed are the development of broadcast journalism, the impact of globalization, the rise of the military-industrial complex, the politics of scandal, education-reform movements, the fallout shelter craze, modern architecture, the social impact of high-tech medicine, the massive growth of prisons, stock-market booms and busts, and the social and cultural factors that impinge on the lives of working women and mothers. In addition, the chapter bibliographies, illustrations, and photographs have all been updated.

We welcome a new coauthor, Karen Anderson, to the *Present Tense* team. A specialist in the history of women, work, family, and minority groups, Karen has written extensively on women defense workers during World War II and ethnic women in twentieth-century America, and she is completing a book on the Little Rock school desegregation crisis of 1957.

Friends, colleagues, and students at the universities of Arizona and Colorado have assisted us in conceiving, writing, and improving this book. In addition, many readers have sent along useful suggestions on ways to improve the text. To all, we extend our appreciation. Their interest has helped make this a better book. We also thank the following reviewers who provided many useful comments on the book that guided us in the revision process: Jeffrey Charles, California State University, San Marcos; Walter L. Hixson, University of Akron; Margaret Paton-Walsh, Albright College; Joel M. Roitman, Eastern Kentucky University; and Victoria W. Walcott, St. Bonaventure University.

M.S.   R.D.S.   K.A.

New Deal and World War: Into the Modern Era

Men employed by the Works Progress Administration, a New Deal work relief program, widen a street. / © Bettmann/CORBIS

One day in 1936, Farm Security Administration photographer Dorothea Lange was driving on a California highway trying to reach home before it got very late. She saw a sign that said "Pea Pickers' Camp," passed it, drove for a while, and then turned back. At the camp, she took the most famous photograph of her career and provided the American public with a poignant picture of the devastation wrought by the Great Depression. The photograph, with the caption "Migrant Mother," appeared in the *San Francisco News* the next day to illustrate a story describing the 2,500 migrant farm workers stranded in Nipomo, California, without work, food, or income. The photograph of "Migrant Mother" generated intense public sympathy. On the same page, the *News* ran an editorial entitled "What Does the 'New Deal' Mean for This Mother and Her Child?" The picture of Florence Thompson and three of her children came to represent the suffering, despair, and quiet strength of those victimized by the nation's worst economic crisis. Within a few days, the federal government sent 20,000 pounds of food to the distressed workers. By the time the aid arrived, however, Thompson and her family had left Nipomo in search of work elsewhere.

For many then and since, Thompson has epitomized the plight of rural families displaced by the "Dust Bowl" and the Depression. Her story, however, is much more complex. A native of Oklahoma, Thompson had migrated to California in the 1920s with her Mississippi-born husband and their three children. Her poverty had multiple causes. Although she was widely perceived to be white by those who saw the photograph, Thompson was actually a Cherokee whose family had been displaced from tribal lands. Widowed in 1931 with five small children and a sixth on the way, she supported her family working in the fields by day and in a restaurant at night. After the birth of an out-of-wedlock child, she returned to Oklahoma with her children. By the mid-1930s, she and her family had joined the "Okie" migration to California, where she established a common-law relationship that led to four more children. Eking out a living as farm workers, theirs was a precarious existence. In the postwar period, Thompson married a more stable wage earner and left farm labor.

During World War II, the migration of poor people from the rural areas of Oklahoma, Texas, Arkansas, and Missouri to California continued at a high volume. These "defense Okies" were joined by other migrants seeking work in defense plants. In California, many of those who had come before the war experienced decreased hostility from the local population and economic improvement as they moved from rural work to industrial and construction jobs. No longer seen as a relief burden and valued now for their contributions to the war effort, they overcame much of the stigma associated with their origins as poor rural southerners. For them as others, the defense boom meant higher wages (often in unionized jobs), low unemployment rates, and the labor of wives, which brought many families out of the economic distress of the 1930s.

As Thompson's story suggests, the administration of Franklin Delano Roosevelt, who served as president from 1933–1945, had mixed implications for her and other Americans. Her family's plight indicates the tattered nature of the safety net for poor Americans before and after the New Deal. Indeed, many in the "Okie" migration came because New Deal agricultural policies and politics had cost them their work as tenant farmers. Her photograph was part of a government publicity campaign to generate sympathy and public assistance for those displaced, and it helped prompt a new role for government in the lives of Americans.

Our current powerful federal government, which touches the life of every American in myriad ways, evolved during the years of Roosevelt's presidency. Direct government intervention in the economy, government provision of extensive social services, government involvement in and support for science and industry—all these are by-products of the Great Depression and World War II. For white women and people of color, these years brought some expansions in opportunity, primarily during the war years, along with rising hopes and frustrations that had a great effect on postwar society. Most dramatically, the United States assumed a new, all-important position in international relations. By the end of the Roosevelt era, the United States had become a superpower—a difficult, uneasy role that has shaped the nation's history ever since.

When Farm Security Agency photographer Dorothea Lange took this picture of Florence Thompson and three of her children, she gave a poignant human face to the millions of Americans struggling to survive in Depression-era America. / AP/FSA/Wide World

Economic Crisis

Franklin D. Roosevelt's inauguration in March 1933 occurred in the midst of the Great Depression, with the American economy perched on the threshold of collapse. Following the dramatic stock market crash on October 24, 1929, over 13 million workers—one-fourth of the labor force—had lost their jobs, while many others faced drastic reductions in their wages and work hours. In the same period, industrial production and national income had fallen by half, and foreign trade had declined by two-thirds. The collapse of 5,000 banks wiped out 9 million savings accounts. The ensuing panic created a run on solvent banks as well. Hundreds of thousands of homeowners and farmers faced foreclosure when financial institutions called in loans. On one day in 1932, one-fourth of the land in the state of Mississippi was sold at auction. Millions of homeless throughout the United States slept in makeshift camps derisively called "Hoovervilles," after the incumbent president, Herbert C. Hoover, who seemed paralyzed by this national crisis. The title of a popular song asked plaintively, "Brother, Can You Spare a Dime?"

Unprecedented in its magnitude and duration, the Great Depression forced the American people and their elected officials to face the problems of poverty more directly than at any time in the country's history. Accustomed to ignoring the destitution and distress of the chronically poor—immigrants, people of color, the elderly, and rural inhabitants—Americans took poverty seriously when millions of urban white men in their prime earning years experienced long-term unemployment and downward mobility. Ironically, their problems also focused policymakers' attention on the plight of those historically consigned to economic marginality. Lorena Hickok, journalist and New Deal insider, wrote to Harry Hopkins, a professional social worker and one of the president's closest confidantes, that their investigation of poor people had "uncovered for the public gaze a volume of chronic poverty, unsuspected except by a few students and by those who have always experienced it."

People of color, for whom poverty had been an enduring problem, faced even more severe destitution as a result of the economic crisis, and at times, as a result of New Deal policies themselves. Before World War II, over three-fourths of all African Americans lived in the South, where they were employed mainly in agriculture or as domestic workers. In the North, they occupied the lowest rung of industrial and service jobs and eked out a precarious living. The Great Depression left them with nowhere to turn because desperate white workers took many of their jobs, many white families fired domestic workers to cut expenses, and New Deal agricultural policies prompted landowners to discharge large numbers of white and black tenant farmers and sharecroppers in the South. In the Southwest, state and local governments "repatriated" 400,000 Mexican and Mexican American workers to Mexico to spare themselves relief expenses and in response to the idea that the jobs these workers held belonged to (white) "Americans." Many middle-class people of color faced ruin, and their hardships increased the economic power of whites in racial ethnic communities. In Harlem, the proportion of property that African Americans owned or managed declined from 35 percent of the total in 1929 to 5 percent in 1935.

White women workers did not experience occupational displacement to the same degree as African American women mostly because many employers were not willing to replace women with men workers and because men were often reluctant to take work labeled "women's" or to settle for the wages that were usually paid to women. Employers believed that certain jobs required skills they assumed to be feminine and were not willing to replace experienced women with inexperienced male workers. This situation did not mean, however, that the jobs held by women were "Depression-proof." Some journalists, business leaders, and public officials even suggested that the "cure" for unemployment was to fire all married female workers to open slots for jobless men! As the Depression deepened, women's unemployment rates increased dramatically. This trend was caused by increased employer discrimination against women workers, especially those who were married; public policies that focused almost exclusively on increasing male employment; cutbacks in public sector jobs, including those of public school teachers; and greater numbers of women seeking jobs to be able to contribute to their families' support. One federal relief official complained, "your average businessman just won't believe there are any women who are absolutely self-supporting." The fact that some Americans believed unemployment would be solved if women relinquished their jobs to men indicates the degree to which women served as scapegoats for the nation's economic woes.

Older workers also faced a critical situation in the economic crisis. Historically, most had worked or relied on relatives for their livelihoods because very few had access to corporate or government pensions. Although many had families to support, they were among the first fired and, as the Depression dragged on, they faced the likelihood that they would never secure full-time employment again. Many of these workers were very frightened and demoralized. Harry Hopkins concluded that they had "gone into an occupational oblivion from which they will never be rescued by private industry." When Francis Townsend, a California doctor, mobilized older citizens to secure government pensions, his grassroots movement scared policymakers into support for a much less drastic plan that became part of the Social Security Act of 1935.

The Depression had significant effects on family life. Unable to support families, young people deferred marriage. In many cases, economic hardship heightened family stress and conflict by disrupting customary divisions of labor and authority within families, exacerbating dissension over economic issues, and forcing relatives to move in together and thus pool resources. When male breadwinners lost their jobs, wives and children often provided income for their families. In some cases, they assumed some of the prerogatives Americans had associated with the provider role, provoking conflict. One jobless man reported that there "certainly was a change in our family . . . —I relinquished power in the family. I think the man should be boss in the family. . . . But now I don't even try to be the boss. She controls all the money. . . . The boarders pay her, the children turn in their money to her, and the relief check is cashed by her or the boy. I toned down a good deal as a result of it." At times, wives refused sex to unemployed husbands because they worried about bringing more children into a household already in grim economic circumstances and convinced that they did not owe sex to a mate who was not meeting his traditional family responsibilities. Conflicts over money, power, and sex sometimes escalated to domestic violence.

The decline in marriages caused by the Depression was mirrored by a decline in the birth rate. The economic crisis, in fact, occasioned a substantial change in public, medical, and political views regarding birth control and abortion. Some Americans, saw their difficulties as deriving in part from poor family planning. "I could have avoided my present status," one man noted, "if I had taken precautions to have fewer children. Before the depression I never gave a thought to birth control. Both my wife and I were against it, and let the children come as they would. Had we been able to foresee the depression, we would have felt differently about it. I'm convinced now that birth control is a good thing." The demand for reproductive services led the American Birth Control League and the federal government to open birth control clinics in large numbers. Although official medical authorities continued to condemn abortion, many doctors changed their views and added economic circumstances to medical indicators as legitimate reasons for abortions. Abortions remained illegal throughout the United States, but increasing numbers of women obtained them in the 1930s. In Chicago, one doctor performed abortions for over 18,000 women between 1932 and 1941. Reflecting changed medical attitudes, over 200 other physicians in the area referred women patients to her for the illegal procedure.

Women responded to their families' material and emotional problems in other ways, too. In all social groups, women used their labor to reduce family expenses. They grew and processed food, made and mended family clothing, learned how to prepare meals more economically, and exchanged goods and services with their neighbors. They also used their interpersonal skills to reduce the stresses of new family arrangements and reduced incomes. Extended families may appear idyllic when viewed through the lens of nostalgia, but having large numbers of relatives occupying crowded households often led to conflict.

Not all families managed to weather their crises. In the early years of the Depression, divorces declined because unhappy spouses could not afford the legal costs of a formal divorce. Desertions increased, however, followed later by rising divorce rates and a related growth in the number of female-headed families. These families and many others would find that the traditional institutional practices of the economy and those of government and private charities would be inadequate for ensuring their survival.

The Roosevelt Revolution

In the United States, "good government" had traditionally meant "minimal government," with the greatest authority remaining in the hands of state and local officials. Unlike the developed nations of Europe, the United States had no tradition of a federal government actively committed to solving social and economic problems. Yet minimal government had failed to stem the ravages of a massive depression with both national and international origins. Reliance on state and local governments and private charities—a favorite solution of Hoover and other conservatives—could not begin to counter the effects of the Depression. Faced with declining tax revenues, most local governments fired workers and cut already meager assistance programs. In Chicago, unemployment cost workers approximately $2 million per day in lost wages, and public and private local and state agencies there provided about $100,000 per day in assistance.

In Roosevelt's view, the time had come when government had to save capitalism from its own folly by ensuring every American the "right to make a comfortable living." He predicted that a violent revolution of the Right or Left "could hardly be avoided if another president failed as Hoover has failed." His apprehensions may have been exaggerated. American citizens, in the words of one contemporary observer, appeared more in the grip of "fathomless pessimism" than of revolutionary fervor. Still, it seemed likely that disillusion with democracy and capitalism would spread rapidly if government failed to combat the Depression. The fear that desperate times might lead to desperate measures prompted policymakers to provide more rights and benefits to workers than they would have done otherwise.

Accepting the Democratic presidential nomination in 1932, Roosevelt promised a "new deal" for the American people, and in his inaugural address the next March, he sought to break the mood of despair. "The only thing we have to fear," he proclaimed, "is fear itself." He made it clear that he intended to deliver what the nation demanded: "action and action now." Should Congress fail to respond to the challenge, he would seek "broad executive power to wage a war against the emergency, as great as the power that would be given to me if we were in fact invaded by a foreign foe."

As Roosevelt's words hinted, his "new deal" required a federal government that would take a direct and prominent role in the economy and American society. Roosevelt favored an active federal government that would safeguard the public welfare within a vibrant system of free enterprise. Throughout the 1930s, he sought to rescue capitalism by curbing its excesses through reform and regulation. This approach was a new phenomenon in American history—it was almost a revolution. Within a few years, Roosevelt's administration enlarged the federal government's size and scope to an extent previously unimaginable. The new federal government touched more people in more ways than ever before.

Until 1933, the only routine interaction between the federal government and most citizens was the delivery of mail by the post office. Policies set in Washington rarely affected the everyday lives of ordinary people. There was no pension system, no federal unemployment compensation, no aid to dependent children programs, no federal housing support, no stock market or banking regulations, no farm subsidies, no withholding of payroll taxes, and no minimum wage—to name only a few federal activities now taken for granted.

The New Deal reflected Roosevelt's complex personal background. Born an only child to a socially prominent Anglo-Dutch family in upstate New York, Roosevelt never had to struggle for money, status, security, or dignity. Like many young men of patrician roots, he viewed self-made millionaires and industrialists as unscrupulous. Roosevelt had an easy self-assurance that disarmed almost everyone he met. Although not a deep thinker, he relished fiery intellects and recruited them as his advisers. His broad but undisciplined mind sought practical solutions rather than detailed theoretical analyses of vexing social problems. Supreme Court Justice Oliver Wendell Holmes succinctly described Roosevelt as a "second-class intellect, but a first-class temperament."

After serving Woodrow Wilson as assistant secretary of the navy during World War I and running unsuccessfully as the Democratic nominee for vice president in 1920, Roosevelt suffered a crippling attack of polio. Several years of therapy beginning in 1921 failed to restore the use of his legs, but his struggle with polio "humanized" Roosevelt. Previously considered something of an upper-class dandy who dabbled in politics as a hobby, Roosevelt had now suffered the kind of tragedy that afflicts ordinary people. When he re-entered politics to run for governor of New York in 1928, he related to people in an intimate way. His emotional vigor overshadowed his physical handicap. He could stand only with the aid of braces and generally sat in a wheelchair, but his handicap never emerged as a serious liability, even in an age when such disabilities often ended public careers. He charmed the press corps so effectively that they refrained from writing about or taking pictures of his legs.

Unlike the cautious Hoover, Roosevelt was determined to take quick action to meet the national emergency. During the so-called First Hundred Days following his inauguration in March 1933, Roosevelt mobilized the federal government. He worked with an eclectic group of university professors, socially conscious lawyers, and social workers known as his "Brain Trust," and the new administration rapidly drafted legislation and figured out how to administer it. Although not anticapitalist, most members of the Brain Trust believed that, in a complex economy dominated by large industrial corporations, government must force big business to share its power and, in Roosevelt's words, "distribute wealth more equitably." Congress gave the president most of what he sought, and even initiated some programs of its own.

Within a short time, the New Deal produced a score of recovery programs that boosted prices and employment while shoring up banking and financial institutions. The National Industrial Recovery Act (NIRA) encouraged businesses to form associations that would raise prices and profits, in the hope that this move would create new jobs. The Agricultural Adjustment Act (AAA) sought to raise farm prices by limiting crop production in return for cash subsidies. Other new laws regulated banking and provided federal insurance for individual deposits, supervised the stock market, provided funds for refinancing home mortgages, and insured private loans for new construction projects. To preserve basically sound industries that faced ruin unless assisted by the government, the Reconstruction Finance Corporation (started by Hoover) loaned about $10 billion to the private sector. This influx of capital saved millions of jobs and kept factories operating. The Tennessee Valley Authority (TVA)—an ambitious and unique new agency—undertook vast flood-control and electrical-power projects in the Upper South. Various government bureaucracies launched massive dam-building ventures in the West, thus remaking the economy and ecology of the entire region.

In the next few years, the new administration would break dramatically with the laissez-faire tradition, crafting its policies in a context of persisting economic crisis and recurring popular mobilizations. The latter ranged from the anti-eviction actions of urban Unemployed Councils to union drives and strikes by rural and industrial workers alike. In Arkansas and Texas, for example, impoverished tenant farmers and sharecroppers formed the Southern Tenant Farmers' Union (STFU) to increase their power relative to the planters who had exploited them economically and politically for many decades. Because they had used racial divisions to secure their power and profits in the past, the planters understood that the STFU's ability to bring black and white farmers into its fold posed as much of an economic threat to their interests as it did its goal of claiming a larger share of the proceeds from farm production. Ultimately, the planters relied on violence and their right to evict tenants to destroy the STFU.

The growth and transformation of the American labor movement in the 1930s reveals the reciprocal relationship between the changes in public policies and the grassroots organizing efforts that sometimes developed during the New Deal. In 1933, section 7(a) of the NIRA provided ground rules for labor relations and attempted to establish the federal government as a mediator between workers and employers, which was a change from its past position as the ally of management. Under the law, however, the government had no legal authority to act when management intimidated or fired workers for supporting unions or broke other NIRA rules designed to secure workers' right to organize. Despite this lack of federal intervention, militant union drives occurred in many industries, encouraged by workers' conviction that Roosevelt and his administration supported their efforts. John L. Lewis, president of the United Mine Workers, capitalized on this belief by urging his organizers to tell coal miners that "the President wants you to join a union."

By 1934, workers across the country had organized to address long-term grievances against their employers and to counter the Depression's devastating effects. In most cases, management fought bitterly to retain its power over workers by using its traditional repertoire of tools: violence, blacklisting and firing of union activists, and other forms of intimidation. From California to the Carolinas, union activists fought pitched battles against employers' security forces, police, and National Guardsmen, which sometimes resulted in serious injuries and deaths. The federal government was occasionally able to encourage mediation, as in the case of the San Francisco longshoremen's strike. When a businessman there requested federal intervention, charging that the strikers wanted to "destroy our most sacred institutions and traditions," Secretary of Labor Frances Perkins responded that "the only 'sacred tradition' which the strike leaders sought to destroy were low wages and graft-ridden hiring halls."

In the textile industry, long a bastion of low wages, long hours, and child labor, the United Textile Workers of America mobilized hundreds of thousands of workers in New England and the South for an industrywide strike in 1934. In addition to their desperate poverty, the workers particularly objected to the "stretch-out," a practice requiring workers to attend several machines at a time. One worker described the physical exertion this practice required: "When you get out, you're just trembling all over." Local police in the South brutalized union leaders, driving some out of town, while employers surrounded the plants with machine guns to fend off union activists, most of whom were women and children. Embracing the violent strategies of industry leaders, a textile trade publication declared that "a few hundred funerals will have a quieting influence." Company officials evicted strikers from company housing. Although federal policies permitted the provision of public assistance to striking workers, local welfare officials denied support to union members. One observer reported, "Some of these folks are literally starving." In the end, the workers gained nothing because they were overcome by the employers' power and the federal government's timidity and lack of authority.

Faced with a militant workers' movement and aware of the inadequacies of the labor provisions of the NIRA, Congress passed the National Labor Relations Act, also known as the Wagner Act, in 1935. The act recognized the right of workers to organize into unions and to bargain collectively with employers as a means of improving their wages and working conditions. Even so, it took a series of strikes and other militant actions for the new Congress of Industrial Organizations (CIO) to organize in basic industries such as steel, coal, and automobile manufacturing. Because the CIO organized on an industrywide basis, it was able to incorporate more women and minority workers than the American Federation of Labor (AFL), which organized only skilled crafts workers. It also mobilized workers at the grassroots level, a tactic that encouraged women to participate. However, union leadership remained in the hands of white men, who often failed to recognize that unions had a responsibility to address race and sex discrimination in the workplace.

With local agencies overwhelmed by the number of unemployed, the New Deal replaced reliance on private, local charity for the needy with a system of social rights, or entitlements. The Social Security Act (SSA) of 1935 created a national system to administer pensions, unemployment insurance, and aid for the blind and handicapped. It replaced the mothers' pension laws passed in some northern and western states with a program of Aid to Dependent Children (ADC). For the first time, the federal government took primary responsibility for alleviating the impact of unemployment and poverty on individual Americans.

The benefits of the SSA were not extended equally to all citizens. The unemployment compensation and pension programs excluded workers in agriculture, domestic service, government, and other occupations held disproportionately by white women and people of color. Almost 90 percent of African American women workers were ineligible for these sources of support. The unemployment compensation and pension programs were not means tested and did not regulate the lives of their recipients. The ADC program, which mainly benefited single mothers and their children, gave great discretion to the states in determining stipend levels and administering eligibility requirements and provided a lower level of federal contribution. The result was very low stipends for these families and a systematic pattern of racial discrimination in southern and western states. Local officials used casework methods to monitor the lives of recipients to ensure that they kept clean houses, sent their children to church, and did not keep company with men. The policies designed for men did not incorporate oversight of their morals, a fact that prompted historian Linda Gordon to conclude that policymakers responsible for those programs "considered the supervision inherent in casework unneeded, demeaning, [and] an attack on a (largely unconscious) masculinity."

Eager to alleviate economic hardship and to jump-start the economy, the Roosevelt administration also broke new ground by adopting programs to assist the unemployed. A host of agencies, such as the Federal Emergency Relief Administration (FERA), the Works Progress Administration (WPA), and the Civilian Conservation Corps (CCC), provided grants to states for welfare benefits or directly employed the poor in federal works projects. These programs hired the unemployed to build highways, municipal buildings, schools, seaports, airports, zoos, parks, and dams throughout the United States. Artists were commissioned to paint murals in public buildings; writers were commissioned to write travel guides. In New York City alone, the WPA employed more people than the entire American army. At its peak, the WPA had a national work force of 3 million.

African American schoolchildren in an art class sponsored by the WPA in Florida. / Franklin D. Roosevelt Library

The Roosevelt administration broke with a century-long tradition of government interference in the private lives of Native Americans by instituting the Indian New Deal in 1934. Under the leadership of John Collier, who became the new commissioner of Indian Affairs in 1933, the government abandoned the policy of allotment that had been central to its assimilation efforts since 1887. Under the old policy, the government divided communal Indian lands into small individual holdings and sold much of the remaining Indian lands to white settlers at bargain basement rates. In the 1930s, the federal government tried to stimulate economic development on the reservations by encouraging crafts production and other market-based strategies. These tactics did little to alleviate the destitution that haunted the reservations, however. Still, Collier tried to undo the legacy of indifference and exploitation that had previously characterized federal policies. Christian ministers criticized him bitterly for lifting the ban on traditional Indian religious ceremonies and for dropping efforts to force cultural and religious assimilation.

Many in Roosevelt's inner circle justified their vigorous government action by citing the theories of an iconoclastic British economist, John Maynard Keynes. Keynes believed that active state intervention was fundamental to the success of mature capitalism. The depression of the 1930s had so shaken business confidence, he argued, that recovery without government intervention was unlikely. Corporations and entrepreneurs would not make new investments until consumer demand reappeared. To increase consumer demand, public money had to be pumped into the economy.

Government money could enter the economy in several ways. By hiring unemployed workers to build bridges or roads, for example, the government could generate demand for raw materials and machinery. Workers receiving government paychecks would be able to pay for rent, food, and clothing, thus creating a market for consumer goods. This government intervention would create sufficient consumer purchasing power to restore the confidence of the private sector and to enable government to collect higher taxes when economic conditions improved. As the economic system returned to normal, the government could withdraw its participation from the marketplace.

Orthodox economists and political conservatives bristled at the idea of government intervention in the economy, and they considered deficit spending a heresy. Even Roosevelt hesitated to support the massive federal spending and central planning that Keynes and his followers believed were necessary to overcome the depression. Roosevelt also feared making citizens too dependent on the government as an employer of last resort. Nevertheless, his pragmatic approach to the crisis brought profound changes to the American economy and government.

Many of the New Deal programs and agencies had expired by the end of World War II. Several, including the Securities and Exchange Commission, the Federal Deposit Insurance Corporation, the TVA, and the Social Security Administration, survive today. Most important, the New Deal established the principle that the federal government should intervene in the country's economic and social life on behalf of its citizens.

    Along with the revolution in the size and scope of government came a change in the profile of federal appointees. Most federal officials had been white, Anglo-Saxon men from the business community. The New Deal reached out to Catholics, Jews, African Americans, and women with professional experience in social work, labor unions, and universities. Some of Roosevelt's closest advisers, such as Thomas Corcoran, James Farley, Henry Morgenthau, Jr., and Felix Frankfurter, came from Irish or—even more controversial—Jewish backgrounds. Labor Secretary Frances Perkins, the first woman in a presidential cabinet, played a critical role in promoting new social legislation. Harry Hopkins, the first professional social worker to serve a president, became a frequent and influential adviser on both domestic and foreign affairs. First Lady Eleanor Roosevelt, a political activist who represented a national network of progressive women, also influenced Roosevelt's views on social issues. Between 1933 and 1945, she transformed the role of First Lady as she vigorously promoted the New Deal agenda. Unfettered by the political restrictions that bound her husband, she pushed various progressive measures. Trade unionists, sharecroppers, and women's groups considered her their pipeline into the government. She also emerged as the administration's leading advocate for the rights of African Americans. At a segregated meeting in Alabama, she insisted on sitting in the "colored only" section. When the Daughters of the American Revolution refused to rent a concert hall to African American singer Marian Anderson, Eleanor Roosevelt resigned from the organization in protest. She then secured the grounds of the Lincoln Memorial for the performance.

    African American employment at all levels in the federal government tripled between 1933 and 1945, with most of the gains made during the war years. Roosevelt's new federal agencies caused a sensation by abolishing segregated cafeterias and offices in their Washington headquarters. An informal "Black Cabinet" of prominent African American citizens consulted regularly with agency heads and, on occasion, with the president. Eleanor Roosevelt, especially, championed the efforts of racial minorities. She met regularly with African American leaders like Mary McLeod Bethune, an official of the National Youth Administration; invited them to the White House; and legitimized their concerns. She supported civil rights legislation and federal laws against lynching and the poll tax. Her more cautious husband, fearful of the power exercised by southern Democrats in Congress, refused even to speak on such issues.

    This multiplicity of voices enriched Roosevelt's presidency and brought the concerns of diverse groups and classes to national attention. For women and African Americans, however, the politics of representation employed in the New Deal had important limitations. Almost all policymakers, men and women alike, believed that a family wage economy, in which men supported women and children, would ensure women's economic well-being. They ignored the historic multiple-earner strategy in working-class families and women workers' need for increased opportunities and higher wages, in part because they were reluctant to help women become economically independent from men and because they assumed that women took jobs that legitimately belonged to men. By 1940, many African Americans were beginning to believe that the "Black Cabinet" strategy of the administration offered them symbolism rather than substantive change in state policies.

To a large degree, Roosevelt relied on his appeal to the "forgotten man" to stimulate widespread interest in New Deal programs. Part of his effectiveness stemmed from his ability to speak to the American people en masse. Few national leaders have used the mass media—in his case, radio—as effectively to bond with the public. Roosevelt initiated "fireside chats": live radio broadcasts through which he addressed millions of listeners in their living rooms. His audience considered the president a guest in their homes and planned their evening activities around his broadcasts.

Roosevelt's appeal transcended traditional factions and was particularly strong for working-class people. The New Deal coalition included not only the traditional Democratic Party machine but also labor unions and voters from almost every ethnic and minority group. The children of immigrants and minorities, helped by New Deal social programs, developed a greater sense of belonging and self-worth. These supporters contributed to Roosevelt's landslide re-election in 1936 and then to his re-election in 1940 and 1944.

Millions of Americans experienced tangible benefits from New Deal programs. Some people were put to work; others received farm support payments or were able to refinance mortgages. Rural residents could recall the day on which electric power, funded by the federal government, first came to their homes and farms. Above all, Roosevelt's programs and personality restored hope to vast numbers of Americans and countered the lure of fascism and communism. Yet there were signs, even in the heady early days of the New Deal, that it would not be an unqualified success. Although the unemployment rate fell dramatically from its high of 25 percent in 1933, it still hovered at 16.9 percent in 1936 (compared to just 3.2 percent before the stock market crash in 1929) and continued at an unacceptably high level throughout the 1930s. And many people fell through the gaps in the New Deal assistance programs.

Because federal programs operated through and depended on the cooperation of local authorities, government administrators often bowed to local racial prejudices and distributed benefits in blatantly unequal proportions. This situation created more hardship and inequity in the South, where local officials ensured that agriculture, relief, and jobs programs maintained racial and class inequalities. Although federal regulations stated that landowners were to share their federal subsidies for crop reductions with their tenant farmers and sharecroppers, the dominance of local AAA positions by southern white landowners meant that this distribution did not occur. The displacement of many poor farmers from the land occasioned by crop reductions meant that poor whites and blacks had nowhere to turn for other work in the underdeveloped South. Racial discrimination in relief worsened the already desperate situation of African Americans. Local white officials also fought to ensure that the money gained through federal relief and jobs policies did not exceed the very low pay usually accorded to Mexican Americans in the Southwest and African Americans in the South. In Mississippi, where over half the population was African American, 98 percent of the jobs with the Civilian Conservation Corps went to whites. In 1938, the president declared that the South was "the nation's number 1 economic problem."

Organizations like the National Association for the Advancement of Colored people (NAACP), the National Urban League, and the National Negro Congress protested the denial of work-relief benefits to African Americans and fought against the delegation of power to local authorities. They lobbied politicians and mobilized African American voters in the North to demand change. They found important supporters among left-wing political groups, the CIO, and white liberals. But Roosevelt was not willing to anger the southern wing of the Democratic Party, which held disproportionate power in Congress and was already wary of the liberal bent of New Deal programs, even though some of those programs enriched the planters who controlled Democratic officeholders from the South. Because of disfranchisement in the South, most African Americans could not vote, and southern Democrats controlled key committees in Congress.

The New Deal civil rights record gradually improved. Top federal work-relief administrators hired growing numbers of minorities. Although officials in the South resisted these moves and segregation in federal programs remained common, African Americans appreciated these efforts by Democratic New Dealers. As one leading black newspaper commented, "[W]hat administration within the memory of man . . . had done a better job . . . considering the imperfect human material with which it had to work? The answer, of course, is none."

The positive effect of New Deal policies on the racial climate in the United States, however incomplete, attracted millions of new voters into the Democratic coalition. In the 1932 presidential election, over two-thirds of African American voters (nearly all in the North) supported the Republican candidate, Herbert Hoover, over Franklin Roosevelt. In 1940, over two-thirds of them voted for the Democratic ticket, and this number grew in later decades.

Throughout the 1930s, groups and individuals on both the Left and the Right promoted radical alternatives to FDR's reforms. These groups and individuals included the American Communist Party as well as demagogues like Father Charles Coughlin, Gerald L. K. Smith, Francis Townsend, and Louisiana senator Huey Long. Each blamed "conspirators"—industrialists, bankers, Jews or other minorities—for America's problems. In the end, however, none offered a credible alternative to the New Deal.

Despite Roosevelt's landslide re-election in 1936 and the establishment of large Democratic majorities in Congress, the New Deal's struggles increased in the president's second term. Roosevelt caused one problem himself with a bungled attempt to pack the Supreme Court. Through 1937, a group of four conservative justices, joined by Chief Justice Charles Evans Hughes and Justice Owen Roberts, formed a majority that struck down New Deal legislation such as the NIRA and the AAA and thus threatened the entire New Deal program.

The conservatives insisted that not even a national economic emergency justified government interference in private economic matters such as the setting of wages and the sanctity of contracts. In fact, the Supreme Court had been the most conservative part of the American government since the 1780s, defending slavery and big business against almost all challengers.

Fearing further judicial assaults on his programs, Roosevelt asked Congress in 1937 for the authority to appoint up to six additional Supreme Court justices. It refused to do so. In mid-1937, however, one justice who usually voted with the conservatives switched sides, and another announced plans to retire. An emerging liberal majority on the Court upheld the Wagner Act, the minimum wage law, and key provisions of the Social Security Act. The Court had turned a decisive corner. From 1937 on, the federal government exercised broad regulatory power over private contracts and commerce without fear of judicial intervention.

Roosevelt's judicial appointments had a lasting impact on civil rights. With the exception of James F. Byrnes, Roosevelt's eight appointees to the Supreme Court sympathized with efforts to dismantle legal segregation. By the late 1940s, they had struck down state laws excluding minorities from juries, established the rights of workers to picket against discrimination in employment, outlawed racially restrictive covenants in housing, challenged segregation on interstate public transportation, forbade the peonage of farm workers, and outlawed the system that barred nonwhites from voting in the all-important southern Democratic primaries. These Supreme Court rulings provided momentum for additional legal challenges to segregation and for the civil rights movement of the late 1940s through the 1960s.

But just as the Supreme Court began affirming the right of the government to intervene extensively in the economy, a severe recession in 1937 and 1938 caused an increase in unemployment and shook popular confidence in Roosevelt's leadership. Roosevelt's influence with Congress had waned, and he barely managed to shepherd the landmark Fair Labor Standards Act through Congress in mid-1938. The act banned child labor, established a federal minimum wage, and limited the workweek to forty hours for many occupations. It exempted agricultural, retail, clerical, domestic, and other service workers—groups that were represented disproportionately by white women or people of color—from its wages and work hours provisions. Until the 1960s, when social movements forced changes in the law, significant numbers of employed white women and people of color routinely received below-minimum wages for their labor.

In the 1938 congressional elections, Republicans picked up eighty-one House and eight Senate seats. They joined conservative Democrats in blocking additional New Deal innovations. They demanded balanced budgets, curbs on labor unions, and—under the banner of states' rights—no federal help for racial minorities. Many of the additional goals of the Roosevelt administration would not be addressed until the 1960s.

The conservative bloc in Congress created the House Un-American Activities Committee, which later achieved notoriety in the postwar years. The committee charged that Roosevelt's "left-wing followers in the government are the fountainhead of subversive activities." Under attack from politicians whose support he needed to deal with growing threats from Germany and Japan, and hoping to repair his tattered relations with business leaders, Roosevelt backed away from reform. Soon the outbreak of war pushed social progress even further into the background.

America and the World Crisis

Until the late 1930s, the focus on the Great Depression limited public concern with foreign affairs. Roosevelt barely mentioned world events in his first inaugural address in 1933. He did promise that the United States would act as a "good neighbor," especially in dealing with Latin America, and this policy resulted in the removal of occupation troops from Haiti, the lowering of tariffs, and the extension of trade credits to Latin American countries.

Early in his first term, Roosevelt extended diplomatic recognition to the Soviet Union. Since the Russian Revolution in 1917, the United States had refused to recognize the Soviet government. Public school teachers had been urged not to mention the name Soviet Union, and many maps showed the country as a blank spot. The president hoped that recognition would boost trade with the newly industrialized country and ally the Soviets with the Western democracies against Nazi Germany and Imperial Japan. Lingering suspicions of communism, disputes over payment of Czarist debts, and revulsion toward Joseph Stalin's brutal collectivization of agriculture and his political purges prevented much cooperation before 1941.

By the mid-1930s, the spirit of isolationism was widespread. Many Americans, including a substantial number in Congress, believed that the United States should have little to do with conflicts between foreign countries. Congressional hearings of the mid-1930s focused on charges that British and French propagandists and U.S. arms manufacturers (the "merchants of death") had hoodwinked the United States into entering World War I. These charges increased the public's distaste for foreign affairs and led Congress to pass neutrality acts between 1935 and 1937. These acts restricted the president and private Americans from giving economic assistance to foreign nations at war.

These laws, which did not distinguish between aggressor and victim, coincided with belligerence by Germany, Japan, and Italy. All three countries were ruled by Fascist or ultranationalist regimes that claimed special rights, frequently on the basis of race, to conquer their neighbors. The Italian invasion of Ethiopia in 1935, the Italian and German support of the 1936 Fascist revolt in Spain, German remilitarization, Germany's annexation of Austria from 1936 to 1938, and Japan's invasion of China in 1937 evoked little more than tongue-clicking from the U.S. government.

In September 1938, when Adolf Hitler demanded the partition of Czechoslovakia, Roosevelt supported the decision by the British and French governments to appease Hitler's appetite, delay war, and possibly turn the German dictator's wrath toward the Soviet Union. After the fateful meeting in Munich, in which the British and French sealed the fate of the Czechs by agreeing to Hitler's demands, Roosevelt cabled two words to British Prime Minister Neville Chamberlain: "Good man." Only later, when Hitler turned his fury on the West, did the Munich agreement and the term appeasement take on the aura of cowardly capitulation.

Like most Americans (and many Europeans), Roosevelt hoped to preserve the world balance of power while taking as few risks as possible. He hoped that other nations would take the responsibility for containing the advances of aggressor nations. After Hitler violated the Munich agreement by seizing all of Czechoslovakia and then demanded Polish territory, the British and French finally abandoned their policy of appeasement. In the months after Munich, Roosevelt got Congress to increase funding for a critical buildup of American air and naval forces.

In September 1939, after signing a nonaggression pact with the Soviet Union, Hitler invaded Poland. Britain and France responded by declaring war on Germany. By June 1940, Germany's Blitzkrieg ("lightning war") victories in Western Europe had left only Britain resisting Nazi power. (Russia remained neutral until it was attacked by Germany in June 1941.) Japan, which by then occupied large portions of China, joined Germany and Italy in the Axis Alliance and began threatening European and American colonies in Asia.

Just weeks after the outbreak of war in Europe, the president received a stark indication of the growing German threat. Nuclear physicist Albert Einstein, himself a Jewish refugee from the Nazis, sent Roosevelt a letter warning that German scientists had taken the first steps toward harnessing atomic power for military use. If German scientists developed an atomic bomb, Einstein predicted, Hitler would win the war.

Roosevelt authorized a group of high-level officials to begin an atomic weapons program, later code-named the Manhattan Project. By 1945, about 150,000 people were working on some phase of the $2 billion project to construct the ultimate weapon. Many of the project's participants realized that the bomb would have a profound effect on the world, both during and after the war. The massive development project also marked a coalition of government, science, and industry that became a hallmark of post-1945 national security policy, as well as a force for social transformation of the nation.

As Germany stepped up its attacks against Britain, Roosevelt stretched his constitutional powers to the limit. He transferred warships to the British and ordered the American navy to prevent German submarines from entering a large portion of the Atlantic. The American army at that time was comparable in budget ($500 million) and size (185,000 men) to the Bulgarian army and desperately needed to expand. Prodded by Roosevelt, Congress reluctantly passed the nation's first peacetime draft in 1940, despite charges from his opponents that labeled him a warmonger.

Roosevelt promised the voters in 1940 that he would not send America's youth into any foreign wars. After his election to an unprecedented third term

(cont. on page 21)

The Rise (and Fall) of Broadcast Journalism

World War II almost created broadcast journalism. Radio news reports, especially from overseas, barely existed before Edward R. Murrow signed up with the fledgling Columbia Broadcasting System (CBS) to cover London during the 1940–1941 German air force *blitz* that tried to bomb Britain into surrender. Speaking in a deep, reassuring voice, with air-raid sirens and audible explosions in the background, Murrow began his radio reports with the line "This . . . is London." For millions of Americans, his description of the resilience of ordinary Londoners was proof that the Nazi war machine had not crushed the one nation that stood between Hitler and the United States.

With the rise of television in the early 1950s, Murrow became the driving force in the CBS news division. Nightly network news remained a brief, fifteen-minute summary of events until it expanded to a half hour in 1963. Before then, Murrow pioneered the use of television documentaries to bring weighty issues to a mass audience. During the 1950s, he hosted *See It Now,* television's first weekly show with a news magazine format and the forerunner of shows such as *60 Minutes.* Produced in partnership with Fred Friendly, *See It Now* explored complex and controversial issues. In 1954, for example, Murrow broke the taboo on critical coverage of Senator Joe McCarthy by examining both the brutal methods and dubious results of the senator's anticommunist crusade. In 1955, Murrow (himself a chain smoker) devoted two shows to a special investigation of the several recent scientific studies linking cigarette smoking and lung cancer. Other episodes examined the development of the Salk polio vaccine, the environmental threat posed by pesticides, the impact of the Red Scare on American life.

Murrow and his corporate sponsors also recognized the market for "middlebrow" entertainment. His *Person to Person* show featured interviews with actors, sports figures, and creative artists. Walter Cronkite, a Murrow protégé, made his mark at CBS with a show called *You Are There* that featured mock interviews with historical figures, such as Brutus in the Roman Forum at the moment he assassinated Julius Caesar or George Washington at Valley Forge.

In 1960, Murrow and Friendly began a new documentary series called *CBS Reports.* An early episode, "Harvest of Shame," chronicled the harsh lives and miserable working conditions of migrant farm laborers. Its impact has been compared to John Steinbeck's classic novel, *The Grapes of Wrath.* Murrow's popularity prompted the NBC and ABC networks to upgrade their news divisions to compete with CBS.

In 1961, President John F. Kennedy appointed Murrow to head the U.S. Information Agency (USIA), the bureau that presented government news and information programs abroad. Although he generally shared Kennedy's outlook, Murrow chafed at the escalation of the Vietnam War and found the role of official propagandist limiting. Shortly after Kennedy's death, the veteran newsman resigned so that he could return to broadcast journalism. Ironically, the journalist who did so much to alert the public to the risks of smoking fell ill with lung cancer and died in early 1965.

In some ways, Murrow's legacy lived through his successors. Walter Cronkite became the CBS evening news anchor in 1963 and was soon described by pollsters as "the most trusted man in America." In 1968, in the wake of the Tet Offensive in Vietnam, when he publicly questioned the value of continuing the war, President Johnson was stunned. "If I've lost Cronkite," he lamented, "I've lost middle America."

Beginning in the 1970s and accelerating after 1990, broadcast journalism faced a wide range of commercial and technological challenges. Corporate conglomerates pur-

CBS wartime correspondent Edward R. Murrow in London, 1940. His live broadcasts reassured Americans that Hitler's air force had not subdued England. / AP/Wide World

chased most locally owned radio and television stations while giant corporations such as Disney, General Electric, and Viacom acquired the ABC, NBC, and CBS networks. New corporate owners, their stockholders, and financial analysts cared less about the content of news and entertainment shows and more about their immediate profitability. Broadcast executives had to minimize costs (by lowering production expenses) and maximize advertising revenue (by expanding audience size or attracting more "desirable," i.e., younger, viewers) to keep their jobs. The proliferation in the late 1980s first of cable news stations such as CNN and then of Internet news sites meant that the number of people watching traditional network news shows was steadily dwindling. In the early 1980s, for example, the evening news shows on the three networks attracted 84 percent of the viewing audience. By 2002, that number fell to barely 43 percent. Even more troubling, television audiences became more demographically fragmented as cable and Internet outlets siphoned off groups of younger, older, male, and female viewers most interested in, say, sports, financial news, health matters, music, and so on.

Americans who remained tuned to network news averaged about sixty years old and were considered just a step away from the grave by youth-centered advertisers fixated on the eighteen- to twenty-four-year-old market. The commercial products advertised during network news—Pepcid, Viagra, Polident, and Depends—illustrate the point. Market fragmentation, the loss of a wider viewing audience, and pressure for profits made radio and television news divisions desperate to hold onto what remained of their viewer base, even if it required "dumbing down" their coverage.

Technological change also reshaped the news. Previously, a news show might feature a discussion of the root causes of a war or refugee crisis abroad. Now, a small crew with a mobile video camera fed to a satellite link could show starving refugees or a volcanic eruption in nearly real time. The effect was dramatic. In 1993, for example, CNN broadcast video that showed eighteen U.S. soldiers who were part of a peacekeeping mission being killed by a mob in Somalia. This incident, the basis of the book and film *Black Hawk Down,* prompted a public outcry that led the Clinton administration to withdraw troops from the U.N. peacekeeping mission. The images and the public outrage they fostered, not the real value to the national interest of the intervention, shaped policy.

Closer to home, technology drove news coverage in other ways. In the late-1970s, as mobile minicameras mounted on helicopters became available, television stations in Los Angeles calculated they could afford either to maintain traditional news bureaus in the state capital, Sacramento, or buy the camera-equipped aircraft. While testing the cameras, one helicopter happened upon a police chase on an L.A. freeway. The helicopter tracked and simultaneously broadcast the chase. Other local television stations promptly reduced the number of reporters in the field and acquired camera-equipped helicopters that roamed the sky in search of the "chase of the day." O. J. Simpson's celebrated freeway drive was merely the best known of these incidents. As live video of fires, crime scenes, and car chases proliferated, broadcasters cynically adopted the phrase "if it bleeds, it leads."

Network executives engaged in the equivalent of buying camera-equipped helicopters by shifting news budgets from "hard" to "soft" coverage. At first, this change meant promoting more programs with news magazine formats and reducing the number of journalists stationed abroad. *60 Minutes* segued into *48 Hours.* From there, it was a short jump to the tabloidlike *Dateline, 20/20,* and *Entertainment Tonight.* In place of Edward R. Murrow, Geraldo Rivera became the most visible "investigative journalist" on television. Soon, hucksters like Jerry Springer put Geraldo to shame with "investigations" that consisted of social deviants pummeling each other in front of cheering audiences. One network promoted celebrity boxing matches as part of its public affairs offering. Not all of these shows found a large audience, but each appealed to a segment of the fragmented media market.

Cable and Internet news faced a special challenge. Because they broadcast continuously, they required a constant stream of words and images to fill the screen. Programmers relied on celebrity gossip and sex scandals. For a decade beginning in 1991, scandals involving O. J. Simpson, the murder of Jon-Benet Ramsay, Bill and Hillary Clinton, Paula Jones, and Monica Lewinsky dominated the airwaves. In 2001, obsessive coverage of an affair between California Congressman Gary Condit and a missing intern, Chandra Levy, seemed poised to replace the Clinton-era sex scandals until it was preempted by the terrorist attacks on the World Trade Center and Pentagon. In the "new economy," news had become just another commodity.

---

in 1940, however, he declared that if England or China surrendered, Americans would be "living at the point of a gun." To prevent this predicament, he proposed a massive aid program, called Lend-Lease, that would make America the "arsenal of democracy." In a "fireside chat," the president compared the aid to lending a fire hose to a neighbor whose house was in flames to keep the sparks from spreading. In March 1941, Congress passed legislation, by a lopsided vote, to provide $7 billion in military aid for nations resisting Germany and Japan.

This aid package was nearly as large as the entire federal budget at that time. Secretary of War Henry Stimson referred to the Lend-Lease bill as a "declaration of economic war" against Berlin and Tokyo.

Roosevelt sent American troops to occupy Greenland and Iceland and ordered navy ships in the Atlantic to hunt down German U-boats. By the autumn of 1941, the German and American navies were engaged in an undeclared war that led to the sinking of an American destroyer. When Nazi armies invaded the Soviet Union in June, Roosevelt quickly approved Lend-Lease to the Soviets. He did so despite earlier American fury at Stalin for signing the 1939 nonaggression pact with Hitler, which freed the Soviets to seize the Baltic republics and eastern Poland.

With American attention turned toward the crisis in Europe, Japan took the opportunity to seize southern French Indochina, demand special access to oil from the Dutch East Indies, and insist that Washington stop military aid to China. In response, Roosevelt shifted naval units to the Pacific and imposed a trade embargo on Japan, leaving Tokyo with only a few months' reserve of petroleum. Roosevelt insisted that Japan had to quit the Axis Alliance with Germany, withdraw its forces from China and Indochina, and make a nonaggression pledge before he would lift the oil embargo. Japan, under the de facto leadership of General Tojo Hideki, demanded the immediate resumption of oil sales and a cutoff of aid to China before considering any pullback.

When discussions broke off on November 26, 1941, American officials expected a Japanese attack in Southeast Asia or on the American-controlled Philippines; they sent warnings to commanders there and in Hawaii. American intelligence had been intercepting Japanese diplomatic communications, but they were unaware of Japan's plan to target the Pacific fleet at Pearl Harbor, Hawaii.

On December 7, 1941—a date, Roosevelt said, would "live in infamy"—Japan mounted a surprise air attack on the U.S. fleet and airfields at Pearl Harbor. The assault killed over 2,400 sailors and soldiers, damaged or sank eight American battleships, and destroyed a large number of planes. Suddenly, war had come to the United States. At Roosevelt's request, Congress promptly declared war on Japan. On December 10, Japan's allies—Germany and Italy—declared war on the United States. As Japan rolled to a string of easy victories in Southeast Asia, shock and humiliation shook an American citizenry that had previously felt immune from the war. But Germany and Japan had sown the seeds of their own doom by engaging America's vast military-industrial potential. Within a short time, America was producing more ships and planes each month than were lost to the Japanese during the sneak attack on Pearl Harbor.

Pearl Harbor ended domestic dissent over participation in the war. On New Year's Day in 1942, the United States, Great Britain, the Soviet Union, and twenty-three other partners issued a "Declaration of the United Nations," a pledge to fight for victory against the Axis. Roosevelt and his military advisers resolved that the United States would provide additional Lend-Lease aid to Britain, Russia, and China to help them carry the bulk of the fighting against Germany and Japan. As soon as possible, British and American armies would open a second front to invade Western Europe and relieve the pressure on the Soviets (who would face about two-thirds of all German forces alone until 1944). Roosevelt's "Europe-first" strategy anticipated that once the Allies crushed Germany, the Soviets would then join in the final assault on Japan.

Supply problems, British stalling, the competing demands of the war against Japan, and other factors delayed the Allied entry into France until June 6, 1944. The massive invasion of Normandy on that date (see Map 1.1) quickly broke the power of the Nazis in Western Europe. By then, the Soviets had pushed German forces out of Russia and into Poland, at a cost of more than *20 million* civilian and military dead. Given the Western allies' long delay in opening the second front, Stalin remained deeply suspicious of them. He believed they would fight Germany to the last Russian and then move to control Europe themselves.

The behavior of Soviet leaders tended to arouse similar fears in London and Washington. Beginning in 1942, for example, Stalin demanded that Roosevelt and Churchill approve the transfer of parts of prewar Poland and southeastern Europe to the Soviet Union. Although Western leaders believed such a concession would violate the rights of Poland and the other nations involved, they also recognized that the Soviets had a justified interest in creating a security zone in Eastern Europe, the route of two German invasions since 1914. Churchill and Roosevelt eventually accepted the Soviet demands in return for Stalin's promise to respect the political independence of the rest of Eastern Europe. Some American policymakers believed that at times Churchill seemed more interested in safeguarding British interests in the Mediterranean than in defeating Hitler. Like the Soviet Union, Britain also worried about America's power in the postwar world.

Roosevelt hoped that wartime trust and cooperation would create support for a new world political order. At a series of summits held between 1941 and 1945, the president sketched plans for a postwar international organization, the United Nations, to be monitored by what he sometimes called the "Four Policemen"—the United States, the Soviet Union, Great Britain, and China. Each nation would police a particular sphere of interest that was important to it and would work toward opening up world trade, decolonizing its own empire, and rehabilitating Germany and Japan to encourage their formation of democratic societies. The United Nations was chartered in 1945, shortly after Roosevelt's death. By then, however, growing mistrust between the United States and the Soviet Union frustrated efforts to have the United Nations serve as an international peacekeeper.

Although the diplomatic and strategic logic of the war often seemed confused, a pattern had emerged by 1945. As Stalin remarked, "[W]hoever occupies a territory also imposes on it his own social system." Thus, the Western Allies gradually established pro-Western, anticommunist regimes in North Africa, Italy, Greece, France, western Germany, Japan, and southern Korea. As American forces advanced across the Pacific, Washington took possession of hundreds of islands formerly in the possession of Japan, declaring them "strategic trusteeships." The United States also became more involved in the

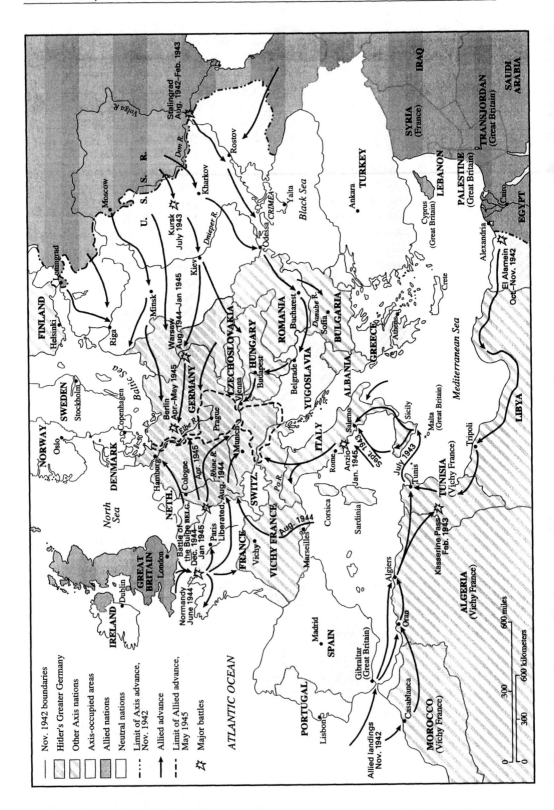

Middle East, an area of immense petroleum reserves. Roosevelt met with the ruler of Saudi Arabia, King Ibn Saud, in 1943 and began a cooperative relationship that provided American access to Saudi oil for the rest of the twentieth century.

In truth, all the Allies looked after their own interests, even while pursuing common goals. The British, French, and Dutch rushed to recolonize Southeast Asia as Japan retreated (see Map 1.2). As Russian forces pushed the Nazis toward Berlin, Stalin similarly imposed pro-Soviet regimes in most of Eastern Europe. Roosevelt, who was hardly naïve, preferred delaying most bargaining until the war's end, when he thought the U.S. position would be stronger.

But by February 1945, the Allies could no longer defer discussing postwar issues. Roosevelt and Churchill joined Stalin for a crucial meeting at Yalta, a Soviet city on the Black Sea. There the "Big Three"—Great Britain, the United States, and the Soviet Union—agreed to participate in the new United Nations and to exact industrial reparations from Germany. They also agreed that the Soviets would enter into the war against Japan three months after Hitler's defeat. In exchange, Roosevelt granted Stalin certain concessions. Critics of the Yalta agreements later charged that Roosevelt acceded to Stalin's demands out of naïveté, deteriorating health, or perhaps even communist sympathies. Why else would he sanction a dominant Soviet role in Poland or grant Stalin special economic privileges in Manchuria? "Yalta" became shorthand, especially among Republicans, for appeasement of Soviet territorial demands.

In fact, the Yalta agreement merely recognized what Stalin had already taken in Eastern Europe and the Baltic states. The Soviets were poised to invade Germany and would soon be able to attack Japan through Manchuria. Thus, Roosevelt did not give away anything. Furthermore, American military leaders feared high casualties in the last stages of the war against Japan and pressed Roosevelt to make concessions to Stalin to get Stalin into the Pacific War. The three leaders pledged cooperation in restoring democratic government in the liberated territories.

Roosevelt believed that the accord was the best he could do under the circumstances. Without continued Soviet cooperation, Roosevelt knew the Western Allies would face a far bloodier road to Berlin and Tokyo. Soviet domination of Eastern Europe and northeast Asia—which Stalin could impose with or without Western permission—seemed a reasonable price for saving American lives and shortening the war. Even American hard-liners did not seriously recommend fighting the Soviets to move them out of Poland. Most Americans rejoiced, in fact, when the Russians captured Berlin and when Germany surrendered on May 8, 1945. On the basis of earlier agreements, the Soviet Union turned over part of the German capital and other territory to its allies.

It is important to realize that when the war ended, the United States and its Western Allies dominated most of the industrialized world. The Soviets occupied much of Eastern Europe and a fourth of Germany, but their spoils did

◀ **Map 1.1**
   The Allies on the Offensive in Europe, 1942–1945

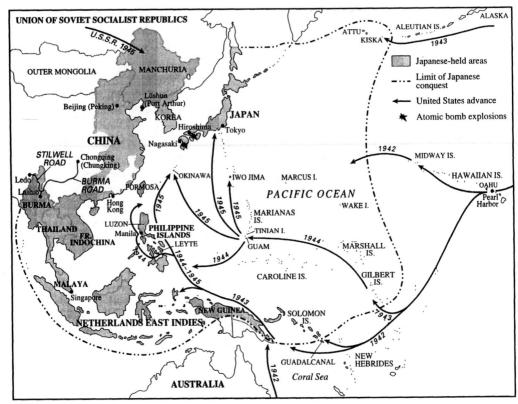

Map 1.2
The Pacific War

little to enhance their industrial or economic power. This fact, more than any other, ensured American supremacy after 1945. Among the warring powers, the United States had made the smallest human sacrifice—about 400,000 dead, compared to a worldwide total approaching 50 million—and had gained the most. Russian civilian deaths during the three-year siege of Leningrad— just one city—exceeded the total number of military deaths sustained by the United States. The United States emerged from the war with the world's strongest economy and armed forces, as well as a monopoly on atomic power. When the killing stopped, the United States, with only 6 percent of the world's population, produced half the world's goods. This relative level of power and economic well-being was not surpassed in the subsequent half-century. As one contemporary noted, "[W]hile the rest of the world came out bruised and scarred and nearly destroyed, we came out with the most unbelievable machinery, trade, manpower, and money."

War on the Home Front

The war years brought most New Deal social programs to a halt. Even though the New Deal was gone, the war itself acted as a catalyst for far-reaching social and economic change. In 1941, the United States still had many characteristics of a rural and small-town society. Of 132 million Americans, only about 74 million lived in cities with more than 10,000 inhabitants. About one-third of dwelling units lacked indoor plumbing, and two-thirds lacked central heating. Only 40 percent of adults had an eighth-grade education. One-fourth had graduated from high school; one-tenth had attended college, and only half of these had completed a college degree. Over half of all wage-earning men and three-fourths of wage-earning women earned $1,000 per year or less. In January 1941, about 9 million workers, or 15 percent of the labor force, still had no job. Private investment stood 18 percent below the 1929 level. The gross national product (GNP) barely surpassed the 1929 figure.

All of this changed dramatically during the war years. Unemployment almost disappeared, and ordinary Americans felt the shadow of the Great Depression finally lift from their lives. Private investment quickly surpassed the 1929 level and then continued to soar. GNP swelled from a prewar level of $90 billion per year to over $212 billion in 1945. Mass population shifts occurred as millions of Americans moved to cities. By the end of the war, the United States had taken a giant leap from its lingering small-town past toward the urbanized, high-tech present.

The most obvious economic effect of the war was the surge in federal spending. The Lend-Lease program alone, which cost a total of $50 billion during the war years, was an enormous sum compared to the total federal budget of $9 billion in 1939. The annual federal budget increased tenfold, to more than $95 billion, between 1939 and 1945. Not surprisingly, this budget increase led to a rapid rise in the national debt, despite efforts to fund a significant proportion of war costs through increased taxes.

In addition to raising money, the government had to mobilize U.S. industry for war. For this task, Roosevelt turned to the business executives he had once denounced as selfish plutocrats. Thousands of corporate executives agreed to guide the national economy; they were called "dollar-a-year men" because they kept their business salaries and received only a token payment from the government. These "war lords of Washington," as one critic called them, exercised unprecedented control over the national economy by deciding what should be built, where, and by whom.

Corporations were initially reluctant to invest the huge amounts of money needed to convert from civilian to military production. For example, it would cost General Motors a fortune to retool plants to produce tanks and jeeps instead of cars. Who would pay for conversion (and reconversion when the war ended), and how could profits be guaranteed? Should private businesses invest in costly, experimental technology that might have no peacetime application? To encourage industrial production, the Justice Department relaxed antitrust enforcement. Washington offered manufacturers the innovative "cost plus a fixed fee" contract whereby the federal government paid research and production costs and purchased items at a guaranteed markup. As a result, corporate after-tax profits swelled from $6.4 billion in 1940 to $10.8 billion in 1944.

Defense mobilization led to other innovations. Before 1941, the federal government spent little on scientific research. By 1945, Washington funneled $1.5 billion annually into research and development, not counting the $2 billion spent on atomic bomb research and the billions more used to construct plants to manufacture steel, synthetic rubber and other products. Radar, electronic computers, jet engines, synthetic fibers, wonder drugs like sulfas and penicillin, nuclear weapons, napalm, and ballistic missiles were all products of wartime research. The government used the war to justify experiments on American citizens, including injecting unwitting people with radioactive substances as part of the research connected to the Manhattan Project.

The War Department's Office of Scientific Research and Development (OSRD) poured $2 billion into the vast, highly secret atomic bomb project. In three new "atomic cities"—Oak Ridge, Tennessee; Hanford, Washington; and Los Alamos, New Mexico—nearly 150,000 people conducted research, refined uranium, and produced weapons. The facilities rivaled the entire automobile industry in size. In 1950, Congress created the National Science Foundation to institutionalize its basic research, especially research related to defense.

Overall, the administration's policies spurred military production that was little short of miraculous. In recognition of the importance of industrial output to Allied victory, Soviet leader Joseph Stalin once toasted Roosevelt by remarking that "Detroit was winning the war." Aircraft plants, which had produced barely 2,000 planes a year before the war, turned out nearly 100,000 in 1944. By 1945, American industry had produced over 100,000 tanks, 87,000 ships of all types, 2.5 million trucks, 5 million tons of bombs, and 44 billion rounds of ammunition. As a result, Allied soldiers had a three-to-one advantage in arms over their Axis enemies. A story was told at the time of a ship christening at which a woman at dockside was handed a bottle of champagne to do the honors. "But where is the ship?" she asked. "Just start swinging, lady," a worker remarked. "We'll have the ship there in time."

On the negative side, the war production gave birth to what later critics, including President Dwight D. Eisenhower, would call the military-industrial complex. In 1940, the hundred largest American companies produced only 30 percent of the goods manufactured in the United States. But wartime spending on high technology benefited large firms more than small ones. By 1945, the "Big 100" American companies produced 70 percent of the country's defense output, and the ten largest corporations accounted for nearly one-third of all war production. The close relationship between the military and large defense contractors would continue after the war, and the economic health of many U.S. communities would depend on military appropriations.

As big business prospered during the war years, so did its traditional antagonists, the labor unions. For both patriotic and practical reasons, most labor leaders worked closely with government and business leaders. Buoyed by rising wages, most major unions took a no-strike pledge during the war, and this willingness to cooperate enhanced their emerging role as part of the economic and political establishment. Among factory workers, union membership increased dramatically, from 10.5 million in 1941 to 15 million in 1945. This number represented one-third of the nonfarm work force and the all-time peak of union membership.

At first, the combination of defense spending, full employment, and shortages of civilian goods fueled inflation. Agencies like the National War Labor Board and the Office of Price Administration imposed various wage and price controls, along with rationing. Consumers needed ration coupons to buy items like gasoline, meat, and sugar. Children were encouraged to collect old cans, tires, and fat, which could be recycled into war goods. City dwellers cultivated millions of tiny victory gardens to supplement their diet.

While ordinary people conserved sugar and saved cans, a remarkable process was occurring. The war years brought about the most dramatic rise in income for working Americans in the twentieth century. With adjustment for inflation, real factory wages rose from $24 to near $37 per week during the war, largely because the greatest growth in employment occurred in unionized, high-wage manufacturing jobs. The share of the national wealth held by the richest 5 percent of Americans declined from 23.7 percent to 16.8 percent. The number of families with an annual income below $2,000 fell by half, while the number with annual incomes over $5,000 increased fourfold.

In addition to its economic impact, the war had a dramatic effect on where Americans lived and worked (see Map 1.3). The most obvious change was the fact that 16 million men and 250,000 women entered military service between 1941 and 1945. Almost all eligible men between the ages of eighteen and thirty-five served in the armed forces. Over 12 percent of the total American population spent time in uniform. Many GIs were sent to parts of the country they had never seen before, and often they liked what they saw. The military thus broke down regional barriers.

An upheaval among civilians also took place. Six million rural Americans headed for war work in the cities, while as many urban residents moved to jobs in new cities. Many of the migrants were African Americans who left the states of the old Confederacy in the South for jobs in the North and West. With shipbuilding, aircraft manufacturing, and other war industries concentrated on the east and west coasts and in the upper Midwest, these areas grew rapidly. Many cities, however, could not readily absorb such rapid increases in population, which led to severe overcrowding caused by housing shortages. As white officials, realtors, and residents sought to retain prewar patterns of segregation in housing, racial conflicts increased and African Americans faced extreme overcrowding and neighborhood deterioration. The federal government's housing program for war workers built few projects for blacks.

The Sunbelt—the warm states of the South and Southwest—began its rise during the war years. Not only war workers but tens of thousands of military personnel migrated to cities in the West—like San Diego, Los Angeles, and Seattle—and decided to remain there as permanent residents. California's population grew by over one-third during the war, when 2 million people came from the South and from rural areas to work in the aircraft and

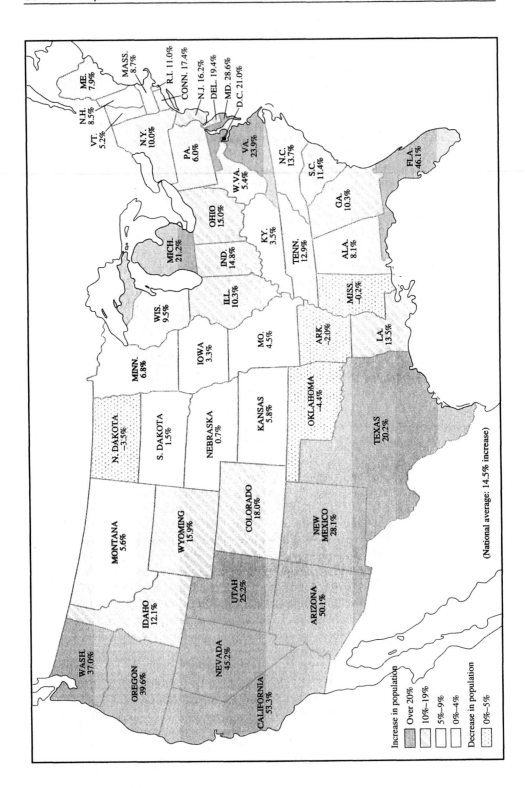

N.H. 8.5%
VT. 5.2%
ME. 7.9%
MASS. 8.7%
R.I. 11.0%
CONN. 17.4%
N.J. 16.2%
DEL. 19.4%
MD. 28.6%
D.C. 21.0%
N.Y. 10.0%
PA. 6.0%
VA. 23.9%
W.VA. 5.4%
N.C. 13.7%
S.C. 11.4%
FLA. 46.1%
OHIO 15.0%
KY. 3.5%
GA. 10.3%
MICH. 21.2%
IND. 14.8%
TENN. 12.9%
ALA. 8.1%
WIS. 9.5%
ILL. 10.3%
MO. 4.5%
MISS. -0.2%
LA. 13.5%
MINN. 6.8%
IOWA 3.3%
ARK. -2.0%
N. DAKOTA -3.5%
S. DAKOTA 1.5%
NEBRASKA 0.7%
KANSAS 5.8%
OKLAHOMA -4.4%
TEXAS 20.2%
MONTANA 5.6%
WYOMING 15.9%
COLORADO 18.0%
NEW MEXICO 28.1%
IDAHO 12.1%
UTAH 25.2%
ARIZONA 50.1%
WASH. 37.0%
OREGON 39.6%
NEVADA 45.2%
CALIFORNIA 53.3%

(National average: 14.5% increase)

Increase in population
Over 20%
10%–19%
5%–9%
0%–4%
Decrease in population
0%–5%

shipbuilding industries. The population of the West grew by 40 percent between 1940 and 1950, with much of that explosive growth a direct result of the war.

Women's roles changed dramatically during the war, too, even though gender-based inequality remained deeply ingrained. In 1940, about 27 percent of all women worked outside the home, but only 15 percent of married women did so. Most women in the labor force held low-paying jobs in light manufacturing, service, and clerical areas. Employers justified the exclusion of women from many occupations on the basis of stereotypes about women workers, including the belief that they could not handle work that was technical, physically arduous, or managerial.

With the wartime labor shortage came a shift in public policy and private attitudes toward women in the labor force. Women were encouraged to work and to take jobs traditionally held by men—at least for the time being. A War Department pamphlet put it succinctly: "A women is a substitute—like plastic instead of metal." The Office of War Information (OWI), an agency that produced radio plays, films, and posters in an attempt to mold public attitudes, added its encouragement for women to join the work force. Such appeals swayed public opinion. Before the war, 80 percent of surveyed Americans opposed wives working outside the home; in 1942, 80 percent approved.

By 1945, over 6 million additional women, including 4 million who had been housewives before the war, had entered the industrial work force and accounted for one-third of the total. They worked as riveters, welders, assembly line workers, aircraft fabricators, and in numerous other positions previously held only by men. Steelyards, shipyards, and aircraft plants employed almost no women before 1942, but three years later women made up as much as 40 percent of the work force in key defense plants. Despite the persistence of racism in employment, African American women contributed to the trend, entering manufacturing and clerical work in significant numbers for the first time.

Despite the wartime labor shortage, women were often assigned to gender-segregated tasks, received lower wages than men for the same work, and found few support services such as daycare for children. In a few cases, social workers discovered babies sleeping in cars outside defense plants because their working mothers had nowhere else to leave them. Business and political leaders offered various rationalizations for denying women equal pay and access to daycare. Women were encouraged to think of factory work as a temporary expedient, to keep their sights on the home, and to be prepared to resume the roles of housewife and mother when the war ended.

Many of these women, however, had different expectations. Surveys by the Labor Department found that, although many women resented unequal pay and sexual harassment on the job, they found the new opportunities and

◀ **Map 1.3**
   Americans on the Move During the 1940s

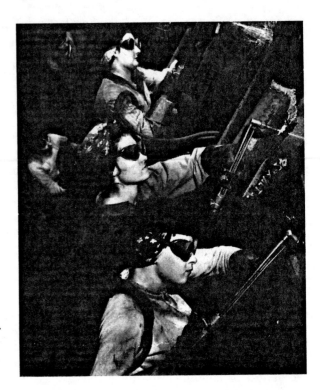

Women welders at a Gary, Indiana, steel plant prepare armor plating for tanks. / Margaret Bourke-White, © Life Magazine, Time Inc.

responsibilities exciting. Women enjoyed spending and saving their higher earnings, valued the independence and self-confidence that came with earning an income, and liked acquiring new skills. Most employed women hoped to continue working when peace returned—but they did so, as we will see in Chapter 3, under changed rules. Some men found the wartime changes unsettling. Max Lerner, a popular columnist, voiced a common male complaint that war work had created a "new Amazon" who could "outdrink, outswear, and outswagger the men."

When they sought defense work, women of color faced additional obstacles stemming from racist treatment by management and coworkers. In the Southwest, Mexican American women achieved their greatest access to defense jobs in the aircraft industry of southern California. Elsewhere in the region, discrimination confined most to service work and traditional industrial work, especially in garment production. Similarly, Native American women left reservations in large numbers but found jobs primarily in service work. African American women entered defense work in large numbers mostly outside the South and did so in part as a result of their own activism. When denied defense work, they held protests at plant gates, worked with civil rights organizations and unions to combat discrimination, and filed complaints with the federal government.

As men entered military service, women's responsibilities increased in many ways beyond that of wage earner. Women became the center of family life as never before. They also assumed responsibility for critical unpaid work in service to the wartime state. They served as Red Cross nurses, canteen volunteers, and actresses on tours sponsored by the United Service Organizations (USO). These contributions were celebrated in films like *Stage Door Canteen*, the tale of three USO hostesses who struck up romances with soldiers on leave. Hollywood's romanticized images of women's unpaid work notwithstanding, most women discovered that their domestic labor was more difficult and time-consuming as a result of consumer shortages, overcrowded housing, the need to do volunteer work for the war effort, and inadequacies in public services.

The war also fostered important changes in race relations because minority communities' dissatisfaction with the pace of change increased. The United States was fighting enemies who proclaimed the right to enslave or exterminate "inferior" races. Presumably, American citizens were united in detesting such hateful ideologies. Yet minorities in the United States and in the armed forces still faced discrimination and abuse. Law and tradition segregated them in school, at the workplace, and in numerous aspects of social life.

In 1941, as defense orders poured into factories, African American leaders expressed outrage that employment on military production lines opened new opportunities almost exclusively for white workers. A. Philip Randolph, head of the Brotherhood of Sleeping Car Porters, a union composed mostly of African Americans, challenged racial economic discrimination directly. That spring, he announced plans for a mass march on Washington to demand equal employment rights.

To avert a racially explosive protest march, Roosevelt issued Executive Order no. 8802, which created a presidential Fair Employment Practices Committee (FEPC) to investigate complaints of discrimination in the defense industry. Even though the FEPC lacked enforcement power, it pressed formerly segregated industries to hire about 600,000 additional African American workers by 1945. The lure of these new jobs contributed to the migration of about 2 million African Americans from the South to other regions during the 1940s.

African American leaders supported the war effort, seeking what they called a double victory—a victory over Nazi racism abroad and discrimination at home. The NAACP urged its members to "persuade, embarrass, compel, and shame" the federal government into acting against racism. Migration, employment in industry, and military service created a strengthened desire among African Americans for the full rights of citizenship long denied them. Higher wages and the wartime activism of African American women in particular also led to tremendous growth in the membership of the NAACP. Nevertheless, segregation and racism remained the norm, both in the military and in civilian life, during and after the war.

Ironically, the shared experience of war helped remove old ethnic barriers between whites. On the battlefields and in the canteens, white Americans from various ethnic and religious backgrounds mingled and got to know one another. But the black-white barrier was much harder to crack. Although the military drafted 1 million African Americans, it segregated them and placed most of them in menial positions such as cook, driver, or laborer. The Red Cross maintained segregated blood banks. African American troops were often stationed in the South and commanded by Southern white officers who treated them harshly.

Still, African American soldiers pressed ceaselessly for greater responsibilities and often challenged the racism they encountered in the military and in the communities adjacent to military bases. For example, a young lieutenant named Jackie Robinson—who would later become the first black player in major league baseball—refused to sit in the segregated section of a bus. He was court-martialed for his defiance, but he successfully defended himself and the charge was dismissed. Although his rebellion was not at all unusual, he was fortunate in his treatment. Throughout the war years, hostile white communities responded to the concentration of large numbers of black soldiers in their area with limitations on the soldiers' access to off-base recreation and freedom of movement. When they fought back against racist treatment, black soldiers faced violence at the hands of military and civilian police, which often led to bloody encounters that sometimes involved people from local African American communities. As General Benjamin Davis, the highest ranking black army officer, noted, "[M]ilitary training does not develop a spirit of cheerful acceptance of Jim-Crow laws and customs." Unwilling to desegregate the military, the War Department responded with more on-base recreation for African Americans and better training for military police. Ultimately, only the transfer of large numbers of black troops to combat areas abroad reduced the military's racial tensions.

At home, African American anxieties were confirmed by several violent wartime race riots, most notably in Detroit in 1942 and in Harlem in 1943. In Detroit, a black-white fight at a park sparked the riot; in Harlem, the violence started with the shooting of a black soldier by a policeman. White resentment of blacks seeking homes in white-only neighborhoods and applying for factory jobs previously reserved for whites contributed to the intensity of these conflicts.

In spite of such outbreaks of racial hatred, the war years generally had a positive effect on the struggle for equality and civil rights largely because war occasioned shifts in the consciousness and political mobilization of people of color. Military service, even in a segregated system, brought soldiers from minority communities a certain sense of empowerment. New employment opportunities, exposure to the world outside the rural South and Southwest, migration to new places, and growing membership in civil rights organizations also gave a tremendous boost to people of color. The wartime generation was unwilling to suffer silently in the face of discrimination; both their militancy and their expectations were on the rise. These people and their children would play a critical role in the postwar challenge to segregation.

Mexican immigrants and Mexican Americans also experienced hardship during the war. Since the early twentieth century, Mexicans had migrated in large numbers to the United States. After 1941, as large numbers of agricultural workers entered the armed services or sought more lucrative defense work, farm managers experienced severe labor shortages. In 1942, the federal government negotiated a contract labor program with Mexican authorities that continued, in various forms, until 1964. Under this so-called *bracero* (laborer) program, the U.S. government promised to supervise the recruitment, transportation, and working conditions of large groups of Mexican farm workers. During the war, this agreement brought in about 1.75 million farm and railroad laborers. However, the proposed supervision of working conditions was incredibly lax, *braceros* were paid as little as 35 cents per day (despite a mandated minimum wage of 30 cents an hour), and many lived under miserable conditions. The program did not stem the continued migration of many undocumented workers during and after the war.

The nearly 2.7 million Mexican Americans faced additional problems. Living mostly in the Southwest, they were confronted with segregation in schools, housing, and employment. New social tensions flared in communities such as Los Angeles, where rapid growth inflamed latent racism. Mexican American youth gangs members dressed in flamboyant clothes called zoot suits. They were frequently harassed by the police and by white servicemen, who often cruised the barrios in search of zootsuiters and attacked and humiliated them by stripping off their clothes. Police often charged the zootsuiters instead of the servicemen with disturbing the peace. To many Chicanos, the distinctive clothing was a way to assert their ethnic identity and to flout white culture.

The tensions exploded in June 1943, when hundreds of sailors and marines went on a several-day rampage, attacking Mexican Americans, African Americans, and Filipinos in East Los Angeles. Because local police participated in the attacks, military police were needed to quell the riot. The *Los Angeles Times* reported the incidents with headlines such as "Zoot-Suiters Learn Lesson in Fight with Servicemen." When Eleanor Roosevelt suggested that long-standing discrimination against Mexican Americans might have provoked the riots, the paper accused her of promoting racial discord.

The consequences of racism were, of course, nowhere more savage during the war than they were for European Jews. The Holocaust was a tragedy the United States did little to avert. In November 1938, after the German government had stripped German Jews of most civil and economic rights, Nazi mobs attacked Jewish businesses, synagogues, and homes, smashing and looting in an orgy that quickly became known as *Kristallnacht*, or Night of the Broken Glass. Shortly after that incident, German police sent 20,000 Jews to concentration camps, which later became the sites of mass extermination. Roosevelt remarked that he could "scarcely believe that such things could occur in a twentieth-century civilization." As the Nazis conquered Eastern Europe, the murder escalated.

European Jews who attempted to flee confronted legal barriers everywhere. Since 1924, the United States' National Origins Act had restricted nearly all immigration from Eastern and southern Europe. Even Jews who qualified under the unfilled German quota faced a maze of bureaucratic red tape that made it nearly impossible to obtain an entry visa.

Fear of competition for scarce jobs added to anti-Semitism in the United States, creating little sympathy for, and much agitation against, the immigration of even token numbers of Jewish refugees. Roosevelt, who worked closely with many Jewish advisers, was already the target of anti-Semitic remarks. Bowing to this pressure, he allowed the State Department to place impediments in the path of would-be immigrants seeking sanctuary.

Evidence surfaced in 1942 and 1943 that the Nazis planned to exterminate millions of Jews with poison gas. Yet even after the plans became known, U.S. and British strategists rejected the idea of bombing the death camps and the rail lines leading into them. Such diversions from more important missions, Allied leaders argued, would delay victory. Congress rebuffed efforts to allow Jewish children into the United States. American officials even opposed granting temporary refuge to the few thousand European Jews who had slipped away from Nazi control.

In 1944, Roosevelt finally created a War Refugee Board to establish camps in neutral countries and U.S.-occupied territory overseas. These centers eventually helped save the lives of a few hundred thousand refugees. Only 1,000

The liberation of the Bergen-Belsen concentration camp—Americans confront the Holocaust. / Imperial War Museum

refugees were admitted directly into the United States. As one scholar wrote, "Franklin Roosevelt's indifference to so momentous an historical event as the systematic annihilation of European Jewry emerges as the worst failure of his presidency."

Roosevelt's failure to champion the cause of Jewish refugees must be seen in light of the strong anti-Semitism in American culture. An opinion poll taken in 1942 found that many U.S. citizens believed that Jews posed nearly as great a threat to national security as did Germany and Japan. Leaders of the American Jewish community anguished over the horrors of Nazi persecution but feared a backlash among Christian Americans if they spoke out forcefully. As a result, most Jewish organizations refrained from pressing politicians to rescue Holocaust victims. Instead, they called for creating a Jewish homeland in Palestine for those lucky enough to survive.

Meanwhile, the Japanese American community was singled out for special persecution in the United States. Not only was Japan a wartime enemy, but the United States also had a century-long tradition of anti-Asian agitation and hysteria. The surprise attack on Pearl Harbor, followed by Japan's initial victories in the Pacific, spurred exaggerated fears that Japanese Americans would conspire to aid the enemy. Although almost no members of the Japanese American community committed sabotage or illegal acts before or after 1941, their mere existence aroused public hysteria. Journalists such as Westbrook Pegler demanded that every Japanese man, woman, and child be placed under armed guard. Congressman Leland Ford of California insisted that any "patriotic native-born Japanese, if he wants to make his contribution, will submit himself to a concentration camp." General John DeWitt, head of the Western Defense Command, declared that Japanese of any citizenship were enemies. A popular song was entitled "We're Gonna Find a Feller Who Is Yeller and Beat Him Red, White, and Blue."

In February 1942, President Roosevelt issued Executive order no. 9066, which was quickly backed by Congress. The order declared that parts of the country were "military areas" from which any or all persons could be barred. Nearly every politician in the West applauded the move. Although the regulations also targeted German and Italian aliens (most Italians were later exempted), all persons of Japanese ancestry, regardless of their citizenship, were affected. In May, the War Relocation Authority ordered 112,000 Japanese to leave the West Coast in a matter of days. In Hawaii, unlike California, the dangers of a Japanese invasion were much more real, but residents of Japanese descent made up such a large portion of the Hawaiian population and were so vital to the economy that only a few individuals were interned.

Nearly all those affected by the forced relocation orders complied without protest, abandoning their homes, farms, and personal property to speculators. Bleak internment camps were hastily established in several Western states. While not equivalent to incarceration in the Nazi death camps, this mass imprisonment marked the greatest violation of civil liberties in wartime America.

Japanese American families at the Manzanar War Relocation Center in California line up for "mess call." / AP/Wide World

Families lived in rudimentary dwellings and were compelled to do menial work under armed guard.

In 1944, the Supreme Court addressed the policy of forced relocation in a case against Fred Korematsu, a citizen who had refused to leave a designated war zone on the West Coast. The Court's decision in *Korematsu* v. *United States* affirmed the government's right to exclude individuals from any designated area on the basis of military necessity. The majority claimed that the defendant's race was irrelevant because the government could, if it chose, exclude groups besides those of Japanese ancestry. In a powerful dissent, Justice Frank Murphy denounced the *Korematsu* verdict as a "legalization of racism" based on prejudice and unproven fears.

Despite the restrictive relocation orders and the degradation of life in the internment camps, Japanese Americans contributed significantly to the U.S. war effort. Many male internees volunteered for military duty and served in Europe, achieving recognition for their bravery in action. Others worked in the Pacific theater as translators, interpreters, or intelligence officers. A few Japanese American men chose to resist the draft, declaring that they would not assume the obligations of citizenship until they had been given their full rights as citizens. As the war progressed, some internees were permitted to leave the relocation camps if they agreed to settle in eastern states. By the summer of 1945, all could leave. A fortunate few found that friends had protected their homes or businesses; the rest lost the work of a lifetime.

Despite growing recognition that internment had been a grave error, Congress and the courts hesitated to make formal redress. Congress offered a token payment in 1948, but it was not until the 1980s that several Japanese Americans convicted of wartime offenses successfully reopened their cases. Files from the Justice Department and the Federal Bureau of Investigation revealed that prosecutors had withheld evidence showing that no danger existed to justify relocation. Congress then made a formal apology and offered compensation of about $20,000 per surviving internee.

Wartime Politics

As the wartime economic boom gradually erased memories of the Great Depression, many Americans felt that the reform programs of the New Deal no longer mattered. The 1942 congressional elections increased the number of seats held by Republicans and conservative southern Democrats. The new Congress proceeded to end several New Deal agencies, including the WPA and the CCC.

The president's chief of mobilization, James F. Byrnes, gloated that the war had helped elbow the "radical boys out of the way [and] more will go." His prediction proved accurate, and nervous Democratic Party leaders blamed electoral losses on the left-leaning vice president, Henry A. Wallace. Unlike his more cautious boss, Wallace actively promoted civil rights and had called for postwar economic intervention by the government. Witnessing Roosevelt's obvious physical decline, the party barons feared that Wallace might assume the presidency after Roosevelt's death or retirement. Bowing to their complaints, in mid-1944 Roosevelt agreed to replace Wallace with Senator Harry S Truman, a moderate from Missouri. The Democratic candidates faced a Republican ticket headed by New York Governor Thomas E. Dewey. Roosevelt won easily, though by his smallest majority yet (53.4 percent). He got significant assistance from organized labor, which created the first political action committee, or PAC, to raise campaign funds.

Despite the political challenges and his own concentration on winning the war, Roosevelt made some effort in his last years to impart a vision for postwar reform. In his 1944 State of the Union address, he called for drafting a "second Bill-of-Rights under which a new basis of security and prosperity can be established for all." He described a government committed to providing jobs, housing, education, and health and retirement insurance for all Americans.

In a draft speech dictated on April 11, 1945, and as victory in Europe loomed, Roosevelt appealed to the American people to "conquer the fears, the ignorance and the greed" that made the horror of world war possible. But the next day, April 12, the president died of a cerebral hemorrhage. Roosevelt's death and the imminent victory over the Axis forces marked the threshold of the postwar era.

Conclusion

The Roosevelt years, stretching from the Great Depression to the last months of World War II, brought vast changes to the nation and increased its role on the world stage. Those years molded the postwar world in fundamental ways that continue to affect us today.

Both the Depression and the war prompted rapid growth in the federal government's size and scope of action. For the first time in the nation's history, the U.S. government had a direct and frequent effect on the daily lives of ordinary citizens. The government managed the economy to an unprecedented degree. It began to provide relief to the needy and the elderly, but it did so within the limits imposed by an economy that discriminated against white women and people of color. It funded scientific research that changed U.S. industry and made possible the high-tech society in which we now live.

The Great Depression and the war put Americans on the move, literally as well as figuratively. During the war, millions of rural and small-town Americans packed their bags and headed to the major industrial cities. African Americans left the rural South in huge numbers, many making their new homes in the North and West. The *bracero* program, and the high level of immigration by undocumented workers that accompanied it, contributed to a substantial influx of Mexican workers. The Sunbelt and the West Coast began their rise to prominence.

For women, the years of the Depression and war meant the continuation of labor discrimination and of the idea that women's identities and work should be particularly focused on home and family. The war tested those patterns, however, giving women a chance to take jobs traditionally reserved for men and to demonstrate their capacity for work in heavy industry. This change constituted a first step toward the revolution in women's lives that is still occurring today. For ethnic minorities, these years were times of mingled hope, fear, and disappointment. The wartime internment of Japanese Americans left a blot on the nation's record that no later compensation could remove. The government's failure to help European Jews escape the Holocaust seemed almost incomprehensible to later generations. Yet the Roosevelt era also brought a rising concern for the rights of minorities and new hopes that protest could lead to improvement—crucial ingredients for the civil rights movement of the postwar years.

The generation dubbed America's "greatest" by journalist Tom Brokaw thus left a mixed legacy for the future. Its economic reforms and assistance programs saved capitalism in the United States, while leaving those Americans most vulnerable to private-sector discrimination—people of color and white women—outside its most important protections. Those reforms owed as much to the pressures provided by grassroots activists as to the political capacities of politicians in Washington. The military victory in World War II was hardly won single-handedly by the United States, which relied heavily on its Allies to carry the burden before it entered the war and to bear the brunt of the fighting in Europe throughout the war. The most important military contributions provided by the United States were its industrial production and technical advances in warfare, most notably the development of nuclear weapons.

Finally, as a direct consequence of the war, the United States emerged in 1945 as the world's leading military and economic power. Europe was devastated. The Soviet Union, though a mighty wartime ally and future competitor, had suffered terrible losses. In the postwar world, the history of the United States would be shaped by its demanding new role as a superpower and by the conflicting ideas of it citizens about how that role should be played.

F   U   R   T   H   E   R   •   R   E   A   D   I   N   G

On the Depression and New Deal, see Michael A. Bernstein, *The Great Depression: Delayed Recovery and Economic Change in America, 1929–1939* (1988); Anthony J. Badger, *The New Deal: The Depression Years, 1933–40* (1980); William E. Leuchtenberg, *Franklin D. Roosevelt and the New Deal* (1963); Kenneth S. Davis, *FDR: The New Deal Years, 1933–1937* (1986); Suzanne Mettler, *Dividing Citizens: Gender and Federalism in New Deal Public Policy* (1998); Alan Brinkley, *Voices of Protest: Huey Long, Father Coughlin, and the Great Depression* (1982); Harvard Sitkoff, *A New Deal for Blacks* (1978); James N. Gregory, *American Exodus: The Dust Bowl Migration and Okie Culture in California* (1989); Lizabeth Cohen, *Making a New Deal: Industrial Workers in Chicago, 1919–1939* (1991); Susan Ware, *Holding Their Own: American Women in the 1930s* (1982); Steven Fraser, *Labor Will Rule: Sidney Hillman and the Rise of American Labor* (1991); Steve Fraser and Gary Gerstle, eds., *The Rise and Fall of the New Deal Order, 1930–1980* (1989). **On American society during World War II,** see Doris Kearns Goodwin, *No Ordinary Time: Franklin and Eleanor Roosevelt: The Home Front During WWII* (1994); Daniel Kryder, *Divided Arsenal* (2000); John M. Blum, *V Was for Victory: Politics and American Culture during World War II* (1976); Karen Anderson, *Wartime Women (1981)*; Susan Hartmann, *The Homefront and Beyond* (1980); Peter Irons, *Justice at War: The Story of the Japanese-American Internment Cases* (1982); Roger Daniels, *Prisoners Without Trial* (1993); Gerald D. Nash, *The American West Transformed: The Impact of the Second World War* (1985); Studs Terkel, *"The Good War": An Oral History of World War II* (1984). **On military strategy and foreign policy,** see Robert Dallek, *Franklin D. Roosevelt and American Foreign Policy* (1979); Warren Kimball, *The Juggler: Franklin D. Roosevelt as Wartime Statesman* (1991); Russell D. Buhite, *Decisions at Yalta* (1986); David Wyman, *The Abandonment of the Jews: America and the Holocaust, 1941–45* (1984); Michael Sherry, *The Rise of American Air Power* (1987); John Dower, *War Without Mercy: Race and Power in the Pacific War* (1986); Martin J. Sherwin, *A World Destroyed: The Atomic Bomb and the Grand Alliance* (1975); Michael C. C. Adams, *The Best War Ever: America and World War II* (1994); William O'Neill, *A Democracy at War: America's Fight at Home and Abroad in W.W. II* (1993). **On broadcast journalism,** see A. M. Sperber, *Murrow: His Life and Times* (1998); Steven M. Barkin, *American Television News: The Media Marketplace and the Public Interest* (2003); Leonard Downey, Jr., and Robert J. Kaiser, *The News About the News: American Journalism in Peril* (2002); Eric Alterman, *Sound and Fury: The Triumph of the Punditocracy* (2002), and *What Liberal Media? The Truth About Bias and the News* (2003).

2

From Atomic War to Cold War: Victory and Containment at Home and Abroad, 1945–1952

The death of a city and the birth of a symbol: Atomic bomb destroys Nagasaki, Japan, August 9, 1945. / © CORBIS

J ack Short of Poughkeepsie, New York, was barely twenty years old when he landed in France soon after D-Day in June 1944. Over the next ten months, the men in his unit raced toward Berlin, pushing the German army back across the Rhine. On the eve of the Nazi surrender in May 1945, Short and his comrades came upon a concentration camp at Nordhausen, Germany. The bodies of the dead and dying, he recalled, were "stacked up like cordwood." Decades later, he sometimes reviewed the photographs he took that day as a testament to the horrors he encountered.

In spite of this painful memory, Jack Short told interviewer Studs Terkel how the war had actually improved his life. Born into a working-class family, all Short's relatives worked in factories. None had ever gone beyond high school. But after three years in the military and meeting people from different backgrounds, Jack aspired to more. Almost miraculously, the government's new GI Bill helped turn his dream into reality. "It paid for 99 percent of your college expenses and gave you money each month to live on," the veteran explained. In 1950, Jack Short became the first of his family to graduate from college, and he took a job with the emerging computer giant, IBM. "Everything in my life since the war," he believed, "has been positive."

World War II transformed Jack Short's life and the lives of most Americans, whether or not they served in the military. Although no one intended or expected it, the most destructive, human-caused event in history revitalized the nation's economy and propelled it into the position of the world's leading power. The year 1945 would also witness the death of Franklin Roosevelt, the birth of the nuclear age, and the beginning of the so-called Cold War that defined international relations for the next half century.

Truman Takes Charge and Prepares for the First Atomic War

On April 12, 1945, Vice President Harry S Truman relaxed with congressional friends in the office of House Speaker Sam Rayburn. After chairing a tedious Senate debate on a water treaty, the vice president savored a stiff bourbon. Abruptly, a phone call from presidential press secretary Steve Early summoned him to the White House. There, Eleanor Roosevelt delivered a somber greeting: "Harry, the president is dead." Truman asked if there was anything he could do for her. "Is there anything we can do for you?" she replied; "you are the one in trouble now."

Since 1933, Franklin D. Roosevelt had dominated public life in America. To millions of working men and women, he personified their restoration of faith in democracy and capitalism; he steered the country through the shoals of depression and war, only to be struck down cruelly on the threshold of victory over evil. Even those who resented Roosevelt's political accomplishments, especially his expansion of the power of the federal government, recognized him as a giant whose passing left a void in American public life. An ordinary soldier spoke for millions when he remarked, "America will seem a strange place without his voice, talking to the people when great events happen." Nearly everyone recognized that FDR was a tough act to follow.

Truman, a former haberdasher, county judge, and senator and widely disparaged as a political nobody, was suddenly in charge of concluding the war, preserving the Grand Alliance, converting the war economy to peacetime production, and nurturing the liberal goals of a still unfulfilled New Deal. Organized labor, ethnic Americans, racial minorities, and women hoped to expand the vistas of opportunity partially opened to them by Franklin Roosevelt. Business interests and conservatives in both the Democratic and Republican parties celebrated Roosevelt's passing as a chance to reassert their traditional power over society.

The new president came from a modest farming family near Independence, Missouri. During World War I, he commanded an artillery battery in Europe. After the armistice, he returned to Missouri, married Bess Wallace, and opened a clothing store in Kansas City. When the business failed, he turned to politics.

For most of the 1920s and early 1930s, Truman served as an elected judge in Jackson County, adjacent to the area controlled by "Boss" Tom Pendergast's corrupt Kansas City political machine. Despite his friendship with Pendergast, Truman earned a reputation for competence and honesty. In 1934, riding the early crest of Roosevelt's popularity, he won election to the U.S. Senate as a Democrat.

The future president's youthful social outlook mirrored the bigotry common in midwestern border states. "I think one man is just as good as another," he wrote his fiancé, "so long as he's honest, and decent, and not a nigger or a Chinaman." As a senator and president, he modified these views and expressed support for civil rights and liberties.

Truman left few footprints in the Senate before he achieved modest fame for investigating war profiteering. During the three months he served as vice president, he had little contact with Roosevelt. Either because he could not reckon with his own mortality or because he had a low regard for Truman, Roosevelt had kept his deputy in the dark about the development of the atomic bomb, the growing strains among the Allies, and his postwar plans. Truman resented the fact that he was surrounded by better-informed men reluctant to admit him into Franklin Roosevelt's inner circle. Commenting on the staff and cabinet he inherited, Truman lamented that there was not a "man on the list who would talk frankly." The "honest ones were afraid and the others wanted to fool me."

During his first year in the Oval Office, Truman pushed out nearly all Roosevelt's intimates, replacing many old New Dealers with advisers closely linked to big business and the military. Even though Truman later proposed several New Deal–style reform programs, many rank-and-file progressives considered him a lukewarm liberal. By the same token, Republicans and conservative Democrats criticized him as too liberal and shook the political tightrope on which he wobbled, hoping to make him tumble.

As Allied armies neared Berlin in April 1945, Truman had to respond rapidly to military and diplomatic problems he knew little about. In his determination to appear as a forceful leader, he sometimes made snap judgments. Just hours after taking office, for example, he asserted to aides that, unlike his former boss, he would "stand up to the Russians," implying that Roosevelt had been too easy on Stalin.

Several of Roosevelt's more anti-Soviet advisers, including ambassador to Moscow Averell Harriman, Secretary of the Navy James Forrestal, chief of staff Admiral William Leahy, and Undersecretary of State Joseph C. Grew encouraged Truman's suspicions of Stalin. All had urged Roosevelt to demand a larger role for non-Communists in the new governments of Poland and Eastern Europe. Truman accepted their advice more readily than his predecessor.

Following Roosevelt's death, Harriman had flown from Moscow to Washington to brief Truman on Soviet behavior. The ambassador blamed the tensions between the allies on Stalin's effort to expand the Soviet sphere in Eastern Europe, in violation of the Yalta accords. Harriman condemned the advance of Russian armies as a "barbarian invasion of Europe." Communism, he told Truman, confronted America with an ideological threat "just as vigorous and dangerous as Fascism or Nazism." Truman accepted at face value Harriman's warning that failure to resist Stalin would resemble the nearly fatal appeasement of Hitler in the 1930s.

On April 23, 1945, the president used what he called "words of one syllable" to accuse visiting Soviet foreign minister Vyacheslav M. Molotov of violating pledges to allow free elections in Poland. When the envoy complained about the president's language, Truman recalled that he gave Molotov a "straight one-two to the jaw," yelling, "[c]arry out your agreements, and you won't get talked to like that." In private, however, he wondered if he had done right.

Verbal fireworks had little impact on Soviet policy, in Poland or elsewhere. Stalin responded to Truman's charge of treaty violations with a blunt statement: "Poland borders with the Soviet Union," he observed, which "cannot be said of Great Britain or the United States." The Soviet dictator noted that just as the Western allies imposed friendly governments in areas they liberated from the Nazis, he would forge a security zone in Eastern Europe, even if it caused a rupture in the Grand Alliance. British Prime Minister Winston Churchill complained that Stalin had erected an "iron fence" (anticipating the term *iron curtain*) across Europe by installing brutal puppet regimes in Poland, Bulgaria, and Rumania—much as Hitler had done before him.

In the time-honored tradition of Russian czars, Stalin measured Soviet security by the weakness of neighboring states and the degree of control that Moscow exercised over them. Also, like most Russians, he really did fear a revived Germany and Japan. Because most Eastern Europeans resented Soviet pressure, they would, if allowed free elections, form governments that sought Western protection. This resentment further complicated matters and convinced Stalin that nothing short of total Soviet control could ensure that Eastern Europe remain a buffer against a revived Germany. By imposing harsh control over Eastern Europe, however, Stalin aroused the very hostility he feared from the capitalist West—including the eventual decision to rebuild western Germany and Japan. When Germany formally surrendered on May 8, 1945, the Allies partitioned Germany and its capital into occupation zones. No one yet knew whether these divisions would be temporary or permanent. The German problem became more complicated when the Soviet Union annexed a swath of land along the Soviet-Polish border and compensated Poland by grafting on to it a portion of eastern Germany. This swap moved the Soviet border closer to Central Europe. Meanwhile, the expulsion of ethnic Germans from Poland and Czechoslovakia in 1945 forced 11 million refugees into occupied Germany.

As the jockeying for power in Europe began, the conflict with Japan raged on. Despite American hopes and aid, Nationalist China under Jiang Jieshi (Chiang Kai-shek) contributed little to the war against Japan. Instead, U.S. navy, army, and marine forces fought their way across the Pacific, seizing islands from which to mount additional naval and air attacks. By early 1945, Japan was surrounded, cut off from its several million troops in China and Southeast Asia, running out of raw materials, and subject to relentless air attack. In March, for example, army air force planes launched incendiary raids on Tokyo, which killed over 100,000 civilians and burned much of the city. Japanese troops on islands close to the homeland, such as Iwo Jima and Okinawa, fought desperately, often using suicide *kamikaze* tactics to resist the Americans.

By the summer of 1945, Japan was defeated, but the militarists in power refused to surrender. They clung to the belief that by continuing to fight, they could win better terms of surrender. Although many civilian leaders wanted to negotiate a cease-fire, the Japanese emperor wavered. U.S. military planners dreaded the prospect of invading either China (where several million Japanese troops remained) or the Japanese home islands. They urged Roosevelt and then Truman to seek Soviet help, even if it meant that Stalin gained an Asian foothold.

Allied leaders held what proved to be their final wartime summit conference in mid-July 1945. Truman, Churchill, and Stalin met in Potsdam, the once opulent suburb of bombed-out Berlin. (Midway through the conference, voters in Britain tossed Churchill out of office and replaced him with Labor Party leader Clement Attlee. The new prime minister promised a better life for British workers but shared Churchill's strong anticommunist views.) Amid the rubble of what was to have been Hitler's Thousand-Year Reich, the "Big Three" spent nearly two weeks arguing over German and Polish boundaries, the make-up of eastern European governments, and reparations from Germany to the Soviet Union. Truman came to Potsdam hoping to get a renewed Soviet pledge to join the war soon against Japan. Stalin agreed to do so by mid-August.

On July 16, amidst these discussions, Truman received a coded message that an atomic bomb had been tested successfully at the Trinity site in New Mexico—a remote location near the Los Alamos laboratory. The news cheered Truman considerably because the new weapon might end the war quickly, thus saving American lives and reducing the Soviet role in the defeat of Japan. Truman casually mentioned to Stalin that American scientists had developed a powerful, new weapon. Although the term *atomic bomb* was not used, Stalin understood. His Western Allies had tried to keep the atomic project secret from him, but Soviet spies had learned about it and Stalin had already begun his own nuclear program. The Soviet leader's outward calm led Truman to gloat mistakenly that he had "fooled Mr. Russia."

At the conclusion of the conference, British and American officials issued the Potsdam Declaration. Unless Japan surrendered promptly, they warned, "[I]t may expect a rain of ruin from the air the likes of which has never been seen on this earth." Still hoping to negotiate better terms, the Japanese government vowed to fight on.

Truman ordered that the two available atomic bombs, code-named Fat Man and Little Boy, be used as soon as possible. On August 6, a B-29 named *Enola Gay* (for pilot Paul Tibbets's mother) flew from the island of Tinian and dropped the first bomb on the city of Hiroshima. Residents had rejoiced over their having been spared the conventional bombing attacks inflicted on most other cities. In fact, war planners had purposely kept Hiroshima "virgin," as they put it, to demonstrate more forcefully the power of the new weapon. Two days later, the Soviet Union declared war on Japan and sent the Red Army into Japanese-occupied Mongolia and Manchuria. On August 9, an American plane obliterated Nagasaki with a second atomic bomb. About 150,000 civilians, including many Korean laborers and a few American POWs, perished in the attacks. Radiation sickness later claimed more victims.

Since these events, scientists, historians, politicians, and ordinary citizens in Japan and the United States have debated the decision to use the atomic

The devastation of Hiroshima after the use of the atomic bomb. / © Dennis Brack/Black Star

bombs. Critics wondered if anti-Asian sentiment played a role, along with Truman's desire to keep the Soviets out of Asia and to force them to back down in Eastern Europe. Many speculated that a desperate Japan would have soon quit fighting anyway, if only the United States had offered better terms or demonstrated the bomb's power on, say, an uninhabited island off Japan's coast. Others disputed claims by Truman and his aides that using the bomb averted one-half million or more U.S. invasion casualties. (Actual estimates projected 50,000 deaths.)

While critics raise valid questions, most historians have come to accept the logic of Truman's decision to use the atomic bombs. Publicly, Truman never voiced doubt about his motives. In announcing the first attack, he thanked God for giving him a weapon that saved "thousands and thousands of American lives." Privately, Truman criticized "crybaby" scientists who had wanted to inform Japan in advance of an atomic attack. At the time he decided to go forward, Truman privately called the Japanese "savages, ruthless, merciless and fanatic." When "you have to deal with a beast," he wrote, "you have to treat him like a beast." Other prominent Americans issued calls for "gutting the heart of Japan with fire," killing "about half the civilian population," and even "sterilizing every damn one of them so that in a generation there would be no more Japs."

Truman and advisers like Secretary of State James F. Byrnes did hope that the impact of the atomic bomb would end the war before Soviet armies gained a foothold in China or Japan. When news of the atomic test reached Byrnes at Potsdam, he told an aide that the president no longer needed to haggle with Stalin over details. He could issue an ultimatum "giving the Japs two weeks to surrender or face destruction." A "secret weapon" would be ready by then.

Truman and those closest to him had multiple rationales for using the bomb. Even if the president did not expect a half million casualties from an invasion, he probably believed that even one avoidable American death justified an atomic strike. The United States possessed only three or four atomic bombs in August, so it seemed risky to chance a "demonstration shot" that the Japanese might well ignore. If Truman could end the war quickly, reduce American deaths, and limit Soviet expansion in Asia, he saw no reason *not* to seize the opportunity. After all, how could he justify having spent $2 billion constructing the weapon if he hesitated to use it?

Although anti-Japanese sentiment was rampant, U.S. strategists had planned to use the atomic bomb against German targets if the weapon had been available before the Nazi surrender. British and American firebombing of German and Japanese cities was as deadly to civilians as the new weapon. The indiscriminate slaughter of civilians had become so common by 1945 that few moral objections were raised in public. Truman and his aides believed that, given the structure of Japan's government, probably nothing short of combat use of the bomb would compel surrender on acceptable terms.

American officials knew that military hard-liners in Japan rejected even the most minimal surrender terms insisted upon by the United States. These terms included military occupation and disarmament, the trial of war criminals, and strict limits on the Japanese emperor's power. Secretary of War Henry Stimson, although deeply troubled by the moral dimensions of the bomb, favored its use because he thought it would "produce exactly the kind of shock on the ruling Japanese oligarchy" that would "strengthen the position of those who wished peace" and would "weaken . . . the military party." Recent evidence suggests that he guessed correctly. The bomb, one high-ranking Japanese official remarked just after its use on Hiroshima, "drastically altered the whole military situation and offered the military [in Japan] grounds for ending the war."

Following the destruction of Hiroshima, the Japanese emperor and his civilian aides agreed that Japan "must now bow to the inevitable," especially if it hoped to avoid a revolt by ordinary Japanese. The Soviet declaration of war on August 8 reinforced their belief. Even after these events, however, the Japanese army high command still believed that Japan could secure better surrender terms by hanging tough. The destruction of Nagasaki on August 9 broke the deadlock by creating a "psychological shock" that allowed both the Japanese emperor and Japan's militarists to save face. Several of Japan's key army leaders convinced themselves that America's "scientific prowess," not its military skills or bravery, had overwhelmed them. "We lost a scientific war," explained one of Hirohito's army aides. Under this circumstance, "the people will understand" and be forgiving. In a letter to his son shortly after the surrender, the emperor complained that his generals had placed "too much significance on spirit, and were oblivious to science." Rationalizing defeat as a surrender to "science" also served as a prelude to Japan's postwar emphasis on science, technology, and trade.

On August 10, a day after the destruction of Nagasaki, the emperor acted decisively. "Since the appearance of the atomic bomb," he told his cabinet, "continuation of the war spelled needless suffering for his subjects and Japan's ruin as a nation." He ordered his aides to accept the Potsdam Declaration, with the proviso that he remain on the throne. Anxious to end the war and slow the Soviet advance in China, Truman agreed on August 14 to modify the original peace terms. If the emperor personally ordered his troops throughout Asia to surrender, the United States would permit him to remain on the throne, subject to the authority of the American occupation commander, General Douglas MacArthur. The next day, Hirohito addressed his country via radio and called on all Japanese to cease resistance.

The awful destruction of Hiroshima and Nagasaki may have had an unintended positive consequence. Pictures and descriptions of what happened to these cities and their inhabitants, such as John Hersey's harrowing account of nuclear death in *Hiroshima* (1946), appeared around the world. Despite the saber-rattling of the Cold War, Soviet and American leaders recognized the special nature of nuclear weapons and used their atomic arsenals as a deterrent and as weapons of last, not first, resort.

Victory over Japan ended nearly a decade and a half of world lawlessness and confirmed the United States' place as the world's leading economic and military power. With a mere 6 percent of the earth's population, the United

States produced over half of the world's goods and controlled more than half of its wealth. Not surprisingly, Americans celebrated their wartime accomplishments, and many shared the view articulated by Henry Luce, the influential publisher of *Time* and *Life* magazines. The "American experience," Luce wrote in 1945, "is the key to the future. America must be the elder brother of the nations in the brotherhood of man." The notion that this country had a special historic mission was not new. Now, however, the nation had a uniquely powerful position. To the Soviets—and to other critics of U.S. policy in the postwar years—an attitude of the sort expressed by Luce smacked of arrogance and provoked a volatile mix of gratitude and hostility.

Demobilization and Building Peace: The GI Bill and New Deal Legacy

In 1946, Hollywood released a film with the ironic title *The Best Years of Our Lives*. It told the poignant story of three veterans—one actor was an actual GI who lost his hands in the war—returning home and making a sometimes painful readjustment to civilian life. Although the film won the Academy Award for best picture, within a few years several artists who worked on the project were accused of being Communists and using the movie as a vehicle to undermine society. For most Americans, the early postwar years were uncertain but compared to the previous period of depression and war, the postwar period really turned out to be the best years of their lives.

After Japan surrendered, Americans were eager to turn their attention to domestic matters. Young people looked forward to obtaining peacetime jobs and starting new families. With money in their pockets, they began moving to new suburbs and having children in record numbers. After a decade and a half of privation, they also went on a spree of consumer buying, snapping up home appliances, automobiles, and new gadgets called televisions.

Americans hoped that victory in World War II would ensure prosperity, not a return to depression. Many worried that the mustering out of 12 million men from military service, along with the abrupt cancellation of war orders that displaced 2 million workers, might create massive unemployment. Soldiers and sailors stationed around the world demanded to be shipped home as soon as possible. They sometimes demonstrated to protest delays. A point system, based on length of service, brought order to the process. In less than two years, the number of men in uniform fell by 90 percent.

Veterans had less difficulty finding jobs than many experts anticipated. A large number of veterans replaced women workers, 3 million of whom were laid off in the aftermath of victory. Both bosses and labor leaders took their lead from a senator who called on Congress to force "wives and mothers back to the kitchen." Private employers and civil service boards gave veterans preference over other job seekers. Even though 75 percent of women who wished to continue working eventually found postwar jobs, they often had to settle for clerical, sales, and light assembly work rather than the more lucrative skilled factory labor available during the war. In 1950, about 33 percent of women held paying jobs, up from 27 percent before the war. Their wages decreased from a wartime level of about $50 to $37 per week for white women, and to half that for African American women. Men experienced only a small drop in pay.

The American economy performed better than most people predicted. Between 1945 and 1952, the gross domestic product (GDP) rose an average of 4 percent annually. A huge savings pool built up during the war fueled an inflationary surge during 1945–1946, but the conversion of war plants soon began to satisfy consumer demand for a range of goods that had been in short supply before 1945 or, in many cases, had not existed earlier. The number of working Americans increased from a wartime high of 53 million to 60 million in 1948, and to 64 million by 1952.

Many labor unions came out of the war determined to push for both wage increases and a greater say in company policy. The United Automobile Workers (UAW), for example, staged a long strike against industry giant General Motors during 1946. In addition to higher wages and more benefits, the UAW wanted a seat on the GM governing board in order to influence corporate policy. Ultimately, the UAW, like many other industrial unions, settled for a contract that provided more money but little say over workplace rules. Because labor unions won a bigger slice of the pie, and as the Cold War intensified and government and employers brought pressure on the labor movement to cooperate, most labor unions became less militant and more accommodating.

Before 1945, the American government had never treated its war veterans generously. Aside from token pensions for the disabled or their widows, the federal government lost interest in its soldiers once they had finished serving their country. The sheer dimensions of World War II changed that pattern. Sixteen million men and about 350,000 women served in the armed forces, which meant that nearly every American family had a son, father, or close relative in service. In 1944, President Roosevelt and the otherwise anti–New Deal American Legion formed an alliance to push Congress to reward military service through a comprehensive entitlement program. FDR and liberals saw this as a unique opportunity to enact one last great New Deal reform. Conservatives considered the expanded aid a patriotic obligation. Together, the coalition outmaneuvered opponents such as Democratic Representative John Rankin of Mississippi, who feared that federal aid to African American veterans would challenge segregation. Ultimately, the 1944 Servicemen's Readjustment Act, or GI Bill of Rights, as everyone called it, benefited millions of veterans and their families and influenced where they worked, lived, and studied. In the next chapter, we will see how government and private financing of veterans' home mortgages literally reshaped the urban and suburban landscape.

The GI Bill provided unemployment pay for veterans, hiring preferences in civil-service jobs, new hospital and health benefits, low-interest loans to start businesses and purchase homes, and tuition and living stipends for college and vocational education. Demobilized soldiers unable to find work received $20 per week—more than the minimum wage of 40 cents per hour—

for up to one year. Participation in the so-called 52-20 club put spending money in veterans' pockets, gave them a sense of dignity, and enabled them to search for jobs as they readjusted to civilian life. This program paid out nearly $4 billion in the postwar years.

Except for those attending religious or teacher training schools, few Americans of moderate means attended college before 1945. The GI Bill offered students who enrolled in college or a trade school $110 per month to live on, plus additional money for books, fees, tuition, and dependents' support. The resulting surge of veterans into both public and private universities created a far larger and more democratic system of higher education—a change with great social consequences for the rest of the century. In the late 1940s, over 2 million students, half the total male enrollment at institutions of higher learning, attended college on the GI Bill. Nearly half the veterans in school were married, which forced colleges to drop their prohibitions or strict control over married students. Family housing units replaced all male dormitories; diapers, rather than team pennants, hung out of windows. Freshman hazing, a common experience before the war, almost ceased. One battle-hardened veteran of the Iwo Jima campaign recalled how he and his friends handled demands from younger upperclassmen that they wear beanies and perform menial chores: the veterans formed a platoon and chased the would-be hazers off campus. College professors judged the GI generation, which was determined to get degrees quickly and begin careers, as the most motivated students they had ever encountered.

As students flooded into crowded facilities, state legislatures were pressured to fund public universities more generously. By 1947, the total federal outlay for veterans' education reached $2.25 billion. When the program ended in 1956, the Veterans Administration (VA) had spent $14 billion. The professionals and technicians trained during these years earned far higher incomes than unskilled laborers, thus allowing the government to recoup much of its outlay in increased tax revenues.

Because only a small number of women had served in uniform, they received modest benefits from the GI Bill. Still, the number of women attending college increased after 1945. They were often steered away from careers that placed them in competition with men, however. Tacit or explicit sex discrimination and quotas led to a drop in the number of women enrolled in law, medical, and business schools. Harvard Business School did not admit a female student until 1963.

These attitudes were often bolstered by experts who insisted that women had to leave the work force and return to the home, for their own good and for the health and well-being of the nation. As sociologist Ferdinand Lundberg and psychiatrist Marynia Farnham explained in their 1947 bestseller, *Modern Woman: The Lost Sex*, "[W]omen are the pivot around which much of the unhappiness of the day revolves, like a captive planet. To a significant extent they are responsible for it. . . . Women as a whole (with exceptions) are maladjusted, much more so than men. For men have appropriate means to social adjustment: economic, political, and scientific power, and athletic prowess." Farnham and Lundberg saw no point in eliminating the employment and professional barriers that inhibited women. Instead, they urged women to seek happiness in the domestic realm by pursuing the traditional rolés of homemaker and mother.

Popular Culture and the Age of Television

During the first half of the twentieth century, mass-circulation periodicals, motion pictures, and the radio dominated popular culture. When the war ended, most adult Americans read daily newspapers (usually in the evening); 34 million households (out of 38 million) owned at least one radio that they used to listen to music, comedy, sports, and soap operas; and the average American still went to a movie theater at least once each week. Soon, however, a new electronic medium—television—began to displace other forms of popular entertainment.

Because its large size made it difficult to distribute a newspaper widely, the United States lacked any truly "national" newspapers before the technological revolution in printing in the 1970s. In the years just after World War II, most households subscribed to local newspapers. Aside from a few big city dailies, reporting focused on local social events, sports, weather, crime, and gossip. Except for the staff members of a handful of newspapers that served black communities in cities like New York, Chicago, and Pittsburgh, nearly all journalists were white males. In the 1950s, the *Washington Post* hired its first African American reporter, but forced him to use a segregated washroom. The few female journalists were usually assigned to cover fashion and homemaking.

Radio remained more popular than newspapers or movies until the early 1950s. People tuned into four national networks and numerous local stations. Most programming consisted of popular music, sporting events, radio dramas that focused on romance or adventure, quiz shows, and situation comedies.

Since the 1920s, five major Hollywood studios dominated the movie production industry and owned most of the theaters that showed films. Hollywood also dominated the global movie industry before World War II and for decades afterward. Domestic audiences grew larger during the war, and by 1945, the typical urban American viewed two movies per week. Industry production codes regulated the sexual and moral content of films, stipulating how long a kiss might last, and meted out punishment to those who broke the law or acted immorally. Films typically portrayed people of color as servile and lazy, Asians as suspicious, and women as the "weaker sex" whose lives should revolve around husbands and families.

Beginning in 1948, television revolutionized popular culture, eclipsing radio, motion pictures, newspapers, and magazines. Although the technology had been pioneered in the 1920s—and Franklin Roosevelt had even appeared in an experimental broadcast in 1939—television did not flourish until the price of receivers was reduced as a result of wartime production techniques, and broadcasters received permission to charge for commercials. In 1946, the Federal Communications Commission (FCC) licensed twenty-six television stations, which began airing shows the next year. In 1948, both the Democrats and the Republicans held their presidential nominating conventions in Philadelphia because the city possessed a cable hookup that allowed viewing by an audience of 10 million. By 1949, about 1 million homes, mostly in large cities, watched television on sixty-nine local stations. After that, the number of viewers increased exponentially. The percentage of homes with TV sets grew from 0.4 percent in 1948 to 9 percent in 1950, from 23.5 percent in 1951 to 34.2 percent the next year.

At first, most TVs were purchased by taverns and wealthy families. Bars took out newspaper notices encouraging patrons to come and watch television while drinking. Well-off families often flaunted their wealth by hosting neighborhood "TV parties" for those unable to afford sets of their own. By the early 1950s, prices declined and television ownership became common. Parents with young children were especially eager to acquire the new technology, either as a form of in-house babysitting for the kids or evening relaxation for the exhausted adults.

Airwaves were soon filled with visual versions of radio shows. Comedy-variety, situation comedies, westerns, soap operas, quiz shows, sporting

Television's first star, "Uncle Miltie" (Milton Berle), hoofs it with Ethel Merman, about 1950. / © Bettmann/CORBIS

events, and police dramas became—and have remained—standard TV fare. Uncle Miltie (Milton Berle), starred in the first big television hit, *The Milton Berle Show*, which debuted in 1948. The show was so popular that stories spread of water pressure in cities plummeting during commercial breaks when millions of viewers rushed to the bathroom. Although television was not the sole cause, its radically growing popularity cut deeply into the size of audiences that attended vaudeville and movies or read newspapers. Films and television shows, especially in the 1950s, both reflected and perpetuated various cultural stereotypes.

The Origins of the Cold War and the Birth of Containment

In September 1946, a year after the Japanese surrendered aboard the battleship *Missouri* in Tokyo Bay, former vice president and Commerce Secretary Henry A. Wallace addressed a crowd in New York's Madison Square Garden. The escalating war of words between Washington and Moscow deeply troubled Wallace. President Truman, he feared, had fallen under the spell of anti-Soviet hard-liners such as Secretary of State James F. Byrnes and Navy Secretary James Forrestal, both of whom urged a get-tough policy. But "getting tough," Wallace declared, "never brought anything real and lasting—whether for school yard bullies or businessmen or world powers. The tougher we get, the tougher the Russians will get." Instead, he urged both nations to modify their behavior, perhaps by adopting a spheres-of-influence approach that accepted each other's special interests.

Whether right or wrong, Wallace sought a middle ground where none existed. His audience, which included many members of the American Communist Party, booed him for suggesting that the Soviet Union had any need to mend its ways. Truman similarly rejected the notion that the United States bore any blame for tensions with its former ally. The president fired Wallace from his cabinet, complaining to an aide that the "Reds, phonies, and 'parlor pinks' . . . seem to be banded together and are becoming a national danger. I am afraid they are a sabotage front for Uncle Joe Stalin."

Months before this incident, the president ruminated that he was "tired of babying the Soviets." Unless "Russia is faced with an iron fist and strong language," he reasoned, "another war is in the making." With considerable insight, he told his wife and daughter that a "totalitarian state is no different whether you call it Nazi, Fascist, or Communist." In fact, he claimed to see no difference between the Soviet regime, its Czarist predecessor, "or the one Hitler spoke for."

As World War II ended, the national security policies of Washington and Moscow were on a collision course. Stalin was determined to forge a security sphere around the Soviet Union by dominating Eastern Europe. He crushed all political movements he could not control. Although Stalin offered little encouragement to communists outside this sphere, his prediction of a coming world revolution terrified Western audiences, who had looked forward to a world of political pluralism, reduced trade barriers, and reconciliation with the defeated Axis powers.

At the same time as Americans came to fear Soviet expansion abroad, an anticommunist hysteria erupted at home. Fueled by legitimate worries about the Soviet Union as well as by political opportunism, the domestic Red Scare distorted national politics and culture for almost a decade. Even at the time, it was clear that communism was no threat *in* the United States. Prodded by political demagogues, however, the federal and state governments as well as private industry conducted a political witch hunt in search of real and imaginary Reds. This activity frustrated efforts by progressives—including, to some degree, President Truman himself—to expand social reforms of the New Deal. It also led to political intolerance and the suppression of civil liberties. The outbreak of the Korean War in June 1950, and its bloody but inconclusive nature, invigorated the Red Scare and set the stage for the Republican Party's return to national power.

The Cold War dominated American foreign policy from 1945 until the Soviet Union collapsed in 1991. It produced a high level of tension between the United States and its communist rivals. It also spurred a nuclear arms race, divided much of the world into antagonistic alliances, and led to competition for influence in the poor, postcolonial nations of Africa, Asia, the Middle East, and Latin America, collectively known as the Third World. The Cold War shaped the foreign and domestic policies of the two superpowers, including their political, economic, and military institutions. It provided justification for American leaders to exercise power far away from home, and gave Soviet leaders, from Joseph Stalin to Mikhail Gorbachev, an external enemy that justified their internal repression. Wars fought by the United States in Korea and Vietnam were in part proxy contests to frustrate perceived threats from the Soviets and Chinese communists.

Although six great industrial powers (the United States, Germany, Japan, France, Great Britain, and the Soviet Union) fought World War II, only the Soviet Union and the United States emerged from the conflict with enhanced strength or additional territory. The United States was powerful, judged by economic, technological, and military measures and by the fact that it controlled much of the world's energy supply. The Soviet Union controlled more territory in 1945 than it had in 1941, but its devastating wartime losses—of at least 25 million people and much of its farm equipment and factories—gave it an economic base only one-quarter in size compared to the United States. Like those of the United States, the Soviet armed forces demobilized rapidly after 1945. The Soviet Union also lacked much of an air force or navy and, until 1949, did not possess atomic bombs. In terms of power, the Soviet Union was a distant second to the United States.

American anxiety about Soviet intentions in 1945 and 1946 derived in part from the fact that the Red army occupied much of Eastern Europe and Germany and well as northeastern China. These positions placed Soviet power close to the industrial heartland of Western Europe and Japan. Few American

(cont. on page 60)

The Rise of the Gunbelt

When Japanese troops surrendered on August 15, 1945, journalist Edward R. Murrow remarked that "seldom, if ever, has a war ended leaving the victors with such a sense of uncertainty and fear, with such a realization that the future is obscure and that survival is not assured." The threat of nuclear annihilation made the half-century of peace after World War II a uniquely uncertain period. In the 1954 film *Strategic Air Command*, actor Jimmy Stewart personified the sacrifices demanded of Americans in the Cold War. Stewart's character, "Dutch" (also Ronald Reagan's nickname), abandoned a promising career as a major league baseball pitcher to serve in the Air Force. When his wife protested, arguing that no war was being fought, Dutch spoke for a generation of Americans: "But there is a kind of war. We've got to stay ready to fight without fighting. That's even tougher. That's why I made this decision."

On the eve of the war, U.S. military spending would hardly count as a "rounding error" in today's federal budget. Massive defense outlays during World War II segued into the forty-year-long Cold War arms race, punctuated by hot wars in Korea and Vietnam. Before the collapse of the Soviet Union in 1991, military spending peaked at around $300 billion. After a small decline during the 1990s, spending rose sharply under President George W. Bush. Following the September 2001 terrorist attacks on the United States, Bush requested a $400 billion defense budget. By comparison, America spends about $10 billion annually on foreign aid.

Military spending has never been about only national security or the size of the armed forces. Nuclear weapons, computers, and aerospace technology required close cooperation among the Pentagon, private industry, and universities. Astronomers, mathematicians, computer programmers, physicists, and oceanographers played as large a part in modern warfare as generals and foot soldiers.

The huge sums of money directed toward specific technologies, industries, and regions have reshaped the political and economic landscape of post–World War II America. Just as journalists and geographers refer to the Sunbelt, Frostbelt, and Rustbelt to characterize the climate and economic conditions in different regions, defense spending has created wholly new industrial complexes in parts of California, the Pacific Northwest, New England, Texas, Arizona, New Mexico, Georgia, Florida, Utah, and Colorado. This flow of dollars into what some have called America's Gunbelt contributed to the deindustrialization of what, in earlier times, had been the nation's Midwest industrial heartland. President Eisenhower voiced concern over this phenomenon when he left office in 1961, cautioning Americans about the costs and risks of an immense "military-industrial complex."

During and after World War II, the federal government recognized the value of pure and applied research by establishing several national laboratories such as those in Los Alamos and Sandia, New Mexico; Livermore, California; Brookhaven, New York; Oak Ridge, Tennessee; and Argonne, Illinois. Defense research money also flowed into institutions such as the Massachusetts Institute of Technology (MIT), the California Institute of Technology (Cal Tech), the University of California, and the University of Chicago. During World War II, these universities created special units that focused on the development of atomic power, radar, rocketry, and proximity fuses. During the 1950s and 1960s, government funds allowed MIT and Cal Tech to create major research programs in defense-related areas such as particle physics, materials science, and optical sciences. By the 1970s and 1980s, the Defense Department, National Science Foundation, and Energy Department sponsored university research in areas such as recombinant DNA, superconductors, supercomputers, and robotics.

Nike missile production line in Santa Monica, California, 1955. With so many defense plants, southern California became the "buckle on the Gunbelt." /
© Bettmann/CORBIS

Most defense dollars—especially the lucrative aerospace and electronics contracts—flowed to New England, the South, the Southwest, and the West. Until the 1990s, about a dozen large defense contractors dominated the field. Then, many merged; in effect, only a handful of giant companies actually build planes, missiles, ships, and other equipment for the Department of Defense. Winning or losing a contract to build a new fighter plane can make or break the fortunes of both a contractor and a community like San Diego, Seattle, or Houston.

Moreover, defense spending had a significant impact on gender, race, and class relations. Military production for items like rockets and airplanes tends to be more capital than labor intensive—requiring more money and a smaller number of highly trained workers than equivalent civilian production. As a consequence, defense spending often channels money away from industries relying on less skilled blue-collar workers. As recently as 1990, women made up only 15 percent and minorities just 3 percent of the aerospace work force.

Corporations have invested more of their own resources in technology and plants likely to attract defense dollars. This, in turn, meant less investment in older plants in midwestern and northeastern cities that employed a more diverse industrial work force. Contributing to the loss of blue-collar jobs in older cities, the flow of military contracts and employment to the Gunbelt had an especially negative effect on African American workers in cities like Detroit, Philadelphia, Cleveland, Chicago, and Milwaukee.

Los Angeles and southern California boast the nation's biggest concentration of military contractors and defense-supported universities. In 1941, barely 5 percent of America's academic and other research scientists received federal grant money. By the early 1960s, about half of the nation's scientists relied on government research support. These funds had a huge impact on local business conditions. In the early 1990s, for example, following the collapse of the Soviet Union, the decline in military procurement dealt a sharp blow to the California economy.

Defense contractors, university researchers, military leaders, and politicians have promoted increasingly complicated and expensive weapons systems. The two most costly and controversial programs of the past few decades have been the Stealth, or B-2 bomber, and the antimissile system (called the Strategic Defense Initiative [SDI] by supporters and Star Wars by critics). Both systems were conceived in the late 1970s. Eventually, the Air Force acquired a few dozen Stealth bombers at a cost of about $1 billion per plane. Difficult to fly and expensive to maintain, the B-2 is combat-ready barely one-third of the time. Although designed as a strategic weapon for use against the Soviet Union, it found a niche role as a tactical bomber in the military operations in Kosovo and Afghanistan. In the two decades since President Reagan proposed building an antimissile shield, the government has spent $100 billion on missile defense but has yet to deploy a workable system. If the technological problems can be solved, a missile defense will cost several hundred billion dollars more to deploy.

The best known, most cost-effective, and longest lasting Cold War weapon, the B-52 bomber, was conceived at the inception of that struggle and continues to play a key role in military operations. The plane has "starred" in several films, including *Dr. Strangelove*. The B-52 "Stratofortress," as its manufacturer called it, was conceived over a weekend in 1947, when Boeing engineers responded to a call to design a plane capable of reaching the Soviet Union from the United States and delivering a massive nuclear payload. The swept-back wing design for the long-range bomber was eventually applied to a new generation of large commercial jets such as the 707.

The first B-52s rolled off assembly lines in 1952 and the last models were built a decade later. The plane's immense dimensions made it appear like some flying prehistoric creature as it rumbled down extralong runways. Forty feet tall and 185 feet from wingtip to wingtip, the B-52's eight jet engines allowed it to fly at 650 miles per hour, and as high as 50,000 feet or as low as 300 feet. It could deliver a 70,000-pound nuclear or conventional payload a distance of 9,000 miles. The planes were produced for the remarkably cheap price tag of $8 million each (about $50 million in today's dollars), and Boeing built 744 of the aircraft, of which nearly 100 are still flying. Originally, the plane was designed to last for about five thousand hours of flying before metal fatigue set it. The use of upgraded components has more than tripled its life expectancy. The B-52 has received three major overhauls, and its avionics and electronics are periodically upgraded. These modifications led wags to joke that Boeing figured out how to sell the same plane to the Air Force three times.

Air Force and civilian planners recognized the awe-inspiring physical and psychological power of the B-52. Originally on alert twenty-four hours a day to deter or retaliate against an aggressor, the warplane was never used for its intended mission—dropping hydrogen bombs on the Soviet heartland. But it has played major roles in every regional conflict since the 1950s. The B-52 was used extensively to drop conventional bombs during the Vietnam War. It served as a workhorse during the conflicts in the Persian Gulf in 1991, in Kosovo in the late 1990s, in Afghanistan after September 2001, and in the war with Iraq in 2003. When a B-52 is deployed, a pilot recalled, "the other side knows you're serious."

Military officials have mothballed many of the more expensive weapons systems built since the 1980s, but the B-52 remains airworthy and can be kept operational until 2037, more than eighty years after the first models flew. In fact, the B-52 may be the first operational warplane that the *grandchildren* of the original pilots might fly in combat. When Eisenhower cautioned about the influence of the military-industrial complex, he also called for weapons that delivered "more bang for the buck." The B-52 certainly fit the bill.

leaders expected Stalin to seize these areas by force. Instead, they worried that the physical, economic, social, and political weakness in Asia and Europe would create a vacuum into which Soviet power would inevitably flow. To make matters worse, radical nationalist groups were competing for power in parts of Asia and the Middle East, areas that had or soon would gain independence from the British, French, Dutch, and Japanese. U.S. officials worried that if the Soviet Union controlled the industrial potential of Western Europe and Japan or the resources of the Third World, it could become strong enough to alter the global balance of power.

Although both the United States and the Soviet Union nursed mutual fears extending as far back as the Bolshevik Revolution of 1917, leaders in neither Washington nor Moscow had a master plan for world domination after 1945. Nevertheless, each side defined security in ways that threatened the other. Thus, Stalin's determination to extract reparations from Germany and to protect Soviet borders by forcibly creating puppet buffer states in Eastern Europe struck many Americans as both brutal and provocative. Similarly, American desires to rebuild the economies of Europe and Japan and to construct overseas military bases looked to Stalin like a plan to encircle and threaten the Soviet Union. During 1946, when Washington blocked the flow of industrial reparations from western Germany to the Soviet Union, Moscow responded by squeezing resources out of eastern Germany and its new satellites in Eastern Europe. Stalin invoked the fear of "capitalist encirclement" in a speech to the Russian people in February 1946, when he called for greater sacrifices to meet the outside threat.

Political leaders on both sides of what soon became called the Iron Curtain often found it useful to overdramatize the immediacy of the threat. For example, former British prime minister Winston Churchill encouraged anti-Soviet sentiments as part of a campaign to secure a multibillion-dollar loan from the United States. Speaking to an audience that included President Truman in Fulton, Missouri, on March 5, 1946, Churchill declared that "from Stettin [Poland] in the Baltic to Trieste [Italy] in the Adriatic, an Iron Curtain has descended" that separated the free and slave world. He proposed an alliance of all English-speaking peoples, backed by the atomic bomb that "God has willed to the United States."

Churchill ignored the fact that while brutal, the Iron Curtain was as much a defensive barrier for a weak Soviet Union to hide behind as a starting block for future expansion. In fact, Stalin used the rigid division of Europe in part to hide from the people of Eastern Europe and Russia the truth about the backwardness of the Soviet empire. This isolation allowed Stalin to pump up the threat of "capitalist encirclement" and call on his subjects to work harder for defense in place of seeking greater liberty or more consumer goods.

In the aftermath of these accusations, the Soviet Union rejected membership in two American-sponsored international economic organizations: the World Bank and the International Monetary Fund. These institutions were designed to stabilize currencies and to promote world trade and economic development. The U.S. dollar, redeemable for gold at $35 per ounce, served as the world's benchmark currency until 1971.

Stalin, who pushed his scientists to develop an atomic bomb, also rejected the so-called Baruch Plan, an American proposal made to the United Nations in 1946 for placing all forms of nuclear power under a U.S.-controlled international commission. In the midst of the U.N. debate over the plan, the United States conducted a series of dramatic atomic bomb tests on the Pacific atoll of Bikini, a name quickly popularized by a French bathing suit designer. Even though the odds of a nuclear deal at the United Nations were slim to begin with, the provocative Bikini tests made them almost impossible.

The two sides exchanged accusations, and each jockeyed for position. As noted above, the Americans halted the dismantling of German and Japanese industry for shipment as reparations to Russia. At Nuremberg, Germany, and Tokyo, Japan, the Soviets and Americans joined in the trial and punishment of a small number of Axis leaders as war criminals. But cooperation soon faded. Washington had initially refused to employ Nazis for scientific work. But soon Americans began recruiting hundreds of German rocket scientists, physicists, and physicians to work in or for the United States. "Operation Paperclip," the project's code name, found a home for physicians who had conducted horrible medical experiments on concentration camp inmates, as well as for engineers like Wernher von Braun, who worked slave laborers to death while he supervised the development of the deadly V-1 and V-2 rockets. Japanese doctors who conducted germ warfare tests on Allied POWs were given immunity from prosecution after they provided their data to American scientists. The Soviets, who had suffered so gravely under the Nazi assault, adopted similar recruitment practices.

In 1946, the Americans responded to what they saw as Soviet threats against Iran and Turkey. During World War II, the Allies had deposed the pro-Nazi shah and jointly occupied Iran. British and American forces departed early in 1946, but the Soviets lingered, demanding oil concessions like those held already by the British. To force action, they backed a separatist movement in northern Iran. Moscow also pressed Turkey to grant it joint control over the Dardenelles, a strategic strait connecting the Mediterranean and Black seas. Some American diplomats feared a Soviet sweep across Turkey and Iran, which would give it control over much of the Middle East and its oil reserves.

Declaring that the United States might as well find out now rather than later whether Stalin was bent on world conquest, Truman issued tough warnings against Soviet meddling and sent a naval task force into the Mediterranean. In fact, Stalin had limited goals in the region and no desire to fight the far stronger United States. When he backed off, some Americans leaders concluded that the Soviet dictator had expansionist goals that could only be curbed with superior strength. Meanwhile, American oil companies used the opportunity to muscle in on the British and gain concessions in Iran, Saudi Arabia, and Kuwait.

. In spite of angry rhetoric and regional disputes, both the Soviet Union and the United States sharply reduced the size of their armed forces and their military budgets after 1945. Americans possessed an atomic monopoly but built few atomic bombs in the immediate aftermath of the war and mothballed many of its long-range aircraft. The Soviets retained a larger ground force than the Americans and the British but devoted much of it to internal police duties. American pressure may have influenced Soviet actions in Iran and Turkey, but Stalin also voluntarily withdrew troops from Manchuria, parts of Norway, Finland, Hungary, and Czechoslovakia. As of 1947, the two antagonists probably lacked the capacity or desire to initiate a major war.

During the two years following the end of the war, economic chaos and political instability afflicted much of the world. In Europe and Japan, the physical destruction of war; the uncertainties of military occupation; and a shortage of money, fuel, and raw materials stalled economic recovery. Rebellions and civil war in French Indochina, India, the Dutch East Indies, and China impeded the flow of raw materials to Western Europe and Japan. A nearly bankrupt Great Britain had to abandon India and Palestine. To stem starvation in occupied Germany and Japan, the United States spent nearly $1 billion per year. Even though the Soviet Union did not cause these problems, Americans feared Stalin would benefit from them.

George F. Kennan, then second in command at the U.S. embassy in Moscow, sent his superiors a report early in 1946 analyzing the worsening world situation. In his so-called long telegram (that he published as an article anonymously in 1947), Kennan argued that Stalin purposely provoked tension with the West to justify his harsh repression of the Soviet people and the captive eastern Europeans. Although Soviet power remained "impervious to the logic of reason," it was "highly sensitive to the logic of force." Rather than trying to placate the Kremlin, Kennan asserted, Washington should implement a policy of "long-term, patient but firm and vigilant containment." This suggestion soon became the operating principle behind American foreign policy.

Like several of Truman's advisers, Kennan recognized that the immediate threat to Europe and Japan was not Soviet military power but a growing economic crisis or "dollar gap." This gap constituted the difference between the value of American exports and the amount of dollars that foreign customers had available to pay for them. As 1947 began, the gap stood at about $8 billion and threatened to halt world trade. Foreign trade—including American exports—could continue only if the U.S. government and private lenders provided credit. They would risk doing so only as long as Europe and Japan showed signs of recovery. Once credits disappeared, foreign nations would be unable to trade with the United States or import the industrial raw materials they needed to spur recovery. This could quickly bring on the kind of global economic collapse that fed the Great Depression and led to World War II. The Soviets, American leaders feared, might take advantage of such chaos by using the carrot of economic assistance and the stick of military intimidation to gain control of vulnerable areas of Europe and Asia. If the Soviets harnessed European and Japanese industry and Middle Eastern petroleum to their own economy, Kennan warned, they could tip the balance of world power in their favor.

Containment, in short, depended on the reconstruction of the German and Japanese economies, what Undersecretary of State Dean Acheson called the "great workshops of Europe and Asia." Yet Congress, controlled by Republicans since 1946, balked at long-term foreign aid, which was a new idea at the time. When GOP critics accused Truman of promoting New Deal–type welfare programs abroad, the plan stalled.

Since 1944, a brutal civil war had raged between conservative Greek monarchists and the left-wing National Liberation Front (EAM). EAM included both communists and noncommunists. Britain had supported the monarchists, but on February 21, 1947, the financially hard-pressed government in London informed Washington that it could no longer aid Greece. The State Department's Dean Acheson took charge of selling a Greek aid program to Congress, with the hope that it would pave the way for a far larger, more comprehensive assistance package.

In discussions with the president and members of Congress, Acheson insisted that the United States and the Soviet Union were divided by an "unbridgeable ideological chasm." In this battle between democracy and dictatorship, any shirking of responsibility would prove fatal. If the United States walked away from Greece, then like "apples in a barrel infected by one rotten one," the "corruption . . . would infect Iran and all to the east." Greece's struggle was portrayed as a proxy battle between Soviet and Western interests.

Republican Senator Arthur Vandenberg, chairman of the Foreign Relations Committee, urged Truman to make a dramatic case to Congress if he wanted GOP support for foreign aid. According to legend, Vandenberg declared that if the Democrats wanted to provide a WPA-style welfare program to Greece, Truman needed to "scare the hell out of the American people."

When Truman spoke to Congress on March 12, 1947, he highlighted the "global struggle between freedom and totalitarianism." Portraying all communists as Soviet-directed enemies of economic and political freedom, the president declared that it must be the "policy of the United States" to "support free peoples who are resisting attempted subjugation by armed minorities or by outside pressure." Galvanized by this so-called Truman Doctrine, Congress approved $400 million for aid to Greece and Turkey.

As it turned out, Joseph Tito, the Communist leader of Yugoslavia—rather than Stalin—was the main supporter of the Greek rebels. Tito hoped to build his own mini-empire by adding parts of Greece to his proposed Balkan federation. Stalin took a dim view of empire-building by his puppets and had discouraged support for the Greek communists in order to avoid provoking the United States. Angered by his underling's provocative actions, the Soviet leader denounced Tito as a renegade and tried to topple him. The desperate Tito cut off support to the Greek rebels and soon solicited American aid. The lack of support from Tito for their rivals coupled with U.S. military assistance led to victory by the conservative Athens government.

The real impact of the Truman Doctrine, however, was felt elsewhere. On June 5, 1947, speaking at Harvard University, Secretary of State George C. Marshall proposed an ambitious plan for economic recovery that soon took his name. To prevent the Soviets from taking advantage of economic collapse, Marshall called on Congress to fund a multiyear reconstruction program for Western Europe and Japan. During the next few months, this idea evolved into a $27 billion aid request.

The Republican-controlled Congress hesitated to fund what became known formally as the European Recovery Program (informally as the Marshall Plan). Fortunately for Truman, Stalin helped ensure positive action. The Soviet leader worried that if U.S. aid succeeded in rebuilding Western Europe and Japan, pressure would build in communist-controlled and nonaligned parts of Eastern Europe to join an American-led trade and military bloc. To discourage this development, Stalin pressed the large communist parties and labor unions in France and Italy to oppose the aid scheme. In February 1948, when the Czech government showed interest in aid through the Marshall Plan, Stalin ordered a coup by local communists that pulled neutral Czechoslovakia behind the Iron Curtain. In March, the commander of American forces in Germany warned of a "subtle change in Soviet behavior" that might indicate plans to launch a war with "dramatic suddenness." Truman then called on Congress to fund the Marshall Plan quickly, before Moscow gobbled up Europe (see Map 2.1).

Congress passed a trimmed-down aid program that included funds to rebuild the Japanese economy. Over the next several years, the United States provided more than $15 billion in reconstruction aid (around $100 billion in 2003 dollars) in the form of credits, raw materials, and agricultural commodities. The American commitment also spurred greater regional cooperation among European and Japanese leaders.

At this time, Congress also enacted the National Security Act of 1947, which reformed the squabbling military and intelligence agencies. The act created a unified Department of Defense, led by a civilian cabinet secretary, and a National Security Council (NSC) to advise the president on foreign policy matters. It also provided for a Central Intelligence Agency (CIA) to gather and analyze information and conduct secret, or covert, missions abroad. Along with a new military draft, Congress authorized expansion of the atomic arsenal from fifteen weapons to over two hundred bombs by 1950.

Stalin reacted to these events by imposing tighter economic and political controls in areas under his rule. He purged the few independent-minded leaders in Eastern Europe and also tried to drive the Western powers out of Berlin by blockading land routes into the city. A prosperous West Berlin, located deep inside the Soviets' East German occupation zone, shone as a tempting beacon of liberty. When the United States announced a currency reform for the Western zones of Germany and Berlin, Stalin attempted to force the Western powers out of the city. Claiming that the currency reform violated earlier agreements, he voided Western rail and road access privileges into West Berlin. However, the Soviets did not impede air corridors into the encircled city because these access routes were guaranteed in a separate agreement.

During the1948 Berlin Blockade, children cheer a U.S. cargo plane carrying supplies. Some pilots dropped candy as they landed. / © Bettmann/CORBIS

Occupation commander General Lucius Clay feared the imminent fall of Berlin and warned that "western Germany will be next." He urged Truman to allow him to shoot his way through Soviet barriers. Truman made a symbolic show of force by sending sixty atomic capable B-29 bombers—without nuclear weapons—to airfields in Britain. But rather than challenge the Soviet blockade directly, he opted to airlift food and fuel into Berlin. The president guessed, correctly, that Stalin did not want war. In fact, Soviet forces did not impede the airlift.

To Stalin's disappointment and Truman's delight, the yearlong Berlin blockade and airlift proved a public relations disaster for Moscow. On their final landing approach to Berlin, American pilots threw Hershey bars and chewing gum to children gathered at the ends of the runways, and the city and its people were transformed from former Nazi enemies into symbols of resistance to Soviet bullying. In May 1949, the United States convinced western Europeans to support the creation of a powerful new west German state, the Federal Republic of Germany. Even Stalin realized that his actions were counterproductive. Belatedly, the dictator called off the blockade and a month later, in June 1949, created a puppet German Democratic Republic in the former Russian occupation zone.

At this point, the United States was well on the way to winning the Cold War. As reconstruction aid poured into Western Europe and Japan, the European and Japanese economies came to life. American policy promoted regional

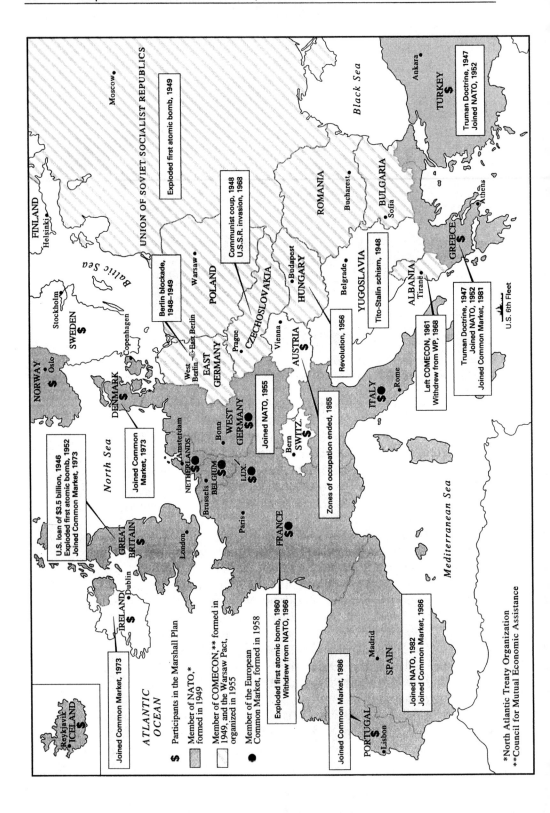

economic and political cooperation that broke down many of the barriers between West Germany and its neighbors. As living conditions improved, the influence of communist parties in France, Italy, and Japan declined. Stalin's effort to keep Europe and Japan weak, divided, and isolated from the United States had backfired. In April 1949, now Secretary of State Dean Acheson oversaw the creation of the North Atlantic Treaty Organization (NATO), which bound Britain, France, Belgium, the Netherlands, Italy, Portugal, Denmark, Iceland, Norway, and Canada to the United States in a common defense against Soviet attack. Over the following decades, Greece, Turkey, West Germany, and Spain joined the alliance. After the collapse of the Soviet Union, several of its former East European satellites joined as well. As Acheson boasted to Congress, America now enjoyed a "preponderance of power" over the Soviet Union.

It seems a cruel irony that charges of "softness on communism" stuck to the Democratic Party and the Truman administration. As historian Stephen Ambrose observed, the president and his party "forced the Russians out of Iran in 1946, came to the aid of the Greek government in 1947, met the Red Army's challenge in Berlin and inaugurated the Marshall Plan in 1948, joined the North Atlantic Treaty Organization in 1949, and hurled back the Communist invader of South Korea in 1950, all under the banner of the Truman Doctrine which had proclaimed American resistance to any advance of Communism anywhere."

National Politics in the Early Cold War and the Origins of the Red Scare

Many Americans felt politically adrift after Roosevelt's death in April 1945. As noted earlier, Truman assumed the presidency almost unknown to the public. Just weeks after Japan surrendered, Truman asked Congress to enact twenty-one domestic programs, including an increase in the minimum wage; more expenditures for hospitals, small businesses, and agricultural price supports; and a full-employment bill. A coalition of Republicans and southern Democrats buried most of these proposals. The full-employment bill would have committed the federal government to a policy of economic planning and management designed to ensure jobs for all. When finally passed, the Employment Act of 1946 created a presidential Council of Economic Advisers but merely endorsed the goal of maintaining full employment and production.

During the first year and a half of peace, most Americans were more troubled by inflation than unemployment. Wartime savings and veterans benefits, along with new jobs in the private sector, sustained purchasing power and prevented high levels of unemployment. But shortages of food and consumer goods such as automobiles and vacuum cleaners drove up prices. Major strikes

◀ **Map 2.1**
   Divided Europe

in the automobile, electrical, coal, and transportation industries created additional bottlenecks. Truman flip-flopped on the question of maintaining wartime price controls, and many Americans blamed him for the combination of shortages and high prices.

On the eve of the November 1946 congressional election, pollsters reported that only one-third of the public approved of Truman's job performance. Republicans captured the nation's mood in a campaign slogan that asked "Had Enough?" Most voters had. They elected eleven new Republicans to the senate and fifty-six to the House. For the first time since 1930, the GOP controlled both houses of Congress. Republican presidential prospects seemed bright. One poll taken in 1947 found that only 3 percent of Americans listed Truman among the most admired leaders of recent decades.

Despite promises by Republican leaders such as Ohio Senator Robert Taft to unravel the New Deal, Republicans made only tepid efforts to restore an unregulated economy. They did roll back some important labor rights by passing the Taft-Hartley Act of 1947. Enacted over Truman's veto, the law abolished the closed shop (which compelled workers to join a union), barred secondary boycotts, made unions liable for monetary damages, established procedures to decertify unions, and gave the president power to impose an eighty-day cooling-off period in labor disputes before a strike could be called. The Taft-Hartley Act also required union officers to take a noncommunist oath.

The law bolstered conservative labor leaders and made union-organizing drives more difficult, especially in the South. The Taft-Hartley Act encouraged state legislatures in the Sunbelt to pass right-to-work laws that barred making union membership a requirement for employment. To get out of union contracts, many labor-intensive industries, such as textiles, relocated to the Sunbelt.

In the run-up to the 1948 election, Truman seemed almost as unpopular within his party as he did among Republicans. When asked who the Democrats might run in 1948, some joked, "[W]e'll dig somebody up," a grim reference to Franklin Roosevelt. The president found comfort in an analysis prepared by his young adviser, Clark Clifford. In November 1947, Clifford urged Truman to step up his attack on Republican efforts to unravel New Deal reforms while offering a liberal program of his own.

During 1948, Truman vetoed sixty-two Republican-sponsored bills, damning them as efforts to kill the New Deal. He rallied the New Deal coalition by proposing programs to aid small farmers, raise the minimum wage, liberalize immigration policy, enhance civil rights, reduce taxes for workers, and increase Social Security benefits. As Republicans voted down each proposal, Truman's standing rose among key Democratic voting blocs. Organized labor appreciated his depiction of the Taft-Hartley Act as a "slave labor act." Jewish Americans and others of east European origin applauded his support for the Displaced Persons (immigration) Act and his prompt recognition of Israel. African Americans cheered his creation of an advisory Committee on Civil Rights and his endorsement of its call for federal laws against lynching and the poll tax and the creation of a Fair Employment Practices Commission. Small farmers admired his effort to raise commodity price supports. The president's sponsorship of the Truman Doctrine, Marshall Plan, and Berlin airlift convinced the public that he offered the right mix of liberalism at home and resistance to communism abroad.

At the same time as Truman reached out to labor and minorities, liberal Democrats moved closer to the political center by taking a stand against communism. Labor leaders such as Walter Reuther and David Dubinsky; public figures such as Eleanor Roosevelt and her son, Franklin, Jr.; and influential theologians and academics such as Reinhold Niebur and Arthur Schlesinger, Jr., organized the Americans for Democratic Action (ADA) in 1947. Although many ADA members did not especially admire Truman, they preferred him to Henry Wallace, whom they dismissed as a misguided apologist for the Soviet Union.

At the Democratic nominating convention in July 1948, Truman hoped to mollify both African Americans and southern Democrats by endorsing a bland civil rights platform. But liberals, led by Minneapolis mayor Hubert H. Humphrey, insisted on a stronger civil rights agenda. This infuriated segregationists, such as Senator James O. Eastland of Mississippi, who accused Humphrey of trying to "mongrelize" America and complained that Truman was "kissing the feet of minorities."

Some outraged southern delegates bolted the convention and organized their own States' Rights, or "Dixiecrat," party. They nominated Governor Strom Thurmond of South Carolina as their presidential candidate. Thurmond, like many who gravitated to his party, combined populism with bigotry. For example, they complained that Truman's support for foreign aid made him a tool of Wall Street millionaires and monopolists, while his advocacy of civil rights made him a pawn of communists, Jews, and African Americans. The Dixiecrats, Thurmond declared, stood for the "deepest emotion of the human fabric—racial pride, respect for white womanhood, and superiority of Caucasian blood." He condemned civil rights as a Red plot.

While segregationist Democrats attacked Truman from the right, Henry Wallace and his supporters accused Truman of abandoning New Deal principles and provoking a Cold War with the Soviet Union. Wallace ran for president on the ticket of the Progressive Party. With the Democrats split three ways, it seemed likely that Progressive voters in the North and Dixiecrats in the South could tip enough states to push the election into the House of Representatives or ensure a GOP victory.

Republicans maximized their appeal by moving toward the political center. Instead of the party's most prominent conservative, Senator Robert Taft, they nominated a moderate, New York Governor Thomas Dewey. The GOP candidate began the 1948 campaign with a fifteen-point lead over Truman in the opinion polls. One prominent Republican ridiculed Truman as a "gone goose." Dewey and his team felt so certain of victory that they spent more time planning his inauguration than outlining an agenda of their own or rebutting Truman's campaign rhetoric.

In a spirited campaign mounted on a special train that crisscrossed the country, Truman delivered hundreds of combative speeches. Relieved of any need to placate the Wallace or Thurmond factions of the party, Truman appealed to anticommunists as well as black urban voters. Boasting that he did not want the support of "Henry Wallace and his Communists" or Thurmond and avowed racists, Truman blasted the GOP-led "do-nothing Eightieth Congress." These "gluttons of privilege" stuck a "pitchfork in the back of the farmers" and "tried to enslave totally the working man." Republicans, he bellowed, would do a "real hatchet job on the New Deal" and bring back the Depression. Crowds at whistle-stops cheered, "Give 'em hell, Harry!"

Although most pollsters and many journalists had lost interest in the campaign, Truman's appeals took hold. When the tally came in November, Truman beat Dewey by 24 million votes to 22 million, one of the most dramatic upsets in the history of presidential contests. Wallace and Thurmond each received around 1 million popular votes. Even though the Dixiecrats won the electoral votes of four states (South Carolina, Louisiana, Alabama, and Mississippi), they and the Progressive Party faded away.

Now elected in his own right, Truman emerged from Franklin Roosevelt's shadow by introducing his own reform program, the Fair Deal. During 1949, he called on Congress to pass legislation providing national health insurance, public housing, expanded Social Security benefits, a higher minimum wage, support for civil rights, higher support payments for small farmers, and the repeal of the Taft-Hartley Act. Even though Democrats reclaimed control of the House and Senate in 1948, few of these measures even came to a vote in Congress. The enduring coalition of Republicans and southern Democrats tied up most Fair Deal proposals in committee. Only a modest expansion of Social Security and a weak public housing bill passed. Truman's new administration had barely begun before the expanding dimensions of the Cold War at home and abroad inflamed public suspicion of liberal social policies.

During the decade following World War II, a growing anticommunist movement convulsed American politics. It was linked to, but somewhat separate from, the Cold War confrontation between the two superpowers. American anticommunism stretched back to the Bolshevik Revolution of 1917. It revived in the 1930s, when left-wing elements of the Democratic Party, the labor movement, and American intellectualism squared off against centrists and conservatives who abhorred the Soviet Union and anyone who defended it. Before the Pearl Harbor attack ended debate, Republicans tried to make political headway against New Dealers by accusing them of an affinity for communism and disloyalty. Cold War anxieties after 1945 fed a Red Scare that reached a fever pitch by the end of the decade. Eventually, Joseph McCarthy, a Republican senator from Wisconsin, gave his name to the movement, but it was well under way by the time he emerged as a national figure in 1950.

Communism had a small but growing following in the United States during the 1930s. The American Communist Party reached its zenith during World War II, when nearly 100,000 people paid membership dues. Within a few years, party rolls declined by 50 percent, and by the mid-1950s, only about 25,000 Americans remained formal Communists. Most rank-and-file American Communists supported Soviet policy and ignored evidence of Stalin's brutality. But few advocated violence to overthrow the U.S. government and most were really more reformers than revolutionaries. Party leaders were more rigid apologists for Stalin and had a cynical view of democratic civil liberties, except in defense of their own activities. In any case, the FBI had infiltrated the party so thoroughly that it could barely organize a picnic, no less a revolution, in secrecy. European democracies, such as France and Italy, had far larger communist parties and lived much closer to the Soviet "threat." Although they excluded communists from a role in government, their societies experienced no comparable Red Scare. In the United States, government and private anticommunist efforts were wildly disproportional to the actual danger posed.

During and right after the war years, Republican political leaders, business groups, opponents of civil rights, and other conservatives discovered the advantage of linking Democratic liberals and progressive policies to "the Reds." Labeling someone or their ideas as communist effectively discredited them. In 1946, the chair of the Republican National Committee told voters that in the upcoming congressional election, they would have to choose between "Communism and Republicanism." In 1950, Senate candidate Richard Nixon charged that Helen Gahagan Douglas, his Democratic opponent, was "pink right down to her underwear." The American Medical Association denounced Truman's 1948 proposal for national health insurance by labeling it a "monstrosity of Bolshevism."

As early as 1942, southern Democrats were fearful of a postwar push for civil rights and condemned as communist those opposed to segregation. Representative Martin Dies, Democrat of Texas, deplored the fact that "throughout the South today, subversive elements are attempting to convince the Negro that he should be placed on social equality with white people." J. Edgar Hoover's FBI promoted this alleged link throughout the Cold War. In 1951, for example, the FBI chief approved a script for the film *I Was a Communist for the FBI* that included party members taking credit for inciting race riots in Detroit and New York. "To bring about Communism in America," one party boss asserts, "we must incite [more] riots." Soviet officials, the film explains, used African Americans as pawns.

In 1948, *Life* magazine highlighted the alleged nexus between communism, race, and sex in a report on smart "party girls" dangled in front of maladjusted young men by Communist leaders. These decoys preyed upon sexually inadequate males by flattering their vanity and providing sexual gratification. "The party girls were wonderful," *Life* explained. They talked, recruited, and "went to bed" with their marks. Worse still was the ploy of using white party girls to "enfold likely Negroes," even arranging interracial marriages to recruit blacks.

In 1946, the committee on socialism and communism of the U.S. Chamber of Commerce called for barring not just communists, but liberals, socialists, and other undesirables from teaching in schools, working in radio or television, or working in any "opinion forming agencies." In an effort to blunt union drives, the committee also recommended barring people with unacceptable ideas from large factories. After this position became formal U.S. Chamber of Commerce policy in 1952, the group called on local volunteers to monitor the ideas and actions of public officials.

There were, of course, real subversives, spies, and traitors in the United States. To acquire technology and military information, the Soviets utilized professional agents, disgruntled employees, and occasionally communist sympathizers or actual party members. Based on VENONA, the code name for FBI intercepts of Soviet communications during the 1930s and 1940s, historians estimate that a few hundred American citizens provided classified information to Moscow. American Communist leaders knew about these activities, even if most ordinary party members did not. Politically motivated spies were especially active during the 1930s and early 1940s, when democracy appeared on the ropes and the Soviet Union was an ally in the fight against fascism. After 1945, Soviet spies found it difficult to recruit communist sympathizers in the United States. By 1950, a top Soviet intelligence official reported to the Kremlin that because of the shortage of American recruits, he was forced to rely on newspaper clippings for information.

Most of the real traitors unearthed during the Red Scare had actually ceased spying at the end of World War II, and many of their names were already known to the FBI. Nevertheless, grandstanding politicians made few distinctions between past and present subversion and ignored the fact that most espionage was carried out by Soviet professionals utilizing Americans with a personal grudge against an employer or the government. College professors, actors, or even most diplomats were of little use or interest to Moscow.

Congress, especially the House Un-American Activities Committee (HUAC), played a large role in stirring up the Red Scare. The most strident committee members during the 1940s were conservative southern Democrats and like-minded Republicans. Democrats such as John S. Wood (Georgia) and John Rankin (Mississippi) used HUAC as a platform to criticize New Deal programs, especially those relating to civil rights. Rankin took pride in bringing to the nation's capital a law modeled on those in twenty-two states that banned interracial marriage. He condemned the Red Cross for "mongrelizing" the nation by removing racial labels from blood bank bottles, and warned of conspiracies among "alien-minded communistic enemies of Christianity," his code for Jews.

Truman attempted to deflect charges that he waffled on the Red threat by creating a Temporary Commission on Employee Loyalty in November 1946 and, the following March, a Federal Employee Loyalty Program. These organizations required all federal employees to undergo an investigation to determine if they posed a risk to national security. Hearsay, wiretaps, and anonymous denunciations could be used to discredit someone. Aside from the Communist Party itself, Attorney General Tom Clark compiled a list of eighty-two suspect organizations linked to subversion. Congressional committees identified over 600 such groups. Membership in any one of these organizations could, by itself, justify dismissal of "pinkos" and "fellow travelers" from government service. Communists, Clark warned, "are everywhere—in factories, offices, butcher shops, on street corners, in private businesses—and each carries with him the germs of death for society."

Investigations of federal employees were conducted by FBI agents, whose long-serving director, J. Edgar Hoover, had been chasing Reds since 1919. Hoover and many of his agents despised communists, African Americans, homosexuals, and most kinds of political or social nonconformity. By the early 1950s, over 5 million government employees had undergone some form of security check. Several thousand quit in protest, and a few hundred were fired for belonging to groups on the attorney general's list. Yet these probes uncovered almost no bona fide spies.

Anticommunists often viewed sexual "perversion" as linked to disloyalty, a handy option because there were few actual communists to catch. Senator Kenneth Wherry, Republican of Nebraska, considered it nearly impossible to "separate homosexuals from subversives." As a leader of the so-called Lavender Purge, Wherry urged action to secure major coastal cities "against sabotage through conspiracy of subversives and moral perverts in government establishments." Like many Americans, Wherry feared that "deviants" not only lacked patriotic fiber but also were susceptible to Red blackmail. A 1950 Senate report on the "Employment of Homosexuals and Other Sex Perverts in Government" warned that 3,750 gays worked for the federal government in Washington, D.C., including 400 in the State Department, and that "one homosexual can pollute a government office." Between 1947 and 1953, over 400 employees of the Department of State were dismissed or forced to resign for being homosexuals, a rate nearly double that of those fired as subversives. "Commies and queers," as Senator Joe McCarthy put it in 1950, were fair game.

Several memoirs by ex-communists connected their secret political and illicit sexual lives. The most important of these, Whittaker Chambers's *Witness* (1952), explicitly linked homosexuality and treason, and portrayed religious faith as the key to redemption. None of the confessionals, however, had the raw power or generated the mass appeal of novelist Mickey Spillaine. Beginning with his first novel *I the Jury* (1947), which introduced private detective Mike Hammer, Spillaine published seven books in six years that sold over 17 million copies. Hammer, a fictional World War II veteran, becomes a private eye to escape the "pansy" bureaucracy that emasculates real police work. He despises intellectuals, homosexuals, communists, and the Mafia and does his best to exterminate them. The hero boasts of killing "commies, queers, and dames" who "should have died long ago." The string of bestsellers stopped in 1952, when Spillaine became a Jehovah's Witness and dedicated himself to church work.

Nearly every case of actual espionage prosecuted in the 1940s and 1950s was the product of criminal investigations by the FBI, not congressional probes. J. Edgar Hoover was no civil libertarian, but unlike some members of Congress, he retained at least a minimal commitment to notions of evidence and cause and effect. Headline-grabbing politicians did little but sow confusion and fear. Still, a few high-profile cases of alleged treason involving communists, their sympathizers, and members of the Roosevelt administration created the impression among the public that a cabal of disloyal Americans threatened the nation.

When Republicans won control of Congress in 1946, Representative J. Parnell Thomas of New Jersey became HUAC's chair, and the committee soon announced that the Red plot against America "had its headquarters in Hollywood." The movie industry provided an almost irresistible target to the publicity-seeking committee. East European, Jewish immigrants headed most of the major film studios. Although they anglicized their names and made movies that celebrated American life, anti-Semites on HUAC, especially Representative John Rankin, were anxious to pillory them. The films produced by Hollywood studios dominated popular culture, and Rankin, like chair Thomas, realized the public would savor a glimpse at the private lives of celebrities.

There were, of course, "real" communists in Hollywood. A small number of writers, for example, formed the left-wing Screen Writers Guild that battled studio executives over salary and creative issues. In retrospect, what stands out about their scripts is the lack, not abundance, of political messages. Nervous studio bosses, such as Jack Warner and Sam Goldwyn, hoped that by cooperating with HUAC's probe they could demonstrate their own patriotism and crush the bothersome union.

HUAC held hearings in both Hollywood and Washington at which "friendly witnesses," such as Warner and actor Ronald Reagan, were encouraged to pledge their cooperation by instituting procedures to bar the employment of self-professed communists or of those who refused to tell Congress what it wanted to hear. When pressed for examples of Red messages in films, studio executives cited the sympathetic treatment of Apache chief Cochise in "Broken Arrow," kindly black servants, and the smiles depicted on the faces of Russian soldiers in a film produced during World War II.

The committee focused on a group of ten "hostile" writers and directors, including Dalton Trumbo, Ring Lardner, Jr., and John Howard Lawson. Several in this group were past or current communists. All ten refused to answer the committee's questions about their political beliefs, citing the First Amendment's protection of free speech and political association. They were cited for contempt and later jailed after the Supreme Court upheld HUAC's right to inquire into communist activities. Meanwhile, publications such as *Red Channels* and *Counterattack* soon appeared. They contained the names of hundreds of actors, writers, and directors accused of left-wing leanings who found themselves unemployable due to an informal blacklist. Following the HUAC probe, Hollywood studios produced a few dozen stridently anticommunist films, including *The Iron Curtain* (1948), *The Red Menace* (1949), *The Red Danube* (1949), *Conspirator* (1950), *My Son John* (1952), and *Big Jim McLain* (1952). With wooden plots and moral posturing, all these films were critical and commercial flops.

HUAC launched its most famous inquiry in 1948. For several years, Whittaker Chambers, an editor at *Time* magazine, had told various government officials that in the 1930s he had been part of a Soviet spy ring that received material from members of the Roosevelt administration. After 1937, Chambers explained, he broke with communism, became a devout Christian, and finally confessed his sins to Representative Richard Nixon, Republican of California, and other members of HUAC.

In 1950 Congressman Richard Nixon took grim satisfaction from learning that a federal jury had convicted Alger Hiss of perjury. / © UPI/Bettmann/CORBIS

In his first public appearance before the committee in August 1948, Chambers claimed that Alger Hiss, a former high official of the State Department, had been a fellow communist, although not a spy. Later, when Hiss filed a libel suit, Chambers upped the ante and named Hiss as a coconspirator. Unlike the sinister-looking Chambers, Hiss seemed a paragon of charm, eloquence, and professional accomplishment. He had worked for several New Deal agencies, had attended the wartime Yalta conference, and after the war became head of the prestigious Carnegie Endowment for International Peace.

When Hiss persuasively denied knowing Chambers, several HUAC members decided to drop the case. But Nixon, a freshman who had won election in 1946 by charging that his Democratic opponent, Jerry Voorhees, was procommunist, refused to give in. He arranged a face-to-face meeting between Chambers and Hiss, and coaxed an admission from Hiss that he had indeed met his accuser in the 1930s but knew him then by a different name.

After Truman's unexpected election victory in November, frustrated Republicans pushed the case with renewed vigor. Chambers, with FBI prompting, recalled additional details of his past misdeeds. He now charged that Hiss had passed secret documents to him as late as 1938. To prove this claim, he and Nixon brought reporters to Chambers's Maryland farm, where they produced a hollowed-out pumpkin that held documents and several rolls of microfilm. The FBI determined that the material (dubbed the pumpkin papers), were actually secret reports, some of which had been copied on a typewriter that matched a machine in the Hiss household. Because the statute of limitations on espionage had lapsed, Hiss was indicted only for perjury: lying to Congress about his communist affiliations and relationship with Chambers.

A trial in 1949 resulted in a hung jury, but in January 1950, a second jury found Hiss guilty. He went to jail for several years and spent the next forty years of his life maintaining his innocence and blaming the FBI for framing him. Chambers went on to a highly public career as a professional anticommunist. In his bestselling memoir, *Witness*, Chambers boasted that "when I took up my little sling and aimed at Communism, I also hit something else . . . that great socialist revolution, which, in the name of liberalism . . . has been inching its ice cap over the nation for two decades." Ronald Reagan, then in the process of changing his own political stripes from liberal to conservative, credited Chambers for helping him see the light. Thirty years later, President Reagan designated Chambers's farm and pumpkin patch a "national historic site" and Cold War shrine. Nixon parlayed his fame into winning a senate seat in California in 1950 and two years later won election as vice president.

Most historians now believe that Hiss did pass information to Moscow and lied about his actions. But the Chambers-Hiss case became more important as a political morality play. Republicans felt they had proved the link between New Dealers and the communist conspiracy. When Truman and Secretary of State Dean Acheson initially defended Hiss, Republicans went wild. Nixon called their actions "disgusting," adding that Acheson suffered from "color blindness—a form of pink eye toward the Communist threat in the United States."

In February 1950, a month after Hiss's conviction, British police arrested a German émigré scientist, Klaus Fuchs, who confessed to participating in a spy ring at the nuclear lab in Los Alamos, New Mexico, during World War II. Many suspected that Fuchs not only helped the Soviets get the atomic bomb but also may have given them data on the still undeveloped hydrogen bomb. In the summer of 1950, the FBI arrested a New York couple, Julius and Ethel Rosenberg, and charged them with conspiring to steal the "secret" of the atomic bomb.

The Rosenbergs had been Communist Party members in the 1940s. Unlike Fuchs, they denied their guilt, even when Ethel's brother, David Greenglass, who worked at Los Alamos, admitted his role in the conspiracy. After sifting the evidence for years and gaining access to Soviet materials, historians generally agree that Julius Rosenberg plotted to pass both atomic and other technological data to Moscow. The evidence against his wife was less clear, and fifty years after her conviction, Ethel's brother David admitted he had concocted some of his testimony about her role. She was the mother of two young sons, and it appears the government charged her in an effort to force her husband to confess. Ultimately, both Rosenbergs were convicted and died in the electric chair in 1953. Fuchs and several other confederates went to prison.

While Congress probed for spies, a federal jury convicted twelve leaders of the American Communist Party in October 1949 of violating the Smith Act.

This 1940 law made it a crime to advocate the overthrow of the government by force or to belong to a group advocating such action. The verdict, upheld by the Supreme Court in 1951 in *Dennis* v. *United States*, was handed down despite the fact that no evidence tied the party leaders to efforts to overthrow the government.

By the time the Supreme Court decided that communism was a violent and illegal conspiracy, Congress had passed new, restrictive laws. The Internal Security Act of 1950 (called the McCarran Act after Senator Pat McCarran, a Nevada Democrat) declared that communism was an international conspiracy posing an immediate threat to the United States. The law stopped short of outlawing the Communist Party but ordered "Communist affiliated" groups and individuals to register with a Subversive Activity Control Board or face a $10,000 fine and five years in prison. Communists were denied passports and barred from working for the government or in the defense industry. The law permitted the deportation of naturalized citizens and the detention, without trial, of people considered security threats in time of emergency.

In the climate of the early Cold War, immigration was perceived as a potential threat. The quota system adopted in the 1920s favored immigrants from Western Europe and excluded nearly everyone else. After 1945, the tragic condition of more than a million displaced persons in Europe evoked concern. These refugees included several hundred thousand Jewish Holocaust survivors and even more ethnic Germans, Latvians, Estonians, and Lithuanians who had fled Soviet control in Eastern Europe. After intense lobbying by citizens' groups, in June 1948 Congress passed the Displaced Persons Act, opening two hundred thousand special immigration slots for these people. An extension of the law in 1950 let in an equal number.

Congress deferred dealing with broader immigration problems until 1952, when it passed the McCarran-Walter Act. Senator McCarran believed that the country already had too many "indigestible blocs" and fought efforts to liberalize the strict quotas passed in the 1920s. The new law repealed the almost complete ban on Asian immigration but set an absurdly low annual quota of one hundred persons from each Asian-Pacific nation. It continued to favor Western Europe and to exclude most eastern Europeans. The law barred suspected communists, along with homosexuals and other "undesirables," from even visiting the United States. Naturalized citizens were subject to deportation if they were accused of subversive acts. Passed over Truman's veto, the law set basic immigration policy until 1965.

Thirteen states followed Congress's lead and established their own HUAC-type committees. They spent much of their efforts castigating labor unions and civil rights organizations, and imposing a web of loyalty oaths. Several southern state legislatures labeled even centrist civil rights organizations like the NAACP as Red fronts and barred their members from serving as public school teachers or working in civil-service jobs. Many states required public employees or those seeking licenses to pledge their loyalty. Loyalty pledges were often required to get a driver's license or even a business permit. Pharmacists in Texas, professional wrestlers in Indiana, and those seeking fishing permits in New York were required to affirm their opposition to communism and loyalty to the United States. Texas required that authors of school textbooks not only sign anticommunist oaths but also include in their books accounts of "our glowing and throbbing history of hearts and souls inspired by wonderful American principles and tradition."

The Expanding Dimensions of the Cold War

Despite the success achieved by American efforts in Western Europe and Japan, the Cold War overflowed its early boundaries. Soviet development of an atomic bomb led Washington to reassess its own security needs. Communist victories in China and Vietnam prompted demands for more extensive involvement in Asia. Meanwhile, the Republican drumbeat about spies and subversives grew louder.

In September 1949, American reconnaissance planes collected air samples that revealed an atomic explosion had recently occurred inside the Soviet Union. Coming several years earlier than many Americans expected, the detonation spurred fears that Stalin would be emboldened to challenge the United States. The Soviet bomb triggered both a search for spies who may have given away nuclear secrets as well as a debate over whether to build a super-, or hydrogen, bomb a thousand times more powerful than the weapons used against Japan. Whereas atomic bombs derived their energy from the splitting, or fission, of uranium atoms, the proposed new weapon would use the energy released by the fusion, or bonding together, of hydrogen atoms.

Some powerful voices protested this new venture. J. Robert Oppenheimer, a central figure in the creation of the atomic bomb, and diplomat George Kennan both argued against expanding the arms race. They did not believe that the Soviet atomic bomb gave Stalin much of an advantage, especially because atomic bombs could be made much more powerful anyway and the Soviets lacked the means to deliver a weapon directly against the United States. Before rushing into an expensive race to build a hydrogen bomb, they urged a renewed effort to negotiate an arms control pact with Moscow. If Stalin balked, the United States could still build a hydrogen bomb (an H-bomb).

The politically charged atmosphere in Washington poisoned debate. Truman's advisers used Oppenheimer's opposition to the hydrogen bomb as an excuse to remove him from his position as a government weapons consultant. Later, he was declared a "security risk" and barred from doing any classified work. Kennan, the so-called Father of Containment, was also sidelined. Secretary of State Acheson replaced him as head of policy planning with hard-liner Paul Nitze, an advocate of building the superweapon and sharply increasing military spending. Truman approved development of the H-bomb in January 1950. The United States tested a prototype device in November 1952, and the Soviets followed with their own the next August.

In October 1949, just a month after confirming the Soviet atomic test, Communist leader Mao Zedong established the People's Republic of China

Jiang Jieshi and Mao Zedong at an American-sponsored peace conference in 1945. Civil war soon followed. / Jack Wilkers, © Life Magazine, Time Inc.

(PRC). Jiang Jieshi's Nationalists fled to the island of Taiwan. The "loss of China," as Republicans described it, disheartened Americans who remembered the World War II alliance with Jiang and thought of China as America's favorite charity. Even though the United States had provided over $2 billion in military and economic aid to Jiang since 1945, his government's corruption and unpopularity nullified its effect. As one American military observer put it, Nationalist troops abandoned positions "they could have defended with broomsticks." In 1946, Truman had sent General George C. Marshall to mediate the conflict, but he abandoned the effort in 1947, criticizing both the Nationalists and Reds.

When Marshall returned to Washington to become secretary of state, the Truman administration largely washed its hands of China. Military aid seemed pointless because Nationalist commanders either fled or sold their weapons to the Communists. Privately, Truman called Jiang a "crook" and even Republican senators agreed in private that aid to China was "money down a rat hole." The president hoped that once Mao took power, he would distance himself from the bullying Soviets and act flexibly toward the United States.

In August 1949, Truman and Secretary of State Acheson tried to calm Americans by issuing a massive report, *The China White Paper*, detailing how Jiang's government, not the United States, had "lost" China. The administration criticized the Communists as well but made it clear that it would not defend Taiwan and would consider establishing diplomatic ties with the Communist regime once the "dust had settled" in China's civil war.

In January 1950, Acheson announced that the Truman administration would turn its attention away from China and concentrate on securing the "Great Crescent," the Asian-Pacific lands that stretched from Japan through Southeast Asia to India. Japan's industrial capacity and the raw materials of Southeast Asia, he explained, were much more important to American and European economic security than was the vast poorhouse of China. Ignoring this strategy, Republicans labeled *The China White Paper* a whitewash and criticized the administration for not offering military protection to either Taiwan or South Korea.

Early in 1950, the United States began to assist French forces fighting a Communist-led uprising in French Indochina (Vietnam, Laos, and Cambodia). During World War II, Vietnamese guerrilla leader Ho Chi Minh—a Communist but also a dedicated fighter against colonial rule—had cooperated with Americans against Japan. In 1945, he appealed for U.S. support in gaining Vietnamese independence. Earlier, Roosevelt had pressed the French to loosen their grip on Vietnam, but Truman worried more about keeping France a strong, anticommunist, and pro-American ally in Europe and Asia. Although some junior American diplomats sympathized with Ho Chi Minh's Vietminh independence movement, Secretary of State Acheson ended debate when he declared that in colonial areas, "all Stalinists masquerade as nationalists."

In an effort to undercut Ho Chi Minh's nationalist appeal, the State Department urged Paris to appoint a Vietnamese to lead their colony and to promise eventual independence. France selected Bao Dai, a dissolute playboy descended from Vietnamese royalty, as their puppet emperor. One irreverent U.S. diplomat complained that Bao Dai's entire political following in Vietnam consisted of "a pimp and three prostitutes." Nevertheless, in February 1950, after China and the Soviet Union recognized Ho Chi Minh's insurgent government, U.S. officials held their noses and extended official recognition to Bao Dai's puppet regime. That spring, the first American military aid and advisers were sent directly to Vietnam, a down payment on what would become a multibillion-dollar investment that eventually cost 58,000 American lives.

In the wake of the Soviet A-bomb and the Chinese Revolution, Truman ordered a comprehensive review of security policy. Acheson tapped his aide, Paul Nitze, to coordinate the study. The resulting top-secret document, given to Truman by the National Security Council (NSC) in April 1950 and known as NSC-68, presented a grim outlook. In a departure from Kennan's argument that the Soviet challenge was primarily economic and political, Nitze warned that the Soviets posed a real military threat and that Stalin's "fanatical" actions showed a new boldness that "borders on the reckless." By 1954, the report claimed, the Soviets would possess the nuclear capacity to destroy the United States. To counter Moscow's attempt to "impose its authority on the rest of the world," NSC-68 proposed a steep increase in both nuclear and conventional military spending.

Even Acheson described the report privately as overkill. But he defended it as required to "bludgeon the mass mind of government" into action. Some of the president's economic advisers argued that larger defense expenditures would supplement the Marshall Plan and boost industrial output and employ-ment, both at home and among America's allies. Truman endorsed NSC-68 in principle but worried about its enormous price tag. With the administration under Republican attack and uncertain how to meet perceived communist threats, policy gridlock gripped Washington. But then, one high official later recalled, "Korea came along and saved us."

Conclusion

"I suppose," Truman told the American people a few days before he left office in 1953, "that history will remember my term . . . as the years when the Cold War began to overshadow our lives. I have had hardly a day in office that has not been dominated by this all encompassing struggle—this conflict between those who love freedom and those who would lead the world back into slavery and darkness."

During the Truman years, the basic outlines of American Cold War pol-icy, at home and abroad, were established. The United States committed itself to the containment of Soviet power globally and to the promotion of world trade. It had established the principle that America would intervene with aid, advisers, or troops wherever it appeared that the Soviet Union, China, or any of their clients were trying to extend communist influence. Stalin and Tru-man, while certainly not moral equivalents, both oversimplified complex prob-lems and blamed each other for many of the uncertainties of the post-1945 world order. In Western Europe and Japan, the United States largely succeeded in "winning" the Cold War by 1950. But soon, the frustrations of the Korean conflict, along with the fierce anticommunism spawned by both Truman and his Republican opponents, contributed to the Democrats' fall from power in 1952 and passed on a legacy of global competition between the United States and the Soviet Union.

F U R T H E R • R E A D I N G

On the Truman presidency and early postwar years, see Lizabeth Cohen, *A Consumers' Republic: the Politics of Mass Consumption in Postwar America* (2003); Robert J. Donovan, *Conflict and Crisis: The Presidency of Harry S Truman, 1945–1948* (1977) and *Tumul-tuous Years: The Presidency of Harry S Truman, 1949–1953* (1982); Alonzo S. Hamby, *Man of the People: A Life of Harry S Truman* (1995); David McCullough, *Truman* (1992); Norman D. Markowitz, *The Rise and Fall of the People's Century: Henry A. Wallace and American Liberalism, 1941–48* (1973); Zachary Karball, *The Last Campaign: How Harry Truman Won the 1948 Election* (2000). **On the origin of the Cold War,** see Melvyn Lef-fler, *A Preponderance of Power: National Security, the Truman Administration, and the Cold War* (1991); Arnold Offner, *Another Such Victory: President Truman and the Cold War, 1945–53* (2002); Martin Sherwin, *A World Destroyed* (1975); Gregg Herken, *The Win-ning Weapon* (1981); Paul Boyer, *By the Bomb's Early Light* (1990); David Holloway, *Stalin and the Bomb* (1994); John L. Gaddis, *The United States and the Origin of the Cold*

War, 1941–1947 (1972), *Strategies of Containment: A Critical Appraisal of Postwar American National Security Policy* (1982), and *We Now Know: Rethinking Cold War History* (1997); Norman Naimark, *The Russians in Germany: A History of the Soviet Zone of Occupation, 1945–1949* (1995); Carolyn Eisenberg, *Drawing the Line: The American Decision to Divide Germany, 1944–1949* (1996); Michael J. Hogan, *The Marshall Plan* (1987); Daniel Yergin, *A Shattered Peace* (1977); Walter Isaacson and Evan Thomas, *The Wise Men: Six Friends and the World They Made* (1986); Robert D. Dean, *Imperial Brotherhood: Gender and the Making of Cold War Foreign Policy* (2001). **On domestic communism and the Red Scare,** see William L. O'Neill, *A Better World: Stalinism and American Intellectuals* (1983); Harvey Klehr and John Earl Haynes, *The American Communist Movement: Storming Heaven Itself* (1992); Harvey Klehr, John Earl Haynes, and Kyrill M. Anderson, *The Soviet World of American Communism* (1998); John Earl Haynes and Harvey Klehr, *Venona: Decoding Soviet Espionage in America* (1999); Harvey Klehr and Ronald Radosh, *The Amerasia Case: Prelude to McCarthyism* (1996); Allen Weinstein, *Perjury: The Hiss-Chambers Case* (1997), and *The Haunted Wood: Soviet Espionage in America: The Stalin Era* (1999); Sam Tanenhaus, *Whittaker Chambers: A Biography* (1997); Ronald Radosh and Joyce Milton, *The Rosenberg File* (1997); Sam Roberts, *The Brother: The Untold Story of Atomic Spy David Greenglass and How He Sent His Sister Ethel Rosenberg to the Electric Chair* (2001); David Caute, *The Great Fear* (1977); Athan Theoharis, *Seeds of Repression: Harry S Truman and the Origins of McCarthyism* (1971); Richard Gid Powers, *Secrecy and Power: The Life of J. Edgar Hoover* (1987), and *Not Without Honor: The History of American AntiCommunism* (1995); Richard M. Freeland, *The Truman Doctrine and the Origins of McCarthyism* (1972); Richard Fried, *Nightmare in Red: The McCarthy Era in Perspective* (1990), and *The Russians Are Coming! The Russians Are Coming! Pageantry and Patriotism in Cold War America* (1998); David M. Oshinsky, *A Conspiracy So Immense: The World of Joe McCarthy* (1983); Thomas C. Reeves, *The Life and Times of Joe McCarthy* (1982); Ellen W. Schrecker, *No Ivory Tower: McCarthyism in the Universities* (1986), and *Many Are the Crimes: McCarthyism in America* (1998). **On immigration policies,** see David M. Reimers, *Still the Golden Door: The Third World Comes to America* (1992); Leonard Dinnerstein, *America and the Survivors of the Holocaust* (1982). **On the Korean War and the expanding dimensions of the Cold War,** see Bruce Cummings, *The Origins of the Korean War*, 2 vols. (1981, 1990); William W. Stueck, *The Road to Confrontation: American Policy Toward China and Korea, 1947–1950* (1981), and *The Korean War: An International History* (1995); Burton I. Kauffman, *The Korean War* (1986); Michael Schaller, *The American Occupation of Japan: The Origins of the Cold War in Asia* (1985), and *Douglas MacArthur: The Far Eastern General* (1989); John W. Dower, *Embracing Defeat: Japan in the Wake of World War II* (2000); Mark Bradley, *Imagining Vietnam and America: The Making of Post Colonial Vietnam, 1919–1950* (2000); Robert M. Blum, *Drawing the Line: The Origin of the American Containment Policy in East Asia* (1982). **On the military industrial complex,** see Ann Markusen, Peter Hall, Scott Campbell, and Sabina Deitrick, *The Rise of the Gunbelt: The Military Remapping of Industrial America* (1991); James Fallows, *The National Defense* (1981).

3

America at Home, 1953–1960

This scene of workers emptying moving vans in a new suburb of Los Angeles captures the mobility, materialism, and family norms that transformed postwar America's urban and social landscapes. / J. R. Eyerman, © Life Magazine, Time Inc.

In 1955, thousands of invited guests walked down Walt Disney's vision of Main Street for the first time as Disneyland opened in Anaheim, California. Imagined as a new kind of amusement park, it offered its visitors an entertaining and idealized view of nature and society. Its planners called that view "Disney Realism," explaining that they intended to "program out all the negative, unwanted elements and program in the positive elements." Their efforts started in their publicity, which targeted middle-class American families who embraced the consumer and domestic values that dominated the postwar period. They continued at the gates, where ticket prices and security guards ensured that only those who met the standards for appearance and demeanor would be admitted.

Once inside, visitors could enjoy the rides and marvel at their experiences in Tomorrowland, Adventureland, Frontierland, and Fantasyland. These park areas incorporated familiar characters and themes from Disney's films and television shows. Guests encountered Mickey Mouse, Donald Duck, and other favorites from Disney's cartoons on Main Street and in Fantasyland. They also attended exhibits provided by corporate sponsors, who were assured by Disney's promoters that "in this environment, visitors are more susceptible to the messages" they sought to convey. The amusement park touted nationalism and Cold War values, claiming "Disneyland could happen only in a country where freedom is a heritage and the pursuit of happiness a basic human right." In 1959 its managers reinforced the "Americanism" of such values when they defied the government's request to close the park to the public for a day to accommodate a visit by Soviet premier Nikita Khrushchev.

Disneyland's embrace of the corporate and consumer culture of the postwar period also extended to its personnel policies, which were designed to ensure a wholesome and pleasant experience for the customers. Disneyland employees learned at the outset that the company's culture required close conformity to its rules. The company handbook made this clear, expressing to its workers the "hope that you enjoy thinking our way." According to film critic Richard Schickel, Disney's employees had to "spend a few hard days in the 'University of Disneyland,' which [trained] them in the modern art forms—pioneered by the airlines—of the frozen smile and the canned answer delivered with enough spontaneity to make it seem unprogrammed." Indeed, Disney workers had to display the other-directed personality of the organization men described by the social critics of the time. Workers who had contact with the public were all white, prompting historian John Findlay to conclude that "race relations inside the theme park were far from futuristic."

As the success of Disneyland suggests, Americans in the 1950s accelerated the trends they pursued in the immediate aftermath of the war. The economy continued to grow. With money in their pockets, Americans rushed to new homes in suburbia, had children in record numbers, and went on a consumer buying spree, snapping up home appliances, automobiles, televisions, and a plethora of other goods and services. Most Americans believed they had entered an era of well-deserved stability and prosperity, a message widely reinforced in popular culture. Dwight D. Eisenhower was a popular president who brought a sense of security to American life. Especially for the white middle class and unionized blue-collar workers, confidence in material progress and the perfectibility of American society coexisted alongside a fervent anticommunist ideology and anxiety about nuclear destruction.

Beneath the surface stability, however, the 1950s were years of change and upheaval. Continued population movement and the automobile, television, and advanced technology weren't the only factors to change the face of American life. Critics began to complain that the apparent consensus of American society was hollow. In the age of *Father Knows Best* and trips to Disneyland, American youth developed its own subculture centered on rock 'n' roll music, which alarmed their elders. Meanwhile, the civil rights struggle erupted in the South, which forced Americans to confront issues that had too long been ignored.

The Affluent Society

Beginning in the late 1940s and continuing well into the 1990s, the most dramatic population growth occurred in American suburbs, the new rings of residential communities outside larger cities. Until the 1960s, people of color were barred by custom, law, or restrictive lending practices, but white Americans flocked in growing numbers to large subdivisions built on former farmland. Americans had begun leaving cities in the nineteenth century, but only after 1945 could the United States be called a suburban nation. Between 1940 and 1970, the proportion of suburban dwellers increased from 19.5 to 37.6 percent (see the table). An associated phenomenon was the rise in suburban shopping centers, or malls; their number increased from eight to four thousand in the first postwar decade.

Until 1945, the housing industry had focused on building custom homes or urban multifamily buildings. During the Depression and war years, housing construction almost ceased. Now, 16 million veterans and their new families clamored for homes and apartments. These homes did not exist, however, or cost more than most could afford. In New York City, for example, several

Geographic Distribution of U.S. Population, 1930–1970

Year	Central Cities	Suburbs	Rural Areas and Small Towns
1930	31.8%	18.0%	50.2%
1940	31.6	19.5	48.9
1950	32.3	23.8	43.9
1960	32.6	30.7	36.7
1970	31.4	37.6	31.0

Source: Adapted from U.S. Bureau of the Census, *Decennial Censuses, 1930–1970* (Washington, D.C.: U.S. Government Printing Office).

veterans and their brides slept each night in the beds in the show windows of Macy's department store. Their plight was only partly a publicity stunt because little affordable housing was available. More typically, new couples roomed with relatives.

Meanwhile, the National Association of Home Builders and the National Association of Realtors were lobbying to shape federal housing policies. By tradition, banks and other private lenders had followed restrictive mortgage procedures, often demanding 50 percent of the purchase price as a down payment and repayment of the balance within ten years. Following the war, however, the Federal Housing Administration (FHA) began insuring thirty-year bank mortgages with only a 5 to 10 percent down payment. Under the GI Bill, qualifying veterans could often take title for a token $1 down payment. By guaranteeing loan repayment, the FHA and Veterans Administration (VA) persuaded private lenders to relax mortgage terms.

The result was a housing boom, particularly in suburbia, where large areas of inexpensive land could be developed. Housing starts jumped from 114,000 in 1944 to 1.7 million in 1950. By then, federal agencies insured more than one-third of all mortgages. In addition to FHA and VA loan guarantees, the government's tax policy promoted housing growth by allowing a deduction for mortgage interest. Veterans' demands and the new federal policies meshed with a new trend in the construction industry: the increasing dominance of large construction firms, which had discovered that they could operate profitably by building a great number of similar homes on large tracts of land.

Levittown, named after builder William Levitt, became a synonym for suburban development. Levitt, a builder of luxury homes before 1941, pioneered prefabrication techniques for navy housing during the war. In 1947, he decided to mass-produce private homes that GIs would be able to afford. The first Levittown, a planned community of 10,000 homes, sprang from a 1,200-acre potato field on Long Island, New York. Larger projects followed in Pennsylvania and New Jersey.

Levitt harnessed mass-production techniques to home construction, making a "factory of the whole building site." Materials were precut and preassembled by teams of semiskilled laborers and moved to lots when needed. Instead of hiring union painters and carpenters, Levitt trained workers to do specific tasks, such as spray painting or using power tools, on an assembly-line basis. The company bought its own forests, milled its own lumber, and convinced appliance companies to manufacture new, standard-size washers, dryers, and refrigerators at reduced prices. At the height of Levittown construction, a house was completed every sixteen minutes. Construction costs were $10 a square foot, 30 percent below the industry standard. With a VA loan, a veteran could move into a new home for $56 per month, which was often less than the cost of renting an apartment. When one subdivision opened in 1949, 1,400 units sold in a single day.

The Levittown house, like Henry Ford's Model T, set an affordable standard that made homeownership a reality for the postwar middle class. But

Levittown was only the most conspicuous example of a widespread trend. Surrounding cities across the United States, new suburbs of similar, middle-class houses began to appear. In a chaotic world, the freestanding, single-family, self-contained, all-electric suburban home was presented as a refuge in which the female homemaker could take charge of housework and childcare, while appliances did the hard work.

Architectural critics condemned the cookie-cutter appearance of these new communities. Social commentators worried about conformist pressures, such as the rule that lawns be mowed weekly or that homes could be painted only with approved colors. But most new residents who had shared cramped quarters with resentful in-laws were thrilled to move into a three-bedroom house equipped with luxuries such as a washer, dryer, and refrigerator. Suburbia also homogenized white society by mixing ethnic, social, and political groups that formerly had lived in separate urban neighborhoods. New institutions such as churches and civic clubs replaced extended families and kinship networks.

Levittown and its many imitators made homeownership a reality for the white postwar middle class. Houses originally priced in the $7,000 range would be worth $300,000 or more fifty years later. Some "Levittowners" used their home equity gradually to trade up to fancier homes; others held on to their homes for decades and used the equity to finance college for their children or to fund their own retirement.

Suburbs tended to be ethnically diverse but racially segregated. Suburbanization actually increased the separation of races in most parts of America. In 1950, for example, only 1 million of the 20 million Americans living in suburbs were nonwhite. During its first several years, Levittown, like many planned subdivisions, barred "members of other than the Caucasian race" from buying homes. Meanwhile, in cities where most racial minorities were concentrated, federal agencies and private lenders provided few loans to build or improve homes.

By 1946, the nation was experiencing a baby boom that would last into the 1960s. The average number of children born to an American family increased from 2.4 to 3.2 between 1945 and 1957, when the boom peaked (see Figure 3.1). The American population surged by 30 million in the 1950s, reaching 180 million by the end of the decade. When births peaked at 4.3 million in 1957, one-third of all Americans were age 14 or younger. This demographic feature created exceptional demands for new housing, appliances, toys, and schools. Between 1950 and 1960, total school enrollment in kindergarten through twelfth grade increased from 28 million to 42 million.

In previous decades, parenting manuals had described infants as nasty tyrants who would grow up with grave character disorders if they were indulged or overstimulated. Pediatrician Benjamin Spock challenged these assumptions in his 1946 *Book of Baby and Child Care*. Spock urged parents to have fun with their kids. He encouraged physical contact and emotional nurturing as keys to healthy development. The book sold over 20 million copies in ten years, and 40 million copies by 1990.

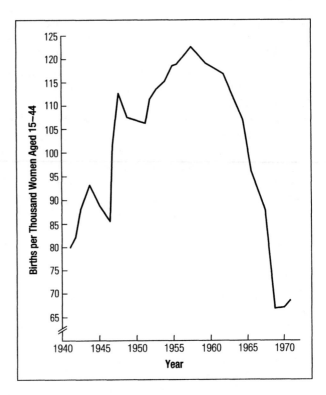

Figure 3.1
Birth Rate, 1940–1970

As young parents in suburbia read Dr. Spock and enjoyed their electric kitchens, the same policies that promoted suburban growth were causing serious problems for cities, the poor, and minorities. The FHA gave preference to subsidizing single-family, detached homes in the $7,000 to $10,000 range. Until the 1960s, the FHA provided few loans to assist buyers in racially mixed neighborhoods or to improve existing multifamily housing. In making these decisions, the FHA followed the color-coded rating system devised by the federal Home Owners Loan Corporation, which classified neighborhoods (from green to red) according to the loan default risks they were presumed to pose for mortgage lenders. These redlining practices kept many African Americans and other people of color out of the housing market and living in older, decaying urban neighborhoods. Meanwhile, minorities were barred from most suburban homes.

Public and private discrimination contributed to drawing a "white noose" around the increasingly nonwhite cities. As businesses and white families left the cities for the suburbs, they took with them the jobs and income that had contributed to urban tax revenues and employment. The growth of suburbs around a city usually resulted in the decline of the city's economy. By 1960, the suburban population of 60 million equaled that of all urban areas. Except for the South and West, where rural-to-urban migration continued, most large cities either lost population or barely held steady during the 1950s.

At first, almost all suburbanites commuted to jobs in central cities, but by 1960 many worked closer to home. Suburban employment and manufacturing rose dramatically, while employment in the twenty-five largest U.S. cities declined about 7 percent during the decade. Downtown commercial districts lost business to suburban shopping centers surrounded by acres of parking lots.

The American population continued to shift west and south, with California, Florida, and Texas attracting many newcomers. The gains in urban population in the West and suburban population in the Northeast came partly at the expense of rural America. The number of agricultural workers fell to barely 6 percent of the population, down two-thirds since America entered World War II.

The rise of the suburbs had other lasting effects as well. One was the increased demand for cars and better roads. Between 1946 and 1950, domestic automobile production jumped from 2 million to 6 million annually. By 1960, America had nearly 70 million vehicles on the road. In Los Angeles County alone, more cars traveled the freeways than in all of Asia or South America. By the 1950s, the highway lobby—an umbrella group of automakers, highway construction companies, and trucking firms—began to pressure the federal government for a national highway system. Nine out of ten suburban families owned a car, compared to only six out of ten urban households. Women driving station wagons full of children became emblems of suburban life.

These cars were not the staid models of the 1940s. Detroit built bigger, gaudier, more expensive machines than ever before. The public adored two- and three-tone models, tail fins, and wraparound windshields. Innovations like

By the 1950s, American culture was car culture. / Picture Research Consultants

power steering, automatic transmission, and air conditioning made cars more comfortable and convenient. Auto tourism became a major form of family leisure. Bobby Troupe's hit song "Get Your Kicks on Route 66" reflected Americans' love of the road. Families took cross-country trips to national parks and new amusement parks like Disneyland. Motel chains proliferated. So did other spin-off industries such as fast-food restaurants and drive-in theaters.

Responding to demands from business, local governments, and automobile owners, the federal government decided to upgrade the nation's inadequate highways. By 1956, a bipartisan movement in Congress, supported by organized labor, the highway lobby, and civil-defense advocates (who argued that better roads would speed the evacuation from cities in times of war), won passage of the National System of Defense Highways. This massive building program authorized the construction of forty thousand miles of new highways. Washington paid 90 percent of the initial $50 billion tab through excise taxes levied on tires and fuel, and the states paid the rest. The massive road-building program prompted one leading Democrat to quip that "the New Dealers had been replaced by the car dealers."

The interstate highway system dwarfed anything built by the New Deal. And although the title of the bill suggested that highways were needed primarily for defense purposes, the most important effects of interstate highways were social. By subsidizing the car culture with six thousand miles of city-to-suburb freeways, while denying funds for inner-city mass transit, government promoted suburban development at the cities' expense.

The public's enthusiasm for the automobile allowed manufacturers to ignore the poor safety records and nonexistent fuel efficiency of their products. The mounting highway death toll (forty thousand in 1959) elicited little concern, although a young Harvard law student, Ralph Nader, worried enough to begin investigating auto safety as early as 1957. But the big Detroit automakers either ignored their few critics or dismissed them as deviants.

By the early 1960s, many urban planners and ordinary Americans began to question the wisdom of chopping up cities with smog-producing freeways while permitting mass transit to decay. But during the 1950s, nearly everyone celebrated public road subsidies for private automobiles. Gasoline was cheap, highways were "free," and America's future was on the road.

Leisure and entertainment in general were becoming big business. Television's influence on American life was soon evident in ways both large and small. The television industry expanded quickly in the early 1950s, when the Federal Communications Commission (FCC) sped up licensing procedures. As the size of televisions increased, quality improved and prices fell to an average of $200. By the time Eisenhower took office in 1953, half of all American homes had a television. For the rest of the decade, sales ranged between 5 million and 7 million units annually. By 1956, two-thirds of all American homes had one or more televisions, and Americans viewed programs on over 600 stations, nearly all of which were affiliated with a national network. By the early 1960s, 90 percent of all homes had at least one receiver. As early as 1956, Americans spent more time watching television than working for wages.

Some early comedy-variety offerings, like Sid Caesar's *Your Show of Shows* (1950–1954), provided quality writing and acting. A fair amount of sophisticated live drama aired through the mid-1950s on shows such as *Kraft Television Theater*, *Playhouse 90*, and *Studio One*. But toward the end of the 1950s, Hollywood began selling old movies to television and producing low-budget, made-for-TV movies. This switch effectively removed most original drama from television.

Among the most successful comedy shows of the 1950s was *I Love Lucy*, which became a model for many subsequent situation comedies, or sitcoms. Lucille Ball played Lucy Ricardo, the scatterbrained wife of Cuban-born bandleader Ricky Ricardo, played by Desi Arnaz, her real-life husband. Each week Lucy and her friend Ethel Mertz schemed to get jobs, impress their husbands, and achieve respect. Their plans usually backfired, forcing Ricky and Fred Mertz to rescue their wives. Although the show's endings reinforced the assumption that traditional gender roles best suited the capacities of women and men, Lucy's ambition, energy, and resourcefulness came through strongly, undermining the psychological explanations of women's discontent that dominated other media.

Because of technical limitations on live broadcasts and remote filming, news coverage was not a staple of television until the early 1960s. Still, Edward R. Murrow, a pioneer of radio and TV investigative journalism, produced some exceptional work for CBS, including an exposé of Senator Joseph McCarthy on *See It Now* and a pioneering probe of the link between smoking and lung cancer in 1955. But most television news came in a fifteen-minute format. As innovations such as the video camera made it possible to follow breaking stories, the networks expanded nightly news coverage to half-hour broadcasts in 1963 and promoted the programs heavily to win audience share.

Television generally provided entertainment, not intellectual enlightenment. *Howdy Doody*, a lighthearted romp using marionettes and mock Indians, set the tone for children's programming. Westerns like *Hopalong Cassidy* and *The Lone Ranger* played to young viewers before adult westerns such as *Gunsmoke* and *Maverick* came into vogue. Soap operas and quiz shows dominated the daytime airwaves. Inexpensive to produce, they appealed to busy housewives, who could break up the household routine with television viewing. *Queen for a Day*, in which bedraggled women told hard-luck stories in return for prizes, merged the soap-opera and quiz-show formats.

In the evening, family-oriented sitcoms proliferated. The decade's big hits included *The Adventures of Ozzie and Harriet*, *Leave It to Beaver*, *Father Knows Best*, and *The Honeymooners*. Except for the last, in which bus driver Ralph Kramden (Jackie Gleason) and his sewer-worker buddy Ed Norton (Art Carney) schemed to get rich, these were middle-class fables in which white suburban families with a homemaker mother and a breadwinning father lived pleasant lives. People of color appeared only as servants. Television's need to attract mass audiences and thus earn advertising revenue ensured that its content would appeal to the greatest possible number and that complex social or economic issues would not be discussed.

The rarity of African Americans on television made the inclusion of any blacks noteworthy. Henry Louis Gates, Jr., who was raised in West Virginia in the 1950s, remembers that the neighbors would shout, "Colored, colored, on Channel Two," from their front porches or get on the phone to tell their friends. Even *Amos and Andy*, widely criticized for its stereotypical black characters, was popular in his neighborhood because the world of the show "was *all* colored, just like ours." The inclusion of black professionals on the show gave African Americans images of different lives. Like other Americans, blacks found that the "TV was the ritual arena for the drama of race" unfolding in American society, from Montgomery to Little Rock and beyond.

A quiz-show scandal in 1959 tarnished television's reputation as the purveyor of clean values. In 1955, a few prime-time quiz shows with large cash prizes, such as *The $64,000 Question* and *Twenty-One*, captured the public's fancy. In dramatic encounters, one or more contestants, isolated in glass booths, competed for cash prizes. To heighten the suspense, the questions were kept in bank vaults and brought to the studio by armed guards. Each week's winner proceeded to a new round, tougher questions, and bigger prizes. These shows attracted huge audiences and earned large profits for both the networks and sponsors. Producers often coached contestants on how to smile, grimace, fidget, and knit their brows while pondering the questions. Some contestants secretly received additional help, including the answers to questions.

In 1956, Charles Van Doren, a young, articulate English professor at Columbia University, won $129,000 on *Twenty-One*—a great improvement on his $4,400 academic salary. NBC hired him as a consultant for $50,000 annually. Parents and teachers wrote to praise Van Doren as a role model for children. Two years later, the bubble burst. In 1958, the man dethroned by Charles Van Doren complained to New York journalists that Van Doren had received the answers in advance. Both a grand jury and a congressional subcommittee investigated the scandal. Van Doren first maintained his innocence, but eventually he broke down and gave the investigating committee details of his cheating. The prospect of wealth and fame had corrupted him, Van Doren explained. In the wake of this scandal, networks canceled most of the quiz shows.

The scandal made some question the value of television. After all, TV had invaded the American home, taking center stage in the American living room. What happened when this new focus of family life lied to viewers? Should it be admired as a source of entertainment and information, despised as cultural pabulum, or feared for its demagogic potential? Just as social commentators disagree about television's worth in today's society, historians have mixed feelings about its contribution to the 1950s. Newton Minow, newly appointed chair of the Federal Communications Commission (FCC), shocked a gathering of broadcast executives in 1961 by describing their industry as a vast wasteland. Forty years later, quiz shows, sitcoms, sports, and police dramas (rather than westerns) still dominated television programming.

Nowhere was the impact of television on popular culture clearer than in the area of sports. After World War II, professional and college sports assumed a growing significance in American life. By the late 1940s, professional leagues in basketball and ice hockey had joined those in baseball and football to provide increasing sports entertainment for an avid public. Sports took on the trappings of a secular religion as people gave vast significance to the fortunes of their favorite teams. In the suburbs, Little League baseball and football, modeled on the professional leagues, enrolled millions of boys.

Television was part of this change because it elevated players to unprecedented fame and gave fans a new and closer look at their idols. Initially, TV cameras worked best in small arenas and other venues in which a single camera could pan the playing area. Boxing, wrestling, and roller derby fared well on TV, as did baseball. As the technology evolved, multiple and remote cameras improved the coverage of football and basketball, and sports occupied a growing portion of the TV schedule. By the 1960s, sports had become a major part of broadcasting. Television also became the key to sports profits because television payments soon exceeded the revenue from ticket sales.

Desegregation proceeded slowly in professional and college athletics. After Jackie Robinson broke baseball's color line in 1947, professional teams began to hire black athletes, but the pace varied from one sport to another. Some southern college basketball teams refused to recruit African Americans or play against teams that did. Because the segregated sports programs gradually became uncompetitive, they were eventually forced to recruit blacks as well as whites.

As the nation's population shifted toward the West and the Sunbelt, the owners of professional teams began to move franchises to these areas, often provoking outcries from loyal fans. When baseball owner Walter O'Malley took his Brooklyn Dodgers to Los Angeles after the 1957 season, New Yorkers decried his betrayal and demanded a congressional investigation. But during the next decade, many teams relocated. The old fans protested, but fans in the new cities hastened to the stadiums and arenas or watched the games on television.

The Politics of Moderation

By the beginning of the 1950s, it was clear that national politics were swinging to the right. The question was, how far right? General Dwight D. Eisenhower, widely known by his nickname Ike, chose politics as a second career at age sixty-two. Despite this late beginning, he became one of the most popular and successful presidents of the postwar era. The public was reassured by his calm, grandfatherly style and seldom questioned his rather disengaged stewardship of domestic policy. Veteran journalist Walter Lippmann remarked, "Ike could be elected even if dead. All you would need [to do is] to prop him up in the rear seat of an open car and parade down Broadway."

Eisenhower was born in 1890 in Denison, Texas, into a large, pious, and poor family. He grew up in Abilene, Kansas, and attended West Point despite his parents' pacifism. He graduated in 1915, but because few promotions were available during the interwar period, he had risen only to the rank of major by 1939. With the start of the war in Europe, however, Eisenhower quickly ascended to prominence, helped by army chief of staff General George C. Marshall, who considered him among the most promising men in the army. By 1944, Eisenhower was a four-star general and commander of the Allied forces in the European theater. His ability to manage and conciliate the Allied armies sped victory and won him acclaim as a talented and humane leader.

After the war, Eisenhower served successively as army chief of staff, president of Columbia University, and the first supreme commander of NATO during the Korean War. Ambitious but wary of politics, he rebuffed both Democratic and Republican invitations to seek the presidential nomination in 1948. Four years later, he still coveted the White House but disdained the idea of campaigning for office, seeking instead a "draft" that would nominate him by acclamation.

Despite Eisenhower's wartime ties to Roosevelt, he held fairly conservative views on economics and social programs, favoring private enterprise over government intervention as a solution to most problems. He was at the same time a confirmed internationalist who supported the containment of communism, the Marshall Plan, and the "Europe-first" orientation of the Truman administration. Eisenhower resented and feared the anti-NATO, Asia-first ideas of Republican presidential aspirants such as senators Robert Taft and Joseph McCarthy and General Douglas MacArthur. Early in 1952, Eisenhower made his decision: he resigned his NATO command and entered the Republican primaries, securing enough delegates to defeat his chief rival, Taft, at the party's nominating convention. Eisenhower placated the Republican right by tapping California senator Richard M. Nixon as his vice-presidential running mate.

Cracks in the Picture Window

While Eisenhower exuded his aura of political stability, American life was changing in significant ways. Technology continued the boom begun during World War II, and the economy reached new heights of prosperity in spite of three recessions. The home and family were increasingly the center of popular values, reinforced by a widespread revival in church membership. But critics surveying the social landscape began to insist that important flaws lay beneath the surface of prosperity and contentment.

Economic growth during the 1950s averaged more than 4 percent annually, despite recessions in 1954, 1958, and 1960. Inflation remained below 2 percent and unemployment remained below 5 percent. The gross national product (GNP) nearly doubled between 1950 and 1960, to $500 billion (see Figure 3.2). Measured in constant 1954 dollars, this represented a per capita increase of about 25 percent (from $2,096 to $2,536). Median family income grew from about $3,000 to $5,657. Real wages rose by 30 percent.

With high employment and higher incomes, Americans found more ways to spend their wages. Lenient bank lending policies and the advent of the credit card also stimulated consumer spending. The Diners Club and American Express credit cards were both introduced during the 1950s, followed by oil company, hotel chain, and department store credit cards. Sears promoted its cards

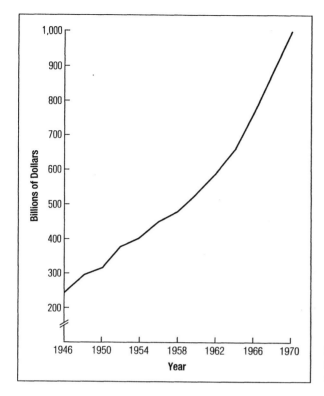

Figure 3.2
Gross National Product,
1946–1970

so aggressively that by 1960, over 10 million Americans held them. As a record number of young families furnished homes and clothed children in the 1950s, private debt climbed from $73 billion to $200 billion. That debt financed a mountain of consumer goods as Americans sought the new, the disposable, and the modern. Encouraged by advertising to equate consuming with personal freedom and "the good life," Americans used natural resources as though the supply was infinite and littered newly created landfills with tons of disposable goods. The 1950s witnessed the creation of the throwaway society, complete with TV dinners in aluminum containers or "boil-in bags," and a plethora of paper products—from napkins to dresses—that could be discarded after one use. In 1951, *House Beautiful* asked women "Is Your Grandmother Standing Between You and Today's Freedom?" while offering them information on the use of new household products. At the end of the decade, *Look* provided similar training and extolled the new "kitchen freedom" being offered to women.

The profile of industry and business also changed. Mergers accelerated, with the result that the two hundred largest corporations controlled over half of all business assets by the end of the decade. Some corporations were beginning to expand across national borders. Traditional industries such as iron, steel, textiles, and mining shrank, while chemicals, aviation, drugs, plastics, fast-food chains, discount retailers (such as Kresge's, later Kmart), and electronics expanded. Overall, heavy industry and manufacturing declined, partly a result of automation, which cost an estimated 1.5 million jobs from 1953 to 1959. New job growth clustered in the service, clerical, and managerial sectors. By 1956, white-collar workers outnumbered blue-collar workers for the first time.

Throughout the 1950s, the number of American farm families continued to decline. Increased mechanization, cheap chemical fertilizers, and new herbicides and pesticides allowed farmers to boost crop yields significantly. The increased production of grains, vegetables, and dairy products benefited urban consumers but created a surplus that drove agricultural commodity prices down. Congress responded by adopting a complex price support system that paid some farmers to grow less, paid others a subsidy to cover their costs, and promoted agricultural exports through subsidies or as food aid to poor countries. But even as the number of farmers declined in the decades after World War II, productivity grew and, as in industry, a growing proportion of farms were owned by corporate agribusiness and worked by employees. Small farmers found it increasingly difficult to compete against these conglomerates and foreign producers.

Meanwhile, the labor movement struggled, with only partial success, to hold its own. Once the war was over, it pushed for a law making the federal government responsible for securing employment for all job seekers who were able to work. The 1946 Full Employment Act, gutted in passage by Congress, promised only "maximum employment," an ambiguous term that left plenty of room for shifting views of what represented an acceptable unemployment rate. In 1955, the American Federation of Labor and the Congress of Industrial Organizations overcame their long-time rivalry and merged to form the AFL-CIO. But congressional investigations into union ties to organized crime, along with the federal conviction of Teamsters Union president Dave Beck, tarnished labor's image and led to the passage of the Landrum-Griffin Act of 1959. It created new legal restrictions on the labor movement, including additional limits on boycotts and picketing.

Although the number of union members remained fairly steady, the unionized proportion of the total work force declined with the loss of jobs in heavy industry, and unions faced new challenges as they sought to extend their power in the blue-collar sector. Corporate leaders used relocation and automation to reduce the power of unions. The automobile industry, for example, moved many plants to suburban locations, some in the Detroit area, and to new areas in the Midwest and California. In the South, redbaiting, management pressures, and local hostility to unions made growth difficult in a region where new service and manufacturing jobs (mostly for whites only) were rapidly replacing jobs lost in the rural areas. The unions that managed to penetrate the white-collar sector, such as the American Federation of State, County, and Municipal Employees (AFSCME), accounted for a growing percentage of union membership.

Throughout the decade, some progressive business leaders and economists boasted of creating a "people's capitalism" that ensured the equal distribution

(cont. on page 100)

High-Tech Medicine

The baby-boom generation was raised by three doctors: Dr. Spock, Dr. Salk, and Dr. Seuss. Dr. Benjamin Spock's advice to anxious parents alleviated stresses of childcare. Dr. Seuss (Theodore Geisel) wrote miraculous stories such as *The Cat in the Hat* and *Green Eggs and Ham* that put a generation of children to bed while instilling in them a love of reading. Dr. Jonas Salk's vaccine banished the terror of paralytic polio, a disease that had haunted America since the 1920s. The biotechnological revolution of the 1940s and 1950s ushered in an era when Americans looked to science and medicine to eliminate infectious disease, regulate birth, and mitigate the effects of aging. They also heard frequent warnings from public health authorities about the risks of smoking and obesity.

Today, Americans suffering from a diversity of maladies treat the problem with a pill or shot. Before World War II, few such treatments existed, and aspirin was about as high-tech as medicine got. World War II spurred a revolution that transformed the treatment of illness and produced the modern pharmaceutical industry.

Most physicians accepted the germ theory of disease, but science had produced few treatments before 1930. In 1929, British bacteriologist Arthur Fleming reported that the common *penicillium notatum* mold produced a substance that killed bacteria in a laboratory dish. But for a decade, no one followed up on this observation. In 1939, as war began in Europe, British and American researchers began to study the antibiotic, or germ-killing, properties of the mold.

Penicillin, as scientists called the mold's active ingredient, proved difficult to extract. It took a year to gather one-tenth of a gram of penicillin, just enough to test on an infected mouse. A human treatment required at least 30 grams. But, spurred on by the war, in 1941 a team of researchers discovered that penicillin could be produced through a bulk fermentation process that utilized a molasses-like by-product of corn. They enlisted private industry to start a massive production effort, and by 1942, several companies opened "bottle plants" that contained 100,000 one-liter fermentation containers. A federal "penicillin czar" oversaw the production and distribution of millions of doses of the miracle drug that destroyed the germs that caused such common killers as pneumonia, tuberculosis, and staphylococcus. After the war, many of the penicillin pioneers left government for university or private laboratories, where they developed new antibiotics.

Initially, few researchers realized that by killing off natural forms of bacterium, antibiotics cleared the path for the emergence of new drug-resistant strains. As drug-resistant "staph" and "strep" proliferated, pharmaceutical companies raced to develop new antibiotics. These new drugs, in turn, opened the bacteriological environment for new resistant strains in a never-ending antibiotic war.

Americans alive in the 1940s and 1950s dreaded few things more than the annual spring onset of the polio season. Each summer since 1916, the disease struck tens of thousands of victims, killing or paralyzing several thousand. In a futile effort to stop the plague, municipal pools and beaches closed and parents kept children at home. Everyone knew someone who, like Franklin D. Roosevelt in 1921, had gone to bed with a headache and never walked again. Their tragedy was captured in poignant photographs in *Life* and *Look* magazines that displayed hospital wards full of children and adults in bulky metal breathing devices called iron lungs. The most severe polio outbreak occurred in 1952, when 60,000 Americans fell seriously ill. About 3,000 died and about 9,000 suffered some degree of paralysis. Influenza, heart disease, and cancer took a higher toll, but no disease conjured up more fear than polio.

97

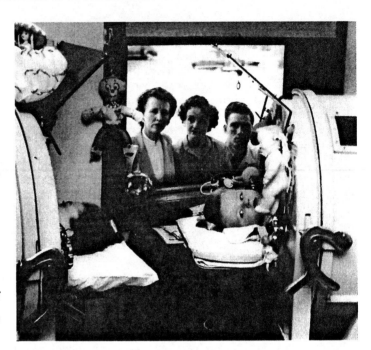

As polio epidemics grew more severe in the early 1950s, every parent's nightmare was that his or her child might die or end up in an "iron lung." / ©Bettman/CORBIS

Until the twentieth century, the virus that caused poliomyelitis afflicted relatively few people. Most babies were exposed to the virus shortly after birth, when it caused only a mild infection and conferred lifelong immunity. But in the United States, improved sanitation often delayed exposure to the virus, whose symptoms became more virulent as age increased. Babies raised in middle- and upper-class homes were more likely to avoid exposure in infancy and thus suffer from later infection.

The fight against polio became an American obsession during the 1930s to 1950s, in part because Franklin D. Roosevelt, whose legs were crippled by the disease in 1921, became president in 1933. Roosevelt projected a new public vision of the polio survivor as someone who triumphed over adversity through struggle. He and his former law partner, Basil O'Connor, organized the National Foundation for Infantile Paralysis in 1938. Although a private organization, it benefited from a close association with FDR's New Deal. The foundation's "March of Dimes" annual fundraiser selected a poster child whose image helped bring in as much as $67 million each year by the 1950s for polio treatment and research.

The postwar baby boom intersected with a rising incidence of polio. The disease struck at the very essence of a middle-class, child-centered society, and at a faith that science could vanquish all problems. If scientists could harness nuclear power and build rockets and computers, surely they could conquer a primitive virus.

In 1949, Dr. Jonas Salk, a research physician based at the University of Pittsburgh (also home to Dr. Spock), received support from the National Foundation for Infantile Paralysis to develop a polio vaccine. Salk applied techniques developed by others who had discovered how to grow poliovirus in a test tube. He concentrated on creating a vaccine derived from "killed" viruses, while other researchers favored a vaccine from weakened, or "attenuated," live viruses.

After a small-scale test showed promise, Salk and his foundation sponsors launched a massive field trial. In 1954, 220,000 volunteers, 20,000 physicians, and 64,000 public health workers recruited 2 million elementary schoolchildren, called "polio volunteers," for the largest test ever of an experimental drug. To ensure accuracy, children from all races had to be included in the experiment. Segregation remained so strong in southern states, however, that black children were denied entry into the white-only schools where the shots were given. Instead, they lined up in parking lots for the test.

By April 1955, the results were conclusive. Newspaper headlines trumpeted "Polio Threat Conquered by Salk Vaccine." Salk became a global hero. He was featured on Edward R. Murrow's television show *See It Now* and was given a congressional medal. Although it would cost only $140 million to inoculate all Americans under age twenty-one, both the Eisenhower administration and the American Medical Association (AMA) opposed full public funding as a dangerous move toward "socialized medicine." The AMA distrusted Salk when he refused to claim sole ownership of the vaccine, saying to do so would be like "patenting the sun." After much squabbling, federal, state, and private funds supported a mass-vaccination campaign that almost banished paralytic polio and the terror that accompanied it.

In the early 1960s, country music diva Loretta Lynn recorded a hit entitled "The Pill." She crooned how "All these years I've stayed at home while you've had all your fun/And every year that's gone by another baby's come/There's gonna be some changes made right here on Nursery Hill/You've set this chicken your last time 'cause now I've got the Pill." The lyric reflected the fact that starting in 1960, for this first time in history, women had access to a relatively safe, effective, and legal oral contraceptive. The Pill was added to the list of American scientific triumphs by many—and blamed by some for the nation's "moral decline."

Three male scientists (Drs. Gregory Pincus, Chang Min-chueh, and John Rock) are credited with developing and testing the Pill. But they were prodded, inspired, and funded by two remarkable women, Margaret Sanger and Katherine McCormick. Sanger, the founder of the Planned Parenthood Federation of America, had long crusaded for legal, effective birth control. She challenged many state and federal laws dating from the 1800s that barred birth-control counseling or even the sale of diaphragms and condoms. McCormick, one of the first women to earn a science degree from the Massachusetts Institute of Technology (MIT), was active in the women's suffrage movement. She used her fortune (from marrying into the McCormick farm implement family) to fund research on several illnesses as well as on human fertility.

Sanger believed a birth-control pill would ensure voluntary motherhood in advanced countries and control the so-called population explosion in poor countries. Her views were tinged with eugenics (the notion that society should limit the breeding of inferior humans) as well as Cold War concerns that overpopulation in the Third World would breed communism.

Sanger and McCormick turned for help to Dr. Pincus, a specialist in mammal physiology, who set up a private research institute after being denied tenure at Harvard University in the 1940s. The G.D. Searle pharmaceutical company had funded his effort to synthesize the hormone cortisone. But when another scientist won the race, Searle cut Pincus off. Sanger and McCormick then offered him support to develop a pill to prevent unwanted pregnancy. Federal agencies refused to fund contraceptive research.

Pincus, along with Chang and Rock, focused on the role played by the female sex hormones progesterone and estrogen in regulating fertility. Some early tests on humans were performed on involuntary female mental patients. Field trials took place among women on Puerto Rico and Haiti in the late 1950s.

Once the Pill showed promise, companies like G.D. Searle eagerly marketed the discovery. Searle received Food and Drug Administration (FDA) approval for Enovid, the brand name for the oral contraceptive, in 1960, even though thirty states still outlawed or severely restricted contraceptives. Women rushed to their physicians to get prescriptions for the Pill and it quickly became the most commonly used contraceptive in the United States. Partly because of the expense and the need for a doctor's referral, white, middle-class women have always been the biggest users of the pill. Despite opposition from their Church, about 30 percent of Catholic women of childbearing age used the Pill within a few years of its appearance.

By the close of the twentieth century, researchers developed an arsenal of medicines to treat not only infections, but also chronic health conditions. Pharmaceutical companies spend about $30 billion annually on research and development. It takes about eleven years to take a drug from the laboratory to the market.

The cost of drug treatment has grown not just because a single dose of medicine is expensive. Rather, a patient with high blood pressure now treats the condition with medicine that he or she will take for decades. In 2001, Americans spent $155 billion on prescription drugs. Nearly $80 billion went for just a few drugs that alleviate the symptoms of depression, allergies, diabetes, hypertension, and sexual dysfunction. Twelve percent of each health dollar now goes for drugs, an amount likely to double in ten years.

The high cost of long-term drug treatment is a growing burden to elderly patients and the healthcare system. When Congress passed the Medicare program for seniors in 1965, it did not include a prescription drug benefit because few medications existed to treat age-related illness. Today, drugs constitute one of the most expensive components of healthcare, especially among the elderly. Congress has refused to defray their cost for them or for the nearly 25 percent of working Americans with no health insurance.

---

of abundance and erased class divisions. Others, however, stressed economic growth, not income redistribution, as the means to economic well-being. They engaged in a sustained campaign using the media and economic "education" programs for their employees to persuade workers and the general public that Americans could rely on corporate leadership, unfettered by the countervailing power of unions or by government regulation, to create the material abundance they sought. This campaign characterized unions as obstacles to consumers' goals, discrediting their participation in strikes, in corporate decisions, and in national political life. It equated state action with communism, charging that state intervention led to tyranny and inefficiency.

Despite business leaders' protestations that increased productivity would benefit all, wealth remained highly concentrated, as it had throughout the century. In 1960, the richest 1 percent of the population possessed one-third of the nation's wealth, and the top 5 percent controlled over half its wealth. Half of all families had no savings account, and almost one-fourth of the population lived near or below the poverty line (then figured as an income of $3,000 per year for a family of four). The poverty rate was especially high among the elderly, racial minorities, and rural Americans.

Superficially, Americans seemed a content lot, and they became increasingly devout. By the end of the decade, two-thirds of the population claimed formal church membership, up from 48 percent before World War II. Ninety-seven percent professed a belief in God. Religious popularizers like Billy Graham became media celebrities, appearing in newspapers, on radio and television, and on bestseller lists. A new translation of the Bible sold millions of copies. For those without time to read it, *Reader's Digest* issued an abridgment. Congress added the words *under God* to the Pledge of Allegiance and put the motto "In God We Trust" on the nation's paper money.

Christianity, like parenthood and the suburban nuclear family, became a measure of Americanism and a rejection of atheistic communism. Surveys revealed that a large majority of Americans considered atheism a subversive threat. Like Eisenhower, few people stressed doctrinal differences or weighty theological issues; rather, religion served to unify society. As Will Herberg, a professor of Judaic studies, noted in his incisive 1955 study *Protestant-Catholic-Jew*, the nation's religions, especially in suburbia, tolerated almost any content in their observances—or lack thereof. Rather than reorienting life to God, religion served a social function in the new communities.

Religious and secular opinion leaders agreed emphatically on one issue—the need for a strong American family founded on traditional values. There was as much novelty as tradition in postwar family values, however. The conviction that the nuclear family could meet all the emotional and practical needs of its members was new, although the idea that women were responsible for seeing that it did so successfully derived from older beliefs. According to popular media, when a woman subordinated her needs and ambitions totally to her family's well-being, she would ensure that families would be happy and stable.

Reinforcing this view, advice columns, television shows, and schools emphasized traditional gender roles, placing the husband at work and the wife in the home. Indeed, the popular media used its version of Freudian psychology to urge women to accept their femininity, meaning subordination to men, domesticity, and economic dependence. To do otherwise was understood as a socially dangerous form of emotional maladjustment. Indeed, experts interpreted women's dissatisfaction with these prescriptions as unhealthy masculinist strivings, code language for penis envy. In some cases, women were institutionalized and subjected to electric shock treatments for failure to conform their values and behavior to these precepts.

Clearly, experts in the 1950s produced a great deal of advice literature designed to repress women's discontent by labeling it deviant. Those women who found society's expectations impossible to meet or unrewarding felt compelled to deny, hide, or seek panaceas for their unhappiness. One suburban housewife later described her life in these years as one of "booze, bowling, bridge, and boredom." When *Redbook* magazine asked its readers to explain "Why Young Mothers Feel Trapped," the editors received an astonishing twenty-four thousand replies. The popularity of a new drug—tranquilizers—marketed in the mid-1950s attested to women's sense of uneasiness with their lives. In 1959, Americans, mostly women, consumed 1.15 million pounds of the pills.

At the same time, American women appeared to embrace the domesticity touted by 1950s popular culture. During the decade, they reversed a hundred-year trend by marrying younger and having more babies. Changes in courtship and sexual practices contributed to these trends. In the postwar period, young couples radically changed dating practices, shifting from an emphasis on popularity, evidenced by casual dates with different people, to going steady. The development of emotionally intense and sexually freighted long-term relationships among teenagers frightened their parents, who worried particularly about premarital pregnancies. Their fears were well placed because the 1950s spawned the highest teen pregnancy rates in U.S. history and witnessed an increase of more than 100 percent in the proportion of white brides who were pregnant on their wedding day. As historian Stephanie Coontz concluded, "Young people were not taught how to 'say no'—they were simply handed wedding rings."

Pregnant women who did not marry faced constrained choices. Parents and public officials strongly encouraged white women to leave town for the duration of their pregnancies, usually spending that time in homes for unwed mothers, and then to put their babies up for adoption. Doing so enabled the young women to undergo a kind of moral rehabilitation, first, by hiding the pregnancy from public view at home and, second, through counseling. These policies enabled many white couples to fulfill their family goals by becoming adoptive parents. Most white officials, however, viewed African American women as incapable of moral change and expected them to keep their babies. Few adoption services were available to them, and the enduring poverty of African American families meant that most did not meet the economic standards for adoption developed by whites. The women's families generally offered assistance and acceptance to them and their children. African American women's increasing use of Aid to Families with Dependent Children to help support their children prompted a backlash among whites, who saw the mothers as immoral and the children as economic liabilities.

Abortion remained illegal but had become somewhat safer with the introduction of antibiotics in the 1940s. Escalating police crackdowns on abortion providers, often accompanied by sensationalist coverage by the local press, made securing the illegal procedure more difficult. Even so, large numbers of women had abortions and many, especially those who were poor, died as a result. The situation was hardly invisible because big-city hospitals created special wings to treat women suffering from infections and other complications. Middle-class women could sometimes secure safe, legal abortions if a hospital committee agreed that continuing the pregnancy would cause them serious physical or emotional harm. Those who tried to do so, however, were likely to be turned down on the grounds that their desire for an abortion might itself be a symptom of a profound maladjustment whose cure would include motherhood.

Despite society's conviction that women, men, and children were happiest when women focused on full-time homemaking, the domestic authority exercised by women generated cultural anxieties about "the overfeminization of schools and households." In 1954, *Life* magazine announced "the domestication of the American male" and worried that it might lead to emasculation. Family experts saw a solution to this threat in men's greater involvement with their children, particularly their sons. In an article urging men to take a more active role in their sons' lives, *Better Homes and Gardens* worried about whether Americans were "staking our future on a crop of sissies" and sympathized with fathers' fears: "You have a horror of seeing your son a pantywaist, but he won't get red blood and self-reliance if you leave the whole job of making a he-man of him to his mother." *Rebel Without a Cause*, a film starring James Dean that focused on a young man's alienation and rebellion, associated juvenile delinquency and children's unhappiness with inverted general roles in a family where the mother had too much authority and the father (seen at one point wearing an apron) too little.

A fear of sexual chaos, brought on by the Cold War, also emerged as a common theme. Popular literature discussed the dangers posed by "loose women" and "sex perverts" who might be in league with the Soviet Union. Senator Joseph McCarthy, whose close aide Roy Cohn was a closeted homosexual, joined Republican Party chair Guy Gabrielson in warning that "sexual perverts [had] infiltrated our government" and were "perhaps as dangerous as real Communists." Even the admirable Joseph Welch, counsel to the army in the hearings that finally exposed McCarthy's mania, was not above gay-baiting. When confronted with evidence obviously doctored by McCarthy's associates, he taunted Cohn, "Do you suppose fairies put it there?"

The dominant domestic ideology of the period, which Betty Friedan dubbed "the feminine mystique" in her 1963 book of that title, defined women as wives and mothers. But in fact, one-third of all women worked for wages, and total female employment grew in the 1950s from 16.5 million to 23 million, a number representing one-third of the work force. The rapid growth of the clerical and service sectors of the economy created many new jobs for women. Not only were employers dependent on women's paid labor, many working-class families pieced together a livelihood and others achieved middle-class status because of the income added by working wives. In many households, economic necessity and postwar consumerism trumped domesticity as women made decisions about work and family. Nevertheless, in popular thinking, women belonged at home, raising children and erecting a bulwark of social stability.

Despite warnings from self-declared experts that higher education inhibited fertility, a growing number of women attended college. Educated women, however, still faced discouragement. Adlai Stevenson exhorted women at Smith College not to feel frustrated by their distance from the "great issues and stirring debate" for which their education prepared them. A woman could be a good citizen, he claimed, by helping her husband find value in his work and by teaching her children the uniqueness of each individual. Increasingly, critics insisted that women be taught primarily those subjects designed to prepare them for domesticity and assumed that a college education was more important for men. Indeed, male high school graduates were twice as likely to earn a college degree as their female counterparts.

Prodded by such assertions from civic leaders and the media, it is not surprising that the average mother of the 1950s had between three and four children, usually by age thirty. As noted earlier, the birth rate continued to rise until 1957. At the same time, contraception, accepted by all the major faiths except the Roman Catholic Church, became common as a method for spacing pregnancies and limiting births.

Sexual Anxieties, Popular Culture, and Social Change

In spite of the formal sexual orthodoxy of the era, there were portents of a more emancipated future. Notably, sex was more openly discussed and displayed during the 1950s than in most earlier periods. Popular science provided a vehicle for sexual openness in 1953 when Dr. Alfred C. Kinsey published his bestselling *Sexual Behavior in the Human Female*, which suggested that women, like men, engaged in a wide variety of sexual acts, both before and after marriage. In the climate of the times, many people considered this finding "dirty" and offensive. Many had reacted similarly to his earlier finding that homosexual encounters were common and that many gay men did not look or act in stereotypical ways.

Kinsey's reports did not reduce prejudice against gay men and lesbians, who formed an urban subculture and their own political organizations in the postwar years. They did so in the face of political attacks from anticommunists and heightened police harassment that were enabled, ironically, by the proliferation of bars and other public areas frequented by gays and lesbians. In 1951, a small group of leftist gay men formed the Mattachine Society and in 1955, Del Martin and Phyllis Lyon created the Daughters of Bilitis, the first lesbian organization. Although the formation of gay and lesbian communities and political groups enabled mutual support and some efforts at public education, the conviction that homosexuality was dangerous and abnormal retained its hold on the general public.

Sexual conservatism did not prevent artistic representations of sex from becoming more open in the 1950s. In the film industry, for example, the Hollywood Production Code had long barred the use of words like *virgin* and *seduction* and restricted the sexual content of films. Even married couples were shown sleeping in separate beds. By the mid-1950s, the code was relaxed. The movies did not necessarily improve, but the sex in them became more graphic than before.

During the same years, the Supreme Court overturned several state laws restricting publication of serious erotic literature, such as D. H. Lawrence's *Lady Chatterley's Lover*. Such books became more widely available, and writers of less renown also offered some steamy reading. The decade's most popular novel, *Peyton Place* (1956), sold almost 10 million copies. The book jacket promised that author Grace Metalious, a young housewife, "lifted the lid off a small New England town, exposing lust, rape, incest, alcoholism, murder, and hypocrisy."

Playboy magazine was surely the most influential erotic publication of the decade. Its glossy centerfolds brought bare-breasted women into millions of homes, displaying them like one more consumer product. When Hugh Hefner first published *Playboy* in December 1953, he featured the rising starlet Marilyn Monroe as "Playmate of the Month." Slick, upscale, and replete with the hedonist Playboy philosophy, selections from serious writers, and airbrushed photographs of busty women, *Playboy* represented a quantum leap from the grimy "girlie" magazines of the past. By 1956, its circulation had reached one-half million per month.

Besides pressuring women into domestic roles, the massive profamily propaganda of the fifties stifled many men, who found that *Playboy*, which described marriage as a trap for unwary men, provided a rationale for their avoidance of family. Hefner pitched his magazine to college students and young status-conscious men who wanted to date, not marry, the centerfold models. Willing to spend their salary on the expensive stereos and pricey liquor advertised in *Playboy*, they dreamed of worry-free sex with no mortgages or children to complicate their lifestyle.

Young girls, by contrast, were urged to develop the bodies and behaviors that would inspire young men to date and eventually marry them. Advice literature in the popular media told adolescents and young women the taboos of dating. For girls, they included going "dutch" (letting each person pay his or her own expenses), opening your own doors, showing too much intelligence, and ordering your own food in a restaurant. In a letter to *Scholastic Magazine*, a boy from Missouri summed up the rationale for codes designed to reinforce the idea that men were in control in heterosexual relationships: "[P]aying the girl's way gives me a responsible and important feeling. It makes me feel superior to my date." Women also had to present acceptable bodies to signify their conformity to 1950s gender prescriptions. Encouraging and capitalizing on the popularity of Marilyn Monroe, American advertisers promoted devices and creams designed to increase breast size, while the clothing industry propelled young women into "training bras" and girdles in the name of "junior figure control." Historian Joan Jacobs Brumberg concluded that these practices constructed young girls as sex objects and "foreshadowed the ways in which the nation's entrepreneurs would accommodate, and also encourage, precocious sexuality."

The emerging art form of rock 'n' roll touched a deep chord in American youth. Before the advent of rock, mainstream 1950s music featured fatuous songs like "How Much Is That Doggie in the Window?" But as television gave radio increasingly stiff competition, radio stations became less profitable, and this prompted many of them to change their formats. In some large cities, radio stations began targeting a new audience, African Americans. African American popular music of the time, often called "race music," vibrated with religious and sexual energy. But white audiences had little exposure to it. To make the distinctive black style more acceptable, some disc jockeys called it rhythm and blues, or R&B. After 1945, R&B began to influence southern hillbilly and western cowboy music, creating the hybrid country-and-western style. And by the mid-1950s, increased exposure of R&B paved the way for its evolution into rock 'n' roll. This dynamic new musical form, along with improved recording technologies and the emergence of a large cohort of teenagers with money to spend, created a vast new commercial market in music.

In 1952, Cleveland disc jockey Alan Freed premiered an R&B radio show called "Moondog's Rock 'n' Roll Party." Like the term *jazz, rockin' and rollin'* originally referred to sexual intercourse. To appeal to his white audience, Freed downplayed this reference, connecting the words *rock 'n' roll* to the style of dancing associated with the music. From then on, the barriers between white and black music began to tumble. White audiences heard black music at the same time the civil rights movement was challenging the racism of white society.

In 1954, Bill Haley, a portly, nearly middle-aged white bandleader, recorded "Rock Around the Clock," an exuberant tune that became the theme song of the popular film *Blackboard Jungle* (1955). The movie chronicled the struggle of a young teacher in a run-down inner-city high school who tried to motivate alienated, poor youth. It touched on problems of race, class, and delinquency—unusual themes in commercial art of the time. The film's message—crime does not pay, and middle-class values are a salvation—is scarcely remembered. But "Rock Around the Clock," critics and audiences agreed, gave *Blackboard Jungle* its "insurrectionary power" and brought white middle-class youth to their feet. Theater owners reported spontaneous dancing in the aisles.

The record industry was especially eager to appeal to white youth because they represented an enormous market. Teenagers, a relatively recent term for those who enjoyed a prolonged adolescence before entering the labor force, formed an expanding group during the 1950s. Their numbers and economic impact grew steadily, so that by 1959, the teenage market—including money spent by parents on teenagers and by teenagers on themselves—topped $10 billion per year. With so much at stake, record producers hustled to find more white recording artists who employed the black sound in a form acceptable to white teenagers.

The biggest find was a nineteen-year-old part-time truck driver from Tupelo, Mississippi—Elvis Presley. Born poor, he had taught himself the guitar and learned the R&B style. His first record in 1954 earned him appearances on regional radio shows, and within a year he was a star throughout the South. In live performances, he aroused his fans, both female and male, by undulating his body and thrusting his hips in a style he attributed to revivalist preachers. Presley almost created the image of the hypersexed male rock star, replete with long hair, leather jacket, a sneering expression, and a sultry demeanor.

By 1956, Presley had become a national sensation. He released a series of hits, including "Heartbreak Hotel," "Don't Be Cruel," "Love Me Tender," and "I'm All Shook Up," that sold over 14 million records that year. He appeared on Ed Sullivan's popular TV variety show, where the cameras focused above the waist to conceal the young man's suggestive thrusts. Over 80 percent of all American viewers watched this performance, a number unsurpassed until the Beatles made their television debut in 1964.

Between early 1956 and March 1958, when the army drafted him, Presley released fourteen consecutive million-seller records. By 1966, he had sold 115 million records. Presley's success not only set a standard for other white rock singers, but also spurred white acceptance of African American artists such as Ray Charles, Chuck Berry, Little Richard, and Fats Domino.

While the young went wild over rock 'n' roll, parents recoiled at its influence. Some rock lyrics made fun of middle-class values. Besides its generally sensual, even sexual emphasis, rock music ridiculed work ("Get a Job"), downplayed schools ("Don't Know Much About History"), mixed religion with sex ("Teen Angel"), scoffed at authority ("Charlie Brown, He's a Clown"), and celebrated irresponsibility ("Rock Around the

Elvis Presley in 1956. His exuberant singing style shocked adults and excited youths. / UPI/Bettmann/CORBIS

Clock"). Popular music had never before so blatantly defied social mores or so distinguished youth from older generations.

Adult fears, and the discontents that gave rise to concern, emerged plainly in films like *The Wild One* (1953), *Rebel Without a Cause* (1955), and *Blackboard Jungle* (1955). These three movies featured actors Marlon Brando, James Dean, and Sidney Poitier, respectively, as young toughs who oozed anger, sexuality, and contempt for their elders. Their fictional characters presented an even stronger challenge to the social order than did Holden Caulfield, the alienated teenage hero of J. D. Salinger's popular novel *Catcher in the Rye* (1951). Despite the films' overt messages that violence and immorality were wrong, most teenagers who flocked to see Brando, Dean, and Poitier cheered the unrepentant rebels, not the characters who accepted their elders' advice.

Among parents who had just experienced World War II, peace and quiet seemed a good bargain. Young people, however, wanted something more. A youth subculture was emerging, and many parents worried about it. They blamed its music, movies, books, and comics, and even the television programs that would seem so innocent to later generations. Some people invoked the communist specter. Early in the decade, Justice Department officials helped one Hollywood studio produce a film warning that "throughout the

United States today, indeed throughout the free world, a deadly war is being waged." The "Communist enemy," the film declared, was trying to subvert American youth by spreading drugs and encouraging obscenity in the mass media.

Education and Mass Society

Many political liberals and professional educators attributed juvenile delinquency and a host of other social ills to the lack of federal aid to public schools. Without more money for buildings, equipment, and libraries, they argued, teachers could not cope with surging enrollments and the constant accumulation of new information. Only higher salaries, paid for by taxes, would lure talented college graduates into teaching. Many academics also criticized the schools for emphasizing social adjustment and conformity, rather than skepticism and individuality, and for inadequate attention to the traditional, subject-based academic curriculum.

Conservatives, on the other hand, were wary of plans to increase the federal government's role in education. They blamed the educational establishment itself, including teacher training colleges and unions, for poor student performance. The right wing believed that John Dewey's popular ideas of "progressive education," with their emphasis on social relevance, democratic ideals, and pragmatism, had undermined respect for the acquisition of basic skills, traditional values, and culture. They called for a return to basics, more classroom discipline, and the teaching of religious values. These debates were not new and would continue to the present day.

Neither liberal nor conservative critics fully acknowledged that part of the problem lay in the changing nature of mass education. Before World War II, relatively few students finished high school, and even fewer went to college. Public primary schools sought merely to instill some basic discipline and rudimentary reading and arithmetic skills. The wealthy attended private schools, middle-class students received a standard liberal arts curriculum in public high schools, and most working-class children dropped out to help support their families or sought vocational training.

Postwar prosperity resulted in many more working-class youths attending high school. As blacks and Hispanics migrated to urban areas, they became a major presence in public schools, increasing the cultural and social diversity there. Tension within this newly varied population, combined with the baby boom and the rapid expansion of the suburbs, put education at all levels under stress. Schools were expected to teach job skills, citizenship, and a sophisticated science, math, and literature curriculum to a broader cross section of students than ever before.

In the postwar period, educators adapted to these developments by locating schools carefully to ensure that student populations came from homogeneous class and racial backgrounds; using standardized tests to assign students to different tracks (college or vocational) in secondary schools; and emphasizing education for citizenship and social adjustment, rather than academic training, for students on the vocational or general tracks. Under this system, educators assumed that tests accurately reflected academic promise and interests and that students who came from disadvantaged groups should generally be prepared for blue-collar jobs. They also hoped that their focus on adjustment would prevent working-class alienation from schools and other social institutions and practices and thus help to prevent crime and radicalism.

Whatever their level of performance on IQ and achievement tests, girls found themselves increasingly relegated to commercial curricula designed to prepare them for clerical and service jobs. In the mid-1950s, only 48 percent of high school girls, compared to 66 percent of boys, were in academic or general curricula. Encouraged by guidance counselors, the girls chose clerical work or marriage as their desired occupations and took typing, shorthand, and other vocational classes. Among those whom the Educational Testing Service rated as able to do college work, 78 percent of the boys and only 62 percent of the girls planned to attend college.

By tradition, American schools are locally funded and controlled, making it difficult to promote change at the national level. Criticism of American education reached new heights after October 1957, however, when the Soviet Union launched the first artificial satellite, Sputnik I (see Chapter 4). Anxiety over the Cold War added fuel to the crisis in education. Journalists and politicians described the Soviet Union as the model of successful mass education. Communism, it seemed, had won the space race by winning the education race. What would Moscow win next?

In fact, Soviet success in education was greatly exaggerated. Nevertheless, Sputnik forged a national consensus in the United States in favor of federal aid to education. Before the crisis, southern Democrats opposed federal spending for education, fearing it would erode local control and spur integration. Northern liberal Democrats worried about opening public coffers to parochial schools. Parochial schools feared that higher school taxes would affect parents' ability to pay tuition and would thus erode their client base. Most Republicans simply opposed spending money on social programs. But the clamor to catch up with the Russians changed the debate.

Senator Lyndon B. Johnson of Texas, Democratic majority leader and presidential aspirant, chaired an investigating committee assessing the impact of Moscow's space coup. Long an advocate of federal support for education, he now warned of a widening science and technology gap. Congress and President Eisenhower cooperated in September 1958 to pass the National Defense Education Act (NDEA), a billion-dollar package, supplemented by state grants, to provide aid to schools and universities. It granted funds for construction; student loans and scholarships; and the teaching of science, mathematics, and foreign languages. In the following two decades, the NDEA and successor programs had a huge impact on American education at all levels, from the primary grades through graduate and professional schools. As with the GI Bill of the decade before, loans and fellowships allowed many more students to pursue advanced degrees. By 1960, the United States granted ten thousand doctorates annually, three times the pre–World War II number. Foreign students flocked to American universities, making the United States a world center of higher education.

With educational assistance provided by the NDEA, a record number of students enrolled in college during the 1960s. The large group of confident, intellectually curious students hitting college campuses coincided with growing American military involvement in Vietnam. Not surprisingly, this generation of college students would play a major role in challenging the Vietnam War in the 1960s.

The 1950s role models for college rebels were the Beats, a small, loosely defined group of iconoclastic writers who captured the public attention late in the decade. Their defiance of social and literary convention, as well as their dabbling in drugs, Eastern mysticism, and homosexuality, outraged the middle class and excited many teenagers and young adults. Beatniks, as they became known, disparaged Christianity, work, materialism, family life, patriotism, and interest in winning the Cold War.

The Beat writers included poets Allen Ginsberg and Gregory Corso and novelists Jack Kerouac and William S. Burroughs. Most began writing in New York City early in the decade and later drifted toward San Francisco. Ginsberg gained national attention in 1956 when San Francisco police charged him with obscenity for publishing his poem *Howl*, a highly personal cry against American materialism. The Beats achieved additional fame in 1957 with Kerouac's bestseller *On the Road*, a raucous, thinly fictionalized account of the author's cross-country travel with his unconventional friends.

Despite such rumblings of rebellion, most social commentators agreed that the United States had solved the major problems afflicting society. Persistent pockets of poverty, such as among African Americans, were seen as minor embarrassments rather than as major problems. An influential analysis published by Daniel Bell near the end of the decade, *The End of Ideology*, argued that the passionate ideological crusades of earlier years no longer had relevance. The United States had mastered the production of abundance and now had only to decide how to allocate the wealth.

Nevertheless, some critics began to question the social mores and culture that arose from this decade of calm prosperity. Books such as David Riesman's *The Lonely Crowd* (1950), Sloan Wilson's *The Man in the Gray Flannel Suit* (1955), William H. Whyte, Jr.'s *The Organization Man* (1955), John Keats's *The Crack in the Picture Window* (1957), and Richard Gordon's *The Split Level Trap* (1960) turned a critical eye on the 1950s and its definition of successful masculinity. Riesman and Whyte discussed the eclipse of the inner-directed personality that they deemed appropriate for men. Instead of relying on internal drives and values, they charged, Americans had become other-directed: little more than sheep who sought approval and rewards from their peers and the corporate hierarchy. Wilson worried that corporate success required that men develop the arts of ingratiation and subordination (usually associated with femininity) not those of individuality. According to Whyte, the bureaucratic structure of big business stifled a healthy competitive spirit in men. No longer spurred by drive and vision, the organization man looked to "the group as the source of creativity."

Critics also attacked the pervasive consumer culture. In a trilogy of bestsellers criticizing the advertising industry—*The Hidden Persuaders* (1957), *The Status Seekers* (1959), and *The Waste Makers* (1960)—journalist Vance Packard blamed mass marketing and the concept of planned obsolescence for turning citizens into insatiable consumers of overpackaged, unnecessary, and often shoddy products. According to Packard, American families spent an average of $500 a year just for packaging costs. He singled out the automobile industry in particular for its reliance on new models each year to increase car sales and for creating bigger and bigger cars that used increasing amounts of steel and other materials, guzzled gas and oil, and wore out parts at an accelerated pace. When economists from MIT, the University of Chicago, and Harvard examined his charges, they found that more than one-fourth of the price of new cars could be accounted for by the costs of designing and producing new models each year.

Only a few social critics claimed to find basic structural flaws in American society. One of these was sociologist C. Wright Mills, whose book *The Power Elite* (1956) asserted that a small group of military, business, and political leaders controlled the country in such a way that the majority of Americans were left powerless. Herbert Marcuse, a German émigré philosopher, blended Freudian psychology and Marxism in his *Eros and Civilization* (1956), which argued that a tiny minority manipulated the lives of most people and developed unique forms of psychological repression. In *Growing Up Absurd* (1960), Paul Goodman criticized schools and other institutions for stifling creativity and individualism. These critics offered evidence that America's problems had not disappeared or been forgotten. Their dissent foreshadowed the radical challenges that emerged in the 1960s.

Continuing Struggles: Civil Rights and Civil Liberties

At a time when so many Americans enjoyed abundance, African Americans were still denied basic human rights and opportunities. In the rural South, farm mechanization pushed black sharecroppers off the land. Because the Social Security Act excluded farm laborers from its benefits, these displaced workers were not eligible for unemployment compensation. Desperate for employment, some went to southern cities like Atlanta and Birmingham. More went north and west (see Map 3.1). They entered urban labor markets at the bottom, as unskilled laborers and service workers.

The migrants did not find residential integration in their new communities. Just as they arrived, white Americans were leaving the cities for the suburbs. By 1960, over half of all African Americans lived in the largely poor and mostly black inner cities. There, they faced great shortages of affordable housing, caused in part by restrictive covenants that forbade occupants to sell to people of color as well as federal mortgage loan policies that excluded black

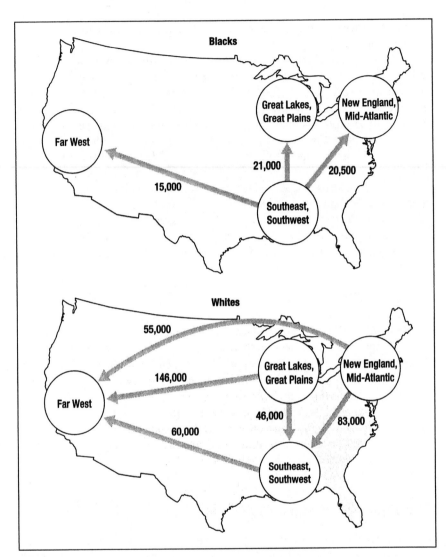

Map 3.1
Average Annual Regional Migration, 1947–1960

neighborhoods from coverage. Landlords in these neighborhoods subdivided units, leading to greater overcrowding; refused to make repairs; and charged exorbitant rents for the scarce housing. Blacks generally paid more than whites for worse housing. As the cities deteriorated, the new suburban communities remained nearly all white. The poor housing conditions in black communities convinced many whites that integrated neighborhoods would deteriorate and many bankers that home loans to blacks were high risk. In the North, whites organized protests when they thought homes in their areas would be sold to blacks.

In the South, segregation came under sharp attack from African American activists. Court decisions, boycotts, and new laws undermined the legal and social pillars of racism. Led in many cases by war veterans, African Americans organized voter-registration drives in the South, where they encountered white hostility and sometimes outright violence. After hearing reports of blacks killed for daring to assert their voting rights, President Truman acted. Even though he privately rejected social equality among the races, he established the President's Committee on Civil Rights in late 1946 to recommend steps for the federal government to take to ensure basic civil rights for all Americans. The panel urged government action to guarantee equal opportunity in education, housing, and employment. It called for federal laws against lynching and poll taxes, the creation of a permanent Fair Employment Practices Commission, and a strong Civil Rights Division within the Justice Department.

When Congress declined to act, Truman used executive authority to bolster civil rights enforcement by the Justice Department. He also appointed a black federal judge and made several other minority appointments. When labor leader A. Philip Randolph threatened in July 1948 to organize a boycott of the draft to protest the segregated armed forces, Truman issued an executive order calling for desegregation in the services. Still, the armed services moved so slowly that desegregation took another six years.

As the government inched forward, African Americans pursued nonviolent direct action inspired by India's Mohandas Gandhi. Two women staged the first sit-in in Washington, D.C., during the war. (One of them, Patricia Harris, later became a cabinet secretary in the Carter administration.) After the war, the Congress of Racial Equality (CORE) carried out sit-ins at lunch counters in northern cities and organized a "swim-in" at Palisades Park in New Jersey. Although mobs beat the participants, the amusement park and many lunch counters were desegregated as a result of these demonstrations. These small and hard-won victories convinced activists of the importance of direct action for mobilizing their communities and maintaining political pressure on the white establishment.

In the legal realm, too, progress was being made. In *Smith* v. *Allwright* (1944), the Supreme Court overturned the whites-only primary system that prevailed in many southern states. Two years later, in *Morgan* v. *Virginia* (1946), the Court held that racial segregation on interstate buses violated federal law. In 1947, CORE organized the first freedom ride to test the ruling. The group made it as far as Durham, North Carolina, before being arrested and sentenced to thirty days on a chain gang. In *Shelley* v. *Kraemer* (1948), the justices ordered that state courts could not enforce restrictive clauses in private contracts. On hearing of the new ruling, a furious congressman declared "there must have been a celebration in Moscow last night."

Nothing symbolized the unequal status of African Americans more powerfully than school segregation. At the time, 53.9 percent of white college students in the South attended state universities supported by taxpayers, while only 8.9 percent of black college students did so. The region provided only three law schools for African Americans but had thirty-one for whites.

In various decisions, the U.S. Supreme Court did not outlaw segregation or overturn the separate-but-equal rule dating from 1896 (*Plessy* v. *Ferguson*). But a majority of justices seemed willing to chip away at segregation by forcing states to honor the "equal" part of the "separate but equal" doctrine. Their rulings encouraged Thurgood Marshall, chief counsel of the National Association for the Advancement of Colored People (NAACP), to escalate the attack on school segregation, placing the system under constant judicial siege. By 1952, the NAACP was pressing five suits before the Supreme Court against public school segregation.

These five suits were eventually combined under the heading of one key case involving Linda Brown of Topeka, Kansas. Each morning, she had to walk past a nearby white-only school to catch the bus that would take her to a colored-only school. Marshall decided to abandon his piecemeal strategy. He likened the "separate-but-equal" doctrine to the "black codes" established after the Civil War to restrict the rights of African Americans. The doctrine could be sustained, Marshall argued, only if the Supreme Court agreed "that for some reason Negroes are inferior to all other human beings." Marshall insisted that segregation violated the Fourteenth Amendment, and he submitted research by psychologist Kenneth Clark suggesting that African American children educated in single-race schools suffered lasting emotional and intellectual damage.

The Supreme Court heard arguments in *Brown* v. *Board of Education* late in 1952, but they delayed ruling. Chief Justice Fred Vinson, like several associate justices, had misgivings about segregation but thought states had a right to set their own school policies, discriminatory though they may be. In September 1953, in the midst of the Court's deliberations, Vinson died. Associate Justice Felix Frankfurter privately quipped that Vinson's timely demise was "the only proof I've ever seen of the existence of God." A year before, presidential candidate Eisenhower had secured support from Governor Earl Warren of California by promising him the first opening on the Supreme Court. Eisenhower had some qualms about appointing Warren to the most influential seat on the Court, but he honored his promise. Neither Eisenhower nor most other Americans imagined how fateful this appointment would become. Warren viewed the Supreme Court as a unique force for protecting the weak, the oppressed, and the disadvantaged. His vision and activism brought the Court into the center of national politics and made him the most influential chief justice in over a century.

Warren ordered a rehearing of *Brown* in December 1953. Then he persuaded all eight associate justices to join him in a unanimous opinion, issued in May 1954, that struck down segregation in public education. Warren rejected the *Plessy* decision of 1896 and put forth an essentially new interpretation of the Fourteenth Amendment. For Warren, the issue was simple justice. To segregate schoolchildren solely on the basis of race, he wrote, "generates a feeling of inferiority . . . that may affect their hearts and minds in a way unlikely ever to be undone. . . . Segregation with the sanction of law, therefore, has a tendency to retard educational and mental development of Negro children." In education, he declared, "separate but equal has no place. Separate educational facilities are inherently unequal."

Critics charged that the ruling misconstrued the Constitution and relied on dubious sociological data. Others accused the Supreme Court of usurping congressional and state power by making, rather than interpreting, the law. A young minister in Lynchburg, Virginia, named Jerry Falwell claimed he saw "the hand of Moscow" behind the *Brown* decision. He further stated that "[i]f Chief Justice Warren and his associates had known God's Word, I am confident that the . . . decision would never have been made." According to Falwell, the Bible taught that blacks "were cursed to be the servants of the Jews and Gentiles" and not their constitutional equals. Warren's defenders retorted that the *Brown* decision yielded the morally correct verdict. In fact, the Supreme Court had taken action—reluctantly—to resolve a moral, legal, and political issue that neither Congress nor the president would confront. Civil rights had been stuck in a political gridlock that only the Supreme Court seemed capable of unraveling.

In practice, the *Brown* decision affected only public schools, not the comprehensive web of segregation laws that prevailed in twenty-four states and the District of Columbia. The Supreme Court delayed implementing its ruling and called for consultation between local authorities and judges. During 1954 and 1955, while the Court heard the NAACP demand "integration now," southern states requested delays and demagogues called for "segregation forever." During this interim period, the Court's delay and President Eisenhower's uneasiness over the desegregation ruling helped fuel a massive resistance movement.

Warren again spoke for a unanimous Court in May 1955 when he ruled in a case called *Brown II* that school segregation must be ended everywhere in the nation. Although desegregation should begin with "all deliberate speed," the Court issued no timetable. Southern officials hoped that federal district judges would wink at delays and, as a Georgia official remarked, define a "reasonable time as one or two hundred years." When district judges insisted on early action, however, segregationists dug in their heels. In several southern states, white citizens' councils sprang up to intimidate black parents and white school boards attempting to integrate the schools. Designed to provide a respectable form of resistance, these groups of middle-class citizens—the "uptown Ku Klux Klan"—formally disavowed violence while tacitly encouraging it. Indeed, they took out newspaper ads providing the names of blacks who had registered to vote or engaged in other civil rights activities. Southern politicians hurried to inform white citizens that the Court's decision was illegitimate, and therefore white southerners would not have to comply with it. Over one hundred members of Congress signed a Southern Manifesto opposing the *Brown* decision. Senator Harry F. Byrd, a Democrat from Virginia, called for massive resistance, and several state legislatures in the South declared that they would defy the "unconstitutional" Supreme Court rulings.

In the next few years, these states passed over 450 laws designed to interpose state authority between the federal government and local school officials, forbid officials to carry out any action that would mix races in public schools, and provide state money (usually in the form of vouchers) to support all-white private academies. In addition, several states curtailed or abolished public schools. At one point, Mississippi and South Carolina actually amended their state constitutions to abolish public education, and Virginia closed public schools for several months. In 1957, their efforts received support from conservative spokesperson William F. Buckley, who wrote in the *National Review* that "the White community in the South is entitled to take such measures as are necessary to prevail, politically and culturally, in areas where it does not predominate numerically. . . ." It had the right to do so, he argued, because "for the time being, it is the advanced race . . . It is more important for any community, anywhere in the world, to affirm and live by civilized standards, than to bow to the demands of the numerical majority."

In the short run, the passage of these laws enabled southern politicians to delay implementation of school desegregation by creating enormous legal confusion, to cost the NAACP and other litigants a great deal of time and money as they challenged the laws in court, and to claim that the laws represented legitimate public authority—unlike the Supreme Court's decisions—because they reflected the popular will of the South. While doing so, they clogged the courts with cases involving laws that would eventually be declared unconstitutional. Because of this resistance and hostility, most schools in the South and many in the North remained as segregated in 1960 as before. Far from being resolved, the issue would become the focus of public debate again and again in later decades.

President Eisenhower did little to promote the Supreme Court rulings. As army chief of staff in 1948, he had defended military segregation, arguing that "if we attempt to force someone to like someone else, we are just going to get into trouble." Of course, equality under the law, not the "liking" of minorities, was the real issue. Pressed by the contending factions to endorse or denounce the *Brown* ruling, Eisenhower privately blamed Earl Warren for the crisis and called his appointment of the judge "the biggest damn fool mistake I ever made." Although the president accepted the desegregation decision, he declined to endorse it. He told Booker T. Washington's daughter, "We cannot do it by cold law-making, but must make these changes by appealing to reason, by prayer, and by constantly working at it through our own efforts." NAACP executive director Roy Wilkins reacted to the president's hesitant approach by observing that "President Eisenhower was a fine general and a good, decent man, but if he had fought World War II the way he fought for civil rights, we would all be speaking German today."

One of Eisenhower's earliest tests came in 1955, when a fourteen-year-old African American boy named Emmett Till was murdered in Mississippi for violating southern racial mores. Till, who lived in Chicago, had come to the delta area of Mississippi to visit relatives there. In an attempt to impress local black children, he claimed to have had white girlfriends in the North. In response, they goaded him to prove himself by flirting with a white woman named Carolyn Bryant, who was working in her family's store in the town of

Money, Mississippi. In the South, where whites assumed that black men were sexual aggressors determined to pursue white women, the defense of white women's sexual and racial purity was the defense of the color line itself. Although Bryant did not tell her husband, Roy, of the incident, he heard of it from others. With his half-brother, J. W. Milam, he took Till from the home of the boy's uncle, brutally murdered him, and dumped the body in the Tallahatchie River.

Although southern white officials initially condemned the murder, Mississippi whites rallied around the accused when northerners reacted with horror to the event. That horror was intensified when Till's mother, Mamie Till Bradley, declared that she wanted "the world [to] see what they did to my boy" and kept the casket open at the funeral. Initially published in *Jet* magazine, the photograph of his body, which had been mutilated almost beyond recognition, was soon reprinted widely in white publications. At the trial in Sumner, Bradley testified that the victim was her son, while lawyers for the defense argued that the body was not that of Till. They also wanted to include testimony from Carolyn Bryant regarding the incident in the store, which would invite the jurors to conclude that Till had "asked for it," but the judge forbade her to testify in front of the jurors on the grounds that the information she presented was not relevant. The sheriff, Harold Strider, testified that the body had been in the water too long to be that of Till, leaving it to the defense attorneys to try to explain the presence of Till's ring on the body in question. After the jury had acquitted the defendants, Strider said that he wanted to "tell all of those people who've been sending me those threatening letters that if they ever come down here, the same thing's gonna happen to them that happened to Emmett Till."

Till's murder occurred in the poorest region of the poorest state in the union. African Americans, who were a majority of the area's population and the backbone of its plantation labor force, counted no registered voters in their ranks. Mississippi was the birthplace of the white citizens' councils. Through the use of violence and economic threats and reprisals, their members had significantly reduced the already small number of blacks on the voting rolls in the state and elsewhere and had created a climate of terror for any who sought racial change.

The national media attention focused on the murder combined with national outrage at the acquittals put the Eisenhower administration in a difficult position. The president refused public comment on the case. Convinced that only state laws had been violated in the case, administration officials claimed that they were powerless to act. The Civil Rights Acts of 1866 were the only ones on the books at the time designed to provide federal protection for civil rights. They had been eroded by conservative Court decisions in the 1940s and were always hindered by the refusal of white jurors in the South to convict whites accused of crimes against blacks. Even so, the administration had little enthusiasm for using them when it had strong legal grounds or for strengthening them in order to protect the lives and civil rights of African Americans. In 1955, local U.S. attorneys received orders from the Justice

Department not to investigate disorders that impeded the execution of federal integration decrees, even though federal jurisdiction was clear in these cases. A year later, FBI director J. Edgar Hoover, who had believed that the outcry over the Till case had been communist inspired, argued against strengthening the civil rights laws on the grounds that to do so would impair social harmony in the South.

Eisenhower's greatest effort on behalf of change came in response to a direct challenge to federal authority in Little Rock, Arkansas. In 1957, the Little Rock school board, which had voluntarily put forward its own desegregation plan in 1955, began implementation by choosing nine African American students to enroll in the city's Central High School. But Governor Orval Faubus called out the National Guard to block them. When a federal court ordered the troops to withdraw, a white mob surrounded the school, taunting and threatening the blacks attempting to enroll. Faced with massive local revolt against a federal court order and unable to persuade the defiant Faubus to offer state assistance in protecting the black students, Eisenhower reacted as he would to an insubordinate junior officer. Embarrassed by Soviet propaganda publicizing American racism—which found a wide audience in the Third World—he sent one thousand army troops and ten thousand National Guardsmen to ensure the students' safety, maintain order, and support the authority of the federal government.

Fifteen-year-old Elizabeth Eckford endured the taunts and threats of hostile white students as she attempted to desegregate Little Rock's Central High School in September 1957. Under orders from Arkansas governor Orval Faubus, National Guard troops barred her entrance. / Bettmann/CORBIS

The troops stayed a year, although their presence in the school did not deter a systematic campaign of harassment of the African American students orchestrated by a group of segregationist white students. In an effort to prevent integration, Governor Faubus closed the Little Rock public high schools in September 1958 under a new state law that required voters to approve the continuation of integration or close the affected schools. Despite the efforts of local African Americans, a few ministers, and some white women activists, voters strongly rejected integration. A year later, a federal court disallowed this move and local voters, disillusioned with closed schools, removed the segregationists who had opposed reopening the schools from the Little Rock school board. The whole episode, including vivid pictures of the howling mob and the frightened but dignified African American students, became an international embarrassment to the United States.

The administration tried to mollify critics by introducing a civil rights bill to Congress in 1957. Attorney General Herbert Brownell pushed the legislation while Eisenhower recuperated from an illness. Brownell had political motives for pressing a civil rights bill: he hoped that a debate on the question would divide the northern and southern wings of the Democratic Party and curb the influence of presidential hopeful Lyndon Johnson. The ploy failed when Johnson used his talents of persuasion to convince a majority of Democrats to support the Civil Rights Act of 1957, an amended version of the administration's bill that declared support for black voting rights but left enforcement in the hands of southern juries.

In passing the 1957 Civil Rights Act, Congress was responding to a rising tide of grassroots activism on the part of African Americans. Shortly before Christmas in 1955, Rosa Parks, a tailor's assistant in Montgomery, Alabama, who was also secretary of the local NAACP branch, boarded a bus to ride home. When ordered to move to the rear so that a white passenger might sit, she refused. Parks declared that she had decided to discover "once and for all what rights I had as a human being and, a citizen." Besides, she added, "my feet hurt." For her trouble, she was arrested for violating the law requiring the separation of whites and blacks on public buses.

Rosa Parks was not the first black woman to be arrested for breaking this law; in three recent cases, the city of Montgomery had dropped charges to avoid a legal challenge. The Women's Political Council, a group of African American professional women, knew of Parks's good reputation in the community and her support for civil rights causes. They considered her case an ideal test case. The council conferred with other community leaders, including E. D. Nixon, a local NAACP official, and decided to mobilize grassroots support for a challenge to the law. They enlisted the help of Baptist ministers, including Ralph Abernathy and Martin Luther King, Jr., in organizing a black boycott of Montgomery buses.

King, then a twenty-seven-year-old preacher, was new to the community. He came from a prominent family in Atlanta. His father, Martin Luther King, Sr., ministered to a large congregation and encouraged his talented son to pursue a broad education, including a doctorate in theology from Boston University.

This woman joined about fifty thousand other African Americans in Montgomery, Alabama, who walked to work, to stores, and to church for over a year to protest the city's segregated bus system. / Don Cravens, © Life Magazine, Time Inc.

Martin Luther King, Jr., did not initiate the challenge to racism in Montgomery, but he gradually emerged as its leader because of his talents and passionate oratory. He told local and national audiences that "there comes a time when people get tired . . . of being segregated and humiliated, tired of being kicked about by the brutal feet of oppression." The time had come for his people to cease tolerating "anything less than freedom and justice." Influenced by his reading of Thoreau and Gandhi, King applied the principles of nonviolent civil disobedience to the boycott. He would soon become the nation's most prominent African American leader.

For a year, about fifty thousand African Americans walked or rode in car-pools rather than ride the segregated buses of Montgomery. Led by JoAnn Gibson Robinson, African American women sparked, organized, and staffed the Montgomery campaign. Boycott leaders did not insist on full integration, asking only that passengers be seated on a first-come, first-served basis, with blacks seating themselves from the rear to the front and whites from the front to the rear. Despite the modest nature of this request, city officials responded by indicting protest leaders for violating state antiboycott laws and by banning car-pools as a public nuisance. Terrorists bombed churches and the homes of activists, including King's. But in November 1956, the Supreme Court overturned the Alabama bus segregation law under which Parks had been arrested. This decision left the city and the bus company no legal recourse and a financial disincentive to resist integration. Thus, the combination of grassroots and judicial activism achieved victory.

The boycott illustrates the critical role that churches and ministers played in the early civil rights crusade. Because segregation excluded blacks from political activity, churches offered the one permissible setting for community organization. They provided a base of support, local leadership, some financial resources, a common language and culture, and a sense of empowerment that could be turned toward meeting political goals. Ministers such as King and Abernathy molded African American religions into a political weapon by portraying heroes like Moses and Jesus as social revolutionaries. Just as the biblical Jews reached the Promised Land after long tribulation, African Americans could win freedom, these ministers told their congregations, through faith and a commitment to struggle.

Many other African Americans had challenged segregation, independently and collectively, by the end of the decade. College students in the South took the boldest initiative. In February 1960, four students from the North Carolina Agricultural and Technical College, after shopping in a Greensboro, North Carolina, Woolworth's, sat down at the lunch counter to order coffee. When the manager refused to serve them, they stayed there until the store closed, when they were arrested.

This tactic spread quickly. Lunch counter sit-ins occurred in over thirty cities in seven states. Many protesters were arrested, and some were beaten. Most adopted a strategy of nonviolence in the face of assaults. The effort yielded notable successes, with many national chains integrating their lunch counters. Some of the student activists followed Ella Baker into the Student Non-Violent Coordinating Committee (SNCC), which she organized in 1960. Over the next few years, SNCC would play a major role in challenging segregation.

Despite these important achievements, most African Americans still attended predominantly segregated schools and lived in single-race neighborhoods at the close of the 1950s. Few blacks in the South could vote. Many more personal sacrifices by civil rights activists, and the intervention of a sympathetic federal government, would be necessary to effect real change.

The civil rights movement brought together diverse Americans who had fought long and hard against discrimination. Mexican Americans also organized on their own behalf in the postwar period. Groups such as the League of United Latin American Citizens (LULAC) and the GI Forum resisted discrimination and segregation in the West, mounting legal challenges that overturned school segregation in California and banned the exclusion of Mexican Americans from Texas juries. Such organizations emphasized the rights of Mexican Americans to be treated as full citizens, but they distanced themselves from Mexican immigrants coming into the country—both legally and illegally.

At the same time, many western Mexican Americans, Native Americans, and other people of color resisted Anglo calls for cultural assimilation. They sought to maintain the languages and traditions that made their groups distinctive. The tension between the desire for equal rights and the demand for legal and cultural distinctiveness remains an issue for people of color in the West today.

Even as the federal government and the courts began to support African Americans, the Eisenhower administration and Congress imposed several well-intentioned but ultimately calamitous policies on Native Americans. Reversing New Deal efforts to expand assistance to American Indian tribes, the federal government adopted the policy of termination: gradually eliminating many Indian reservations and social services. Native American nations were also required to turn properties held communally by the respective tribes into private holdings in the hands of individuals or corporations. The administration and Congress justified these measures as ways to reduce costs, protect states' rights, and expand the rights of individual Native Americans. Indeed, congressional supporters of the policy routinely referred to it as one that would offer freedom to American Indians. This freedom, however, was understood in terms of autonomy from certain forms of government rather than as self-determination. Indeed, most Native Americans opposed termination, and government regulation of their economic activities and personal lives increased.

Between 1954 and 1960, the federal government withdrew benefits from sixty-one tribes. Many reservations were absorbed by the states in which they were located, becoming new counties. The tribes now had to pay state taxes and conform to state regulations. To raise the cash required for taxes, many tribes and individuals had to sell land and mineral rights to outside interests. For example, the Klamaths of Oregon, enticed by offers from lumber companies, sold off most of their ponderosa pine forests. The Menominees of Wisconsin sold much of their reservation to wealthy Chicagoans, who built vacation cabins on former tribal land.

The financial gains from these deals proved fleeting. The loss of returns from tribal enterprises to white economic interests and the persistence of Native American poverty took their toll. Individuals who needed assistance through Aid to Families with Dependent Children had to liquidate their assets, including the bonds they had received as compensation for termination, in order to qualify for benefits. Within a few years, the tribes were worse off than before. An increasing number of American Indians abandoned the former reservation lands. By the end of the 1960s, half the Native American population had relocated to urban areas, assisted by a federal program that provided them with one-way tickets to various cities. There, the Native Americans found the same limited opportunities encountered by other people of color entering urban economies.

Starting in 1956, the Supreme Court began unraveling the restraints on free speech and political action that had been spun during the Red Scare. The Court nullified antisubversion statutes in forty-two states with the 1956 *Pennsylvania* v. *Nelson* decision. Speaking for the majority, Chief Justice Warren ruled that only federal, not state, laws could make it a crime to advocate the overthrow of the federal government. In 1957, in *Jencks* v. *United States*, the Court dealt a blow to government witch hunts by insisting that accused persons had the right to examine the evidence gathered against them. That same year, in *Yates* v. *United States*, the Supreme Court overturned the conviction of fourteen midlevel Communist Party officials sentenced for violating the Smith Act. The justices ruled that verbal calls for toppling the government did not constitute a crime. To be illegal, an act must involve the attempt to "do something now or in the future."

The Court, however, did not extend its liberal premises to sex discrimination cases. In the 1961 case of *Hoyt* v. *Florida*, it upheld states' rights to limit women's participation on juries to ensure that they did not neglect their domestic responsibilities. In Florida, women were exempted from jury service unless they registered their willingness to serve with the court and passed the subjective criteria on jury service applied by local officials. The defendant in the case, Gwendolyn Hoyt, was accused of murder in the death of her husband, whom she accused of infidelity and physical abuse. Her lawyers argued that hers was a crime of passion and that she could not receive a fair trial if she were "forced to trial by jury with an all-male panel who do not have the same passions and understanding of females and their feelings as other women would have." The state of Florida contended that the defendant was seeking not a fair jury, but one that included "female friends," and defended the state law on the grounds that women were the "only bulwark between chaos and an organized and well-run family unit. . . ." The Supreme Court agreed that Florida's law was reasonable because the Constitution "does not entitle one accused of crime to a jury tailored to the circumstances of the particular case, whether relating to the sex or other condition of the defendant" and because ". . . woman is still regarded as the center of home and family life."

Eisenhower's Second-Term Blues

As Eisenhower entered the final year of his first term, the public seemed at ease with his casual style of leadership. The Korean War had ended, Senator McCarthy was a spent force, Stalin's successors called for peaceful coexistence, and the economy was robust. Only Eisenhower's health worried voters. He suffered a serious heart attack in September 1955 and a disabling attack of ileitis, followed by surgery, the next June. His speedy recovery, however, quieted most fears. Eisenhower decided to run again.

Eisenhower harbored doubts about keeping Vice President Richard Nixon on the ticket. He had never liked the brash young man, and now he pondered ways to ease Nixon out. When Nixon balked, Eisenhower relented rather than provoke the wrath of the Republican right. But his misgivings about Nixon undermined the vice president's stature and hurt his presidential candidacy in 1960.

The Democrats renominated Adlai Stevenson, following a challenge from Senator Estes Kefauver, who then beat Senator John F. Kennedy for the vice-presidential slot. Stevenson raised serious questions about poverty, the lack of a national health program, and the administration's refusal to fund public schools. Stevenson also favored ending the draft and halting the open-air testing of atomic weapons; however, he condemned Eisenhower for losing half of Indochina to communism and for not building as many long-range bombers as the Soviets. Nevertheless, as one journalist commented, "The public loves Ike. . . . The less he does the more they love him."

On Election Day in November 1956, Eisenhower gathered 58 percent of the popular vote, over 35 million ballots to Stevenson's 26 million. The public liked Ike far more than it liked his party, however. The Democrats maintained a four-seat majority in the Senate and a twenty-nine-seat majority in the House.

In November 1957, Eisenhower suffered a mild stroke. Although his mental powers were intact, his slurred speech made his public communication less effective than before. That autumn, several foreign and domestic events called his leadership into question. After his dispatch of troops to Little Rock, Arkansas, to protect the black students at Central High School, critics called his actions either too great or too modest a response. The clamor over Sputnik prompted Democrats to ridicule Eisenhower for starving education and for spending too little money on space and defense projects. The new Soviet leader, Nikita Khrushchev, began making whirlwind tours of the Third World, offering aid and winning praise for his country's support of emerging nations. In 1958, Eisenhower's powerful chief of staff, Sherman Adams, resigned amid allegations that he had accepted expensive fur coats from a contractor. Democrats in Congress took the lead in funding the NDEA and space research. To many Americans, Eisenhower began to seem disengaged.

By 1960, political discontent was percolating just beneath the surface. The third recession since Eisenhower took office along with new challenges from Moscow, a communist revolution in Cuba, and a sense that America needed younger, more dynamic leadership gave the Eisenhower administration a tired, somewhat shabby appearance. Yet Eisenhower remained a hero to most Americans. They credited him with ending the Korean War and delivering peace and prosperity. His bland, comfortable stewardship, like that of the typical father in the era's sitcoms, had reassured most middle-class Americans that they would be allowed to get on with their lives.

Conclusion

In the postwar period, American society changed in significant areas of social and cultural life: greater numbers of Americans went to college, including particularly white, working-class men; many white, middle-class Americans moved from cities to suburbs; minorities concentrated in the inner cities largely because of housing and employment discrimination at the hands of private economic interests and public policymakers; interest in consumer products such as home appliances and televisions surged; and Americans of all social groups created a baby boom that, by the late 1950s and 1960s, would lead to an increasingly youth-oriented culture.

For women, the heroic wartime days of Rosie the Riveter were gone. Once government no longer needed her workplace services, experts and the media transformed the working woman from a patriot to a subversive threat with dizzying speed. This switch justified a return to discriminatory practices in the workplace and the insistence that women were to stay home with their families. Although many women managed to return to work, they generally had to settle for lower-paying jobs. More women attended college than before the war, but men's educational advantage increased and women faced especially high barriers in fields such as law and business.

For ethnic minorities, these years brought similarly mixed results. Native Americans faced difficulties brought on by the policy of termination. Mexicans continued to migrate to the United States, but like the Mexican Americans already in the country, they faced persistent discrimination. Mexican Americans and Native Americans grappled with the tension between seeking equality and maintaining their cultural distinctiveness. African Americans made significant progress in establishing civil rights through voter-registration drives, legal challenges, nonviolent demonstrations, and symbolic acts like sit-ins and freedom rides. Sometimes the activists encountered bloody resistance, and the legislative and executive branches took only small and slow steps to help. Yet crucial court victories set the scene for the major civil rights victories of the 1960s.

In retrospect, the 1950s seem a curiously contradictory period in American life. Eisenhower practiced the politics of moderation, churches increased their membership, and conservative family values appeared dominant. Middle-class suburban families embraced the trappings of prosperity—the automobile, home appliances, television, sports, jet travel, and other new miracles of consumerism. But young people, inspired by their own emerging subculture, entered a period of ferment. Despite the emphasis on traditional family structures, sex was discussed more openly. Women went to work in greater numbers, not quite fulfilling their idealized role as housewives and mothers. Intellectuals challenged the era's conformity and consumerism, and the Beat writers dared to suggest that drugs, sex, and alternative religious experiences might be more important than patriotism.

Perhaps the biggest contradiction of all was that despite the overall prosperity, one in four Americans lived near or below the poverty line at the end of the decade. And despite government inaction, some economists had begun to pay serious attention to this problem. By then, too, the civil rights revolution was under way; the African American struggle to end segregation and claim equal rights was in the process of transforming the social landscape. American women's discontent with constrained lives was also coming to the surface, posing a threat to all fundamental institutions. With all of these developments interacting, the 1950s was a period of considerable change beneath a guise of security and stability.

F U R T H E R • R E A D I N G

On Eisenhower, business, and the politics of the 1950s, see Charles Alexander, *Holding the Line* (1975); Stephen E. Ambrose, *Eisenhower: The President* (1984); Barbara B. Clowse, *Brainpower for the Cold War: The Sputnik Crisis and the National Defense Education Act of 1958* (1981); Fred L. Greenstein, *The Hidden Hand Presidency* (1982); Elizabeth A. Fones-Wolf, *Selling Free Enterprise: The Business Assault on Labor and Liberalism, 1945–60* (1994). **On social change and popular culture,** see Keith W. Olson, *The G.I.*

Bill, the Veterans, and the Colleges (1974); Kenneth Jackson, *Crabgrass Frontier: The Suburbanization of the United States* (1985); Herbert J. Gans, *The Levittowners* (1967); John M. Findlay, *Magic Lands: Western Cityscapes and American Culture After 1940* (1992); Richard Schickel, *The Disney Version: The Life, Time, Art and Commerce of Walt Disney* (1968); Erik Barnouw, *Tube of Plenty* (1982); Mark H. Rose, *Interstate: Express Highway Politics, 1941–56* (1979); Susan Strasser, *Waste and Want: A Social History of Trash* (1999). **On gender, families, and sexualities,** see Elaine T. May, *Homeward Bound: American Families in the Cold War Era* (1988); Rickie Solinger, *Wake Up, Little Susie* (1992); Leslie J. Reagan, *When Abortion Was a Crime: Women, Medicine, and Law in the United States, 1867–1973* (1997); Stephanie Coontz, *The Way We Never Were: American Families and the Nostalgia Trap* (1992); Beth Bailey, *From Front Porch to Back Seat: Courtship in Twentieth Century America* (1988); Joan Jacobs Brumberg, *The Body Project: An Intimate History of American Girls* (1997). **On civil rights,** see Stephen J. Whitfield, *A Death in the Delta: The Story of Emmett Till* (1988); Nicholas Lemann, *The Promised Land: The Great Black Migration and How It Changed America* (1991); Mark V. Tushnet, *The NAACP's Legal Strategy Against Segregated Education* (1987); Taylor Branch, *Parting the Waters: America in the King Years, 1954–63* (1988); David J. Garrow, *Bearing the Cross: Martin Luther King, Jr., and the Southern Christian Leadership Conference* (1986); Richard Kluger, *Simple Justice* (1975); Michal Belknap, *Federal Law and Southern Order: Racial Violence and Constitutional Conflict in the Post-Brown South* (1987); Mario Garcia, *Mexican Americans: Leadership, Ideology, and Identity, 1930–1960.* **On high-tech medicine and polio,** see Jane S. Smith, *Patenting the Sun: Polio and the Salk Vaccine* (1990); Andrea Tone, *Devices and Desires: A History of Contraception in America* (2001).

Generals and Presidents: U.S. Foreign Policy in the 1950s

4

They liked Ike: President Dwight D. Eisenhower flashes his trademark smile. /
© Bettmann/CORBIS

Shortly after the arrest in England of spy Klaus Fuchs in February 1950, Senator Homer Capehart, an Indiana Republican, rose from his seat in the Senate chamber to ask, "How much more are we going to have to take? Fuchs and Acheson and Hiss and hydrogen bombs threatening outside and New Dealism eating away at the vitals of the nation. In the name of Heaven, is this the best America can do?" In a speech before the Republican Women's Club of Wheeling, West Virginia, on February 9, Capehart's colleague from Wisconsin, Joseph McCarthy, explained why the nation faced such grim prospects. America risked defeat in the Cold War, McCarthy asserted, because Secretary of State Acheson, a "pompous diplomat in striped pants and a phony British accent," employed over two hundred communists in the State Department. These miscreants had already "lost" China and were poised to betray the remainder of the free world.

As we saw earlier, during the first months of the 1950s, the American public was whipsawed by countervailing claims of victory and defeat in the Cold War. President Truman and his top aides insisted that the Marshall Plan and the NATO Alliance had stabilized Western Europe and Japan, effectively denying Stalin the real prizes he sought. Republicans countered that the Truman administration, riddled with security risks and spies, looked the other way while Soviet and Chinese agents gained ground in Asia, Africa, the Middle East, and Latin America. As politicians traded charges, ordinary citizens worried that traitors had penetrated the nation's vital institutions. Truman and Secretary of State Acheson tried to refute these charges, but events at home and abroad soon overwhelmed them. Amid lurid claims of what he called "twenty years of treason," Senator McCarthy added his name to the rogue's gallery of American politics. A relative latecomer to the Red Scare, he so dominated public attention from 1950 to 1954 that *McCarthyism* became a catchword for the era. A stalemated war in Korea and growing doubts about Truman's leadership contributed to the election of the first Republican president since Herbert Hoover. Although General Dwight D. Eisenhower campaigned on a pledge to clean out the federal government and to liberate people in the "enslaved nations of the world," he presided over an administration characterized by moderation at home and abroad. In fact, Eisenhower worked behind the scenes to restrain the arms race and explore cooperation with a new generation of Soviet leaders.

McCarthyism and the Korean War

Joseph McCarthy served as a county judge in Wisconsin before entering the Marine Corps during World War II. While a desk officer stationed in the Pacific, McCarthy flew a few routine missions in the tail gunner's seat of a combat aircraft. In 1946, campaigning as "tail gunner Joe," he won election to a seat in the U.S. Senate. During his first years in Washington, both colleagues and journalists considered him an affable buffoon, quick with a joke or a drink. In 1950, in search of a hot issue, McCarthy pieced together information provided by friends such as Representative Richard Nixon into an indictment of the Truman administration.

The speech he gave on February 9, 1950, in Wheeling, West Virginia, with its claim that Secretary of State Acheson employed hundreds of communist agents bent on betraying America, catapulted McCarthy from obscurity to international prominence. Over the next few months, McCarthy often changed the number of traitors and their exact roles. In an unguarded moment while drinking with several reporters, he confided that he had no idea if there were two or two hundred spies in Washington. "What I have," he gloated, "is a bucket of shit, and I know just where to spread it." Ultimately, he labeled as spies and traitors the "whole group of twisted-thinking" New Dealers who "led America to near ruin at home and abroad."

McCarthy was a cynic and opportunist who came to believe his own ravings. During a Senate probe into his charges, he clowned and bullied his way around the evidence. His sensational claims were shown to be either fantasies or recycled information. McCarthy quibbled over the number of alleged Reds in government because it suggested that the Democrats questioned only his details, not the basic facts of his case. Several leading Republicans in Congress saw through his antics but valued him as a wrecking ball who undermined public faith in the Democratic Party. Many ordinary Americans found comfort in McCarthy's conspiracy theories, which provided simple answers to complex

As lawyer Joseph Welch (hand on brow) listens, Senator Joseph McCarthy lectures a special Senate committee about the supposed Communist conspiracy in the United States. / UPI/Bettmann/CORBIS

questions. The country had no need for expensive aid programs and entangling foreign alliances such as the Marshall Plan and NATO. A purge of Reds at home would set everything right.

Journalists such as George Reedy felt guilty about devoting coverage to McCarthy. Reedy recalled that "Joe couldn't find a Communist in Red Square" and "didn't know Karl Marx from Groucho." But as a senator, he commanded a degree of attention from the press. Blessed with a good sense of timing, McCarthy often made inflammatory charges just before radio, TV, or press deadlines. This timing put his accusations in front of the public for a day or more, while his hapless victims struggled to play catch-up.

The North Korean invasion of South Korea on June 25, 1950, transformed the Cold War into a hot one. By the time the fighting stopped three years later, U.S. defense spending had quadrupled, over forty thousand Americans (and many more Koreans and Chinese) had been killed, and U.S. forces were stationed around the globe. Violence within and between the rival Koreas killed tens of thousands even before the outbreak of formal war.

In August 1945, the United States and the Soviet Union had divided Korea, a Japanese colony since the early twentieth century, into temporary occupation zones north and south of the 38th parallel (see Map 4.1). Plans to unify the country collapsed as the Cold War intensified. The Soviets sponsored a communist regime, the Democratic People's Republic of Korea led by Kim Il Sung, in the north. South of the 38th parallel, the United States promoted a conservative government, the Republic of Korea, led by Syngman Rhee, a prominent Korean nationalist who had lived in the United States for decades. Soviet and U.S. forces departed in 1949, leaving behind advisers to rival regimes that each claimed the right to rule all Korea.

Korea had no special strategic importance, but American officials worried that abandoning the South Korean government might be seen as deserting an ally. Despite their own doubts about Rhee's authoritarian regime, Truman and his advisers reacted quickly to the North Koreans' attack. They considered the invasion a Soviet test of U.S. resolve, not a bona fide civil war. The relationship between Stalin and North Korea's Kim Il Sung, one U.S. official remarked, was "the same as that between Walt Disney and Donald Duck."

The facts were murkier. The Soviets, and to a lesser extent China, had provided support and advice for the North Korean assault. But Stalin approved the venture largely in response to Kim's pleas for assistance and his assurance that northern forces would be welcomed as liberators. They would sweep to victory, Kim insisted, before the United States could respond. Stalin and Mao viewed the attack as a low-risk move to create a unified, communist-friendly Korea that would help counterbalance nearby Japan, then being rebuilt and rearmed by the United States. No one anticipated a major war.

Once fighting began in 1950, the Truman administration rushed to support the beleaguered South Korean government. The U.N. Security Council

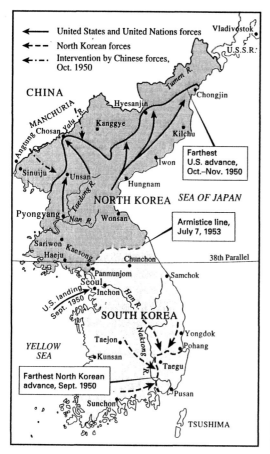

Map 4.1
The Korean War

(which the Soviets were boycotting to protest its refusal to seat a delegation from the People's Republic of China) adopted an American resolution that called upon member states to assist South Korea. On June 27, Truman ordered U.S. air and naval forces into action. Fearing a wider threat to the Asia/Pacific area, Truman also expanded aid to French forces fighting communist guerrillas in Indochina (Vietnam) and sent the U.S. 7th Fleet to protect the Chinese Nationalist–held island of Taiwan from Chinese communist assault. Three days later, he dispatched ground combat forces to Korea under the command of General Douglas MacArthur, who already served as occupation commander in nearby Japan. Congress was informed of these actions but not asked to declare war. Truman soon referred to the intervention as a police action. American soldiers made up the large majority of U.N.-sponsored troops in Korea.

For two months, U.S. and South Korean forces struggled to maintain a toe-hold around the city of Pusan on the southern tip of the Korean peninsula. On September 15, 1950, MacArthur assembled a large force that mounted a daring amphibious assault at Inchon, a port in South Korea behind North Korean lines. In barely two weeks, triumphant American soldiers had cleared South Korea of Northern invaders and achieved the U.N. and U.S. goal of re-establishing the South Korean government.

The deceptively easy victory at Inchon gave MacArthur the appearance of infallibility and prompted Truman to expand American goals. In place of restoring the prewar border, Truman ordered MacArthur to cross the 38th parallel to destroy the North Korean army and to unify the country under the Rhee regime. The strategy of rolling back communist influence had wide appeal. Truman hoped it would send a tough message to Stalin as well as to Republicans at home who questioned his leadership. MacArthur guessed that a victory in Korea might open the way for a wider crusade against communism in China and, possibly, clear a path for him to the White House. The president worried about the general's loose talk of a bigger war and several times considered firing him. But as a World War II hero and the darling of the Republican Party who had twice sought the GOP presidential nomination, MacArthur could not be removed without provoking a backlash among many Americans who considered him a living legend.

Truman sought a military victory in Korea without provoking a wider war with China or the Soviet Union. Yet he discounted several warnings from China during October that American forces should not move north of the 38th parallel or approach the Yalu River, which separated North Korea from Manchuria, China's industrial heartland. Truman took China's threats to intervene more seriously than did MacArthur—who may well have wanted to provoke a major conflict—and flew to Wake Island in the Pacific to confer with the general. MacArthur claimed the war was nearly over and that if the Chinese dared to intervene, there would be the "greatest slaughter." The prophecy proved true, but not exactly as he supposed.

In late November, MacArthur ordered an all-out push to the Yalu River, predicting that American troops would be "home by Christmas." Chinese soldiers stunned the U.S. commander by crossing into North Korea and launching an offensive that drove American forces back to and then south of the 38th parallel. MacArthur responded by accusing Truman and the Joint Chiefs of Staff of tying his hands in this "entirely new war." After China entered the fighting, the American commander demanded massive reinforcements, called on Truman to seek help from anticommunist Chinese on Taiwan, and proposed attacking China, perhaps with atomic bombs.

Truman and nearly all his civilian and military advisers rejected these ideas. They wanted to defend South Korea, not start World War III by provoking an even bigger fight with Moscow and Beijing. Nor did they see any role for the atomic bomb on Korean battlefields or against Chinese cities. Because the real Cold War prizes remained in Europe and Japan, it made no sense to get sucked into a major war in a strategic backwater. Instead, Truman reverted to the original war aim of restoring separate North and South Korean regimes.

Still, many Americans were intoxicated by MacArthur's grandiose rhetoric and had difficulty understanding why American soldiers should "die for a tie." After less than a year of fighting, two-thirds of the public disapproved of how Truman handled the war. In March 1951, MacArthur sabotaged the president's attempt to start truce talks with China. He followed this tactic by sending a letter to Republican congressman Joseph Martin, in which he implied that by not fighting for a clear win, Truman was responsible for the pointless murder of American boys. MacArthur asserted, "[T]here is no substitute for victory."

Truman finally had enough. On April 11, 1951, he sacked MacArthur, whom he privately called a "flim-flam artist" and a "bunko man." The president named General Matthew Ridgway, the respected commander of the 8th Army in Korea, as theater commander as well as MacArthur's replacement in Japan. Republicans condemned the president and predicted that firing MacArthur would lead to a communist conquest of all Asia. Senator Nixon claimed Truman had made the communists "the happiest people in America." Senator McCarthy insisted that Truman must have been drunk when he fired the general. Crowds in several cities burned effigies of Truman, and many newspapers demanded his impeachment.

MacArthur returned to a series of parades in his honor, followed by an invitation to speak before Congress. In his memorable speech of April 19, 1951, the general repeated his charge that Truman was an appeaser and called for military victory in Korea and all Asia. He closed with the lyrics of an old army song, "Old Soldiers Never Die, They Just Fade Away." As one seasoned journalist noted of the audience, there was not a "dry eye among the Republicans, nor a dry seat among the Democrats."

Obviously, MacArthur hoped he would not fade away. But, in fact, he did so rather quickly. Lengthy Senate hearings into the military situation in Korea revealed that no senior U.S. military commanders agreed with MacArthur's strategy. As General Omar Bradley, chairman of the Joint Chiefs, put it, expanding the conflict in Korea or fighting China would be the "wrong war, in the wrong place, against the wrong enemy." Unable to score political points in his testimony, MacArthur began a nationwide speaking tour, paid for by a pair of conservative Texas oil millionaires. Crowds at arenas where he spoke cheered the general. But when he began calling for a rollback not only of Asian communism but also of petroleum taxes paid by his patrons, the crowds thinned and he soon cancelled the remainder of the tour. A year later, Republicans nominated a heroic World War II general as their presidential candidate, but his name was Eisenhower, not MacArthur.

The public's love affair with MacArthur also lapsed because his successor, General Ridgway, halted China's offensive in Korea and restored the battle lines near the 38th parallel without using atomic weapons or widening the war. In July 1951, China and North Korea began armistice talks with the United States. The talking, and fighting, continued for two more years.

Political and Economic Consequences of the Korean War

When the Cold War turned hot in Korea, conservatives of both parties escalated their attacks on liberalism. Senator Pat McCarran, a Nevada Democrat, competed with Joe McCarthy for the title of chief Red hunter. After giving his name to the anticommunist McCarran Act (discussed in Chapter 2), he took over the chair of the new Senate Internal Security Subcommittee (SISS), which launched a series of lengthy political probes into the alleged loss of China by subversive diplomats and organizations. Some State Department officials specializing in Asian affairs were subjected to as many as ten loyalty hearings and then finally fired. Within a few years, so many China experts were purged that a senior official called the Far Eastern Division of the State Department a "disaster area filled with human wreckage."

Energized by the Korean stalemate, the Red Scare continued through the late 1950s. Between 1950 and 1956, various House and Senate committees launched over 100 probes of alleged communist activity by public employees, labor unions, and voluntary organizations, and within particular industries such as Hollywood. Left-leaning unions—such as the Mine, Mill and Smelter Workers; the Longshoreman's Union; the United Electrical Workers; and the New York Teachers Union—were favorite targets. Several corporations that were eager to rid themselves of bothersome demands for higher wages and improved working conditions used allegations of communist control to refuse to negotiate contracts with suspect unions. They sometimes justified this stance by saying that the federal government would refuse to place military orders with industries whose workers were represented by communists or "fellow travelers."

Individuals suspected of political unorthodoxy or who simply refused to sign loyalty oaths could be fired by local, state, and federal agencies. In New York, for example, 300 public school teachers were fired for political reasons during the 1950s. Nationally, about 100 college professors lost their jobs. As noted earlier, several thousand federal employees quit or were fired in the face of loyalty hearings.

In 1956, America's most prominent playwright, Arthur Miller, was indicted for contempt of Congress when he refused to tell the House Un-American Activities Committee (HUAC) the names of people whom he had seen at communist meetings decades before. Miller, whose play about the Salem witch trials, *The Crucible*, was a thinly veiled allegory of Cold War political hysteria, had refused a deal offered by HUAC. If he permitted his wife, actress Marilyn Monroe, to pose in suggestive photographs with the committee chair, he would be let off with a slap on the wrist. Fortunately for Miller and Monroe, a judge later quashed the indictment.

Popular expressions of anticommunism appeared on television and in magazines, film, and popular books. Herbert Philbrick's 1952 memoir, *I Led Three Lives*, aired as a weekly TV show from 1953 to 1956. In 1956, J. Edgar Hoover assisted the publication of a bestselling history of his agency, *The FBI Story*, written by Don Whitehead, which also ran in 170 newspapers and was made into a movie. Hoover published his own bestselling exposé of communism, *Masters of Deceit* (1958), which went through twenty-nine printings by 1970.

The Korean War also had other, lasting economic and political consequences. Defense spending at home and abroad fueled rapid economic growth that lasted nearly two decades. Before the war began, American defense expenditures were just under 5 percent of the annual gross national product (GNP). After the fighting erupted in Korea, military spending rose to over 13 percent of GNP in 1953 and averaged 10 percent for the rest of the decade. This high rate of military spending forged a consensus that joined Democrats and Republicans in support of big government spending. The defense budget served as a kind of national economic policy for the United States, promoting advances in electronics and aerospace technology. It also continued the process begun during World War II of shifting the country's manufacturing base from the Northeast and Midwest to the South and West. By 1957, for example, over one-half of all industrial jobs in southern California were linked to military production. Later, when geographers began using the term Sunbelt to refer to much of the South and the West Coast, some argued that these areas really ought to be called the Gunbelt.

War-generated spending also spurred economic growth in Western Europe and Japan, where the United States placed military orders. Prosperity promoted closer economic and political integration in Western Europe. Six western European countries established a coal and steel community in 1951, eliminating trade barriers in these basic commodities. In 1957, the six-nation Treaty of Rome created the European Economic Community (EEC), the forerunner to the Common Market. A decade of strong growth in Europe and Japan undercut the waning appeal of left-wing political parties.

The economic growth promoted by military spending lay in the future. As of 1952, the political mood in the United States remained sour. The stalemate in Korea, the redbaiting by both Republicans and conservative Democrats, and the charges of petty corruption in Washington doomed the Truman administration as the 1952 election neared. The GOP campaign slogan that denounced the Democrats as the party of "Korea, Communism, and Corruption" proved brutally effective.

Eisenhower Takes Command

Shortly after taking office in 1953, President Dwight D. Eisenhower gathered a group of military and diplomatic specialists in the White House sun parlor and asked them to reassess Cold War strategy. In a project dubbed Operation Solarium, the experts weighed the policy of containment against more radical proposals, including threatening Moscow with nuclear war should it cross a demarcation line, and attempting to push back existing areas of Soviet control through political, psychological, economic, and covert military pressure. Discussion even touched on launching a pre-emptive attack on the Soviet Union.

As a candidate, Eisenhower had pledged he would never rest until he had liberated the "enslaved nations of the world." John Foster Dulles, the newly appointed secretary of state, had denounced the existing containment policy as a "treadmill, which at best might keep us in the same place until we drop exhausted." Both men had criticized Truman's foreign policy because it was not designed to win a conclusive victory, and Republican campaign rhetoric had castigated the Democrats for "abandoning people to Godless terrorism."

Nevertheless, the new president approved continuation of the containment policy much as it had been received from his predecessor. With the campaign's rhetoric behind him, Eisenhower pursued a relatively moderate foreign policy during his two terms in office. His precise approach to foreign affairs was not easy to categorize. Although he had declared that America could never rest until the communist yoke had been lifted from Eastern Europe and China, he resisted calls from the Pentagon and Congress to increase defense spending, fearing that large budget deficits would be as destructive as war in the long run. He was willing to threaten other countries with nuclear weapons, but he avoided full-scale conflict and never employed America's expanded nuclear arsenal against an enemy. Under Eisenhower's leadership, the United States and the Soviet Union gradually learned how to coexist.

Eisenhower's choice for secretary of state, the formidable John Foster Dulles, seemed a marked contrast to the avuncular president. A powerful corporate lawyer active in the Presbyterian church, Dulles had long been touted as the Republicans' chief foreign policy expert. He often wore a sour expression, and he delivered frequent lectures on Christian virtue and communist sin. He was so noted for his toughness against communism—in Asia and elsewhere—that Winston Churchill joked he was the only "bull" who carried around his own "China closet."

During Ike's two terms, Dulles and Vice President Richard Nixon made frequent bellicose and controversial statements, creating the impression that they, not Eisenhower, were the real forces behind the administration's foreign policy. In fact, as historians have come to realize, Eisenhower kept both men on a short leash. He used them to float controversial ideas, warn adversaries, and appease Republican hard-liners. They acted as lightning rods to draw criticism away from the president, whose views were less extreme.

The administration's 1953 strategic plan, called NSC 162/3, placed a greater emphasis than before on the use of atomic bombs, both as weapons and as bargaining chips in the Cold War. For the president, this approach had economic as well as military benefits. By relying more on nuclear weapons and the air force, the United States could slash the size of its costly ground forces. Unlike military officials who wanted enough troops, ships, and conventional munitions to achieve a decisive superiority over the Soviet Union, Eisenhower favored sufficient striking power to deter or, if necessary, destroy the Soviet Union, but no more than was needed. Attempting to match the Soviets "man for man, gun for gun," he warned, would lead to national bankruptcy. On one public occasion he noted that "every gun that is made, every warship launched, every rocket fired, signifies, in a final sense, a theft from those who hunger and are not fed, those who are cold and are not clothed." Eisenhower managed to reduce military expenditures from about $52 billion annually to about $36 billion at the end of his first term, even if none of the savings went to the hungry, the cold, or the poorly clothed. During his second term, military spending increased again because of congressional pressure and renewed competition with the Soviet Union.

Eisenhower and Dulles christened their strategy the New Look. The strategy depended on what Dulles called the threat of "massive retaliation" against Soviet or Chinese provocation. The administration had inherited a nuclear arsenal of about one thousand bombs. Over the next eight years, this stockpile grew to eighteen thousand weapons. An important addition to the military's arsenal was the huge, eight-engine B-52 bomber. Small, tactical nuclear weapons as well as intercontinental ballistic missiles (ICBMs) and sub-

Cartoonist Herblock depicted the anxiety many Americans felt about the Eisenhower-Dulles foreign policy. / From *Herblock's Special for Today,* Simon & Schuster, 1958

marine-launched missiles were under development. By the time Eisenhower left office in 1961, the United States had enough air-, sea-, and ground-launched nuclear weapons to destroy Soviet targets many times over—far surpassing Eisenhower's own goal of sufficiency. The Soviets played catch-up and soon acquired their own "overkill" capacity.

Some critics, especially Democratic politicians and career army officers, argued that the New Look and the doctrine of massive retaliation locked the United States into an all-or-nothing response to foreign threats. Eisenhower and Dulles responded with three measures designed to meet the all-or-nothing dilemma. First, the administration entered into anticommunist military alliances with numerous countries, promising American materiel support for local troops fighting in small wars. Second, for situations short of war, the president authorized the CIA to carry out covert military operations against unfriendly regimes or groups. Finally, the administration pushed the development of tactical atomic weapons for battlefield use. These explosives, small enough to be fired in artillery shells, were intended to counter a conventional attack by Soviet or Chinese forces without escalating to global thermonuclear war. The army even developed a 58-pound atomic bomb that commandos could carry in their packs and use to blow up bridges, factories, or military depots.

Eisenhower saw no reason why atomic artillery shells should not be used "exactly as you would use a bullet or anything else." He approved a policy stating that, in the event of hostilities with the Soviet Union, the United States would "consider nuclear weapons to be as available for use as other munitions." In part because of his military background, however, Eisenhower was wise enough to fear a nuclear showdown. In 1954, when South Korean strongman Syngman Rhee wanted him to threaten Russia and China with war in order to unify Korea, Eisenhower replied that "if war comes, it will be horrible. Atomic war will destroy civilization." Clearly, the president hoped to avoid a nuclear conflict, and he saw the atomic arsenal as a deterrent. If deterrence failed, however, Eisenhower was prepared to "push the button."

The policy of relying more heavily on the nuclear threat received its first test in Korea, where fighting continued near the 38th parallel despite two years of peace talks. A major unsettled point was China's demand that the United States observe international law by returning all Chinese and North Korean prisoners of war (POWs) held in South Korea, including several thousand who had sought asylum. Like Truman before him, Eisenhower feared a domestic backlash if he agreed to repatriate POWs to China against their will.

Determined to break the deadlock, Eisenhower ordered a study to consider the use of tactical atomic weapons in Korea. To his surprise, most military and diplomatic experts doubted that atomic weapons would do much good. As the Truman administration had realized, there were few suitable targets to bomb in North Korea. Inconclusive use of the bomb might "depreciate the value of our stockpile," strategists warned. Attacking urban and industrial targets in China would cause huge civilian losses, something Eisenhower opposed. In a bluff, American officials spread the rumor that Eisenhower planned to use the atomic bomb. When an armistice was achieved in July 1953, Dulles claimed that he had made it known to the Chinese that they faced a nuclear threat, and that fear of it compelled them to accept the U.S. demand for voluntary prisoner returns.

In reality, several factors contributed to the breakthrough. Joseph Stalin's sudden death from a stroke on March 5, 1953, brought to power Soviet leaders eager to improve relations with the United States. China had grown weary of the costly war and sought better ties with the West. Even before Washington had dropped hints about escalating the war, Chinese and American negotiators had made progress on a partial exchange of sick and wounded prisoners. They then compromised on the broader issue. POWs resisting repatriation would be remanded to a neutral commission to determine their ultimate fate. When South Korean president Syngman Rhee opposed this deal, an enraged Eisenhower threatened to depose him. Thus, diplomacy and Stalin's death, as much as atomic threats, led to the Korean cease-fire.

During the dictator's final years, Stalin had expanded Soviet military power and initiated bloody new purges to stamp out imagined conspiracies within his inner circle. After his death, a triumvirate composed of Georgi Malenkov, Nikolai Bulganin, and Nikita Khrushchev assumed power. The three new leaders promised Soviet citizens a better life. Despite their rivalries, they agreed to do away with Stalin's network of terror and to seek improved relations with the West. Malenkov announced that no dispute—even with the United States—was so bad it could not be settled peacefully through negotiations.

By 1955, Khrushchev's skills at inner-party intrigue allowed him to oust his colleagues and emerge as the first among equals. In 1956, he shocked his country and the world by denouncing Stalin's crimes. Downplaying his own role as one of the dictator's henchmen, the new party boss charged that Stalin's "personality cult" had distorted communism and led to the slaughter of several million loyal Bolsheviks and Soviet citizens.

Changes within the Soviet Union posed challenges. Should Washington trust Soviet talk of "peaceful coexistence," or should it increase pressure on Moscow now that a less oppressive regime held power? Did the new Kremlin leaders really seek cooperation with the West? Should the United States try to break up the Sino-Soviet alliance? If so, should it maintain a rigid policy toward China or act more flexibly? Some Western leaders, such as Winston Churchill, urged Eisenhower to meet with the new Kremlin bosses and to allow commercial ties with China; restrained by Dulles, Eisenhower at first reacted cautiously to changes in the communist camp. Either from fear of a political backlash, a preference to wait passively for the demise of communism, or conflicting advice from his aides, the president hesitated to open a dialogue with Soviet leaders.

The Ebbing of McCarthyism

The Red Scare at home also influenced Eisenhower's approach to foreign policy. During 1953 and 1954, Senator Joseph McCarthy continued to attack supposed Reds in American government. Although Eisenhower personally found McCarthy vile, he had done little during the presidential campaign to alert the public to McCarthy's excesses. Even when McCarthy labeled General George C. Marshall a traitor who had perpetrated "a conspiracy so immense as to dwarf any previous such venture in the history of man," Eisenhower refused to condemn the senator or defend the general—the World War II chief of staff, architect of the Marshall Plan, and the man who raised Ike from military obscurity to the heights of wartime command. Eisenhower merely told aides he would not "get into the gutter" with McCarthy.

Eisenhower made other concessions to Republican extremists. In 1953, he refused to block the execution of Ethel and Julius Rosenberg, who were convicted of espionage for Moscow, even though he harbored doubts about Ethel's guilt. In another high-profile case, Eisenhower approved stripping physicist J. Robert Oppenheimer of his security clearance in retaliation for his opposition to the development of the hydrogen bomb. Eisenhower allowed Dulles to appoint Scott McLeod, a McCarthy protégé, to purge China specialists in the State Department who had predicted victory by Mao's communist forces in 1949. Foreign Service officers had to demonstrate "positive loyalty,"—an indefinable quality—to keep their jobs. Dulles ordered that books by "Communists, fellow travelers, et cetera" be removed from U.S. Information Agency libraries abroad. "Et cetera" included works by such "radicals" as Mark Twain. During Eisenhower's administration, about fifteen hundred federal employees in various agencies were fired as security risks, and another six thousand were pressured to resign.

But McCarthyism was on the wane after 1954, the year McCarthy began to self-destruct. Early in that year, piqued at the army's refusal to give his staff aide David Schine a draft deferment and other special treatment, McCarthy charged the army with coddling communists. The bizarre allegation focused on a dentist, Irving Peress, who had been drafted, promoted, and honorably discharged despite his admitted communist sympathies. When high-ranking army officials, acting on the president's orders, refused to apologize or give personnel records to the senator, McCarthy charged them with incompetence and treason. The Wisconsin Republican declared he "did not intend to treat traitors like gentlemen."

With Eisenhower's backing, army leaders countercharged that McCarthy had tried to blackmail them into giving David Schine special treatment. In April 1954, the Senate launched an inquiry. At this time, television journalist Edward R. Murrow aired a segment of his show *See It Now* that highlighted some of McCarthy's most unsavory actions. Soon several members of the Senate began to question their colleague's behavior. During a dramatic, televised Senate inquiry known as the Army-McCarthy hearings, 20 million viewers had their first close look at McCarthy's vicious attacks on the loyalty of all who resisted him. Army counsel Joseph Welch, the soul of telegenic respectability, parried McCarthy's shrill tirades and refused to be provoked by the slashing attacks of Roy Cohn, the senator's legal aide.

Although only a small number of observers realized it at the time, a sexual undercurrent was present in an exchange between Cohn, a closeted homosexual who ridiculed gay men as perverts and subversives, and Welch. When Cohn could not explain how certain evidence he had placed in the record had been tampered with, Welch taunted Cohn by suggesting that "fairies"—common slang for gay men—had been responsible. By hinting broadly that Cohn was homosexual, Welch implied that McCarthy's villainy even extended to hiring deviants. In the timbre of the times, homosexuality was considered so unsavory that even liberals and civil libertarians felt free to use allegations of it to attack the redbaiters.

After weeks of failing to prove any Red plot within the army, a frustrated McCarthy charged that Frederick Fisher, a young lawyer who worked for Welch's Boston firm but was not a member of the army's legal team, had communist leanings. Welch, who had anticipated the accusation, responded to McCarthy's mudslinging with a sad shake of the head, saying, "I think I never really gauged your cruelty or your recklessness." Unable to stop himself, the senator resumed his attack on Fisher. Finally, Welch could tolerate McCarthy's slander no more. He declared that McCarthy's forgiveness would "have to come from someone other than me." The lawyer then issued a historic query: "Have you no sense of decency, sir, at long last? Have you left no sense of decency?"

Even though the Army-McCarthy hearings rendered no formal verdict, the senator had failed a critical media test. Opinion polls taken during and after the televised sessions revealed a dramatic slide in McCarthy's approval rating, from nearly 50 percent at the beginning of 1954 to only 30 percent in June. By December, the Senate voted to censure him for "unbecoming conduct." Eisenhower, who took a bit more credit for the senator's humiliation than was warranted, hosted Welch at the White House and remarked that "McCarthyism had become McCarthywasim." The senator's slide gave Eisenhower more freedom to maneuver. McCarthy never recovered from these public defeats. Shunned by old friends, he increased his legendary drinking, lost political influence, and died of alcohol-related illness in 1957.

America and the Challenges of the Third World

In the fifteen years following the end of World War II, thirty-seven nations emerged from colonialism to independence, eighteen during 1960 alone. Most of these new states were nonwhite, poor, nonindustrialized, and located in Asia, Africa, or the Middle East (see Map 4.2). Many had gained independence through armed struggle; in some, the violence continued after independence. They had much in common with other poor nations, especially those in Latin America, where political unrest often became armed rebellion. During the 1950s, at least twenty-eight prolonged guerrilla insurgencies were under way.

Most of these emerging and underdeveloped nations, loosely called the Third World, existed outside the bloc of the industrialized democracies (the First World) and the communist nations (the Second World). Few had democratic governments. Most sought to remain neutral in the Cold War while pursuing economic development and soliciting aid from both sides. Poor nations both envied and resented American power. They often employed the rhetoric of socialism, even as they sought the material rewards of capitalism. Under Stalin, the Soviet Union had ignored or criticized most noncommunist liberation movements. Khrushchev proved more adroit, offering economic and military assistance to emerging nations whether or not they adhered to Moscow's line.

The United States shared Moscow's concern with the Third World. The emerging nations contained vast raw material wealth and a huge population. Eisenhower and Dulles worried that the Third World's criticism of imperialism and capitalism would provide a wedge for Soviet influence. And many Americans mistrusted any model of national development that deviated from the U.S. experience.

Competition for influence in the Third World also affected domestic policy. For example, American diplomats and intelligence officials reported that communist propagandists had a field day publicizing racial violence in the United States. Stories and pictures of lynchings, Klan rallies, and race riots during the 1950s were frequently distributed by the Soviets in Asia and Africa. Several times in the 1950s, African Americans filed appeals with the United Nations demanding international action to defend the basic rights of black Americans.

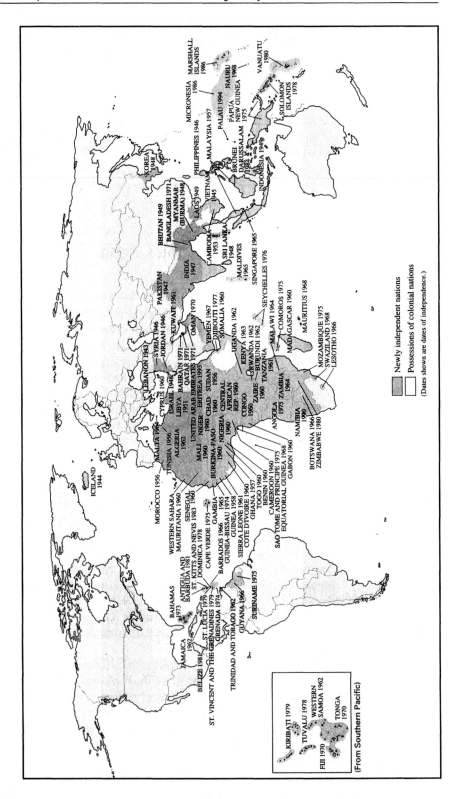

(From Southern Pacific)

Significantly, the first meeting between Vice President Nixon and Martin Luther King, Jr., took place in 1957 in Ghana, one of the newly independent African nations. The violent reaction in 1957 to court-ordered integration of Central High School in Little Rock, Arkansas, was front-page news in the Soviet press, which showed pictures of a mob surrounding black teenager Elizabeth Eckford and screaming "Lynch her." President Eisenhower, who had tried to avoid taking any direct stand in defense of civil rights, finally acted by dispatching federal troops to enforce the integration order lest it become a propaganda victory for America's Cold War rival.

To avoid embarrassment, the State Department urged officials in southern states to treat visiting African and Asian diplomats, tourists, and students as "honorary whites" exempted from Jim Crow laws. Partly to counteract communist charges of American racism, during the 1950s government agencies began sending abroad prominent African Americans, such as jazz musician Louis Armstrong and the Harlem Globetrotters basketball team, as informal "ambassadors of goodwill."

The main strategy of the Eisenhower administration to halt communist inroads in the Third World included forging numerous anticommunist alliances based loosely on NATO. These alliances included the Central Treaty Organization (CENTO) in the Middle East and the Southeast Asia Treaty Organization (SEATO), as well as bilateral defense agreements with Taiwan, South Korea, Spain, and the Philippines. Unlike NATO, most of these pacts committed Washington to provide only aid and consultation in cases of aggression. The agreements had more psychological and political than military value because when American interests abroad were threatened, the United States usually acted on its own.

Foreign aid also played a growing role in the administration's effort to influence the Third World. Under Truman, nearly all foreign economic assistance had been sent to Western Europe and Japan. Eisenhower first called for eliminating most aid, offering two-way trade as the best way to help poor countries. But because the poorest nations had little to export and no money to buy foreign goods, two-way trade would not substantially help them. Eventually the Eisenhower administration not only increased overall aid levels but also sent most of its assistance—surplus food, credits to buy American products, military equipment, construction loans—to emerging nations.

Critics pointed to faults in the aid programs for developing nations. For example, providing surplus grain under the Food for Peace program fed the hungry and helped American farmers dispose of surplus crops, but it also undermined enactment of sound agricultural policies in needy countries. Construction loans were frequently squandered on glamorous projects like sports arenas, while basic necessities like rural irrigation systems and clinics went unfunded.

◀ **Map 4.2**
Nations Achieving Independence, 1943–1980

In 1958, writers William J. Lederer and Eugene Burdick highlighted these problems in their bestselling novel, *The Ugly American.* They described a fictional Southeast Asian country (one resembling Vietnam) in which arrogant American diplomats knew nothing about their host nation and lived in an isolated "golden ghetto." They contemplated grand development schemes but ignored the plight of the peasant farmers. The unconventional hero defied the stereotype by learning the local language, associating with ordinary people, discovering their real needs, and successfully defending the nation against communism.

When aid programs did not suffice, the Eisenhower administration countered communist influence in the Third World by supplying military advisers and authorizing covert actions by the CIA. During the 1950s, Eisenhower deepened American involvement in Vietnam, and soon the United States was intervening in Iran, Guatemala, the Congo, and Cuba as well.

During his first term, Eisenhower appointed General James Doolittle to chair a secret study of the CIA's ability to counter Soviet activities. The resulting report warned that America faced "an implacable enemy whose avowed objective is world domination by whatever means and at whatever cost." There were "no rules in such a game," because "previously acceptable norms of human conduct" no longer applied. Americans "must learn to subvert, sabotage and destroy our enemies by more clever and sophisticated and more effective methods than those used against us."

Using the CIA to conduct secret operations had a strong appeal to American leaders. Covert actions provided the opportunity to achieve foreign policy goals without the direct costs of war or the scrutiny of public debate. The secrecy of CIA operations also permitted the government to act in ways that the American public found too uncomfortable to admit or to discuss, be it overthrowing governments or testing mind-altering drugs on unsuspecting citizens.

Eisenhower inherited the war in French Indochina and passed it on to his successors. In 1953 and 1954 (and in later years), policymakers worried that if the communist Vietminh guerrillas won in Vietnam, first all of Southeast Asia and then resource-starved Japan would "fall like dominoes." After this fall, Eisenhower predicted, the Pacific Ocean would "become a Communist lake."

Since 1950, the United States had spent over $1 billion in Vietnam, providing about 70 percent of the cost of France's war against the Vietminh and its leader, Ho Chi Minh. As American analysts admitted, however, French rule was unpopular in Vietnam and unlikely ever to be accepted. Eisenhower and Dulles hoped that if the French granted real power to noncommunist Vietnamese rather than the puppet emperor Bao Dai, the war would change from a colonial struggle to a battle against communism. Defending the "freedom" of an independent Vietnam would prove more popular among Americans—and presumably Vietnamese—than saving a colony.

In the spring of 1954, the war in Indochina reached a climax. Vietminh guerrillas trapped twelve thousand French troops at Dienbienphu, a valley in northern Vietnam. Washington again urged the French to grant Vietnam independence as a way of building support for expanded American and British military aid. Eisenhower compared the threat in Vietnam to the dangers posed by the Axis powers before World War II. As in the 1930s, he complained, the French were "a hopeless, helpless mass of protoplasm."

As the battle for Dienbienphu climaxed late in April, Dulles, Nixon, and the heads of the armed services formulated plans for American air strikes against the Vietminh. General Nathan Twining proposed dropping three small atomic bombs around the battle zone to clean out the communists. Eisenhower urged restraint, declaring, "You boys must be crazy. . . . We can't use those awful things against Asians for the second time in ten years." Eisenhower did consider a conventional air strike, however, and he allowed Dulles to threaten atomic retaliation if China sent combat troops to help the Vietminh. But when Britain declined to commit troops to aid the French and congressional leaders proved unenthusiastic, Eisenhower refused to intervene.

Early in May 1954, the Vietminh overran Dienbienphu. In Paris, a new prime minister, Pierre Mendes-France, pledged to negotiate a quick end to the Indochina war during talks that summer at an international conference in Geneva. Eisenhower sent an American observer to the Geneva talks, and Dulles also attended briefly. When asked if he planned to meet with Chinese representative Zhou Enlai, Dulles responded, "[O]nly if our cars collide." The United States feared that whatever arrangement emerged from Geneva would merely enhance communist power and prestige.

To the surprise of Americans, China and the Soviet Union actually played a moderating role at the Geneva talks. Eager to win points with the West, the major communist states pressed Ho Chi Minh to accept a temporary division of Vietnam rather than taking immediate total control. The Geneva Accords, reached in July, drew an armistice line, intended as a temporary military division, along the 17th parallel, with French forces moving to the South and Vietminh troops to the North. The key provision called for the departure of all French forces from Vietnam by 1956, followed by free national elections. No foreign forces were to replace the French. As the French withdrew from Indochina, they also granted independence to Laos and Cambodia, which bordered Vietnam.

American leaders were hopeful about the two-year hiatus before the proposed elections, which Ho Chi Minh would probably win. Dulles warned European leaders that the West must never surrender Southeast Asia. To bolster the wobbling dominoes, he flew to Manila in September 1954. There, he signed the SEATO alliance, essentially a Western pact to police Asia. Only two southeast Asian nations, Thailand and the Philippines, were signatories. Dulles also negotiated a defense treaty with Taiwan.

Meanwhile, the United States began providing substantial economic and military assistance, as well as military advisers, directly to noncommunist groups in southern Vietnam. As the French departed, American personnel, many working for the CIA, backed Ngo Dinh Diem, a Vietnamese Catholic (in a largely Buddhist nation) who had lived for several years in Europe and the United States. Attracted by his pro-Western rhetoric, his Christianity, and his anticommunism, army and CIA officers helped Diem organize a government and army in Saigon. To expand Diem's base of support, the CIA encouraged

Vietnamese Catholics, many of whom lived north of the 17th parallel, to move south. About 1 million did so.

In 1956, with American approval, Diem canceled the scheduled national unity election. Instead, he staged a pair of elections below the 17th parallel that deposed Emperor Bao Dai and substituted himself as president of the new Republic of Vietnam. Washington recognized this republic, better known as South Vietnam, as an independent nation. American diplomats and journalists applauded Diem's "one man democracy" and sent another $1 billion in aid to the regime. By 1960, however, a powerful communist-led guerrilla movement was threatening to topple what Senator John F. Kennedy called "our offspring."

Fear of the People's Republic of China (usually called Red China in the 1950s) boosted America's interest in the fate of Vietnam. In 1954 to 1955 and again in 1958, the United States and China came close to war over the fate of several small Nationalist Chinese–held islands in the Taiwan (Formosa) Strait. The most important of these, Quemoy and Matsu, lay only a few miles off the coast of China. The pro-American Chinese Nationalist government on Taiwan (Formosa) stationed troops on these islands and often used them as staging areas for commando raids against the mainland. In retaliation, and in hope of taking over Taiwan, the Chinese began shelling Quemoy in September 1954. The United States responded by signing a mutual security pact with Taiwan.

In private, both Eisenhower and Dulles had little respect for Jiang Jieshi (Chiang Kai-shek) and ridiculed his claim to the Chinese mainland. Yet both felt compelled to assist Jiang, in part because they had criticized the Democrats for deserting him but also because they feared additional Chinese expansion if Taiwan fell. The administration convinced Congress early in 1955 to approve the Formosa Strait Resolution, which empowered the president to use force to protect the security of Taiwan and "related positions and territories in that area." The president and secretary of state also issued a veiled warning of atomic retaliation if Chinese forces invaded Quemoy or Taiwan.

The 1955 crisis ended when China seized a few minor islands in the Taiwan Strait but abandoned efforts to capture Quemoy. Washington and Beijing then began diplomatic talks in Warsaw and Geneva that continued, sporadically and with little success, for fifteen years. Tensions resumed in 1958 when China renewed its shelling of Quemoy and Eisenhower ordered the American navy to resupply Nationalist troops on the island. After some tense moments, the Chinese declined to shoot at the American ships. The Americans convinced Jiang to stop provoking China. The Chinese artillery gradually abated, first firing only on odd-numbered days and soon after that substituting shells filled with propaganda leaflets.

Eisenhower used the CIA to deal with various threats in both the Middle East and Central America. The agency played an especially important role in deposing regimes that challenged American or Western domination of raw materials and in situations where the Soviets were not directly involved. Examples of these situations occurred in Iran, Guatemala, and Cuba.

During World War II, American oil companies began to displace British, French, and Dutch control of Arab and Persian Gulf petroleum. Inexpensive oil played a major part in the postwar economic growth of the United States, Western Europe, and Japan. When Eisenhower took office, he inherited a smoldering dispute over control of Iranian oil. In 1951, Iran's nationalistic (but noncommunist) prime minister, Mohammed Mossadeq, seized the holdings of the Anglo-Iranian Oil Company without fully compensating its (mostly British) owners. In retaliation, major European and American oil companies organized a boycott, refusing to purchase, transport, or refine Iranian petroleum. In May 1953, as the boycott caused economic havoc in Iran, Mossadeq cabled Eisenhower that, unless the boycott ended, he might seek Soviet assistance. Eisenhower rejected Iran's request for support and urged Mossadeq to reach a "reasonable settlement" along the lines demanded by the British.

Shah Mohammed Reza Pahlavi, Iran's nominal monarch, had played only a minor role in the nation's politics since succeeding his father during World War II. The young shah resented Mossadeq's influence and saw the crisis as an opportunity to gain power by playing up the Soviet threat. His interests coincided with those of American diplomats and oil companies, who hoped to preempt Britain's dominant role in the Iranian oil industry. To prevent any Soviet role in Iran and to preserve access to the region's petroleum, Eisenhower authorized the CIA to cooperate with British agents in a coup to topple Mossadeq and put the shah in control.

Kermit Roosevelt, grandson of Theodore Roosevelt and a veteran spy, played a key role in the coup. Arriving in Teheran in August 1953, he contacted the shah and a general in the Iranian army, Fazollah Zahedi. Roosevelt financed violent demonstrations against Mossadeq, enlisting mobs led by circus performers along with army and police personnel. The shah fled briefly to Rome while the army moved to restore order. Zahedi's forces stormed the parliament and arrested Mossadeq, and the general became prime minister. The shah returned to power, and Washington promptly extended $45 million in aid to his government.

An American delegation sent by Eisenhower mediated a deal between Iran and the British oil companies. The settlement allowed Iran to retain control of its oil fields as long as it agreed to market its petroleum at a low price through a consortium, in which American companies were granted a 40 percent stake. The British discovered that the cost of calling in the United States included losing a large measure of its oil monopoly.

Aside from Iran, the Middle East remained in political turmoil throughout the 1950s. Arabs felt humiliated by Israel's military victory in 1948 and the continued ability of the tiny Jewish state to defeat its numerous Arab neighbors. Although at the time Britain and France, rather than the United States, provided most of Israel's weapons, American Jews, with Washington's blessing, made substantial private contributions to Israel. Many Arabs considered Israel a vestige of Western colonialism; they also found it a useful scapegoat for their own problems.

(cont. on page 151)

Oil

Oil for planes, ships, tanks, and trucks helped the Allies win World War II. Petroleum became even more important after 1945 as Americans drove cars, flew in commercial aircraft, ate food produced by industrial agriculture, and used a vast array of plastics crafted from petroleum. Throughout the post–World War II era, Americans developed an almost unquenchable thirst for oil and petroleum-based products. At the same time, they regularly distrusted and feared, and they occasionally loathed, large oil companies and their executives.

Led by the United States, worldwide demand for oil encouraged the growth of the biggest, richest business on the planet—the petroleum industry. In the postwar period, the rising demand for oil-based products and the increasingly complicated relationships among multinational oil companies, petroleum-producing nations, and world powers like the United States and the Soviet Union set the tone for much of international relations and domestic political and economic affairs.

Before the 1950s, the oil industry had been relatively simple, even though it had always been a central player in the world economy. The United States produced and consumed much of the world's oil domestically, and a small number of American (Amoco, Esso [later Exxon], Mobil, Texaco, and Chevron), British (British Petroleum), Dutch (Shell), and French (Total and Elf) multinationals controlled the international oil industry.

In the decade after World War II, American cars rode for ten miles on a gallon, but with the price of gasoline at only 20 cents per gallon, few people worried about the efficiency of internal combustion engines. Although gas was cheap and plentiful, Americans did resent the influence of the oil companies. These behemoths managed to avoid paying corporate income taxes.

If the driving public was blissfully unconcerned about the future of oil supplies dur-

ing the 1950s, oil-company executives and government officials believed that expanding American access to cheap, reliable sources of foreign oil was vital to the country's prosperity and power. In the race for influence, the United States and the Soviet Union eyed oil-rich nations such as Saudi Arabia, Iraq, Iran, and Libya as key to long-term success.

More than most industries, the petroleum industry has been closely intertwined with governments and international affairs. For oil-producing nations, their economies and international status depended on their success at extracting the "black gold" and setting its price. By the time Eisenhower took office, the first postwar oil crisis had erupted over who controlled Iranian oil. Iran's new prime minister, Mohammed Mossadeq, seized control of oil production, and major British and American oil companies responded with a well-orchestrated boycott that wreaked havoc on the Iranian economy. Mossadeq turned to President Eisenhower for help ending the boycott in 1953, suggesting that, without it, he might be forced into the arms of the Soviets. Eisenhower ignored him. Instead, he authorized a CIA-sponsored coup to oust Mossadeq and return to power Shah Mohammed Reza Pahlavi. Once the coup succeeded, Eisenhower offered the Shah financial aid and mediated a settlement between British oil companies and the Iranian government. The deal, which called for a consortium to market the country's petroleum, assured American companies a significant portion of future Iranian oil profits.

America's need to maintain its oil supply continued to shape its relationship to countries in the Middle East. In 1956, for example, the dictator of Egypt, Colonel Gamal Abdel Nasser, sparked a global crisis when he appropriated the Suez Canal from Anglo-French control in an attempt to rid his country of the lingering influence of its former colonial rulers. The canal provided Western

Europe with vital access to the majority of its oil supply, and Great Britain and France loathed the idea of relinquishing control to Nasser. Along with Israeli forces, British and French troops temporarily seized the waterway. The invasion failed when the United States, motivated by its own need to maintain a steady supply of oil, cut off emergency oil reserves from Britain and France and suspended financial support for Israel. The three powers withdrew their armies from the canal and the Sinai Peninsula.

In 1960, five oil-rich countries—Iran, Iraq, Kuwait, Saudi Arabia, and Venezuela—met in Baghdad and formed the Organization of Petroleum Exporting Countries (OPEC) in an attempt to wrest pricing power from the multinationals who had controlled the industry until that time. They demanded that companies consult with member countries on all future pricing matters. Over the next decade, OPEC and the multinationals negotiated the price of oil for the world market. In 1970, a barrel of oil sold for $2.00 on the world market, about the same as ten years before. At the end of the 1960s, however, the OPEC countries had raised the royalty payments they demanded and received from the multinationals to the point where $0.50 of every dollar went to OPEC members.

OPEC seized international attention in 1973 when the member states raised the price of oil from $2.00 to $8.00 a barrel after the outbreak of the Yom Kippur War. It followed this surprising action with an even bolder one, however, one that changed the balance of power in the region and wiped away all remaining vestiges of the notion that corporations and superpowers were in control: OPEC instituted an embargo against the United States and other countries supporting the Israelis in the war. The effects were devastating: lines formed at gasoline stations; motorists cursed each other, government officials, and oil industry leaders. Americans began demanding more fuel-efficient cars. They turned away from cars made by the Big Three domestic man-

Refinery pipeline: America's dependence on oil has increased steadily since World War II. Well over half of the oil now consumed—mostly by automobiles—is imported. / © Hulton-Deutsch Collection/ CORBIS

ufacturers (General Motors, Ford, and Chrysler) and scrambled to buy Japanese and German vehicles. Executives of the Big Three waited until it was almost too late to roll out their own smaller, lighter, more fuel-efficient vehicles.

For the next several years, OPEC decisions dominated the direction of international oil markets and, by extension, the world economy. Industrialized nations worked to diminish their dependence on OPEC products. Beginning in the late 1970s, the development of oil production on Alaska's North Slope, in Mexico, and especially in the North Sea (sites that had been identified as new sources of oil but not developed prior to 1973) offered some alternatives in the international marketplace.

The scramble to identify and exploit other new sources of oil consumed the industry in the decades that followed as multinational oil companies redirected their exploration efforts to stable, westernized areas. This trend only increased as political instability took hold in Middle Eastern nations and sparked additional panic in world markets following the 1979 Iranian revolution. The price of oil shot up once more—to $32.00 dollars a barrel. A gallon of gasoline cost over $1.00, and long gasoline lines appeared again in the United States. The federal government restricted car owners to buying gas no more than four days a week. The old popular disdain for the oil industry, symbolized by the contempt that many Americans had held for John D. Rockefeller, the founder of Standard Oil in the early twentieth century, intensified. *Dallas,* a prime-time soap opera featuring a family of crude, conniving oil billionaires, became the most popular show on television for several years in the late 1970s.

The rise of the environmental movement—the green movement—beginning in the 1970s affected the American oil industry. In some paradoxical ways, the green movement has encouraged the growth of the petroleum industry. The movement's focus on clean air and water provided an impetus for American corporations and consumers to switch from coal- to oil-based fuel. More often than not, however, environmentalists have adversely affected the industry and its reputation. When the supertanker *Exxon Valdez* ran aground in Alaska's Prince William Sound in 1989 and spilled over 240,000 barrels of oil into the water, environmentalists seized on the event as evidence that the world needed to focus on environmental protection over energy consumption, and people around the world responded.

Oil remained a constant element in U.S. foreign and domestic policy. During the Gulf War of 1991, the United States led a multinational force of thirty-seven countries to reverse Iraq's attempt to annex the tiny, oil-rich country of Kuwait. Oil remained cheap throughout the rest of the 1990s. The price of gasoline fell to about $1.10 per gallon.

When inflation was taken into account, fuel in the late 1990s was cheaper than at any time since 1960. After the oil crises of 1973 and 1979, Congress mandated a doubling of the efficiency of internal combustion and electric engines. By 1995, everything from cars to boats to airplanes to refrigerators to furnaces required less than half the fuel that they had used in 1975 to produce the same amount of work.

Unfortunately for the hopes of energy conservationists, Americans inevitably forgot their earlier concern about fuel efficiency with the onset of low gasoline prices in the mid-1990s. Passenger cars remained efficient, but consumers deserted the sedan and rushed to buy heavy sports utility vehicles (SUVs), many of which got less that 12 miles per gallon. SUVs offered comfort; they seemed safer than smaller cars; and owners thought their rugged good looks made the occupants look tough, outdoorsy, and free spirited. The auto manufacturers loved them too. The Big Three and Japanese automakers earned three times as much on every SUV sold than they did on the average car. Because of a quirk in the federal fuel-efficiency standards, regulators considered SUVs to be light trucks, not cars, and therefore exempted them from the strictest fuel-economy standards. America's dependence on foreign oil reached 60 percent of annual consumption.

By 2000, energy policy became an issue in the presidential election campaign. The Republican candidates George W. Bush and Dick Cheney both had close ties to the Texas oil industry. They proposed drilling for oil in the Arctic National Wildlife Refuge (ANWR), a vast area of pristine wilderness adjacent to the nearly played-out oil field of Prudhoe Bay. Al Gore, the Democratic candidate, advocated conservation and a major research effort to wean Americans from dependence on the internal combustion engine.

In 2001, the Bush administration put Vice President Cheney in charge of a task force charged with developing a new national energy policy. Cheney's task force met in secret for months. Oil-industry executives found an open door, while environmentalists had little influence. By the time the Bush administration unveiled its energy plan in the summer of 2001, public opinion had once more turned sharply against the oil industry. Following a wave of mergers in the oil industry in the late 1990s, oil prices rose again—to an average of about $1.75 per gallon. In San Francisco and Chicago, prices hit $2.40 per gallon in the summer of 2001. As a result of these mergers, Exxon had gobbled up Mobil, and Chevron bought Texaco. In the previous fifteen years, Amoco, Gulf, Diamond Shamrock, and Sinclair had all disappeared as independent companies. Americans believed that the major oil companies colluded to keep supplies tight and prices high. Public anger at big oil surged even more when the Houston energy-trading firm Enron collapsed under a mountain of bad debt and shady accounting practices in 2001.

Congress declined to endorse additional drilling in ANWR, but it also declined to demand higher fuel-efficiency standards for SUVs. The 280 million people living in the United States, about 4 percent of the world's population, consumed about 25 percent of the world's oil production. Americans continued to fret about the price and availability of oil, a commodity they desperately needed and whose suppliers they often despised.

Such was the situation when Gamal Abdel Nasser, an Egyptian army officer, toppled the inept, pro-British King Farouk in 1952. Nasser emerged as a popular and ambitious leader who envisioned Egypt as the center of a revived Arab world. He bought arms from the Soviet bloc; but at the same time he sought economic assistance from the West to finance construction of the immense Aswan Dam across the Nile. The dam was designed to provide electricity and water for Egyptian farmlands. Dulles initially favored American financing for the project, but he canceled the aid in July 1956 when Nasser extended diplomatic recognition to communist China. By this time, the Eisenhower administration feared that Nasser's appeal to pan-Arab nationalism would destabilize the oil-rich region—even though Egypt had little oil of its own—thus opening a path for Soviet influence or endangering the West's supply of cheap petroleum.

Nasser retaliated for the withdrawal of American support by nationalizing the British-owned Suez Canal, through which much of Europe's oil supply passed. Egypt's seizure of the canal enhanced Nasser's image among Arabs and provided tolls that would help pay for the Aswan Dam. The British and French governments decided to send forces to recover the canal (and, they hoped, topple Nasser). They coordinated their plans with Israel, which feared the popular Egyptian's influence on other Arabs.

In accordance with the joint plan, on October 29, 1956, the Israeli army attacked and defeated the Egyptian army on the Sinai Peninsula and camped just east of the canal. Britain and France then announced the dispatch of troops, with the stated goal of protecting the Suez Canal from destruction. The European powers demanded that both Egyptian and Israeli armies withdraw from either side of the waterway and return it to European control.

These actions by America's allies infuriated Dulles and Eisenhower. They feared that European intervention in the Suez dispute would strengthen Arab radicals and distract world attention from the crisis in Hungary, where Soviet forces were crushing an uprising. The fact that America's two close friends, England and France, had acted secretly both embarrassed and angered the American leaders. The United States therefore joined the Soviet Union in condemning the Suez attack, and the otherwise rival superpowers supported a U.N.-mandated cease-fire. With sunken vessels blocking oil shipments through the canal, Dulles pressed Latin American exporters to embargo petroleum sales to Britain and France until the European forces left Egypt. Washington also threatened to block private American aid to Israel. By December 1956, the invaders had left Egypt, Nasser had claimed a victory over imperialism, and British prime minister Anthony Eden had resigned in disgrace.

Following this fiasco, Britain and France moved to accommodate Arab sentiment by distancing themselves from Israel, and the United States took a more active role in the Middle East. In January 1957, Eisenhower got Congress to approve a resolution giving him the power to use force, if necessary, to "block Communist aggression" in the region. Washington hoped to woo conservative Arab rulers in Saudi Arabia, Jordan, and Iraq by posing as their protector against both Soviet influence and Nasser's radical followers.

The so-called Eisenhower Doctrine held that the United States would intervene in the Middle East if any nation there requested help to resist a communist takeover. During 1957, a series of plots, coups, and countercoups swept Syria, Jordan, and Iraq. In 1958, Nasser forged an alliance among Egypt, Syria, and Yemen, creating the United Arab Republic. In July, a pro-Nasser officer, General Abdel Karim Kassim, toppled the pro-Western King Faisal of Iraq and considered allying his new government with Egypt.

American officials feared that Nasser and his followers throughout the region would block the world's access to Middle Eastern oil, forcing the United States, Europe, and the Soviet Union to bargain with them for petroleum. Determined to block Nasser's influence, the Eisenhower administration made a show of strength in the tiny country of Lebanon, where a political crisis had shaken the government for months.

Before abandoning control of Lebanon during the 1940s, France imposed on the Lebanese a constitution that gave greater political power to the Maronite Catholic minority than to the Muslim majority. As the number of Muslims grew, so did their resentment at their second-class status; many were attracted to Nasser's vision of a unified, Arab Middle East. In July 1958, Lebanese president Camille Chamoun, a Maronite, outraged Muslims by suggesting he might stay in office when his term expired a few months later. Egypt urged Muslims to depose the Christian-dominated government in Beirut, and rioting erupted. When Chamoun looked to the United States for assistance, Eisenhower saw an opportunity to intimidate Nasser.

The president believed that Nasser's true aim was to gain control of vital Middle East petroleum supplies in order to destroy the Western world. Dulles feared that unless American forces intervened in Lebanon, all governments in the Middle East not affiliated with Nasser would be overthrown. The impact would be felt worldwide, he worried, as people surmised that the United States was "afraid of the Soviet Union."

On July 14, 1958, Eisenhower ordered fourteen thousand marines, with tactical nuclear capability and backed by a large fleet, to suppress what he called a "Communist-inspired" threat to Lebanon. Ironically, by the time the marines landed in Beirut, most of the rioting had ended. Sunbathers gaped in awe as landing craft disgorged troops prepared to fight their way ashore.

The operation achieved its basic aim of limiting Nasser's influence over Middle East oil supplies. The Lebanese factions patched together a compromise, and Chamoun surrendered his office to another Christian. Iraq dropped plans to ally with Egypt and promised to protect Western-owned oil facilities. Even Nasser backed off after receiving word from Khrushchev that the Soviet Union would not assist him in any direct challenge to the United States. Although the Middle East remained chronically unstable and the Arabs and Israelis would fight several more wars, Eisenhower's show of force held the line through the end of the decade.

The Eisenhower administration was also greatly concerned about blocking communist influence in Latin America. In Senate testimony in 1953, the secretary of state described a growing communist conspiracy in the region. In the past, Dulles explained to his brother Allen, director of the CIA, Washington could afford to ignore turmoil in Latin America. Now, however, unrest and upheaval would lead to control by communists.

Most U.S. aid to Latin America took the form of military advice and equipment. For example, the army established special training programs in Panama and elsewhere for Latin American military officers. By paying lip service to democracy, ignoring the region's social problems, and aligning itself with repressive regimes, Washington showed that it opposed communism in Latin America, but it turned a blind eye to the dictatorships and poverty there. In 1953, Eisenhower and Dulles identified the major crisis in Latin America as the "Communist infection" in Guatemala, one of the region's poorest nations.

In 1944, a group of reform-minded Guatemalan army officers had overthrown long-time dictator Jorge Ubico. After a relatively fair election in 1945, reformer Juan Jose Arevalo became president. He inherited a desperately poor country in which the European-descended elite held nearly feudal control over the large Indian population. About 2 percent of the population controlled 70 percent of the land. In addition, the American-owned United Fruit Company, a banana grower, held vast tracts of farmland, much of which remained uncultivated. United Fruit also controlled railroads, ports, and communications infrastructure. Although United Fruit was not the most exploitative employer in Guatemala, its American employees lived in relative luxury while its peasant workers eked out a living on a dollar a day. Arevalo abolished forced Indian labor, extended voting rights, imposed a minimum wage, and began a modest land-reform program. In 1951, Arevalo's elected successor, President

Jacobo Arbenz Guzman, ordered the redistribution of large uncultivated land-holdings to the poor and sponsored new labor and wage reforms. In the Guatemalan context, these actions were revolutionary. Arbenz drafted plans to build new roads and ports that would break United Fruit's monopoly over the transportation system. He also expropriated 400,000 acres of uncultivated company land, offering compensation of $3 per acre, a figure based on the declared tax value of the property.

United Fruit demanded $75 per acre and got the Eisenhower administration to intercede on its behalf. The State Department—several of whose top officials had past business associations with United Fruit—claimed that the issue was neither social justice nor land reform but a communist assault on private property. American officials cooperated with United Fruit publicists in a propaganda campaign that labeled Arbenz a communist dupe. By casting the dispute over compensation for banana plantations as a battle between communism and Western-style democracy, the administration and United Fruit created a pretext for intervention. By removing Arbenz, Dulles told the president, Eisenhower would achieve a "Czechoslovakia in reverse." He was referring, of course, to the Soviet military pressure that toppled the noncommunist government in Prague in 1948. Washington prodded several key Latin American nations to join it in a declaration that no nation in the Western Hemisphere had a right to a communist government.

In the summer of 1953, Eisenhower authorized a CIA plan to stage a coup in Guatemala. To undermine Arbenz's support within the military, Washington cut off aid to the Guatemalan army and increased assistance to neighboring states. From bases in Honduras and Nicaragua, the CIA organized a small Guatemalan exile force under Carlos Castillo Armas. It began a disinformation campaign, using pamphlets and radio broadcasts to confuse the Guatemalan people. The broadcasts declared that a large rebel army would soon attack. When Arbenz purchased a small arms shipment from communist Czechoslovakia in May 1954, American officials immediately described it as part of a "master plan of world communism" that threatened the Panama Canal.

In June, one thousand or so CIA-directed exiles entered Guatemala and set up a base camp. CIA radio stations broadcast reports of a massive invasion. A few small planes dropped anti-Arbenz leaflets in the capital while the pilots threw sticks of dynamite out of their cockpits. In a panic, Arbenz tried to arm a peasant militia. The regular army feared fighting the United States or being supplanted by peasants. Fooled into thinking he faced a large invasion and deserted by his army, Arbenz resigned on June 27, 1953. As the CIA had planned, Castillo Armas and his comrades took over.

Eisenhower considered the Guatemalan coup a model Cold War triumph. At a dinner in their honor, Eisenhower told a gathering of key CIA participants that, thanks to them, America had averted the establishment of a Soviet beachhead in the Western Hemisphere. The new Guatemalan rulers restored United Fruit's lands and rolled back most other reforms. Over the next three decades, a succession of military governments slaughtered an estimated

100,000 Indians, labor organizers, students, and intellectuals who challenged the ruling elite.

Eisenhower later approved CIA operations to overthrow President Sukarno of Indonesia, General Rafael Trujillo of the Dominican Republic, and Premier Patrice Lumumba of the Congo. Although Sukarno survived a botched coup attempt, Trujillo and Lumumba both fell to assassins' bullets. American agents encouraged these assaults but did not take a direct role.

The Cuban Revolution of 1959 presented a greater challenge than had Guatemala. Since Franklin Roosevelt, American presidents had tolerated Cuba's long-lived military dictator, Fulgencio Batista, because he protected foreign investments and supported the United States in the Cold War. As a reward, Cuban sugar producers enjoyed privileged access to the American market. This profited wealthy landowners, among them many Americans, but few benefits trickled down to plantation workers.

Batista's regime collapsed in January 1959 when Fidel Castro led a guerrilla army into Havana. The son of a well-to-do Cuban family, Castro had lived for a time in New York, where he dreamed of pitching for an American baseball team. Trained as a lawyer, he led a failed rebellion in the early 1950s, spent time in a Cuban prison, and launched a second revolt in 1956. Castro called initially for socialist reform but had no specific Marxist program or links with the Soviet Union.

At first, Washington took a wait-and-see attitude. Castro legalized Cuba's small Communist Party, made anti-American speeches, ousted moderates

Fidel Castro with Richard Nixon in April 1959 during his visit to the United States. / AP/Wide World Photos

from his movement, postponed promised elections, and publicly executed about five hundred of Batista's henchmen. During a visit to Washington in April 1959, Castro insisted he wanted good relations with America. But he later signed a trade deal with Russia and expropriated foreign-owned plantations, paying the owners with bonds rather than cash at a price based on deflated tax valuations. Eisenhower decided the Cuban leader was a dangerous pro-Soviet puppet.

Although Castro lost his popularity among the wealthy, many poor and nationalistic Cubans admired his bold challenges to Uncle Sam. Castro's spunk in standing up to the United States also made him something of a hero elsewhere in Latin America. To counter his appeal, Eisenhower approved long-term economic aid to Latin America, a program President John F. Kennedy later dubbed the Alliance for Progress.

After cutting trade and diplomatic ties with Cuba, Eisenhower decided in mid-1960 to eliminate Castro. He authorized the CIA to undermine Castro's image and regime covertly and to train an army of exiled Cubans to invade the island. Mindful of the overthrow of Guatemala's Arbenz, Castro organized a popular militia armed with Soviet weapons. A year later, the CIA plan led to the disastrous Bay of Pigs invasion, for which the next president, John F. Kennedy, took the principal blame.

The Hungarian Uprising and Refugee Politics

Although the Eisenhower administration intervened in Third World countries to counter communist influence, it avoided challenging the Soviets in regions they already controlled. This fact was clear during the 1956 uprising in Hungary. Inspired by Khrushchev's recent speech denouncing Stalin, Hungarian citizens as well as local communist officials revolted against Soviet domination in the autumn of 1956. A reformist faction gained control of the Hungarian Communist Party and began to dismantle the totalitarian apparatus. Moscow held back at first but intervened brutally when reformer Imre Nagy declared that Hungary intended to quit the Warsaw Pact, the military agreement that bound eastern European states to Moscow. Early in November, in the middle of the Suez crisis, Khrushchev sent Russian tanks into Budapest to crush this heresy.

Although CIA-supported Radio Free Europe had urged eastern Europeans to revolt, when the Hungarians did rise against the Soviets, Washington refused to help. Eisenhower feared that American intervention would destroy Hungary rather than free it. "[The] Russians are scared and furious," he noted, and "nothing is more dangerous than a dictatorship in that frame of mind." The president even barred sending to Hungary a group of CIA-trained exiles prepared for guerrilla operations.

The uprising in Hungary created a major refugee problem for the United States. About 200,000 people, mostly noncombatants, fled the reimposition of

Soviet control. Because the 1952 McCarran-Walter Act barred most immigration from Eastern Europe, few could enter the United States. As President Truman had predicted, the law was a slap in the face to those "fleeing barbarism."

In 1953, Eisenhower had persuaded Congress to enact the Refugee Relief Act. This law allocated about 200,000 special visas outside the quota system, with half reserved for "escapees" from "Communist-dominated" areas of Europe. A few Chinese also came under its provisions. Except for this one-time relaxation, however, strict immigration quotas remained in place. Senators William Revercomb of West Virginia and Pat McCarran of Nevada warned that refugees might be Communist "sleeper agents," and many Americans complained that too many foreigners had already entered the country. In 1954, Eisenhower responded to complaints about large numbers of illegal Mexicans by authorizing the deportation of 1 million undocumented migrants during a nationwide sweep called Operation Wetback.

The mass Hungarian exodus prompted the United States to bend its rigid immigration policy. Eisenhower found a loophole in the existing law that permitted the attorney general to grant refugees "parole," a legal status that allowed them to enter the United States "for emergency reasons or for reasons deemed strongly in the public interest." This provision had been written to accommodate individual hardship cases, not large groups. Nevertheless, Congress approved use of the parole power to admit 38,000 Hungarians; it also voted special aid for them. Most of the 160,000 others who fled Soviet reprisals settled in Europe.

Lawmakers and the public showed selective compassion toward this group. The Hungarians were seen both as victims of Soviet oppression and as an easily assimilated group. The situation repeated itself in 1959 and 1960, when over 125,000 middle- and upper-class Cubans fled Castro's revolution. By utilizing the special parole provision, Congress avoided pressure to liberalize restrictive immigration quotas.

Policymakers viewed refugees from communist regimes not merely as victims but as public relations assets in an ideological struggle. Mexicans were deported as unworthy "economic refugees," while Hungarians and Cubans were welcomed as symbolic freedom fighters. The situation repeated itself in later decades when the federal government routinely welcomed Cuban "boat people" while simultaneously towing boatloads of desperate Haitians out to sea.

The Space Race

In October 1957, the Soviet Union captured world attention by launching a basketball-size satellite, Sputnik 1. A White House spokesperson dismissed the achievement as an "outer space basketball game." A month later, however, the Russians launched the one-thousand-pound Sputnik II carrying a dog into orbit. Senator Lyndon Johnson of Texas, chair of the Armed Services Committee's Preparedness Subcommittee, expressed astonishment that another nation achieved a technological victory over the United States. Like millions of Americans, he wondered what it would mean if a Sputnik satellite carried a nuclear bomb instead of a dog. Senator Henry Jackson of Washington called for a National Week of Shame and Disgrace. *Life* magazine added to the panic when it described the Soviet satellite as a major defeat for the United States.

The space and missile race had begun during World War II with the German V-2 rocket. After 1945, both Moscow and Washington eagerly recruited German scientists—including some guilty of terrible crimes against humanity—to help develop rocket programs. After a slow start, Eisenhower's New Look strategy, with its stress on atomic weapons, provided a budget and mission boost for the American rocket program. The new president was also keen to use rockets for launching reconnaissance satellites capable of providing reliable visual intelligence on Soviet capabilities. By observing what the Russians really had, the United States could avoid arming too lightly or too heavily.

But even with increased funding, spy satellites would take years to develop. As a stopgap, Eisenhower approved constructing the secret U-2 spy plane. A brilliant team of aircraft engineers designed and built the U-2 prototype in only three months at a secret site run by Lockheed Aviation. In 1956, the high-flying spy plane began crisscrossing the Soviet Union at 80,000 feet, photographing rocket test sites and allowing intelligence analysts to keep close tabs on their rivals' progress.

The U-2, Eisenhower explained, produced intelligence "of critical importance to the United States." Besides revealing what the Soviets *did* have, it revealed what they did *not* have. The spy plane, Eisenhower said, "provided proof that the horrors of the alleged 'bomber gap' and the later 'missile gap' were nothing more than the imaginative creations" put forth by irresponsible Americans who wanted to build more weapons than U.S. security needs required.

When Sputnik 1 went aloft, Eisenhower assured his cabinet that it posed no threat and hinted at a closely guarded secret: U-2 pictures revealed that, despite the success with Sputnik, the Soviets possessed only a small and unreliable rocket arsenal. The president urged his colleagues to play down Sputnik, lest public hysteria force an unnecessary boost to America's space budget.

Administration spokespersons therefore belittled the Russian achievement as a gimmick and attributed it to the skills of German scientists working for the Soviets rather than communist technological superiority. But this talk did little to quell public anxiety. Democrats, educators, journalists, and military contractors alike charged in the media that the Russians had humiliated the United States and threatened its national security. Each of these groups used Sputnik as leverage to achieve its own agenda: to embarrass the administration, to secure more funding for education, or to force an increase in defense spending. At the Senate committee hearings chaired by Lyndon Johnson, a parade of critics claimed that the Soviets had achieved the scientific equivalent of the Japanese attack on Pearl Harbor. On television, stand-up comics asked what the first Americans to reach the moon would discover: "Russians," came the punch line.

In response to this pressure, Eisenhower advanced the date for launching an American satellite. In December 1957, in the middle of the Senate hearings on the space race, a hastily prepared Vanguard rocket exploded on takeoff as live TV caught the mishap. Critics promptly dubbed it Flopnik. Eisenhower then approved the use of a military rocket, which launched a satellite a few months later.

As the Senate hearings wound down, Johnson warned of widening gaps between the United States and the Soviet Union in aircraft, missiles, submarines, and high technology. Because the United States stood on the verge of losing the "battle of brainpower," he called for increases in space and military appropriations as well as massive federal funding for education. Eisenhower responded by appointing a White House science adviser and increasing funding for the National Science Foundation. He worked with Congress to create the National Aeronautics and Space Administration (NASA), with an initial budget of $340 million. As noted earlier, he also supported passage of the National Defense Education Act (NDEA), a billion-dollar package of federal grants for schools and universities.

Shortly after Sputnik's launch, a high-level advisory panel, the Gaither Commission, reported to Eisenhower on the expanded Soviet threat. Hoping to force Eisenhower's hand, the authors used inflammatory language like that contained in the NSC-68 report of 1950 and leaked their conclusions to journalists. Headlines warned that the United States was about to become a second-class power exposed to immediate danger from a Soviet Union bristling with missiles. The Gaither report predicted that the Soviets would soon deploy hundreds of nuclear-tipped, long-range missiles, thus threatening America's survival. The authors called for accelerating American missile production, increasing military spending by 25 percent, and building a massive system of fallout shelters (at a cost of $30 billion) to protect civilians. Democratic presidential hopefuls, among them senators Stuart Symington, John F. Kennedy, and Lyndon Johnson, warned that the administration ignored a perilous "missile gap." This charge was bogus because the United States possessed a far more advanced technology base and was about to deploy a new array of land- and sea-based missiles.

Stirrings of Détente

Even as the space race joined the arms race in heightening public anxiety in America and creating new reasons for disagreement with the Soviets, a countervailing trend began to emerge. Eisenhower and Khrushchev took significant steps toward détente, talking with each other at summit meetings and establishing a temporary moratorium on nuclear tests. Although these efforts produced no lasting agreement, they did set a precedent for future negotiations.

The relaxation of tensions stemmed in part from the fact that by 1955, the Soviets possessed a substantial atomic arsenal. The Cold War rivals had struck a balance of power, or of terror: either side could greatly damage or destroy the other. Eisenhower acknowledged that under these circumstances, there was little possibility of victory, only varying degrees of mutual devastation, in a full-scale war. In spite of Dulles's boast that his willingness on several occasions to go "to the brink of war" had forced China and the Soviet Union to back down, Soviet leader Nikita Khrushchev probably hit the mark when he explained that Dulles "knew how far he could push us, and he never pushed us too far."

By the mid-1950s, growing prosperity in Europe and the changing of the Kremlin guard had taken some of the edge off the Cold War. The creation of an independent West German army and its inclusion in NATO in 1955 formalized the postwar division of Europe. The Soviets responded by creating their own military alliance, the Warsaw Pact, which was mostly a mechanism for controlling, not defending, Eastern Europe. But otherwise they accepted Western moves. The Soviets surprised the United States in 1955 by accepting American terms for a treaty ending the joint occupation of Austria that had begun in 1945.

Prodded by the NATO allies and his own desire to lessen the nuclear threat, Eisenhower agreed, in July 1955, to meet the Soviet leadership at a summit conference in Geneva. At the gathering, Eisenhower stunned the Soviets by calling for a policy of "open skies," whereby each side would be free to conduct aerial reconnaissance of the other's military facilities. The United States had little to lose and much to gain from such an arrangement. The Russians dismissed the proposal as a "bald espionage plot," and it went nowhere. Eisenhower, of course, soon approved development of the U-2 spy plane. Despite the lack of formal agreement, both sides left the summit praising the "spirit of Geneva"—a willingness between opposing blocs to talk.

During Eisenhower's final three years as president, he tried harder to reach some form of accommodation with the Soviet Union. For example, the perennial problem with Berlin re-emerged in 1958. Since the early 1950s, about 300,000 East Germans had fled communist rule annually, most of them through Berlin. Faced with this population hemorrhage, Khrushchev demanded the withdrawal of Western forces and the creation of a "free" (meaning East German–controlled) city. He announced a six-month deadline for the removal of Western troops, prompting members of Congress to demand an increase in defense spending. Eisenhower told the Soviets that American forces would stay in Berlin; at the same time, however, he informed Khrushchev that if the deadline for Western withdrawal were set aside, a superpower summit could be arranged. Khrushchev dropped his threat and accepted an invitation to visit America in the fall of 1959.

In July, before the scheduled visit, Eisenhower sent Vice President Richard Nixon on a goodwill trip to the Soviet Union. During an impromptu debate with Khrushchev, held in a model American kitchen at a Moscow trade fair,

Nixon proposed shifting the terms of the superpowers' competition. During what journalists dubbed the kitchen debate, the vice president boasted that most Americans owned houses stocked with appliances that made life easier for homemakers. A flustered Khrushchev dismissed these "useless gadgets" but insisted that Soviet housewives had even better washing machines. Confident that America had the edge in the appliance race, Nixon asked, "Would it not be better to compete in the relative merits of washing machines than in the strength of rockets?" Influential Democrats lambasted this effort to encourage nonmilitary competition. Senator John F. Kennedy, positioning himself as a presidential candidate, ridiculed what he labeled Nixon's femalelike "experience in kitchen debates" as a prime example of the administration's weakness and the reason for its failure to build more missiles.

A few months later, the Soviet leader visited the United States. When he conferred with Eisenhower at Camp David, Maryland, the absence of the hard-liner Dulles, who was terminally ill with cancer, lightened the atmosphere. As in the earlier summit meeting between Eisenhower and Khrushchev, no formal agreements emerged. But the two leaders found it useful to take each other's measure, and both spoke of a "spirit of Camp David," which observers took to mean an informal reduction in tensions. Khrushchev accepted the president's idea that he travel through the United States. Among other places, he visited a Hollywood movie studio and an Iowa corn farm. Although angry that security concerns blocked a stop at Disneyland, where Mrs. Khrushchev had hoped to meet Mickey Mouse, the Soviet leader enjoyed himself and agreed to meet Eisenhower in Paris the following spring.

To Eisenhower, these summits offered a chance to reduce the danger of nuclear war and to slow the development in America of a garrison state obsessed with security. The president believed that massive defense spending had contributed to America's emerging international trade deficit and to the economic recession of 1958. Khrushchev hoped that a reduction in tension would improve his ability to hold off Soviet hawks, including members of the military establishment who demanded greater missile production. For both Khrushchev and Eisenhower, one of the central issues was an agreement to limit nuclear testing.

In December 1953, Eisenhower had proposed an Atoms for Peace program to secure international cooperation in expanding the peaceful use of atomic technology. Congress passed legislation assisting construction of domestic nuclear power plants, but the proposal had little effect on curbing the arms race. In fact, for the rest of the decade, both the United States and the Soviet Union produced tens of thousands of additional nuclear weapons. In the United States, this increase required a crash effort to expand uranium mining, plutonium production, and weapons testing, mostly in western states, in Alaska, and on Pacific islands.

In the red rock mesas and valleys of Arizona, for example, government engineers descended on Navajo villages and convinced sheepherders to take up uranium mining "in defense of the nation." Hundreds of small mines, employing over 1,500 Navajos, were opened during the 1950s and 1960s. The miners were offered good wages, but they were never warned about the dangers of breathing uranium dust. By the 1970s, many of the miners were ill with various fatal cancers. In some families, two or three generations of fathers and sons died from mining-related cancers.

Uranium ore was turned into weapons-grade material at processing facilities in Hanford, Washington, and Rocky Flats, Colorado. Many small subcontractors, like the Albecroft Machine Shop, which was located in a residential neighborhood of Oxford, Ohio, also built bomb components. Under pressure to produce enriched uranium and plutonium at an accelerating pace, such facilities observed few environmental safeguards. Radioactive residue was dumped into streams, vented into the air, or buried in the ground. When Albecroft closed in the 1960s, it left behind polluted ponds that local children used as swimming holes. Five of six girls in one family living adjacent to the abandoned plant died of cancer. As one Defense Department official admitted in 1980, "[T]he army considered what was inside the fences [of the nuclear facilities] our problem, and no one should know about that."

Between 1945 and 1963, atmospheric test blasts were conducted at sites in Nevada and the South Pacific. During these tests, thousands of soldiers and sailors were stationed as close as three miles from ground zero. In Nevada, infantry units were often marched to the detonation point within an hour of the explosion; the intent was to "train military units to become familiar with new weapons and their characteristics." Soviet troops underwent similar training. From a present-day perspective, the ignorance of the hazards of radiation is astounding.

Atomic dummies at Yucca Flat, November 1955. To study the effects of an atomic blast on suburbia, weapons designers placed lifelike dummies inside Levittown-style homes at nuclear bomb test sites. / Loomis Dean, © *Life Magazine*, Time Inc.

Thousands of Americans living in small towns in Nevada, Utah, and Arizona—the so-called downwinders—were exposed to high levels of wind-blown fallout following each test. In 1955, the government distributed brochures to people living near the test sites. It informed them that "you are in a very real sense active participants in the nation's atomic test program." Many residents recall having family picnics outdoors to watch the giant plumes of colored clouds from the explosions. Little did they know that "active" participation would eventually be measured by high rates of leukemia and other cancers from radioactive fallout.

Similar misfortune plagued the Bikini islanders, whose Pacific atoll was selected as the location for the first full-scale hydrogen bomb test in 1954. The Defense Department moved the population to another island, but this relocation failed to protect them when the unexpected power of the bomb and shifting winds dusted them with radioactive debris. Fifty years later, Bikini remains uninhabitable. A Japanese fishing boat, the *Lucky Dragon*, sailed too close to the test area and was contaminated by what its crew called "the ashes of death." This incident caused a crisis with the Japanese government after one of the sailors died. The dramatic mushroom cloud from the Bikini explosion was featured in the 1954 Japanese horror film *Godzilla*, designed as a parable for adults about the dangers of nuclear weapons. When released and re-edited in the United States two years later, the film's antinuclear message was toned down in order to attract a teenage audience.

While most early cases of radioactive contamination were caused by ignorance, accident, or the desire to cut corners and thus speed weapons production, cases of willful injury also occurred. Beginning in 1945 and continuing through the early 1970s, medical scientists at government laboratories and in prominent research institutions subjected unsuspecting patients to injections of plutonium and other radioactive substances. Generally these patients were poor prison inmates and minorities or were already suffering from grave illnesses. Most had no idea of the risks involved. Several hundred pregnant women, for example, were offered free prenatal "care" that included injections of small amounts of plutonium to determine its effects on fetal development. The purpose of many of these experiments was to determine "safe" radiation dosages for workers in the nuclear industry.

Before the 1970s, the Atomic Energy Commission (AEC), citing national security, downplayed the danger from all forms of radiation, even though by the late 1950s, its own studies had confirmed the injury to the miners, soldiers, and downwinders. The AEC actually promoted routine use of X-rays in shoe stores to fit children. Soldiers at the Nevada test site were instructed merely to avoid breathing sand. The downwinders were told to dust off their clothes and brush off their shoes if debris fell on them. The best action, according to the AEC, was "not to be worried about fallout." Navajo miners and workers at Rocky Flats and other weapons plants were not even provided with paper face masks when digging ore or sweeping plutonium dust. Cartoons featuring Bert the Turtle assured American schoolchildren that they would be safe from nuclear bombs if they remembered to "duck and cover" beneath their desks.

In 1990, as medical evidence mounted about the devastating health effects of exposure to radiation, Congress passed the Radiation Exposure Compensation Act. Under its provisions, uranium miners, military personnel, workers in government nuclear arsenals, and downwinders who had suffered certain types of cancer were eligible for between $50,000 and $100,000 in compensation. In many cases, however, the eligibility criteria were so complex that victims had difficulty making a case. For example, by 1990, most of the Navajo uranium miners had died. Many of their widows could not produce marriage certificates or employment stubs from forty years earlier and were barred from collecting damages. After long delays, Congress and the Energy Department moved to rectify some of these problems in 2001.

By the late 1950s, growing public anxiety over nuclear fallout led a growing number of scientists and citizen activists to urge a halt to nuclear tests. Eisenhower sympathized with some of their concerns but would not agree to a test ban unless the Soviets permitted on-site inspection. When Moscow hinted that it might relent, American hard-liners panicked. Dr. Edward Teller told Eisenhower that if he were allowed to conduct tests a while longer, he could build a fallout-free weapon. Although misleading, Teller's claim slowed negotiations on a ban. In 1958, however, the president changed tack when his newly appointed science adviser, James Killian, introduced him to several scientists who refuted Teller's views. They argued that atmospheric testing was not needed to maintain a nuclear arsenal, especially if underground testing continued. To assuage fears that the Soviet Union might sign a test-ban treaty and then continue testing secretly, American scientists assured Eisenhower that a network of seismic stations could detect most nuclear explosions, even those underground. While their subordinates worked on the terms of a treaty, Khrushchev and Eisenhower agreed to an informal test moratorium, effective in October 1958. To placate hardliners, both leaders approved a round of massive test explosions just before the moratorium.

Eisenhower proposed banning fallout-producing atmospheric explosions but allowing small underground tests. The smaller tests were difficult to detect and, as American hard-liners noted, they were useful in designing new types of weapons. Khrushchev surprised American negotiators by proposing a comprehensive ban on all testing, coupled with limited on-site inspection within the Soviet Union to guard against cheating. Although uncertainties remained, a compromise agreement at the upcoming Paris summit seemed possible.

However, the May 1960 Paris summit proved a fiasco. On the eve of the conference, an American U-2 spy plane crashed inside the Soviet Union. It was brought down by a combination of engine failure and a Soviet missile. Eisenhower had approved this risky mission in the hope of gathering photographic evidence confirming that, despite Khrushchev's bluster, the Soviet Union had not deployed many long-range rockets. Such data would give the president greater flexibility in arms control discussions. The failed U-2 mission proved disastrous for this cause.

After American officials released a cover story about a missing weather aircraft, Moscow announced that in fact it had brought down a spy plane.

The Soviet trial of captured U-2 plane pilot Francis Gary Powers. Powers was later exchanged for a Soviet spy, only to die in a crash while flying a traffic helicopter. / © Bettmann/CORBIS

The CIA had assured Eisenhower that neither the aircraft nor its pilot could survive a crash. This assertion led Ike to deny that any such aircraft existed. Khrushchev then stunned Washington by displaying the well-preserved wreckage of the U-2. He then trotted out a live and contrite U-2 pilot, Francis Gary Powers, who confessed to espionage. The president was so depressed about this turn of events and their undermining détente that he considered resigning.

When the two world leaders met in Paris a few weeks later, Khrushchev demanded that Eisenhower apologize to the Soviet people for the U-2 mission. Eisenhower refused, and the summit broke up. An important opportunity to limit nuclear testing and slow the arms race had slipped away. The informal moratorium on nuclear testing lasted until the fall of 1961, when both the Soviets and the Americans resumed their tests.

Conclusion

By the end of his presidency, Eisenhower sensed the limitations of his achievements in foreign policy. He also worried that American society would face increased regimentation as the nation remained shackled to its huge and growing defense budget. His reflections on these matters were evident in his remarkable farewell address of January 1961, which has been quoted repeatedly ever since. Eisenhower warned against the temptation to solve domestic problems through "some spectacular and costly action" abroad. The old general deplored the view that a large increase in defense spending would create a miraculous solution to the nation's troubles. The greatest threat to democracy, he observed, came from a new phenomenon, the "conjunction of an immense military establishment and a large arms industry." Americans needed to guard against the unwarranted influence of this "military-industrial complex." With this turn of phrase, the former military man had sounded a warning that would ring down the decades. It had little immediate effect, however, on the administrations that followed.

Eisenhower began his presidency proclaiming the New Look, which emphasized the use of nuclear weapons and the doctrine of massive retaliation. Accordingly, he presided over a dramatic buildup of the nuclear stockpile, including the development of ICBMs. He also intervened repeatedly in Third World conflicts, often employing the CIA to undermine governments that he considered dangerous. He deepened the American involvement in Vietnam, which would have tragic consequences in the 1960s and 1970s.

Nevertheless, most historians see Eisenhower as a president who basically kept the peace. After ending the Korean War, he avoided direct conflicts with the Soviet Union or China. Although he and Dulles brandished nuclear weapons as the ultimate threat, he never authorized a nuclear attack. In the early years of his administration, he made significant efforts to restrain defense spending, and in his second term, he took steps toward détente with the Soviet Union. The next chapter will examine how his immediate successor, John F. Kennedy, handled issues such as the space race, missiles, détente, and unrest in the Third World.

F U R T H E R • R E A D I N G

On foreign policy, the arms race, and the Cold War during the 1950s, see Stephen E. Ambrose, *Eisenhower: The President* (1984), and *Ike's Spies* (1981); H. W. Brands, Jr., *The Cold Warriors* (1988); Robert A. Divine, *Eisenhower and the Cold War* (1981); Richard Immerman, *John Foster Dulles and the Diplomacy of the Cold War* (1990), *John Foster Dulles: Piety, Pragmatism, and Power in U.S. Foreign Policy* (1999), and *Waging Peace: How Eisenhower Shaped an Enduring Cold War Strategy* (1998); Richard Rhodes, *Dark Sun: The Making of the Hydrogen Bomb* (1995); Howard Ball, *Justice Downwind: America's Nuclear Testing Program in the 1950s* (1986); Robert A. Divine, *Blowing on the Wind: The Nuclear Test Ban Debate, 1954–60* (1978); Tad Bartimus, *Trinity's Children: Living Along America's Nuclear Highway* (1991); Jonathan Weisgall, *Operation Crossroads: The Atomic Tests at Bikini Atoll* (1994); Carole Gallagher, *American Ground Zero* (1993); Kenneth D. Rose, *One Nation Underground: The Fallout Shelter in American Culture* (2001); Walter A. McDougall, *The Heavens and the Earth: A Political History of the Space Age* (1985); Ellen Schrecker, *No Ivory Tower: McCarthyism and the Universities*

(1986) and *Many Are the Crimes: McCarthyism in America* (1998); Mary Dudziack, *Cold War Civil Rights: Race and the Image of American Democracy* (2000); Thomas Borstelmann, *The Cold War and the Color Line: American Race Relations in the Global Arena* (2002); Philip Taubman, *Secret Empire: Eisenhower, the CIA, and the Hidden Story of America's Space Espionage* (2003). **On recent studies of the Soviet Union and China in the Cold War,** see V. M. Zubok, *Inside the Kremlin's Cold War: From Stalin to Khruschev* (1996); Chen Jian, *China and Mao's Cold War* (2001). **On U.S. policy in the Third World,** see Stephen G. Rabe, *Eisenhower and Latin America: The Foreign Policy of Anti-Communism* (1988); Nick Cullather, *Secret History: The CIA's Classified Account of Its Operations in Guatemala, 1952–1954* (1999), and *Illusion of Influence: The Political Economy of United States—Philippine Relations, 1942–1960* (1994); Mark Bradley, *Imagining Vietnam and America: The Making of Post-Colonial Vietnam, 1919–1950* (2000); George McT. Kahin, *Intervention: How America Became Involved in Vietnam* (1986); Robert Schulzinger, *A Time for War: The United States and Vietnam, 1941–1975* (1997); David L. Anderson, *Trapped by Success: The Eisenhower Administration and Vietnam* (1991); John Gaddis, *The Long Peace* (1987); Michael Beschloss, *Mayday* (1986); Thomas Paterson, *Contesting Castro: The United States and the Triumph of the Cuban Revolution* (1994); Qiang Zhai, *China and the Vietnam Wars, 1950–1975* (2000); Gordon Chang, *Enemies and Friends: The United States, China, and the Soviet Union, 1948–1972* (1989); Michael Schaller, *Altered States: The United States and Japan Since the Occupation* (1997); Barry M. Rubin, *Paved with Good Intentions: The American Experience and Iran* (1981); Robert McMahon, *The Cold War on the Periphery* (1994); Elizabeth Cobbs, *The Rich Neighbor Policy* (1992); Richard Immerman, *The CIA in Guatemala* (1982); Douglas Little, *American Orientalism: The United States and the Middle East Since 1945* (2002). **On the growth of the oil industry,** see Hooshang Amirahmadi, ed., *The Caspian Region at a Crossroad: Challenges of a New Frontier of Energy and Development* (2000); Michael Economides and Ronald Oligney, *The Color of Oil: The History, the Money and the Politics of the World's Biggest Business* (2000); Roger Owen and Sevket Pamuk, *A History of Middle East Economies in the Twentieth Century* (1999); Ahmed Rashid, *Taliban: Militant Islam, Oil, and Fundamentalism in Central Asia* (2000); Daniel Yergin. *The Prize: The Epic Quest for Oil, Money and Power* (1991).

5

The New Frontier at Home and Abroad, 1960–1963

President John F. Kennedy and Soviet leader Nikita Khrushchev meet in Vienna, June 1961. / © Bettmann/CORBIS

On a sweltering Monday afternoon in late July 1962, President John F. Kennedy, Secretary of State Dean Rusk, and National Security Adviser McGeorge Bundy spent a few minutes discussing the qualities the president wanted in the officials who would represent the United States abroad. "You never want to generalize," the president cautioned, but he could not get over what he thought was an appalling lack of "spine" among Foreign Service officers. He disliked one ambassador because he did not present "a very virile figure." Kennedy chuckled that "maybe that work doesn't require it." Yet he clearly believed that diplomats needed to be forceful in arguing the American case. "These days," he told his key foreign policy lieutenants, "you're talking to so many people who are dictators, who sort of come off in a hard and tough way [and] I don't think it makes much of an impression on them if some rather languid figure" from the Foreign Service presents the American point of view. Not that Kennedy wanted to rely on brute force. "I know that you get this sort of virility over at the Pentagon and you get a lot of . . . admirable nice figures, without any brains." He wanted something else—tough-minded, disciplined, intelligent, and curious representatives to explain the American cause.

He was not alone. By 1960, many Americans wanted something more. Not only had President Eisenhower's grandfatherly style begun to seem unexciting, but social and political attitudes were also evolving. Among many young people, the ideal of a stable, secure, middle-class family in the suburbs was giving way to a desire for more adventure, a greater challenge, and service to people or causes greater than themselves. Among African Americans, who represented approximately 10 percent of the country's population, the degrading system of legal segregation had become intolerable. A new civil rights movement spread across the South, where more than half the African American population lived. In politics, many people admired a style of action and engagement rather than the cautious consensus of the 1950s. Americans who embraced these new challenges and sense of promise found a leader to suit their tastes in the wealthy, witty, and optimistic John F. Kennedy.

Often known informally as Jack or JFK, the young Massachusetts Democratic senator was elected as the nation's first Catholic president by a tiny margin in 1960. Kennedy embodied urbane masculinity. He combined a dazzling smile, a youthful appearance, a probing intelligence, and abundant curiosity with what his admirers called toughness—the ability to act decisively without expressing agonizing self-doubt. The Kennedy style captivated the mass media and, through them, the public. Kennedy's presidency raised the expectation that problems could be solved by wit, intelligence, knowledge, energy, and skillful management. Many middle-class Americans felt more optimistic about their country's social, spiritual, and economic prospects during the one thousand days of Kennedy's presidency than they did for years thereafter. His murder on November 22, 1963, permanently wounded the American outlook.

Seen in retrospect, however, Kennedy's administration loses some of its luster. In the decades after 1963, more and more of the dark side of the Kennedy years came to light. The president's sunny optimism sometimes seemed to be reckless risk taking. His compulsive womanizing and his disregard for civil liberties were judged more critically in later years. Kennedy's toughness, knowledge, and energy alone could not meet many of the challenges facing the country. His principal skills were those of technique and style. He had less success outlining a compelling vision for the future. Kennedy was a splendid public official. He connected with people; he made them look forward to the future. But he was not an advocate of any particular cause. He and his supporters considered it a source of strength and a sign of their maturity that they treated public affairs coolly and dispassionately.

In domestic affairs, Kennedy's often detached, pragmatic attitude made the federal government slow to respond to important emerging issues. During his presidency, an energetic civil rights movement gathered strength across the American South. Scenes of bloody attacks on black and white Freedom Riders sickened many people across the country. The effort to integrate the University of Mississippi led to another violent confrontation. The demand for civil rights pushed the Kennedy administration into supporting legislation banning legal discrimination. Public concern over the desperate conditions of the one-quarter of Americans living in poverty also revived in the early 1960s. Kennedy responded with some sensitivity to the problems of the poor, but his legislative agenda remained unfulfilled at the time of his death. Some of Kennedy's reluctance to passionately embrace causes of social reform stemmed from the narrowness of his electoral victory over Republican Vice President Richard M. Nixon in 1960. Kennedy did not want to get too far in front of public opinion. But he also remained deeply suspicious of expressing too much passion for any social cause.

In foreign policy, the United States continued the policy of containment that had been established more than a decade earlier. Kennedy's belief in the need for toughness with the Soviet Union encouraged him to take more risks about the possibility of nuclear war than his predecessors had done. Although the public backed him at the time and remembered him fondly for decades afterward, historians have taken a more measured view of his foreign policy. They have balanced admiration for his intelligence, engagement, and energy with disappointment over his assertive waging of the Cold War. If only he had dared to think more imaginatively about improving relations with the Soviet Union, or if he had had more time, the United States and the world might have been spared decades more of anxiety.

American Society and Politics in 1960

Americans expressed a yearning anxiety about their lives in 1960. The post–World War II economic boom was real, but it also left many people looking for something more. By 1960, Americans were more educated than ever before. In 1960, females stayed in high school through the eleventh grade; males stayed in high school through the tenth. (Ten years earlier, males and females had left school in the tenth and ninth grades, respectively, on average.)

In 1950, about 1.56 million men were enrolled in higher education, compared with 721,000 women. In 1960, 2.26 million men and 1.3 million women were in college. Graduation rates for the genders were far different, though. About 37 percent of women graduated, compared with 55 percent of men. Even starker differences between the genders showed up when one considers the attainment of postgraduate degrees. In 1960, 8,000 men received doctorates, compared with 1,028 women.

Women continued to enter the work force in the 1950s, reversing the trend of the immediate post–World War II years. In the decade between 1950 and 1960, 5 million more women worked outside the home, raising the percentage of working women to 38 percent (from 34 percent at the beginning of the decade).

About 50 percent of African Americans lived in poverty in 1960. Throughout the 1950s, blacks continued to leave the South, where the demeaning system of legal segregation remained the norm. By 1960, only about 53 percent of African Americans lived in the states of the Old Confederacy. In the South, African Americans experienced daily humiliations. Schools, restaurants, buses, beaches, drinking fountains, and swimming pools were segregated. Whites addressed African American men as "boy," or "George," or "Jack." African American women were called "Aunt" or by their first names. Whites in the South never addressed African Americans as Miss, Mrs., or Mr. Racial discrimination was more subtle in the North, but it still ran deep.

Unemployment rates among blacks were twice as high as for whites. Employers discriminated against African Americans in hiring, wages, and promotions. Housing discrimination intensified in northern cities. The major cities of the North designed massive urban-renewal projects that tore down black neighborhoods and forced African Americans into dilapidated neighborhoods or huge, forbidding, high-rise housing projects. By 1960, social critics began characterizing African American neighborhoods in northern cities as ghettos. Blacks who sought to migrate to the suburbs were blocked at almost every turn.

In 1960, social critic Paul Goodman published *Growing Up Absurd*, a series of essays decrying what he characterized as the mindless consumerism of the 1950s. Like many cultural critics in the late 1950s, Goodman complained about the conformity, blandness, sameness, and lack of adventure of suburban life. The election of 1960 crystallized many of the hopes Americans had for the new decade. It demonstrated how much American politics had changed since World War II. Democrats expected that the New Deal coalition of liberals, working-class people, Catholics, southerners, and racial minorities would continue to give them an advantage in presidential elections. They believed that the idea of an activist government, promoted by the New Deal, had been accepted by a majority of Americans. They explained away the popularity of Dwight D. Eisenhower as a reflection of his personal appeal rather than an endorsement of the Republican Party. However, the 1960 election results revealed serious limits to the New Deal coalition and the public's acceptance of government activism. The Democrats barely won with John F. Kennedy, a moderate candidate from the party's center. Richard Nixon, the Republican candidate, did so well that he remained an important figure in American politics. White southerners continued their flight from the Democratic Party, preparing the way for future Republican and conservative triumphs.

Only forty-two years old when he announced his candidacy for the presidency in January 1960, Massachusetts senator John F. Kennedy shook up Democratic Party professionals, who dismissed him as a brash outsider. But these leaders were unaware of the advantages Kennedy's celebrity would bring to the 1960 election. He was already well known to the public thanks largely to the tireless efforts of his father, former ambassador to Great Britain Joseph P. Kennedy. The Ambassador, as he liked to be called, had amassed a fortune in real estate and the movies in the 1920s. A fiercely proud Irish American Catholic, Joseph Kennedy took various positions in the New Deal. He hoped to succeed Roosevelt and become president in 1940. That ambition dashed, he planned to have his first-born son, Joseph, Jr., elected the first Catholic president, but Joe, an Army Airs Corps pilot, died when his plane was shot down over France in 1944. The Ambassador then decided that his second son, John, would carry the family's ambitions to the White House. Joseph Kennedy helped plant laudatory stories about his son John in newspapers and magazines in the 1950s. He helped garner the 1957 Pulitzer Prize for his son's 1956 book *Profiles in Courage*. John Kennedy made a favorable impression by nearly winning the Democratic Party's nomination for vice president in 1956. His fresh, youthful appearance stood in sharp contrast to Eisenhower's age and apparent passivity—a difference Kennedy planned to emphasize in his campaign. Kennedy looked like the picture of good health—his face tanned, his hair abundant, and his teeth a radiant white. Appearances told only part of the story, though. Kennedy suffered from a disorder of his adrenal gland, for which he took a mixture of cortisone and amphetamines. The pills produced a mild euphoria, which heightened the sense of hope and optimism he wanted to project.

Kennedy also believed that his moderate stance on the controversial issues of the 1950s would distinguish him favorably in voters' minds from the party's liberal wing. He astutely concluded that the public mood had become more conservative since the New Deal, and that voters would respond best to a candidate who projected energy and managerial competence rather than passionate commitment to causes. The growing influence of television bolstered Kennedy's approach. He mastered the medium, appearing in people's living rooms as intimate, friendly, and approachable. His father's Hollywood background helped. "We're going to sell Jack like soap flakes," Joseph Kennedy declared. Some observers marveled at the young senator's command of the small screen. The journalist Stewart Alsop, one of FDR's greatest admirers, thought Kennedy was his equal. "Kennedy is his own secret weapon," Alsop wrote. Others thought Kennedy was shallow. The independent leftist journalist I. F. Stone complained about the "phony smell of advertising copy" hanging over the Kennedy campaign.

Although party professionals and most liberals had their doubts about the young candidate, they could not agree on an alternative. Kennedy dashed the

Enthusiastic crowds greeted Massachusetts Democratic senator John F. Kennedy wherever he campaigned for president in 1960. / © Bettmann/CORBIS

hopes of the older men by winning victories in seven presidential primaries. His victory in West Virginia, an overwhelmingly Protestant state, proved that his Catholicism would not provoke a significant voter backlash. By the time the Democratic convention met in July, only Senate majority leader Lyndon Johnson of Texas could mount a last-ditch campaign against Kennedy.

Johnson's bid came so late, and Johnson had opposed so many liberal initiatives, that his attempt to gain the nomination fizzled. Kennedy won on the first ballot. He then astonished his own staff—and disturbed party liberals—by offering the vice-presidential nomination to Johnson. Much to Kennedy's surprise, Johnson accepted. Two days later, Kennedy addressed fifty thousand Democrats at the Los Angeles Coliseum. He announced that "we stand on the edge of a New Frontier—the frontier of the 1960s—a frontier of unknown opportunities and perils—a frontier of unfulfilled hopes and threats." The crowd cheered when he offered not "a set of promises [but] a set of challenges." Kennedy's New Frontier came with "the promise of more sacrifice instead of more security," and the public was intrigued.

Nevertheless, Richard Nixon, the Republican candidate, had the advantages of experience in national office and the inherited mantle of the popular president Eisenhower. Nixon's steadfast loyalty to the president helped him win the Republican nomination over a last-minute challenge from New York governor Nelson Rockefeller, who had spent the previous two years on ambitious public works projects in the Empire State. Shortly before the Republican nominating convention, Nixon met Rockefeller and agreed to lead a much more activist government than Eisenhower had directed.

To win the presidency, Kennedy had to demonstrate that he was Nixon's equal. A key element in the campaign was a series of four face-to-face televised debates. The first Kennedy-Nixon debate proved crucial because most voters had never seen Kennedy before, whereas Nixon had been a familiar figure for the last eight years. Instead of seeing an inexperienced youth easily defeated by his opponent, viewers saw Kennedy as a knowledgeable, self-assured, handsome candidate. His crisp, fact-filled delivery made him appear Nixon's equal, erasing experience as an edge for the incumbent vice president. Nixon, on the other hand, looked tired and haggard. Sweat poured down his face. Each candidate's appearance affected audience perceptions of who had won the debate. People who watched the debate on television considered Kennedy the clear winner, whereas those who listened to it on the radio thought Nixon did a better job.

During the campaign, each man tried to convince voters that he would confront the communist threat with greater conviction than his opponent, and both indicated that they would oppose the Soviet Union more vigorously than had Eisenhower. Nixon vowed to defend Quemoy and Matsu, two small islands off the coast of the People's Republic of China, which Eisenhower and Dulles had protected. Kennedy responded with an attack on Eisenhower and Nixon for tolerating a "Communist outpost" in Cuba, just ninety miles from Florida. Shortly before the final debate, Kennedy's office released a statement promising "to strengthen the non-Batista democratic anti-Castro forces." Nixon, aware that the CIA had already developed plans for an invasion of Cuba, feared that Kennedy had deliberately revealed a plot to overthrow Castro. Nixon characterized such a plan as a violation of international law that would rouse anti-American passions throughout the Western Hemisphere.

No Catholic had ever been elected president. In 1928, the Democratic Party had nominated New York's governor Al Smith, who had gone down to an ignominious defeat. Millions of Protestants, who customarily voted for Democratic candidates, deserted Smith. They expressed the fear that a Catholic president would show greater allegiance to the pope than to American interests. Kennedy deftly turned the issue of his Catholicism to his advantage, neutralizing anti-Catholic sentiments and winning the hearts of his fellow Catholics. He gave a brilliant televised performance before the Houston Ministerial Association—a highly skeptical audience of several hundred Southern Baptists—telling them, "I am not the Catholic candidate for President, I am the Democratic candidate, who happens to be Catholic." He promised to resign if he was ever forced to choose between violating his conscience and violating the Constitution.

Another brilliant gesture helped him secure the votes of blacks. African Americans had been cool toward Kennedy because of his noticeable lack of interest in civil rights legislation during his years in Congress. Kennedy and his brother Robert melted the animosity with two telephone calls in late October 1960. Civil rights leader Martin Luther King, Jr., had been sent to a rural Georgia jail to serve a four-month sentence on trumped-up charges involving a demonstration against a segregated lunch counter at an Atlanta department store. John Kennedy called the prisoner's wife, Coretta Scott King, to express his interest in her husband's welfare. His brother and campaign manager Robert secured King's release by calling the judge and telling him that the harsh sentence made the state of Georgia look bad. The judge relented and ordered King's release. In gratitude, King's father, Martin Luther King, Sr., a Baptist minister, withdrew his earlier endorsement of Richard Nixon and proclaimed that the mostly Protestant African Americans had no reason to fear the election of the Catholic Kennedy. The Kennedy campaign then distributed 2 million copies of a booklet describing the Kennedy brothers' efforts on King's behalf.

In the November election, Kennedy won a razor-thin plurality, beating Nixon by only 118,574 votes out of a total of 68,334,888 votes cast. And even that narrow victory was tainted by charges of voter fraud in several key states where Kennedy won by a small margin. Sixty-four percent of Americans cast votes, the largest proportion since 1920. The issue of Kennedy's religion reduced his popular-vote margin, but it actually helped him win electoral votes. Although he lost the backing of about 1 million Protestants who had supported Democrats in earlier elections, these people were concentrated in midwestern farm states that customarily voted Republican anyway. Among Catholics, Kennedy won 80 percent of the vote, up from the approximately 63 percent who had voted for Democratic candidates since Roosevelt, and this gain proved important in the electoral college. African Americans also helped Kennedy win key northern industrial states such as New York, Pennsylvania, and Michigan. Although most blacks still could not vote in the South, those who did provided crucial victory margins in North Carolina, South Carolina, and Texas. The presence of Texas senator Lyndon Johnson on the ticket also helped the ticket carry traditionally Democratic states of the Old Confederacy.

The Kennedy Presidency

Kennedy took the oath of office under a brilliant blue sky on a bitterly cold January 20, 1961. The handsome young president captured his listeners with his stirring phrases and his calls to sacrifice in his inaugural address. The speech included what were probably Kennedy's most famous words: "And so my fellow Americans, ask not what your country can do for you—ask what you can do for your country."

The stylish inauguration set the tone for the one thousand days of the Kennedy administration. He and his family projected a sexy image of vigor and refinement to which the nation responded. The president's staff participated in bone-wearying fifty-mile hikes; the nation's public schools began requiring physical education. Intellectuals felt valued, in sharp contrast to the harassment they had experienced during the McCarthy era. Jacqueline

Kennedy touched a similar nerve with her efforts to refurnish the White House with authentic antiques.

At every opportunity, Kennedy sought to distinguish his freewheeling management approach from the military-style hierarchy of the Eisenhower years. The new president sought advice from anyone in or out of government. His brother Robert operated a running seminar on public policy at his sprawling home across the Potomac in Virginia. Many old Washington veterans heard echoes of the exciting days of the early New Deal. Some people thought the newcomers were far too brash. "They've got the damned bunch of boy commandos running around," complained former Democratic presidential candidate Adlai Stevenson.

In choosing his advisers and key administrators, Kennedy appointed a group that writer David Halberstam would later call "the best and the brightest." Relatively young, often educated in the most distinguished colleges and universities, many of them boasting fine records in business or academia, these new stars in Washington added to the Kennedy aura. Kennedy assembled a cabinet of men who shared his view that managerial competence, not commitment to any particular program, mattered most in the conduct of public affairs. Feeling the need for continued counsel from his closest adviser, he named his thirty-six-year-old brother Robert as attorney general. He included two Republicans in his cabinet: C. Douglas Dillon as treasury secretary, to reassure business leaders, and Robert S. McNamara, the young president of Ford Motor Company, as secretary of defense. McNamara—ferociously intelligent, impatient with ignorance, a numbers-and-facts kind of man—set the tone of the New Frontier. If information could not be summarized numerically, McNamara would not use it.

Kennedy also chose a Republican to fill an important post outside the cabinet. McGeorge Bundy, forty-one-year-old dean of the faculty at Harvard and a long-time friend, became national security adviser. Kennedy believed that Eisenhower's disengaged style had hampered the nation's conduct of foreign affairs; he wanted to elevate the importance of the national security adviser to help make the president the central figure in foreign policy. Under Kennedy, the influence of the secretary of state—a cabinet position—declined. After a long search for a secretary of state, Kennedy settled on Dean Rusk, formerly Truman's assistant secretary of state for Far Eastern affairs.

At the same time that he sought to strengthen his control of foreign policy, Kennedy limited his options in domestic affairs by retaining J. Edgar Hoover as director of the Federal Bureau of Investigation. From the beginning, Hoover and Robert Kennedy fought bitterly. Hoover refused to acknowledge the existence of the Mafia; Robert wanted the FBI to infiltrate it. The attorney general also pressed Hoover to obtain evidence against Jimmy Hoffa, president of the Teamsters Union, but Hoover resisted that idea as well. The FBI director, in turn, forced Robert into approving wiretaps on African American civil rights leader Martin Luther King, Jr., whom Hoover detested and suspected of ties to the Communist Party of the United States. With these tapes, Hoover compiled lurid evidence of King's many extramarital sexual encounters. Yet the Kennedys had to keep Hoover in office because the FBI chief had in his files damaging tape recordings that proved a 1941 sexual liaison between twenty-three-year-old navy lieutenant John F. Kennedy and a woman who may have worked for Nazi intelligence. Although President Kennedy often seemed to flaunt his extramarital encounters, he feared that Hoover's files could destroy him.

Kennedy's Foreign Policy

Like his predecessors, Kennedy pursued a policy of containing the Soviet Union and opposing revolutionary change in the Third World. In 1961 and 1962, the United States confronted the Soviet Union and its Third World clients as assertively as ever before, hoping for a decisive Cold War victory. In the Cuban missile crisis of October 1962, the world came close to a nuclear war. In the aftermath of the missile crisis, ordinary citizens and policy planners looked for alternatives to their permanent competition. This early détente, or relaxation of tension, did not last, however.

Fidel Castro was like a toothache to the new president: the pain would not get better and Kennedy could not take his mind off the Cuban dictator. In 1960, under President Eisenhower, the CIA had begun planning an invasion of Cuba by armed exiles. By the time Kennedy took office, the operation was nearly ready. When the CIA presented its plans for the invasion, most of Kennedy's inner circle of advisers approved. CIA chief Allen Dulles informed the president that the prospects for success in an invasion of Cuba were greater than they had been in 1954, when the agency had sponsored an invasion of Guatemala. Dulles predicted that once the exile force landed, a general uprising would sweep over Cuba, expelling Castro from the island.

Kennedy's main concern was for the administration's ability to maintain "plausible deniability" of its involvement. In response, the CIA changed the proposed landing site to the remote, swampy Bay of Pigs, and the president banned the U.S. Air Force from providing cover to the invaders. Some analysts later claimed that these alterations doomed the operation but, in fact, the plan was flawed from the beginning. Castro was broadly popular among poor Cubans throughout the island. Castro's large, well-supplied army of peasant supporters was ready for an attack. Indeed, some of Kennedy's own advisers doubted that the plan would work. The invasion went forward anyway because it seemed easier to continue than to cancel an advanced plan. The president feared looking weak should word leak out that he had scrapped a plan prepared by the Eisenhower administration. He worried that if the members of the brigade were forced to return to the United States from their bases in Guatemala, they would inform the media of the plan, making it appear that Kennedy's toughness was just a pose for the election.

The invasion began at first light on April 17, 1961 (see Map 5.1). The brigade hit the beaches shortly after a CIA broadcast from Honduras entreated Cubans to rise against Castro. That plea had no effect, but Castro's own call to arms for his 200,000-man militia worked perfectly. The Cuban defenders sank

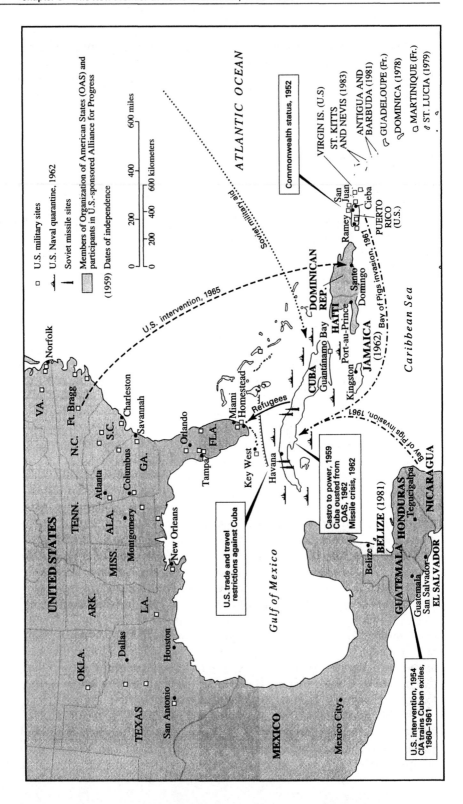

many of the invaders' landing craft. Attackers who made it ashore became easy targets for Castro's tanks and fighter planes. By the evening of the first day, officials in Washington knew that the operation had failed. Within seventy-two hours, the Cuban army had captured 1,189 invaders and killed 114; only about 150 escaped death or capture.

In the aftermath of the Bay of Pigs debacle, Kennedy set about restoring the image he had tried to craft of a decisive, successful, active leader. He embarked on a public relations offensive against Castro, implying that the United States would look for other ways to end Castro's regime. In a speech before the American Society of Newspaper Editors, Kennedy blamed the victim, explaining that American "restraint" toward Cuba was "not inexhaustible." He pledged never to "abandon . . . the country to communism." The public loved Kennedy's tough reaction. A Gallup poll taken the week after Kennedy's speech revealed that 71 percent approved of his overall handling of the presidency, and over 80 percent backed his Cuban policy.

Kennedy's obsession with Cuba continued after the failure of the Bay of Pigs invasion. The American government ransomed the approximately twelve hundred captured Cuban exiles with $120 million worth of drugs, medical supplies, trucks, tractors, and agricultural implements. Veterans of the brigade were given a tumultuous reception in Miami's Orange Bowl. Kennedy accepted one of their battle banners and promised to return the flag "in a free Havana." All the while, his administration proceeded with efforts to discredit, overthrow, or kill Fidel Castro and drafted plans to invade the island once more.

In late 1961 the CIA initiated Operation Mongoose, the code name for various schemes to oust or assassinate the Cuban leader. The CIA developed a series of fantastical plans. Psychological warfare experts suggested that a full beard represented sexual potency in Cuban culture, so agents tried to drop depilatory powder in Castro's boots. Another scenario involved agents slipping him cigars either laced with LSD to make him incoherent or injected with poison to kill him. At various times, would-be assassins tried to poison him, spear him with harpoons as he snorkeled in the Caribbean, or induce him to don a wet suit rigged with explosives. None of these attempts worked.

In frustration, the CIA turned to the Mafia, hoping to tap its assassination expertise. Mafia chiefs had helped the Eisenhower administration in its efforts to kill Castro because they hoped to regain control of the casinos closed by the revolutionaries. Eventually, the connection between the U.S. government and the criminals became too hot for top Kennedy administration officials, and the partnership was severed. One of the president's several mistresses also shared a bed with the boss of the Chicago Mafia. FBI director Hoover knew of this bizarre triangle, and he ultimately persuaded Robert Kennedy that any exposure of this connection could severely embarrass the administration. Kennedy stopped the affair. Castro learned of the American-sponsored plots on his life and sought

◄ **Map 5.1**
   The United States in the Caribbean and Central America

help from his patrons in Moscow. Nikita Khrushchev responded with Soviet troops equipped to repel another U.S. invasion. In mid-1962, the Soviets also agreed to station in Cuba a few dozen intermediate-range ballistic missiles (IRBMs) armed with nuclear bombs. This action soon provoked a major crisis.

Elsewhere in the developing world, the Kennedy administration used various methods—some far gentler than Operation Mongoose; some equally violent—to encourage people and governments to support the United States in its global competition with the Soviet Union. During the election campaign of 1960, Kennedy accused the Eisenhower administration of indifference to poverty in Latin America and a lack of support for independence movements in Africa and Asia. Eisenhower, he said, had ignored the winds of change sweeping the Third World and had opened the way for the Soviet Union to gain advantages there. The new administration sought to restore America's prestige among the poor or newly independent states of Latin America, Africa, and Asia by helping to build modern societies in those areas of the world.

Fearing that many Latin American states, racked by poverty, social inequality, and political repression, stood on the verge of revolutions similar to Cuba's, the Kennedy administration developed a foreign assistance program called the Alliance for Progress. Kennedy obtained from Congress a down payment of $500 million to eradicate illiteracy, hunger, and disease in the Western Hemisphere. Over the next eight years, the United States provided about $10 billion in assistance to Latin American governments; an additional $8 billion came from private agencies. Kennedy also promised to advance political and social reform in Latin America by pressuring the region's political leaders to revise tax and land laws that favored the rich.

The hopes inflated by the Alliance for Progress made disappointment almost inevitable. Creating just and prosperous societies in the Western Hemisphere proved far harder than restoring modern, industrial European countries to the prosperity they had enjoyed before World War II. Throughout Latin America, economic growth stalled at an unimpressive average of 1.5 percent per year during the 1960s. Unemployment rose, and the average figures for life expectancy, infant mortality, adult illiteracy, and the amount of time that children spent in school remained the same.

The Kennedy administration found it harder to practice concern for democracy and social justice than to preach it. Kennedy produced a mixed record in his efforts to promote popular, elected governments. The administration did hasten the end of Rafael Trujillo's dictatorship in the Dominican Republic, and it supported constitutional regimes in Venezuela, Colombia, and Mexico. But it allowed military coups in Argentina, Guatemala, Honduras, and Haiti. The CIA also secretly funded moderate and conservative candidates in Chile to undermine the Socialist candidate, Salvador Allende Gossens, in the presidential race of 1964. In most cases, a government's attitude toward Castro determined the American response to it. Governments that opposed Castro received American aid. Those that expressed sympathy for him or questioned U.S. actions in the Bay of Pigs were suspected of leftist sympathies and denied Alliance for Progress funds.

Another program, which did not involve covert actions, had a more lasting benefit. The Peace Corps, a project arising from the Kennedy administration's desire to encourage active commitment among American young people, became one of the most popular government programs in recent history. Like the Alliance for Progress, the Peace Corps originated from Cold War preoccupations and a sense that Eisenhower had done too little to oppose communism abroad. The day after his inauguration, Kennedy asked his brother-in-law, Sargent Shriver, to organize the Peace Corps. Congress created the new organization in September 1961. In the remaining twenty-seven months of the Kennedy administration, about seven thousand Peace Corps volunteers, most under age twenty-five, went to work in forty-four countries in Asia, Africa, and Latin America. More than half worked in education, fighting adult illiteracy and teaching children. The rest helped with community development, public works, healthcare, and agricultural programs.

A Peace Corps volunteer in the West African nation of Mali helps with the planting. / Courtesy of the Peace Corps

Most recipients of the aid admired the earnest young Americans, but to the surprise of some Peace Corps volunteers, they did not choose to transform their culture into one based on an American model. Peace Corps members learned from the exchange of ideas that the Peace Corps promoted. The personal impact of their service lasted for decades. Service in the Corps became a grand adventure. A volunteer wrote home: "Well, I got it—malaria!" He carried a secret microphone in his breast pocket when he met his hero, President Kennedy. "I got it all on tape," he wrote his parents. His eyes were opened to the appalling poverty of rural Colombia. He carried a small boy down a mountainside from a remote village to a doctor who would operate on his crushed foot. ("Have you ever tried to convince a little boy that he really doesn't need his little toe?") Sophisticated volunteers returned home with a heightened appreciation for other cultures. Many came to question the anticommunist assumptions that had created the Peace Corps in the first place. Instead of seeing the problems of poorer lands in terms of the competition between the United States and the Soviet Union, many returning volunteers believed that the United States should try to understand poorer countries in terms of their own culture and history.

Africa was only a slightly higher priority to Kennedy than it had been to Eisenhower. And when the administration did act decisively in Africa, it assisted conservative elements. For example, in the former Belgian Congo, a nation that had been independent since mid-1960, the Kennedy administration spent two years trying to install an anticommunist labor leader as head of the government. The CIA bribed the Congolese legislature into electing Washington's choice, a move Rusk hailed as a "major Soviet defeat." The victory proved ephemeral, however, and the Congo sank into civil war. During this conflict, the United Nations tried to arrange cease-fires and create stability, but Washington resented these efforts, fearful that they would interfere with American efforts to promote an anticommunist faction.

Obsessive anticommunism and preoccupation with events elsewhere also hampered American efforts to advance independence in Portugal's African colonies of Angola and Mozambique. At first, the Kennedy administration backed a U.N. resolution condemning Portuguese rule. Later, however, Portugal's dictator threatened to tear up the lease for American military bases on the Azores, a group of islands in the mid-Atlantic. Portugal's friends in the United States argued that the bases were vital outposts in the Cold War. Faced with stiff opposition, the Kennedy administration gradually dropped its support for self-determination and independence from European rule for the remaining colonies in Africa.

In addition to challenging Fidel Castro and attempting to fend off further leftist gains in the Third World, the Kennedy administration also intensified direct American opposition to the Soviet Union. The frigidity in U.S.-Soviet relations that began with the U-2 incident and the collapse of the Paris summit in May 1960 continued throughout the first year of the new administration. Hoping to demonstrate his mastery of foreign affairs, Kennedy met Soviet Communist Party General Secretary Nikita Khrushchev at a hastily arranged summit conference in Vienna in June 1961. The meeting took place less than two months after the catastrophe at the Bay of Pigs. Although the American public had rallied around their young president after the Cuban debacle, Kennedy's standing abroad had suffered. Earlier reservations among world leaders regarding his youth and lack of experience in foreign affairs seemed to have been borne out by the fiasco in Cuba. Thus, Kennedy went to Europe in June to reassure French president Charles de Gaulle that he could recover from his blunder and also to impress Khrushchev with how tough he could be.

The stop in Paris buoyed the president. The First Lady charmed the aging President de Gaulle, and Kennedy's knowledge and his ability to speak clearly and cogently relieved French suspicions. But in Vienna, instead of the get-acquainted session he had expected, the president found himself caught up in a dangerous conflict with Khrushchev over the future of Berlin.

The former capital of the Third Reich had been occupied by the four victorious Allies (the United States, the Soviet Union, Great Britain, and France) since 1945. Emerging Cold War tensions had blocked progress on a formal peace settlement with Germany, leaving the future of Berlin unresolved. The city was divided into eastern and western sectors, and the entire municipality was completely surrounded by the German Democratic Republic (East Germany). Created by German Communists in 1949, East Germany maintained its capital in the part of Berlin controlled by the Soviet Union. The Western powers, however, refused to recognize the sovereignty of the German Democratic Republic or its control over East Berlin. The Federal Republic of Germany (West Germany), also established in 1949, had installed its capital in the quiet Rhine town of Bonn. Since its inception, West Germany had insisted that the two Germanys must eventually be reunited and that East Germany was a puppet of the Soviet Union. Meanwhile, the Western powers had retained their rights to supervise the affairs of Berlin.

At the Vienna summit, Khrushchev raised the issue of Berlin as a way of bolstering the sagging legitimacy of East Germany. He had complained about the West's refusal to acknowledge East German sovereignty at the Camp David summit with Eisenhower in September 1959, but the situation had persisted. In the interim, the East German government had pressed the Soviets to do something to boost its prestige. Now, at his meeting with Kennedy in Vienna, the Kremlin leader insisted that the Allies finally resolve the German problem by signing a peace treaty recognizing the legitimacy of East Germany, with a capital at East Berlin. If no progress occurred soon, he threatened, the Soviet Union would sign a separate peace treaty with East Germany, ceding to that government control over land and air access to Berlin. Under such a treaty, East Germany would be in a position to strangle West Berlin because the city's economy depended on trade with the rest of West Germany, 120 miles away. The Western powers had been strongly committed to West Berlin's existence ever since they had airlifted supplies to the city in 1948. The loss of West Berlin, many feared, would erode faith in Washington's ability to defend other friendly areas challenged by the Soviet Union.

In addition to his tough stand on Berlin, Khrushchev surprised Kennedy by affirming Soviet support for what he called "wars of national liberation" in Southeast Asia and Latin America. Kennedy responded to Khrushchev's unexpected demands by expressing hopes for friendly relations with the Soviets, but he clearly had been caught off guard. Robert Kennedy felt that his brother's failure to crush Cuba had led Khrushchev to believe Kennedy was a weak president.

In the aftermath of the Vienna summit, the United States came close to war with the Soviet Union over Berlin. Within hours after returning to the United States, Kennedy delivered a somber, televised report on his encounter with Khrushchev. He told the public that meeting the Soviet leader had been a frightening experience. He explained that Khrushchev believed "the tide of history was moving his way" and "the so-called wars of national revolution supported by the Kremlin would replace the old method of direct aggression and invasion."

Behind the scenes, Kennedy prepared U.S. forces for a showdown with the Soviets over Berlin. He recognized that Khrushchev had manufactured the Berlin crisis in order to demonstrate his own toughness to the Soviet military and to assure the East German government of his support. Nevertheless, the United States behaved as if the crisis could turn into a war. To prevent the

Soviets from making good on their threat to limit access to Berlin, Kennedy let them know that Washington no longer felt bound by its pledge not to unloose a preemptive nuclear strike. He decided that Khrushchev "won't pay attention to words. He has to see you move."

On July 25, 1961, Kennedy further defied the Soviets with a bellicose speech. "If we do not meet our commitments to Berlin, where will we later stand?" he asked the American public. He reactivated some reserve units, which were to go immediately to Germany, and increased the armed forces by over 200,000 troops by doubling draft calls and dropping the exemption for married men. The next day, he asked Congress for an additional $3.5 billion for military outlays. Included in that figure was $207 million more for civil defense—an amount that prompted morbid speculations among ordinary citizens about the likelihood of nuclear war. Seventy-one percent of those questioned in a Gallup poll agreed that Americans should fight their way into Berlin if access were blocked.

While American anxieties grew, events in Germany in early August changed the course of the crisis. The constant stream of refugees from East to West Germany became a flood in July. That month, more than thirty thousand of the best-educated and most skilled East Germans left their dreary police state for the robust economic opportunities of the West. The East German government responded to the exodus on the night of August 13 by beginning construction of a concrete and barbed wire fence between East and West Berlin. Within three days, the Berlin Wall became an almost impenetrable barrier that prevented East Germans from fleeing to West Berlin. The wall would remain in existence for almost three decades, and hundreds of East Germans would be shot trying to escape through it or over it. Yet in 1961, despite the moral outrage in the West, construction of the Berlin Wall actually defused the crisis. It allowed the Soviets and East Germans to stop the flow of refugees without a diplomatic confrontation with the West. Khrushchev spoke no more about a separate peace treaty.

The Berlin Wall caught the Kennedy administration completely by surprise. Its construction demonstrated that the American military buildup had not intimidated the communists. Nor had it left the United States with the kind of flexible options that the Kennedy administration had wanted. On the other hand, many of Kennedy's advisers privately accepted the logic of the solution. Although Kennedy drew cheers from hundreds of thousands when he spoke at the wall in June 1963, declaring "Ich bin ein Berliner" ("I am a Berliner"), it is clear that his Berlin policy did not present the flexible, skeptical approach to world politics that his intellectual supporters expected from him.

The Kennedy administration adopted a more complex mixture of military threat and diplomatic bargaining during the Cuban missile crisis of October 1962, one of the most pivotal and dangerous episodes of the Cold War. In the end, the United States forced the Soviet Union to remove missiles and manned bombers from Cuba, but for thirteen days, from October 15 to 28, 1962, the United States and the Soviet Union approached the brink of thermonuclear war.

(cont. on page 188)

Nuclear Fallout Shelters—A Blast from the Past

In the wake of the September 11, 2001, terrorist attack against the World Trade Center and the Pentagon, and amidst fears that the nation's enemies might next use biological or atomic weapons, the Bush administration dusted off an emergency plan devised at the height of the Cold War. In the event of Washington's destruction, it provided for a shadow government in secret locations staffed by key officials. The largest of nearly one hundred underground facilities, built in White Sulfur Springs, West Virginia, could accommodate the 535 members of Congress and support staff. Although conceived to stymie a Soviet nuclear barrage, the shadow government took shape again after the September 11 attacks.

Since the first atomic bombs were used against Japan, numerous American writers speculated on how a nuclear attack might affect the United States. Three of the best-selling novels in the 1950s, Nevil Shute's *On the Beach* (1957), William M. Miller, Jr.'s *A Canticle for Liebowitz* (1960), and Pat Frank's *Alas, Babylon* (1959), contained apocalyptic themes of nuclear war that threatened all life on earth.

The anxiety over atomic war grew more intense after 1954, when the newly tested hydrogen bomb produced a vastly more powerful explosion than its atomic cousin. The accidental irradiation of a Japanese fishing boat in 1954 and later of several small towns in southern Utah from test explosions added to the widespread fear that radioactive strontium-90 had contaminated the nation's milk supply.

In response, some Americans formed citizens groups such as the Committee for a Sane Nuclear Policy to demand an end to nuclear testing. Filmmakers in Hollywood and Tokyo produced dozens of "creature features" like *Godzilla* and *Them* that depicted rampaging monsters created by nuclear tests. The federal government, acting through the Federal Civil Defense Administration (FCDA), tried to reassure the public that nuclear weapons were not so terrible.

Among its most celebrated actions was OPERATION ALERT, a series of mass evacuations begun in 1954. The best-known drill occurred in Washington, D.C., in 1955, when President Dwight D. Eisenhower and fifteen thousand federal employees were taken to thirty-one secret sites in a mock evacuation. Another demonstration took place in Mobile, Alabama, where civil defense officials transported thirty-seven thousand schoolchildren to secure locations. Most of these exercises proved so chaotic that officials privately admitted that civil-defense agencies "couldn't cope with a brushfire threatening a dog house in the backyard." None of the tests treated the threat of radioactive fallout seriously and many urban officials dismissed the notion of evacuating large cities as "so much moonshine."

During the 1950s and 1960s, public school students routinely performed "duck and cover drills." After watching a Walt Disney film about *Our Friend the Atom*, pupils read a pamphlet or viewed a cartoon featuring Bert the Turtle. He reassured children that they would be safe if they hid beneath a school desk and tucked their heads between their knees. Some young cynics subverted the exercise by chanting, "Now we put our head between our knees and kiss our ass goodbye." Their skepticism was justified. Federal blueprints for "nuclear-safe" schools included plans for large morgues in each building. A secret 1958 Defense Department *Emergency Plans Book* concluded that a Soviet nuclear and/or biological-chemical attack, even if directed only against military and industrial targets, would kill 30 million Americans outright, with at least 10 million more soon dying of radiation exposure. In the wake of such an attack, the planners concluded, the economy, law and order, and healthcare would collapse.

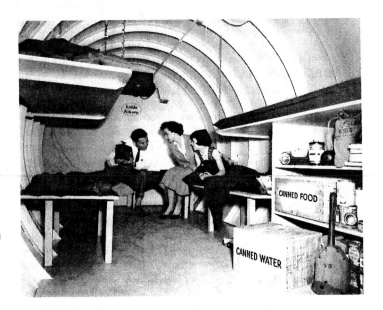

The nuclear family: the federal government encouraged families to build fallout shelters such as this prototype. Despite fears of nuclear war, very few did so. / © Bettmann/CORBIS

President Eisenhower and Congress dealt with these threats by utilizing them to build support in 1956 for the largest federal construction program ever: the National System of Defense Highways. The new coast-to-coast interstates, designed to accommodate the public's love of the automobile, were also promoted as a network to speed the movement of military vehicles and the evacuation of urban areas.

The Soviet Union's launch of the Sputnik satellite in October 1957 rekindled public fear of sudden nuclear attack and prompted resumed calls for defense. Reports issued by two blue-ribbon panels, the Gaither Committee and the Rockefeller Brothers Fund, urged the Eisenhower administration to spend billions of dollars to construct a vast network of blast and fallout shelters. The RAND Corporation, a private think tank linked to the Defense Department, proposed building an immense shelter under Manhattan to house 4 million people. Defense expert Herman Kahn, author of the controversial book *On Thermonuclear War* (1960) and the model for Dr. Strangelove in Stanley Kubrick's 1962 film of that name, insisted that most Americans could survive a

nuclear conflict if they had shelters. In a short time after the bombs fell, he claimed, life would return to "normal." New York governor (and presidential hopeful) Nelson Rockefeller pressed his state legislature to make fallout shelters mandatory in new homes and buildings. Shelter advocates argued that besides saving lives in a war, civil-defense measures would deter an enemy attack.

These claims failed to sway President Eisenhower or the American public. Eisenhower balked at the immense expense and dubious value of shelter construction. If individuals wanted to build their own shelters, he told aides, they should do so. The government should offer advice (like the quaintly named Grandmother's Pantry program of guidelines for stockpiling food) but no funding. Eisenhower insisted that a credible threat of "massive retaliation" remained the best way to deter a Soviet attack.

The public also resisted calls to go underground. Many intellectuals publicly criticized the notion of retreating underground as barbaric, war mongering, or a poor use of money. Ordinary Americans focused on the "gun-thy-neighbor" problem. Journalists, teachers, theologians, and television scriptwriters speculated over how to handle people without a shelter trying to gain entry into one built by their neighbor or a stranger. Would a shelter owner be justified in shooting intruders? The press printed threats by some of the few people who actually built shelters to blast away at interlopers. By the end of 1960, only about 1,500 home shelters had been constructed.

In 1961, President John F. Kennedy tried to breathe new life into the civil-defense crusade. That May, JFK spoke of shelters as "insurance." In July, he responded to a Soviet threat to drive the Western powers out of Berlin by announcing that he would defend the divided city. He also called on Congress to fund a shelter system. In a crisis mode, Congress appropriated over $200 million for a crash program to identify and stock existing structures as temporary fallout shelters while a new Office of Civil Defense developed a broader program.

Kennedy persuaded the editors of *Life* magazine to rally support for his plan. *Life* devoted its September 15, 1961, issue to promoting shelters, claiming that they could save the lives of 97 percent of all Americans. In December, the Office of Civil Defense printed millions of copies of a pamphlet entitled "Fallout Protection: What to Know and Do About Nuclear Attack." A nuclear war would be "terrible beyond imagination," the writers admitted. Then, in a shift of tone, they assured Americans that with proper precaution, "it need not be a time of despair."

Kennedy endorsed the creation of a vast shelter construction industry and proposed federal funding for community and school shelters. Cheered on by Herman Kahn, physicist Edward Teller ("father of the H-bomb"), and Governor Rockefeller, public agencies placed prototype shelters on display in parks, schools, and at state fairs.

Critics raised many of the old moral objections and argued that only middle- and upper-class homeowners could afford private shelters. Willard Libby, former head of the Atomic Energy Commission, retorted that a "poor man's shelter" could be built with railroad ties and bags of dirt for less than $100. To prove his point, he constructed a prototype near Los Angeles, only to have it destroyed almost immediately by a brushfire. Atomic scientist turned peace activist Leo Szilard described this incident as "proof not only that there is a God, but that he has a sense of humor."

To Kennedy's consternation, support for a federal shelter program faded in 1962 as the Berlin crisis abated. The whole idea, one critic noted, led to "more introspection than excavation." As talk turned to the basic question of whether survivors' lives would be worth living, shelter advocates recanted. In January 1962, *Life* retracted its earlier claim that civil defense could save nearly all Americans. Shelters, the magazine now advised, "would somewhat increase the chances of survival" under "certain ghastly circumstances." The New York legislature, which in November 1961 adopted Governor Rockefeller's plan for mandatory shelters in new buildings, reversed course a few months later when the press reported that several state politicians had financial ties to construction companies. Congress rejected Kennedy's proposal that the federal government underwrite the cost of school and community shelters. Not even the brief terror stoked by the Cuban missile crisis of October 1962 revived interest in civil defense. With the signing of the limited nuclear test ban treaty in 1963, most Americans turned their attention away from the issue of civil defense. As of 1965, private homeowners had built only about 200,000 fallout shelters, most of them little more than reinforced corners of existing basements.

In 1982, as part of his plan to confront the Soviet Union, President Reagan revived talk of bomb shelters. He claimed—incorrectly—that the Soviets had invested heavily in civil defense in order to survive a nuclear war. Deputy Undersecretary of Defense T. K. Jones predicted that the United States could easily protect its population and recover quickly from an all-out nuclear war if people simply took time to "dig a hole, cover it with a couple of doors, and then throw three feet of dirt on top. . . ." Everybody, he proclaimed, is "going to make it if there are enough shovels to go around."

Again, the public balked at the notion of going underground. Jones's remarks provoked congressional hearings, angry editorials, and a revived antinuclear movement. Jonathan Schell's 1982 bestseller, *The Fate of the Earth*, retold what would happen if a hydrogen bomb hit New York. In 1983, 100 million viewers tuned into an ABC docudrama, *The Day After*, that portrayed the gruesome aftermath of a nuclear war in a midwestern town. The public's refusal to embrace civil defense prompted Reagan to shift direction in favor of an antimissile system that he called the Strategic Defense Initiative, and that critics dubbed Star Wars.

Until the 2001 terrorist attacks on American soil, civil defense had faded as an issue. President George W. Bush then revived the antimissile program as a pillar of his defense agenda. The president also created an Office of Homeland Security to defend against both terrorists and "rogue states" armed with atomic, biological, or chemical weapons. The next step, some have speculated, may be a call for construction of underground shelters.

In the summer of 1962, the Cubans believed that another American-sponsored invasion of their island might be launched at any time. Their fears were realistic: the Defense Department had already drafted plans for a second, larger attack on Cuba. In July, Raul Castro, Fidel's brother and Cuba's minister of defense, visited Moscow and pleaded for Soviet help against the CIA's Operation Mongoose. In response to this plea, Khrushchev supplied Cuba with intermediate-range ballistic missiles (IRBMs) and the technicians to operate them. The missiles were capable of delivering nuclear warheads to targets in the eastern third of the United States. By this time, the Soviets had also stationed manned bombers and an estimated ten thousand to forty thousand troops in Cuba to repel another invasion.

Missiles offered little effective protection against the small-scale harassment of Operation Mongoose, but the weapons served Soviet interests in several ways. They retaliated against the United States, which had stationed its own IRBMs, aimed at the Soviet Union, in Turkey. The weapons would probably make Castro feel safer and more grateful than ever for Moscow's help. Most of all, Khrushchev believed that sending the missiles to Cuba had little cost. They really had not increased the threat to the United States, a fact noted at the height of the crisis by Secretary of Defense McNamara. "A missile is a missile," he said at the time. "It makes no difference if you are killed by a missile fired from the Soviet Union or from Cuba." Applying the same reasoning, Khrushchev did not expect that the United States would risk world war to force the missiles out.

Khrushchev did not reckon on America's obsession with Cuba and the emphasis that would be placed on the Cuban missile crisis as the fall congressional campaigns approached election day. Even before Kennedy knew the exact extent of the missile buildup, some Republicans, led by Senator Kenneth Keating of New York, claimed that the Soviets had installed IRBMs capable of launching a nuclear attack at any moment. (Keating's information came from a group of anti-

Castro Cubans.) On October 10, 1962, Keating declared that the Soviets in Cuba had the "power to hurl rockets into the American heartland." Fearful of a public outcry and of charges that the Democrats were "soft," Congress passed a resolution promising "by whatever means may be necessary, including the use of arms . . . to prevent in Cuba the creation or use of an externally supported military capability endangering the security of the United States."

On the night of October 15, the CIA developed photographs taken by a U-2 spy plane that showed the construction fifteen miles south of Havana of a launching site for missiles with a range of about two thousand miles. The president saw the pictures at nine o'clock the next morning and exploded, saying that he had been "taken" by the Soviets, who had assured him in September that only defensive anti-aircraft missiles would be situated in Cuba. The missiles had to be removed, he said. Otherwise, the United States would be vulnerable to attack, the public would be terrified, and "Ken Keating will probably be the next president of the United States."

An executive committee consisting of the administration's principal foreign policy and defense officials met secretly over the next twelve days. Their task was to force the Soviets to back down without igniting a world war. Robert Kennedy chaired most of the meetings. The president attended some of them, but he usually kept quiet to allow uninhibited deliberations. The

In October 1962, U.S. ambassador to the United Nations Adlai Stevenson presents to the Security Council photographs showing Soviet missile installations in Cuba. / © Bettmann/CORBIS

president was keenly aware of the historic significance of the executive committee meetings, and he ordered secret tape recordings of the proceedings. When the tapes were made public in the 1990s, they revealed Kennedy's probing intelligence. Throughout the crisis, the president and his brother sought the removal of the Soviet missiles without resorting to war. From the beginning, the participants agreed that the missiles presented an unacceptable threat. Allowing them to stay in Cuba would represent a humiliating setback for an administration committed to waging the Cold War more aggressively than the apparently cautious Eisenhower had.

Although the advisers were united in their refusal to tolerate the missiles, they were divided on tactics. They weighed the risks and potential opportunities offered by a blockade of Cuba or air strikes against the missile installations. As the discussions proceeded, a majority of the executive committee members, prodded by Robert Kennedy, began to endorse the idea of a quarantine of Cuba as a way of forcing the Soviets to remove the missiles. The committee eventually recommended a blockade.

By Sunday, October 21, 1962, the Washington press corps was abuzz with speculation. On Monday, the blockade began; 108 U.S. Navy ships patrolled the Atlantic Ocean and the Caribbean Sea, intercepting and inspecting the cargo of any vessel bound for Cuba to make certain it was not carrying offensive weapons. At 7 P.M. that evening, Kennedy appeared on television to deliver one of the most somber speeches any president had ever given. He announced the existence of the CIA photographs, explaining that they showed "a series of offensive missile sites . . . now in preparation on that imprisoned island."

Americans anxiously waited out the next several days. When the president received news that Soviet ships were steaming toward the navy's blockade line, the tension seemed too much to bear. Robert Kennedy remembered that his brother's face was drawn, his eyes squinting in anguish. A few hours later, however, navy officials radioed that the Soviet vessels had stopped without challenging the blockade. The U.S. navy allowed only tankers and passenger ships through. As a symbolic gesture, sailors from two U.S. destroyers boarded a cargo ship chartered by the Soviets. Finding no forbidden weapons, the navy allowed the ship to pass through to Cuba.

The blockade succeeded in preventing movement of additional weapons to Cuba because neither the Americans nor the Soviets wanted the situation to deteriorate into war. The quarantine did not, however, settle the matter of the missile sites already under construction. In a series of telegrams to Khrushchev and in several secret, face-to-face meetings in Washington between U.S. and Soviet representatives, Kennedy pressured the Soviet leader to demolish the sites and remove the missiles already in Cuba. At one point, a Soviet representative in Washington offered to remove the missiles and bombers. Khrushchev confirmed the offer in a telegram, but he added a condition: he would act only if the United States removed its IRBMs from Turkey. Kennedy ignored the offer of an exchange, and he also did not respond when Khrushchev seemed to reverse himself in a later telegram. Instead, Kennedy repeated that the Soviet missiles had to be eliminated, and he focused on Moscow's initial offer to remove them. Faced with overwhelming American military might and astonished that the young American president would actually risk a nuclear war over a largely symbolic issue, Khrushchev capitulated. He wired Kennedy that he had instructed his officers to "discontinue construction of the . . . facilities, to dismantle them, and to return them to the Soviet Union."

It appeared to relieved Americans that Kennedy had won a great victory. In the aftermath of the crisis, the United States quietly removed its missiles in Turkey. Washington also promised never to invade Cuba. In return, the Soviets took their manned bombers out of Cuba and pledged never to install offensive weapons on the island.

Fidel Castro felt betrayed by Khrushchev's surrender; the suspension of Operation Mongoose a few days after the end of the crisis did little to mollify him. He believed that the United States still wished him dead and that now he had no protector. His anxieties had a factual basis. The next spring, the State Department created a secret Cuban Coordinating Committee to bring down Castro's government. In October 1963, the committee approved sabotage operations against twenty-two targets on the island.

During the crisis and for years afterward, Kennedy won high praise for his grace under pressure and the way he sifted conflicting advice and made decisions. By skillful diplomatic initiatives that allowed Khrushchev room to maneuver, he forced the Soviet Union to retreat without a fight. The eventual removal of American missiles from Turkey offered the Soviets a small satisfaction. Yet Kennedy had risked nuclear war to show his toughness toward Khrushchev and Castro. The missiles in Cuba never threatened the security of the United States to the extent the president had indicated at the time. As his trusted aide Theodore Sorensen later observed, "[T]he United States was already living under the shadow of Soviet missiles, which could be launched from Soviet territory or submarines, and, therefore, there was no real change in our situation that required any kind of drastic action."

The Cuban missile crisis sobered both the Americans and the Soviets, encouraging officials and ordinary citizens in both countries to look for ways to avoid future confrontations. In the aftermath of the showdown, relations between the superpowers began to improve. In the next six months, the two governments agreed to install a direct communications link—a Teletype hot line—connecting the Kremlin with the White House. Kennedy abandoned some of his harsh anticommunist rhetoric and urged other Americans to do the same. Americans and Soviets had a mutual interest in ending the arms race, the president declared: "We all breathe the same air. We all cherish our children's future."

In 1963, the United States and the Soviet Union signed the first limited test ban treaty, ending the aboveground nuclear tests that had resumed in 1961. The treaty banned explosions of atomic devices in the atmosphere, in outer space, and under the ocean. The two sides promised to work on a more comprehensive treaty banning underground nuclear explosions as well.

New Frontiers at Home

On the domestic front, the Kennedy administration tried to shake the torpor of the Eisenhower years by promoting an expanding American economy. Kennedy's efforts to improve economic conditions began slowly, but they gained momentum over time. Administration officials initially resisted endorsing efforts to redistribute wealth, fearing that such programs would provoke antagonism from wealthy and middle-class Americans. At first, the Kennedy administration paid more attention to the economic and social concerns of the white middle class than to the deprivation of the poor or the hardships endured by people of color. In 1963, the last year of his life, Kennedy adopted a more liberal position, calling for aggressive government action to eliminate poverty.

The president's curiosity and his wide reading eventually made him alert to the previously hidden crises of widespread poverty and the degradation of the environment. Kennedy and his principal advisers had come of age politically in the late 1940s and 1950s—a time when leaders were expected to stress the positive aspects of American society as it confronted the Soviet Union in the Cold War. In the early 1960s, however, Americans looked more critically at their country's shortcomings. Kennedy had spoken eloquently during the 1960 presidential campaign about the need for vigorous action both at home and abroad, and although he did not develop many specific details for a domestic program, it was to his credit that he grew intellectually as president by recognizing the flaws and inequities in American society. By late 1962, the Kennedy administration had begun to lay the foundations of the major domestic reforms that would be undertaken by his successor.

When Kennedy promised in 1960 to get the country moving again, to a large extent he was promising to engineer an economic recovery. Economic growth had averaged about 3 percent annually from 1953 to 1960, but the averages masked wild yearly swings, from declines of 2 percent in some years to growth of 5 percent in others. And although prices had increased little during the Eisenhower years, the country had suffered sharp recessions in 1954, 1958, and 1960. Rising unemployment had helped Kennedy win some important industrial states in the Midwest in the presidential election of 1960.

Kennedy's efforts to bolster economic growth worked slowly, but eventually the economy expanded robustly. Rather than stimulating the economy directly by creating government programs to aid depressed areas, as liberal advisers urged, the Kennedy administration decided that a safer course was to adjust taxes to encourage private investment. In April 1961, Kennedy urged Congress to eliminate the complicated system of tax deductions, or loopholes, that had arisen since 1945. At the same time, he stated that businesses would invest more if Congress enacted investment tax credits to encourage businesses to modernize their plants and equipment. At first, the proposed legislation received little attention because concern over the Bay of Pigs and heightened tensions with the Soviets preoccupied Congress. When Congress resumed work on the tax issue in the summer of 1963, it preserved most of the tax loopholes while giving more preferences to corporations than Kennedy had originally requested. The revised bill finally passed in the early months of the Johnson administration.

The economy improved overall in the Kennedy years, though its performance fell short of what had been promised. In contrast to the fluctuations of the 1950s, economic growth was steady at 3 percent per year. Unemployment began to decline from 6 percent to under 5 percent. In 1961 and 1962, inflation, as measured by the consumer price index (CPI), fell to a nearly negligible rate of 1 percent per year. Business leaders were reassured by the administration's resistance to policies designed to redistribute wealth and income.

Public concern grew over the plight of one-fifth of the American population—approximately 25 million people—living in poverty. Largely forgotten since the end of World War II, the poorest Americans lived in decaying cities and remote rural areas. Eighty percent of them were white; the remainder were ethnic minorities. The poorest of the poor were people over the age of sixty-five living in rural areas. The Democrats of the 1950s and early 1960s, heirs of the New Deal but eager for acceptance from the business community, had mostly ignored their needs. In 1962, Michael Harrington, a former social worker, challenged this indifference in his book *The Other America*. Harrington decried a vicious cycle in which "there are people in the affluent society who are poor because they are poor; and who stay poor because they are poor." He spoke directly to the country's leaders, explaining to them, "the fate of the poor hangs on the decisions of the better off."

The Other America made a deep impression on intellectuals and opinion makers. Kennedy found in Harrington's book a troubling critique of his own timid efforts to revitalize the American economy and to make the New Frontier reach everyone in the country. He asked the chair of the Council of Economic Advisers to develop plans for a more vigorous assault on poverty. Before a program was ready, however, Kennedy was murdered.

The Push for Civil Rights

The popular movement to eliminate discrimination based on race reached its peak in the 1960s. By the end of the decade, the efforts of thousands of African Americans and their white allies ended the degrading system of legal segregation. America underwent a revolution in race relations. This so-called Second Reconstruction altered the American racial landscape even more than the first Reconstruction, which took place in the decade after the Civil War. African Americans had mobilized against segregation for years; by the 1960s, their efforts commanded the attention of most white Americans, provoking both support and resistance. As public officials gradually realized how important it was to end legally sanctioned segregation, the Kennedy administration began to take steps to aid the effort.

In 1961, six years after the Supreme Court ruled that segregation in the public schools had to end "with all deliberate speed," separation of the races remained a fact of life across the nation, especially in southern and border regions (including Washington, D.C.). Not only were many public schools and universities closed to blacks, so were many public transportation vehicles, bathroom facilities, and parks, as well as privately owned restaurants and hotels. The National Association for the Advancement of Colored People (NAACP), the most prominent of the black civil rights organizations, had sought to build on the victory in the landmark *Brown* v. *Board of Education* case by persuading the courts to order quicker desegregation and encouraging Congress to pass civil rights legislation protecting black voters. The NAACP desegregated some school districts and saw passage of a civil rights law in the late 1950s, but progress was painfully slow. As noted in Chapter 4, President Eisenhower did not speak out against racial discrimination, and he only belatedly ordered federal troops to Little Rock, Arkansas, in 1957 to ensure the safe admission of black students to that city's Central High School. The modest Civil Rights Act passed that year did not outlaw discrimination in public or privately owned accommodations as African Americans had hoped it would. After the sit-in at a Greensboro, North Carolina, lunch counter in 1960, the sit-in movement spread, along with marches, demonstrations, and other protests against legally sanctioned discrimination. Many of these actions involved the newly formed Student Non-Violent Coordinating Committee (SNCC). Participation in demonstrations, sit-ins, and mass marches sent waves of energy through African American young people. "You find out," said one, "the difference between being dead and alive." Poor blacks were thrilled to see African American college students take the lead. "We were all excited about these young people," a woman recalled, "because they treated us so nice." Martin Luther King, Jr., said that the civil rights workers were "trying to save the soul of America."

As a senator, John Kennedy had taken few positions on racial discrimination. During the presidential campaign of 1960, he became somewhat bolder, but he continued to walk a narrow line on civil rights, hoping to retain the support of traditional white southern Democrats while also winning the votes of blacks. He refrained from endorsing new civil rights laws but condemned Eisenhower for his timidity in not putting the moral authority of the presidency on the side of victims of racial prejudice. The president, Kennedy said, could end discrimination in public housing "with the stroke of a pen" by signing an executive order. He promised that his protection of minorities would be more vigorous, and blacks believed that the Kennedy brothers' telephone calls on behalf of the jailed Martin Luther King, Jr., signaled sympathy with their cause.

At first, however, Kennedy's administration did little to advance civil rights. Particularly galling to those blacks who had supported him was Kennedy's failure throughout 1961 to sign an executive order ending discrimination in public housing. By the end of the year, the Congress of Racial Equality (CORE), a rival of the NAACP that favored more militant action, sought to shame Kennedy into making good on his promise. CORE organized the Ink for Jack campaign, in which supporters of civil rights mailed thousands of ballpoint pens to the White House. Eventually, in 1962, Kennedy signed an executive order outlawing racial discrimination in public housing.

The Ink for Jack campaign represented only a small part of the civil rights effort. Many ordinary citizens believed that much more was required to achieve civil rights and that the government would not act unless pressured from below. In the spring of 1961, blacks and whites joined together in a campaign of civil disobedience to force the federal government to take a more aggressive stand. In early May, two busloads of blacks and whites left Washington, D.C., bound for New Orleans, with interim stops scheduled along the way throughout the South. Calling themselves Freedom Riders, the travelers demanded the enforcement of a 1960 Supreme Court decision striking down state laws prohibiting mixed seating on interstate buses and requiring public accommodations along the way to maintain whites-only and colored-only facilities. In practice, such laws meant nonwhites could not enter most restaurants or relieve themselves in most public restrooms.

At first, the Freedom Riders encountered icy stares from white people and found bus stations mysteriously closed when they arrived. This silent resistance was difficult enough, but when the travelers reached Alabama, the opposition proved much more dangerous. In Anniston, Alabama, a mob of two hundred whites attacked one bus with pipes, slashed the tires, and demanded that the Freedom Riders leave the bus. Although the local police escorted the bus and its passengers out of town, the gang continued its pursuit in fifty cars. After the bus's tires went completely flat, the mob surrounded it, and someone threw a bomb through the window. When the Freedom Riders ran out of the bus, the mob beat them. One white Freedom Rider was punched in the face while others stomped on his chest until he lost consciousness. A Howard University student on the bus said, after being hit in the head, "I see what Martin Luther King means when he says suffering *is* redemption."

When the buses reached Montgomery, the police gave a howling mob of five hundred to one thousand fifteen to thirty minutes to run rampant. They first went after TV and newsweekly crews, smashing their cameras. Then they turned their fury on the Freedom Riders. Women screamed, "Kill the nigger-loving son of a bitch," at the first white man to leave the bus. John Siegenthaler, President Kennedy's personal emissary, tried to help two women escape. He was then knocked unconscious and lay on the ground for thirty minutes because no white ambulance would pick him up. FBI agents also did not intervene. Siegenthaler later complained, "[I]t galls me to think that the FBI stood there and watched me get clubbed."

This inexcusable refusal by public authorities to protect U.S. citizens goaded Kennedy into action. The violence had been photographed and shown in newspapers and on television, shocking many Americans. Scenes of the howling mob attacking unarmed Freedom Riders also offered a propaganda boost to the Soviet Union on the eve of the Vienna summit. The president, sickened by the sight of this violence, ordered U.S. marshals to Alabama to protect the Freedom Riders, and the Justice Department enjoined racist organizations from further interference with the buses.

At the same time, the reluctance of the administration to take decisive action was evident. Only 24 percent of Americans said that they supported the

During the violence against the Freedom Riders in Montgomery, Alabama, Attorney General Robert F. Kennedy consults with Byron White, a Justice Department official he had sent to Montgomery to head a force of four hundred U.S. marshals to restore calm. / © Bettmann/CORBIS

Freedom Riders, but 70 percent said that they approved of Kennedy's sending marshals to keep the peace in Montgomery. No matter how offensive the attacks on Freedom Riders became, Washington officials remained reluctant to antagonize southern whites, who had been an essential element of the Democratic Party's coalition. Robert Kennedy asked for a cooling-off period of 100 days to let tempers subside. James Farmer, executive director of CORE, acidly replied, "We've been cooling off for one hundred years. If we got any cooler we'd be in the deep freeze." Accordingly, CORE ignored advice to stop the demonstrations and continued to arrange Freedom Rides for the rest of the summer of 1961. Federal marshals offered protection against physical assaults on the buses and riders. At the same time, Robert Kennedy sought unsuccessfully to persuade the Freedom Ride organizers that voter registration, rather than public demonstrations, would do more for the cause of civil rights.

Like many other white northerners, the Kennedy brothers gradually developed greater concern over racial discrimination as the demonstrations continued. They expressed their greatest commitment to civil rights in September 1962, during a confrontation with Mississippi governor Ross Barnett over the enrollment of James Meredith, a black man, at the state's university in Oxford. Meredith, an air force veteran, had applied for admission to the University of Mississippi in January 1961. A high school graduate and resident of Mississippi, he was entitled to admission to the state university, but it refused to enroll him. He appealed the decision in federal court, and on September 13, 1962, Supreme Court Justice Hugo Black, a native of Alabama and former member of the Ku Klux Klan, ordered the university to admit him. Mississippi's state legislature responded by making Governor Barnett a temporary registrar of the university. Playing to strong racist sentiments throughout the state, Barnett vowed not to surrender to "the evil and illegal forces of tyranny." He promised that Meredith would never register.

The president and attorney general spoke several times on the telephone to Barnett. For a while, it appeared that a compromise had been arranged: the governor would save face by resisting the federal marshals who had been sent to Oxford to escort Meredith into the university, but Meredith would be allowed to register later. That deal fell through, however, as hundreds of whites converged on the college town, intent on chasing Meredith away. When Meredith and his escort of federal marshals finally reached the campus, over one thousand white demonstrators blocked their path, screaming, "Go to Cuba, nigger lovers, go to Cuba!" They threw rocks and bottles at the line of marshals. Then several members of the mob, now numbering over two thousand, opened fire with shotguns and rifles, killing an English reporter and wounding a marshal and a U.S. border patrolman.

In the midst of this violence, Kennedy addressed the nation. He spent more time calming the fears of white Mississippians than explaining the evils of racial discrimination. He appealed to that state's "great tradition of honor and courage, won on the field of battle." He urged the university's students, most of whom had not been involved in the demonstrations, to continue to stay on the sidelines, because "the eyes of the nation and the world are upon you and upon all of us." At the same time, Kennedy ordered 23,000 army troops to Oxford to quell the rioting and to ensure that Meredith could enroll for classes and study in relative peace. Five hundred troops remained stationed in Oxford until Meredith graduated in June 1963. Martin Luther King, Jr., thought the Kennedy brothers had helped the cause of civil rights but that they did not fully appreciate how much work remained to be done.

In 1963, Martin Luther King, Jr., sought to increase the momentum of the civil rights movement. In May, he helped organize demonstrations for the end of segregation in Birmingham, Alabama. The protesters found the perfect enemy in Birmingham's police commissioner, Eugene "Bull" Connor, whose beefy features and snarling demeanor made him seem a living caricature of a racist southern sheriff. Connor's police used clubs, dogs, and fire hoses to chase and harass the demonstrators. Kennedy watched the police dogs in action on television—along with the rest of the country—and confessed that the brutality made him sick. He later observed, "the civil rights movement should thank God for Bull Connor. He's helped it as much as Abraham Lincoln." The president dispatched the head of the Justice Department's civil rights division to Birmingham to try to work out an arrangement between King's demonstrators and local business leaders that would permit desegregation of lunch counters, drinking fountains, and bathrooms. The president made several calls to the business leaders himself, and they finally agreed to his terms.

Birmingham, Alabama, police use dogs against civil rights marchers, May 1963. / AP/Wide World

On June 10, 1963, during a national address focusing on civil rights, Kennedy acknowledged that the nation faced a moral crisis. He rejected the notion that the United States could be the land of the free "except for the Negroes." Reversing his earlier reluctance to request civil rights legislation, he announced that he would send Congress a major civil rights bill. The law would guarantee service to all Americans, regardless of race, at all establishments open to the public—hotels, restaurants, theaters, retail stores, and the like. It would also grant the federal government greater authority to pursue lawsuits against segregation in public schools and universities and would increase the Justice Department's powers to protect the voting rights of racial minorities.

African American leaders found Kennedy's commitment to legislation encouraging, but they wanted assurances that the president would follow through. To maintain pressure on Congress, several civil rights leaders revived the idea, first presented in 1941, of a march on Washington to promote civil rights. The Kennedy administration was not in favor of such a march. Already public opinion polls indicated that a plurality of voters thought the president was pushing integration too fast, and Kennedy worried about the political cost of endorsing the black push for equality.

The March on Washington went forward anyway, on August 28, 1963. A crowd of about 300,000 people, mostly black but including people of all races, filled the mall facing the Lincoln Memorial. Led by folk singer Joan Baez, they sang the spiritual "We Shall Overcome," which had become the unofficial anthem of the civil rights movement. They heard other songs and listened to speeches. John Lewis, a leading Freedom Rider, prepared a militant address that was toned down by march organizers before he delivered it. He spoke of "blacks" rather than "Negroes," a change in terminology that took hold over the next few years.

The climax came when Martin Luther King, Jr., offered to the watching world an inspiring vision of the future: "I have a dream that one day all God's children, black men and white men, Jews and Gentiles, Protestants and Catholics, will be able to join hands and sing in the words of the old Negro spiritual, 'Free at last! Free at last! Thank God Almighty, we are free at last!'" Although he had invoked these images many times before, much of white America was listening to him for the first time. President Kennedy watched on television and told an aide in admiration, "He's damn good." But within three months, Kennedy was dead, and the civil rights legislation advocated by the March on Washington needed the support of a new president.

Scientific, Technological, and Cultural Changes in the Early 1960s

Americans had developed a new appreciation for the benefits of technology by the early 1960s. They believed that much of their prosperity came from exciting new developments in electronics, space research, medicine, and transportation. By the time Kennedy was murdered in November 1963, however, fears had grown about the potential negative impact of modern science and engineering on everyday life. In April 1961, days before the defeat at the Bay of Pigs, a Soviet cosmonaut, Yuri Gagarin, became the first man to orbit the earth. Americans felt ashamed and frightened. The shock of the 1957 Sputnik launch was still fresh in everyone's mind. Members of the joint congressional committee on space demanded that the Kennedy administration make good on its campaign pledge to restore the country's flagging prestige. One member of the committee told the director of the National Aeronautics and Space Administration (NASA), "[T]ell me how much money you need, and this committee will authorize all you need." A newspaper concluded that Soviet successes in space had "cost the nation heavily in prestige" and that "neutral nations may come to believe that the wave of the future is Russian."

In this atmosphere, the Kennedy administration wanted to act quickly. NASA's own reports indicated that the United States led the Soviet Union in every area of space science, but in the tense aftermath of Gagarin's flight and the Bay of Pigs, Americans wanted a definitive victory in the space race. The president told a press conference that he was tired of the United States being second best. He made Vice President Lyndon Johnson chair of the Space

Council and instructed him to look for ways of "beating the Russians." In late May, the president went before Congress to announce a goal of "landing a man on the moon, and returning him safely to earth . . . before the decade is out." Privately, Kennedy expressed doubts about whether the race to the moon would yield many scientific breakthroughs, but he remained convinced that getting to the moon before the Soviets carried its own rewards.

To fulfill this lunar mission, Congress encouraged NASA to create the Apollo program. Johnson made certain that friends in Texas and nearby states received the lion's share of the scientific and construction contracts for Apollo. The Apollo complex followed the contours of the Gulf of Mexico, from Texas to Florida, providing jobs, income, and a stake in federal projects to traditionally poor but fast-growing southern states. Johnson called it a "second Reconstruction" for the area. In four years, the number of workers employed directly by NASA had grown from 6,000 to 60,000. Another 411,000 scientists, engineers, technicians, and clerical staff flocked to the region to work for private firms under contract to NASA.

While the Apollo scientists worked feverishly preparing for the moon mission, NASA tried to top Gagarin's orbital flight. In the summer of 1961, two astronauts, Alan Shepard and Virgil Grissom, made space flights lasting about fifteen minutes in capsules launched by Atlas ICBMs. Then, in February 1962, ten months after Gagarin's orbit, Marine Lieutenant Colonel John Glenn was strapped into Friendship 7 and blasted into orbit. In the next five hours, Glenn made three trips around the globe. His success buoyed Americans, who had seen too many events that seemed to point to a decline in U.S. power, influence, and scientific preeminence. Glenn was a guest at the White House and enjoyed a ticker-tape parade down Manhattan's Broadway, the likes of which had not been seen since Charles Lindbergh returned in triumph after his solo flight from New York to Paris in 1927.

Americans also began to focus on another concern, which would become increasingly important in later years: the quality of the environment. In 1962, science writer Rachel Carson published *Silent Spring*, a lengthy indictment of the damage done to the environment by the pesticide industry. Use of synthetic pesticides, a product of technology developed during World War II, had increased 400 percent between 1947 and 1962. The United States now sprayed 650 million pounds of deadly chemicals per year over farms, gardens, and homes. As Carson wrote, these poisons did not distinguish among their victims and "should not be called insecticides but biocides." The chemicals remained in the environment, filtering through the soil, entering the groundwater, and eventually finding their way into the food chain, where they contaminated animals and humans alike.

Carson's work alarmed the American public. About 200,000 copies of her book were snatched up within a month, and members of Congress and newspapers were deluged with letters demanding federal action. Kennedy met Carson, and he instructed the President's Science Advisory Committee (PSAC) to study the pesticide problem. In May 1963, the PSAC reported that pesticides had done extensive damage to fish, birds, and other wildlife and that traces of toxic chemicals had been found in humans. The report urged elimination of the use of toxic pesticides. Pesticide manufacturers opposed the recommendations, but seven years later, the newly formed Environmental Protection Agency (EPA) banned the use of DDT, the most harmful pesticide, in the United States. A new environmental movement arose in the West in response to the explosive growth of cities. Western environmentalists tended to be city people who wanted to protect the wilderness areas where they sought recreation and renewal. In the 1960s, they often focused on issues involving water and the wilderness. The Sierra Club, led by David Brower, successfully fought the construction of a dam at Echo Park on the Colorado River, which would have flooded part of Dinosaur National Monument in Utah, and managed to prevent the construction of dams that would have flooded parts of the Grand Canyon. Their victories, however, were sometimes Pyrrhic.

Instead of building a dam at Echo Park, for example, the Bureau of Reclamation built one that flooded Glen Canyon, a place of such extraordinary grandeur that its loss would become the cardinal symbol of environmental degradation to a later, more militant generation of wilderness advocates. And when the Sierra Club argued against the Grand Canyon dams, they insisted that developers could instead garner electrical generating capacity by building coal-fired and nuclear power plants. As a consequence, the Black Mesa on the Arizona Navajo and Hopi reservations was strip-mined, and the coal-burning Navajo Power Plant was built at Page, Arizona. Such tradeoffs convinced more and more advocates of environmental protection that they would have to take a more systemic, ecological view of their cause.

For all of the excited talk about the new decade of the 1960s representing a sharp break with the supposed dullness of the 1950s, people's personal lives changed slowly. Theodore Sorensen, Kennedy's aide, joked that "this administration is going to do for sex what the last one did for golf." The first birth-control pill was approved for use in May 1960. A sexual revolution was on its way, but it took its time gathering momentum. The same year, a poll of college women reported that over 50 percent of them were virgins. The same poll reported that 70 percent of male college students expected to marry virgins. Homosexual acts were against the law in nearly all states and municipalities. Abortion was illegal in every state. The words *rape* and *abortion* could not be spoken on NBC news. The *Saturday Evening Post* ran a story on abortion in 1961, and it received hundreds of letters condemning both abortion and the *Post*'s decision to carry the story.

Some attitudes toward sex, childhood, and family life did change in the early 1960s. In 1962, Helen Gurley Brown published *Sex and the Single Girl*, a manifesto for an end to the sexual double standard. She then took over the editorship of *Cosmopolitan* and altered its format to stress the pleasure of sex for young women. About the same time, Hugh Hefner, who had started *Playboy* in 1952, began publishing "The Playboy Philosophy" as a monthly column. No one would have mistaken Hefner's opinions about the joys of sex and the repressive outlook of traditional sexual morality for the deep thoughts of classic or contemporary philosophers, but he did capture a moment. The young women who read *Cosmopolitan* and the young men who looked at *Playboy* sensed that some of the truths of togetherness and suburban happiness of the 1950s were sheer hypocrisy.

It became fashionable in the Kennedy years to puncture the pretensions of the powerful. In 1961, Joseph Heller published *Catch-22*. This comic send-up of the absurdities and petty abuses of power in military life in World War II attracted a huge following among young readers. The phrase *Catch-22*, with its sense that many, if not most, rules in large organizations were developed by fools to humiliate decent people, caught on with young people. The next year, Ken Kesey published *One Flew Over the Cuckoo's Nest*, a novel set in a mental hospital where a brutal staff enforced a series of absurd rules. Kesey's young readers responded to his outrage at the arbitrary exercise of raw power.

The 1950s had seen its share of criticism of the banality of suburban life. Social critics had nearly ignored cities in that decade, possibly because few people thought cities interesting. But now cities seemed once more to hold out promise—if only the heavy hand of officialdom could be lifted. In 1961, Jane Jacobs published *The Death and Life of Great American Cities*. The book celebrated cities, not suburbs, as the centers of vibrant civilization. But Jacobs assailed generations of city planners, who had drained the natural vitality of the American urban landscape since the 1920s with their grandiose projects. She wrote that urban renewal had leveled living communities and replaced them with spiritually dead blocks of high-rise sameness where no one knew anyone. Her vision of urban blight sounded a warning for the decade. While many Americans appreciated Kennedy's optimism and sense of managerial expertise, more unruly, ecstatic, and rambunctious spirits were spreading. In the later years of the 1960s, this new exuberance, so challenging to authority, became a central feature of American life. (See Chapter 8.)

Assassination

Kennedy's endorsement of the civil rights movement during the fall of 1963 complicated his re-election chances in the South. As in 1960, a key state was Texas, where the Democrats feuded over policies and patronage. Governor John Connally, leader of the Texas Democrats' conservative faction, opposed Kennedy's plans for a civil rights bill. The governor was not on speaking terms with the state's liberal senator, Ralph Yarborough, and both Connally and Yarborough distrusted Vice President Lyndon Johnson, whose shifting positions did not satisfy either liberals or conservatives. Seeking to bolster his own standing in his home state, Johnson persuaded several prominent national officeholders, including the president, to visit Texas in the fall.

When U.N. ambassador Adlai Stevenson spoke in Dallas in October, he encountered ugly demonstrations organized by vocal conservatives. Handbills appeared with pictures of Kennedy labeled "Wanted for Treason." The mob swarmed around Stevenson, someone hit him in the face with a sign, and only the protection of a police squad got him out of the hall safely. The attack on

Stevenson was only the most recent in a series of violent protests against the administration. The Secret Service had compiled thirty-four credible threats on the president's life from the Dallas area since 1961. Many came from those who espoused extreme right-wing views, but the Secret Service also documented threats from leftists, anti-Castro Cubans, Puerto Rican nationalists, black militants, and several mentally disturbed individuals.

One month after Stevenson's encounter with the mob of Dallas demonstrators, on November 21, 1963, Kennedy flew to San Antonio with Jacqueline to begin a three-day swing through the Lone Star State. Johnson joined them later that day in Houston and the next day in Fort Worth, where the president addressed businesspeople about the importance of Texas defense contractors to the nation's military strength. At 11:20 A.M., Air Force One took off from Fort Worth for the brief flight to Dallas. The presidential jet landed in Dallas at noon, and Governor Connally, his wife Nellie, and President and Mrs. Kennedy entered an open-air limousine for a trip downtown, where Kennedy was scheduled to speak before another business group. The motorcade route had been published days before to ensure the largest crowd possible. Thousands lined the route, and most were smiling, cheering, and waving. Mrs. Connally told the president, "You can't say Dallas doesn't love you." Kennedy replied, "That's obvious." Seconds later, at 12:33 P.M., three shots rang out. Two bullets hit the president; one passed through his throat and the other exploded through the back of his head. In shock, Mrs. Kennedy rose and climbed onto the rear hood of the car. The motorcade raced to nearby Parkland Hospital, where Kennedy was pronounced dead at 1:00 P.M.

Later that afternoon, police arrested twenty-four-year-old Lee Harvey Oswald in a movie theater. A Marine Corps veteran and lonely drifter, Oswald had recently returned from a long stay in the Soviet Union. He worked in the Texas Book Depository, the building from which the shots were fired. Oswald had flitted among political causes of the left and right, making it difficult for later investigators to determine his motives. He had contacted the Cuban embassy in Mexico City earlier in 1963, but the Cubans had refused to speak with him, fearing that he was a provocateur sent by the CIA. To complicate matters further, Oswald had family ties to a Mafia member who had spoken of his desire to kill Kennedy in order to halt the Justice Department's investigations of organized crime.

The chances of ever discovering Oswald's true allegiances probably disappeared two days after the Kennedy assassination. That Sunday, most Americans sat glued to television sets, watching hundreds of thousands of grief-stricken mourners file past a closed casket in the Capitol rotunda. When the networks cut away to the basement of the Dallas police station to show Oswald being escorted to another jail, millions of viewers saw nightclub owner Jack Ruby step out of a crowd and kill Oswald with a bullet to the abdomen.

In December 1963, President Johnson appointed a special commission, chaired by Chief Justice Earl Warren, to investigate the assassination. Less than a year later, the Warren Commission filed a report concluding that

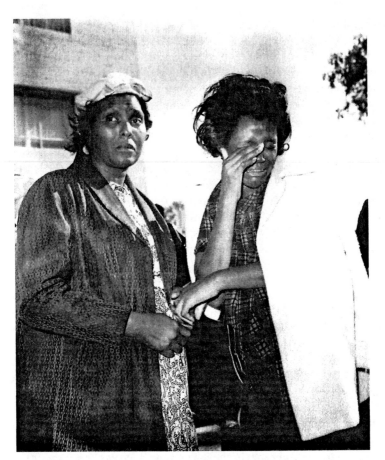

Two women stand grief-stricken outside Parkland Hospital in Dallas on the
afternoon of November 22, 1963, after learning of President Kennedy's death.
© Bettmann/CORBIS

Oswald, acting alone, had killed Kennedy. The Warren Commission worked
hastily because it believed a speedy report would still rumors of a conspiracy,
but that did not happen. For years afterward, many Americans, at times a majority of them, believed that a conspiracy was behind Kennedy's murder. The
list of suspected conspirators was varied and shifted from year to year: extreme
conservatives, the Mafia, the CIA, Fidel Castro, conservative Vietnamese, even
Lyndon Johnson. In 1979, a House committee concluded that more than one
person had fired shots at Kennedy's limousine, but FBI scientists rebutted the
committee's findings. In the decades after the Warren Commission's report, little tangible evidence has come to light to demonstrate that its conclusions
were flawed.

      The persistence of the belief that Kennedy died at the hands of conspira-
tors represented an effort to make sense out of a shocking act that deeply
shook many Americans' faith in their institutions. In the years following

Kennedy's death, other prominent figures fell to assassins, and shots were fired at other presidents in 1975 and 1981. Within five years of that fateful November afternoon, Americans had come to see their society as dangerous, violent, and led by people who lacked Kennedy's ability to inspire the nation. Many traced the beginning of their sense that America's public institutions did not work properly to the day Kennedy died.

Conclusion

After his death, Americans quickly elevated John Kennedy to martyrdom. His optimism, wit, intelligence, and charm—all of which encouraged the feeling that American society could accomplish anything its people wanted—were snuffed out in an instant. He was only forty-six years old. Within six months of his murder, journalist Theodore White bestowed on his administration the name Camelot. Popularized by the 1962 Broadway musical of that title, the term referred to the mythical kingdom of Arthur and his knights of the Round Table. In this view, Kennedy's 1,037-day administration represented a brief, shining moment during which the nation's political leaders spoke to Americans' finest aspirations.

The reality was more complicated. Kennedy and his advisers had been formed by the experiences of the postwar world. They represented a new generation, nurtured by the Cold War, an activist government, and the military-industrial complex. Skeptical of ideology and serenely self-confident, officials of the Kennedy administration and their circle of friends believed problems could be mastered and managed. That was their strength because it encouraged their curiosity about people, trends, and ideas. They learned from their setbacks and mistakes, and by 1963, their skepticism even extended to the beliefs they expressed in 1960 that the United States could vanquish the Soviet Union through sheer willpower. Their self-confidence offered Americans hope.

Yet the style of cool self-reliance favored by Kennedy and his advisers also betrayed their primary weakness. Their resistance to emotion and passion stunted their ability to empathize with groups that had been excluded from the bounty of American society. The Kennedy administration did more for civil rights than his predecessor had, but its principal efforts in this area came as a result of intense pressure and dramatic events that could not be ignored. On the questions of poverty and the environment, Kennedy took important first steps; whether his administration would have accomplished significantly more if he had lived longer, historians can only speculate. Overall, his domestic program reflected the politics of consensus, much like his predecessor's.

In foreign affairs, he also continued an earlier trend, the reflexive anti-communism of the Cold War, but with a particularly aggressive twist. His propensity for tough confrontation with the Soviets led the world to the brink of nuclear holocaust. Only after the near-disaster of the Cuban missile crisis did he begin to move toward détente.

Advocates of the New Frontier had promised the country a new youth and vigor in the White House, and the Kennedy administration provided these qualities in abundance. It was less successful in offering substance and new solutions. The burden of resolving many problems fell on Lyndon Johnson, a very different man, who was suddenly elevated to the presidency.

F U R T H E R • R E A D I N G

On politics and policies in the Kennedy administration, see Maurice Isserman and Michael Kazin, *America Divided: The Civil Wars of the 1960s* (2000); James N. Giglio, *The Presidency of John F. Kennedy* (2003); Robert Caro, *The Years of Lyndon Johnson*, Vol. 3, *Master of the Senate* (2002); Allan Matusow, *The Unraveling of America: A History of Liberalism in the 1960s* (1984); Philip Zelikow and Ernest May, eds., *The Presidential Recordings: John F. Kennedy, The Great Crises* (2001); Richard Reeves, *President Kennedy: Profile in Power* (1993); Thomas C. Reeves, *A Question of Character: A Life of John F. Kennedy* (1991); Theodore Sorensen, *Kennedy* (1965); Arthur M. Schlesinger, Jr., *A Thousand Days* (1966) and *Robert F. Kennedy and His Times* (1978); Theodore H. White, *The Making of the President, 1960* (1961); David Knapp and Kenneth Polk, *Scouting the War on Poverty: Social Reform Politics in the Kennedy Administration* (1971); Robert Dallek, *An Unfinished Life: John F. Kennedy, 1917–1963* (2003). **On Kennedy's assassination,** see Gerald Posner, *Case Closed: Lee Harvey Oswald and the Assassination of JFK* (1993). **On space policy,** see Walter A. McDougall, . . . *The Heavens and the Earth: A Political History of the Space Age* (1985). **On civil rights,** see Taylor Branch, *Parting the Waters: America in the King Years, 1954–1963* (1988) and *Pillar of Fire: America in the King Years, 1963–1965* (1998); David Garrow, *Bearing the Cross: Martin Luther King, Jr., and the Southern Christian Leadership Conference* (1986). **On environmentalism,** see Samuel P. Hays, *Beauty, Health, and Permanence: Environmental Politics in the United States, 1955–85* (1987); Marc Reisner, *Cadillac Desert: The American West and Its Disappearing Water* (1993). **On changing sexual mores,** see Lara V. Marks, *Sexual Chemistry: A History of the Contraceptive Pill* (2001); and Andrea Tone, *Devices and Desires: A History of Contraceptives in America* (2001). **On foreign policy,** see Thomas Zeiler, *Dean Rusk: Defending the American Mission Abroad* (2000); Ernest May and Philip Zelikow, *The Kennedy Tapes: Inside the Kennedy White House During the Kennedy Administration* (2001); Thomas Paterson, *Contesting Castro: The United States and the Triumph of the Cuban Revolution* (1994); Michael Beschloss, *The Crisis Years: Kennedy and Khrushchev 1960–1963* (1991); Montague Kern, Patricia W. Levering, and Ralph B. Levering, *The Kennedy Crises: The Press, the Presidency and Foreign Policy* (1983); Elizabeth Cobbs Hoffman, *"All You Need Is Love": The Peace Corps and the Spirit of the 1960s* (1998); John Lewis Gaddis, *Strategies of Containment* (1981); Trumbull Higgins, *The Perfect Failure: Kennedy, Eisenhower and the Bay of Pigs* (1987); Richard D. Mahoney, *JFK: Ordeal in Africa* (1983). **On nuclear fallout shelters,** see Kenneth D. Rose, *One Nation Underground: The Fallout Shelter in American Culture* (2001); Andrew W. Grossman, *Neither Dead Nor Red: Civil Defense and American Political Development in the Early Cold War* (2001); Paul Boyer, *Fallout: A Historian Reflects on America's Half-Century Encounter with Nuclear Weapons* (1998); Margo Henriksen, *Dr. Strangelove's America: Society and Culture in the Atomic Age* (1997).

6

The Dream of a Great Society

A mother holds her daughter in front of their home in poverty-stricken Appalachia. /
© Wally McNamee/CORBIS.

By the early 1960s, many Americans believed that the apparent prosperity of the postwar years masked serious flaws in their society. At least one-quarter of the population remained mired in grinding poverty. Racial segregation remained the law of the land. Some middle-class white college students caught glimpses of the brutality encountered every day by African Americans in the South. Allard Lowenstein, a civil rights activist, told an audience of thousands of rapt students on the Stanford University campus in the fall of 1963 that Mississippi was "a foreign country in our midst." It was a place where "you can't picket, you can't vote, you can't boycott effectively, can't mount mass protest of any kind, and can't reach the mass media."

Many African Americans already knew what Lowenstein was talking about. Throughout the South, blacks demanded an end to legal segregation, and they pressed for the right to vote. In the midst of the outpouring of grief over Kennedy's assassination, Robert Moses, a leader of the Student Non-Violent Coordinating Committee (SNCC), commented that most white people in the country did not comprehend how strong was the resistance to voting rights for African Americans in the Deep South. The daily violence—beatings, clubbings, and jailings—against civil rights workers was terrifying. Moses told a SNCC conference on the Howard University campus over Thanksgiving weekend in 1963 that volunteers across the South every day confronted "the problem of overcoming fear."

On Thanksgiving morning, Martin Luther King, Jr., preached in Atlanta. He referred only briefly to Kennedy's murder before surveying the history of two hundred years of slavery. "A low dirty, evil thing," he called it. He described "[m]en and women chained to ships like beasts. . . . They knew the rawhide whip of the overseer. Sizzling heat. Long rows of cotton." The congregation shouted, "Preach on." King did—with a high note: "We've broken loose from the Egypt of slavery!" Continuing the biblical metaphor, he said, "Caleb and Joshua have come back with a minority report. They are saying we *can* possess the land."

The new president, Lyndon Johnson, acknowledged the deeply felt desire to distribute the benefits of affluence to those who had been left behind. He had witnessed deprivation firsthand during the Great Depression and was strongly moved to erase it. Addressing Congress five days after Kennedy was shot, he said, "We have talked long enough in this country about equal rights. We have talked for a hundred years or more."

As president, Johnson articulated a vision of a "Great Society." And for a while he captured the public mood. He rode the crest of a wave of earnest popular demands to bring an end to racial discrimination, provide equal opportunity to all people, eliminate poverty, and provide all Americans with adequate healthcare. Yet the scale of this undertaking was so vast that disappointments were almost inevitable. Also, by 1966, the popular consensus in support of these goals began to erode under the weight of the war in Vietnam and a white backlash against government efforts on behalf of African Americans. Johnson's own shortcomings—his abrasiveness, untruthfulness, and manipulation of others—made him an unsuitable leader, however, for such times of political discord. When he lost congressional support for his initiatives, Johnson turned his back on the Great Society he had so eloquently promoted in his first years in office. He withdrew on occasion into passivity and a brooding paranoia.

The successes and failures of the Great Society reflected the triumphs and disappointments of political liberalism in general. From the time of the New Deal until the mid-1960s, the liberal ideal—expanding government power in order to improve social and economic conditions—dominated much of American political and social life. By the end of the 1960s, however, many Americans no longer believed that government programs, agencies, or officials delivered tangible benefits. The early 1960s were years of enormous hope and promise for many; by the end of the decade, however, a more somber mood prevailed. America's faith in liberalism became a casualty, to some extent, of liberalism's most ambitious endeavor.

Lyndon Johnson: The Man and the President

Lyndon Johnson went to Washington in 1931, during the depths of the Great Depression, as an aide to a newly elected Texas congressman. The congressman let Johnson run his office and decide how he should vote; within months, the young aide was congressman in everything but name. In 1933 Johnson persuaded his boss to drop his entrenched conservatism and support the New Deal. Two years later, in 1935, Johnson used the contacts he had made within the Texas congressional delegation to win appointment as the Texas director of the newly created National Youth Administration. In 1937 Johnson won a special election to Congress as a New Dealer. He took the courageous step for a Texas politician of courting black and Mexican American voters, telling the black leaders of Austin, Texas, that if they supported him he would someday back voting rights and perhaps a hot-lunch program.

Back in Washington, he mastered the rules of the House and faithfully voted for Roosevelt's programs. By 1948 Johnson wanted to be a senator. In keeping with the Truman administration's ambivalent attitude toward New Deal reforms, he tempered his earlier populism, ran a viciously negative campaign as a moderate against a conservative former governor, stuffed ballot boxes in some key precincts, and won the election by eighty-seven votes. From that point, he rose fast, becoming the majority leader in the Senate by 1955.

For the remaining six years of the Eisenhower administration, Johnson ran the Senate as no one had before him. He perfected the "treatment," a combination of flattery, cajolery, threats, empathy, blackmail, and horse trading, to get his way. His relations with the Eisenhower administration were excellent, but liberal Democrats came to distrust him as a Texas wheeler-dealer. He eliminated references in the 1957 civil rights bill to equal treatment in public accommodations, and he sided with business interests against labor unions in the debate over the Landrum-Griffin Labor Reform Act of 1958. Liberals were offended, seeing such actions as the work of a compromiser and perhaps even a reactionary.

Johnson toyed with the idea of a presidential run in 1960, but he hesitated. After Kennedy had won the nomination, Robert Kennedy, the candidate's brother and campaign manager, relayed word to Johnson that Kennedy wanted him as vice president. Eventually the senator from Texas, reviled by many of Kennedy's most ardent backers as a southwestern political fixer and manipulator, became the Democratic vice-presidential candidate. He accepted the nomination in order to win the election for the Democrats; his job during the campaign was to carry Texas and as much of the South as possible.

Johnson helped Kennedy carry Texas by forty-six thousand votes. His service during the campaign temporarily warmed the hearts of Kennedy's inner circle, but for Johnson it proved to be a curiously joyless victory. Johnson feared, with good reason, that he would have little power as vice president. When there were important decisions to make—on Berlin, Cuba, Vietnam, taxes, civil rights—Kennedy and his inner circle made them without consulting Johnson. Instead, the vice president chaired the newly created National Aeronautics and Space Council and the Presidential Committee on Equal Opportunity. In 1961, these positions seemed remote outposts of the New Frontier. They were, however, important proving grounds for Johnson's own presidency.

Johnson found solace in travel. When he left Washington for trips to Africa, Europe, and Southeast Asia, he was like a man released from jail. But by 1963, even the delights of travel had paled. Kennedy's staff could not stand Johnson, and he knew it. In the summer of 1963, some of Kennedy's aides

President Lyndon B. Johnson herding cattle on his Texas ranch. / © Bettmann/CORBIS

openly expressed the wish that Johnson—"Uncle Corn Pone," they called him—would voluntarily step down from the Democratic ticket in 1964. In early November 1963, a dispirited Johnson confided to an aide that his future as vice president seemed bleak, and he mused about a new career. It came in an unexpected way. On November 22, Kennedy was shot in Dallas, on a trip arranged to quell the endemic feuding among Texas Democrats.

Johnson took the oath of office aboard Air Force One with a stricken Mrs. Kennedy, her clothes splattered with the blood of the slain president, looking on. Many of Kennedy's most ardent supporters viewed Johnson as unworthy of the office held by a fallen hero. Unlike Harry Truman, who became president following the death of Roosevelt in 1945, Johnson asked his predecessor's staff to stay. But it was nearly impossible to cultivate harmony between Kennedy's circle and the assistants who had served Johnson in the vice presidency. The more inconsolable of the Kennedy people resented Johnson as a usurper. Johnson's aides believed Kennedy did not deserve his posthumous golden reputation. After all, Kennedy's domestic agenda had made little progress in Congress, but a legislative master like Johnson might turn the dreams of racial justice and expanded economic opportunity for the poor into law.

Initially Johnson rose above such pettiness. Immediately after Kennedy's funeral, he addressed Congress, calling for unity, consensus, and the continuance of Kennedy's vision. A few weeks later, he stood before Congress to deliver his first State of the Union address. In it, he pledged to continue Kennedy's program, but with a distinctly activist and legislative stamp. Along with civil rights—the basic moral issue of the day—he emphasized the need to eliminate the blight of poverty. "This administration today, here and now, declares unconditional war on poverty in America. . . . It will not be a short or easy struggle, but we shall not rest until that war is won."

After his stirring words to Congress, Johnson plunged immediately into the effort to pass the landmark civil rights bill advocated by the demonstrators in Washington in August 1963. Despite Johnson's best efforts, the bill languished in the Senate in the fall. The provisions outlawing segregation in privately owned restaurants, overnight lodgings, and transportation were anathema to southern senators, who complained that they interfered with property rights. Nevertheless, in 1964, the House of Representatives, with the assistance of the Johnson administration, added two additional provisions to the bill. One empowered the Justice Department to intervene and file suit when a person's civil rights had been violated. The other created the Fair Employment Practices Commission, giving it the power to enforce equal opportunity in hiring and promotion in firms employing more than one hundred people. The House also added a provision forbidding discrimination based on gender as well as race; this provision later had a dramatic impact in reducing discrimination against women. The bill sailed through the House on February 10, 1964, by a vote of 290 to 130. Representatives explained their votes as a tribute to John Kennedy.

Things were more difficult in the Senate, however, where southerners and other opponents of the bill threatened to defeat it with a filibuster. Johnson went to work with his legendary "treatment" to force senators to vote for cloture (an end to debate), in order to bring the legislation to a vote on the floor. With the aid of Minnesota Democrat Hubert Humphrey, he wooed Everett Dirksen, the Republican minority leader. They convinced Dirksen that the party of Abraham Lincoln could not afford to be responsible for the defeat of civil rights legislation. Finally, on July 2, 1964, two and a half months after the filibuster began, the Senate passed the law by a vote of 73 to 27.

The act banned discrimination based on race in public accommodations—restaurants, theaters, hotels, motels, and rooming houses. State-supported institutions such as schools, libraries, parks, playgrounds, and swimming pools could no longer be segregated. The Justice Department now had the right to intervene to protect those whose civil rights had been violated. The Fair Employment Practices Commission could bring suit to end discrimination in private employment.

Johnson looked forward to signing more civil rights legislation after the election of 1964. He told the new attorney general, Nicholas deB. Katzenbach (who took over in the summer of 1964 after Kennedy resigned), "I want you to write me the goddamndest, toughest voting rights act that you can devise." Before submitting a voting-rights bill, however, Johnson wanted to be elected president in his own right. He hoped not just to win, but to demolish the Republican nominee. As "president of all the people," he could emerge from the shadow of John Kennedy's legacy. He believed that winning a wide majority would enable him to preside successfully over a legislative program as rich as the New Deal.

Johnson's task appeared to be made easier by recent changes within the Republican Party. Since the New Deal, Republicans had suppressed their most conservative inclinations during presidential campaigns, nominating nonideological, centrist candidates they hoped could win. Whatever else they believed in, Republican presidential candidates Dewey, Eisenhower, and Nixon all accepted the basic premise of the New Deal: that the federal government had a role to play in managing social and economic affairs. Party conservatives complained, but they were regularly outvoted at convention time.

By 1964, however, the more conservative Republicans, including Senate minority leader Everett Dirksen, House minority leader Charles Halleck, old supporters of Senator Robert Taft, members of far-right groups like the John Birch Society, and various newcomers to the party (among them Ronald Reagan, a former president of the Screen Actors Guild), had had enough. Enraged by what they considered the arrogance of "the Eastern Establishment," they railed against Wall Street, international finance, Madison Avenue, Harvard, the *New York Herald Tribune*, and Ivy League prep schools. One advocate of this militant new conservatism, Phyllis Schlafly, complained that in the past "a small group of secret king-makers, using hidden persuaders and psychological warfare techniques, [had] manipulated the Republican national convention to nominate candidates who had side-stepped or suppressed the key issues." Never again, vowed the conservatives, promising to nominate one of their own for the presidency.

For their part, eastern Republicans such as governors Nelson Rockefeller of New York and William Scranton of Pennsylvania were contemptuous of the backwardness and ignorance of the people they called "primitives"—midwestern, southern, and western politicians who had never valued the role of government in modern society. Fighting for the nomination were Rockefeller, a man whose pedigree and career proclaimed "Eastern Establishment," and Senator Barry Goldwater of Arizona, standard-bearer for the new conservatives.

Goldwater was a product of the Sunbelt, the fast-growing region that had gained wealth, power, and population since World War II. He grew up in Phoenix, a city that had swelled from thirty thousand inhabitants in his youth to over eight hundred thousand by the 1960s. Freed, they hoped, from the crowding, dirt, crime, and zoning regulations of older cities, the residents of the Sunbelt adopted new political habits. They distrusted government—especially the federal government, which controlled hundreds of thousands of acres of land in the western states—and they resented easterners. Few of them publicly acknowledged that federally funded roads, dams, and electric power grids had made the Sunbelt's agricultural, industrial, and population growth possible.

Goldwater capitalized on the Sunbelt's animosity in his 1964 campaign. He sealed his nomination for the presidency with a narrow win over Governor Rockefeller in the California primary in early June. Goldwater quickly dashed moderate Republicans' hopes that he would soften his rhetoric and run as a centrist. His speech accepting the Republican nomination gave no quarter,

Arizona senator Barry Goldwater accepts the Republican Party's nomination for president in San Francisco, July 1964. / © Bettmann/CORBIS

saying that "those who do not care for our cause, we don't expect to enter our ranks." Finally, he dismissed party moderates with his famous pronouncement, "Extremism in the defense of liberty is no vice! . . . Moderation in the pursuit of justice is no virtue!"

In Goldwater, Lyndon Johnson found the perfect opponent. Choosing Senator Hubert Humphrey of Minnesota as his running mate, Johnson campaigned as a unifier and a builder of consensus. In contrast to Goldwater, who seemed sharp, divisive, and ultimately frightening to the public, Johnson looked conciliatory. The Arizona senator alarmed voters with talk of giving control over nuclear weapons to battlefield commanders. His proposals to make Social Security private and voluntary and to sell the Tennessee Valley Authority confirmed suspicions that he was a radical who wanted to dismantle the most popular programs of the New Deal.

Democrats capitalized on these fears with a series of hard-hitting television advertisements designed to portray Goldwater as untrustworthy. The most famous of the TV spots showed a young girl counting the petals on a daisy. The image of the girl faded as a solemn announcer counted backward from 10. The sight of a mushroom cloud rising from an atomic explosion filled the screen, and Johnson was heard in a voice-over: "These are the stakes. We must learn to love one another, or surely we shall die." Johnson refused to debate Goldwater, letting the mushroom cloud and other TV ads carry his message instead, with devastating effect.

Johnson summarized his goals as moving "not only toward the rich society and the powerful society, but upward to the Great Society." He defined the Great Society as "abundance and liberty for all . . . an end to poverty and racial injustice . . . a place where every child can find knowledge to enrich his mind and to enlarge his talents." Johnson drew huge, responsive crowds throughout the country, and a wide coalition—whites and blacks, business and labor, liberals and moderates, Democrats and Republicans—supported his campaign.

Johnson's victory represented the greatest presidential landslide since the previous century. He carried forty-four states and 60.7 percent of the popular vote (see Map 6.1). Nevertheless, there were some ominous signs for the Democratic Party when it came to the distribution of the popular vote. Throughout the South—the base of the Democrats' success in presidential elections since 1932—Johnson received only 51 percent of the white vote, a signal that his party's control of that region had slipped. In fact, this election would be the last time a Democratic presidential candidate would win a majority of the southern white vote. In the Deep South, Goldwater's conservative appeal was especially effective. In addition to his native Arizona, Goldwater carried South Carolina, Georgia, Alabama, Mississippi, and Louisiana. White voters in those states were enraged by the Civil Rights Act, and grave fissures had appeared in the New Deal coalition.

But in the aftermath of Johnson's dramatic victory, it was hard to predict any difficulties for the Democrats. Alongside the Johnson landslide, the Democratic Party added thirty-seven seats in the House and two more seats in the Senate. When the new Congress convened in January 1965, House Democrats

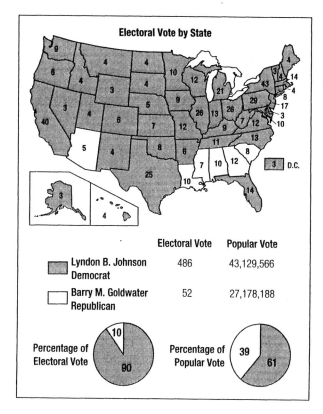

Electoral Vote by State

	Electoral Vote	Popular Vote
Lyndon B. Johnson Democrat	486	43,129,566
Barry M. Goldwater Republican	52	27,178,188

Percentage of Electoral Vote

Percentage of Popular Vote

**Map 6.1
Presidential Election of 1964**

outnumbered Republicans by 295 to 140. In the Senate were sixty-eight Democrats and only thirty-two Republicans. Not since Franklin Roosevelt's election of 1936 had either party assembled such massive majorities in Congress. Johnson appeared to have the congressional backing he needed to use the government to revitalize American society.

The Great Society: Success and Disappointment

Spurred by Lyndon Johnson, in 1965 and 1966, Congress enacted the most sweeping social reforms since the New Deal. Designed to win the War on Poverty and create the Great Society that Johnson had promised, these programs enhanced the role of the federal government in promoting.health, economic welfare, education, urban renewal, and civil rights. The scope and content of the Great Society programs originated in the work of numerous social thinkers, reformers, and activists. In the late nineteenth and early twentieth centuries, progressive social reformers believed that the poor were mostly immigrants whose culture did not conform to that of the dominant white Protestant majority. The poor could be helped to achieve a stable position in American society by extending down to them the hands of the well-to-do and the intellectuals who studied their problems. In the 1960s, the federal government revived this approach. Intellectuals studied the conditions of poor Americans and sought solutions to their problems. Consultants came to Washington to help draft laws reflecting the ideas of social scientists from the past twenty years.

The Great Society was not limited to programs designed to eliminate poverty among the poorest quarter of the population; Great Society programs also served the needs of the three-quarters of Americans who were not poor. The creators of the Great Society hoped to give everyone a stake in its success. They wanted to avoid policies that appeared to take resources from one group and give them to another. By steering clear of redistribution of wealth, the Great Society was able to gain the support of white, middle-class Americans. Many, perhaps most, middle-class, white Americans endorsed the goals of the Great Society while the economy expanded, as it did for most of the 1960s. Even during the boom, however, middle-class whites began to worry about their own place in society. The effort to maintain a consensus carried substantial costs, and eventually support for the War on Poverty faded in the middle class.

These ambitious initiatives not only increased government spending but also required a greater number of government officials to administer them. In contrast to the 1930s and 1940s, however, the greatest need for new government employees was at the state and local levels (see Figure 6.1). Some of the new programs were very successful, but others left a legacy of disappointment and controversy.

Extending federally funded healthcare benefits was one of the first and most popular of the Great Society initiatives. In 1965, heeding the president's call to improve access to healthcare for elderly Americans, Congress enacted the ambitious program known as Medicare. Fulfilling a pledge made first by the Truman administration, the legislation created universal hospital insurance for Americans over age sixty-five who were covered by Social Security. Congress also included voluntary insurance to cover doctors' fees and nursing-home charges. Medicare did not, however, cover the cost of medicines prescribed outside hospitals. At the time, few medicines other than antibiotics and a limited number of pills for high blood pressure were in widespread use. Three decades later, medicines prescribed outside hospitals provided at least as much medical care as did hospital visits. A complementary program, Medicaid, was enacted in 1966; it allowed participating states to receive matching federal grants to pay the medical bills of welfare recipients of all ages. After a slow start, all states but Arizona agreed to participate in Medicaid. The creation of Medicare and Medicaid coincided with growing awareness of environmental and other human threats to health and well being. For example, public health concerns over the risk of cigarettes grew steadily after the January 1964 widely reported release of the Surgeon General's report that corroborated the long discussed links between smoking, lung cancer and heart disease.

Medicare and Medicaid gained wide popularity because they covered nearly everyone at one time or another in their lives. The programs substantially reduced the gap in medical treatment between the poor and the rich. By

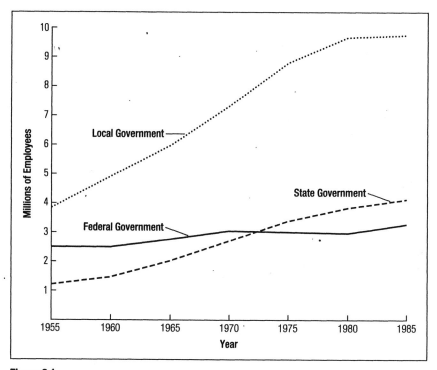

Figure 6.1
Growth of Government, 1955–1985

1970, the proportion of Americans who had never visited a physician fell from 19 percent to 8 percent. Prenatal visits increased, which helped lower the infant mortality rate by 33 percent. Among African Americans, the change in infant mortality was especially noticeable, declining from 4 percent of live births in 1965 to 3.1 percent in 1970 and 2.4 percent in 1975.

One problem, however, was the cost of these medical programs, which far outstripped original estimates. To overcome resistance from many medical doctors, the administration had agreed that medical services would continue to be provided by private doctors chosen by the patients themselves. Hospitals and physicians would receive "reasonable and customary" payments for their services. When the inflation rate climbed during the late 1960s, medical charges rose even faster. Partly as a result, the annual cost of these government programs soared from $3.4 billion to $18 billion in ten years. As the financial resources of Medicare became strained, the government encouraged medical professionals to restrict the amount of time that patients spent in hospitals. At the same time, numerous pharmaceutical innovations made it easier to treat ailments such as heart disease, diabetes, anxiety, depression, and even cancer outside hospitals. By the late 1970s, many private insurance plans included payments for prescription drugs, but Medicare did not.

In 1965, Congress also passed a spectacular array of measures aimed directly at reducing poverty. Many of these programs were designed to alleviate the urban poverty that had led to race riots in numerous American cities in the summer of 1965. Congress created the Office of Economic Opportunity (OEO) to supervise the War on Poverty. Johnson appointed Sargent Shriver, who had successfully headed the Peace Corps, as the first director of the OEO. Congress also created the food-stamp program, which provided assistance to people whose income fell below a level set by the government. The program worked well: ten years after its enactment, research indicated that government efforts were "almost fully effective in reducing flagrant malnutrition."

Because experts considered education a key element in helping young people climb out of poverty, Congress created the Head Start program to reach the preschool children of impoverished families. This program was also successful. Later studies revealed that Head Start children gained substantial advantages over poor children who did not enroll. They gained an average of seven points on IQ tests and were half as likely as nonparticipants to repeat grades in school or to be assigned to special-education classes. Long-term studies suggested that, as teenagers and young adults, Head Starters completed more years of school, worked more steadily, and engaged in less criminal behavior. Congress also provided grants to school districts with large numbers of poor children, and scholarships and loans for underprivileged college students.

Another step was the creation of the Job Corps, which was patterned on the Civilian Conservation Corps of the New Deal. Reformers believed Job Corps members would develop effective work habits that they would continue to use once they gained employment outside the government. The corps employed one hundred thousand young men and women from poor families. Eight years later, in 1973, Congress expanded the Jobs Corps with the Comprehensive Employment and Training Act (CETA). CETA provided on-the-job training for the chronically unemployed. For those who could not find positions with private employers, the government created full-time public service jobs for them. Although costly, this program met its goals.

To aid urban renewal, Congress created the Model Cities program, but this endeavor was less successful. Planners had originally hoped to concentrate on a few targets, mobilize local leadership, and try various methods to invigorate dying communities. If a few cities could be revitalized—their slums renewed and their residents provided with useful work—these demonstration projects would act as beacons for other places. Powerful members of Congress channeled the lion's share of the benefits to their own districts. The program could not even begin to fulfill the vision of its founders.

To oversee the distribution of grants for Great Society programs, Congress established the cabinet-level Department of Housing and Urban Development (HUD) and Department of Transportation (DOT). These departments made a start in reducing the grinding poverty in urban centers, but Congress did not fund them fully in the period from 1965 to 1967. By the time the Johnson administration asked for a new housing act in 1968, much of the enthusiasm for the Great Society had ebbed. The costs of the Vietnam War made Congress reluctant to fund programs designed to replace dilapidated inner-city tenements. Consequently, the president's request to build 6 million low-income dwellings was slashed to less than one-quarter of the original proposal.

Funding problems also bedeviled the OEO, headed by Sargent Shriver, who left the Peace Corps to take on the vastly more complicated job of directing the War on Poverty. The OEO was supposed to coordinate several other programs, including the Job Corps; Volunteers in Service to America (VISTA), a domestic version of the Peace Corps; and the Community Action Program (CAP). Despite Shriver's best efforts, the OEO had to oversee a vast proliferation of programs, with little increase in funds. There were organizational troubles as well. One task of CAP was to encourage recipients of government assistance to participate in administering government programs; the goal was defined as "maximum feasible participation." But this goal provoked clashes between local authorities and the neighborhood activists assisted by the OEO.

Such conflicts undermined congressional support for the OEO after 1966. The CAP's difficulties typified some of the Great Society's larger problems. The Johnson administration was trying to satisfy irreconcilable groups and factions. Johnson truly believed in building a consensus—a legacy of his congressional career—and he thought the way to foster consensus was to satisfy competing interest groups. But the antipoverty programs, as the historian Allan Matusow observed, "sought to appease vested interests that had resisted reform or occasioned the need for it in the first place." As time went on, administrators of Great Society programs came to believe that they had been underfunded and could not possibly meet the vast needs of the country's poor. Opponents of the programs, on the other hand, came to believe that they gave too much power to groups who previously had not had a voice. However modest this empowerment of the poor was, it threatened the political and social position of the people who had previously been dominant.

Despite the many flaws of the antipoverty programs and the resistance they sparked, they had some real successes. They helped reduce the percentage of people living in poverty by about 50 percent in a decade. Standards of medical care improved dramatically. Education reached impoverished rural and urban children in ways that had never before seemed possible. Job training provided a means of breaking out of the cycle of poverty. If the Johnson administration did not vanquish poverty in the United States, it at least gave many Americans an opportunity for a better life.

The issue of reform became inextricably bound up with race. Some of the most far-reaching changes created by the Great Society involved expanding the voting rights of people who had been persistently excluded from the polls because of their race. A series of demonstrations in Alabama helped set the stage for congressional action. For six weeks in early 1965, Martin Luther King, Jr., and the Student Non-Violent Coordinating Committee (SNCC) organized demonstrations in Selma for the right to vote. A city of 29,000 people, Selma had 15,000 African Americans of voting age. In 1965 only 355 of them were registered to vote. The board of registrars, which determined voting eligibility, met for a few hours, twice a month. It took great courage for any

African American to appear before the registrars, and when they did so, they found a board determined to keep them from the polls. African Americans were denied a place on the voting rolls for failing to cross a *t* or dot an *i* on the voter registration form. The registrars routinely asked African American applicants convoluted questions like, "What two rights does a person have after being indicted by a grand jury?"

In January and February 1965, demonstrators demanding the right to vote in Selma were clubbed and tear-gassed by Alabama sheriff's deputies who arrested and jailed over three thousand people. Sheriff Jim Clark wore a button reading "NEVER." At one point, deputies threw a woman to the ground and Sheriff Clark beat her with a club. The deputies used electric cattle prods on the demonstrators, singeing their skin and forcing them to their knees, vomiting in agony.

King and John Lewis of SNCC then organized a fifty-six-mile march from Selma to Birmingham. On Sunday, March 7, 1965, six hundred black demonstrators walked to the Edmund Pettis Bridge at the edge of town. State troopers and sheriff's deputies gave the marchers two minutes to turn back. A phalanx of uniformed officers then flew into the marchers. Swinging their clubs and hurling tear gas at the demonstrators, the officers advanced to the cheers of a white mob standing nearby. Sheriff Clark then ordered horse-mounted deputies to plunge into the crowd. They hit the demonstrators with bullwhips and rubber tubes wrapped in barbed wire. Seventy demonstrators went to the hospital. As he was carried off on a stretcher, SNCC leader Lewis said, "I don't see how President Johnson can send troops to Vietnam . . . and can't send troops to Selma." Television news ran film of the massacre that Bloody Sunday repeatedly. Across the country, editorials denounced the Alabama authorities and demanded congressional action on a voting-rights act. For the culminating march to Montgomery on Tuesday, March 9, thousands of people flew in.

Johnson seized the opportunity to deliver a moving speech before Congress on March 15. He recalled the poverty of the rural school where he had taught in 1928: "My students were poor and they often came to class without breakfast, hungry. They knew even in their youth the pain of injustice. . . . Somehow you never forget what poverty and hatred can do when you see its scars in the hopeful face of a young child." He had never expected to be in a position to do much about the problem. But now that he had the chance, he told Congress, he meant to use it: "I mean to be the president who educated young children . . . who helped to feed the hungry . . . who helped the poor to find their own way." He then linked these memories with a call for passage of the voting-rights act. If African Americans did not gain equal voting rights, Johnson declared, "we will have failed as a people and a nation." He asked his fellow citizens to "overcome the crippling legacy of bigotry and injustice." Adopting the slogan of the civil rights movement, he insisted "we shall overcome."

Congress obliged with the Voting Rights Act of 1965, which empowered the Justice Department to register voters directly in localities where discrimination existed. If fewer than 50 percent of the citizens of a district voted or were registered to vote in 1964, the Justice Department assumed that there had been discrimination at the polls. Literacy tests for voter registration were also outlawed. Over the next three years, the law resulted in the registration of an additional 740,000 black voters (see Map 6.2). The overall rate of registration among African Americans rose from 31 percent to 57 percent. About 70 percent of whites registered. The law eventually produced an increase in black officeholders as well. The number of blacks in the House of Representatives rose from five to seventeen in the next twenty years, and the total number of black public officials in the entire nation increased from 103 to 3,503. In the 1970s and 1980s, African Americans were elected to the mayor's office in cities ranging from Newark, New Jersey, and Gary, Indiana, to New York, Los Angeles, and Chicago. The change was even more startling in the Deep South: Atlanta, New Orleans, Birmingham, and even Selma elected black mayors.

Although the Great Society is remembered for its attempts to erase poverty and discrimination, it also sponsored programs that appealed directly to the American middle class. By funding the arts and humanities, promoting

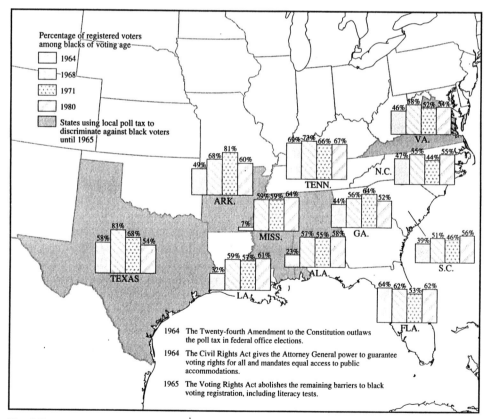

Map 6.2
Voting Rights for African Americans, 1964–1980

nonprofit television, and helping to clean up the nation's highways, the Johnson administration produced benefits even the wealthy could appreciate.

To fulfill his promise to "build a richer life of mind and spirit," Johnson sent Congress legislation to create the National Foundation for the Arts and Humanities, a smaller version of the National Science Foundation, which had been in existence since 1950. The new foundation consisted of two divisions: the National Endowment for the Arts (NEA) and the National Endowment for the Humanities (NEH). The Federal Council on the Arts and Humanities was created to supervise the two endowments. Both directly and through state councils, each endowment offered grants to individuals and to institutions such as universities, museums, ballet companies, and local arts centers.

The NEA and NEH sponsored conferences, produced films, offered fellowships for scholars and creative writers, and funded university courses and new curricula. In the beginning, the endowments grew slowly, from a budget of $2.5 million each in 1966 to roughly $6 million each in 1970. But ten years later, each endowment was spending $106 million per year. Together, the NEA and NEH had a profound effect on the arts and humanities throughout the nation. The proliferation of local theater and dance companies, the development of many young artists and writers, the expansion of scholarly research—all of these were made possible by the NEA and NEH.

The Great Society influenced American television, too. To offer American people an alternative to commercial programming, Congress in 1967 reserved 242 channels on the nation's airwaves for local public, noncommercial TV stations. It also provided direct federal subsidies for public programming with the creation of the Corporation for Public Broadcasting (CPB). Governed by a presidentially appointed board, the CPB distributed grants to produce TV shows and helped with the operating budgets of local public TV stations. Programs such as *Sesame Street*, an educational hour for preschoolers, and *Nova*, a highly regarded series on science, received support from the CPB. Five years later, in 1972, Congress added National Public Radio, a network of noncommercial radio stations. Those stations, and some of the programs they aired, received support from the CPB.

The Great Society also demonstrated a concern for the natural environment. Congress enacted legislation mandating improvements in air and water quality. The president's wife, known to the nation as Lady Bird Johnson, took the lead in fostering a more pleasant environment along the nation's roads. Deathly afraid of air travel, she commuted between Texas and Washington on the nation's highway system. She was appalled by the junkyards and unsightly billboards lining the interstates. She pressed her husband to submit to Congress the Highway Beautification Act, which was passed in 1965. By increasing the federal contribution to interstate highway construction from 85 to 90 percent for states that joined the program, the law encouraged states to ban billboards and remove roadside junkyards. Because the law allowed billboard companies wide latitude in adhering to regulations, it resulted in only minor improvements. Nevertheless, this early gesture toward beautification, along with the measures designed to clean up the air and water, set the stage for stronger environmental laws in the 1970s.

Johnson's Great Society had a profound influence on immigration as well. When Johnson took office, an immigration quota system dating from the 1920s was still in effect. In setting limits on entry for many foreign nationals, the quotas reflected deep-rooted racial and ethnic biases against Asians, Eastern Europeans, Catholics, and Jews. Hoping to erase the inequities of this system, President Kennedy had presented Congress with an immigration-reform package abolishing discrimination against immigrants on the basis of national origin.

The bill languished until Kennedy's death, but Johnson resubmitted it to the reform-minded eighty-ninth Congress in 1965. When it passed that year, it seemed only a moderate modification of America's immigration policy. It phased out the national quota system over the next three years. After 1968 there would be a total of 290,000 slots available each year, divided into 170,000 visas for immigrants from the Eastern Hemisphere and 120,000 for immigrants from the Western Hemisphere. In place of quotas based on national origin, Congress created seven categories to set priorities for granting entry. Two categories of immigrants received the highest priority: those holding desirable job skills and those with close relatives (parents and siblings) in the United States. Political refugees were given the lowest priority and accounted for the smallest number of visas. This situation was largely overlooked at the time but generated controversy later.

Because the law gave first preference to family members, Congress expected that the new mix of immigrants would closely resemble the old one. Although this reasoning made sense at the time, it failed to anticipate a profound change in immigration patterns in the next decade. For a few years, the law worked as planned, admitting immigrants from southern and Eastern Europe in large numbers.

By the middle of the 1970s, however, immigration patterns had changed due to worldwide economic trends. Job prospects brightened in Europe, making America less attractive. European immigrants made up 45 percent of the total in 1965 but only 15 percent in the late 1970s. During this period, immigration from Asia, the Caribbean, and South America shot up. Residents of these lands found the American economy extraordinarily attractive compared to the opportunities available in their own countries. This situation was especially true for educated people, whose skills qualified them for special preference under the terms of the 1965 law.

Congress did not envision that the family reunification provision would create an immigration chain. For example, a foreign student attending college in the United States could gain the skills needed to qualify for immigration preference. Within a short time, he or she could use the family reunification provision to bring over his or her parents, spouse, and children. As these relatives attained citizenship, they too became eligible to sponsor relatives. Thus, an ever wider network evolved, bringing many additional immigrants to the United States.

This pattern, which held true for immigrants from nearly every Asian nation except Japan, actually reduced poverty in the United States. Many Asian immigrants came from upper-class, highly educated backgrounds. Within a decade of the new law's passage, tens of thousands of Asian physicians and nurses entered the United States. They became the backbone of many public hospitals' staffs. So many professionals emigrated from South Korea, Taiwan, the Philippines, India, Pakistan, and the British colony of Hong Kong that officials in these countries sometimes accused the United States of promoting a "brain drain" of talent that they needed for progress at home.

By 1979 the seven largest groups of immigrants were all of non-European origin:

Mexico   52,000

Philippines   41,300

China, Taiwan, and Hong Kong   30,180

Korea   29,348

Jamaica   19,714

India   19,708

Dominican Republic   17,519

Refugees and undocumented aliens swelled these figures even further. All in all, the 1965 immigration act resulted in an unprecedented boom in non-European immigrants to the United States during the 1970s.

Changes in the National Economy

In the early years of his administration, when his Great Society programs were springing into action, Johnson's efforts were bolstered by the greatest peacetime economic boom since the end of World War II. The administration's strategy—adjusting government spending to encourage employment and growth and to dampen inflation—seemed to work. Unemployment fell to 3.7 percent of the labor force, its lowest level since the Korean War. Economic activity, as measured by changes in the gross national product (GNP), grew by over 4 percent per year from 1964 to 1966. (*Gross national product* was the term used in the 1960s to measure total output of goods and services. In the 1990s, the term was changed to *gross domestic product*.) Government expenditures and receipts were roughly in balance for these years.

The boom hastened the rise of the Sunbelt. Spending for the military and the space program continued to flow to the South and the West. California consolidated its position as the premier defense contracting state (it became known as "the buckle on the Sunbelt"), while Texas surpassed New York as the second. By the end of the 1960s, the federal payroll in the ten Sunbelt states amounted to $10 billion per year, double the amount in all other states combined.

Business prospered in the Sunbelt as well. For example, the oil industry, long headquartered in the Northeast, began to relocate to Texas, Oklahoma, and California. Getty, Union, Occidental, and Signal Oil, all based in Los Angeles, grew to prominence. Phillips Petroleum of Bartlesville, Oklahoma, and Tenneco, in Houston, challenged New York–based companies such as Mobil and Texaco.

The sixties also saw an explosion in banking in the Sunbelt. North Carolina National Bank grew the fastest, earning more money than any other bank in the country. San Francisco's Bank of America became the country's largest, with hundreds of branches serving retail customers. It heavily promoted its BankAmericard, the first bank credit card, sparking a new trend in consumer spending. In 1965, four big Chicago banks started MasterCard; two years later, four California banks created Master Charge. Ads urged consumers to use their plastic to purchase everyday items—gasoline, clothing, meals, televisions, lawn mowers. The banks made money from these cards in three ways: charging interest for purchases not paid for within a specified grace period, collecting fees from merchants accepting the cards, and licensing other banks to issue their own cards bearing the now famous BankAmericard, MasterCard, and Master Charge names. Bank of America eventually sold its credit-card business to a consortium of other banks, who changed the name of the card to VISA, and Master Charge merged with MasterCard, retaining the latter name.

Sunbelt banks also took the lead in developing bank holding companies, financial concerns that bought small local banks. The new entities, among them the United Bank of Los Angeles, Valley National Bank of Phoenix, and Columbia Savings and Loan of Los Angeles, had assets of over $1 billion each, a large sum for the time. They were able to provide loans for large real-estate and industrial-development programs, which had previously been forced to rely on major Wall Street firms for financing.

Wall Street also did well. Between 1963 and 1966, the New York Stock Exchange enjoyed its greatest growth since the 1920s, with prices more than doubling. One effect of this bull market was the development of industrial conglomerates. Audacious dealmakers, often from the Sunbelt, arranged for one firm to buy another in an unrelated industry. The parts of the resulting merged enterprise had little to do with one another economically, but the balance sheets showed increased profits. As if to emphasize the company rather than the product, the combined firms took names that had little intrinsic meaning. American Tobacco became American Brands. Ling Temco Vought became LTV. Some of these business arrangements joined highly unlikely partners. Litton Shipyards, renamed Litton Industries, acquired the Stouffer food company; the renamed LTV, a defense contractor, bought the Wilson meatpacking corporation.

But celebrations of the economic boom were premature. By 1966 the growing war in Vietnam (see Chapter 7) had unleashed unexpected and uncontrollable inflation. The inflation rate began to fluctuate between 2.5 percent and 4 percent per year. For people accustomed to the many years of price stability since the Korean War, this development was frightening. Keynesians explained the rise as a result of too much business demand in the wake of the

(cont. on page 230)

Big Dreams, Big Buildings

The Cold War was as much about culture as it was about international conflict. Americans sought to show people around the world the freshness, cleanliness, and openness of American society. In the 1950s, the government created the United States Information Agency (USIA) and expanded Voice of America and Radio Free Europe to broadcast American music and news over the radio to a global audience. The Eisenhower administration launched a new trade-fair program aimed at promoting American business interests abroad. The most famous occurred in Moscow in the summer of 1959. Vice President Richard M. Nixon and Soviet Communist Party General Secretary Nikita S. Khrushchev engaged in a heated impromptu debate over the merits of an all-electric kitchen installed by General Electric (GE). Nixon explained that Americans lived better than anyone. Khrushchev replied that Americans were too materialistic and lived in isolation.

By 1960, ninety-seven trade exhibits had been seen by more than 60 million people in twenty-nine countries. Visitors gaped at the vast array of postwar consumer products, from huge cars to electric ranges, automatic dryers, toasters, stereos, and TVs. Some overseas critics bemoaned the intrusion of American consumer culture as unsophisticated and threatening to local traditions. But the scoffers rarely came to the fairs. The millions who did mostly liked the bright smiles on the faces of the young American women and men who demonstrated the contemporary wares.

American businesses transmitted American culture and beliefs to host countries through other avenues, some quite unintended. Products as different as Hollywood movies, TV shows, Coke and Pepsi-Cola, McDonald's hamburgers, and Ford Mustangs and Chevrolet Corvettes created larger-than-life visions of the United States that veered from powerful and generous to free and fresh, to wasteful and arrogant. Architecture too transmitted ideas about the American style to an international audience.

Buildings constructed by Americans abroad conveyed the idea that the United States was a new, modern, rich, and powerful country. Following the end of World War II, the State Department commissioned no fewer than two hundred projects in seventy-two countries. Most of these structures, developed for embassies and consulates, were designed like modern corporate architecture. Between 1954 and 1959, over fifty different architectural firms developed about fifty-eight high-profile buildings, including U.S. embassies in India, England, and Norway. The designers favored huge, open entryways. The façades used white stone and a lot of glass. While some criticized the results of the State Department's building program as ostentatious and others praised them as cutting-edge artistry, few could fail to see that these massive new structures transmitted the image of a thoroughly modern, glamorous, commanding, and rich United States. The London embassy project, for instance, was elevated from the street level on stilts and featured a controversial stone eagle with a thirty-five-foot wingspan perched atop its main entrance.

These public buildings drew their inspirations from the glass-and-steel skyscrapers built in American cities in the 1950s and 1960s. Philip Johnson, a prominent modern architect, set the tone with his design for New York's Seagram Building. When Seagram's headquarters opened, critics lauded it for its apparent weightlessness. The green glass seemed to float above the noisy, crowded city below. Modern buildings, like modern American, seemed unbounded, free, and clean. Architectural magazines hailed the new American embassies as admirable examples of the progressive-minded, friendly

The World Trade Center under construction in lower Manhattan, February 1971. / © Charles E. Rotkin/CORBIS

spirit of America, and contrasted them with the classic and pretentious architectural style of Soviet embassies that seemed as heavy as Russian food and unstylish as the suits favored by the stolid bureaucrats of the upper echelons of the Soviet government.

Commentators especially appreciated the way that the planners appropriated local architectural styles and transformed them into modernized, distinctly American structures. Such was the case in Ireland in 1959. Developers capitalized on that country's Celtic motifs and round building designs to deliver a trendy structure that included floor-

to-ceiling windows separated by precast concrete sections and the most up-to-date amenities. Buildings like this one, which offered updated versions of antiquated styles, successfully transmitted the idea that Americans were innovative—and in control.

While policymakers may have welcomed such a reputation, the designs of the new embassies were as likely to convey less flattering images of the United States. For instance, the new embassy in Morocco, completed in 1961, made a mockery of American innovation when it proved unlivable thanks to a long list of flaws: it was too hot in summer,

227

drafty and cold in winter; the roof leaked; stone floors and plazas cracked. Designers placed some of the windows in out-of-the-way crannies that made it impossible to clean the glass. An eight-foot-high wall and fence surrounded the enormous American embassy in Saigon, Vietnam, making it nearly impossible to see the buildings from the street. The American-designed presidential palace in Saigon opened in 1965. Its façade of gilt-colored, anodized aluminum looked cheap, and the palace itself resembled a Sunbelt municipal building.

On a broader level, critics condemned the grandiose scale on which the embassies were built, finding them out of step with the new attitudes of self-determination and frugality in ascendance around the world. By the mid-1960s, the State Department, having exhausted earlier funds and facing withering criticism from Congress, stepped back from its ambitious building program. The State Department building program then concentrated on low-profile embassies. By the 1980s, architectural styles had changed too. The most sought-after architects had tired of the open, glass-and-steel, high-rise style. Where once it appeared clean, architects now considered it sterile. Tall buildings soaring above the streets below now appeared isolated and lacking the human touch.

Structures erected by American businesses during the Cold War also conveyed the idea of a privileged, powerful United States through their architectural style. The physical presence of the sixteen glittering new Hilton hotels erected in sixteen cities—including Istanbul, Berlin, Tel Aviv, Cairo, and Athens—became beacons of the American way of life. Conrad Hilton makes clear in his autobiography, *Be My Guest*, that he viewed the internationalization of his hotel chain as an effective way to spread the American message of freedom and democracy around the world. The hotels featured luxurious amenities like wall-to-wall carpeting, high-speed express elevators, air con-

ditioning, bars and restaurants on upper floors with views of the surrounding cities, and outdoor swimming pools where waiters brought Cokes, American beer, and hamburgers to lounging guests. These hotels provided an enviable American contrast to the traditional and sometimes dilapidated buildings of the host cities. In Athens, for instance, the imposing and luxurious Hilton proved a dramatic contrast to the crumbling Acropolis, leaving no doubt as to which country was currently on the rise.

The view of America as exceptional extended inside the hotel as well, where interiors offered sanitized versions of local art and culture so that guests could "experience" the unfamiliar. In Istanbul, for instance, the Hilton featured Turkish-vaulted architecture, a ladies' sitting area garnished with divans and lavish draperies to create an Arabian Nights effect, a mini-mall with locally produced items for purchase, and local cuisine. These attempts to re-create the local flavor stood in stark contrast to the glimmering coffee shops, green lawns, and American soda fountains that were prominent features of the usual international Hilton experience. Together, the juxtaposition of American modernity and native tradition created an idealized, Americanized version of foreign lands for Western consumption. Hilton hotels provided Americans safe havens from which to view foreign lands. For the most skeptical critics, a stay in an overseas Hilton was like a trip to Disneyland. Everything was clean and safe—and deeply false and misleading. But the guests appreciated a familiar setting in a strange land. Locals also started to use the American hotels as meeting places with visiting business executives. The Egyptians, Turks, Israelis, or Germans who used the hotels began to enjoy the comfort and efficiency they found there. They might become slightly annoyed by their own country's slower pace, but at the same time they became interpreters of the United States to their own countries, and vice versa.

Other U.S. corporations overseas sent an even more exclusivist message with the structures they developed. Oil conglomerates extracting oil from Middle East land, for instance, created elite compounds for their American employees that were strictly off limits to native workers. The California-based Arabian American Oil Company created a sprawling oasis of Americanism in Dhahran, Saudi Arabia, that featured a bowling alley, a golf course, air conditioning, cinemas, and elaborate landscaping. Its ostentation stood in stark contrast to the dirt floors, flimsy huts, and stinky latrines forced on the majority of the local work force. Some U.S. military installations took a similar approach, creating spaces that exuded a message of modernity and exclusivity. The bungalows at China Beach, about ten miles north of Da Nang, Vietnam, and a popular rest and recreation area for Americans during the Vietnam War, were an exact replica of an American beach club, with one exception, however. The eight-foot-high brick wall that ran along the beach was topped with rolls of barbed wire to keep out local Vietnamese, any one of whom the military feared might be a dangerous Viet Cong guerrilla. In the Middle East, the Sinai Field Mission, erected in 1976 as a permanent base for American troops charged with patrolling a U.N. buffer zone between Israeli and Egyptian forces, featured trendy, prefabricated, concrete modules like those used by a major hotel chain. As if to illustrate that American soldiers were a breed apart, the mission offered luxurious amenities such as tennis courts, carpeting, and air conditioning.

Since at least the 1960s, American structures have served as targets for those disgruntled with American policies and privileges. In 1969, for instance, right-wing militants bombed the Athens Hilton as a way of expressing their displeasure with American support of a rival political group. Embassies have repeatedly suffered attacks by militants hostile to American interests, from the 1975 chaotic takeover of the U.S. embassy in Saigon through the violent assault on the Tehran embassy by Iranian students in November 1979 and the 1998 bombings of U.S. embassies in Tanzania and Kenya by Islamic fundamentalists.

No buildings better symbolized the complex story of American architecture's place in global economics and culture than did the 110-story twin towers of the World Trade Center (WTC). When the WTC opened in 1972, the tide had already turned against the minimalist style of post–World War II commercial skyscrapers. Critics savaged the design as "two Kleenex boxes standing on their side." No longer did steel, concrete, and glass mean clean lines and the power of American enterprise. Instead, the critics said that the WTC was barren and dull. The whole idea of building a vertical city where 40,000 people would work every day appeared to be artificial. The windswept plaza of the entryway to the WTC seemed devoid of the vibrant street life it had replaced. But over the years, workers and tourists alike grew fond of the WTC. The food at Windows on the World might have been uninspired, but the view at night was breathtaking. So was the vista from the observation deck. The Islamic terrorists who tried to bring down the WTC in February 1993 by parking a bomb-laden Ryder truck in the basement perceived the building as a central symbol of American financial and commercial power. That bombing attempt failed. But on September 11, 2001, another group of terrorists succeeded when two commercial jetliners crashed into each of the twin towers in a span of twenty minutes. Within ninety minutes of the last plane crash, first the north and then the south tower collapsed in giant fireballs. Two thousand eight hundred people died. Tens of millions of shocked television viewers saw the buildings fall. The reverberations will last for years.

war in Vietnam. They urged the president to raise taxes in 1966 in order to pay for the war and to stem inflation. Johnson refused, fearing that if he emphasized the need to pay war bills, conservatives would force him to squeeze his Great Society budget. Liberals criticized him too when they saw how much the war hurt the reform effort. Wanting to satisfy everyone, Johnson believed that the country could afford both guns and butter. The administration did monitor price and wage increases, and it established guideposts for business and labor to follow. But it had little success in rolling back the increases that it considered excessive.

Interest rates soared in 1966. Banks began paying more than 5.5 percent interest on passbook accounts, more than savings and loan institutions were legally permitted to offer. Thereafter, owners of savings and loans lobbied Congress to relax the ceilings on what they could pay depositors. Rates on government securities, consistently below 3 percent in previous years, rose to 6 percent. The credit crunch, as it was called, also sent the stock market sprawling in 1966. All of this was supposed to slow the rise in prices, but it did not. In 1966 and 1967, prices rose by more than 4 percent per year; in 1968, inflation hit 6 percent.

Inflation hurt pensioners living on fixed incomes and small savers whose return was kept low by regulation. But in the beginning, it helped those poor people who had obtained jobs during the boom because wages for marginal workers rose faster than those for skilled workers. Businesses lost to inflation, however, as higher wages reduced profits, from 10.6 percent of the nation's income in 1966 to 7.2 percent in 1970. Inflation also took its toll internationally. Since 1945 the dollar had been the standard currency of international trade. As prices rose in the United States, European holders of dollars began redeeming their currency for gold. The United States Treasury obliged, but by 1968 the $20 billion U.S. gold reserve represented less than one-third of all dollars held by foreigners.

What seemed the worst about inflation were its persistence and its tendency to increase over time. A 3 percent rate of inflation might be tolerable if it went no higher. In the last years of the Johnson administration, however, the annual rate of inflation rose steadily, discouraging savings, making long-term investment difficult, and souring the public on additional costly programs to aid the poor.

The Supreme Court and Civil Liberties

While Lyndon Johnson promoted his Great Society, the Supreme Court was engaged in another sort of liberal reform: the expansion of constitutionally guaranteed rights. Still led by Chief Justice Earl Warren, the Court expanded on its work of the 1950s: protecting the rights of individuals, altering criminal law, and regulating national and state voting systems. Together, presidents Johnson and Kennedy appointed four justices to the Supreme Court. Byron White (1962–1993), named by Kennedy, became one of the more conservative members. But Arthur Goldberg (1962–1965), Abe Fortas (1965–1969), and

Thurgood Marshall (1967–1991) joined with Warren, Hugo Black, William O. Douglas, and William Brennan to consolidate the Court's liberal majority.

While acknowledging that the freedoms of speech, assembly, press, and religion guaranteed by the First Amendment sometimes had to be balanced against other interests, the Court's liberal majority required the government to show a compelling need to restrict liberty. If it could not, citizens' freedoms could not be abridged.

In *Bond v. Floyd* (1966), for example, the Court ruled that the Georgia House of Representatives could not refuse to seat an elected representative of the people, even though he expressed admiration for those who had opposed conscription for the war in Vietnam. A unanimous Court held that neither public officials nor private citizens could be punished for opinions that did not violate the law. The Court also offered protection to "symbolic speech." In *Tinker v. Des Moines School District* (1969), the Court ruled that students could not be expelled for wearing black armbands protesting the war in Vietnam. Writing for the majority, Justice Fortas argued that students did not lose their rights when they entered a schoolroom.

In *New York Times v. Sullivan* (1964), the Court loosened restraints on what the news media could write or broadcast about well-known figures. The Court ruled that public officials could not win a judgment of libel against a publication merely because a statement was untrue. The libel laws covered only "recklessly false statements" made with "actual malice." Justice Brennan held that "even a false statement may be deemed to make a valuable contribution to public debate." The decision emboldened the press, but it also resulted in a complete lack of privacy for public figures.

Nothing produced more public debate and more confusion on the Court than its efforts to define obscenity. From 1957 to 1968, the Court decided thirteen obscenity cases, issuing fifty-five separate opinions. It never did satisfactorily resolve the questions of what is obscene and how much latitude the government should have in restricting such material. Justice Brennan thought he had found an answer in *Roth v. United States* (1957), when he observed that expressions containing "the slightest redeeming social importance" could be protected by the First Amendment. The Court agreed that government could regulate as obscene any materials that "the average person, applying contemporary community standards," would regard as appealing to "prurient interests." For the next decade, the Court tried to write rules determining what materials fit that definition. It failed to do so, acknowledging that the process had to be subjective. Obscenity would remain a controversial issue for subsequent justices on the Supreme Court. Under Chief Justice Warren Burger (1969–1986), the Court changed the definition of obscene materials from "utterly without redeeming social value" to "lacking serious literary, artistic, political or social value." This definition permitted more government regulation, but it was no more successful than the earlier definition in creating a universally accepted standard.

The Warren Court won praise from civil libertarians and stirred opposition from traditionalists with a series of decisions interpreting the First Amendment's

Earl Warren, chief justice of the United States from 1953 to 1969, presided over a Supreme Court that greatly expanded individual rights. / © Bettmann/CORBIS

ban on the establishment of a state religion. In *Engel v. Vitale* (1962), the Court banned states and localities from instituting prayers in public schools. Justice Black, writing for the majority, said, "[I]t is no part of the business of government to compose official prayers for any group of American people." Over the next several years, the Court ruled that schools could not require devotional reading of the Bible. The justices also revived memories of the famous 1925 "monkey trial" of John Scopes in Tennessee when they struck down an Arkansas law requiring the teaching of "creation science" as a valid alternative to the theory of evolution. Such a law, the Court decided, was an unconstitutional attempt to establish a state religion.

Conservatives denounced these cases as examples of judicial lawmaking. One member of Congress complained that "they put the Negroes in the schools, and now they have driven God out." To a substantial minority of Christians, the Court's rulings were highly offensive. From 1963 through the mid-1980s, opponents of the rulings tried to pass constitutional amendments permitting prayers or Bible-reading in public schools. Although these efforts failed, they were a key element in the conservative tide that rose in the late 1970s. Many religious men and women who had once voted Democratic became ardent supporters of Ronald Reagan and the Republicans in 1980.

The Court also expanded the rights of citizens accused of crimes and set new procedural standards for law enforcement officers. In *Mapp v. Ohio* (1961), the Court forced all states to conform to the exclusionary rule, which holds that evidence gathered outside the specific terms of a search warrant cannot be used against a defendant. In another landmark case, *Gideon v. Wainwright* (1963), the Court observed that Clarence Earl Gideon, a man who had spent over half of his adult life in jail or prison, had never had a lawyer to defend him. The decision affirmed that a "fair trial" meant a right to qualified legal counsel. If a defendant could not afford an attorney, a state had to provide one.

In a more controversial, 5-to-4 ruling in *Miranda v. Arizona* (1966), the Warren Court extended the Fifth Amendment's ban against self-incrimination. Ernesto Miranda, arrested for burglary in Phoenix, had been coerced into confessing by police, who told him that if he remained quiet, judges would sentence him harshly. In its opinion on this case, the Warren Court set standards for police to follow when arresting suspects. Accused persons had to be informed in clear language (later called the Miranda warnings) that they had a right to remain silent and that anything they said could be used against them in a court of law. Police officers had to tell suspects that they had a right to a lawyer and that if they could not afford to hire one, legal counsel would be provided free by the state.

The Warren Court also enhanced the right to privacy in a decision that had profound reverberations both for individual behavior and for legal reasoning and scholarship. In 1965 the Court struck down an 1879 Connecticut law prohibiting the use of any contraceptive device and penalizing anyone giving advice on birth control. The law had long been ignored, but Planned Parenthood managed to bring it before the Court as a test case. In *Griswold* v. *Connecticut*, Justice Douglas held that the state's ban on contraception violated a long-established right to privacy. Although such a right is not specified in the Constitution, Douglas inferred it from other rights that are specified in that document. Three other justices—Brennan, Goldberg, and Warren—concurred, but they were troubled by what they saw as Douglas's invention of a new right. Instead of following Douglas's reasoning, therefore, they relied on the rarely used Ninth Amendment, which reserves for the people any rights not enumerated in the Bill of Rights. They argued that the right of privacy was ancient, older than the Constitution, and that the framers intended to incorporate it through the Ninth Amendment. One of the Court's liberals, Hugo Black, dissented. Black considered himself a strict constructionist, and he could find no specific guarantee to a right of privacy contained in the Constitution. Black's reservations gave some legal scholars pause, but the popular reaction to the *Griswold* decision was highly favorable—few people wanted state intrusion into their bedroom.

The Court also established new rules for elections, making them more representative and democratic. In *Baker* v. *Carr* (1962), the Court overruled earlier precedents when it declared that it and lower courts could decide if the boundaries of state congressional districts were fair. In many states, legislatures had not reapportioned the districts for decades. As a result, rural districts often contained fewer than one-fifth the population of their urban or suburban counterparts. City dwellers complained, but they were reminded that the U.S. Senate also did not represent voters proportionally. But after *Baker* v. *Carr*, underrepresented voters had a wedge with which to sue. They based their appeals on the simple rule of "one person, one vote," and the Court agreed with them.

By 1968 Earl Warren had been chief justice for fifteen years. He was seventy-seven years old and had presided over some of the most far-reaching decisions in the Court's history. In March of that year, Lyndon Johnson announced that he would not seek re-election. Because Warren wanted Johnson to have the opportunity to appoint a chief justice, he told the president that he intended to resign as soon as his successor could be confirmed. The president had a candidate in mind—Abe Fortas. An associate justice since 1965, Fortas was a long-time friend who had continued to give Johnson political advice after his appointment to the Court, often violating the tradition of judicial impartiality. During those three years, Fortas had become a stalwart member of Warren's liberal majority.

Fortas's nomination faced immediate difficulties in the Senate. Democrats still had a majority, but Republicans used several delaying tactics throughout the summer. They expected Richard Nixon to win the upcoming presidential election, and they wanted him to appoint the chief justice. Fortas's support for the Vietnam War, as well as his intimate ties to the now unpopular Johnson, had made him unattractive to some Democrats as well. During the confirmation hearings, the Senate Judiciary Committee learned that Fortas had received $15,000 for teaching some summer law courses; the money had been paid by men who might have had cases before the Court. Faced with charges of cronyism, Fortas asked Johnson to withdraw his nomination in October. Warren remained chief justice until 1969, when President Nixon named Warren Burger, a conservative federal judge from Minneapolis, to replace him. Fortas remained an associate justice until the spring of 1969, when further allegations of financial impropriety forced him to resign.

The end of the Warren Court marked the conclusion of a sixteen-year era of expanding individual rights and the curtailment of arbitrary government power. At the beginning of this period, the Court outlawed segregation in public schools; by the end, it had expanded First Amendment protection in ways that affected the daily lives of most Americans. It had validated the growing pluralism in American life. Yet its endorsement of social changes exacted a substantial price, in effect eroding the Court's own authority in the years that followed. Traditionalists who bemoaned the very pluralism that the Court had affirmed attacked the justices' work. Over the next twenty years, conservatives gained an advantage by deriding what they characterized as the social engineering and judicial activism of the Warren Court. While the subsequent Burger and Rehnquist Courts did not reverse most of the decisions of the Warren years, they curtailed many of their applications.

Decline of the Great Society

Despite the high hopes raised in 1964 and the amazing spate of Great Society legislation in 1965 and 1966, the good feelings lasted barely eighteen months. By late 1966, the impetus behind the Great Society had dwindled. Among the principal reasons for this decline were the war in Vietnam and a white backlash against the extension of civil rights.

Johnson's efforts to secure equality for all races peaked with the Voting Rights Act of 1965. That act, together with the Civil Rights Act of 1964, allowed the Johnson administration to put the weight of the federal government behind efforts to end formal, legal discrimination against racial minorities. Yet most observers realized that ending social and economic inequality between the races would require more than removing the legal barriers.

In the summer of 1965, while addressing the graduating class at predominantly black Howard University in Washington, D.C., Johnson spoke of the vicious cycle of "despair and deprivation" among African Americans. He explained that the Voting Rights Act was "the beginning of freedom . . . but freedom is not enough." He noted that the unemployment rate for blacks was now double that for whites, although thirty-five years earlier it had been the same. The unemployment rate for black teenage boys was 23 percent, compared to 13 percent for whites. The poverty rate for whites had fallen 27 percent, while that of blacks had diminished by only 3 percent.

The reasons for the increasing economic gap between whites and blacks were complex, Johnson said, mostly deriving from "ancient brutality, past injustice, and present prejudice." But Johnson placed some of the responsibility for black poverty on the current cultural norms of African Americans themselves. Drawing on a report called *The Negro Family: The Case for National Action*, by Assistant Secretary of Labor Daniel Patrick Moynihan, he emphasized the dreadful effects of "the breakdown of the Negro family structure." Assuming that this structure should consist of an adult male wage earner and a female homemaker, his argument implied a sentimental, idealized view of the family, hardly representative of the reality for either black or white Americans. Yet both Moynihan and Johnson ignored the complexity and variety of family life in their effort to demonstrate links between culture and poverty. "When the family collapses," Johnson said, "it is the children that are usually damaged," because of the absence of a strong father figure. "When it happens on a massive scale," the president explained, "the community itself is crippled."

Johnson's speech and Moynihan's report were supposed to set the agenda for additional government action to reduce poverty. Moynihan had expected that by concentrating on cultural reasons for African American poverty, the administration would be able to secure better antipoverty programs. But that was not to be. A White House conference met in November with the goal of expanding earlier civil rights legislation, but it broke up in acrimony over the Moynihan report. Some African Americans, expressing new feelings of racial pride and resenting what they perceived to be condescending meddling by white liberals, denounced Moynihan's conclusions as racist. Several critics concluded that the report blamed the victims of discrimination for their plight. Analysts found flaws in Moynihan's methods and described unique strengths in African American families and culture.

Despite its apparently condescending tone, the Moynihan report represented a serious attempt to address a complex problem. But the early criticism undermined support for it. The report left a contradictory legacy. Some people noted its attention to black male unemployment and advocated jobs and training programs. Conservatives and some moderates seized on the report's bleak condemnation of African American family structure to justify dismantling antipoverty programs, notably Aid to Families with Dependent Children. At the same time, Johnson was distracted by the growing problem in Vietnam. In July 1965, he committed U.S. ground forces to the war, and over the next years, as the war consumed more and more of the government's resources and the administration's attention, the problems of poverty and racial inequality received less priority.

Another problem also intervened. In the summer of 1964, race riots struck New York City and several other cities in New York and New Jersey.

Police responded to these outpourings of African American rage with gunfire. Dozens of mostly young black men were shot dead. These violent incidents proved to be only preludes to what was to come. In August 1965 a major uprising erupted in Watts, a predominantly African American section of Los Angeles. The insurrection sprang from economic frustration and black rage at the brutality of the all-white police force. Nevertheless, the events in Watts shocked moderate whites, who only five months before had been moved by the nonviolence and moral force of the demonstrators at Selma, Alabama. White support for racial equality began to erode.

Over the next year, whites began to resent the efforts of Martin Luther King, Jr., and other civil rights leaders to desegregate housing in northern cities. Suspicion was also aroused by the Supreme Court's extension of the rights of people accused of crimes. The race riots spread from one city to another after 1965; by 1968, Detroit, Newark, Washington, Cincinnati, and many other cities across the country had experienced major rioting. Whites were further alienated by the militancy of a newer generation of black leaders (see Chapter 8). By the time of the 1966 congressional elections, white anger at blacks was a key underlying issue.

In 1966, a Gallup poll reported that 52 percent of whites believed the administration was pushing too hard on civil rights, 20 percent more than four years ago. Some Republican candidates denounced "crime in the streets," a term for the African American uprisings. They opposed the Great Society's plans to desegregate public housing. Democrats, too, fanned white fears of blacks. The unsuccessful Democratic candidate for governor of Maryland ran on the slogan "Your home is your castle—protect it." One Democratic congressman from Chicago ruefully reported that in "any home, any bar, any barber shop" you will find people "talking about Martin Luther King and how they are moving in on us and what's going to happen to our neighborhoods."

The white backlash, along with voter dissatisfaction over the administration's handling of the Vietnam War (see Chapter 7), propelled a Republican gain of forty-seven seats in the House and three in the Senate in 1966. The backlash also had an effect at the state level. In California, conservative Republican Ronald Reagan, who condemned the Watts rioters, won the governorship with a margin of nearly 1 million votes. After the election results were in, the defeated Democratic governor, Edmund G. Brown, concluded that "whether we like it or not, people want separation of the races."

Over the next two years, white distrust of social reform grew. Working-class whites, many descended from eastern or southern European immigrants, came to despise the Johnson administration. As prices rose and the government seemed powerless to stop inflation, these white ethnics believed that their needs had been overlooked in the effort to end poverty and forge a Great Society. The urban riots and the Supreme Court's extension of protections to criminal defendants particularly infuriated white ethnic groups. Johnson seemed bereft of ideas to reconstruct his shattered consensus. After the U.S. Army had quelled the Detroit riots in July 1967, at a cost of forty-four lives, the president called for a day of prayer for "order and reconciliation among men." He created a presidential commission, headed by former judge Otto Kerner, to study the causes of urban violence. Yet when Kerner submitted his report in 1968, describing the emergence of "two nations, separate but un-equal, white and black," Johnson refused to receive it.

Johnson's aides told him he needed more than prayer to restore his public standing. By the fall of 1967, his public approval rating had slipped below 33 percent, the lowest figure since Truman's dismal rating at the end of the Korean War. Assistants suggested that Johnson might revive his standing in the polls by showing support for police. In an address to the International Association of Chiefs of Police, Johnson drew prolonged applause with an attack on African American rioters: "We cannot tolerate behavior that destroys what generations of men and women have built here in America—no matter what stimulates that behavior and no matter what is offered to try to justify it."

From that point on, the Great Society ground down. The flood of legislation begun in 1965 slowed to a trickle after the new Congress assembled in 1967. The only major law passed was a housing bill, submitted in 1968, designed to replace the dilapidated dwellings devastated by riots in northern cities. This law also banned racial and religious discrimination in the sale or rental of housing. Modified during the Nixon administration, the law ultimately led to the construction of 1.3 million low-income housing units, but the building program benefited rich developers and investors more than poor people.

Other Great Society programs withered at the end of the Johnson administration. Unwilling to fund both the war in Vietnam and the War on Poverty, Congress cut back on the latter. The president lost heart too at the end of his term, when he saw his support for the poor become a liability among whites. This reduction of support for the War on Poverty further fueled the backlash over the next decade. Conservative opponents of government assistance to the poor now pointed to the failure of the Great Society to eliminate poverty as proof that such programs could not work. In fact, these programs were under-funded, often mismanaged, and had little input from poor people themselves.

Foreign Affairs in the Shadow of Vietnam

The excitement and controversy created by the Great Society, and the dramatic escalation of the war in Vietnam, left government officials with neither the time nor the inclination to think deeply about relations with the rest of the world. Essentially, the administration continued the efforts begun earlier in the Cold War to project American power around the globe. Not comfortable with foreign affairs himself, the president relied on advice from the national security experts he had inherited from Kennedy. Together with men like Secretary of State Dean Rusk, national security advisers McGeorge Bundy (1961–1965) and Walt Whitman Rostow (1965–1968), and Secretary of Defense Robert McNamara (1961–1968), Johnson involved the United States in a series of regional disputes in Latin America, the Middle East, and Europe. These controversies produced little success, and they strained relations with long-time friends. By 1968, experts inside and outside government were calling for a new direction in foreign affairs. At that point, the administration attempted to dampen the passions of the Cold War and relax tensions with the Soviet Union. But its efforts at détente were cut short, and it remained for the succeeding Nixon White House to put them into effect.

The Johnson administration reversed its predecessor's halting efforts to foster social reform in the Western Hemisphere. In March 1964 the director of the Alliance for Progress announced that the alliance would change its emphasis; instead of focusing on land reform and reducing the gap between rich and poor, it would encourage economic growth. Henceforth, he said, the United States would be neutral on social reform and would protect its private investments. The United States would not force Latin American governments to adopt democracy if they faced communist or other revolutionary movements. This policy served as an excuse for relying on Latin American military regimes to protect U.S. interests.

Besides its suspicion of social reform in Latin America, the United States also displayed insensitivity to issues of national pride and identity in the region. Early in 1964, for example, the administration had to confront a host of angry Panamanians. For sixty years, Panama had resented U.S. domination of the Canal Zone. The 1903 treaty granting the United States the rights to the zone "as if it were sovereign" offended Panamanian pride. In 1964 the Panamanians became upset when American high school students in the Canal Zone tore down the Panamanian flag and U.S. authorities refused to raise it again, despite promising to do so. Four days of rioting in Panama left twenty-four Panamanians and four American soldiers dead. Thousands of Panamanians were forced to flee their homes. Johnson took matters into his own hands. Speaking to the Panamanian president personally, he promised to discuss Panamanian grievances in detail at an upcoming summit. But when talks opened between the two nations, Washington downplayed the issue of the offensive canal treaty. Most Panamanians believed Washington was merely stalling.

Elsewhere in the hemisphere, the United States reverted to direct military intervention in the Dominican Republic. That impoverished Caribbean country had long been dominated, directly or indirectly, by the United States. A dictator, Rafael Trujillo, had ruled with American connivance from 1940 to 1961. Toward the end of his regime, however, Washington lost patience with his brutality. In May 1961 he was assassinated, and the Kennedy administration backed the democratic election of a successor. In December 1962 the Dominicans elected Juan Bosch as president. Bosch, a leftist but not a communist, soon ran afoul of the Dominican military, which overthrew him in the fall of 1963.

In April 1965 young army officers sympathetic to Bosch ousted the military-backed government. Their more conservative seniors panicked and appealed to the American ambassador for help. Shooting broke out on the streets of Santo Domingo, and the U.S. envoy wired Washington that a communist revolution was at hand. The embassy published a false press release stating that fifty-eight "identified and prominent Communist and Castroite leaders" were directing the pro-Bosch forces. President Johnson decided to send the marines and the army to quell the uprising and install another conservative government. At first, the president justified the intervention as necessary to preserve American lives and property. Two days later, on April 30, he explained instead that "people outside the Dominican Republic are seeking to gain control."

U.S. forces trounced the leftists and eventually helped put a conservative, Joaquin Balaguer, in power. But the intervention produced a furious reaction. Bosch complained that "this was a democratic revolution, crushed by the leading democracy in the world." At home, liberal opinion was discouraged that the United States had reverted to force, intervening in a way repugnant to most Latin Americans.

While the intervention in the Dominican Republic helped to dampen additional domestic consensus over foreign affairs, the war in Vietnam dealt it a fatal blow when it grew into a major controversy. At the same time, strains appeared in the NATO alliance, considered the cornerstone of American foreign policy since 1949. French president Charles de Gaulle attempted to restrain what he considered Washington's high-handed control of the alliance. Europeans were unhappy about the Cuban missile crisis of 1962, when the United States and the Soviet Union had approached the brink of war without consulting their allies. In the aftermath of the crisis, France went forward with its own atomic bomb project, and in 1966, the French president announced that his nation's forces would no longer participate in the military arm of NATO. He forced the alliance to move its headquarters from Paris to Brussels. The Johnson administration dismissed de Gaulle as a bitter old man making a futile attempt to restore France's faded glory.

Events outside Europe also challenged American leadership in international affairs. In June 1967 the Six-Day War between Israel and the Arab states of Egypt, Syria, and Jordan further strained America's foreign relations and created a bitter legacy. For ten years, Egypt had smarted from the military embarrassment it suffered at the hands of Israel during the October 1956 Suez conflict. Egypt's president Gamal Abdel Nasser wanted to restore his standing at home by erasing the stain of the Suez loss. With his army resupplied by the Soviet Union and goaded into action by other Arab states, Nasser looked for ways to threaten Israel in the spring of 1967.

He did so by demanding that the United Nations remove its emergency forces from the Sinai Peninsula, which separated Israel and Egypt. Much to his surprise, the United Nations agreed. The Soviet Union urged caution, but Nasser was trapped by his own inflammatory rhetoric. He closed the Strait of Tiran to ships bound for Israel's southern port of Eilat. At this point, the United States stepped in to head off a war. Johnson begged the Israelis not to respond to Nasser until the United States could organize an international flotilla to break the blockade. But the Europeans, fearful that the Arab states would cut off their oil, declined to join the effort.

Faced with what they believed to be a halfhearted American effort on their behalf, the Israelis took matters into their own hands on the morning of

June 5, 1967. In a pre-emptive strike, the Israeli air force destroyed Egyptian planes on the ground while Israeli tanks knifed across the Sinai. Later that day, Jordan's King Hussein ordered his artillery forces to shell the Jewish sector of Jerusalem; in response, the Israelis turned on Jordan and two days later attacked Syria as well. Within six days, Israel had taken the Sinai from Egypt, the West Bank (an area composed of the western bank of the Jordan River and the eastern part of Jerusalem) from Jordan, and the Golan Heights from Syria. After the war, the United Nations called for Israeli withdrawal from captured territories to secure and recognized borders in return for Arab recognition of Israel's right to exist. The United Nations also asked the combatants to settle the Palestinian problem, a constant source of conflict since Israel replaced the British administration in Palestine after World War II. Hundreds of thousands of Palestinians were now left homeless by Israel's conquest of the West Bank and Gaza. Neither Israel nor the Arabs implemented the U.N. resolutions, and the dispute among Israel, the Arab states, and the Palestinians, who wanted a state of their own, became more bitter than ever.

Two weeks after the Six-Day War ended in 1967, Soviet prime minister Alexei Kosygin visited New York for a special session of the U.N. General Assembly, which was called to discuss peace in the Middle East. While in New York, Kosygin accepted Johnson's invitation to meet him at Glassboro State College in southern New Jersey to discuss U.S.-Soviet relations. At this meeting, the first superpower summit since the melancholy conversations between John Kennedy and Nikita Khrushchev in May 1961, the president sought the Soviet leader's

President Lyndon B. Johnson and Soviet premier Alexei Kosygin confer at Glassboro, New Jersey, June 1968. / © Bettmann/CORBIS

help in arranging an end to the war in Vietnam. Kosygin refused because he wanted to show the North Vietnamese that the Soviet Union could do more for them than the People's Republic of China, now the Soviets' rival.

The two men did agree to begin arms control negotiations. However, steps toward détente went no further in the remaining eighteen months of the Johnson administration. In August 1968, Secretary of State Rusk planned to announce that Johnson would repay Kosygin's visit with a trip to the Soviet Union to begin talks on limiting strategic arms. But on August 20, Soviet tanks rumbled into Prague, Czechoslovakia, to crush a Czech experiment in liberalized socialism. Moscow feared that Czech leader Alexander Dubcek secretly wanted to dismantle the one-party state. *Pravda*, the newspaper of the Soviet Communist Party, explained that Communist states could not stand idly by as one of their number fell "into the process of antisocialist degeneration." Western journalists quickly dubbed this position the Brezhnev Doctrine, after Soviet party chair Leonid Brezhnev. In the climate of hostility evoked by the Soviets' crushing Czechoslovakian freedom, Johnson decided he could not afford the political risk of meeting Soviet leaders to discuss arms control. As in previous administrations, genuine détente with the Soviet Union remained only a tantalizing possibility.

Conclusion

By the end of 1968, it appeared that Lyndon Johnson's administration could be characterized largely by its failed aspirations. Johnson had done more than any other president since Franklin Roosevelt to spur Americans to reform their society. The Civil Rights Act of 1964 and the Voting Rights Act of 1965 had helped remove the legal barriers facing African Americans. The War on Poverty reduced hunger and suffering, and Medicare improved access to healthcare. Meanwhile, Johnson's appointees to the Supreme Court helped the Court expand civil liberties and ensure that electoral districts were correctly apportioned. By 1968, however, most of the public's early enthusiasm for Johnson's agenda had been lost. The Vietnam War was draining the government's funds and energy. Too many Great Society programs were underfunded or mired in administrative troubles. Race riots had erupted across the country, and a white backlash arose to block further attempts at social reform.

But it was foreign policy, not domestic affairs, that ultimately led to Lyndon Johnson's personal downfall and to the discrediting of liberalism. As demonstrated by his administration's intervention in the Dominican Republic, Johnson believed in the usefulness of military power for suppressing leftists and communists in the Third World. In this respect, he was fundamentally no different than his predecessors. As Chapter 7 explains, however, Johnson dramatically raised the stakes in Vietnam and received most of the blame for America's failure there.

F U R T H E R • R E A D I N G

On the personalities and policies of the Johnson administration, see Robert Caro, *The Years of Lyndon Johnson: The Path to Power* (1983), *Means of Ascent* (1989), and *Master of the Senate* (2002); Robert Dallek, *Lone Star Rising: Lyndon Johnson, 1908–1960* (1991) and *Flawed Giant: Lyndon Johnson and His Times, 1961–1973* (1998); Doris Kearns, *Lyndon Johnson and the American Dream* (1977); Michael Beschloss, *Taking Charge: The Johnson White House Tapes, 1963–1964* (1997) and *Reaching for Glory: The Secret Johnson White House Tapes, 1964–1965* (2001); Allan M. Matusow, *The Unraveling of America: A History of Liberalism in the 1960s* (1984); Maurice Isserman and Michael Kazin, *America Divided: The Civil Wars of the 1960s* (2000); Robert Alan Goldberg, *Barry Goldwater* (1995). **On Great Society programs,** see James M. Sundquist, *Politics and Policy: The Eisenhower, Kennedy and Johnson Years* (1968); Daniel P Moynihan, *Maximum Feasible Misunderstanding* (1970); David Reimers, *Still the Golden Door: The Third World Comes to America* (2001); John E. Schwarz, *America's Hidden Success: A Reassessment of Public Policy from Kennedy to Reagan* (1988); Michael Katz, *The Undeserving Poor: From the War on Poverty to the War on Welfare* (1989); Taylor Branch, *Pillar of Fire: America in the King Years, 1963–1965* (1998); Nicholas Lemann, *The Promised Land: The Great Black Migration and How It Changed America* (1991); David M. Chalmers, *And the Crooked Places Made Straight: The Struggle for Social Change in the 1960s* (1991); William L. Van Deburg, *New Day in Babylon: The Black Power Movement and American Culture, 1965–1975* (1992). **On the Supreme Court,** see Melvin Urofsky, *The Continuity of Change: The Supreme Court and Individual Liberties, 1953–1986* (1991); Bernard Schwartz, *Super Chief: Earl Warren and His Supreme Court* (1983); Fred Graham, *The Due Process Revolution: The Warren Court's Impact on Criminal Law* (1977). **On foreign affairs,** see H. W. Brands, *Lyndon B. Johnson and the Wages of Globalism: The Limits of American Power* (1995) and *The Foreign Policy of Lyndon Johnson: Beyond Vietnam* (1999); Diane B. Kunz (ed.), *The Diplomacy of The Crucial Decade: American Foreign Relations During the 1960s* (1994); Michael Oren, *Six Days of War: June 1967 and the Making of the Modern Middle East* (2002); Thomas A. Schwartz, *Lyndon Johnson and Europe: In the Shadow of Vietnam* (2003); Thomas Zeiler, *Dean Rusk: Defending the American Mission Abroad* (2000). **On architecture and American culture,** see Lois Craig and the staff of the Federal Architecture Project, *The Federal Presence: Architecture, Politics, and Symbols in United States Government Buildings* (1978); Robert Haddow, *Pavilions of Plenty: Exhibiting American Culture Abroad in the 1950s* (1997); Ron Robin, *Enclaves of America: The Rhetoric of American Political Architecture Abroad, 1900–1965* (1992); Annabel Jane Wharton, *Building the Cold War: Hilton International Hotels and Modern Architecture* (2001).

The Vietnam Nightmare

7

Vietnamese civilians flee the fighting in Hue during the Tet Offensive, February 1968. /
© CORBIS

In May 1964, six months into his term as president, Lyndon Johnson had a heart-to-heart talk about the looming war in Vietnam with Georgia senator Richard Russell, a man he had often relied on for advice when Johnson served in the Senate from 1949 to 1960. The two old friends agreed that Vietnam was "the damn worse mess" they had ever seen. Russell lamented that he did not see "how we're ever going to get out of [Vietnam] without fighting a major war with the Chinese and all of them down there in those rice paddies and jungles." Johnson anguished about the potential human cost of the war. He told Russell that the thought of sending one of his valets, a man with six children, to fight in Vietnam "just makes chills run up my back." But the president saw no way out. His advisers, men with far more experience than he had in foreign affairs, men who had stood beside John F. Kennedy, told him, "[W]e haven't got much choice, that we are treaty-bound [to the government of South Vietnam], that we are there," that a communist victory in South Vietnam "will be a domino that will kick off a whole list of others, that we've just got to prepare for the worst." Seeing nothing but bad alternatives, unsure of his own grasp of foreign affairs, and deathly afraid of appearing weak, Johnson took the fateful steps early in his presidency to commit the United States to fighting a major war in Vietnam.

American involvement in the war in Vietnam grew from a minor issue of little interest to most people into a frightening nightmare, affecting nearly every aspect of American life. The seemingly endless war threw the country into agony, opening deep fissures in many American political, social, cultural, and religious institutions. The war became a major cause of the American people's disillusionment with government and of their abandonment of political liberalism. Chapter 8 explores the culture of protest fostered by the Vietnam War; this chapter focuses on the war itself and its impact on American politics and foreign policy.

From the beginning of America's involvement, during the late 1940s, until the fall of Saigon in 1975, U.S. politicians, diplomats, and military leaders consistently misunderstood the rapidly changing conditions in Vietnam. Their failure to grasp the intensity of revolutionary nationalism in Southeast Asia led to a futile attempt to sustain a noncommunist regime in the southern half of Vietnam. In the devastating war that developed during the 1960s, American bombs, guns, and money ruined Vietnam physically, economically, and socially. The grueling conflict also took a profound toll on many of the American soldiers who fought it.

As the war dragged on, Americans at home became sick of the brutal, inconclusive fighting. The general consensus on U.S. foreign policy that had developed during the early Cold War eroded as the public became increasingly frustrated with the war in Vietnam. Many Americans continued to believe the United States should oppose communism, but they became disillusioned with this war because it made little progress. Other people believed the war should not have been fought at all. These misgivings about Vietnam spread into doubts about the overall principle of containment that had governed American foreign policy since World War II.

In the 1968 presidential election, Americans voted for change, hoping that a new administration could extricate them from the Vietnam morass. But more than four years—and another presidential election—would pass before a cease-fire agreement was signed.

The Growth of America's Commitment to Vietnam, 1945–1964

John Kenneth Galbraith, Harvard economist and U.S. ambassador to India, once asked President John F. Kennedy, "Who is the man in your administration who decides what countries are strategic? I would like to . . . ask him what is so important about this [Vietnamese] real estate in the space age?" The president declined to identify the planner because it was Kennedy himself who attached such importance to Indochina. Like most other high government officials in the years since 1945, Kennedy believed that the containment of communism should be the principal goal of American foreign policy. But because involvement in Vietnam represented only a small part of the larger U.S. strategy of confronting revolutionary nationalists in the postcolonial world, Americans never focused their attention on events in Vietnam until the United States was deeply involved in the war. From Truman through Kennedy, successive administrations gradually enlarged the U.S. commitment to Vietnam, setting the stage for a dramatic escalation under Lyndon Johnson.

Since 1945, the United States had backed alternatives to the Communist Democratic Republic of Vietnam (North Vietnam), established by Ho Chi Minh in Hanoi on September 2, 1945, the day World War II ended in Asia. The Truman administration, preoccupied with more pressing issues in Europe and other parts of Asia, paid little attention to Ho Chi Minh. The United States declined his pleas for diplomatic recognition. During 1946, war broke out between Ho Chi Minh's Vietminh guerrillas and French troops trying to re-establish French colonial power in Indochina. Despite some uneasiness about supporting colonial rule, the Truman administration backed France and its puppet Vietnamese regime. By the end of 1952, Washington was paying 40 percent of the cost of the war.

During the Eisenhower administration, the French required even more American aid. Despite the confident assertion of Secretary of State John Foster Dulles that an additional infusion of $400 million would help France "break the organized body of Communist aggression by the end of the 1955 fighting season," the Vietminh gained strength. By March 1954, the United States was paying 70 percent of the cost of the war. Nevertheless, the Vietminh surrounded the French military position at Dienbienphu, a strategic outpost in the northwest corner of Vietnam. Eisenhower toyed with the idea of ordering an air strike to relieve the French garrison, but ultimately he decided against it. The Vietminh overran Dienbienphu on May 7, 1954.

Although the fall of Dienbienphu was a catastrophe for France, Washington almost welcomed the defeat as a chance to demonstrate American anticommunist resolve. Unlike France, which was tainted as the colonial power, the United States could sponsor a so-called third force, composed of Vietnamese nationalists who opposed both the Communists and the French. This was the approach Eisenhower had in mind when the peace conference convened at Geneva, Switzerland. Although the United States sent representatives to the conference, it was not a signatory to the Geneva Accords. In fact, it soon helped to undermine them.

After the Geneva Accords partitioned Vietnam along the 17th parallel, the United States became more deeply involved in Southeast Asia than ever. In late 1954, the Eisenhower administration sponsored the creation of the Southeast Asia Treaty Organization (SEATO), a military alliance patterned roughly on NATO. Although the southern part of Vietnam never formally joined SEATO, the United States based its involvement in Vietnamese politics partly on its having accepted protection from the alliance. Washington helped set up Ngo Dinh Diem as prime minister of the southern section. In 1955, Diem proclaimed a new nation, the Republic of Vietnam, with himself as president. Neither the communist North nor the anticommunist South recognized each other. In 1956, the United States supported Diem when he refused to allow the nationwide unification elections, which were to include both North and South and which were promised by the Geneva Accords. The United States further assisted Diem in creating the Army of the Republic of Vietnam (ARVN) and a police force.

Eisenhower espoused what came to be known as the domino theory, which said that if Indochina fell to communism, the rest of Southeast Asia would topple like a row of dominoes. General J. Lawton Collins, the special U.S. representative to Vietnam, recommended in 1955 that Washington withdraw support from the haughty, unpopular Diem, a Catholic in a predominantly Buddhist land, but Secretary of State Dulles declared that "the decision to back Diem has gone to the point of no return."

Vowing to exterminate all vestiges of the popular Vietminh in the South, Diem had his army and police arrest twenty thousand members of the movement, killing over one thousand in a span of three years. These actions won praise from American lawmakers looking for signs of a legitimate third force. Senator John F. Kennedy, for example, glorified the new South Vietnam as "the cornerstone of the Free World in Southeast Asia, the keystone to the arch, the finger in the dike." As U.S. military and economic aid created the appearance of stability, the American government and press celebrated South Vietnam as a "success story" in Asia. It was a forlorn hope.

Despite Diem's harassment, the remnants of the Vietminh in the South, assisted by North Vietnam, managed to mount a campaign of their own. On December 20, 1960, they proclaimed a new National Front for the Liberation of Vietnam (NLF) and began guerrilla attacks against the South. By mid-1961, the NLF forces, referred to as the Vietcong by the South Vietnamese, had succeeded in gaining control of 58 percent of the territory of South Vietnam.

When Kennedy became president, he decided that the Eisenhower administration had not done enough to help Diem. And after the catastrophic Bay of Pigs invasion and his chilly summit meeting with Nikita Khrushchev,

Kennedy especially desired some measure of success against communist movements in the Third World. "How do we get moving?" he asked his staff. They suggested using the army's Special Forces, commonly called the Green Berets, against the Vietcong insurrection.

Kennedy responded with an additional $42 million beyond the $220 million already being spent each year on aid to South Vietnam. He sent hundreds more troops to advise the ARVN on how to fight, and he ordered four hundred Green Berets to lead nine thousand mountain tribesmen in an effort to stop infiltration from North Vietnam. He also had the CIA conduct commando raids against North Vietnam. The United States provided heavy weapons to South Vietnamese provincial civil guardsmen (local militias) to use against the Vietcong in rural areas. By late 1961, there were 3,205 American advisers in South Vietnam; that number rose to 9,000 the next year. The American advisers—who did not limit their activities to advising—helped the ARVN move hundreds of thousands of peasants from their homes to relocation centers, or "strategic hamlets."

The massing of peasants into strategic hamlets—separating them from land their families had tilled for generations—made it easier for the South Vietnamese government to hunt for NLF fighters. But it also gave the NLF a weapon in its propaganda war against the Saigon authorities. Once the rural South Vietnamese were relocated, the ARVN bombed and napalmed the countryside to rout out the NLF. Thousands of civilians, including women and children, lost their lives. The NLF told South Vietnamese peasants that the Saigon government was bombing and burning its own citizens. General Paul D. Harkins, in charge of the American advisory forces, dismissed warnings that this indiscriminate bombing only alienated the population from the government in Saigon, saying that napalm (highly flammable petroleum jelly) "really puts the fear of God into the Vietcong, and that is what counts."

While Harkins kept up a stream of optimistic reports flowing back to Washington, American field advisers grew disgusted with what they considered the cowardice and corruption of the ARVN and the South Vietnamese government. By mid-1963, the Kennedy administration, once so supportive of Ngo Dinh Diem, viewed him and the rest of the Ngo family as obstacles to success against the NLF. The Vietnamese peasantry despised the strategic hamlets and hated Diem's connections to the old landlord class. Leaders of the Buddhist sects, to which over two-thirds of South Vietnam's population belonged, condemned Diem's pro-Catholic policies and demanded his resignation. Buddhists and students led street demonstrations against the government in June; the police responded with clubs and tear gas. On June 11, a seventy-three-year-old Buddhist monk, Thich Quang Duc, turned the Buddhist uprising from a local affair into an international crisis by immolating himself in the middle of a busy Saigon intersection. His ritual suicide was captured on film and broadcast around the world. Americans reacted with horror. President Diem's sister-in-law, Madame Ngo Dinh Nhu, provoked further outrage against herself and her family when she scoffed that she would be "happy to provide the mustard for the monks' next barbecues."

The Kennedy administration decided that General Collins had been right eight years before: Diem's family must either change its ways and broaden its

A Buddhist monk commits ritual suicide to protest the policies of the government of South Vietnam's President Ngo Dinh Diem, June 1963. / © Bettmann/CORBIS

government to include nonfamily members and non-Catholics, or be removed from office. That summer, to secure Republican support for his policies, the president appointed an old Republican rival, Henry Cabot Lodge, as the new ambassador to South Vietnam. Lodge had been Eisenhower's ambassador to the United Nations and Nixon's vice-presidential candidate in 1960. The day after his arrival in Saigon, Lodge encouraged a plot by some of the ARVN's top generals to oust the Ngos, but the generals aborted their plans, fearful that Diem had discovered the plot. Meanwhile, American officials in Washington kept up the pressure for change in Saigon.

Diem refused invitations to go quietly into exile. He dug in his heels and turned on the Americans. His brother Nhu hinted darkly at a deal with North Vietnam that would leave the Ngo family in charge of a neutral South Vietnam. At this point, Ambassador Lodge in Saigon, along with several officials in Washington most concerned with Vietnam policy, decided to encourage the dissident ARVN generals to reactivate their plans for a coup. On November 1, 1963, the plotters seized control of the presidential palace and captured Diem and Nhu. Informed in advance of the coup, Ambassador Lodge made no attempt to protect the Ngos or offer them safe conduct out of the country. They were murdered by the plotters early on the morning of November 2, and a new government took over, headed by General Duong Van Minh. Word of Diem's death shook Kennedy, once one of the Vietnamese president's staunchest backers. He seems to have hoped that Diem would go quietly into exile. When the murder was confirmed, Kennedy turned white and retreated from the room.

At first, the existence of a new South Vietnamese government seemed to present an opportunity to wage war against the NLF with renewed vigor, but by January 1964, American officials in Saigon and Washington had grown impatient with General Minh's inability to subdue the Vietcong. Despite later claims by some Kennedy insiders that, had the president lived, he would have reduced the American commitment after the 1964 election, Kennedy remained dedicated to victory until the date of his assassination, three weeks after Diem's death. But he had not formulated a plan. Although he worried about the complete collapse of the South Vietnamese government, he thought "we'd cross that bridge when we came to it," his brother Robert recalled. The historian Fredrik Logevall concluded the following about Kennedy's intentions in the fall of 1963: "Like many politicians, he liked to put off difficult decisions for as long as possible, and he no doubt hoped that the crisis in Indochina would somehow resolve itself, if not before the 1964 election, then after."

Overall, the Kennedy administration left Lyndon Johnson a terrible burden in South Vietnam. By the time Johnson took office, sixteen thousand U.S. Army, Navy, and Marine Corps "advisers" were conducting daily operations against the NLF. Yet this effort produced diminishing returns because the NLF continued to increase its control over the countryside. The more fighting the American soldiers did, the less the ARVN soldiers and officers seemed willing to do. The government of South Vietnam enjoyed little support except from a coterie of ARVN generals, who preferred the ease of life in Saigon to fighting in the field. In the countryside, where over 80 percent of the population resided, the national government had become at best a nuisance and at worst an enemy. While Kennedy pleaded with the American public not to become weary of the war, many Vietnamese peasants had already lost patience and perhaps hope. The hated strategic hamlets and the government's widespread use of napalm and other defoliants proved powerful recruiting agents for the NLF. Johnson would have a difficult time pursuing Kennedy's vision of a victorious Republic of Vietnam.

Soon the new South Vietnamese government of Duong Van Minh proved no more receptive to American advice than had Ngo Dinh Diem and his family. The resistance of the Saigon government to American suggestions for waging the war presented the new Johnson administration with a painful dilemma, one it never resolved. The South Vietnamese authorities seemed incapable of winning the war without American assistance. Yet the more the Americans helped, the less the South Vietnamese did for themselves, thereby encouraging the Americans to get more deeply involved. The growing U.S. presence, in turn, seemed to validate NLF and North Vietnamese claims that the South Vietnamese authorities were American puppets, not genuine nationalists.

On his one trip to the region in 1961, Lyndon Johnson, then vice president, had called Diem "the Winston Churchill of Southeast Asia." When skeptical reporters questioned him about this strange exaggeration, Johnson responded, "He's the only boy we've got out there." Now new to the presidency and trying to follow Kennedy's policies, Johnson relied on the advice of his predecessor's foreign policy experts. Johnson simply wasn't comfortable with international affairs. "Foreigners," he joked, "are not like the folks I am used to." His own combative personality also led Johnson to a deeper commitment in Vietnam. At his very first meeting about Vietnam, on November 24, 1963, he told his staff: "Don't go to bed at night until you have asked yourself, 'Have I done everything I could to further the American effort to assist South Vietnam?'" A few days later, he told the new deputy chief of mission in Saigon, "Lyndon Johnson is not going down as the president who lost Vietnam." Johnson bullied and cajoled his advisers into reaching a consensus on Vietnam.

Almost to a man, Johnson's advisers believed that the United States needed to increase its presence in South Vietnam; pursue the war more vigorously; and, if necessary, replace General Minh with someone more compliant to Washington's desires. The president, facing the upcoming election, favored delay, hoping to keep Vietnam off the nation's front pages and the evening news. The president would not turn his subordinates away from their militant course, but neither did he want to disrupt the consensus that he expected to carry him to victory in the fall. Johnson had another, darker fear of the consequences of reducing the American commitment in Vietnam: he worried that if he reversed course in Vietnam, his advisers and Robert Kennedy, a man he loathed and distrusted, would accuse him of abandoning President Kennedy's militant policies in Vietnam and desert him in favor of a presidential bid by the slain president's brother.

As Johnson procrastinated, U.S. military planners and diplomatic officials moved to alter the military situation in South Vietnam. In late January 1964, the Pentagon helped engineer another coup in Saigon, replacing General Minh with General Nguyen Khanh, who the Americans thought would aggressively fight the war. Johnson ordered Lodge to do what he could to stiffen Khanh's resolve.

In June 1964 some of the president's principal advisers floated the idea of seeking a congressional resolution supporting American air or ground action against North Vietnam. Six weeks later, after the raucous Republican convention had nominated Senator Barry Goldwater for president, two controversial incidents off the coast of North Vietnam justified introduction of such a congressional resolution and provided an excuse for air strikes by U.S. forces against North Vietnamese naval bases and oil-storage facilities. Two U.S. destroyers, the *Maddox* and the *C. Turner Joy*, had been conducting so-called De Soto patrols in support of South Vietnamese naval operations along the North Vietnamese coast bordering the Gulf of Tonkin (see Map 7.1). During these patrols, American ships sailing inside the twelve-mile territorial limit claimed by North Vietnam conducted surveillance against North Vietnamese coastal radar installations. The surveillance was designed to force the North Vietnamese to activate their radar devices, revealing their location. The *Maddox* and the *C. Turner Joy* would then notify accompanying South Vietnamese patrol boats of the positions of the North Vietnamese installations, and the South Vietnamese boats would attack.

Map 7.1 ▶
Southeast Asia and the Vietnam War

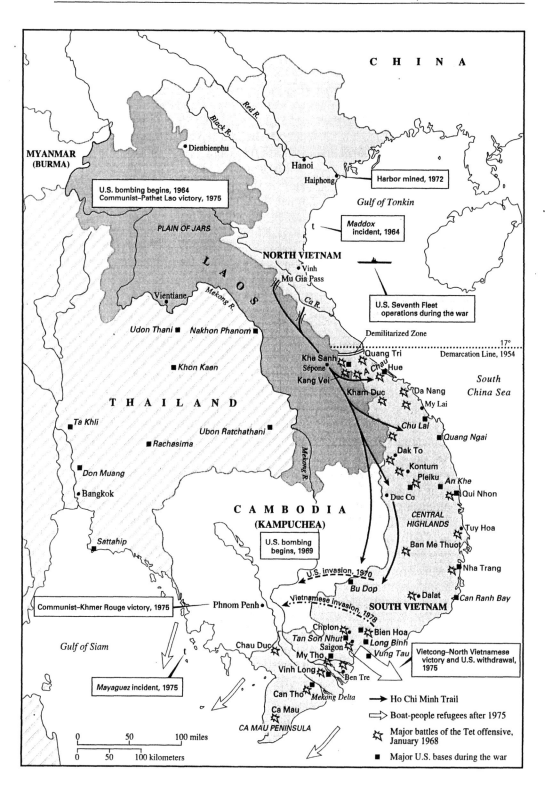

C H I N A

MYANMAR
(BURMA)

Red R.

Black R.

Dienbienphu

Hanoi

Haiphong

Harbor mined, 1972

U.S. bombing begins, 1964
Communist–Pathet Lao victory, 1975

Gulf of Tonkin

PLAIN OF JARS

Maddox
incident, 1964

NORTH VIETNAM

Vinh

Mu Gia Pass

Vientiane

Mekong R.

L A O S

Ca R.

U.S. Seventh Fleet
operations during the war

Udon Thani ■   ■ Nakhon Phanom ■

Demilitarized Zone

Quang Tri

17°

Demarcation Line, 1954

Kha Sanh

Sépone

A Chau

Hue

*South
China Sea*

■ Khon Kaen

Kang Vei

Kham Duc

Da Nang

My Lai

T H A I L A N D

Ta Khli ■

Ubon Ratchathani ■

Chu Lai

Quang Ngai

■ Rachasima

Mekong R.

Dak To

Don Muang ■

Kontum

Pleiku

An Khe

Bangkok

Duc Co

Qui Nhon

C A M B O D I A
(KAMPUCHEA)

*CENTRAL
HIGHLANDS*

Tuy Hoa

Sattahip ■

U.S. bombing
begins, 1969

Ban Me Thuot

Nha Trang

Communist–Khmer Rouge victory, 1975

Phnom Penh ●

U.S. invasion, 1970

Bu Dop

Dalat

Can Ranh Bay

Vietnamese invasion, 1978

SOUTH VIETNAM

Gulf of Siam

Chau Duc

Cholon

Bien Hoa

Tan Son Nhut

Long Binh

My Tho

Saigon

Vung Tau

Vietcong–North Vietnamese
victory and U.S. withdrawal,
1975

Mayaguez incident, 1975

Vinh Long

Ben Tre

Can Tho

Mekong Delta

Ca Mau

CA MAU PENINSULA

→ Ho Chi Minh Trail

⇨ Boat-people refugees after 1975

☆ Major battles of the Tet offensive,
January 1968

■ Major U.S. bases during the war

0   50   100 miles

0   50   100 kilometers

The De Soto patrols provoked the North Vietnamese navy to attack the *Maddox* on the night of August 2, 1964. Two nights later, in heavy seas, the commander of the *C. Turner Joy* thought his ship was under attack and ordered his crew to return fire. They did so, but hit nothing—probably because no North Vietnamese patrol boats were in the area and there had been no hostile fire. The assault on the *Maddox* did actually occur, although Secretary of Defense McNamara was not telling the truth when he claimed, "[T]he *Maddox* was operating in international waters and was carrying out a routine patrol of the type we carry out all over the world at all times."

McNamara's false claims carried the day in Congress, which passed the Tonkin Gulf Resolution on August 7, 1964. The House voted unanimously in favor of this resolution, and in the Senate, only two members voted against it. The resolution authorized the president to "take all necessary measures to repel any armed attack against the forces of the United States and to prevent further aggression." The resolution also called for "all necessary steps, including the use of armed force, to assist" any member of SEATO that asked for American military aid. Although South Vietnam was not in fact a member of SEATO, the alliance had agreed to extend its protection to South Vietnam.

The resolution's extraordinarily broad grant of authority to the nation's chief executive included no time limit. Later, Johnson would use it to justify a greatly enlarged American presence. J. William Fulbright, an Arkansas Democrat and the chair of the Senate Foreign Relations Committee, who presented the resolution on the Senate floor, came to regret his support for the resolution. Within a year, he opposed further U.S. participation in the war. He later lamented that he was "hoodwinked and taken in by the president of the United States, the secretary of state and the chief of staff and the secretary of defense," who had lied to him about what happened in the Gulf of Tonkin.

The Tonkin Gulf Resolution effectively removed Vietnam from the political debate during the 1964 election campaign. Goldwater fully supported the resolution and the limited air raid that Johnson had ordered against North Vietnam. For his part, Johnson stood serenely in the middle of the road on Vietnam. Most people believed that he wanted to keep the United States out of a full-scale shooting war while preventing a communist victory. His major campaign speech on Vietnam sounded moderate but left considerable room for greater American involvement at a later date. He said that "only as a last resort" would he "start dropping bombs around that are likely to involve American boys in a war in Asia with 700 million Chinese." He could not guarantee the future, he said, but "we are not going north and drop bombs at this stage of the game, and we are not going south and run out and leave it for the Communists to take over."

The Americanization of the War, 1965

The year 1965 marked the point of no return for the United States in Vietnam. By July, Johnson had made a series of fateful decisions that transformed the fighting in Vietnam into an American war. Nevertheless, throughout the period of gradually increasing American military involvement in Vietnam, the Johnson administration waged a limited war. Johnson wanted to break the will of the North Vietnamese without provoking a military response from the Soviet Union or China. Officials believed that limiting the extent of the war would lessen the impact on the American public, making it easier to sustain political support for the war. It proved nearly impossible, however, to wage a limited war effectively. Every step up the ladder of escalation alarmed potential adversaries abroad and created anxiety at home. At the same time, efforts to restrict the scope of the war relieved pressure on North Vietnam and generated opposition from a different group of Americans: those who wanted to defeat North Vietnam quickly with the use of massive military force.

In the summer of 1965, Johnson took the final steps toward committing 100,000 U.S. ground troops to the war. The administration would no longer maintain the fiction that American soldiers were acting only as advisers; U.S. forces began conducting large-scale operations on their own, without accompanying ARVN units. As the South Vietnamese government grew continually weaker, the succession of military regimes nearly drove Johnson into apoplexy. News of yet another uprising provoked him to explode, "I don't want to hear any more." One of the president's assistants suggested that the coat of arms of the Saigon government display a turnstile.

In this atmosphere, Pentagon planners concluded that bombing the North would help save the South. General Maxwell Taylor, the ambassador to South Vietnam, told Johnson early in 1965 that air raids would "inject some life into the dejected spirits" of South Vietnam. The president, more prescient than some of his military advisers, worried that "this guerrilla war cannot be won from the air." Sustained bombing of North Vietnam began within a month of Johnson's 1965 inauguration. On February 7, 1965, a company of Vietcong soldiers attacked the American barracks at Pleiku, in the central highlands of South Vietnam, killing eight Americans, wounding 126, and destroying ten planes. Although the assault hardly surprised American officials, they believed that this attack on American forces would further undermine the shaky morale of the South Vietnamese government. Pleiku therefore provided the justification for sustained bombing of the North. Johnson first ordered a single retaliatory mission, similar to the one undertaken after the Gulf of Tonkin incident the previous August. But this retaliatory mission did not stop calls for harsher action. On February 13, Johnson authorized Operation Rolling Thunder, an extensive campaign of sustained bombing against the North. In April, American and South Vietnamese pilots flew 3,600 sorties against targets in the North—fuel depots, railroad yards, bridges, power plants, and munitions factories.

The initial results of the campaign disappointed the air-war advocates. Despite the expectations of Pentagon planners, the North Vietnamese quickly adapted to round-the-clock bombing. There were few industrial targets in the North, and the North Vietnamese quickly rebuilt destroyed bridges. The thick jungle provided cover for thousands of North Vietnamese men, women, and children carrying supplies by hand and bicycle to the South, along what became known as the Ho Chi Minh Trail. The North Vietnamese and NLF fighters did not capitulate, and the South Vietnamese government did not become stronger. American military officers urged even more air attacks. In response, Johnson relaxed restrictions on targets over the next several months.

Since Operation Rolling Thunder resulted in little more than temporary setbacks for the Vietcong, the American commander in South Vietnam, General William Westmoreland, called for direct American ground action throughout the South. There is no solution, he wrote the president, "other than to put our own finger in the dike." But Johnson still resisted a full Americanization of the war, and at a speech at Johns Hopkins University in April 1965, he offered "unconditional discussions" with North Vietnam to end the war.

In early May, McNamara, Taylor, and Westmoreland acknowledged that bombing alone would not win the war. They concluded that the United States had to fight the war on the ground, in the South, if the Saigon government were to have a chance of surviving. Westmoreland wanted another 150,000 troops deployed to fight the ground war throughout the South. Secretary of Defense McNamara cut Westmoreland's request to 100,000 troops and forwarded it to the president. Throughout July, Johnson consulted with his principal advisers on the future course to take in Vietnam. In these meetings, Johnson appeared skeptical of the usefulness of committing additional American troops, but he was unwilling to accept an NLF victory. The only course he could tolerate, therefore, was a continued gradual increase in the American commitment—the very policy that had failed over the previous year.

During the July 1965 meetings, he asked General Earle Wheeler, chair of the Joint Chiefs of Staff, "Tell me this. What will happen if we put in 100,000 more men and then two, three years later you tell me you need 500,000 more? How would you expect me to respond to that? And what makes you think Ho Chi Minh won't put in another 100,000 and match us every bit of the way?" To which Wheeler responded, "This means greater bodies of men from North Vietnam, which will allow us to cream them." Johnson's fear proved prophetic, and Wheeler's reply revealed the folly of the American commanders' war methods.

Eventually, nearly all the president's advisers concurred that adding 100,000 Americans to the 90,000 troops already in Vietnam would help stabilize the situation without causing a backlash in Congress or with the public. Most agreed to reject the request from the Joint Chiefs of Staff to call up the reserves. Such a move would dramatically raise the stakes, both at home and abroad, and would perhaps necessitate a presidential declaration of a state of emergency and a request to Congress for several billion dollars. In that event, Johnson worried, the Great Society would cease, and worse, "Hanoi would ask the Chinese and the Soviets for increased aid."

At the end of July, Johnson announced the plan to send an additional 100,000 troops. That afternoon, Democratic Senate majority leader Mike Mansfield wrote Johnson that most of the public approved of what he was doing because they trusted him as their president, but "not necessarily out of any understanding or sympathy with policies on Vietnam." He thought people backed Johnson for now because they sensed that "your objective [is] not to get in too deeply."

Fighting the War, 1966–1967

During 1966 and 1967, the number of U.S. troops in South Vietnam rose from 190,000 to 535,000 (see Figure 7.1). Yet even this size force could not prevail against the NLF and in fact contributed to the further deterioration of the government and armed forces of South Vietnam. The Americans were trying to apply tactics learned in World War II and Korea to a very different kind of struggle, against a guerrilla force. The "army concept" that had developed over the past twenty-five years held that wars could be won with advanced materiel and technology—aerial bombardment, tank attacks, artillery, electronic detection fences—rather than with soldiers armed with rifles. These principles seemed to make sense for a productive, industrial society that relied on conscripts. If machines could substitute for soldiers, the casualties would decline and public support would continue. But advocates of a high-tech war misunderstood the realities of the war in Vietnam. The army concept removed the

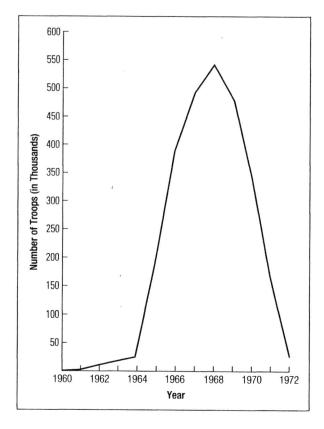

Figure 7.1
Levels of U.S. Troops in Vietnam (at year's end)

American forces from direct contact with the people they were ostensibly helping and ultimately contributed to the loss of the war.

Like most successful officers who had fought in Europe during World War
II, General Westmoreland believed that American military technology could
overwhelm any potential adversary; he therefore followed a strategy of attrition,
or wearing down the enemy by use of massive firepower. Westmoreland never
fully grasped that the NLF and the North Vietnamese fought a guerrilla war, in
which they, not the Americans, determined their level of casualties. Persuaded
that American technology could carry the day, Westmoreland used helicopters
to send American units into the countryside on search-and-destroy missions to
root out and kill enemy soldiers. Americans would fly out in the morning, pursue the Vietcong in firefights, count the dead, and return to their bases in the
evening. The measure of success became "body counts" rather than territory
captured, which was the standard in earlier wars. The tactic encouraged abuses.
Local commanders, hoping to please their superiors in Saigon, inflated the death
figures. Reliance on body counts offered an incentive to shoot first and ask no
questions. One marine remembered that during his first night on patrol, "about
fifty people shot this old guy. Everybody claimed they shot him. He got shot
'cause he started running. It was an old man running to tell his family. . . . Any
Vietnamese out at night was the enemy." Many American GIs expressed contempt for all Vietnamese, regardless of whether they were friendly or hostile.
Thrust into an unfamiliar country with a culture few Americans understood,
troops used racist slurs like "gook," "slope," or "slant-eye" to refer to all Vietnamese. The U.S. army did develop rules of engagement designed to prevent indiscriminate shooting of noncombatants. But the confusion of a war without
clearly defined front lines, with enemy forces who looked like civilians, with the
presence of civilians on the battlefield, and with the demands of producing a satisfactory body count led to atrocities.

Before U.S. troops descended from their helicopters, giant B-52 bombers
and smaller fighter jets pounded the battlefields. The United States dropped
more bombs on Vietnam, a country about the size of California, each month
than fell on all of Europe during all of World War II. But the air raids alerted
the Vietcong and North Vietnamese forces that the Americans were on the
way, giving them time to withdraw or to dive into hundreds of miles of tunnels
to protect themselves from the massive firepower. Also, the Vietcong used unexploded American bombs and artillery shells as weapons against the Americans. The enemy developed shrewd booby traps using these unexploded
bombs, killing or wounding thousands of inexperienced American troops. In
1966, over one thousand American soldiers died of wounds caused by booby
traps, and in the first six months of the following year, 17 percent of all American casualties resulted from mines or booby traps.

The NLF kept gaining strength on the ground, using guerrilla tactics developed earlier by the Vietminh. They avoided firefights where they could, forcing the Americans to waste enormous energy and materiel for meager gains.
They continued political organization in the countryside, even as American
bombers flew overhead. Despite such obvious problems, the United States
Army continued to rely on search-and-destroy operations. The largest oc-

Infantrymen from the 1st Cavalry Division jump from an army helicopter during a search-and-destroy operation in South Vietnam, July 1967. / © Bettmann/CORBIS

curred in late 1966 and early 1967. In one such mission, which lasted from September to November 1966, twenty-two thousand U.S. and ARVN troops, supported by B-52 bombers and massive artillery fire, pursued the NLF northwest of Saigon. In another search-and-destroy operation, from February through May 1967, American B-52s reduced the South Vietnamese landscape to the eerie bleakness of the moon, making hundreds of square miles uninhabitable by the peasants the Americans were supposedly helping. Americans entering villages to root out the Vietcong sometimes carried out so-called Zippo raids, igniting the peasants' thatched huts with tracer bullets, flamethrowers, and cigarette lighters to deny sanctuary to the enemy.

Such actions not only enraged the peasantry but also shocked Americans watching the carnage on the evening news. Yet this enormous firepower failed to eradicate the Vietcong, who would simply melt away until an assault stopped. One reporter likened each blow to "a sledgehammer on a floating cork; somehow the cork refused to stay down."

All the while, North Vietnamese commander General Vo Nguyen Giap, the victor at Dienbienphu, had the Americans playing into his hands as he waged a guerrilla war. Giap, one of the most militantly anti-French members of Ho Chi Minh's inner circle, had created an army of 250,000 in the years 1946–1954. He developed a theory of protracted war, in which a nation could throw off outside domination by patiently wearing down the colonial power, first with guerrilla raids and later with conventional battles. He welcomed the

American search-and-destroy operations, since they took American forces away from the heavily populated coastal plain, where the NLF and the North gained strength among the population. As the Americans engaged in inconclusive battles in the interior, they paid less attention to "pacification," the effort to bind the peasantry to the government in Saigon.

If anything, the Saigon government lost even more support among the South Vietnamese while the American war devastated the countryside. As part of their effort to deny sanctuary to the enemy, American forces used giant transport planes to spray trees with defoliants. Between 1962 and 1972, the Americans dropped over 1 million pounds of toxic chemicals such as Agent Orange over South Vietnam, destroying more than half its forests. Some American crews jokingly adopted the motto Only You Can Prevent Forests. But many crewmembers later suffered serious health problems, probably from contact with the toxins they dropped.

The effect of this tactic on the crops of South Vietnamese farmers—the ostensible beneficiaries of the war effort—was immediate and devastating. Deadly defoliants dropped from planes onto a suspected Vietcong area in the afternoon would soon drift over friendly villages; by the next morning, fruit fell from the trees and the leaves on rubber plants turned brown and broke off. Farmers blamed the Americans for the loss of their crops, and they feared the defoliants would harm animal and human life as well. The birth of a physically or mentally impaired infant was often blamed on the defoliation campaigns. American forces also used poisons to destroy the rice crop grown in Vietcong areas, expecting the hungry enemy to emerge and fight. The theory overlooked the NLF's practice of buying or taking rice from the peasants; in effect, the Americans ruined ten pounds of rice grown by friendly farmers for every pound of Vietcong rice that they destroyed. South Vietnam, once an exporter of rice, began importing it from neighboring countries (and even the United States) as the war ground on.

The havoc in the countryside forced hundreds of thousands of peasants to flee their homes. Between 1964 and 1969, more than 4 million South Vietnamese—one-fourth of the population—were refugees at one time or another. Those who remained on their land often did so only because they feared the Vietcong would redistribute it if they were gone. Many of those who fled the terror from the skies, the defoliants, the artillery barrages, and the Zippo raids swarmed to cities that

Vo Nguyen Giap commanded the Vietminh forces that defeated the French forces in the war from 1946 to 1954. As defense minister of the Democratic Republic of Vietnam (North Vietnam) he refined his theory of protracted war to force the United States to leave Vietnam. / © CORBIS Sygma

had neither room nor facilities for them; others languished in squalid refugee camps.

The population of Saigon, under 500,000 in the 1950s, swelled to 1.5 million by the mid-1960s. The capital and other cities near American installations—Danang, Cam Ranh Bay, Hue, to name a few—changed from Asian commercial centers, conducting business in traditional ways, to army boomtowns. Seedy bars and brothels sprang up near American bases, with women and girls as young as thirteen prostituting themselves for the GIs. Over 100,000 Amerasian children were born of liaisons between American soldiers and Vietnamese women. These children were scorned by the Vietnamese, and after the Americans departed, they suffered terrible privation.

The presence of over 500,000 Americans in Vietnam transformed the Vietnamese economy. Production of food and rubber fell as the Vietnamese concentrated on servicing the newcomers. At first, the GIs paid cash in U.S. dollars. Prices zoomed 170 percent in

American fire sometimes hurt friendly South Vietnamese. A father carries his child wounded by American soldiers who mistook him for a Vietcong fighter. / Phillip Jones Griffiths/Magnum·

1966 and 1967, and many Vietnamese could no longer afford the basic necessities of life. To halt the inflation, the U.S. army started paying its soldiers in scrip, which could only be used to purchase consumer goods on U.S. bases. Vietnamese entrepreneurs responded by importing watches, tape recorders, motorcycles, radios, and the like, to sell to local people who worked for the Americans and were paid in South Vietnamese currency.

Corruption, already a problem before the Americans arrived en masse, vastly increased in 1966. The South Vietnamese government rented space to the Americans at exorbitant prices. South Vietnamese officials took bribes from contractors wishing to do business with U.S. agencies, including military bases and rural development organizations. Others demanded payment for licenses, permits, visas, and passports. Some Saigon officials traded in opium, and many engaged in the flourishing black market. Everything was for sale— U.S. government scrip, South Vietnamese piasters, Scotch whiskey, watches, hand grenades, rifles.

Americans were often aware of the corruption that eroded South Vietnamese society, but Westmoreland thought that curing it would alarm the very government the United States wanted to help. Some midranking American officials wanted to threaten the government of Saigon with loss of aid if it did not remove corrupt officials. Westmoreland overruled such advice, fearing that it would only annoy the government, without producing appropriate changes, or perhaps lead to the government's collapse.

By late 1967, the buildup had not won the war. McNamara's comment in late 1966 that he could "see the light at the end of the tunnel in Vietnam" inspired the rueful rejoinder that what he had glimpsed was the headlight of another train engineered by Ho Chi Minh. Thirteen thousand U.S. servicemen had been killed. Only the lowest American goal—denying a victory to the NLF—had been realized, and continued success was not assured. Other American war aims—creating a stable South Vietnamese government capable of waging the war on its own and winning the loyalty of its people, and forcing the North to quit—had become more elusive than ever. As American involvement intensified, South Vietnamese society dissolved. People either became dependents of the United States or went underground to join the NLF. The South Vietnamese government, once the bedrock of Washington's strategy to defeat communism in Southeast Asia, slipped into dependence and obstructionism.

Working-Class War and the Draft

Although the fighting took place far from the United States, the war deeply affected the way many Americans lived their lives. Military service became an important, life-changing experience for over 2 million American men. Combat soldiers often encountered racial tensions, boredom, drugs, and brutality against the Vietnamese. Some soldiers accepted these unpleasant realities as part of the hardships of military service, but many bore psychological and emotional scars for years after they returned from Vietnam. Nearly 80 percent of the U.S. troops in Vietnam served as support personnel, not combat troops, and their service was far less traumatic. But even those Americans who did not fight were changed by the war. Back home, millions of young men spent a substantial part of their late adolescence or young adulthood wondering whether they would be conscripted and seeking ways to avoid participating in the fighting. Far more men did not go to Vietnam than went, but the war created deep divisions among people of an entire generation. Those who fought in the war often resented those who did not, and people who did not go to Vietnam sometimes treated those who did with scorn, pity, or condescension.

Unlike World War II, for which the armed forces needed nearly every able-bodied American man, the military effort in Vietnam required less than half the eligible population. Of the 27 million available men between the ages of nineteen and twenty-six, 16 million never served in the armed forces. Of the approximately 11 million who did, 9 million enlisted more or less voluntarily, and 2.2 million were drafted under the terms of the Selective Service Act of 1947. A total of about 2.8 million men, along with 6,400 women, actually saw service in Vietnam between 1961 and 1973.

Although the draft took only about 10 percent of the men subject to its call, the Selective Service affected the lives of nearly everybody. As the war became more dangerous and American casualties rose to three hundred dead per week, many young men wanted to reduce the risk to their personal safety. Several options were available: deferments for marriage (dropped in 1965), fatherhood, or student status; enlistment in the National Guard or the reserves; enlistment in the armed forces, with a promise to serve in places other than Vietnam; and service in noncombat zones in Vietnam.

The wealthy and educated, those most aware of the intricacies of the system, knew best how to avoid the most dangerous duty. The military force that the United States sent to Vietnam consisted disproportionately of men from working-class and poor backgrounds. The best estimate indicates that 25 percent of the force was poor, 55 percent were working class, and 20 percent were middle class. Such discrepancies produced a distressing inequity in the make-up of the forces bearing the brunt of the heaviest fighting. They came from inner cities, working-class suburbs, rural areas, and medium-size towns. One enlisted man recalled who served and who did not from his small Kansas hometown: "All but two of a dozen high school buddies would eventually serve in Vietnam and all were of working class families, while I know of not a single middle class son of the town's businessmen, lawyers, doctors or ranchers from my high school graduating class who experienced the Armageddon of our generation." The fighting men were far younger than those who fought in earlier wars. The average age of the American force during World War II was twenty-six; in Vietnam, the average age was nineteen.

The Selective Service system appeared corrupt and demeaning to many of those who faced conscription. One young inductee who had the job of filing case histories at a local draft board had his eyes opened observing the ruses others used to avoid being called up. He telephoned his mother and reported, "The whole set-up is corrupt. I don't need to be here! I don't need to be here! I don't need to be here! I simply didn't need to be drafted!" Nonetheless, he went to Vietnam and became one of the fifty-eight thousand men who died. His feelings that the draft was arbitrary and unfair were common; a Harris poll concluded that most Americans believed the men who went to Vietnam were "suckers, having risked their lives in the wrong war, in the wrong place, in the wrong time."

Three-quarters of the 16 million men who did not serve in Vietnam admitted that they had changed their life plans to stay away from Vietnam, and a majority (55 percent) said that they actively took steps to avoid the draft. Even if drafted, a man had to be physically fit before he could be inducted. Some young men had their family doctor prepare false documents to keep them out of the service

A network of draft counselors, initially sponsored by churches and other pacifist organizations, arose to advise young men of their rights under the Selective Service Act and of legal ways to avoid induction. After the 1965 Supreme Court ruling in *United States v. Seegar* the conscientious objector status was available to anyone with a "sincerely founded reason" for opposing war. Before then, only members of recognized pacifist sects—such as Mennonites, Quakers, Jehovah's Witnesses, Brethren—had been entitled to register as

A man protesting the draft (conscription) stands in the doorway of the national headquarters of the Selective Service system, April 1967. / © Bettmann/CORBIS

conscientious objectors. After *Seegar*, draft counselors advised young men on how to present their antiwar beliefs in a persuasive way:

Some men simply refused induction or tried to evade their draft boards. About 209,000 men were accused of a draft-related offense, but only 25,000 were indicted, and only 4,000 received prison sentences. Even those who entered the military sometimes refused to accept service in Vietnam. About 12,000 men went absent without leave (AWOL) to escape an assignment to Vietnam. About 50,000 deserters or accused draft offenders took flight during the war, with 30,000 of them going to Canada. Many of these men came home quietly over the next decade, but 11,000 remained fugitives until 1977, when President Jimmy Carter proclaimed a pardon.

For the men who went to Vietnam, life in the armed forces bore little resemblance to the experiences of their fathers or older brothers in World War II and the Korean War—and no likeness at all to the idealized versions of those wars presented in movies and television programs. For combat soldiers, Vietnam was sometimes a demoralizing, brutal experience. One day, a young man would be in the relatively familiar surroundings of a stateside military base; the next day, after eighteen hours on an airplane, he would find himself in the alien landscape of Vietnam, in a situation that provoked both frustration and terror. The enemy, often indistinguishable from the local population, could materialize suddenly from the jungle and attack with horrible efficiency. It was especially difficult to maintain the troops' morale when they saw more and more lives lost for little or no gain.

The difficulties were compounded by the military's personnel policy. Unlike earlier wars, in which soldiers served "for the duration," soldiers in Vietnam had a one-year tour of duty, spread over thirteen months, with thirty days' leave for "rest and recreation." A mixture of demographics, politics, and military management techniques prompted this arrangement. Because the pool of available soldiers far exceeded the number needed, keeping 500,000 men at the front while allowing all others to steer free of battle would cause resentment among those who fought and would erode public support for the war. Therefore, the military limited time in service and continually rotated the forces.

According to General Westmoreland, establishing end-of-tour dates helped boost morale and gave each soldier a goal. In fact, however, GIs' goal often became self-preservation: men approaching the end of their tours became reluctant to fight. No one wanted to be killed or wounded, but risking death or injury a few weeks before mustering out appeared especially pointless. One commander called the twelve-month tour "the worst personnel policy in history." To make matters worse, units did not stay together throughout their tours, which increased soldiers' and officers' feelings of isolation. Troops killed or wounded were replaced by newcomers, whose tour of duty expired later than that of the other men in their unit. Men mostly relied on themselves.

The lack of rapport between commanders and soldiers sometimes made personal hostilities difficult to control. The murder of officers by enlisted men—often with a fragmentation grenade or other anonymous weapon—became frequent enough, especially late in the war, to earn its own slang name: "fragging." The armed forces were susceptible to the same racial tensions that plagued American society as a whole. As these animosities grew in the late sixties, racial divisions rose within the armed forces. Many black soldiers had no white friends in the ostensibly integrated units. Inevitably, some of the violence between GIs took on a racial tone. These tensions became especially pronounced after the Johnson administration decided to de-escalate the war and open peace negotiations in 1968. From that point onward, more and more U.S. servicemen and -women came to see the war as pointless.

News of atrocities against the Vietnamese, whom some GIs referred to as "gooks," undermined support for the soldiers back home. In this long war against an enemy that struck without warning and then instantly melted away, soldiers sometimes disregarded the so-called rules of engagement that regulated behavior toward the enemy. Once the body count became the principal means of measuring success in the war, some soldiers became excessive and brutal. A few men chopped off the ears of dead Vietnamese for trophies. They would "take [their] dog-tag chain and fill [it] up with ears," one infantryman recalled. "If we were movin' through the jungle, they'd just put the bloody ear on the chain and stick the ear in their pocket and keep on going. Wouldn't take time to dry it off. Then when we got back, they would nail 'em up on the walls of our hootch, you know, as a trophy." Some GIs gave up the nearly impossible task of distinguishing the Vietcong from uninvolved civilians; besides burning peasants' houses, they shot any Vietnamese they saw. "If it moves, it's VC [Vietcong]" became a common slogan for American soldiers. The most dramatic atrocity of the war occurred in March 1968, when American soldiers massacred more than five hundred unarmed Vietnamese villagers, mostly women and children, at the hamlet of My Lai. The military managed to keep the incident secret until the next year. Americans were uniformly horrified when it was revealed, although like so much else about Vietnam, public opinion about the incident was divided. Some expressed sympathy for the young American soldiers, feeling that they had succumbed to the stress of combat. A smaller but significant group saw My Lai as a symbol of all the reasons why the United States should quit Vietnam.

To escape the fear and absurdity of a war without front lines, leadership, or clear goals, some soldiers turned to drugs. Marijuana, opium, and heroin were freely available and inexpensive in the cities of Vietnam because officials of the South Vietnamese government engaged in the drug trade. So did the CIA, which used profits from drugs to finance a secret counterinsurgency program in the South Vietnamese highlands and along the Laotian border. Soldiers used drugs not only on the base but also in the field. One infantryman who served from mid-1967 to mid-1968 remembered that "in the field most of the guys stayed high. Lots of them couldn't face it. In a sense, if you was high it seemed like a game you was in. You didn't take it serious. It stopped a lot of nervous breakdowns."

Overall, soldiers who experienced combat in Vietnam developed greater psychological and emotional difficulties than did the 80 percent who served in support roles. The latter readjusted relatively readily to American society once they returned home. Surveys taken ten and twenty years after the Vietnam War indicated that the subsequent careers of noncombat soldiers developed similarly to those of men who had not gone to Vietnam. The picture was darker and much more complex for combat veterans. Many experienced post-traumatic stress disorder. Symptoms included drug and alcohol abuse, difficulty sustaining family relationships, trouble finding and maintaining employment, violence, and suicide.

Rising Dissent and the Collapse of the Cold War Consensus

In addition to the soldiers in Vietnam, at least one man in Washington approached nervous exhaustion as the war expanded: President Johnson. The war had gone on longer than his military advisers predicted, and still there was no clear end in sight. Continued war threatened to wreck his cherished Great Society, and it cast doubt on his chances for re-election in 1968.

Johnson's personal crisis was deepened by mounting criticism of the war from former supporters. Arkansas senator J. William Fulbright, chair of the Senate Foreign Relations Committee and an old friend from Johnson's days as majority leader, was among the first moderate public figures to dissent. In late 1965, Fulbright undertook a crash course in American policy toward Indochina, and the following February his committee opened televised hearings on the war. Numerous foreign policy experts told the committee that the administration had headed down the wrong road in Vietnam. George F. Kennan, one of the architects of containment, worried that the "unbalanced concentration of resources and attention" on Vietnam diverted Washington from what he considered to be the proper focus of U.S. foreign policy—Europe. Fulbright expressed disbelief at Secretary of State Dean Rusk's repeated assertions that "this is a clear case of international Communist aggression." Fulbright thought that most of the world viewed the conflict in Vietnam as "a civil war in which outside parties have become involved." Two months later, Fulbright observed that the war had damaged the Great Society and hurt the nation's relations with the Soviet Union and Europe. He lamented "the arrogance of power," which he defined as a "psychological need that nations seem to have to prove that they are bigger, stronger, better than other nations."

While Fulbright and about a dozen other senators dissented from escalation of the war in 1966, more potent opposition to the war arose outside the government in the form of a citizens' peace movement. Diverse groups—peace liberals, pacifists, and social revolutionaries—joined in opposition to the war. Beginning in 1965, these groups organized "teach-ins," in which they lectured college audiences on the evils of the war. The peace movement also sponsored the 1967 "Vietnam Summer" of protests against the war and the 1968 "dump Johnson" campaign, which sought to replace the president with someone who would extricate the United States from the endless war.

Some members of the peace movement agreed with Kennan that Vietnam was diverting American attention from more serious issues. Long-time Socialist leader Norman Thomas acknowledged that more pressing problems were clamoring for attention, "but it is a practical and emotional absurdity to think that the government or people can or will deal with these and other pressing questions until it stops the war in Vietnam." By 1967, even the least radical participants in the peace movement believed that, as Seymour Melman of the Committee for a Sane Nuclear Policy (SANE) put it, "policy change now requires institutional change as well." When Students for a Democratic Society, a New Left group (see Chapter 8), organized the Vietnam Summer in 1967, one Detroit organizer reported, "I find that I am not really working here to 'end the war in Vietnam.' . . . I am working here to make people feel Vietnam, to make them realize that it is part of a pattern which oppresses them, as well as Vietnamese peasants." Along with opposition to the war, a general dissatisfaction with American government began to spread.

Public antiwar activism surged in the spring of 1967. Martin Luther King, Jr., who previously had expressed quiet misgivings about the war, openly broke with the Johnson administration. He called for de-escalation, helped organize a new antiwar group (Negotiation Now!), and endorsed the Vietnam Summer. On April 15, 1967, crowds of one hundred thousand in New York and fifty thousand in San Francisco heard speakers from both the antiwar and the civil rights movements call for an end to the war and a recommitment to the goal of racial equality at home. Johnson grew alarmed at the possibility that King and pediatrician Benjamin Spock, now an antiwar activist, might run for president and vice president, respectively, in 1968.

Federal agencies constantly observed, infiltrated, and harassed antiwar groups. The FBI compared Senator Fulbright's position during the 1966 Vietnam hearings to those taken by the Communist Party. The CIA infiltrated antiwar groups such as Women Strike for Peace, the Washington Peace Center, SANE, the Congress of Racial Equality (CORE), the War Resisters League, and the National Mobilization Committee Against the War. Agents sent phony letters to editors of publications defaming antiwar leaders; other agents infiltrated antiwar groups that called for bombings or violent confrontation with police. Eventually, the CIA opened files on over seven thousand Americans—in violation of its charter, which stipulated that it could not operate inside the United States.

The president became frantic as plans developed for a massive march on Washington in October 1967 to demand a halt to the bombing and the start of immediate negotiations to end the war. In order to discredit the antiwar movement, Johnson asked his attorney general, Ramsey Clark, to leak information about the left-wing and communist affiliations of some of its leaders. Nevertheless, on October 21, a crowd estimated at one hundred thousand assembled on the mall in front of the Lincoln Memorial to hear speeches against the war. Later, a group of about fifty thousand marched to the Pentagon, where scores crossed police lines and were arrested.

These large demonstrations helped change public attitudes toward the war. Equally important were the nightly televised newscasts showing the fighting and the devastation of Vietnamese society. Satellite technology made it possible to air footage of the war the day it was shot. Reporters and camera crews traveled with platoons into firefights in Vietnamese villages. They captured on film the flames of the Zippo raids, the moans of wounded soldiers, and the terror in the eyes of children left homeless by the fighting. What they could not show, because they did not happen, were scenes of GIs liberating villages to the cheers of grateful residents. For a public brought up on the heroic newsreels of World War II, where such images had brought tears of pride to the home front, the sharp contrast between "the good war" of 1941 to 1945 and the quagmire of Vietnam proved especially distressing.

As this "living-room war" ground on without progress, Americans at home, like the soldiers in the field, had trouble distinguishing friendly Vietnamese from the enemy—and wanted no part of either. The fighting appeared pointless, and the public longed for relief from a war it had not anticipated and no longer approved of. Distrust of the government rose sharply in 1967, as observers noted a yawning "credibility gap" between the optimism of the president and his advisers and the continuing violence shown on TV every evening.

Antiwar activities, the failure to achieve victory, and press coverage of the horrors of the fighting altered the way the public viewed the war. Throughout the country, there was a sharp division between "hawks," who supported the war, and "doves," who opposed it. In the beginning of 1967, most Americans were still hawks, willing to escalate the war if it could be

(cont. on page 270)

Wagging the Dog: "The Media-Spindustrial Complex" and American Foreign Relations

Since the Vietnam War, the executive branch of the federal government has been intent on establishing its control over the images of war presented to the American public so that presidents might retain nearly uncontested power over foreign relations decisions. Those same presidents have found that wars often increase their popularity and distract public attention away from issues they wish to obscure. In 1997, Hollywood released a film that raised unsettling questions about how American leaders manipulated public opinion in order to divert attention from the scandals and shortcomings of their public policies and private lives and used wars to create a mandate for incumbent administrations. Entitled *Wag the Dog*, the film's plot centered on a president caught in a sex scandal with a teenager.

In order to keep the president's lechery from impeding his re-election, his managers hired an expensive public relations consultant (spin doctor) to manufacture a foreign policy emergency to divert the public's attention. The consultant in turn enlisted the help of a talented film producer to help him sell the moral necessity for a war to solve a nonexistent crisis in Albania. Together, they created fake "news" footage of a young girl escaping from the violence and cruelty of unspecified "terrorists," hired a songwriter to pen a country-and-western tune hailing the American military for its "contributions" to resolving the crisis, and staged patriotic displays in order to whip the public into a flag-waving frenzy. As they discussed how to generate American fear of Albania, a country once little known to Americans, the spin doctors decided that the president should just say that it had nuclear weapons and could use them to make suitcase bombs.

Intended as parody, *Wag the Dog* seemed only slightly exaggerated, resonating as it did with the tenor of American politics in general and more specifically with

the country's recent history during the Gulf War. In fact, the overt manipulation of public opinion to support the policy and electoral goals of American leaders (corporate and political) has occupied a central role in the drama of postwar America.

In the past fifty years, technology and opinion management have dramatically transformed American politics: the growth of television, with its expansive opportunities for sound-bite journalism and political advertising; the rise of political polling and the public relations industry; and a new cast of characters who exist to aid politicians, from make-up artists to pollsters and spin doctors. Given the costs of these new political props, elected officials now exist in a permanent state of candidacy, their policy decisions and their rhetoric continually focused on the next election. Because the United States has frequently used military interventions to achieve its international goals and because a state of war usually works to the advantage of an incumbent president, the packaging of foreign policy questions, in particular, has intensified in the decades after World War II. The legacy of military defeat in the Vietnam War—the war that cost Lyndon Johnson his presidency and tarnished the prestige of the United States internationally—has only intensified officials' concern with controlling the rhetoric and symbols associated with warmaking.

In 1954, when the CIA orchestrated the overthrow of the reform government of President Jacobo Arbenz Guzman in Guatemala, supporters of the intervention used a public relations campaign developed by the United Fruit Company to persuade Americans that the new policies in Guatemala revealed the communist agenda at work there. The brainchild of Edward Bernays, the public relations consultant later dubbed the "father of spin," the campaign to mold public opinion derived from

Media experts confer with a presidential adviser in a scene from the 1997 movie *Wag the Dog*. / © CORBIS Sygma

his decades of experience promoting the interests of his corporate clients. Beginning in the early 1950s, Bernays hired scholars and writers to provide information and news stories from the point of view of his client, the United Fruit Company (UFC), to American media outlets. The UFC wanted to stop the Guatemalan government's land reforms and its efforts to counter the company's monopoly on transportation facilities in the country (see pages 153–154). Bernays arranged expense paid trips to Guatemala for reporters and then used friendly journalists and editors to publish the accounts he preferred. These accounts stressed two interrelated themes: the purported benefits of the UFC monopoly to the people of Guatemala and

the alleged communist affiliations of the Arbenz government.

When the United States intervened in 1954, Bernays provided major media outlets with news of the brief military struggle. In a later account of the successful CIA coup, the authors determined that "Bernays outmaneuvered, outplanned, and outspent the Guatemalans. He was far ahead of them in technique, experience and political contacts." A *New York Times* reporter concluded similarly that "a hostile and ill-informed American press helped to create an emotional public opinion" that influenced Congress and the State Department. When the American-installed Armas regime failed to bring prosperity to Guatemala, Bernays orchestrated a media campaign designed to blame the previous "communist" government for all its problems.

By the 1990s, the techniques that Bernays and others had pioneered continued to serve various interests, but they did so in a transformed media and policy environment. The rise of cable television, with its all-news networks; the blurring of the boundary between news and entertainment; the importance of ratings to news broadcasts; the increasing technical sophistication of weaponry; and the determination of public leaders to lay to rest the post-Vietnam skepticism of Americans regarding military involvements abroad all shaped the techniques and politics of opinion formation. In that context, many administration officials and congressional representatives believed that the "engineering of consent" that Bernays had advocated in his books was crucial to their policy goals.

They were not the only ones. In 1983, the Reagan administration carefully controlled media access during the brief invasion of Grenada. As a result, about the only image that the public saw of this intervention was the dramatic scene of an American medical student kissing U.S. soil upon his return home. Television networks neglected to report that the Americans studying in Grenada had never been threatened. Through most of the 1980s, the government and the media portrayed Panamanian leader Manuel Noriega as a democratic ally in the war against the Sandinistas. By the end of the decade, however, they represented him as a cocaine-running thug.

Within ten days of its invasion by Iraq in August 1991, the government of Kuwait hired the public relations firm of Hill-Knowlton to manufacture American support for the use of U.S. military forces against Iraq. A powerful and well-connected corporation, Hill-Knowlton had previously represented repressive political regimes from China to Indonesia to Peru. Armed with a $10.8 million retainer from the Kuwaitis, the lobbying firm organized Kuwait Information days at colleges and universities, convinced churches to hold a national day of prayer for Kuwait, and set up meetings between Kuwaitis and newspaper editors. It provided videos for television news outlets and monitored audience reactions to information on the Iraqi-Kuwaiti war.

In one of its most important media moments, the firm arranged for a young woman named Nayirah to testify before the House Human Rights Caucus, an informal group of congressmen whose official-sounding name belied their unofficial status in the House of Representatives. Stating that she feared for her safety, she refused to provide her last name. In tearful testimony broadcast repeatedly by American television news programs, the young woman told of witnessing Iraqi soldiers enter a hospital, where they stole infant incubators and left fifteen babies "on the cold floor to die." Her tale of atrocity was designed to paint the Middle Eastern war in terms of moral absolutes: savage Iraqis fighting blameless and defenseless Kuwaitis. A potent symbol of innocence, the babies made the story morally compelling. Indeed, they helped to swing public and congressional opinion in favor of U.S. intervention in the Gulf War at a time when the administration favored it, but most Americans and a large number of Democratic senators were quite hesitant to support such a policy.

The only dilemma for the architects of the public relations coup was to hide the fact that the story was a total fabrication. Nayirah, as it turned out, was the daughter of the Kuwaiti ambassador to the United States, Sheikh Saud Nasir al-Sabah. Diplomatic immunity and the fact that hers was not official testimony before a House committee (however much it looked like it to American television viewers) meant that she would not have to face perjury charges for her "testimony." As in *Wag the Dog*, the architects succeeded long enough to serve their purposes.

Determined to avoid a repetition of the Vietnam-era antiwar movement, the Bush administration moved to institute strict controls over the reporting of the war. Administration officials allowed only a specified number of reporters, chosen by the officials themselves, to enter the war zone, and they allowed those journalists access (with a government escort) only to the people and places they approved. In particular, they kept reporters away from American soldiers and almost all scenes involving casualties of war. All stories had to pass government censors before they could be published or broadcast. The government provided the media with the images it thought advantageous to administration policies. Anxious to keep their places in the small press pool, journalists provided the administration with the coverage it desired, including (in the words of scholars Susan Jeffords and Lauren Rabinovitz) "'gee-whiz' replications of Pentagon images from the war." Indeed, *Washington Post* reporter Henry Allen concluded that the Gulf War press corps looked like "fools, nit-pickers and egomaniacs . . . a whining, self-righteous upper-middle-class mob jostling for whatever tiny flakes of fame [might] settle on their shoulders."

The result, says historian Daniel C. Hallin, was a media drama of "triumphant technology" in which "the main characters—and heroes—of the [Gulf War] were the experts and the weapons themselves. . . ." Images of Patriot missiles and smart bombs detached from the images of death and injury that they inflicted helped to promote faith in American military prowess and veiled the moral issues raised in a war in which less than 400 coalition soldiers died while somewhere between 100,000 and 200,000 Iraqi soldiers and civilians lost their lives, almost always off camera. Instead of body counts, the U.S. military talked of weapons destroyed, as though the war had been one fought between machines. Even this characterization turned out to be deceptive. It was later revealed that the Patriot missile interceptor shot down almost no Iraqi missiles and that very few smart bombs were actually used in combat.

Unmarred by the images of ground soldiers slogging through the jungles of Vietnam or of little girls burned by napalm and running in terror from American planes, media coverage of the Gulf War conveyed the idea of a war without risks to Americans and without harm to others. One military officer implied that the composition of the U.S. military during the Vietnam War accounted for the differences in the outcomes of the two wars. Marine Corps General George Crist, in a CNN documentary on the Gulf War, compared the soldiers there to those of the Vietnam War. According to Crist, the latter were "an army of draftees, an army taken off the streets of ghettos," but those fighting in the Gulf War were "a professional armed force that had been trained intensely, receiving these new high-tech weapons and learning how to use them and how to use them well. . . ." President Bush, in a speech he made shortly after the American victory, exulted: "We have finally kicked the Vietnam syndrome." American leaders did so, however, with the assistance of the public relations industry and a compliant press.

The politics of spin in a context of "sanitized" war could create unanticipated consequences. The very small number of U.S. casualties in Grenada, Panama, and the Gulf War created an unexpected problem: the American public came to look on this situation as the norm. Thus, Clinton was bitterly criticized when eighteen U.S. peacekeepers were killed in Somalia in 1993. He was reluctant to intervene in Bosnia in the mid-1990s or Kosovo in 1998 because of concern over possible losses. Video cameras and private reconnaissance satellites could provide unauthorized images of war that could spin out of control—as happened in Somalia and in the film *Black Hawk Down*.

The panoply of resources now available to politicians and lobbyists to advance their various agendas—including advertising, polling, speechwriters, and the media—has been labeled the media-spindustrial complex by critic Randall Rothenberg. Whatever it is called, it has been an important component of international relations and domestic politics for some time. As the producers of *Wag the Dog* implied, its control over increasingly sophisticated technologies endows it with great capacities for deception. If George Orwell was right that "political language . . . is designed to make lies sound truthful and murder respectable, and to give an appearance of solidity to pure wind," then those in the media-spindustrial complex exist to make political language sound like the mother tongue.

---

decisively won. Less than one-third of the public believed the war had been a mistake. By July, that figure had risen to 41 percent, and by the time of the march on Washington in October, 46 percent thought the United States should never have entered the war. Yet the number calling for an immediate American withdrawal from Vietnam remained low. Nevertheless, in the fall of 1967, only 28 percent of the public approved of President Johnson's handling of the war. Most Americans saw themselves as neither hawks nor doves;

they simply wanted relief. As the American war entered its third year in 1968, Senator Mansfield's 1965 warning about the shallowness of public support had proved prophetic.

Although no agreement existed about what to do next, the consensus on American foreign policy had shattered. A significant number of people began to question its very basis. Did the principle of containment mean that the United States should take part in any Third World conflict in which one side identified with socialism or communism? Were the communists in places like Vietnam any worse than the regimes that the United States chose to support? Would a triumph by such communists truly weaken the U.S. position with respect to its principal Cold War opponent, the Soviet Union? Did it make sense, in any event, for the United States to fight a war with little chance of victory? Although relatively few Americans had clear answers to such questions in 1967 and 1968, the war led many people to think about them.

By the end of 1967, doubts over further escalation of the war assailed even some of the war's sponsors. The president wondered about the usefulness of bombing North Vietnam. Secretary of Defense McNamara became morose at the lack of progress. At one point, he recommended an unconditional halt to the bombing to get serious negotiations started, but Johnson refused after learning that the Joint Chiefs of Staff had threatened to resign, as one group, if the bombing was stopped. As he began to despair of winning the war through advanced technology, McNamara became emotionally distraught and wanted out. In the fall of 1967, Johnson accepted McNamara's resignation from the Defense Department, replacing him with long-time Democratic Party adviser Clark Clifford in February 1968.

Johnson tried to open negotiations with the North Vietnamese in the fall of 1967. Harvard professor Henry Kissinger secretly relayed to a North Vietnamese official an administration promise to stop the bombing, with the understanding that the pause would lead to prompt discussions. The United States would not demand that the North remove its troops from the South, but it would trust that Hanoi would not take advantage of the hiatus to raise its troop levels. As Kissinger secretly presented these conditions, the bombing continued, suggesting that the military did not know what the Johnson administration was attempting. Suffering from the bombing, the Hanoi government rejected these overtures and called once more for the United States to quit what it described as an "illegal" intervention in Vietnam's civil war.

With this rebuff Johnson sank further into gloom, wary of escalation but incapable of devising a satisfactory alternative. After McNamara announced his resignation, the president's advisers became more hawkish. The president hoped that an optimistic assessment of the war from General Westmoreland, the supreme commander in the field, might buy time with the restless public. In November, Westmoreland returned to Washington and told reporters he was "very, very encouraged" because "we are making real progress." He told Congress that the North Vietnamese and Vietcong could not hold out much longer. He thought U.S. forces had reached a point where the end of the war was in view.

While Westmoreland's rosy scenario made headlines, Johnson's civilian advisers worried about the effect of the war on domestic tranquillity and U.S. prestige abroad. Johnson assembled his so-called Wise Men, foreign policy experts who had served various administrations since 1940, to chart a future path in Vietnam. They supported Johnson's course up until that time, but they warned that "endless inconclusive fighting" had become a "most serious cause of domestic disquiet."

January 1968 brought a military embarrassment elsewhere in Asia, when the *U.S.S. Pueblo*, a navy intelligence ship, was captured off the coast of North Korea. The *Pueblo* crew would remain the North Koreans' captives for almost a year, until negotiations finally produced their release in December. But this incident was minor compared to what the North Vietnamese and the Vietcong had in store.

At 2:45 A.M. on January 30, 1968—on Tet, the Vietnamese New Year—a squad of nineteen Vietcong commandos blasted a hole in the wall protecting the U.S. embassy in Saigon, ran into the courtyard, and engaged the marine guards there for the next six hours. All nineteen Vietcong commandos were killed, but the damage they did to Washington's position in Vietnam could not be repaired. The assault on the embassy was only the most dramatic part of a coordinated offensive by North Vietnamese and NLF forces against South Vietnamese population centers over the Tet holiday. They attacked the Saigon airport, the presidential palace, and the headquarters of the ARVN's general staff. With the benefit of complete surprise, the North Vietnamese and NLF battled with the Americans and ARVN for control of thirty-six of forty-four provincial capitals, five of six major cities, and sixty-four district capitals.

In most areas, the Americans and ARVN repulsed the communists, killing perhaps 40,000 while losing 3,400 of their own. The cost to South Vietnamese civilians ran much higher, with 1 million refugees swelling the already teeming camps in two weeks. One of the most grisly scenes occurred in the old imperial capital of Hue, once noted for its serene beauty. The Vietcong succeeded in controlling the city for three weeks. By the time the battle was over, and the Americans and ARVN had recaptured Hue, their bombs and artillery had left it, according to one soldier, a "shattered, stinking hulk, its streets choked with rubble and rotting bodies." The ARVN uncovered a mass grave containing the bodies of 2,800 South Vietnamese officeholders who had been executed by the Vietcong.

General William Westmoreland, commander of U.S. forces in Vietnam, 1964–1968. Handsome and friendly, Westmoreland got along well with the troops. But his promises of victory in Vietnam gave way to bitter public disillusionment with the war after the Tet Offensive of 1968. / © UPI/Bettmann/CORBIS

The principal American casualty was the cheery fiction of progress in

The frustration of the apparently endless war in Vietnam nearly overwhelmed President Johnson in 1968. / Jack Kightlinger/LBJ Library Collection

the war. After Tet, Westmoreland's recent assertion that an American victory could be achieved within two years sounded hopelessly unrealistic. His claims in the midst of the battle that the United States had defeated the enemy provoked derision. One of the most famous photographs of the war, showing the commander of the Saigon police shooting a Vietcong suspect in the head in the middle of a busy street, outraged the public at home.

Already discouraged by the lack of progress and by Robert McNamara's defection, Johnson grappled with Westmoreland's request for an additional 206,000 men. Failure to provide them, the general implied, meant losing the war. To Johnson, however, sending that many troops seemed a major escalation: it would risk Chinese or Soviet intervention and would shock the American public. After Tet, 78 percent of the public told a Harris poll that they thought the United States was not making progress in Vietnam, and only 2 percent approved of Johnson's handling of the war. Before he would grant Westmoreland's request, the president asked the new secretary of defense, Clark Clifford, to undertake a complete review of Vietnam policy.

Like McNamara before him, Clifford was once a hawk and now doubted whether sending more troops promised any progress. Civilian experts in the Defense Department revived a 1967 proposal by McNamara to change from a strategy of search and destroy to one of "population security." According to this strategy, American forces should protect the bulk of South Vietnam's civilian population while encouraging the ARVN to bear more of the burden of fighting the communists. American casualties would probably decline, reducing public unhappiness at home, but the hope of obtaining a military victory would vanish. Clifford therefore pressed for a negotiated settlement. In early March 1968, Johnson rejected Westmoreland's request for another 206,000 men.

Clifford persuaded the president to reconvene the Wise Men. During the last week of March, these distinguished former officials delivered some shocking opinions to the president. Dean Acheson, secretary of state under Truman, who had endured his own agony during the Korean War, asserted that the United States could "no longer do the job we set out to do in the time we have left, and we must begin to take steps to disengage." Cyrus Vance, former assistant secretary of defense, worried that "unless we do something quick, the mood in this country may lead us to withdraw." Many leading bankers and corporate executives were also in favor of a negotiated withdrawal. Although the war had initially led to an economic boom, by 1968, inflation and a shrinking dollar were causing growing problems for the economy.

Johnson did not like what he heard, but he could no longer ignore the mounting pressure to reverse course. He prepared an address to the nation to be broadcast the evening of March 31, 1968. In it, he promised a partial halt to the bombing, limiting American attacks to the region immediately north of the demilitarized zone at the 17th parallel. He promised to halt all bombing "if our restraint is matched by restraint in Hanoi." He named Averell Harriman, one of the Wise Men, as head of an American delegation to try to open peace talks with North Vietnam. Then, in a passage he wrote himself and kept secret from everyone but his wife, he withdrew from the 1968 presidential race. In order to devote himself to the negotiations he had just promised, he pledged that "I shall not seek, and I will not accept, the nomination of my party for another term as your president."

The Election of 1968

Lyndon Johnson had another reason for not seeking the Democratic nomination for president in 1968: he might not have received it. Anguish over the war had turned the Democrats against one another. For several years, many liberals and Kennedy insiders had stifled their misgivings about Johnson because they supported his domestic reform agenda; now, however, they revolted and looked for someone to challenge him for the nomination. Finding a candidate to run for nomination against a sitting president, even one as unpopular as Johnson, proved difficult. Eventually, an obscure midwestern senator, Eugene McCarthy of Minnesota, allowed himself to be drafted into running in the March 12 New Hampshire primary.

McCarthy's campaign seemed laughable at first. In its early weeks, the senator had few assistants, little money, and almost no press coverage. Everything changed in February, however, as the public reeled from the shock of the Tet offensive. Thousands of college-age volunteers hurried to New Hampshire to help the campaign. Aware that their hippie style would alienate the middle-of-the-road and the middle-aged, they cut their hair, put aside their bellbottoms, and donned coats and ties or skirts and sweaters, becoming "Clean for Gene." McCarthy made Vietnam the issue, demanding a halt to the bombing and immediate negotiations. Johnson's supporters took the bait, running TV ads warning that "the Communists in Vietnam are watching the New Hampshire primary." Johnson denounced McCarthy as "a champion of appeasement and surrender" and predicted that he would receive less than one-third of the vote. On primary day, McCarthy received 42.2 percent, coming within a few hundred votes of defeating Johnson; the Minnesota senator also took twenty of twenty-four delegates to the Democratic convention.

McCarthy's showing rattled the president and shook Robert Kennedy, who reconsidered his earlier refusal to run now that it appeared a challenge to Johnson might succeed. After consulting old supporters and trying unsuccessfully to persuade McCarthy to withdraw in his favor, Kennedy announced his candidacy for the Democratic nomination on March 16, 1968. Two weeks later, Johnson announced his own withdrawal from the race.

Aftershocks from Johnson's March 31 speech were still rumbling when, four days later, on April 4, James Earl Ray killed Martin Luther King, Jr., as King stood on the balcony of the Lorraine Motel in Memphis, Tennessee. King had gone to the city on behalf of striking sanitation workers; almost all of the workers were black, and they represented the abused, overworked, yet politically mobilized people he hoped to include in an interracial Poor People's Campaign. Seemingly prescient about his doom, King nevertheless maintained hope for the movement. The day before his assassination, he gave a speech in which he explained, "I've looked over and I've seen the Promised Land. I may not get there with you, but I want you to know tonight that we as a people will get to the Promised Land. . . . I'm not fearing any man. Mine eyes have seen the glory of the coming of the Lord." The assassination ignited another spurt of black rage. Riots erupted in more than a hundred cities; within a week, the police, the army, and the National Guard had killed thirty-seven people. Several blocks of downtown Washington, D.C., were burned and looted. The war, it seemed, had come home.

Two months later, Robert Kennedy met an assassin's bullet. Early in the morning of Wednesday, June 6, 1968, hours after he had eked out a narrow victory over Eugene McCarthy in the California primary, Kennedy was shot by Sirhan Sirhan, a Palestinian immigrant angry at the New York senator's support for Israel. Once more, the country suffered through a funeral for one of the Kennedys: a Requiem Mass in New York's St. Patrick's Cathedral, followed by a sad train ride south to Washington. Hundreds of thousands of mourners lined the tracks under a blazing sun. One senator on the train recalled that as he looked into their faces, "I saw sorrow, bewilderment." Robert Kennedy was buried next to his brother John in Arlington National Cemetery.

With Kennedy dead, McCarthy continued as the standard-bearer for the antiwar Democrats, who hoped to deny the nomination to Vice President Hubert Humphrey. Humphrey was supported by the prowar faction. The city of Chicago became an armed camp in August 1968 as the authorities prepared for antiwar protests at the Democratic national convention. Barbed wire enclosed the convention center, twelve thousand Chicago police were deployed on twelve-hour shifts, and about six thousand troops of the Illinois National Guard were called out, along with about as many army troops. The overwhelming majority of antiwar activists stayed away. On most days during the convention, there were perhaps four thousand demonstrators, with crowds peaking at possibly ten thousand on August 28. Thus, police generally outnumbered demonstrators by a factor of three or four to one, and federal records suggest that the ranks of the protesters were extensively infiltrated by government agents. Those who did come to protest were hardly a representative cross section of the antiwar movement. For example, male demonstrators at Chicago outnumbered females by eight or ten to one, imparting a particularly macho flavor to the action. The Yippies (the Youth International Party) came prepared to make a farce out of the convention by bringing along their own candidate, a live pig named Pigasus. "Our concept of revolution," said Abbie Hoffman, "is that it's fun." Paul Krassner, a prominent Yippie, terrified city residents by suggesting that demonstrators might attempt to alter people's consciousness by putting LSD into the city's water supply. An infuriated Richard J. Daley, mayor of Chicago, refused to let demonstrators camp in city parks, which guaranteed that plenty of restless people would be looking for conflict. A small minority of demonstrators—perhaps as many as three hundred—representing the extreme Left came to Chicago hoping to provoke violence.

On the same sultry night that Humphrey won the Democratic nomination, the Chicago police force went mad, clubbing and tear-gassing a crowd of ten thousand demonstrators who had come to the city to protest the war. Television cameras caught it all, including the protesters' chant, "The whole world is watching."

After this chaos, the Democratic nomination appeared worthless for Humphrey. Polls put him sixteen percentage points behind the Republican nominee, former vice president Richard Nixon. After losing a 1962 race for governor of California, Nixon had resurrected his political career by traveling the country, supporting local Republican candidates. A third candidate also ran, Alabama governor George Wallace, who had broken with the Democrats over civil rights. Some polls showed Wallace gaining 20 percent of the vote, much of it from formerly Democratic, working-class whites, largely but not exclusively in the South.

Both Nixon and Wallace fed public disgust with Vietnam. The Republican nominee, a hawk when escalation began in 1965, condemned the present stalemate. While presenting no specific way to end the war, Nixon promised an early "peace with honor" and hinted at a plan to reduce U.S. participation. Nixon also pursued a "southern strategy" of seeking the votes of southern white Democrats enraged at blacks. Promising to restore respect for law and order, he decried the race riots Johnson and Humphrey had not been able to stop. His running mate, Spiro Agnew, helped this cause by recalling the angry lecture he delivered to African American leaders after the April riots in Baltimore and on Maryland's eastern shore. George Wallace intimated that he could end the war faster than Humphrey. He named retired air force general

Curtis LeMay, an undisguised hawk, as his running mate, hoping to capitalize on nationalistic feelings. But LeMay's inflammatory remark that he would "bomb North Vietnam into the Stone Age" alarmed voters, and Wallace's campaign began to fade in late September.

Humphrey's campaign languished for six weeks after the Democratic convention. Liberals wanted nothing to do with him, even as he ran against Nixon, their old adversary. Johnson refused to release Humphrey from the political obligation to support the administration's Vietnam policy. Desperate for a way to distance himself from the stalemate in Vietnam, Humphrey announced on September 30, 1968, that he favored a total halt to the bombing "as an acceptable risk for peace, because I believe that it could lead to a success in negotiations and a shorter war." Suddenly, Humphrey began to close the gap with Nixon because many antiwar Democrats decided they preferred him to a man they despised.

Talks in Paris among the United States, North Vietnam, South Vietnam, and the NLF began in the summer, but these talks stalled over the issue of who could participate and the shape of the negotiating table. As the delegations wrangled for months, the seemingly endless talks about the talks came to sym-

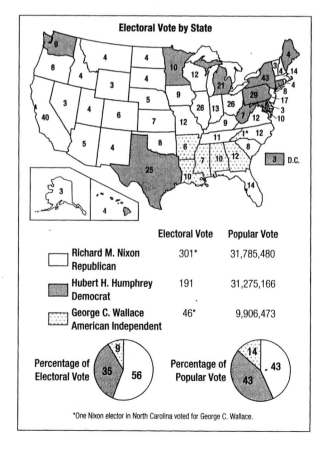

Electoral Vote by State

	Electoral Vote	Popular Vote
Richard M. Nixon Republican	301*	31,785,480
Hubert H. Humphrey Democrat	191	31,275,166
George C. Wallace American Independent	46*	9,906,473

Percentage of Electoral Vote: 35 · 9 · 56

Percentage of Popular Vote: 14 · 43 · 43

*One Nixon elector in North Carolina voted for George C. Wallace.

Map 7.2
Presidential Election of 1968

bolize in the public's mind their frustration with the interminable war. The North Vietnamese refused to grant the Saigon government a separate place at the table, and the United States denied recognition to the NLF. The conversations finally progressed in the days before the November election because the communist side preferred a Humphrey victory to a win by the more hawkish Nixon. The Nixon camp worried that a breakthrough in the Paris talks might give the election to Humphrey. Professor Henry Kissinger, who had ties to both the Humphrey and Nixon organizations, informed the Nixon campaign that Johnson was preparing an "October surprise" to move the negotiations forward, thereby boosting Humphrey's chances. Nonetheless, the weekend before the election, Johnson announced a total bombing halt, along the lines that Humphrey had promised. Serious discussions on ending the war were scheduled to begin immediately after Election Day, on November 5, 1968.

Nixon won by a scant 510,000 votes, taking only 43.6 percent of the vote (see Map 7.2). Humphrey drew 42.9 percent, and Wallace got 13.5 percent. Humphrey's supporters believed that, given another four days, he would have won because he had made up 7 percentage points in the polls in the five days before the election. That may have been wishful thinking: the drop in the Democratic portion of the vote from the 1964 election, when Johnson took nearly 61 percent, represented a striking decline. Nearly all of the 57 percent of the public who had voted for Nixon or Wallace disagreed with Johnson's handling of the war in Vietnam, as did many of those who backed Humphrey.

The story of the events in Vietnam resumes in Chapter 9. Although Nixon took office with an apparent mandate for change, American troops continued to fight in Vietnam for another four years.

Conclusion

By the time of the 1968 election, most Americans wanted to end the Vietnam War, although they still disagreed about how to accomplish that goal. American involvement began quietly under President Truman and was gradually increased by presidents Eisenhower and Kennedy. Lyndon Johnson took the fateful step of committing the United States to a massive air and ground war. Yet the more the United States contributed to the war effort, the more the corrupt government of South Vietnam grew dependent on American support. The result was a cycle of continual frustration.

The war devastated Vietnam—its land, its people, and its society. It also proved tragic for many of the Americans who fought there. By the end of 1968, the war had already cost about thirty-seven thousand American lives, a number that would rise to over fifty-eight thousand by the time the United States withdrew its forces in 1973. And a significant number of American troops who returned physically unscathed suffered long-term psychological and emotional disabilities. Most believed that their efforts in Vietnam had been futile and were unappreciated at home. The veterans' plight contributed to the overall feeling that the nation's public institutions had failed.

At home, disagreement over the war shattered the general consensus about the proper goals of American foreign policy. Opposition became widespread and bitter, ruining Johnson's chances for re-election in 1968 and throwing the Democratic Party into turmoil. Because the war raised doubts about the power of American weapons and technology to mold events around the world, some Americans even began to question the basic doctrine of containment that had guided U.S. foreign policy since the late 1940s.

By dividing the American public, the Vietnam War also opened the deep chasms in American society that were the principal legacy of the 1960s. Chapter 8 describes how opposition to the war merged with other political and social movements to form a full-scale culture of protest. Many people became fundamentally disillusioned with American government and society. They distrusted not only the politicians in Washington, but many other forms of authority as well, and their rebellion stimulated an equally strong conservative backlash.

F   U   R   T   H   E   R   •   R   E   A   D   I   N   G

For overviews of the Vietnam War, see George C. Herring, *America's Longest War: The United States and Vietnam, 1950–1975* (2001); Stanley Karnow, *Vietnam: A History* (1991); Robert D. Schulzinger, *A Time for War: The United States and Vietnam, 1941–1975* (1997). **On the politics and diplomacy of the war,** see Michael Beschloss, ed., *Taking Charge: The Johnson White House Tapes* (1997) and *Reaching for Glory: Lyndon Johnson's Secret White House Tapes, 1964–1965* (2001); David Kaiser, *American Tragedy: Kennedy, Johnson and the Origins of the Vietnam War* (2000); A. J. Languth, *Our Vietnam: The War, 1954–1975* (2000); Fredrik Logevall, *Choosing War: The Lost Chance for Peace and the Escalation of War in Vietnam* (1999); Robert Mann, *A Grand Delusion: America's Descent into Vietnam* (2001); Robert S. McNamara, with Brian VanDeMark, *In Retrospect: The Tragedy and Lessons of Vietnam* (1995). **On fighting the war,** see Mark Clodfelter, *The Limits of Air Power* (1989); William Duiker, *Ho Chi Minh: A Biography* (2000); Neil Sheehan, *A Bright Shining Lie: John Paul Vann and America in Vietnam* (1988); Andrew Krepenevich, *The Army and Vietnam* (1989); Peter G. McDonald, *Giap: The Victor in Vietnam* (1993); Wallace Berry, *Bloods: An Oral History of the War by Black Veterans* (1984); Mark Baker, *Nam* (1982); Don Oberdorfer, *Tet* (1979); Ronald Spector, *After Tet: The Bloodiest Year of the Vietnam War* (1993). **On the home front during the war,** see Christian Appy, *Working Class War: American Combat Soldiers and Vietnam* (1993); Lawrence Baskir and William Strauss, *Chance and Circumstance: The War, the Draft and the Vietnam Generation* (1978); Myra MacPherson, *Long Time Passing: Vietnam and the Haunted Generation* (2002); Melvin Small, *Antiwarriors: The Vietnam War and the Battle for America's Hearts and Minds* (2002); Charles DeBenedetti, with Charles Chatfield, *An American Ordeal: The Antiwar Movement of the Vietnam Era* (1990); Tom Wells, *The War Within: America's Battle Over Vietnam* (1994); Nancy Zaroulis and Gerald Sullivan, *Who Spoke Up? American Protest Against the War in Vietnam, 1963–1975* (1984). **On the political upheavals of 1968,** see James Miller, *"Democracy Is in the Streets"* (1987); Todd Gitlin, *The Sixties* (1987); David Farber, *Chicago '68* (1988); David Caute, *The Year of the Barricades* (1988). **On media relations,** see Larry Tye, *The Father of Spin: Edward L. Bernays and the Birth of Public Relations* (1998); Susan Jeffords and Lauren Rabinovitz, eds., *Seeing Through the Media: The Persian Gulf War* (1994).

8

The Politics and
Culture of Protest

Antiwar protester puts flowers in the guns of military police at a 1967 demonstration at the Pentagon. / Paul Conklin, © Time Magazine, Time, Inc.

In March 1968, when the *New York Times* ran a story entitled "An Arrangement: Living Together for Convenience, Security, Sex," it unleashed a firestorm of criticism at Barnard College, the all-women adjunct college of Columbia University. The article told of the lives of a few college students who were living together as unmarried couples. One interviewee, a student at Barnard, told of her success in evading Barnard's rule that its students live in campus housing, where they were subject to a set of restrictive rules, including the requirement that they be home at a specified hour. As vigilant college officials determined her identity, the newspaper and the college were inundated with letters condemning young couples who chose to "flaunt" their decision to have sex before marriage.

Barnard College charged the student, Linda LeClair, with lying about her housing arrangements and required that she appear before the student-faculty judiciary council. LeClair summarized her position in a letter to the student newspaper: "If women are able, intelligent people, why must we be supervised and curfewed?" The council recommended a minimal punishment (banishment from the college cafeteria), but the president, who was in the middle of a fundraising campaign for the college, threatened expulsion. She did so mostly in response to a barrage of letters and editorials from an outraged public, who understood LeClair's claim to individual freedom and gender equality to be an assault on civilized morals. Many called LeClair a "whore" and claimed that she and her boyfriend were "violating the laws of decency when they flaunt their dereliction in public." Conservative columnist William Buckley said that he was not surprised "that the LeClairs of this world should multiply like rabbits, whose morals they imitate." Before the college reached a final decision in her case, LeClair dropped out of school.

LeClair's challenge to time-honored institutional practices and cultural assumptions reflected the diverse issues touched on by the volatile political and cultural energies unleashed in the 1960s. Within a few years, most colleges and universities had dropped the residence and hours rules that they had applied to women students for over a century, acceding to the demands of the students' and women's movements and recognizing that they were not equipped to monitor the private behavior of their students. Those students, indeed, by that time occupied center stage in some of the most volatile and radical social movements in U.S. history. By 1965, the spirit of protest had spread from young blacks unwilling to tolerate the slow pace of racial progress to young whites angry at government policies and sick of the bland pleasures that middle-class life offered.

Some in the baby-boom generation—those who made up the surge in the national birth rate that began in 1946—followed slightly older dissidents into the civil rights and peace crusades of the early 1960s. Some joined more radical movements, like Black Power and the Weathermen, and a few concluded that only violent revolution could bring the necessary changes. Others sought to extend the boundaries of acceptable everyday behavior, sampling the psychological challenges, sensual pleasures, and physical risks of the emerging counterculture. Many joined women's liberation groups, linking the personal and the political. Their political activism was sometimes enhanced, sometimes enfeebled by the cultural forms they created as they gloried in sexual expressiveness, musical innovation, and experimentation with drugs.

What people in the sixties would call the generation gap—the alienation of the young from the strategies and aspirations of their elders—had been brewing for some time. Among the "baby deficit" generation, born in the 1930s and 1940s, signs of discontent emerged in the 1950s. The pop-culture antiheroes of that decade, from the brooding, doomed James Dean in *Rebel Without a Cause* to the lip-curling Marlon Brando in *The Wild One*, had shown adult America the face of restless youth. Middle-class American parents in the fifties had planned ahead. They knew the price of affluence and were willing to sacrifice and save. Their children took material comfort for granted, but they wondered why so many Americans had to live in poverty. Relieved of the burden of financial worry by the growing American economy of the 1960s, the baby boomers looked to expand the boundaries of peace, justice, and spirituality as part of their quest for an ever better life.

If even the children of privilege felt distant from the American dream, others had more reason to feel disaffected and to raise their voices in increasingly angry protest. African American writer Richard Wright had sounded a note of black rage as early as 1940 with his novel *Native Son*. In the 1960s, other black writers, from Black Panther leader Eldridge Cleaver to poet June Jordan, took up Wright's legacy. From rock singer Janis Joplin to the activists of the women's liberation movement, women also began to find words to defy the restrictions that society placed on them. From these very diverse threads, the sixties wove a new politics and culture of protest.

From Civil Rights to Black Power

For about fifty years, the National Association for the Advancement of Colored People (NAACP) and the Urban League, under the leadership of careful men like Roy Wilkins and Whitney Young, had led the African American campaign for civil rights. They believed that their cause was consistent with democratic and Christian principles, and they saw their movement as instrumental to realizing the promise of American life. They used various methods to secure reforms within the system. By the early 1960s, sit-ins, boycotts, and protest marches had become widespread. But the decade would soon see the emergence of more radical goals and approaches.

By 1964, the civil rights movement had begun to focus on community organization and voter registration as primary tactics in the fight against racism. These methods were used primarily in the South, where racial segregation and hatred were particularly open and entrenched. Rank-and-file civil rights workers in organizations like the Congress of Racial Equality (CORE), founded in 1942; the Southern Christian Leadership Conference (SCLC), begun in 1957; and the Student Non-Violent Coordinating Committee (SNCC), founded at an SCLC conference in 1960, faced potential and actual white violence on a daily basis.

Black Mississippian Anne Moody joined first the NAACP, then SNCC, knowing that doing so entailed grave risks both to herself and her loved ones. One friend had been shot in the back because white townspeople suspected him of belonging to the NAACP; a local clergyman and his family had been run out of town because he had mentioned the NAACP in a sermon. While organizing blacks in the small towns of Mississippi, Moody learned to live with fear. Her uncle and three others were murdered in Woodville, Mississippi, in a campaign of what SNCC leader Robert Moses identified as "terror killings." Those who dared to speak out against the murders became targets themselves; when they asked federal authorities for protection, they were told, "We can't protect every individual Negro in Mississippi." Again and again, FBI and Justice Department officials stood by while demonstrators were beaten and illegally jailed. "I guess mostly the SNCC workers were just lucky," Moody wrote in her autobiography, *Coming of Age in Mississippi.* "Most of them had missed a bullet by an inch or so on many occasions. Threats didn't stop them. They just kept going all the time."

While Congress debated the Civil Rights Act of 1964, the SCLC's Martin Luther King, Jr., courted a national television audience, combining restraint and eloquence with the use of nonviolent boycotts, sit-ins, and demonstrations. A "conservative militant," King was a pivotal figure in the civil rights movement. He retained the support of white liberals, who provided much of the movement's financial backing, while trying to maintain ties with the increasingly frustrated younger African Americans who staffed the front-line positions in the battle. King confronted white violence with dignity, leading peaceful protest marches against segregation and injustice. He dazzled the nation with his "I Have a Dream" speech at the massive 1963 March on Washington. Rank-and-file organizers, however, found King aloof and abstract, and referred to him sarcastically as "De Lawd."

During the summer of 1964, many black and white students spent their college vacations in Mississippi, where white resistance to integration was deep and militant. These student activists sought to break the white monopoly on political power in the South by using weapons dear to the American political system: voters. The Mississippi Freedom Summer Project, organized by the SNCC-affiliated Council of Federated Organizations, attracted more than one thousand students from the North, mostly white, to join veteran black and white southern workers in a campaign to register African American voters for the newly created, racially integrated Mississippi Freedom Democratic Party (MFDP). Volunteers also walked picket lines, attended innumerable meetings, and organized "freedom schools" at community centers to teach remedial reading, government, humanities, and other academic and vocational subjects.

The Mississippi state legislature reacted to the challenge by doubling the state police force, authorizing local authorities to pool their personnel and equipment for riot-control purposes, and introducing an anti-invasion bill intended to keep civil rights workers out of the state. White vigilante groups mounted a campaign of intimidation, ranging from harassment to bombings and killings. In June 1964, civil rights workers Andrew Goodman, Michael

Schwerner, and James Chaney—two northern whites and a southern black—
were murdered. Yet the volunteers kept coming, sleeping in shifts on bare mat-
tresses, living on peanut butter, cranking mimeograph machines, and tramp-
ing the hot streets. Sustained by idealism, SNCC workers wanted not only to
end segregation and political repression, but also to oppose the fury of white
hatred by living out their own vision of a racially integrated "beloved community" based on respect, affection, and a shared commitment to social justice.
To one young, white SNCC volunteer, African American women like Fanny
Lou Hamer, Ella Baker, and Ruby Doris Smith Robinson and men like the
soft-spoken Bob Moses seemed "wise, caring, courageous, honest, and full of
love." Blacks living under the burden of racism inspired younger white college
students from the North with their bravery and their tirelessness.

The beloved community was, however, riddled with tension. Living in fear
of "nightriders," who fired shots through their windows and telephoned bomb
threats, civil rights workers also had to cope with racial friction within their
own ranks. Long-time black workers worried that whites were trying to take
over the movement without facing the risks that blacks encountered daily. Interracial sexual relations caused conflict between black and white women and
between women and men.

SNCC succeeded in mobilizing enough voters to enable the MFDP to
mount a challenge to the all-white delegation that the regular state party
sent to the 1964 Democratic national convention in Atlantic City. MFDP
delegation leader Fanny Lou Hamer electrified a national television audience as she testified before the party's Credentials Committee that she had
been denied the right to vote and had been jailed and beaten in attempting
to exercise that right. "We are askin' the American people," she said, "is this
the land of the free and the home of the brave?" The MFDP demanded that
its delegation be seated in place of the official state delegation. White liberals like Senator Hubert Humphrey of Minnesota and southern conservatives in the party leadership worked out what they termed a compromise:
the white delegation was seated, after promising not to bolt the Democratic
Party later on, and two MFDP representatives received delegate-at-large status. To those who had put their lives on the line all summer, this "compromise" seemed a betrayal, a triumph of expediency over morality. Two disillusioned African American activists, Stokely Carmichael and Charles
Hamilton, wrote that the lesson of Atlantic City was clear: "Black people . . .
could not rely on their so-called allies."

By the time of the Atlantic City convention, African Americans throughout the country were revealing their frustration at the limited success of non-
violent tactics. Martin Luther King, Jr., framed his endorsement of civil disobedience in the language and spirit of Christian forbearance: "One who breaks
an unjust law must do so openly, lovingly, and with a willingness to accept the
penalty." However, the black Christian churches that King represented, which
for a decade had emphasized the necessity of taking the moral high ground,
were losing influence with their congregations. After a church bombing killed
a group of schoolchildren during Sunday school, Anne Moody told her God,

You know, I used to go to Sunday school when I was a little girl. . . . We were taught how merciful and forgiving you are. I bet those girls in Sunday school were being taught the same as I was when I was their age. Is that teaching wrong? Are you going to forgive their killers? . . . Nonviolence is out. I have a good idea Martin Luther King is talking to you, too. If he is, tell him that nonviolence has served its purpose.

Black civil-rights workers had learned through experience that white lawlessness seldom brought penalties. Even King was aware that activists' patience was wearing thin. If nonviolent civil disobedience failed to gain justice, King warned, "millions of Negroes will, out of frustration and despair, seek solace and security in black nationalist ideologies."

King's predictions were fulfilled. Many blacks began to reject Christian forbearance altogether. Some sought new meaning in a black separatist Islamic faith. Malcolm X, the nation's most prominent and eloquent Black Muslim, spoke out for black nationalism, explicitly rejected integration, and advocated meeting violence with violence. Rioting broke out in Harlem in the summer of 1964.

After the Democratic convention, the ranks of SNCC split. One faction, which included black and white southerners and middle-class white college students, believed in participatory democracy and decision making by consensus. The other group, dominated by long-time field organizers like James Forman and Ruby Doris Smith Robinson, wanted to move away from a focus on moral and procedural issues to questions of power. Bitterly disillusioned with the fickleness of their white allies, they argued that SNCC should be black-led and black-dominated.

By the early months of 1965, the concept of "black and white together" in the civil rights movement was being eclipsed. Malcolm X had begun to tone down his antiwhite message and to seek some new solutions to the problem of racism. But he was gunned down in February 1965, allegedly murdered by less conciliatory followers of Black Muslim leader Elijah Muhammad. Ironically, his death convinced some African American activists that power came only from the barrel of a gun. Other civil rights leaders persisted in trying to channel the movement's energies into coordinated, nonviolent action, but their protests seemed inadequate in the face of white brutality. In March 1965, a national television audience watched as Selma, Alabama, Sheriff Jim Clark ordered his men to meet civil rights marchers with clubs and tear gas. Martin Luther King, Jr., and Ralph Bunche led a group of 3,200 people on a fifty-mile march from Selma to the heavily fortified state capitol at Montgomery, Alabama, where they were joined by 25,000 supporters. In the course of the Selma campaign, three activists were killed. Many Americans were struck by the contrast between the violence of the Selma police and the peaceful nature of the march. The Voter Registration Act of 1965, signed in early August, passed partly as a result of the Selma march and partly as a result of President Johnson's revulsion at the accompanying white violence. But the costs of pursuing peaceful tactics were becoming unbearable to movement veterans.

An officer harasses a woman beaten unconscious by public authorities in Selma, Alabama, for marching to protest race discrimination in voter registration. / © Bettmann/CORBIS

Around the nation, African Americans responded to the slow pace of change with increasing fury. In August 1965, five days of looting and rioting broke out in Watts, a black ghetto in Los Angeles. Residents of Watts had reason to be frustrated: although Los Angeles as a whole was booming, blacks in the area were worse off than before. Median income in the area had dropped 8 percent between 1959 and 1965. Many complained that the white-controlled businesses in Watts jacked up their prices and paid low wages to black employees. Thirty percent of adult men in Watts were unemployed, and of those who did hold jobs, many lacked the cars necessary to navigate the nation's preeminent car-culture city. Los Angeles police, mostly white and sometimes openly racist, did little to win this community's trust. By the time the rioting subsided, thirty-four people had died, four thousand had been arrested, and much of the area had been leveled. The Los Angeles police chief blamed civil rights workers; the mayor blamed communists. From the ashes arose a cry of despair that would fuel the revolutionary rhetoric of the Black Power movement and, in turn, the white backlash against African American rights: "Burn, baby, burn." In Los Angeles, a race war seemed a real possibility.

On a march through Mississippi in the summer of 1966, the message crystallized. Those who still supported the goal of integration and the tactics of nonviolence, like Floyd McKissick of CORE and John Lewis, former chair of SNCC, looked on as Stokely Carmichael, bringing news of the founding of the Black Panther Party in Lowndes County, Alabama, announced a new goal—Black Power. To his African American listeners he declared, "It's time we stand up and take over." To society at large, he issued a warning: "Move on over or we'll move on over you."

Within a year, weary veterans of the civil rights movement had been displaced in the public eye by young militants. SNCC became the organizing center of the Black Power movement. Carmichael and the new SNCC chair, H. Rap Brown, viewed the increasingly common ghetto disturbances as a dress rehearsal for revolution. Meanwhile, the federal government offered only a weak response to urban rioting. President Johnson appointed Illinois governor Otto Kerner to head a commission to study the situation. When the Kerner Commission delivered a report concluding that the United States was shot through with racism and was rapidly becoming two nations—one, black and poor; the other, white and rich—Johnson did nothing. He was too preoccupied with the Vietnam War to pursue his promised Great Society.

Urging students at black colleges to "fight for liberation by any means necessary," Carmichael declared, "[T]o hell with the laws of the United States." At a Black Power conference in Newark, New Jersey, held on the heels of a riot in which police killed twenty-five African Americans, one thousand participants approved resolutions affirming black people's right to revolt and calling for a separate black nation and black militia. In 1968, Carmichael, Brown, and SNCC were replaced by the Black Panthers as the most visible militant group. Wearing leather jackets and carrying weapons, the Panthers often resembled an elite paramilitary unit. They aimed their radical rhetoric at the American capitalist system. During the next few years, as the Panthers provoked considerable uneasiness among the white middle class, they became the objects of heavy surveillance by the FBI. They had frequent confrontations with police, including shootouts that left some Panthers dead and others under arrest.

Many African Americans, including those unwilling to embrace violence as a tactic for change, remained sympathetic to the Panthers and the black-power movement. While the vast majority of whites stated in public opinion polls that the killings had been mainly "the result of violence started by Black Panthers themselves," blacks responded that the conclusion that they drew was that "blacks have to stand together." They believed this conclusion because they expected little from whites who condoned government violence against those whom they saw as community leaders. The Panthers' "survival pending revolution" strategies had led them to provide services—including health clinics, breakfast programs for children, employment centers, and visiting programs for families of prisoners—that were of material benefit to people long ignored by white officials and charities and who were left out of significant parts of the New Deal safety net.

The SDS and the Rise of the New Left

As African American groups became more militant, so did other, predominantly white organizations that arose to challenge the structure of American politics and society. Collectively, these groups were soon called the New Left, to distinguish them from the Old Left of the 1930s to 1950s.

In contrast to the liberals and radicals of the fifties, who lived in the shadow of the Holocaust and Stalinism, those who came of age in the early 1960s were the beneficiaries of the new American affluence and the huge postwar expansion of the nation's colleges and universities. Between 1945 and 1965, public spending on higher education rose from $742.1 million to $6.9 billion per year. University life provided the chance for a small but growing group of students to imagine things as they ought to be, rather than as they are. Uneasy in the presence of the world's growing atomic arsenal and ignited by the civil rights movement, they were less wedded to older allegiances than their Old Left predecessors and more optimistic about the prospects for sweeping social change.

Some of those who came of age in the early 1960s founded the most influential and best known New Left group: the Students for a Democratic Society (SDS). At a 1962 SDS meeting in Port Huron, Michigan, Tom Hayden, one of the organization's early leaders, articulated its concerns and goals in his famous Port Huron Statement. Beginning with his Agenda for a Generation, Hayden declared, "We are the people of this generation, bred in at least modest comfort, housed now in universities, looking uncomfortably to the world we inherit." He went on to criticize college students' apathy toward politics and to deplore collegiate complacency. The country's widespread poverty and the unchallenged power of what Eisenhower had called the military-industrial complex threatened the nation's best traditions. Hayden called for a restoration of participatory democracy to make political parties, corporations, and the government more responsive to ordinary people. "America," said Hayden, "should concentrate on its genuine social priorities: abolish squalor, terminate neglect, and establish an environment for people to live in with dignity and creativeness."

Embracing Hayden's hopeful message, white students flocked into civil rights work in the early 1960s. Some SDS members went south. Others in 1964 set up the group's Economic Research and Action Project in northern ghettos, attempting to organize an interracial movement of the poor that focused on issues such as jobs and community control of social programs.

Soon this involvement in the civil rights movement propelled student activists into taking up other issues in new places. Mario Savio and Jack Weinberg, two veterans of the Mississippi Freedom Summer, returned to the University of California at Berkeley in the fall of 1964 to continue recruitment for the movement. When campus authorities forbade their efforts, the Berkeley Free Speech Movement brought active radicalism on campus. Students took over the administration building, declared a strike, and enlisted faculty support for the removal of restrictions on free expression on campus. Free Speech Movement activists expressed both their joy and their anger in words once thought inadmissible in polite company, and conservative Americans began to see Berkeley as an outpost of lawlessness and libertinism. By 1966, California gubernatorial candidate Ronald Reagan was telling campaign audiences that campus activists indulged in "orgies so vile I cannot describe them to you."

Campus protests quickly spread. By 1965, there had been disturbances at Yale, Ohio State, the University of Kansas, Brooklyn College, Michigan State, and St. John's University. Campus disputes often arose over issues of personal conduct rather than national politics. College students of the 1950s had accepted the time-honored doctrine of in loco parentis, which claimed that the institution had the right and the obligation to stand in for parents and regulate students' behavior. But by the mid-1960s, many campus regulations—particularly those attempting to preserve the conservative mating and dating rituals of the fifties—seemed quaint, artificial, and restrictive. Students began to oppose all kinds of limitations on their behavior, from dress codes and anti-smoking regulations to rules governing where they could live, what hours they could keep, and who could visit their rooms. Students at single-sex institutions agitated for coeducation. Returning from summers spent in loosely structured, sexually volatile communal households where they worked for SNCC or SDS, male and female students alike chafed at campus rules.

Even without these lifestyle issues, national politics provided more than enough cause for dissent, particularly as President Johnson escalated the war in Vietnam. As nightly newscasts brought television audiences graphic proof of the bloodiness and futility of the nation's foreign policy, official government pronouncements about the prospects for peace seemed patently false. Berkeley's Jack Weinberg admonished his fellow students not to trust anyone over thirty, and freethinking American journalists began to believe there was no point in trusting anyone in power. On campuses, in cities, and on military bases, underground newspapers sprang up to offer a more radical alternative to conventional news sources.

Even the mainstream press began to mistrust the information released by official sources. Investigative reporters like Seymour Hersh of the *New York Times* looked beyond government press releases to get at the truth of national policy. Jeopardizing his sources in the military, Hersh broke the story of the My Lai massacre in Vietnam. Hersh and other journalists were willing to accept the professional risks inherent in upsetting the previously cozy relationship between reporters and their sources. As a result, they managed to uncover many important stories that government officials had attempted to suppress.

The Vietnam War soon became the main focus of student protest. Because students—male students, at least—were directly threatened by the draft, they represented a huge new constituency for the protest effort. When the SDS endorsed draft resistance, its membership swelled. Draft-counseling centers sprang up across the country. Women joined the protests in support of their male friends. Some in the movement even tried to make resistance sexy; according to one slogan that appeared on protest signs, "Girls say yes to guys who say no." And by the late 1960s, many parents of draft-age men had changed their views on Vietnam as well.

In the spirit of participatory democracy, local SDS chapters and other draft-resistance groups tried various tactics. Some initiated draft-card burnings. Others held sit-ins at Selective Service induction centers, opposed university Reserve Officers' Training Corps (ROTC) programs, protested military recruiters' visits to campus, or demonstrated against corporations involved in defense work. Dow Chemical, the manufacturer of napalm, became a particularly hated target. According to the National Student Association, between January 1 and June 15, 1968, there were 221 major antiwar demonstrations at 101 colleges and universities, involving about forty thousand students.

Across the country, college professors and even high school teachers initiated "teach-ins" to educate curious students about Vietnamese history and politics. There were notable efforts to join student groups with other organizations to orchestrate nationwide protests against the war. In the summer of 1967, twenty thousand people participated in the Vietnam Summer, an effort modeled on the Mississippi Freedom Summer and mounted by a coalition of pacifists, liberals, and radicals to mobilize the middle class against the war. Stop the Draft Week, from October 16 to 21, 1967, culminated in a march on the Pentagon. Fifty thousand people crossed the Arlington Memorial Bridge, some to picket, some to pray, others to attempt to storm the bastion of the military-industrial complex. The march included not only students but also representatives of many other groups ranged against the war. Among those present were Berkeley Free Speech activist Jerry Rubin, childcare expert Dr. Benjamin Spock, linguistics theorist Noam Chomsky, poet Robert Lowell, social philosopher Paul Goodman, and Dagmar Wilson of Women's Strike for Peace. The coalition even had its comic aspects: Ed Sanders, leader of a rock band called the Fugs, proposed a "grope for peace"; Sanders and radical leader Abbie Hoffman coordinated an attempt to levitate the Pentagon.

Sociologist Todd Gitlin, an early president of SDS, noted that as the war became more militant, so too did the antiwar movement. Antiwar demonstrators had often tried to contrast their own peace-loving demeanor with the government's policy of violence, carrying signs reading "Make Love, Not War" and putting flowers in the barrels of the guns pointed at them by police and National Guard troops at demonstrations. By 1967, however, antiwar activists were preaching a harder line, and demonstrators began adopting a tougher posture. In Oakland, California, protests during Stop the Draft Week turned into bloody confrontations with the police.

SDS, its membership swelling, moved beyond the goals articulated at Port Huron. It adopted the slogan "From Protest to Resistance." By 1967, SDS publications had begun referring to the authorities as pigs. Insisting that the cause of justice in Vietnam—which they identified quite simply with the Vietcong and the North Vietnamese—could not get a fair hearing in the United States, some New Leftists declared free speech a sham and shouted down progovernment speakers. National Liberation Front flags began to appear at antiwar rallies, alienating many middle-of-the-road Americans. SDS leader Bernardine Dorn wanted to bring the war home, to make the American people feel Vietnam's torment; such revolutionary tactics confused and angered many Americans, including many who opposed the war. Many sympathized with the radicals' demands but found it hard to accept tactics that included violating property rights.

Nowhere was campus conflict more spectacular than at Columbia University in New York City. Columbia embodied all that campus radicals con-

Columbia University students occupy a professor's office in April 1968. / © UPI/Bettmann/
CORBIS

demned. A bastion of Ivy League privilege in the middle of the ghetto, the
university was both a Harlem landlord and a holder of major defense research contracts. On April 23, 1968, the Columbia SDS chapter joined with
black militants in taking over university buildings, including the president's
office. Columbia students held the buildings for eight days, after which New
York City police moved in with billy clubs. They arrested 692 people,
three-quarters of them students. Though the siege was over, a student strike
forced the university to close early for the year. The stage was set for violent
confrontations between students and authorities on campuses across the nation in the next two years.

   The American student protests were part of an international drive toward
student militancy. The Columbia uprising had its counterpart in Paris, where
angry protesters erected barricades in the streets and battled police. But not
all students—and certainly not all young people—joined the protests. Some opposed only the war and the draft; some sympathized but stayed out of the streets.
Many young people—political conservatives, white southerners, working-
class youths who did not go to college, graduate students who had invested
time and money in pursuit of professional careers—were either unaffected by
the protests or opposed to them. Nevertheless, campus conflicts revealed a
deep gulf between the "straight" social standards of the older generation and
the beliefs of most of those who came of age in the 1960s.

The Counterculture and Mainstream Culture

At the same time that young people were becoming more radical in their political beliefs, they began to experiment with new ways of living. Many had been raised in suburban affluence, yet they condemned the materialism, conformity, and the hypocrisy of their parents' generation. The counterculture they formed derived from, transformed, and posed a threat to mainstream mass culture. Youthful dissenters relied on mass media to popularize new cultural forms and values and to communicate new political ideas. As Yippie Jerry Rubin declared in an underground newspaper, "You can't be a revolutionary today without a television set." The entertainment and communication industries were businesses that sought to sell products, especially to the huge baby-boom generation, while maintaining the economic and social system from which their enterprises had long profited. The counterculture–mainstream culture relationship in the 1960s generated conflict and uneasy accommodations in a context of mutual dependence and contradictory values.

Many young people found inspiration for new lives in the Beat writers of the 1950s. "The only ones for me," author Jack Kerouac wrote in his 1957 novel, *On the Road*, "are the mad ones, the ones who are mad to live, mad to talk, mad to be saved, desirous of everything at the same time, the ones who never yawn or say a commonplace thing, but burn, burn, burn like fabulous yellow roman candles." Along with other Beat writers, Kerouac came to symbolize the rejection of bourgeois comfort and the embrace of a life of sensation-seeking, adventure, and personal authenticity. The Beats also represented a male revolt against the middle-class family and the traditional masculine role of breadwinner. Going on drinking sprees, careening around the country, and embracing freewheeling sexuality, the Beats distanced themselves from the 1950s family man in his gray flannel suits.

While "squares" pursued the American dream in suburban comfort—drinking martinis, listening to *Hit Parade* on TV, raising their kids, and fooling around only if they wouldn't get caught—the Beats, or "hipsters," lived by another set of standards. They lived in bare apartments in urban enclaves like New York City's Greenwich Village and San Francisco's North Beach; expanded the range of recreational drugs from sweet wine to marijuana and heroin; and listened to the incendiary, experimental jazz of Charlie "Yardbird" Parker, Dizzy Gillespie, and Miles Davis. These were the beginnings of a movement that widened by the later 1960s into the counterculture, a loosely defined phenomenon that involved new types of rock music, drugs, sexual freedom, and various other emblems of a liberated lifestyle.

Meanwhile, the popular culture that the Beats despised was undergoing its own transformation. A revival of folk music—identified with the Old Left during the 1950s—meant commercial success in the 1960s for protest singers like Joan Baez and Bob Dylan. Their music sparked a yearning for social change and helped energize protesters. But it was rock 'n' roll that served as the primary musical catalyst for the counterculture.

For millions of American girls, the arrival of the Beatles in the United States in 1964 was a watershed. No musicians before or since have achieved the mass popularity or cultural influence of these four young Englishmen: John Lennon, Paul McCartney, George Harrison, and Ringo Starr. While "Beatlemaniacs" fantasized about romance with their idols, they also found much to identify with in the "Fab Four." Playful, long-haired, wacky, and talented, the Beatles personified both personal independence and a new androgynous sexual ideal. One fan recalled, "I didn't want to grow up and be a wife, and it seemed to me that the Beatles had the kind of freedom I wanted: No rules, they could spend two days lying in bed; they ran around on motorbikes, ate from room service. . . . I wanted to be like them. Something larger than life." Another wrote, "I liked their independence and sexuality and wanted those things for myself."

As they had during the Elvis Presley phenomenon of the late 1950s (see Chapter 3), parents began to worry that their children were getting out of control. But the transformation of rock music and the youth culture it represented was only beginning. By the mid-1960s, the sentimental love songs of the early Beatles gave way to the overt sexual come-ons of groups such as the Rolling Stones and the Doors. "I Wanna Hold Your Hand" gave way to the Stones' "Let's Spend the Night Together," and the Doors' "Touch Me." Many girls and women accepted these ideas, adopting a new, open, and defiant insistence on the right to sexual pleasure, for themselves as well as men. The birth-control pill, first marketed in 1960, made pleasure without procreation possible and galvanized the gradual repeal of state "blue laws" restricting the sale of contraceptives.

The ideal of sexual freedom spread rapidly, galvanized by the rock music that expressed the desires and demands of young people. As the counterculture developed, the music continued to evolve; performers invented new musical forms and hybrids, pushing folk and rock 'n' roll beyond all previous limits. Soon psychedelic music, often known as acid rock, was celebrating the use of mind-altering drugs. Groups like the Grateful Dead and Jefferson Airplane turned their sets into dizzying, deafening swirls of sound. A young white woman named Janis Joplin sang a steamy, screeching, tortured, blues-driven rock that gave her an almost legendary status within the counterculture.

Like Joplin, most of the avant-garde performers were white. Ironically, at a time when many black political leaders were turning from civil rights to Black Power, African American musicians succeeded in reaching a broad commercial audience by taking a fairly cautious approach. The best known black recording artists were associated with Motown, the Detroit music company masterminded by black songwriter-entrepreneur Berry Gordy, Jr. Motown singers like Stevie Wonder and groups like the Temptations and the Supremes combined musical virtuosity with lush production, precise choreography, glittering costumes, and a bland message. One exception to this trend was James Brown, the godfather of soul music, who marked out the frontiers of raw sex appeal. Another black innovator was guitarist Jimi Hendrix, whose incendiary playing defined the psychedelic style.

Along with sex and rock 'n' roll, the counterculture featured the abundant use of drugs. The Beatles took lysergic acid diethylamide (LSD), a psychotropic chemical better known as "acid." Their path-breaking album, *Sergeant Pepper's Lonely Hearts Club Band*, declared, "I'd love to turn you on." "More and more," former SDS president Todd Gitlin observed, "to get access to youth culture, you had to get high." Many people got "stoned" with milder drugs like marijuana, which was said at the time to impair short-term memory but had limited long-term effects. Some, like rock idols Janis Joplin, Jim Morrison, and Jimi Hendrix, sought in drugs a release from deep-seated pain. They combined alcohol with barbiturates, amphetamines, cocaine, and heroin until their drug dependence killed them. At first the term *psychedelic* referred to hallucinogenic drugs that altered perceptions. Counterculture adherents used these drugs as a means of expanding the mind to reach a higher level of experience and understanding. Drug use was also a way of expressing the antimaterialist, anti-authoritarian ethos of the era.

Soon new forms of popular behavior and expression grew up around the music and drug scenes. Adopting the Beats' notion that a posture of hipness constituted a form of social protest, counterculture devotees called themselves hippies. The hippie style, with its flowing hair and bell-bottom jeans, transformed the appearance of American youth. As part of their rejection of Western civilization's "uptight" materialism, devotees of the psychedelic culture adopted some of the trappings of Eastern mysticism, sporting bells, beads, flowing robes, and sandals. They perfumed their homes with incense and festooned them with Indian-print bedspreads. They wove flowers into their hair. They changed their diet, demanding more natural foods to enhance their spiritual health. They embraced the psychedelic art that appeared on rock posters and T-shirts, a style that used saturated colors, swirling calligraphy, and special photographic effects.

By the summer of 1967, hippie neighborhoods had sprung up in most American cities and college towns. San Francisco's Haight-Ashbury district, in particular, had become a magnet for people preaching the virtues of love, drugs, music, sex, and "flower power." While radical political activists proclaimed the summer of 1967 the Vietnam Summer, hippies announced that it was the "Summer of Love." This hedonistic interlude would transform society, not by agitating for widespread social change or an end to the war, but by encouraging individuals to drop out of the rat race and sample the pleasures of the senses. The networks and news magazines predicted the migration of thousands of young people to the Haight that summer, to "crash" in communal "pads"; "groove" at concerts in Golden Gate Park and at the Fillmore; and shower each other and the apprehensive local authorities with peace, love, and flowers. "If you're going to San Francisco," one song's lyrics advised, "be sure to wear some flowers in your hair."

At its root, the counterculture partook of the social problems and prejudices of American society in general. Crash pads, if hospitable, often recreated conventional household hierarchies. One young woman who went with a girlfriend to the Haight for a weekend reported with some disgust that her friend "moved into the first commune we entered and became a 'house-mother,' which means she did all the cooking and cleaning." Racial tensions, like gender hierarchies, persisted among the hip as well as the square. Relations between the predominantly white hippies in the Haight and the nearby black community in the Fillmore were terrible.

Although the Haight-Ashbury experience revealed contradictions in the counterculture, the music persisted, helping to keep the spirit of the cultural revolution alive. Promoters began staging large-scale, open-air rock festivals to attract the faithful. These events reached a high point with the Woodstock music festival of August 1969, a rain- and mud-soaked gathering of 400,000 rock fans in upstate New York. The unexpectedly huge crowd presented many serious problems, particularly in providing sanitation, food, and water. The audience had difficulty actually hearing the music and seeing the stage. Traffic was so bad that state authorities closed down the New York State Thruway. In spite of these troubles, however, many members of the audience would look back on Woodstock as the grandest experience of the 1960s, a demonstration that hundreds of thousands could come together for "three days of peace, love and music." The festival developed an almost mythological aura as the counterculture's finest hour.

By the late 1960s, many hippies had concluded that the only salvation for the counterculture lay in cultivating one's own garden. Across the country, disaffected hippies sought spiritual salvation and physical health by getting back to the land. College students moved out of dormitories and into rural farmhouses, bought sacks of brown rice, and planted organic gardens. Most communes were relatively short-lived, falling apart when faced with issues such as how to share expenses, whom to include or exclude, and how to divide the work. Advocates of "doing your own thing" clashed with those who saw a need for organization, and those who took on the task of collecting money for food or rent were regularly turned away with a haughty admonition to stop being so uptight and materialistic. The communes that lasted tended to be very hierarchical, like The Farm in Tennessee, or devoted to Eastern religious practices, especially various forms of Buddhism.

Hierarchy, of course, did not guarantee stability or virtue. The most infamous of the communes, the murderous Manson family, left Haight-Ashbury to settle, finally, in the dry Santa Susana Mountains of southern California. Charles Manson held his mostly female followers so completely spellbound that by December 1969, they were willing to commit murder at his orders. Even after they had been arrested for multiple homicides, including that of pregnant actress Sharon Tate, Manson's disciples continued to express their loyalty to him from their prison cells.

Hippie communes reflected a fundamental tension in American society: the tension between a longing for connectedness and a desire for personal liberty. If most of these communes lasted only a short time and seemed more dedicated to escapism than to solving the problems of a postindustrial society, they nevertheless represented a desire for a way of life dedicated not to the pursuit of consumer goods but to a vision of a meaningful existence. Often as not, those who experimented with communal living pondered not only hu-man relations, but also the complicated connections between people and the natural world. Some who began by raising organic vegetables became pio-neers of the environmental movement.

While communards sought a place apart from American consumerism and crass materialism, the counterculture spread to mainstream groups as well, becoming part of the everyday world of high school students from the mid-1960s to the mid-1970s, and extending beyond California and New York to other urban areas and even many small towns. As it spread, many people were ready to capitalize on it. Bill Graham grew fabulously wealthy promoting rock concerts. Psychedelic artist Peter Max eventually marketed his talents to about fifty companies, including Sears and General Electric. The countercul-ture spawned new business opportunities for purveyors of dietary and spiri-tual nostrums and proprietors of record stores, head shops, T-shirt stores, health-food stores, and hip clothing boutiques.

Jann Wenner, a particularly canny entrepreneur, spotted the marketing opportunity of the decade when he began publishing *Rolling Stone* magazine, a tabloid that began by covering the rock scene and soon expanded into long feature articles and investigative reporting. Wenner made a fortune while pub-lishing some of the best of the New Journalism. On the pages of *Rolling Stone*, politics and the counterculture came together in extraordinary forms, such as Tom Wolfe's perceptive history of the space program and Hunter S. Thomp-son's brilliant 1972 series on presidential politics, "Fear and Loathing on the Campaign Trail."

Mass Culture and Social Critique

Wenner was not the only one who wanted to capitalize on the opportunities presented by the baby-boom market. More established businesses and their leaders, however, encountered profound challenges as they tried to sell to anti-consumerist consumers. Nowhere did the rebellion of the young create a greater crisis of legitimacy and practice than in the advertising industry. Hos-tile to counterculture values and aesthetics, the industry's leaders vacillated between resisting and condemning change and seeking to co-opt it. Within the industry, the battle played out between the old guard and the "Young Turks," who themselves embraced many counterculture values.

The Young Turks, who criticized 1950s advertisements as boring and unimaginative, pioneered new modes of appeal. In one of the most famous campaigns of the decade, they marketed the Volkswagen Beetle, already popu-lar with the young, by touting its small size and its shortcomings as a status symbol. In one ad, for example, the Volkswagen Beetle, or the VW Bug, was shown sitting alone in a two-car garage with the caption, "It does all the work, but on Saturday night, which one goes to the party?" Another featured two politicians, one in a large 1950s-style convertible complete with fins and the other in the small, ugly German car, which looked the same year after year.

The ad asked: "Which man would you vote for?" The ads' use of humor to criticize consumerist excess typified one successful strategy used by advertisers to accommodate change.

In the 1960s, marketing leaders condemned those who criticized advertising's role in promoting consumption, labeling them subversives who attacked free enterprise and its benefits, while equating consumerism with liberty. As had been true in the 1950s, they singled out women as the purported beneficiaries of this freedom. Many young women began abandoning the use of cosmetics, but Revlon proclaimed that its make-up was "a great new freedom movement." The makers of Nice 'n' Easy hair coloring encouraged women to use the product, while declaring that women were "free to skip the make-up . . . free to dress any way." Increasingly, ads portrayed

A Volkswagen ad touting the small, inexpensive car as a "lemon" typifies the iconoclastic approach taken in the company's innovative ad campaign. / Private collection

women posed provocatively and dressed in miniskirts and other skimpy clothing. The new freedom promised by advertisers stopped short of freedom from objectification or freedom from worry about whether female bodies met contemporary standards for beauty. The new fashions (along with the medical community) contributed to American women's growing obsession with weight. American women joined weight-loss clubs, took amphetamines, and dieted to present themselves as youthful and slim.

Ultimately, the advertising industry decided to appropriate the symbols, music, dress, language, and aesthetics of the counterculture to distance itself from its association with mainstream or "straight" culture. This practice sometimes involved the creative assimilation of new modes and values, but more often it led to the trivialization of those values. An ad for jewelry depicted a young hippie couple with a sign saying "LOVE" in front of them; its caption proclaimed candidly that "What the world needs now is love, sweet love. It'll help our business." More than anything else, advertising sold youth, but more as a state of mind than as a chronological age. Pepsi decided it was for "those who think young," while Oldsmobile urged car buyers to "young it up" in their "youngmobile."

Television also had to accommodate the new youth market and come to terms with its political values, a challenge both to its entertainment and news divisions. CBS, for example, had numerous rural-life shows, including *Green Acres* and *The Andy Griffith Show*, in its prime-time lineup. By the late 1960s, viewers had tired of these shows, and the network decided to add more youth-oriented programs, including *The Smothers Brothers Show*, a variety show featuring two satiric folk singers, Tom and Dick Smothers. At first, CBS scheduled mainstream guests for the show, including Jim Nabors, Jack Benny, Jimmy Durante, and others. Over time, however, the show came to reflect the musical tastes and political values of the hosts.

The show battled with the network censors. Much of the conflict related to antiwar content that offended some viewers and the network brass. The episode that produced the most controversy featured leftist folk singer Pete Seeger on his first television appearance since being blacklisted in the 1950s. Seeger sang "Waist Deep in the Big Muddy," a metaphorical commentary on American involvement in the Vietnam War that includes the line "We're waist deep in the Big Muddy/And the big fool says to push on." CBS cut the song, eliciting a wellspring of protest. An internal memo from the head of Program Practices defending the decision said that a show's content should be "designed for the primary purpose of entertaining rather than to advance a point of view on a controversial subject" and claimed that the song's implication that the president of the United States was a fool was in bad taste. Ultimately, the network reinstated the segment when the show was rerun, but the censors persisted in cutting sections from other episodes, and Tom and Dick Smothers continued to explore the limits of prime-time dissent. In April 1969, CBS cancelled the program, claiming that the censors had not received a print of a forthcoming show in sufficient time to review it. The network scheduled *Hee Haw* in its time slot.

Surprisingly, the segment of the show that involved drug themes—"Share a Little Tea with Goldie"—occasioned much less criticism from viewers and network executives. A parody of afternoon programming directed at women, the segment often began with a greeting from Goldie O'Keefe (comedian Leigh French) such as "Hi! And glad of it." Although network censors cut some of her lines, her use of ambiguous language and drug terms unfamiliar to the general public meant that much of her material reached the air. In a sketch teaching viewers how to make whole-wheat bread, she enthusiastically demonstrated the proper technique: "The more you knead it, the higher it rises. The higher it rises, the lighter you feel. Ohhh—I feel good already! Ladies, ladies, ladies, get it on this way. My bread is getting high. And I'm beginning to rise!"

Despite its controversial content, the show generally had a conventional look. On NBC, however, *Rowan and Martin's Laugh-In* assimilated the counterculture aesthetic to design its sets and write its volley of one-liners. As described by one scholar, the show "abounded in hallucinogenic flashes, zooms, breathtakingly quick cuts, and a barrage of psychedelic colors. . . ." From the jokes written on the bodies of dancing women (including Goldie Hawn) in bikinis to the catchphrases fans loved, the innovative show created stock jokes that appealed to both its more hip viewers and a mainstream audience. Even president Richard Nixon made a cameo appearance, proclaiming "Sock it—to me?" The show's quick pace, which interspersed cultural and political commentary with more mainstream humor, may have defused some of the opposition. In any case, NBC seemed more at ease with its style and content than CBS had been with *The Smothers Brothers Show*.

Television also confronted volatile issues in its news divisions as it brought the Vietnam War into the nation's living rooms and covered the sometimes violent confrontations that marked American politics in these years. Beginning in 1963, the networks extended their nightly news shows from fifteen to thirty minutes, and by the time the war had escalated in the mid-1960s, the authority of well-known anchors, most notably Walter Cronkite, had increased the importance of television as an interpreter of the meanings of the war. Cronkite had almost pronounced benedictions on the war in the mid-1960s, but after the Tet offensive in 1968, he editorialized that the United States could not win and should seek a negotiated peace, and his words carried great clout.

In the print media also, reporters did not challenge political or military leaders' assertions regarding the purposes and prosecution of the war in the early years. Tom Wicker, who covered the White House for the *New York Times*, stated that at first, he did not question the official view that the war was necessary to fight communist aggression, but ultimately he grew increasingly distrustful of the government's claims: ". . . the Secretary of State tells me that, and who am I to argue with him . . . that's the view one had at the time. . . . We had not yet been taught to question the President. . . . We had not been taught by bitter experience that our government like any other in extremis will lie and cheat to protect itself."

The growing skepticism of the war on the part of the press did not mean that it offered sympathetic coverage to the antiwar and other dissident movements. In general, the media depicted opponents of the war as threats to the country's internal security, not as legitimate participants in a foreign policy debate. Indeed, they routinely ignored the political positions advanced by critics of the nation's policies. In a 1968 television feature on American deserters in France, ABC reporter John Rolfson called them misfits and emphasized, not their political objections to the Vietnam War, but the role of a "mysterious" man named Cook (a draft-resistance counselor) in "recruiting" them to desert. He concluded his story by asking rhetorically: "What do you think of the idea of the obligations of citizenship in the United States? Do these ideals mean anything to you? Obviously [these deserters are] being used against the United States."

The media also depicted the antiwar movement as a disreputable threat to social stability and law and order. Television in particular focused on the unusual, the violent, and the flamboyant when it covered dissident political movements. Although reporters tended to cover events held by middle-class people in meeting rooms (like "teach-ins" and Senate committee hearings) with more respect than student protests, they often ignored these forms of middle-class protest because they lacked drama. In the name of balance, television reports often juxtaposed long-haired hippies waving North Vietnamese flags with sober administration spokespersons protesting against the excesses of their critics. In the mid-1960s, when most violence associated with demonstrations was initiated by supporters of the war attacking peaceful marchers, the media still managed to blame antiwar activists. In one such report, CBS anchor Walter Cronkite noted that prowar spectators, angered when demonstrators displayed the NLF flag, had attacked protestors. He explained their attack on the protesters, however, by stating, "Antiwar demonstrators in New York provoked a series of clashes today with counterdemonstrators and police."

1968: A Year of Cataclysm

To some extent, the three movements—Black Power, the New Left, and the counterculture—discussed so far in this chapter represented separate strands of anti-establishment sentiment during the 1960s. They often differed from one another in both goals and methods. For instance, the Black Panthers did not wear flowers in their hair; hippies were frequently indifferent to politics, believing that salvation lay in altering the mind and spirit; and some political radicals of the New Left could not fathom how anyone could smoke marijuana when there was a rally to attend. But the membership of the three movements did overlap, and they generally shared a basic opposition to racism, social injustice, bourgeois consumerism, and the Vietnam War. As the climate of protest intensified in the late 1960s, there were more and more occasions when the various strands of the different movements came together. This was particularly true in 1968, a cataclysmic year for American society and politics.

On December 31, 1967, some important members of the counterculture and the New Left joined forces. Radical leaders Abbie Hoffman and Jerry Rubin, black activist–comedian Dick Gregory, Beat poet Allen Ginsberg, counterculture writer Paul Krassner of *The Realist* (the nation's oldest underground newspaper), and several others founded the Youth International Party, better known as the Yippies. Hoffman, a great believer in employing humor to promote serious causes, was a master at manipulating the media. Applying a combination of militant tactics, freakish pranks, and humor, the Yippies would try to make themselves the national media's front-page story. Their particular goals were sometimes hard to determine. They stood for freedom and for spontaneity; they protested against the Vietnam War, racism, and politics as usual. They planned to turn the 1968 Democratic national convention in Chicago into a "Festival of Life" featuring rock music and elaborate practical jokes, a kind of revolutionary dance party (see Chapter 7).

The Right gained momentum after the convention in Chicago, spurred on by the inflammatory rhetoric of independent presidential candidate George Wallace and Republican vice-presidential contender Spiro Agnew. The Left was transformed but not dead. SDS boomed. Some movement leaders, increasingly seduced by the romance of violent revolution, considered the convention a triumph, believing with Tom Hayden that "our victory lies in progressively demystifying a false democracy." Hayden and seven others, including Hoffman and Rubin, were indicted for conspiring to incite a riot at the Democratic National Convention. Their trial at the hands of reactionary judge Julius J. Hoffman became an emblem of the friction between radical dissidents and repressive authorities. When Judge Hoffman ordered one of the defendants, Black Panther leader Bobby Seale, bound and gagged, newspaper sketch artists had a field day depicting the fulfillment of the order. Seale was ultimately tried separately from the other defendants (all white), a judicial move that underlined the nation's persistent racial polarization.

The jurors, who were overwhelmingly white and middle class, acquitted the seven defendants on the conspiracy charges but convicted five of them of intent to incite riot. The judge added lengthy sentences for contempt of court, which resulted from the defendants' disruptive conduct. Ultimately, a federal appeals court overturned all convictions on the grounds that the judge had acted improperly when he refused to allow defense attorneys to question prospective jurors regarding their cultural biases and because of Hoffman's "deprecatory and often antagonistic attitude toward the defense." In addition, the court noted that the convictions would have also been overturned had it been known at the time of legal arguments that the FBI, with the knowledge of the judge and the prosecution, had bugged the offices of the defense attorneys during the trial.

Sports also served as a site of conflict in 1968, in part the result of the creation of the Olympic Committee for Human Rights (OCHR) by African American sociologist Harry Edwards and others. Their immediate goals were to continue the 1964 ban of South Africa from Olympic competition in protest of its policy of racial apartheid, to secure black representation on the International Olympic Committee (IOC), and to persuade the IOC to remove Avery Brundage as its chair. When the IOC announced its intention to lift the ban on South Africa, the OCHR began planning a boycott by black athletes. Brundage backed down and reinstated the ban, saying that he wanted to prevent violence at the Mexico City games. If that was his goal, however, it failed. When Mexicans demonstrated in protest of the millions spent by the Mexican government to build infrastructure for the international sports event, police opened fire, killing over three hundred people.

At the games themselves, American sprinters Tommie Smith and John Carlos used their first- and third-place finishes in the 200-meter dash as the occasion for protest. As the U.S. national anthem was played, Smith, the gold medalist, and Carlos, the bronze medalist, raised black-gloved hands in the Black Power salute and bowed their heads. In response, the U.S. Olympic Committee suspended them and ordered

As the national anthem played during their Olympics awards ceremony, dissident athletes Tommie Smith and John Carlos raised their hands and looked down in protest of racism. / AP/Wide World them to leave Mexico City. Although many Americans reacted with outrage at the athletes' actions, some athletes and black leaders defended the dissidents. Several American athletes threatened to withdraw from competition after the suspensions. Australian Peter Norman, the silver medalist in the 200-meter dash, wore the official badge of the OCHR when he shared the victory stand with Smith and Carlos.

Smith and Carlos were not the first black athletes to test the limits of dissent in the United States. When world heavyweight champion Muhammad Ali announced that he had embraced the Black Muslim faith in 1965, FBI director J. Edgar Hoover ordered an examination of his exemption from the draft. Ali, who had apparently failed the math sections of his first mental aptitude examination, became the center of a public firestorm led by many sportswriters and politicians. South Carolina congressman L. Mendel Rivers launched a crusade to get the heavyweight champion drafted into the military: "Here he is, smart enough to finish high school, write his kind of poetry, promote himself all over the world, make a million a year, drive around in red Cadillacs—and they say he's too dumb to tote a gun! Who's dumb enough to believe that?" When the Defense Department reduced the mental aptitude percentile that it used for draft eligibility from 30 to 15, Ali (who scored at the sixteenth percentile) was reclassified as 1-A. Declaring that "I ain't got nothing against them Vietcong," Ali refused to serve and was convicted of draft evasion. His case reached the U.S. Supreme Court in 1971, when the Court ruled in his favor on narrow technical grounds.

On American campuses, confrontation became the norm by the late 1960s. In May 1969, police and demonstrators at Berkeley clashed at the battle of People's Park. The park, which belonged to the University of California, had once been a weedy meeting place for dope dealers and their customers but had since been turned into a community garden. The university, claiming that it wanted to build a soccer field on the spot, asked police to seal off the area while bulldozers razed the gardens. When marchers moved in to take back the park, the police fired with buckshot and tear gas. Governor Ronald Reagan sent in three thousand National Guard troops, who occupied the park for seventeen days. People's Park became a symbol of radical struggle and the communal alternative to private property; it also underlined the emerging importance of ecological issues, pitting organic gardeners against bulldozers, tomatoes against tear gas.

Disturbances in the spring of 1969 at Harvard, Stanford, Cornell, and nearly three hundred other campuses included more than a hundred incidents involving arson and attempted or actual bombings. The voice of the counterculture grew more militant. Jefferson Airplane, a San Francisco rock group that had risen to fame by combining powerful vocal and instrumental performances with odes to the mind-expanding power of LSD, turned to celebrating insurrection: "Look what's happenin' out in the streets/Got to Revolution!"

Meanwhile, some activists worked hard to repair the antiwar movement's damaged credibility. The New Mobilization, a coalition of moderate antiwar advocates, organized a nationwide peace demonstration in the fall of 1969, calling for a moratorium on the war. Millions of people responded, holding rallies, teach-ins, marches, and meetings. On the day of the demonstration, one hundred thousand people gathered on Boston Common; in New York City, a series of mass meetings were held, including one on Wall Street. Nationwide crowd estimates for the October 15, 1969, demonstrations ranged from 2 million to 15 million. The following month, more than half a million people gathered in Washington, D.C., for a second demonstration, the largest ever held in that city.

This huge, peaceful outcry against the war did have an impact; it demonstrated that millions of Americans supported neither the war nor the violent tactics of the extreme Left. Yet even moderate antiwar activists became angry and frustrated by their inability to stop the war. The extremists made better copy, and their frequent clashes with police drew attention away from what the moderates regarded as their more serious attempts to affect the nation's policy in Vietnam.

On December 4, 1969, Chicago police raided the local Black Panther headquarters, killing Panther leaders Fred Hampton and Mark Clark in their beds. SDS splintered, and it soon became dominated by a faction calling itself the Weathermen, after a line in a Bob Dylan song: "You don't need a weatherman to know which way the wind blows." Announcing their goal as "the destruction of U.S. imperialism and the achievement of a classless world: world communism," the Weathermen rejected coalition politics of any kind and embraced worldwide revolution. Their heroes included Chinese Communist Party chair Mao Zedong and Central American revolutionary martyr Che Guevara. Their enemies were "the pigs at home"; their vanguard was a revolutionary youth movement. "Kids used to try to beat the system from inside the army or from inside the schools," they said; "now they desert from the army and burn down the schools."

A week before the October 1969 demonstrations, two or three hundred Weathermen street fighters battled Chicago police in a showdown that came to be known as the Days of Rage. In the next year, the antiwar movement's conflicting philosophies were thrown into sharp relief. While thousands assembled to light candles and sing "give peace a chance," a relatively few shock troops fantasized about violence, trained for street fighting, and built bombs. Between September 1969 and May 1970, there were at least 250 bombings at draft boards, ROTC buildings, federal offices, and corporate headquarters. In March 1970, three bombers from the Weather Underground, as the Weathermen now called themselves, died when they blew themselves up in a New York townhouse. The following August, a bomb exploded in the University of Wisconsin mathematics building, killing a graduate student working on a research project in a facility the bombers thought to be empty.

In 1970, there were 9,408 incidents of protest; 731 involved police and arrests, 410 involved damage to property, and 230 involved violence to persons. The confrontations peaked in May, when President Nixon announced that U.S. troops had invaded neutral Cambodia, a state neighboring Vietnam. The announcement set off a wave of student strikes; at least seventy-five

A student screams in horror over the body of an antiwar demonstrator slain by the National Guard at Kent State University on May 4, 1970. In the aftermath of the Kent State killings, college students across the country staged protests and strikes. / © John Filo

campuses shut down for the rest of the academic year, and students at North-western University announced that their institution had seceded from the United States. About thirty ROTC buildings were burned or bombed in the first week of May, including the one at Kent State University in Kent, Ohio. Governor James Rhodes called in National Guard troops to restore order on the Kent State campus; on May 4, nervous troops opened fire on student demonstrators and passersby, killing four and wounding nine. Ten days later, police killed two more students and wounded nine at Jackson State, a predominantly black campus in Mississippi. Torn and bloody, the country seemed to be consuming its young—a cannibalism that some deplored, others embraced.

As radical Left and antiwar protests culminated in these violent confrontations, another protest movement was developing—more quietly at first, but perhaps possessing an even greater potential for long-term impact. This protest movement was for women's liberation, a product of a new feminist consciousness.

The Rise of the New Feminism

Even in the supposedly quiescent 1950s, there had been some organized and articulate attempts to come to grips with women's issues. In the period immediately following World War II, some unions had sought to organize service and clerical workers, who were mostly women, as well as female factory employees like those in California's canneries. Sometimes uniting across ethnic lines, working-class women had pushed for goals such as equal pay for equal work and had begun to consider economic and social questions that would not be articulated fully until the 1980s. Even in the heyday of domestic femininity, the idea that women belonged at home because they were nurturing, timid creatures entirely different from competitive, capable men was questioned. In the 1950s, magazines like *Ladies' Home Journal* and *Good Housekeeping* carried articles celebrating the benefits of paid work for women and featured profiles of successful career women.

By 1960, women's issues had begun to receive attention from the federal government. In 1961, President Kennedy established a Commission on the Status of Women (CSW), headed by Eleanor Roosevelt. Something of an anomaly in the masculine atmosphere of the New Frontier, the CSW took tentative positions, such as recommending new programs in adult education so that women might return to work after raising their children. Such limited goals made it clear that women should not neglect their primary responsibility in the home.

In the early 1960s, Congress began to outlaw some forms of discrimination against working women. The Equal Pay Act of 1963 made it illegal to pay women less than men for doing the same job. However, the decade's most significant piece of legislation in the area of women's rights became law almost serendipitously. As Congress debated the 1964 Civil Rights Act, a reactionary Virginia congressman, Howard W. Smith, attempted to kill the bill by introducing an amendment that he believed would reduce the whole matter of civil rights to absurdity. An amendment to Title VII prohibited discrimination on the basis of gender as well as race, religion, and ethnic background. Encouraged by business- and professional women, liberal northerners led by Representative Martha Griffiths of Michigan pushed the amendment through, and it became law along with the rest of the bill. The Equal Employment Opportunity Commission (EEOC), charged with enforcing the act's bans on workplace discrimination, did not at first take sex discrimination complaints seriously. But under increasing pressure from women's groups it ultimately began to enforce the law.

Meanwhile, as noted in Chapter 3, discontent had been brewing in the tranquil suburbs. Middle-class white women, supposedly fully absorbed in cleaning their houses and raising their children, found domestic life lacking. In 1963 came the publication of Betty Friedan's *The Feminine Mystique*, which lamented the societal waste in isolating educated, talented women in the "comfortable concentration camp" of the American home. Middle-class white American women, Friedan said, felt depressed, useless, and assailed by "the problem that has no name." Speaking for this constituency (and not, for example, for African American mothers, whose families' survival had long depended on their ability to find paid work of any kind), Friedan believed that the solution lay in giving women meaningful jobs outside the home. In 1966, Friedan was among the founders of the National Organization for Women (NOW)—the first national lobby for women's rights since the suffrage era. It was, and still is, dedicated to the goal of achieving for women political and economic opportunities equal to those enjoyed by men.

The women's movement gained momentum because it was rooted in widespread, elemental changes in American society. Among other factors, more and more women were becoming educated. Between 1950 and 1974, college enrollment for men increased 234 percent; for women, it increased 456 percent. Even more important, both married and single women were entering the paid work force. During World War II, employment of adult women increased from 27 percent in 1940 to 36 percent five years later. Female employment dropped off temporarily immediately after the war, but by the beginning of the 1960s, 37.7 percent of women age sixteen and over were employed, and they constituted 33 percent of the total work force. A decade later, 43 percent of women age sixteen and over, representing 38 percent of the civilian work force, were either working or looking for work. The numbers continued to rise steadily. More and more frequently, the working woman was a married woman: by 1962, married women accounted for 60 percent of the female work force. The working woman was also a mother: as early as 1970, one-third of women with children under six years of age held or sought jobs.

At the same time, women workers had fewer job options than their male counterparts. They generally crowded into female-dominated occupations— nursing, clerical work, teaching, domestic work—that paid less than men's jobs. In 1955, the median compensation for women in full-time, year-round employment was 64 percent of men's earnings. In 1960, the figure had dropped to 61 percent, and by 1975, full-time women workers were earning only 58.8 percent of what men earned. Even when they did the same work as men, they were paid less. The EEOC was understaffed and often reluctant to pursue complaints about violations of the Equal Pay Act. Employers could avoid the whole issue by writing slightly different job descriptions or giving different titles to men and women engaged in substantially the same activities.

Most women who worked reported that they did so out of financial necessity or to improve their family's standard of living, although some said they were seeking personal satisfaction. Still, most Americans assumed that even women who held full-time, paid jobs would continue to do most of the housework. According to figures that changed very little between 1955 and the early 1970s, full-time housewives spent between 52 and 56 hours per week doing housework. Wives who worked full-time outside the home still reported spending about 26 hours per week on housekeeping. And whether or not their wives worked, husbands spent about 1.6 hours per day, or 11.2 hours per week, doing household tasks, including yard work. Men helped at times with the shopping, cooking, and laundry, but in general they did not do the cleaning or ironing.

Perhaps most important of all, the myth of the happy nuclear family was crumbling. Greater acknowledgment of the tensions within families (signaled by a rising divorce rate), concern about women who had been widowed or abandoned, and growing alarm over family violence and abuse heralded an urgent need to re-evaluate women's place in American society. If women could no longer count on the family as a protected place, they would have to fashion new ways of making their way in the world.

The dramatic changes in women's roles in society were bound to have political consequences, particularly as civil rights activists were uncovering

(cont. on page 310)

"A Veritable Obsession": Women, Work, and Motherhood

In the spring of 2002, America's mainstream media made Sylvia Hewlett, author of a new book entitled *Creating Life: Professional Women and the Quest for Children*, the center of attention. Appearing on television talk shows from *Sixty Minutes* to *Oprah*, she promoted her new book and warned young professional women that they had to focus on marriage and childbearing if they hoped to have families in the future. Her not-so-new ideas provoked heated debate, prompting columnist Ellen Goodman to conclude that "motherhood [had] become, well, the mother of all controversies." Feminists charged that her advice was part of the larger backlash against new opportunities and enlarged lives for women, a backlash that wanted nothing more than to return women (especially middle-class women) to lives of domesticity. Antifeminists crowed that Hewlett's book had exposed "the feminists' big lie"—the idea that they could win "the war against nature" in which they had purportedly enlisted.

Hewlett's relationship to modern feminism, however, was much more complex than these debates suggested. On the one hand, she did blame "equal rights feminists," as she called them, for encouraging highly educated and ambitious women to enter the workplace and prove themselves by focusing on work in the same ways and on the same terms that high-achieving men had done. The result of this strategy, she stated, was that women either did not marry or faced age-related infertility by the time they decided to have children.

On the other hand, Hewlett credited modern feminism with expanding workplace opportunities for women and thereby giving them new ways to express their creativity and experience challenge, stimulation, and a sense of competence in the public world. She sympathetically related the views of playwright Wendy Wasserstein, who told

her: "I think the women's movement saved my life. In fact, I know it saved my life. . . .The women's movement gave me the right to find my own voice—and the belief that my own voice was worth finding. It's extraordinary—that an idea can do this for someone."

Just as Hewlett's positive views of women's workplace gains generated little media attention, her criticisms of men's self-absorption or of corporate conservatism received relatively little notice compared to her warning to women that they should focus on marriage and childbearing in their twenties and thirties. Hewlett blamed men for not being willing to marry and provide emotional support to high-achieving women, and she blamed corporations for failing to adopt more "family-friendly" policies. According to Hewlett, American men still want to come home and find a nurturing, domestic woman who sees to all their needs, most particularly those needs centered on ego maintenance. As a result, women who require more egalitarian terms for relationships with men are left with poor choices. In addition, Hewlett charged that the conservative values dominating corporate culture limit employers' willingness to accommodate women's family responsibilities through policies that would enable workers to interrupt careers and then return without penalty and through policies providing flexible schedules, paid family leave, and part-time work.

The media, however, zeroed in on her findings regarding the reproductive difficulties of high-income professional women. Citing data showing that such women were much less likely to marry or have children than were men in the same circumstances, she stated her conviction that women should be able to have the same opportunities for work and family that men did. On the basis of her own selective survey of women in high-income jobs, she also concluded that this disparity in their family lives was not something women had chosen and, indeed, that it went up against powerful maternal instincts. As a woman who had spent several years and huge amounts of money so that she could have a fifth child at the age of fifty-one, Hewlett was her own best evidence. Speaking at least as much from her own emotionally-fraught experiences as from her carefully selected evidence (she did not seek women who chose to be childless for her study), she asserted, "If you're over 40, the desire to have a baby before it's too late can kick in with ferocious intensity. It can become a nonnegotiable demand—a veritable obsession—that rides roughshod over every other aspect of life." Her maternal obsession, she asserted, received little social support (even her husband was a reluctant conscript to her cause) and therefore, she concluded that "[a]ll of this must be hardwired."

Sylvia Hewlett touts her book, *Creating a Life,* and its ideas at a meeting on "Maternal Feminism." / AP/Wide World

The biology at the center of her ideas has been expressed in somewhat different ways in different historical periods. In the late nineteenth and early twentieth centuries, anxieties about women and reproduction centered on the rising numbers of women who attended college. One doctor declared, "[S]cience pronounces that the woman who studies is lost"—to reproduction, that is. Cautioning that energy drained in academic work would cost women their reproductive health, doctors and others pointed to the low numbers of college-educated women who married or had children to buttress their case.

The women's decisions, according to the critics, had dire social consequences. Popularizing an idea that developed first in academic circles, President Theodore Roosevelt claimed that the superior races (meaning whites) faced "race suicide" if women from the "better classes" had fewer children than other women. In the 1940s, S. H. Halford alerted eugenicists to "the now undoubted fact that the highly educated woman, as a direct consequence of her adoption of the student habit, very frequently loses the sexual in-

stinct." If she then proceeded to a successful career, she also acquired "a strong economic bias to celibacy, or, if she does marry, against the bearing of children." Instead of passing her intelligence to the children she bore, she contributed to "the impoverishment of the race."

By the 1950s, experts were arguing that women who worked, especially those in demanding professions, were manifesting deep psychological problems ("masculinist strivings") and causing enormous harm to their husbands and children (see pages 101–102). Single women were, if anything, even worse. Marynia Farnham and Ferdinand Lundberg, authors of the much-discussed *Modern Woman: The Lost Sex*, proclaimed that they were "defeminized" and "deeply ill." They also blamed women's growing economic independence for rising divorce rates. Women's magazine headlines reflected the dominant pronatalist view of the period: "Have Babies While You're Young," "Birth: The Crowning Moment of My Life," and "I Will Have Another Baby. I Must Live That Divine Experience Again."

The idea that women "really" wanted domesticity and had been rendered deeply unhappy by the pursuit of careers received renewed attention in the 1980s, when the media focused intensively on the "problem" of single women. The *New York Times*, for example, claimed that single women "suffered from a sickness almost" and were "too rigid to connect." Their unwillingness to settle for just any marriage meant despair and loneliness. The title for a 1987 article in *Harper's Bazaar* provided a common answer to the question of why women were single: "Are You Turning Men Off?: Desperate and Demanding." In a 1986 television special entitled "After the Sexual Revolution," cohosts Richard Threlkeld and Betsy Aaron intoned that successful women were unlikely to have successful relationships. Aaron claimed that feminists had not warned women that the "price of revolution" would be "freedom and independence turning to loneliness and depression." As feminist critic Susan Faludi noted in her 1991 book, *Backlash: The Undeclared War Against American Women*, "It wasn't a trade-off Aaron could have deduced from her own life: she had a successful career and a husband—co-host Threlkeld."

In a highly publicized story that later proved to be greatly exaggerated, *Newsweek* warned in 1986 that single women over forty were "more likely to be killed by a terrorist" than to marry. The reason, they said, was that women were putting high-income jobs over the pursuit of husbands and that they were expecting far too much of prospective mates. Instead, they acted "as though it were not worth giving up space in their closets for anything less than Mr. Perfect." Given the very small number of American women who had managed to secure upper-income jobs, it was quite unlikely that the explanations *Newsweek* provided for national patterns of marriage had any substance. The newsmagazine drew its data from an unpublished study by social scientists at Harvard and Yale that had been severely criticized by de-mographers on the grounds that it was based on faulty numbers. By the late 1980s, media tearjerkers focusing on miserable and apparently penitent single women had become a staple of evening news shows.

At the same time, headlines urged the small number of women holding well-paying jobs to worry that their choices would cost them their fertility and warned millions of others that their hours at work came at the expense of their children. The *Washington Post*, for example, headlined one of its 1987 stories: "The Quiet Pain of Infertility: For the Success-Oriented, It's a Bitter Pill." As with Hewlett, any infertility difficulties experienced by poor women received no notice. To underscore the view that women themselves would be happier at home, newspapers and magazines featured accounts of women who had given up highly successful careers for a happy return to full-time domesticity. While countless such stories appeared in the mainstream media, the labor-force participation rates of mothers (single and married) continued to climb, suggesting that millions of women had in fact combined motherhood and paid employment.

Increasing numbers of married women and mothers have entered the labor force in the postwar period. They have done so for a multitude of reasons. Some have sought employment to supplement family incomes. This is particularly true in working-class families, where the decline in real hourly wages for men (which began around 1970) has been especially steep, and in female-headed households, where women must provide most or all of the support for the family. Married women who have found domesticity isolating, stressful, or routine have sought work that provided them with wider experiences and social contacts, a respite from family pressures, and the opportunity to develop skills and expertise. In a 1997 book entitled *The Time Bind: When Work Becomes Home and Home Becomes Work*, sociologist Arlie Hochschild discovered that many women chose longer hours at their paid work because the emotional work demanded of them at home left them stressed and drained. In the labor force, by contrast, they forged supportive friendships and found human relationships more manageable. This finding occurs despite the persistent discrimination and low wages that many women experience in America's workplaces and despite the stresses and work that women face as they combine long hours at their paid work and at home.

In the meantime, the debate continues, focusing attention on the decisions of individual women rather than on the economic circumstances, corporate practices, cultural values, and political decisions that create the context for their decisions.

---

racial injustice, liberal politicians were embracing social reform, and radical dissidents were questioning the distribution of power in American society. Although the civil rights movement and the New Left fell short of obtaining all their goals, both proved to be seedbeds for a feminist movement of lasting impact and immense scope.

In the fall of 1964, SNCC women, including Ruby Doris Smith Robinson, Casey Hayden, Mary King, and Maria Varela, drafted a paper on women's position in the SNCC. Robinson recognized that, as a woman, she shared some common ground with King and Hayden, both white, but as an African American, she also believed that the organization should be black-led and black-dominated. King and Hayden recognized that the turn toward Black Power would leave no place for them in a movement to which they had devoted years of their lives. Black Power as a political strategy might leave them out, but as an ideology focusing on difference, it provided them with a model for distinguishing the ways in which women's status diverged from men's. A year later, in the fall of 1965, King and Hayden composed "a kind of memo" and delivered it anonymously to women in the peace and freedom movements. They argued that women and blacks both "seem to be caught up in a common-law caste system . . . which, at its worst, uses and exploits women." When they raised the problem of male dominance among their fellow activists, men generally responded by laughing at them. Several months earlier, at an SNCC meeting, where the question of women's position in the movement had been raised, Stokely Carmichael had quipped, "The position of women in SNCC is prone!" Those who heard the remark, including Mary King, "collapsed with hilarity," but when the laughter faded, the serious question remained.

By June 1967, women had found a language to express their grievances. They named the problem sexism (sometimes called male chauvinism); they named the solution women's liberation. NOW activists focused on eliminating wage discrimination and fighting for legal guarantees of equality. They proposed the Equal Rights Amendment to the Constitution and pushed hard for its passage. The radical feminists, who sometimes began as NOW members but more often came out of the civil rights movement and the New Left, identified a new set of political issues, including childcare, abortion, birth control, sexuality, family violence, and the sharing of housework. Meeting in small groups to discuss not only war and racism but also problems that seemed intensely individual and private, they soon developed a new theoretical tool: consciousness-raising. By identifying their common grievances, they came to the fundamental insight of the new feminist movement—namely, that what appeared to be women's individual problems involved much larger questions of social power, or "sexual politics," in the words of feminist theorist Kate Millett. Feminist writer Robin Morgan turned this insight into the slogan, "The personal is political."

From the start, the new feminism, often called "the second wave" to distinguish it from the women's rights movement of the late nineteenth and early twentieth centuries, faced formidable obstacles. All kinds of people felt threatened by the prospect of women's liberation: conservative men, who stood to lose many privileges; middle-class women, especially housewives, who worried that men would simply abandon their breadwinner roles and that women would lose whatever protections they had; fundamentalist Christians, who believed that women's traditional role was biblically ordained; and even leftist men, accustomed to treating women as assistant radicals and sex objects. In the late 1960s and early 1970s, the mainstream press used dismissive language to ridicule the movement. Reporters for *Time* and *Newsweek* who referred to Gloria Steinem and Shulamith Firestone as "women's libbers" never called Eldridge Cleaver or Rap Brown "black libbers."

The task of building a movement based on women's common problems, interests, and objectives was deeply complicated by the very diversity of the women the movement hoped to mobilize. Certainly race made a difference in how women approached feminism. Even in the early days of SNCC, racial differences among women had raised tensions: black women had articulated grievances and goals that diverged from those of their white sisters in the "beloved community." Class, age, sexual preference, and occupational status also divided women. Middle-class housewives who had invested their lives in the idea that their husbands would protect them were far less equipped to face the challenges of economic independence than were college-age women battling discrimination in law school admissions. Lesbian activists saw their interests as diverging in significant ways from those of heterosexual women. Mexican American mothers working as migrant farm laborers or domestics had different needs from the affluent women who bought the produce they picked or hired them to clean their homes.

Some feminist activists, like Robin Morgan, took a page out of the Yippies' book and sought to create splashy media events to gain a national audience. A week after the 1968 Chicago convention, Morgan and almost two hundred other protesters at the Miss America Pageant in Atlantic City crowned a live sheep "Miss America." *New York Times* reporter Charlotte Curtis covered the protest in typically dismissive terms. Media critic Susan Douglas noted that, in Curtis's article, "[C]harges about sexism in the United States were placed in quotation marks, suggesting that these were merely the deluded hallucinations of a few ugly, angry women rather than a fact of life." Print and

The women's liberation movement brought young women into the streets to protest a variety of inequalities. / John Olson, © Life Magazine, Time, Inc.

broadcast media inevitably played up conflicts among women. Curtis devoted a full paragraph of her story to a "counterdemonstration" staged by three women. And they often went even further in demeaning feminist actions and goals. On August 26, 1970, feminists held the Women's Strike for Equality, which featured marches and rallies in major cities across the country. A march down Fifth Avenue in New York attracted between thirty thousand and fifty thousand supporters. ABC anchor Howard K. Smith led the coverage of the event that night with a quotation from Vice President Spiro Agnew: "Three things have been difficult to tame. The ocean, fools, and women. We may soon be able to tame the ocean, but fools and women will take a little longer."

Because of the enormous diversity of issues affecting women, feminists had different views on both long- and short-term goals for the movement. Some argued that the first order of business was to dismantle a capitalist system that especially oppressed women. Others believed that the movement should concentrate first on eradicating male domination. Some believed that men could be reformed and that women had an obligation to maintain relations with men. Shulamith Firestone declared that "a revolutionary in every bedroom cannot fail to shake up the status quo." Others rejected heterosexuality, some for political reasons, some because women's liberation allowed them to act on long-suppressed lesbian feelings. As visions of the women's movement proliferated, so did its tactics, victories, failures, and institutions.

By the mid-1970s, women had made inroads into male-dominated professions, mounted successful challenges to legal and economic discrimination, founded new enterprises, and claimed new rights. Yet much remained to be done. While the privileges of race and class enabled a few American women to "have it all," many more remained highly vulnerable. The wage gap between men and women persisted. If some women made strides in professional circles, many more fell deeper into poverty.

The Legacy of the Sixties

The women's movement has continued, with various shifts in emphasis, to the present day, but the other protest movements of the 1960s gradually faded or evolved into new, less sensational forms. The New Left never recovered from the cataclysmic spring of 1970, when the killings at Kent State capped a surge of bombings and confrontations. After that time, some self-proclaimed revolutionaries went underground. Moderate dissidents seemed dazed by the escalating climate of hatred. Some activists, declaring themselves burned out, retreated from politics altogether. Many left the movement to pursue other political goals. Eventually, peace came to Vietnam, removing the principal issue that had united the many factions of the New Left. But the legacy of the 1960s political protest was not forgotten. Most obviously, future administrations knew that an unpopular war abroad could provoke widespread rebellion at home.

The counterculture saw many of its distinctive attributes absorbed into the mainstream culture. Hippie styles in hair and clothing and psychedelic music became popular enough to lose some of their revolutionary impact. Society at large became more sexually permissive; indeed, the sexual revolution was a primary legacy of the 1960s. Recreational drug use spread beyond hippie enclaves, winning converts in many segments of American society. Some of the erstwhile hippies drifted into more conventional lives, or at least their habits no longer seemed extraordinary. Others founded the New Age movement, reviving ancient religions and joining experimental therapy groups in search of spiritual fulfillment and expanded consciousness. Rooting out one's inner demons—whether through meditation, confrontation, long soaks in seaside hot springs, or hard labor in religious communes—occupied some inheritors of the countercultural tradition. Inevitably, business began to capitalize on nostalgia for the wild and crazy 1960s. Nike launched a TV ad featuring the Beatles' song "Revolution." Tofu, yogurt, herbal tea, and organic rice began showing up on supermarket shelves.

Meanwhile, the civil rights movement, which had been transformed by Black Power, fragmented. Some leaders went into exile; others had died. Still others began to move into the political mainstream. SCLC workers Andrew Young and Jesse Jackson, who had stood with Martin Luther King, Jr., when he was shot in Memphis, Tennessee, led the next generation of activists. Both men became powerful in the Democratic Party. Blacks and women held more and more local and national political offices. Beginning with Carl Stokes of Cleveland, who was elected in 1967 as the first African American mayor of a major American city, blacks moved into positions of power in the nation's urban centers. By 1990, former SNCC president John Lewis would win election to the U.S. Congress, defeating a fellow movement veteran, Julian Bond.

The push for African American rights also spawned a new, multicultural politics of difference. By the late 1960s, Native Americans organized to raise public awareness of the history of their oppression by adopting both militant and moderate tactics. Members of the American Indian Movement (AIM) occupied Alcatraz Island and staged a mass protest at Wounded Knee, South Dakota, the site of a notorious massacre of Lakota (Sioux) Indians in 1890. Other Indian advocates formed organizations such as the Native American Rights Fund to pursue legal change. By 1980, Native Americans had succeeded in forcing the federal government to return some important tribal lands and to provide compensation for other lands that had been confiscated by whites.

Mexican Americans, galvanized by Cesar Chavez's charismatic leadership and his success in organizing the United Farm Workers, pressed for reform in the treatment of Latinos. Latinos shared a heritage based on their Spanish language and culture, but they had come from places as diverse as Mexico, Chile, Nicaragua, Cuba, and Puerto Rico under enormously varied circumstances. As they struggled to articulate common goals—forming organizations like the League of United Latin American Citizens (LULAC)—and to come to grips with differences among themselves, they became an increasingly important part of the American political and economic picture, especially in the Sunbelt. Latino students, particularly Mexican Americans, organized campus groups that continue to play a prominent role at universities across the country.

The protest movements of the 1960s mobilized people to seek racial justice and gender equality; they also created the possibility of a civil rights movement for homosexuals. On June 29, 1969, police raided the Stonewall Inn, a gay bar in New York City's Greenwich Village. Instead of accepting arrest, the patrons fought back with rocks and bottles. This confrontation was heralded as the beginning of the gay liberation movement. Gay and lesbian activists moved quickly to redefine homosexuality not as a perversion but as a legitimate sexual identity. If they did not reach a consensus as to whether sexual preference was inborn or chosen, they enabled millions of homosexuals to come out of the closet, redrew the boundaries of sexual identity, and organized to claim a share of political power in many American cities.

For others who carried on the political legacy of the 1960s, the fate of the earth seemed the most pressing issue. Back-to-the-land hippies became environmental advocates. Others took a more political road to the ecology movement. Peace advocates worried about the environmental threat of nuclear weapons, and activists focused on large corporations that sold shoddy and dangerous products in the United States and the Third World. In 1970, environmental activists held the first Earth Day—part teach-in, part demonstration—designed to promote awareness of the human impact on the natural environment. Books like Rachel Carson's *Silent Spring*, an indictment of the use of pesticides; Paul Ehrlich's *The Population Bomb*, a vision of demographic doom; Barry Commoner's *Science and Society*, a critique of the nuclear power industry; and Ralph Nader's *Unsafe at Any Speed*, an exposé of the automobile business, inspired a new awareness of the connections among technology, politics, personal freedom, and environmental dangers.

A huge and diverse array of organizations would press and expand the environmentalist agenda in the ensuing years. Middle-of-the-road, predominately white organizations like the Sierra Club, the Nature Conservancy, and the Audubon Society mobilized nature lovers on behalf of endangered animals and plants and against development in wilderness areas. More militant groups like Earth First! engaged in what they called "monkey-wrenching," a term taken from the title of a novel by environmentalist writer Edward Abbey. Their tactics included disabling construction equipment and driving metal spikes into trees to destroy loggers' chain saws. Other groups, like the Southwest Organizing Project, which was headquartered in New Mexico, made the connection between racism and environmental degradation. They noted developers' and policymakers' predilection for locating toxic waste dumps in minority communities, and they pointed out the seeming indifference of many white environmentalists to the ecological dangers that minority communities disproportionately faced. In time, these environmental groups became a formidable, national political force; Congress responded to their political clout by establishing the federal Environmental Protection Agency.

Conclusion

In the 1960s and early 1970s, the nation's youth launched a frontal assault on conventional behavior, smashing the barriers between public and private life, and legitimizing new ideas and new behaviors. They exposed the depth of racial oppression in the United States, catalyzed the American withdrawal from Vietnam, began a sexual revolution, helped found a lasting feminist movement, promoted recognition of the pluralist nature of American society, and pressed new concern for the environment.

But these innovations created controversy and carried troubling consequences. A small number of the young radicals contributed to the climate of violence that engulfed American society by the 1970s. By justifying their sometimes outrageous behavior in the name of personal freedom, they paved the way for what historian Christopher Lasch called "the culture of narcissism"—the retreat of many Americans into the pursuit of personal pleasure. By 1980, pundits were referring to the 1970s as the "Me Decade," contrasting that era with the more socially involved 1960s. But the cultivation of "me" was to some extent a legacy of those radical years, an outgrowth of the Yippies, hippies, rock festivals, drugs, and the Summer of Love. Values spawned by movements for social justice, it seemed, could just as easily be deployed on behalf of individualism.

Perhaps inevitably, there was a counterrevolution. President Nixon's attorney general, John Mitchell, looked at the turmoil of the late 1960s and predicted that "this country's going to go so far right, you won't believe it." That old enemy of the Left, Ronald Reagan, ultimately led the triumphal march as the Right seized power in the United States in 1980. It did so by adopting, with immense success, the grassroots organizing techniques developed by the radicals of the 1960s and 1970s.

The politics and culture of protest demanded a great deal from those who took part in the movements, and there were casualties. Drugs ended many careers too soon. Charismatic Panther leader Huey Newton died in a shootout over a drug deal. Some, like Anne Moody, simply wanted to retire from dangerous advocacy and live a quiet life.

However, not all 1960s activists burned out or rejected the politics of their youth. SNCC's John Lewis took his commitment to racial justice to Congress. Another SNCC veteran, Maria Varela, moved to northern New Mexico to create institutions promoting economic self-sufficiency for Hispanic villagers. Tom Hayden of SDS campaigned for economic democracy from the halls of the California state legislature. Feminist lawyer Ruth Bader Ginsburg was appointed to the U.S. Supreme Court. Grateful Dead member Bob Weir became a committed environmentalist, urging fans at Dead concerts to help save the Brazilian rain forest. The unruly, diverse, sometimes shimmeringly beautiful, sometimes corrosively ugly, political and cultural energies unleashed in the 1960s could not be entirely suppressed. A host of genies had been let out of a multitude of bottles.

F U R T H E R   •   R E A D I N G

For an overview of this period, see David Farber, *The Age of Great Dreams: America in the 1960s* (1994). **On civil rights and Black Power,** see Clayborn Carson, *In Struggle: SNCC and the Black Awakening of the 1960s* (1981); William H. Chafe, *Civilities and Civil Rights: Greensboro, North Carolina, and the Black Struggle for Freedom* (1980); David J. Garrow, *Bearing the Cross: Martin Luther King, Jr., and the Southern Christian Leadership Conference* (1986); Harvard Sitkoff, *The Struggle for Black Equality, 1954–1981.* **On the New Left and the antiwar movement,** see Wini Breines, *The Great Refusal: Community and Organization in the New Left* (1983); Todd Gitlin, *The Sixties: Years of Hope, Days of Rage* (1987); James Miller, *"Democracy Is in the Streets": From Port Huron to the Siege of Chicago* (1987); W. J. Rorabaugh, *Berkeley at War* (1989); Kirkpatrick Sale, *SDS* (1973). **On the counterculture and its relationship to mainstream culture,** see Charles Perry, *The Haight-Ashbury* (1984); Theodore Roszak, *The Making of a Counterculture* (1969); Nicholas Von Hoffman, *We Are the People Our Parents Warned Us Against* (1968); Warren J. Belasco, *Appetite for Change: How the Counterculture Took on the Food Industry, 1966–1988* (1989); Hazel G. Warlaumont, *Advertising in the 60's: Turncoats, Traditionalists, and Waste Makers in America's Turbulent Decade* (2001); Aniko Bodroghkozy, *Groove Tube: Sixties Television and the Youth Rebellion* (2001); Melvin Small, *Covering Dissent: The Media and the Anti-Vietnam War Movement* (1994). **On women's changing lives**

and the women's movement, see William H. Chafe, *The American Woman: Her Changing Social, Economic, and Political Role, 1920–1970* (1972); Beth Bailey, *Sex in the Heartland* (1999); Ruth Rosen, *The World Split Open: How the Modern Women's Movement Changed America* (2000); Flora Davis, *Moving the Mountain: The Women's Movement in America Since 1960* (1991); Susan J. Douglas, *Where the Girls Are: Growing Up Female with the Mass Media* (1994); Alice Echols, *Daring to Be Bad: Radical Feminism in America, 1967–1975* (1989); Barbara Ehrenreich et al., *Re-making Love: The Feminization of Sex* (1987); Sara Evans, *Personal Politics* (1978).

Index

AAA, *see* Agricultural Adjustment Act (AAA)
Aaron, Betsy, 309
Abbey, Edward, 315
Abernathy, Ralph, 119, 120
ABMs, *see* Antiballistic missiles systems (ABMs)
Abortion, 201; in Great Depression, 6; in 1950s, 102; *Roe v. Wade* and, 362, 394; Betty Ford on, 407; Carter on, 409; Republican Party and, 450. *See also* Reproductive rights
Acheson, Dean, 63, 67, 76, 78; on Vietnam, 80, 274; McCarthy and, 128, 129
Acquired immune deficiency syndrome, *see* AIDS
Acquisitions, *see* Mergers and acquisitions
Activism: African American, 113, 119–121; of Warren Court, 114–116; antiwar, 265–271; of 1960s, 282, 313–314; of New Left, 288–291. *See also* Antiwar movement; Civil rights movement; Protest(s); Radicalism; specific movements
ADA, *see* Americans for Democratic Action (ADA)
ADC, *see* Aid to Dependent Children (ADC)
Addiction: street crime and, 358–359
Adoption: in 1950s, 102
Advertising: on television, 20; critiques of, 111
AEC, *see* Atomic Energy Commission (AEC)
Aerospace industry, 58
AFDC, *see* Aid to Families with Dependent Children (AFDC)
Affirmative action: for women, 394; neoconservative criticisms of, 401; Carter and, 411; Reagan and, 441
Affluent society, 85–93
Afghanistan: weapons in, 59; Soviets and, 418, 474, 486; U.S. invasion of, 532
AFL, *see* American Federation of Labor (AFl)
AFL-CIO, 96
Africa: image of U.S. in, 141–143; Kennedy and, 182; Nixon, Kissinger, and, 337
African Americans: in Great Depression, 4; WPA and, 11 (illus.); in federal government, 13,

14; migration by, 29; during World War II, 33–34; as newspaper reporters, 53; military contracts and, 58; Truman and, 68; Red Scare and, 71; housing for, 88; on television, 92; unwed mothers and adoption services, 102; music and, 106, 107; poverty of, 110; as displaced workers, 111; segregation of, 112–123; civil rights activism of, 119–121; international image of U.S. and, 141–143; civil rights movement and, 169, 208, 282–287; in 1960, 171; 1960 election and, 174–175; use of term "blacks" and, 199; social reforms and, 219–220; voting rights for, 219–221, 221 (illus.); as officeholders, 221; Johnson on rights of, 234–235; race riots and, 235–236; Olympic protests by, 301–302; political offices held by, 314; Nixon and, 357–358; Burger Court and, 359–360; Hill-Thomas hearings and, 377; in South, 399; backlash against, 405–406; poverty of children and, 437–438; as prisoners, 478, 479; O. J. Simpson verdict and, 513; at RCA, 523
Africans: treatment in U.S., 143
Agencies of government, *see* specific agencies
Agenda for a Generation (Hayden), 288
Agent Orange, 258
Agnew, Spiro, 276, 300, 345; resignation of, 380
Agribusiness, 96
Agricultural Adjustment Act (AAA), 8
Agriculture: in Great Depression, 4; decline of farm families and, 96
AIDS, 442, 451–452, 451 (illus.)
Aid to Dependent Children (ADC), 10–11
Aid to Families with Dependent Children (AFDC), 102, 235; for Native Americans, 122; Nixon and, 354
AIM, *see* American Indian Movement (AIM)
Airplanes: B-52 bomber and, 59, 137; bombing over Scotland, 473
Air-traffic controllers: Reagan and, 430

Alabama: Freedom Riders in, 195; demonstrations in, 219, 220; civil rights marches in, 285
Alas, Babylon (Frank), 185
Alaska: oil production in, 149, 150; federal protection of lands, 415. *See also* Arctic National Wildlife Refuge (ANWR)
Albanians: in Kosovo, 525
Albecroft Machine Shop, 162
Albright, Madeleine, 525
Aldrin, Buzz, 318 (illus.)
Alexander v. Holmes County Board of Education, 361
Ali, Muhammad, 302
Alimony payments, 388
Allen, Henry, 269
Allen, Richard, 467
Allende Gossens, Salvador, 180, 337–338, 338 (illus.)
Alliance for Progress, 180, 238
Alliances: Axis, 18, 22; anticommunist, 143; military, 160. *See also* specific alliances
Allies (World War II), 22–23, 24 (illus.); occupation of Germany by, 46
Alsop, Stewart, 172
AMA, *See* American Medical Association (AMA)
Amazon.com, 501
Ambrose, Stephen, 67
Amendments: for equal rights, 310–311. *See also* specific amendments
America 2000, 446
American Birth Control League, 6
American Brands, 225
American Communist Party, 15, 70–71; prosecution of leaders, 76–77
American Federation of Labor (AFL), 10, 96
American Federation of State, County, and Municipal Employees (AFSCME), 96
American Indian Movement (AIM), 314
American Indians, *see* Native Americans
American Legion: veterans and, 51
American Medical Association (AMA): polio vaccine and, 99
American Psychiatric Association: homosexuals classified by, 395
Americans for Democratic Action (ADA), 69
Americans with Disabilities Act, 456

Amos and Andy (TV program), 92
Anderson, John, 421
Anderson, Marian, 13
Andreesen, Marc, 498
Andropov, Yuri, 470
Anglo-Iranian Oil Company, 147
Angola, 182
Antiballistic missile systems (ABMs), 331, 332
Anti-ballistic missile (ABM) treaty (1972), 470
Antibiotics: penicillin and, 97
Anticommunism: after World War II, 23–24, 70–78; during Red Scare, 134–135; Kennedy and, 182; Reagan and, 426; funding of guerrilla movements, 467
Anticommunist alliances, 143
Anticommunist hysteria, 56
Anticrime statutes: Nixon and, 358
Anti-Defamation League, 447
Anti-establishment sentiment, 300
Antifeminist movement, 388
Antimissile research, 470
Antimissile systems, 59
Antipoverty programs: under Johnson, 218–219
Anti-Semitism: during World War II, 35–37; HUAC and, 74. *See also* Jews and Judaism
Antiwar movement, 289–291; in Vietnam War, 253, 265–271; 1968 Democratic Convention (Chicago) and, 276; protesters during, 280 (illus.), 302–304, 304 (illus.), 324; media coverage of, 299; New Mobilization and, 302–303; Nixon and, 323, 324
Antiwar protests: against Iraq war, 535
Anti-white message: in *civil rights movement*, 285
Anxiety: in 1990s, 499
Apollo program, 200, 318 (illus.), 319
Appalachia: poverty in, 207 (illus.)
Appeasement: of Hitler, 17–18
Appointments: by Roosevelt, 13–14
Arabian American Oil Company, 229
Arab-Israeli wars: Yom Kippur War (1973), 149, 339, 343; Six-Day War (1967), 239–240
Arab oil embargo, *see* Oil embargo (1973)
Arab world: oil industry in, 147; Six-Day War and, 339; Yom Kippur War and, 339. *See also* Islam; Middle East; Muslims; specific countries and issues
Arafat, Yasir, 493, 525–526, 526 (illus.)

Architecture: of U.S. embassies, 226–228; building and, 226–229; of military compounds, 229; of oil company compounds, 229
Arctic National Wildlife Refuge (ANWR), 150; oil drilling in, 530
Arevalo, Juan Jose, 153
Argentina: coup in, 180
Arizona: treatment for drug offenses in, 479–480
Arkansas: in Great Depression, 9
Arkansas Project, 378
Armas, Castillo, 154
Armed forces: World War II and, 18; integration of, 113; in Vietnam War, 247, 249, 253, 254, 255, 255 (illus.), 260–264, 273. *See also* Military
Arms control, 241, 332; SALT II and, 407, 417–418
Arms race, 56; protests against, 78; détente and, 159–160; atmospheric testing and, 164; Reagan and, 466–467, 468–471. *See also* Limited test ban treaty; Nuclear arms race
Armstrong, Louis: as "ambassador of goodwill," 143
Armstrong, Neil, 319
Army-McCarthy hearings, 140–141
Army of the Republic of Vietnam (ARVN), 246, 247, 249, 321–322, 323, 324. *See also* Vietnam War
Arsenal of democracy: U.S. as, 21
Arts: federal funding for, 221–222
ARVN, *see* Army of the Republic of Vietnam (ARVN)
Asia: immigration from, 77, 223, 224, 400, 452; image of U.S. in, 141–143; SEATO in, 143; Southeast, 251 (illus.). *See also* Southeast Asia; specific countries
Asians: treatment in U.S., 143
Asia-Pacific region, 80
Assassination: of John Kennedy, 202–205; of Robert Kennedy, 208, 275; of King, 275, 313; Reagan and, 430
Aswan Dam, 151
Atomic bomb, 42 (illus.), 46–50, 47 (illus.); research on, 28; development of, 46–47; at Hiroshima and Nagasaki, 47, 47 (illus.); debate over, 47–48; testing of, 61; Soviet, 78; Eisenhower on, 136–138. *See also* Nuclear weapons
Atomic Energy Act: of 1946, 340; of 1954, 340
Atomic Energy Commission (AEC), 163, 187, 340

Atomic Industrial Forum (AIF), 341
Atomic power, 18; peaceful uses of, 161
Atomic war: evacuation drills and, 185; fallout shelters and, 186–188
Atoms for Peace program, 161, 340
Attlee, Clement, 46
Audiotapes, *see* Tape recordings
Audubon Society, 315
Austin, Hudson, 476
Austria: German annexation of, 17; occupation ended in, 160
Automobiles and automobile industry: car culture and, 89–90, 89 (illus.); unions and, 96; oil industry and, 148; fuel efficiency and, 149, 150; gasoline and, 150
AWOL (absent without leave) soldiers: in Vietnam War, 262
Axis Alliance, 18; Japan in, 22
Axis of evil: Bush on, 533
Ayatollah. *See also* Khomeini, Ruholla (Ayatollah)
Ayatollah: Iran revolution and, 418
Azores, 182

Babies: Spock on, 87
Baby-boom generation, 87; medicine for, 97–100; activism of, 281–282; mass culture and, 296–299; housing for, 511
Baez, Joan, 199, 292
Baker, Ella, 121, 284
Baker, Howard, 375, 485
Baker, James A. III, 428, 487
Baker v. *Carr*, 233
Bakke case, 411
Bakker, Jim and Tammy Faye, 401, 403, 404, 448, 449
Balaguer, Joaquin, 239
Balance of power, 18, 160
Balkan federation: Tito and, 63
Baltic republics: independence of, 488
"Banana republics," 475
Bangladesh, 334–335
Bank holding companies, 225
Bank of America, 224
Banks and banking: in Great Depression, 3–4, 8; in Sunbelt, 224
Bao Dai (Vietnam), 80, 144
Barak, Ehud, 525–526
Barker, Bernard, 372
Barnett, Ross, 196, 197
Barrios, 35
Baruch Plan, 61
Baseball: desegregation of, 93; movement of franchises, 93; immigrants in, 510

Basketball: immigrants in, 510
Batista, Fulgencio, 155, 156, 174
Battles, *see* specific battles and wars
Bayh, Birch, 428
Bay of Pigs invasion, 156, 177–179
Beatles, 107, 293
Beats (Beatniks), 110, 292
Beautification programs: under Great society, 222
Beck, Dave, 96
Beetle (car), 296–297
Begin, Menachem, 416
Beirut: American embassy bombing in, 472, 472 (illus.)
Belgian Congo, 182
Bell, Daniel, 110
Bell, Terrel, 443–447
Be My Guest (Hilton), 228
Bengalis, 334–335
Bergen-Belsen, 36 (illus.)
Berger, Samuel R. ("Sandy"), 525
Berkeley: Free Speech Movement in, 288; People's Park confrontation in, 302
Berle, Milton, 54 (illus.)
Berlin: Soviets and, 25, 64–65, 160, 182–184
Berlin Blockade, 64–65, 65 (illus.)
Berlin Wall, 184, 463 (illus.), 488 (illus.)
Bernays, Edward: public relations "spin" and, 267–278
Bernstein, Carl, 373, 373 (illus.), 374, 384
Best Years of Our Lives, The (film), 50
Bethlehem Steel Corporation, 398 (illus.)
Bethune, Mary McLeod, 13
B-52 bomber, 59, 137
Biden, Joseph, 460
Big government: defense spending and, 135
Big Three (allies): at Yalta, 25; in World War II, 46
Big Three auto manufacturers, 149, 150
Bikini Islands: nuclear testing in, 61, 163
Bina, Eric, 498
Bin Laden, Osama, 474, 532
Biotechnology, 97, 505–506
Birmingham, Alabama: civil rights movement and, 197, 198 (illus.)
Birth control: in Great Depression, 6; The Pill and, 99–100, 201; Court on information about, 233
Birth rate, 87; in Great Depression, 6; 1940-1970, 88 (illus.); in 1950s, 104; among unmarried women, 389–390, 437
Bishop, Maurice, 476

Black, Hugo, 197, 231, 233
Blackboard Jungle (Hunter): movie, 106, 107; book, 445
Black Cabinet: of Roosevelt, 13, 14
Black codes, 114
Black Hawk Down (book and film), 21, 270
Blacklist: in Great Depression, 9; in 1950s, 298
Black Mesa, 201
Blackmun, Harry, 359, 362
Black Muslims, 285
Black Panthers, 282, 286, 287, 300; Chicago raid on, 303
Black Power, 286–287, 300; 1968 Olympics and, 301–302, 301 (illus.); women and, 310
"Blacks": use of term, 199. *See also* African Americans
Blair, Tony, 535
Blended families, 392
Blinded by the Right (Brock), 377–378, 377 (illus.), 379
Blitzkrieg (lightning war), 18
Blockade: of Cuba, 190–191
Block grants, 353
Blodget, Henry, 501
Bloody Sunday: civil rights demonstration on, 220
Blue-collar workers: in 1950s, 96
Boesky, Ivan F., 435, 436
Boland Amendment, 481
Bolshevik Revolution (1917), 60
Bombings: of Nagasaki, 42 (illus.), 47, 49; of Hiroshima, 47, 47 (illus.); of Vietnam, 253, 256, 274, 322, 328; by antiwar protesters, 303; of American embassy in Beirut, 472, 472 (illus.); in Oklahoma City, 516
Bond(s): high-yield (junk), 503
Bond, Julian, 314
Bond v. Floyd, 231
Bonn, 183
Book of Baby and Child Care (Spock), 87
Boom (economic): in 1990s, 501–505
Border Industries program, 523
Borders, *see* Boundaries
Bork, Robert H., 380, 440, 442
Born-again Christians, 402–404, 448
Bosch, Juan, 238–239
Boschwitz, Rudy, 457
Bosnia, 270; fighting in, 524
Boston: busing and, 405, 405 (illus.)
Boston Common: antiwar demonstration at, 303
Boundaries: German-Polish, 46
Boycott: bus, 119–120
Bracero program, 35
Bradley, Bill, 433, 528
Bradley, Omar, 133

Brain Trust: of Roosevelt, 8
Brennan, William, 231, 233, 457
Brethren, 261
Brezhnev, Leonid, 241, 407; Nixon talks with, 331; SALT II and, 417–418
Brezhnev Doctrine, 241
Bribery: Agnew and, 380
Britain, *see* England (Britain)
Broadcast journalism, 19–21, 91. *See also* Media; News coverage
Brock, David, 377–378, 377 (illus.); homosexuality of, 379
Brokaw, Tom, 40
Brotherhood of Sleeping Car Porters, 33
Brower, David, 201
Brown, Edmund G. (Pat), 236, 427
Brown, Harold, 342
Brown, Helen Gurley, 201
Brown, Linda, 114
Brownell, Herbert, 119
Brown II, 115
Brown v. Board of Education, 114–115, 194, 361
Brumberg, Joan Jacobs, 105
Brundage, Avery, 301
Bryant, Anita, 395–396, 396 (illus.)
Bryant, Carolyn, 116–117
B-2 bomber, *see* Stealth (B-2) bomber
Buchanan, Patrick, 494
Buckley, William F., 116, 281
Buddhism, 246, 247, 295; self-immolation by monks in Vietnam, 247, 248 (illus.)
Budget: during World War II, 27; expenditures and deficits (1976–1992), 434 (illus.); government shutdown (1990) and, 456–457; Clinton and, 516. *See also* Deficit
Buffet, Warren, 502
Building: during Cold War, 226–229
Bulganin, Nikolai, 138
Bull market: in 1960s, 225; in 1980s, 503–504. *See also* Stock market
Bunche, Ralph, 285
Bundy, McGeorge, 169, 176, 237
Burdick, Eugene, 144
Bureau of Land Management, 415
Bureau of Reclamation, 201
Burger, Warren, 234; Supreme Court under, 231, 359–362; Nixon audiotapes and, 381–382
Burroughs, William S., 110
Bus boycott: in Montgomery, 119–120
Bush, Barbara, 493 (illus.)
Bush, George H. W., 404, 493 (illus.); news control under,

Bush, George H. W., *(cont.)* 269–270; 1988 election and, 425, 454–455, 487; 1980 election and, 427–428; education and, 446; religious right and, 448; domestic issues and, 456–459; 1992 election and, 459–461, 494, 495; Soviet dissolution and, 464, 465; Iran-contra pardons by, 483; foreign policy of, 487–491; Noriega and, 491; Gulf War and, 491–493; popularity of, 493–494; Somalia and, 520

Bush, George W.: military spending under, 57; energy policy and, 150; antimissile program, 188; ABM treaty and, 332; nuclear power and, 343; missile-defense system and, 470; 2000 election and, 499, 527–530; stem-cell research and, 506; as Texas governor, 511, 515; Israeli-Palestinian dispute and, 526–527; conservatism of, 530–531; September 11, 2001, terrorist attacks and, 531, 532; on "axis of evil," 533; Iraq war and, 533–535

Bush, Neil: S&Ls and, 440

Business: during World War II, 28; in 1950s, 95–96; in 1960s, 224–225; culture and, 226; tax rate cut for, 429; in 1980s, 436. *See also* Economy; Industry

Busing: Burger Court and, 360–361; backlash against, 405, 405 (illus.)

Butterfield, Alexander, 379, 384

Byrd, Harry F., 115

Byrnes, James F., 16, 39, 48, 55

Cabinet: in New Deal, 13

Caddell, Patrick, 412, 421

Califano, Joseph, 411

California: "Okie" migration to, 2; growth of, 29; defense industry in, 58; divorce laws in, 388; Proposition 13 in, 411–412; Reagan as governor of, 426–427; treatment for drug offenses in, 479–480; Proposition 187 in, 511

Cambodia, 80; independence for, 145; Vietnam War and, 322, 323–324

Camelot: Kennedy years and, 205

Campaigns (political), *see* Elections; specific issues and parties

Camp David: Khrushchev and Eisenhower at, 161; Barak-Arafat meeting at (2000), 525–526

Camp David Accords (1979), 415–416

Campus protests, 288–289. *See also* Activism; Protest(s); Students

Canada: Vietnam draft evaders in, 261

Canticle for Liebowitz, A (Miller), 185

CAP, *see* Community Action Program (CAP)

Capehart, Homer, 128

Capitalism: government and, 7; Keynes and, 12; in 1950s, 96–100; global, 521–524

Capitalist encirclement: Soviet fear of, 60

Caribbean region: U.S. in, 178 (illus.); immigrants from, 223, 452; Grenada and, 476

Carlos, John, 301, 301 (illus.)

Carlucci, Frank, 467, 485

Carmichael, Stokely, 284, 286–287, 310

Carson, Rachel, 200, 315

Carter, Jimmy, 261, 403, 408–422; energy and, 340, 342, 413–415; foreign policy and, 348–349, 415–421; Middle East and, 349; 1976 election and, 408–410; Camp David Accords and, 416–417; SALT II and, 417–418; 1980 election and, 420–421

Carville, James, 461

Casey, William, 467, 481, 485

Castro, Fidel, 155 (illus.), 475; Cuban Revolution and, 155–156; Bay of Pigs and, 177–179; Khrushchev and, 180; Cuban missile crisis and, 191

Castro, Raul, 188

Casualties: in World War II, 26; in Korean War, 130; in Vietnam War, 329; in Iraq war, 534

Catch-22 (Heller), 202

Catcher in the Rye (Salinger), 107

Catholicism: Pill, The, and, 100; in Vietnam, 145–146; in Lebanon, 152; of Kennedy, 169, 172, 174, 175; of Diem, 246, 247; abortion rights and, 362, 394

CBS (Columbia Broadcasting System), 19

CBS Reports (television program), 19

CCC, *see* Civilian Conservation Corps (CCC)

Cease-fire: in Korean War, 138

Celebrity: in 1990s, 513

Censorship: of television, 298

Census: of 2000, 511

CENTO, *see* Central Treaty Organization (CENTO)

Central America: U.S. in, 178 (illus.); intervention in, 475; Iran-contra scandal and, 480–484. *See also* Latin America; specific countries

Central High School (Little Rock): integration of, 118–119, 118 (illus.), 124; international publicity about, 143

Central Intelligence Agency (CIA), *see* CIA (Central Intelligence Agency)

Central Treaty Organization (CENTO), 143

CERN, *see* European Center for Nuclear Research (CERN)

CETA, *see* Comprehensive Employment and Training Act (CETA., 1973)

Chamberlain, Neville, 18

Chambers, Whittaker, 73, 74–76

Chamoun, Camille, 152

Chaney, James, 284

Chang Min-chueh, 99

Chavez, Cesar, 314

Chemical and biological weapons: in Iraq, 533, 534

Chemicals: in Vietnam War, 258

Cheney, Richard ("Dick"), 150, 340, 487, 528, 533

Chernenko, Konstantin, 470

Chernobyl reactor disaster, 342

Chiang Kai-shek, *see* Jian Jieshi (Chiang Kai-shek)

Chicago: Great Depression in, 7; 1968 Democratic Convention in, 275–276, 300–301; Weathermen confrontation in, 303

Chicanos, 35. *See also* Mexican Americans; Mexican immigrants

Child abuse, 393

Childbearing: in 1950s, 102; women's movement and, 307–308, 309

Childcare, 392, 450

Child labor: ban of, 16

Childrearing: by working women, 392

Children: in World War II, 31; Spock on, 87; Head Start and, 218; American-Vietnamese, 259; no-fault divorce and, 388; in female-headed households, 390; poverty among, 437; in single-parent households, 437, 437 (illus.); in poverty, 437–438, 438 (illus.)

Children's Defense Fund, 392

Chile: Nixon and, 337–338

China, 78–79; Japan and, 22, 46; Lend-Lease to, 22; Soviets and, 56–60, 139; communism in, 78–79; Korean War and, 130, 131, 132; Geneva talks (1954) and, 145; Quemoy, Matsu, and, 146; refugees from, 157; Nixon and, 332–336, 335 (illus.); Carter and, 348; Reagan and, 465–466; transformation of, 490–491

China White Paper, The, 79, 80
Chinese Nationalists, *see* Nationalist China
Chomsky, Noam, 290
Christian Broadcasting Network, 403
Christian Coalition, 404
Christianity: evangelical, 401, 402–404
Christian Right: gender issues and, 376
Church, Frank, 324, 331, 428
Church and state: separation of, 447
Churches: membership in 1950s, 101; in *civil rights movement,* 119–120
Churchill, Winston, 45, 46; Iron Curtain speech of, 60; on Soviet Union and China, 139
CIA (Central Intelligence Agency), 64; covert actions by, 64, 144, 467, 475; Central America and, 146; Iran coup and, 146, 147, 148; Guatemala and, 154, 267, 268; coups in Indonesia, Dominican Republic, and Congo by, 155; Cuba and, 156, 179; Bay of Pigs invasion and, 177; in Latin America, 180; in Vietnam, 247; drug trade and, 264; infiltration of antiwar groups by, 266; Watergate break-in and, 326, 373; Chile and, 337; Iran-contra and, 481
CIO, *see* Congress of Industrial Organizations (CIO)
Cities: African American migration to, 29; downtown commercial districts in, 89; in 1960s, 218; race riots in, 235–236; in Vietnam, 259
Civil-defense crusade, 185–188
Civil disobedience: King and, 284
Civilian Conservation Corps (CCC), 11, 15
Civil liberties: Red Scare and, 56; Supreme Court and, 230–234; Nixon and, 358
Civil rights: in New Deal, 15, 16; of Japanese Americans, 37–38; after World War II, 69; Truman and, 70; in 1950s, 111–123; *Brown* decision and, 115; violence and, 115; J. Edgar Hoover and, 118; Kennedy and, 193–199; Nixon and, 357–358; Burger Court and, 359–360; Reagan and, 440–442
Civil Rights Act: of 1866, 117; of 1957, 119, 194, 209; of 1964, 211–212, 234, 283, 305, 359, 361, 440, 457
Civil Rights Division: in Justice Department, 113

Civil rights movement, 119–121, 193–199, 208, 282–287; in 1950s, 125; in 1960s, 169; Kennedy and, 174–175; demonstrations during, 219–220; Mississippi violence during, 283–284; Selma march and, 285, 286 (illus.); fragmentation of, 313–314. *See also* African Americans; King, Martin Luther Jr.; specific individuals
Civil war: after World War II, 62; in Greece, 63; in China, 78–79; in El Salvador, 475–476
Clark, Jim, 220, 285, 498
Clark, Kenneth, 114
Clark, Mark, 303
Clark, Ramsey, 266, 358
Clark, Tom, 72
Clark, William, 467
Clean Air Act: revisions of, 456
Clean Water Act: revisions of, 456
Cleaver, Eldridge, 282
Clergy: in *civil rights movement,* 119–120
Clifford, Clark, 68; Vietnam War and, 271, 273
Clinton, Bill, 21, 368 (illus.), 460, 498–499; Somalia and, 270; sexual scandals and, 377, 517–518; education and, 456; 1992 election and, 459–461, 495, 514; stem-cell research and, 506; presidency of, 514–520; 1996 election and, 516–517; impeachment of, 518–519; foreign policy of, 520–527; Camp David meeting and (2000), 525–526; Middle East peace accord and, 526 (illus.); former Soviet Union and, 527; Gore and, 528–529; 2000 election and, 530
Clinton, Hillary Rodham, 379; Brock on, 377; childcare and, 392; healthcare reform and, 514–515; as senator, 530
Closed shop, 68
Clothing: of counterculture, 294
CNN: Somalia and, 21
Coalition: in New Deal, 14
Cocaine, 443, 477
Cohn, Roy, 103, 140
Cold War: labor and, 51; containment policy and, 55–67, 135–136; U.S. successes in, 65–67; politics in, 67–70; Red Scare and, 70–78; expansion of, 78–81; Truman on, 81; Truman administration and, 128; Korean War and, 130–133; Eisenhower and, 135–139; Third World neutrality during, 141; détente and, 159–165; Kennedy and, 182–183;

shadow government and, 185; architecture and building during, 226–228; culture during, 226–229; Johnson and, 238; Carter and, 415; end of, 489, 495; interventions after, 491–495; foreign affairs after, 520–527. *See also* McCarthyism; Soviet Union
Collectivization: in Soviet Union, 17
Colleges, *see* Universities and colleges
Collier, John, 12
Collins, J. Lawton, 246, 247
Colombia, 180; drugs in, 491
Colonies and colonization: independence after World War II, 141–156; in Africa, 337
Columbia University: antiwar protests at, 290–291, 291 (illus.)
Columbine High School: shootings at, 499
Coming of Age in Mississippi (Moody), 283
Commentary (magazine), 401
Commission on the Status of Women (CSW), 305
Committee for a Sane Nuclear Policy (SANE), *see* SANE (Committee for a Sane Nuclear Policy)
Committee on the Present Danger, 401
Commoner, Barry, 315, 342, 355
Communes: hippie, 295–296
Communism, 15; after World War II, 23–24; Truman and, 45; accusations of, 50; fear of, 55–56; in Greek civil war, 63; unions and, 68; in movie industry, 74; in China, 78–79; government probes of, 134; Latin America and, 153–156, 238–239; suppression of, 241; in Vietnam, 245; Reagan and, 464, 465–466; end in Eastern Europe, 487. *See also* McCarthyism; Red Scare; Soviet Union; Vietnam; Vietnam War
Communist China, *see* China
Communist nations: as Second World, 141
Communist Party: Supreme Court and, 122; in Cuba, 155
Community Action Program (CAP), 219
Comprehensive Employment and Training Act (CETA, 1973), 218, 353
Computers, *see* Internet
Concentration camps, *see* Death camps
Conglomerates, 502
Congo, *see* Belgian Congo

Congress: 1938 election and, 16; 1946 election and, 68; Eightieth, 70; Johnson, Lyndon B. and, 211; parties in, 214–216; Cambodian invasion and, 323–324; War Powers Act and, 346; welfare reform and, 354; Nixon and, 357; 1990 elections to, 457; Gingrich and, 515–516
Congressional districts: boundaries of, 233
Congress of Industrial Organizations (CIO), 10, 96
Congress of Racial Equality (CORE), 113, 194, 196, 266, 282
Connally, John, 202, 345, 363–364, 363 (illus.)
Connor, Eugene "Bull," 197
Conscientious objectors: during Vietnam War, 261–262
Conscription, see Draft (military)
Conservatives and conservatism: New Deal and, 15–16; House Committee on Un-American Activities and, 16–17; education and, 108; in 1960s, 212–213; on religion in schools, 232; on Supreme Court, 234; Reagan and, 236; politics of sexual scandal and, 376–377; Clinton and, 378–379; 1980-1993, 424–462; 1980 election and, 427–428; civil rights and, 440–442; religious right and, 448; George H. W. Bush and, 454, 455–457; George W. Bush and, 528. See also Nixon, Richard M.; specific individuals
Constitution (U.S.), see specific amendments
Construction: industry, 86; during Cold War, 226–229
Consumerism: after World War II, 84–90; in 1950s, 95, 171; critiques of, 111; credit and, 225; of baby-boomers, 296
Consumer price index (CPI): in 1970s, 397
Consumer Products Safety Commission (CPSC), 356
Consumer protection, 356–357
Containment policy, 62–67; Eisenhower and, 135–136; Kennedy and, 170, 177–180
Contraception, 104; oral, 99–100; birth-control pill and, 201; Court on, 233; abortion rights and, 362
Contracts: restrictive clauses in, 113
Contract with America, 515
Conventions, see Political conventions
Coontz, Stephanie, 102
Cooper, John Sherman, 324

Coors, Joseph, 469, 482
Corcoran, Thomas, 13
CORE, see Congress of Racial Equality (CORE)
Cornfield, Bernard, 502
Corporation for Public Broadcasting (CPB), 222
Corporations: during World War II, 27; Disneyland and, 84. See also Industry; specific corporations
Corruption: in South Vietnam, 259–260. See also Scandals
Corso, Gregory, 110
Cosmopolitan magazine, 201, 202
Costanza, Midge, 411
Coughlin, Charles, 15
Council of Economic Advisers, 67
Council of Federated Organizations, 283
Counterculture, 292–296, 300, 313
Coups: in Iran, 147; in Guatemala, 154, 267, 268; in Latin America, 180; in South Vietnam, 248; in Chile, 338
Courts, see Supreme Court
Covert actions: CIA and, 64, 144, 467, 475
Cox, Archibald, 375, 380
CPI, see Consumer price index (CPI)
Crack cocaine, 443, 477
Crack in the Picture Window, The (Keats), 110
Creating Life: Professional Women and the Quest for Children (Hewlett), 307–310, 308 (illus.)
"Credibility gap": in Vietnam War, 266
Credit: after World War II, 62; in 1960s, 230
Credit cards: introduction of, 94–95; BankAmericard as, 224
CREEP (Committee to Re-elect the President), 366, 370, 371, 374
Crime: organized, 96; Nixon and, 358; Reagan and, 441; drugs and, 442–443; prison system and, 477–480, 478 (illus.)
Criminals: rights of, 232
Crist, George, 270
Cronkite, Walter, 19, 299
Crucible, The (Miller), 134
C. Turner Joy (ship), 250–252
Cuba, 174, 475; CIA and, 146; revolution of 1959 in, 155–156; Bay of Pigs invasion and, 156; refugees from, 157; Kennedy and, 177–179; blockade of, 190–191; Marielitos from, 417; Soviets and, 475; al Qaeda fighters in, 533
Cuban Americans: Elian Gonzalez and, 513
Cuban Coordinating Committee, 191

Cuban missile crisis, 177, 184–191; France and, 239
Culture: popular, 53–55, 104–108; corporate, 84; car, 89–90, 89 (illus.); in 1960s, 201–202; in Cold War, 226–229; counterculture vs. mainstream, 292–296; mass, 296–299; in 1980s, 442–454. See also specific issues
"Culture of narcissism," 315
Cuomo, Mario, 515
Curricula: for girls and boys, 109
Curtis, Charlotte, 311, 312
Cyberspace, see Internet
Czechoslovakia: Hitler and, 17, 18; Marshall Plan and, 64; Soviet invasion of (1968), 241

Daley, Richard J., 276, 367
Dallas (television program), 150
Dallas, Texas: Kennedy assassination in, 203–205, 204 (illus.)
Dam-building ventures, 9
Daughters of Bilitis, 104
Daughters of Sarah, 402
Daughters of the American Revolution (DAR): Marian Anderson and, 13
Davis, Benjamin, 34
Day After, The (television program), 188, 469
Daycare, 392; in World War II, 31
D-Day, see Normandy invasion
DDT: ban on, 201
Dean, John W., III, 351 (illus.), 371, 373, 375–379
Death and Life of Great American Cities, The (Jacobs), 202
Death camps: Nazi, 36, 36 (illus.), 43
Deaver, Michael, 428
Debt: in 1950s, 95; under Reagan, 431, 434
"Declaration of the United Nations" (1942), 22
Deep Throat: Watergate scandal and, 374
Defense Department, 57, 58; creation of, 64; on nuclear attack, 185
Defense industry: women in, 31–32, 32 (illus.)
Defense spending, 58 (illus.); in World War II, 27; research and, 57, 109–110; Korean War and, 135; Eisenhower on, 136–137; Reagan and, 428, 431, 435, 464, 468–471
Deficit, 356; Reagan and, 429–430, 434–435, 434 (illus.)
Defoliants: in Vietnam War, 249, 258
De Gaulle, Charles: Kennedy and, 182; NATO and, 239

Deindustrialization: of U.S. economy, 524

Demobilization: after World War II, 50–53

Democracies, *see* First World

Democracy: as ideology, 63

Democratic Leadership Council (DLC), 460, 514

Democratic movements: in Eastern Europe, 489 (illus.)

Democratic National Committee: break-in at headquarters of, 370, 372

Democratic National Convention: in Chicago (1968), 275–276, 300–301; in Atlantic City (1964), 284; in Miami (1972), 367

Democratic Party: after World War II, 67; southern Democrats and, 71; in 1960s, 214–215; in 1970s, 321; in 1976 election, 408–410; in 1980s, 432; in 1990 Congress, 457. *See also* Democratic National Convention; Elections; specific individuals

Democratic People's Republic of Korea, *see* North Korea

Democratic Republic of Vietnam, *see* North Vietnam

Demography: after World War II, 87

Demonstrations: civil rights, 194, 219–220; antiwar, 266, 289–291; at 1968 Democratic Convention, 276. *See also* Antiwar movement

Deng Xiaoping, 490

Dennis v. United States, 77

Department of Transportation (DOT), 218

Deportation: of "undesirables," 77

Deregulation: of S&Ls, 439–440

Desegregation: during World War II, 33; in sports, 93; of schools, 113–116, 118–119, 360–361; by Supreme Court, 113–116; housing and, 236; in Mississippi, 361; education and, 446

Deserters: in Vietnam War, 261

Desert Storm, 492

De Soto patrols: in Vietnam, 250–252

Détente policy, 159–165, 320; Nixon and, 330–332; Ford and, 407; Carter and, 415

Detroit: race riots in, 34, 236

Detroit automakers, 89–90

Developed nations, 141

Developing nations, *see* Underdeveloped nations

Dewey, Thomas, 69; 1944 election and, 39

DeWitt, John, 37

Dictators: Reagan and, 466

Dictatorships: Soviet ideology and, 63; in Latin America, 153

Diem, Ngo Dinh, 145, 246, 247–248

Dienbienphu, 144–145, 245–246

Dies, Martin, 71

Dillon, C. Douglas, 176

Dinosaur National Monument (Utah), 201

Diplomacy: Cuban missile crisis and, 184–191

Diplomats: U..S. treatment of black, 143

Dirksen, Everett: Civil Rights Act of 1964 and, 212

Disabled, 456

Discount retailers, 96

Discrimination: under SSA, 11; in New Deal, 14–15; groups protesting, 15; against African Americans, 33, 34; after World War II, 52; gender, 122–123, 305, 361, 388, 390–391; Kennedy and, 194–199; banning of, 212; in immigration, 223; reverse, 440–441; nonfederal money for, 451. *See also* Civil rights movement; specific groups

Disease: biotechnological revolution and, 97; polio as, 97–99. *See also* AIDS; HIV

Disneyland, 84

Displaced Persons Act (1948), 68, 77

Diversity: in Roosevelt administration, 13; ethnic, 87; gender roles and, 388

Divorce, 6, 388–389, 392

Dixiecrat party, 69, 70

Dobrynin, Anatoly, 321, 331

Dobson, James, 404

Dodd, Christopher, 475

Dole, Elizabeth, 428

Dole, Robert, 515; 1976 election and, 408; 1996 election and, 516–517

Dollar (U.S.), 61; gold reserve and, 230; in 1970s, 346

"Dollar-a-year-men," 27

Dollar gap, 62

Domesticity: in 1950s, 102; men and, 102–103

Domestic policy: international image of U.S. and, 141–143; of Kennedy, 170, 192–193; of Nixon, 352–359; of Carter, 410–411

Dominican Republic, 180; military intervention in, 238–239

Domino effect, 144, 145; Vietnam and, 246

Doolittle, James, 144

Doors (musical group), 293

Dorn, Bernardine, 290

DOT, *see* Department of Transportation (DOT)

Douglas, Helen Gahagan, 71

Douglas, Susan, 311

Douglas, William O., 231, 233

"Doves": in Vietnam War, 266–271, 324

Dow Chemical, 290

Dow Jones Industrial Average, 501–505

Draft (military): in 1940, 18; in Vietnam War, 260–264; resistance to, 261–262, 289, 290; Muhammad Ali and, 302; lottery in, 322; women and, 393; Carter and, 418

Draft resisters: pardon for, 410

Drugs (illegal): in Vietnam War, 264, 323; counterculture and, 294; damage from, 316; crime and, 358–359, 442–443, 477; in 1980s, 442; in Colombia, 491; imprisonment for, 511

Drugs (prescription), 100; penicillin as, 97; Medicare and, 217. *See also* Biotechnology

Drummond v. Acree, 360

Dubcek, Alexander, 241

Dubinsky, David, 69

Duc, Thich Quang, 247

Dukakis, Michael, 487; in Massachusetts, 412; 1988 election and, 454–455

Dulles, Allen, 153, 177

Dulles, John Foster, 136–137, 335; Suez crisis and, 152; Lebanon crisis and, 152–153; Vietnam and, 246

Dust Bowl: in Great Depression, 2

Dylan, Bob, 292

Dyson, Freeman, 342

Eagleton, Thomas, 367–368

Early, Steve, 43

Earth Day (1970), 314–315, 355

Eastern Europe: Soviets and, 25, 45–46, 56–60; end of communism in, 484–485; democratic movements in (1989–1991), 488, 489 (illus.). *See also* specific countries

East Germany, 65; Berlin and, 183; refugees from, 184

East Jerusalem, 526

Eastland, James O., 69

East Pakistan, 334–335

Echo Park, 201

Eckford, Elizabeth, 118 (illus.), 143

Economic Recovery Tax Act (1981), 430

Economy: in Great Depression, 3–6; government intervention in, 12; Keynes and, 12; during World War II, 27–29; after World War II, 51, 60, 62–64,

Economy *(cont.)*
84–85; in 1950s, 94–96; defense spending and, 135; Kennedy and, 192–193; in 1960s, 216, 224–230; immigration and, 223; gap between whites and blacks, 235; of Vietnam, 259; of Japan, 333–334; in 1970s, 345, 397–400; Nixon and, 345, 346, 352; stagnation in, 362–365; in 1980s, 412–413; Reagan and, 428–431, 433–440; George H. W. Bush and, 433–440; in 1990s, 494–495, 500; benefits from, 506–507; Clinton and, 514; deindustrialization of, 524
Edelman, Marian Wright, 392
Education, 108–110; in 1940s, 27; after World War II, 43; under GI Bill, 52; for girls, 109; in sciences, 109–110; federal funding for, 159; in 1960s, 170–171; for women, 306; Reagan and, 443–444; politics of, 444–447; standardized testing and, 445 (illus.); school vouchers and, 446–447; immigrants and, 510. *See also* Schools
Education Act (1972): Title IX of, 390, 444, 450
Edwards, Harry, 301
Edwards, James, 428
EEC, *see* European Economic Community (EEC)
EEOC, *see* Equal Employment Opportunity Commission (EEOC)
Egypt: Nasser and, 148–149, 151; Suez Canal and, 151–152; United Arab Republic and, 152; Israel and, 239–240, 349, 415–416; Yom Kippur War and, 339, 343
Ehrlich, Paul, 315, 355
Ehrlichman, John, 326, 357, 372–373, 372 (illus.), 375
Eightieth Congress, 70
Einstein, Albert: on atomic power, 18
Eisenhower, Dwight D., 28, 57, 59, 93–94, 127 (illus.); as president, 84–85; Earl Warren and, 114; desegregation and, 115, 116, 117–118, 143; 1956 election and, 123–124; moderation under, 128; Cold War and, 135–139; foreign policy of, 136, 144; Soviet Union and, 139, 159–161; foreign aid under, 143; Middle East oil and, 147; oil crisis and, 148; Suez crisis and, 152; Latin America and, 153–156; détente and, 159; farewell address of, 166; fallout shelters and, 186; Viet-

nam and, 245; nuclear power and, 340, 341
Eisenhower Doctrine, 152
Elderly: income for, 354; Social Security benefits for, 430. *See also* Older workers
Elections: of 1932, 7; of 1936, 14, 15; of 1940, 14, 18–19; of 1944, 14, 39; of 1938, 16; of 1942, 39; of 1946, 68; of 1948, 69–70; of 1952, 94, 135; of 1956, 123–124; of 1960, 170, 171–175, 210; of 1964, 213–214, 215 (illus.), 252; of 1968, 233, 245, 274–278, 277 (illus.); of 1966, 236; of 1972, 326, 327–328, 346, 365–370, 369 (illus.); of 1974, 406; of 1976, 407–410, 427; of 1980, 412, 420–421, 427–428, 449–450; of 1988, 425, 454–455, 487; of 1982, 430–431; of 1984, 431–432, 480; of 1992, 459–461, 494, 495, 514; of 2000, 499, 527–530, 529 (illus.); in 1994, 515–516; of 1996, 516–517; of 1998, 518
Electoral college: in 2000, 529–530
Electronics industry, 58, 96
Ellsberg, Daniel, 325–326, 370, 375
El Salvador, 475, 481
Embargoes (oil), 340; by OPEC, 149
Embassies: construction and design of, 226–228; attacks on, 229, 272; bombing in Beirut, 472, 472 (illus.)
Emerging Republican Majority, The (Phillips), 357–358
Emigration: from Soviet Union, 332
Employment: World War II and, 28–29, 67; of African Americans, 34; suburban, 89; of women, 306; in 1970s, 397; in 1980s, 431. *See also* Unemployment
Employment Act (1946), 67
End of Ideology, The (Bell), 110
"Enemies list": of Nixon, 326, 370–371
Energy: crisis in 1970s, 149; nuclear power as, 340–343, 341 (illus.); Carter and, 413–414
Energy Department, 57, 413
Energy policy: in 2000s, 150–151
Energy Research and Development Administration (ERDA), 342
Engel v. Vitale, 232
England (Britain): Hitler and, 17–18; World War II and, 18; Lend-Lease to, 22; Iranian oil and, 147, 148; Suez Canal and, 149; Iraq war and, 534

English language: immigration and, 453–454; as official language, 510
Enola Gay (airplane), 47
Enovid, 100
Enron, 151, 533
Entertainment: after World War II, 90
Entitlements: Social Security Act and, 10
Environmental Protection Agency (EPA), 201, 355, 414, 439; nuclear power and, 342
Environment and environmentalism, 200–201, 296, 314–315, 355; oil industry and, 150; radioactive wastes and, 162; Great Society legislation for, 222–223; nuclear power and, 342; Carter and, 414–415; Clinton and, 520; George W. Bush and, 530
EPA, *see* Environmental Protection Agency (EPA)
Epidemics: of polio, 97–99, 98 (illus.)
Equal Credit Opportunity Act (1974), 391
Equal Employment Opportunity Commission (EEOC), 305, 306, 390–391
Equal pay: for women, 305
Equal Pay Act: of 1963, 305, 306; of 1973, 361
Equal Rights Amendment (ERA), 310–311; passage of, 358; opposition to, 393; Moral Majority and, 404; Republican Party and, 450
Eros and Civilization (Marcuse), 111
Erotic literature: in 1950s, 104–105
Ervin, Sam, 356, 375
Estonia, 488
Estrogen, 99–100
Ethical issues: over genetic research and engineering, 505–506
Ethiopia: Italian invasion of, 17
Ethnic cleansing: in former Yugoslavia, 524–525
Ethnic conflict: in Rwanda, 524
Ethnicity: removal of barriers, 33–34; in postwar suburbs, 87; in 1950s, 125; white ethnics and, 236. *See also* Minorities; specific groups
Eugenics, 99
Europe: Allied offensives in, 24 (illus.); Jews in, 35–36; economic gap in, 62; division after World War II, 66 (illus.); Nixon and, 337
European Center for Nuclear Research (CERN), 498
European Economic Community (EEC), 135

European Recovery Program, *see* Marshall Plan
"Europe-first" strategy: in World War II, 23
Evangelical Christianity, 401, 402–404; politics and, 404; Republican Party and, 448. *See also* Christian Right
"Evil empire": Soviet Union as, 464
Executive Orders: no. 8802, 33; no. 9066, 37
Extended family: in Great Depression, 6
Exxon Valdez (ship), 150

Fair Deal: of Truman, 70
Fair Employment Practices Commission, 68, 113, 211, 212
Fair Employment Practices Committee (FEPC), 33
Fair Labor Standards Act (1938), 16; amendment of, 391
Faisal (Iraq), 152
Falling Down (movie), 494–495
Fallout shelters, 185–188
Faludi, Susan, 309
Falwell, Jerry, 115, 401, 404, 448
Family: in Great Depression, 5–6; during World War II, 32–33; size of, 87; in 1950s, 94, 101; working women and, 103, 306; changes in, 388; blended, 392; nuclear, 392; Reagan, religious right, and, 450; characteristics in 2000, 511
Family Assistance Plan (FAP), 354
Family reunification: immigration and, 223–224
FAP, *see* Family Assistance Plan (FAP)
Farewell address: of Eisenhower, 166
Farley, James, 13
Farm, The, 295
Farmer, James, 196
Farms and farming: Truman and farm aid, 70; decline of, 96; displaced workers and, 111; defoliants in Vietnam and, 258; Carter and, 418; foreclosures and, 430
Farm Security Administration, 2
Farnham, Marynia, 52–53, 308
Farouk (Egypt), 151
Fascism, 17
Fatal Attraction (movie), 449
Fate of the Earth, The (Schell), 188, 469
Fat Man (bomb), 47
Faubus, Orval, 118, 118 (illus.), 119, 446
FBI: Red Scare and, 71, 73; Kennedy and, 176; Watergate break-in and, 373

FBI Story, The (Whitehead), 134–135
FCC, *see* Federal Communications Commission (FCC)
FDA, *see* Food and Drug Administration (FDA)
"Fear and Loathing on the Campaign Trail" (Thompson), 296
Federal appointees: under Roosevelt, 13–14
Federal Bureau of Investigation, *see* FBI
Federal Civil Defense Administration (FCDA), 185
Federal Communications Commission (FCC), 90, 92; television and, 53–54
Federal Council on the Arts and Humanities, 222
Federal Deposit Insurance Corporation, 12
Federal Emergency Relief Administration (FERA), 11
Federal Employee Loyalty Program, 72
Federal government, *see* Government
Federal Housing Administration (FHA), 86
Federal Republic of Germany, *see* West Germany
Federal Reserve Board: Volcker and, 412–413; Greenspan and, 501; stock prices and, 501; interest rates and, 505
Feeney, Helen, 394
"Fellow travelers," 72, 134, 139
Female-headed households: with children, 390
Feminine Mystique, The (Friedan), 103, 305
Feminists and feminism: in 1960s, 304–313; radical, 310–311; Clinton and, 378; gender roles and, 388; conservative fears of, 449. *See also* Women
Feminization of poverty, 389, 437
FEPC, *see* Fair Employment Practices Committee (FEPC)
FERA, *see* Federal Emergency Relief Administration (FERA)
Ferraro, Geraldine, 432
Fertility: working women and, 309
Fertilizers, 96
FHA, *see* Federal Housing Administration (FHA)
Fifth Amendment: criminal rights and, 232
52-20 club: after World War II, 52
Filibuster: against Civil Rights Act of 1964, 212
Films, *see* Movies and movie industry
Finances, *see* Economy; Stock market
Findlay, John, 84

Fine, Benjamin, 445
Fireside chats: of Roosevelt, 14, 21
Firestone, Shulamith, 311, 312
First Amendment: rights under, 231–232; pornography and, 395
First Hundred Days: of Roosevelt, 8
First Lady: Eleanor Roosevelt as, 13
First World, 141
Fisher, Frederick, 140
Fleishmann, Martin, 343
Fleming, Arthur, 97
Florida: all-male jury in, 123; 2000 election and, 530
"Flower power," 294
Focus on the Family, 404
Folk music, 292–293
Food and Drug Administration (FDA), 100
Food for Peace program, 143
Football: immigrants in, 510
Ford, Betty, 382 (illus.), 407
Ford, Gerald R., 382 (illus.), 406; as vice president, 380; assumption of presidency, 383; New York default and, 398; 1976 election and, 408
Ford, Leland, 37
Foreign aid, 57; to Greece, 63; under Truman and Eisenhower, 143; to Latin America, 153; nonmilitary, 466; to El Salvador, 475
Foreign-born Americans, 507–511, 508 (illus.). *See also* Immigrants and immigration
Foreign policy: Roosevelt and, 17–26; in 1950s, 127–165; of Eisenhower-Dulles, 136–137, 137 (illus.); CIA covert actions and, 144; Kennedy and, 169–170, 176, 177; containment and, 170; Johnson and, 237–241, 249–250; toward Vietnam, 271; Kissinger and, 320–346; Nixon and, 320–346, 347–349, 383; of Carter, 348–349, 415–421; Reagan and, 465–495; George H. W. Bush and, 487–491; after Cold War, 520–527. *See also* specific presidents and issues
Foreign Service, 169; McCarthyism and, 139
Foreign trade: after World War II, 62
Forest Service, 415
Formosa, *see* Taiwan
Forrestal, James, 45, 55
Fortas, Abe, 230, 231, 233–234
Forty Committee, 337
401(k) plans, 503
"Four Policemen," 23
Fourteenth Amendment: segregation and, 114
Fragging, 263, 323

France: Hitler and, 17–18; Normandy invasion in, 23; Vietnam and, 144; Indochina and, 145, 245; Suez Canal and, 149; Lebanon and, 152. *See also* Indochina

Frank, Pat, 185

Frankfurter, Felix, 13, 114

Freed, Alan, 106

Freedom fighters: from Hungary and Cuba, 157

Freedom rides and riders, 113, 195

Freedoms: guarantees of, 231. *See also* Civil liberties; Civil rights

Free enterprise: in New Deal, 7

French Indochina, *see* Indochina; Vietnam; Vietnam War

Friedan, Betty, 103, 305

Friedman, Milton, 429

Friendly, Fred, 19

Friendship 7 (space capsule), 200

Friends of the Earth, 342

Frontiero v. Richardson, 362

Frum, David, 379

Fuchs, Klaus, 76, 128

Fuel efficiency: oil and, 150

Fulbright, J. William, 252, 323, 331; Vietnam War and, 264, 265, 266

Full Employment Act (1946), 96; after World War II, 67

Fundamentalism: Christian, 448–449; Islamic, 474, 492

Fusion, *see* Nuclear fusion

Gabrielson, Guy, 103

Gagarin, Yuri, 199, 200

Gaither Commission, 159, 186

Galbraith, John Kenneth, 245

Gandhi, Mohandas, 113

Gary, Indiana: women welders at, 32 (illus.)

Gasoline: price of, 150; costs of, 397. *See also* Oil and oil industry

Gates, Bill, 501

Gates, Henry Louis, Jr., 92

Gay rights: march (Washington, D.C.), 387; campaign, 395–396; Moral Majority and, 404

Gays, 104. *See also* Gay rights; Homosexuals and homosexuality; Lesbians

Gaza Strip, 240, 473

GDP, *see* Gross domestic product (GDP)

Geisel, Theodore, *see* Seuss, Dr. (Theodore Geisel)

Gelb, Leslie, 325

Gender: segregation by, 31; defense spending and, 58; discrimination by, 122–123, 361, 451; changing roles and, 388–396; Reagan and, 450. *See also* Men; Women

General Motors (GM): strike against, 51. *See also* Big Three auto manufacturers

Generation gap, 282

Genetic research and engineering, 505–506

Geneva: Reagan-Gorbachev meeting in, 485

Geneva Accords (1954), 145, 146, 246

Geneva summit (1955), 160

Gephardt, Richard, 433

German Democratic Republic, *see* East Germany

German V-2 rocket, 158

Germany: Hitler in, 17–18; World War II and, 25, 46; Allied occupation of, 46; economy in, 63; cars from, 149; Berlin Wall opened in, 487–488, 488 (illus.); reunification of, 488. *See also* Nazi Germany

Germ theory of disease, 97

Ghana: Nixon-King meeting in, 143

Giap, Vo Nguyen, 257, 258 (illus.)

GI Bill of Rights, 43, 51–52; home mortgages under, 86

Gideon v. Wainwright, 232

GI Forum, 121

Gingrich, Newt, 456–457, 515; Clinton investigation and, 518

Ginsberg, Allen, 110, 300

Ginsburg, Ruth Bader, 316

Girls: educational curricula for, 109. *See also* Women

GIs, *see* GI Bill of Rights; Soldiers; Vietnam War

Gitlin, Todd, 290, 293

Glasnost, 485

Glen Canyon, 201

Glenn, John, 200

Global capitalism, 521–524

Global warming, 520

GNP, *see* Gross national product (GNP)

Golan Heights, 339, 343

Goldberg, Arthur, 230, 233

Goldman, Ron, 512

Gold reserve, 230, 364

Gold standard: Nixon and, 346

Goldwater, Barry, 213, 213 (illus.), 250, 401; 1964 election and, 252

Goldwyn, Sam, 74

Gonzalez, Elian, 513

Gonzalez, Virgilio, 372

Goodman, Andrew, 283

Goodman, Paul, 111, 171, 290

"Gooks": use of term in Vietnam War, 263

Gorbachev, Mikhail, 470, 474; dissolution of Soviet Union and, 464, 490; Reagan and, 484–487; George H. W. Bush and, 487; Yeltsin and, 488–489

Gordon, Richard, 110

Gordy, Berry, Jr., 293

Gore, Al, 460, 513; energy policy and, 150; 2000 election and, 499, 527–530

Government: under Roosevelt, 3, 6–17; as labor mediator, 9; economic intervention by, 12; employees of, 73; defense spending by, 135; purges from McCarthyism, 139–140; costs of, 217; growth of (1955-1985), 217 (illus.); image control by, 267–270; women's issues and, 305; backlash against, 411–412

Graham, Bill (rock concert promoter), 296

Graham, Billy, 101, 402, 403 (illus.), 449

Grateful Dead, 316

Great Britain, *see* England (Britain)

Great Communicator: Reagan as, 431

"Great Crescent," 80

Great Depression: "Okie" migration in, 2–3, 3 (illus.); economy during, 3–6; distribution of wealth in, 8

Great Society, 208–209, 214, 215–224; poverty and, 215–216; Medicare, Medicaid, and, 216; decline of, 234–237

Greece: aid to, 63

Green Berets, 247

Greenglass, David, 76

Green movement, *see* Environment and environmentalism

Greensboro, North Carolina: Woolworth sit-in and, 121

Greenspan, Alan, 501

Green v. Board of Education, 360–361

Gregory, Dick, 300

Grenada: invasion of, 268–269, 432, 475, 476

Grew, Joseph C., 45

Griffiths, Martha, 305

Griggs v. Duke Power and Light Co., 359

Grissom, Virgil, 200

Griswold v. Connecticut, 233, 362

Gross domestic product (GDP), 224; after World War II, 51

Gross national product (GNP): during World War II, 27; in 1950s, 94; 1946-1970, 95 (illus.); defense spending and, 135; in 1960s, 224; foreign aid and, 466

Grove City College case, 451

Growing Up Absurd (Goodman), 111, 171

Guatemala, 481; CIA and, 146; United Fruit in, 153–154; coup

in, 154–155, 180; "spin" cam-
paign and, 267–268
Guccione, Bob, 395
Guerrilla warfare: in Vietnam War,
255–258; funding of anticom-
munist, 467
Gulf of Tonkin incident, 250, 253
Gulf War (1991), 59, 456, 459,
491–493; oil and, 150; news
control during, 269–270
Gunbelt, 57–59
Guzman, Jacobo Arbenz, 154, 267

Haig, Alexander, 328, 467,
471–472
Haight-Ashbury district (San Fran-
cisco), 294–295
Haiti: coup in, 180; refugees from,
417
Halberstam, David, 176
Haldeman, H. R. "Bob," 354,
372–373, 372 (illus.), 374, 375
Haley, Bill, 106
Halford, S. H., 308
Halleck, Charles, 212
Hallin, Daniel C., 269
Hamer, Fanny Lou, 284
Hamilton, Charles, 284
Hampton, Fred, 303
Hanoi, see North Vietnam; Viet-
nam War
Harassment, see Sexual harass-
ment
Harkins, Paul D., 247
Harlem: in Great Depression, 4;
riots in (1943), 34; riots in
(1964), 285
Harlem Globetrotters: as "ambas-
sadors of goodwill," 143
Harriman, Averell, 45, 274
Harris, Patricia, 113
Hart, Gary, 376, 432, 436
Hawaii: Pearl Harbor attack and,
22
"Hawks": in Vietnam War,
266–271, 324
Hayden, Casey, 310
Hayden, Tom, 288, 300, 316
H-bomb, see Hydrogen bomb
(H-bomb)
Head Start program, 218
Healthcare: Medicare, Medicaid,
and, 216–217; reform of,
514–515
Health Education and Welfare, De-
partment of (HEW), 361, 411
Health issues, 442; AIDS, HIV, and,
451–452, 451 (illus.)
Heart disease: smoking and, 216
Heckler, Margaret, 428
Hefner, Hugh, 105, 201
Heller, Joseph, 202
Hendrix, Jimi, 293
Herberg, Will, 101
Herbicides, 96

Herblock (cartoonist), 137 (illus.)
Heroin addicts, 358–359
Hersey, John, 49
Hersh, Seymour, 289
Hershey, Lewis, 322
HEW, see Health Education and
Welfare, Department of (HEW)
Hewlett, Sylvia, 307–310, 308
(illus.)
Hickok, Lorena, 4
Hicks, Louise Day, 405
Hidden Persuaders, The (Packard),
111
Higher education: GI Bill and, 52;
for women, 103; NDEA and,
109–110; in 1960s, 171
High-tech industry, 500–501, 504
Highway Beautification Act
(1965), 222–223
Highways: beautification of, 222
High-yield bonds, 503
Hill, Anita, 377, 458, 458 (illus.)
Hilton, Conrad, 228
Hilton hotels: architecture and
construction of, 228; bombing
in Athens, 229
Hippies, 294–295, 300
Hirohito (Japan), 49
Hiroshima: atomic bombing of, 47,
47 (illus.)
Hiroshima (Hersey), 49
Hispanics, see Latinos
Hiss, Alger, 75–76
Hitler, Adolf, 17–18
HIV, 451–452, 451 (illus.)
HMOs, 515
Ho Chi Minh, 80, 144, 245, 321;
Geneva talks and, 145; Giap
and, 257. See also Vietnam War
Ho Chi Minh City, 407
Ho Chi Minh Trail, 253
Hochschild, Arlie, 309–310
Hockey: immigrants in, 510
Hoffa, Jimmy, 176
Hoffman, Abbie, 276, 290, 300
Hoffman, Julius J., 300–301
Holding companies: bank, 225
Hollywood, see Movies and movie
industry
Hollywood Production Code, 104
Holmes, Oliver Wendell, 8
Holocaust, 35–37; survivors as
refugees, 77
Home front: in World War II,
26–39
Homelessness, 430, 438; in Great
Depression, 4
Home life: in 1950s, 94
Homosexuals and homosexuality:
anticommunists and, 73; in
1950s, 103; Roy Cohn and,
103, 140; Kinsey and, 104; civil
rights movement for, 314;
White Night Riot and, 387;
gay rights and, 395; in military,
514

Honduras, 475; CIA and, 154;
coup in, 180
Honeymooners, The (TV program),
91
Hoover, Herbert C.: Great Depres-
sion and, 4; government and, 7
Hoover, J. Edgar, 71, 73, 302, 322;
civil rights issues and, 118; anticommunist writings and,
134–135; Kennedy and, 176;
Mafia, Cuba, and, 179; sexual
scandals and, 376
Hoovervilles, 4
Hopkins, Harry, 4, 5, 13
Hostage crisis (Iran, 1979), 415,
418–420, 425 (illus.), 473
Hotels: American, 228, 229
Hot line: between Soviets and U.S.,
191
House Un-American Activities
Committee (HUAC), 16–17, 72,
134; movie industry and, 74
Housing, 511; after World War II,
85–87; for minorities, 87, 88,
112; racial discrimination in,
194; desegregation of, 236
Housing and Urban Development,
Department of (HUD), 218
Housing bill (1968), 237
Howl (Ginsberg), 110
How the Good Guys Finally Won,
383
Hoyt, Gwendolyn, 123
Hoyt v. Florida, 122–123
HUAC, see House Un-American
Activities Committee (HUAC)
HUD, see Housing and Urban
Development, Department of
(HUD)
Hudson, Rock: death from AIDS,
452
Hue, Vietnam, 272
Hughes, Charles Evans, 15
Human immunodeficiency virus,
see HIV
Humanities: federal funding for,
221–222
Human rights: Soviets and, 332,
407; Clinton and, 520
Humphrey, Hubert H., 69; Civil
Rights Act of 1964 and, 212;
1964 election and, 214; 1968
election and, 275, 276–277,
278; 1972 election and,
366–367
Hungary: uprising in, 156–157
Hunt, E. Howard, 326, 371, 372,
374
Hunter, Evan, 445
Hussein (Jordan), 240, 339
Hussein, Saddam: Gulf War and,
459, 491–493; George W. Bush
and, 533; Iraq war and, 533,
534
Hyde, Henry, 518–519
Hydrogen bomb (H-bomb), 78

Icahn, Carl, 436, 504
ICBMs, see Intercontinental ballistic missiles (ICBMs)
"I Have a Dream" speech (King), 199, 283
I Led Three Lives (television program), 134
Illegal immigrants, see Undocumented migrants
I Love Lucy (TV program), 91
Images: government control over, 267–270
Immigrants and immigration: Displaced Persons Act and, 68; in Cold War, 77; in 1960s, 223–224; largest groups (1979), 224; violence against, 400; Carter and, 416–417; non-European, 417; after World War II, 452; settlement of, 452–453; since 1980s, 452–454; in 1980s, 453 (illus.); foreign-born population and, 507–511; sports and, 510
Immigration Act (1965), 224
Impeachment: of Clinton, 379, 518–519; Nixon and, 381–382, 384
Imports: of oil, 149 (illus.)
Inauguration: of Kennedy, 175–176
Inchon, Korea, 132
Income: during World War II, 27, 29; in 1950s, 94; for elderly, 354
Income gap, 506–507, 507 (illus.); in 1980s, 436
Income tax: negative, 354; cut in, 430; in 1980s, 432–433
Independence: for Third World colonies, 141–156; nations achieving (1943-1980), 142 (illus.); in Latin America, 180
India: war with Pakistan, 334–335
Indian Affairs, commissioner of, 12
Indian New Deal (1934), 12
Indians, see Native Americans
Individual retirement accounts (IRAs), 503
Individual rights: Warren Court and, 230–234; in 1980s and 1990s, 457–458
Indochina, 80; Japan and, 22; during Korean War, 131; Eisenhower and, 144; Kennedy and, 245. See also Vietnam; Vietnam War
Indonesia: CIA and, 155
Industry: in New Deal, 8; during World War II, 27, 28; in Gunbelt, 57–59; housing, 86; in 1950s, 95–96; in 1970s, 397–398, 398 (illus.); in South, 399; high-tech, 500–501. See

also Business; Economy; specific industries
Inflation, 431; after World War II, 51; in 1950s, 94; in 1960s, 217, 230; Vietnam and, 225–230, 259; Nixon and, 363, 365; in 1980s, 412–413, 435; in 1990s, 505. See also Stagflation
INF missiles, see Intermediate-range nuclear (INF) missiles
Initial public offerings (IPOs), 501
Ink for Jack campaign, 194–195
Inner cities: mass transit in, 90; blacks in, 111–112; housing development and, 219
Insurance: Medicare as, 216
Integration: of armed forces, 113; in Little Rock, 118–119, 143; backlash against busing and, 405, 405 (illus.). See also African Americans; Civil rights movement; Discrimination
Intercontinental ballistic missiles (ICBMs), 137
Interest rates, 431; in 1960s, 230; in 1990s, 505
Intermediate-range ballistic missiles (IRBMs), 180, 188–189
Intermediate-range nuclear (INF) missiles: removal of, 485–486
Internal Revenue Service (IRS): Nixon's use of, 370, 371
Internal Security Act (1950), see McCarran Act (1950)
International affairs, see Foreign policy
International Brotherhood of Electrical Workers, 522
International Monetary Fund: Soviets and, 60–61
Internet, 498; in 1990s, 500; minorities and, 507
Internment: of Japanese Americans, 37–38
Interstate buses: desegregation of, 113
Interstate highway system, 90
Intervention: government economic, 12; Korean War and, 131; in Lebanon, 153; in Guatemala, 154; in Panama, 238; in Dominican Republic, 238–239; by Reagan, 464–465; in Latin America, 475; after Cold War, 491–495; in Somalia, 520; in Yugoslavia, 524–525. See also specific countries
Intifadah, 472–473
Invasions, see specific invasions
Investment: during World War II, 27; in 1980s, 435; in 1990s, 504
Investors Overseas Services (IOS), 502

IPOs, see Initial public offerings (IPOs)
Iran: after World War II, 61; CIA and, 146; oil industry and, 147, 148; in OPEC, 149; 1979 revolution in, 150, 415, 418; Shah in, 338–339; oil prices (1978) and, 397; hostage crisis in, 415, 418–420, 424 (illus.), 473; Iran-Iraq War and, 474
Iran-contra scandal, 480–484; Reagan and, 433, 465
Iran-Iraq War, 474
Iraq, 152; in OPEC, 149; Egypt and, 152, 153; Gulf War and, 491–493; U.S. war with (2003), 527, 533–535
IRAs, see Individual retirement accounts (IRAs)
IRBMs, see Intermediate-range ballistic missiles (IRBMs)
Ireland: American building in, 227
Ireland, Patricia, 378
Iron Curtain, 45, 60
Iron lung, 98 (illus.)
Islam: fundamentalism in, 474, 492. See also Middle East; Muslims
Isolationism: in 1930s, 17
Israel, 147; recognition of, 68; oil crisis and, 149; Suez Canal and, 151; United States and, 152; Six-Day War and, 239–240, 339; Yom Kippur War and, 339; Middle East crises and, 339–344; peace treaty with Egypt, 349, 415–416; Lebanon and, 471–472; Arafat and, 493; Middle East peace agreement and (1993), 525, 526 (illus.)
Italy: Ethiopia invaded by, 17
I the Jury (Spillaine), 73
ITT, 502
I Was a Communist for the FBI (film), 71
Iwo Jima, 46

Jackson, Henry, 158, 331–332
Jackson, Jesse, 313, 432
Jackson-Vanik Amendment (1974), 332
Jacobs, Jane, 202
Japan, 17; World War II and, 22, 25, 55; end of World War II and, 46–50; economy in, 62, 63, 64; military spending and, 135; cars from, 149, 150; China and, 333; Nixon and, 337, 349
Japanese Americans: during World War II, 37–39; compensation for, 39
Javits, Jacob, 344, 347
Jaworski, Leon, 381

Jazz: counterculture and, 292
Jefferson Airplane (musical group), 302
Jeffords, James, 530–531
Jehovah's Witnesses, 261
Jencks v. United States, 122
Jerusalem, 240
Jews and Judaism: Holocaust and, 35–37; Truman and, 68; Red Scare and, 74; Israel and, 147; emigration from Soviet Union, 332; Lieberman as, 528
Jiang Jieshi (Chiang Kai-shek), 46, 79 (illus.), 146
Jim Crow laws, 34; black diplomats exempt from, 143
Job Corps, 218, 219
Jobs: in suburbs, 89; in 1950s, 96; for women, 103
Job training: in 1960s, 219
John Birch Society, 212
Johnson, Lady Bird, 222
Johnson, Lyndon B., 109, 119, 202, 210 (illus.), 240 (illus.); Vietnam War and, 19, 244, 249–255, 264, 273 (illus.); on Sputnik, 157–158; on missile gap, 159; 1960 election and, 173, 175; space exploration and, 199–200, 319; Great Society and, 208–209, 214, 215–224; personal character and presidency of, 209–215; as vice-president, 210–211; assumption of presidency, 211; Civil Rights Act of 1964 and, 211–212; 1964 election and, 214, 252; Voting Rights Act of 1965 and, 220–221; economy and, 224–230; 1968 election and, 233, 274; foreign affairs under, 237–241; Americanization of Vietnam War and, 252–255; military defeat and, 267; Wise Men and, 271, 274; civil rights violence and, 287
Johnson, Philip, 226
Joint Chiefs of Staff: in Vietnam War, 254, 271
Jones, Paula, 378, 518
Jones, T. K., 187–188
Joplin, Janis, 282, 293
Jordan, 152; Six-Day War and, 240; Israel and, 339–343
Jordan, June, 282
Jordan, Michael, 510
Journalism, see Broadcast journalism; News coverage
Judges: Reagan and, 441
Judiciary: Roosevelt, Franklin D. and, 15–16. *See also* Supreme Court
Junk bonds, 503
Junta: in Chile, 338
Jury service: women and, 122–123

Justice Department, 113; civil rights and, 357; Reagan and, 441
Juvenile delinquency: woman's family roles and, 103

Kahn, Herman, 186, 187
Kalmbach, Donald, 371
Kamikaze attacks, 46
Kansas City, 44
Karzai, Hamid, 532
Kassim, Abdel Karim, 152
Katzenbach, Nicholas B., 212
Keating, Charles, 440
Keating, Kenneth, 188–189
Keats, John, 110
Kendall, Donald, 371
Kennan, George F., 62, 78; on Vietnam War, 264–265
Kennedy, Edward M., 334; 1972 election and, 408; 1980 election and, 412, 420; hostage crisis and, 419
Kennedy, Jacqueline, 175–176, 203, 211
Kennedy, John F., 168 (illus.); Murrow and, 19; 1956 election and, 123; Cuba and, 156, 177–179; on missile gap, 159; on "kitchen debate," 161; assassination of, 169, 202–205, 204 (illus.), 211; foreign policy and, 169–170; domestic policy of, 170; 1960 election and, 171–174; presidency of, 175–177; containment policy of, 177–180; Latin America and, 180; Peace Corps and, 181; Africa and, 182; Soviet Union and, 182; Berlin Wall and, 184; Cuban missile crisis and, 184–191; civil-defense crusade and, 186; New Frontier at home and, 192–193; civil rights bill and, 198; space exploration and, 199; assessment of, 205–206; Johnson and, 210–211; Dominican Republic and, 238; Vietnam and, 245, 246–247; Apollo mission and, 319
Kennedy, Joseph P., 172
Kennedy, Robert F., 175, 176, 196, 196 (illus.), 210; Cuba and, 179–180, 189, 190; assassination of, 208, 275; 1968 presidential campaign and, 275
Kent State University: student protests and killings at, 304, 304 (illus.), 323
Kerkorian, Kirk, 504
Kerner, Otto, 287
Kerner Commission, 237, 287
Kerouac, Jack, 110, 292
Kesey, Ken, 202
Keyes v. Denver School District No. 1, 360

Keynes, John Maynard, 12; Nixon and, 365
Khan, Ayub, 335
Khanh, Nguyen, 250
Khomeini, Ruholla (Ayatollah), 418
Khrushchev, Nikita, 84, 138, 139, 168 (illus.); Third World and, 124; Hungarian uprising and, 156; détente and, 159, 160; in United States, 161; Castro and, 180; Kennedy and, 182; Cuban missile crisis and, 188, 190–191; kitchen debate and, 226
Killian, James, 164
Kim Il Sung, 130
King, Coretta Scott, 175
King, Martin Luther, Jr., 208, 283–284; Montgomery bus boycott and, 119–120; Nixon and, 143; Kennedy and, 175, 194; FBI and, 176; in Birmingham, 197; "I Have a Dream" speech of, 199; civil rights demonstrations and, 219–220; resentment of, 236; Vietnam War and, 265; assassination of, 275, 313; on civil disobedience, 284; Selma march and, 285; federal holiday honoring, 441
King, Martin Luther, Sr., 119, 175, 409
King, Mary, 310
Kinsey, Alfred C., 104
Kirkpatrick, Jeane, 428, 432, 466
Kissinger, Henry, 278, 327 (illus.), 348–349, 372 (illus.), 382; Vietnam War and, 271, 320–330; Soviet Union and, 330–331; China and, 332–336; Middle East and, 339–344; economy and, 346
"Kitchen debate," 161, 226
Klamath Indians, 122
Klein, Joe, 378
Kleindienst, Richard, 372
Kmart, 96
Koop, C. Everett, 442
Korean Airlines (KAL) jumbo jet: shooting of, 471
Korean War, 56, 67, 130–133, 131 (illus.); political and economic consequences of, 134–135; peace talks in, 138
Korematsu, Fred, 38
Korematsu v. United States, 38
Kosovo, 270; weapons in, 59; fighting in, 525–526
Kosygin, Alexei, 240–241, 240 (illus.)
Krassner, Paul, 276, 300
Kremlin, *see* Soviet Union
Kristallnacht, 35
Kubrick, Stanley, 186
Ku Klux Klan, 115, 197

Kurds, 493
Kuwait: in OPEC, 149; Gulf War and, 150, 491–493; public relations for, 269
Kyoto agreement, 520

Labor: in Great Depression, 3–4; in 1930s, 9–10; World War II and, 27, 28–29, 31, 68; Truman and, 69; in 1950s, 96–100; Lyndon Johnson and, 209; in 1970s, 345; women of color and, 391; RCA and, 521–524; in Mexico, 523. *See also* Strikes; Unions
Lady Chatterley's Lover (Lawrence), 104
Laffer, Arthur, 429
Laissez-faire: New Deal and, 9
Lakeland, Peter, 344
Land: Native American, 122
Landrum-Griffin Act (1959), 96
Lange, Dorothea, 2, 3 (illus.)
Laos, 80; independence for, 145; Vietnam War and, 325
Lardner, Ring, Jr., 74
Lasch, Christopher, 315, 401
Lasers: as weapons, 469
Latin America: oil sales and, 152; communism in, 153–156; Cuba and, 156; Kennedy and, 180; Soviets and, 183; democracy in, 238; intervention in, 238–239; Nixon and, 337; Carter and, 416, 417; immigrants from, 452; Reagan and, 475–480; Iran-contra scandal and, 480–484
Latinos: protests by, 314; poverty of children, 438; as prisoners, 478, 479; population of, 508; cultural crossover and, 509–510
Latvia, 488
Law enforcement: crime and, 477–480
Lawrence, D. H., 104
Lawson, John Howard, 74
League of United Latin American Citizens (LULAC), 121, 314
Lebanon, 471–472; crisis in, 152–153; Palestinian refugees in, 344
LeClair, Linda, 281
Lederer, William J., 144
Le Duc Tho, 327, 327 (illus.), 328, 330
Leftists: suppression of, 241; at 1968 Democratic Convention, 276; in Latin America, 337. *See also* New Left
Left wing: in 1968, 300
Legal Defense Fund (NAACP), 361
Legislation: Supreme Court and, 15–16; civil rights, 119. *See also*

Great Society; New Deal; specific acts
Leisure: after World War II, 90
LeMay, Curtis, 277
Lend-Lease program, 21–22, 27
Leningrad: in World War II, 26
Lerner, Max, 32
Lesbians, 104; women's liberation movement and, 312. *See also* Homosexuals and homosexuality
Levitt, William, 86
Levittowns, 86
Lewinsky, Monica, 378, 517–518
Lewis, Anthony, 378
Lewis, John (civil rights activist), 199, 200, 314, 316; Black Power and, 286
Lewis, John L. (United Mine Workers), 9
Libby, Willard, 187
Libel, 231
Liberals and liberalism: Red Scare and, 71–72; education and, 108; Kennedy and, 172; in 1960s, 209; Supreme Court, civil liberties, and, 230–234; Vietnam War and, 241
Liberties, *see* Civil liberties; Civil rights
Libya, 473–474
Liddy, G. Gordon, 326, 359, 371, 374, 375
Lieberman, Joseph, 460, 528
Life magazine: Red Scare and, 71; on civil defense, 187
Lifestyle: after World War II, 50–53; of hippies, 294–296; in 1980s, 442; in 1990s, 499; public interests in 1990s, 512–513
Limited test ban treaty, 191
Lincoln Savings and Loan (California), 440
Lindbergh, Charles, 200
Ling-Temco-Vaught, 502
Lippmann, Walter, 93, 444
Literacy tests: for voting, 221
Literature: erotic, 104–105; teen rebellion and, 107; in 1960s, 202; Beats in, 292
Lithuania, 488
Little Boy (bomb), 47
Little Rock, Arkansas: school integration in, 118–119, 118 (illus.), 124, 143, 194, 446
Litton Industries, 225
Livingston, Robert, 518
Loans: by bank holding companies, 225
Local government: New Deal programs administered by, 14–15
Lockheed Aviation, 158
Lodge, Henry Cabot, 248
Loeb, William, 366
Logevall, Fredrik, 249
Lonely Crowd, The (Riesman), 110

Long, Huey, 15
Longshoremen's strike (San Francisco), 9
Lon Nol (Vietnam), 323
Los Alamos: atomic testing at, 46
Los Angeles: defense industry in, 58; suburbs of, 83 (illus.); Watts riot in (1965), 236, 286; immigrants in, 452–453
Love Canal: pollution of, 413–414
Lowell, Robert, 290
Lowenstein, Allard, 208
Loyalty pledges, 72, 77–78
LSD, 293
LTV, 225
Luce, Henry, 50
Lucky Dragon (boat): radioactive contamination of, 163
LULAC, *see* League of United Latin American Citizens (LULAC)
Lumumba, Patrice: CIA operations against, 155
Lunch counters: civil rights demonstrations at, 113
Lundberg, Ferdinand, 52–53, 308
Lung cancer: smoking and, 216
Lynch, Peter, 502
Lynching, 113
Lyon, Phyllis, 104

MacArthur, Douglas, 94; Korean War and, 131–133; removal of, 133
Maddox (ship), 250–252
Maddox, Lester, 408
Mafia: FBI and, 176; CIA, Cuba, and, 179
Magazines: *Playboy*, 105; neo-conservative, 401
Magellan Fund, 502
Malcolm X, 285
Male chauvinism, 310
Malenkov, Georgi, 138–139
Managed care, 515
Management: in Great Depression, 9
Management-labor conflict, 521–524
Manchuria: Soviets and, 25, 47; Korean War and, 132
Manhattan Project, 18; research on, 28
Man in the Gray Flannel Suit, The (Wilson), 110
Mankiewicz, Frank, 367
Mansfield, Mike, 254–255, 334
Manson family, 295
Manufacturing: suburban, 89; in 1970s, 397–398
Manzanar War Relocation Center, 38 (illus.)
Mao Zedong, 78–79, 79 (illus.), 333; Nixon, Kissinger, and, 335
Mapp v. Ohio, 232

March of Dimes, 98
March on Washington: by Randolph (1941), 33; civil rights (1963), 198–199, 283; antiwar (1967), 266
Marcos, Ferdinand, 416
Marcuse, Herbert, 111
Marielitos, 417
Marketing, 111; in 1960s, 296–298
Maronite Catholics: in Lebanon, 152
Marriage: in Great Depression, 6; age at, 102; in 1950s, 105; divorce and, 388–389. *See also* Unmarried couples
Marshall, George C., 94; economic recovery plan of, 63–64; China and, 79; McCarthy on, 139
Marshall, Thurgood, 114, 231, 393–394, 457
Marshall Plan, 64
Martin, Del, 104
Martin, Joseph, 133
Martinez, Eugenio, 372
Marxism: in Grenada, 476
Masculinity: in 1950s, 110–111
Mass culture, 296–299
Mass education, 108–109
Massive retaliation policy, 137, 186
Mass production: of homes, 86
Mass transit, 90
MasterCard, 224
Masters of Deceit (Hoover), 135
Materialism: counterculture and, 296
Matsu, 146, 174
Mattachine Society, 104
Max, Peter, 296
Mayors: black, 221
McCain, John, 528
McCarran, Pat, 77, 134, 157
McCarran Act (1950), 77, 134
McCarran-Walter Act (1952), 77; Hungarian refugees and, 157
McCarthy, Eugene: 1968 election and, 274–275
McCarthy, Joseph, 19, 70, 128–130, 129 (illus.); on sex and sexuality, 73, 103; Eisenhower and, 94; on Cold War, 128; on Truman, 133; Army-McCarthy hearings and, 140–141
McCarthyism, 70, 128–130; end of, 139–141
McCord, James, 371, 372, 373, 374–375
McCormick, Katherine, 99
McFarlane, Robert, 467, 480, 481
McGovern, George, 327, 328, 368 (illus.), 370, 428; 1972 election and, 366–369
McKissick, Floyd, 286

McLeod, Scott, 139
McNamara, Robert S., 176, 237, 325; Vietnam War and, 252, 254, 260, 271
McVeigh, Timothy, 516
Meany, George, 367
"Me Decade" (Wolfe): 1970s as, 315, 401
Media: radio, 14, 19; television as, 53–55; rights of, 231; government "spin" control and, 267–270; Vietnam War and, 298–299; women's movement and, 307, 311–312; evangelists on, 401, 402–404; Pat Robertson and, 404; non-English-language, 509; Jon-Benet Ramsey murder and, 513; O. J. Simpson trial and, 513. *See also* Broadcast journalism; Newspapers; Radio; Television
Mediation: in labor disputes, 9
Medicaid, 216–217
Medicare, 216–217, 430
Medicine: penicillin and, 97; polio vaccine and, 97–99; birth control pill and, 99–100; radioactivity and, 163, 164; Medicare and, 216; innovations in, 505–506. *See also* Drugs (prescription); Healthcare
Mediterranean region: after World War II, 61
Meese, Edwin, 428, 482–483
Melman, Seymour, 265
Men: domestication of, 102–103; sexual relations and, 105; in 1950s, 110–111; roles of, 388–396
Mendes-France, Pierre, 145
Mennonites, 261
Menominee Indians, 122
Meredith, James, 196–197
Mergers and acquisitions: in 1950s, 95; in oil industry, 151; in 1960s, 225; in 1980s, 436, 504; in 1990s, 502
Merman, Ethel, 54 (illus.)
Merrill, Lynch, 502
Metalious, Grace, 104
Mexican Americans, 34–35; in Great Depression, 4; discrimination against, 15; women during World War II, 32; civil rights of, 121; protests by, 314; in California, 511
Mexican immigrants, 34–35, 157
Mexico, 180; "repatriation" to, 4; oil production in, 149; RCA in, 522 (illus.), 523
MFDP, *see* Mississippi Freedom Democratic Party (MFDP)
Microsoft, 501
Middle class: Great Society programs for, 221–222; counterculture revolt against, 292–296

Middle East, 471–474; World War II and, 25; after World War II, 61; CENTO in, 143; oil in, 146–147, 148; Eisenhower Doctrine and, 152; Six-Day War and, 239–240, 339; Nixon, Kissinger, and, 337, 338–344; Yom Kippur War and, 339; Carter and, 349; Ford and, 407; immigrants from, 452; terrorism in, 473; Iran-Iraq War and, 474; Clinton and settlement in (1993), 525, 526 (illus.); violence in, 526–527; peace accord in (1993), 526 (illus.). *See also* specific countries
Midwest, 57
"Migrant Mother" (photo), 2, 3 (illus.)
Migration: in Great Depression, 2–3, 3 (illus.); during World War II, 29–31, 30 (illus.); rural-to-urban, 88; of African Americans, 111–112; average annual regional (1947-1960), 112 (illus.)
Milam, J. W., 117
Milam, Roy, 117
Militants: in civil rights movement, 199, 287
Military: World War II and, 18, 51, 61–62; blacks in, 34; Eisenhower on, 136–137; Kennedy and, 184; compounds of, 229; in Vietnam, 255–264, 323; personnel policy in, 262–263; news coverage of, 267; women in, 362, 393–394; Clinton and, 514. *See also* Armed forces; Defense spending; Veterans; World War II; specific wars and battles
Military coups, *see* Coups
Military-industrial complex, 28, 57, 59; Eisenhower's warning about, 166
Military spending, 57–59
Milk, Harvey, 386 (illus.), 387, 396
Milken, Michael, 436, 503
Miller, Arthur: Red Scare and, 134
Miller, William M., Jr., 185
Mills, C. Wright, 111
Milosevic, Slobodan, 524–525
Milton Berle Show, The (television program), 55
Mineral rights: of Native Americans, 122
Mines and mining: unions and, 9
Minh, Duong Van, 248, 249
Minimum wage, 16; Truman and, 70
Minorities: in New Deal administration, 13; Roosevelt, Franklin D. and, 40; in cities and suburbs, 87; housing for, 88; education and, 444; imprisonment

Minorities *(cont.)*
of, 479; income gap and, 507.
See also specific groups
Minow, Newton, 92
Miracle drugs: penicillin as, 97
Miranda v. Arizona, 232–233
MIRV (multiple, independently
targeted nuclear warheads),
331
Missile gap, 159
Missiles, 331; production of, 58
(illus.); antimissile systems and,
59; nuclear, 137; race for,
158–159; IRBMs, 180,
188–189; controls over,
331–332; new technology for,
332; buildup of, 468–471; in-
termediate-range nuclear (INF)
missiles, 485–486. *See also*
Cuban missile crisis
Mississippi: racism in, 117; segre-
gation in, 196–197; blacks in,
283; civil rights march in, 286
Mississippi Freedom Democratic
Party (MFDP), 283
Mississippi Freedom Summer Pro-
ject, 283
Mitchell, John N., 316, 352, 358,
372; CREEP and, 371
Model Cities program, 218
Moderation: politics of, 93–94
Modern Woman: The Lost Sex (Farn-
ham and Lundberg), 52–53,
308
Molotov, Vyacheslav M., 45
Mondale, Walter: 1976 election
and, 409; 1984 election and,
432, 480
Mongolia: Soviets in, 47
"Monkey trial": of Scopes, 232
Monroe, Marilyn, 105; Arthur
Miller and, 134
Montgomery, Alabama: Freedom
Riders in, 195–196; march to,
220, 285
Moody, Anne, 283, 284–285, 316
Moon landing, 318 (illus.), 319;
Apollo program and, 200
Moral Majority, 401, 404, 448;
sexual values and, 387
Moratorium: on nuclear testing,
164
Morgan, Robin, 311
Morgan v. Virginia, 113
Morgenthau, Henry, Jr., 13
Morocco: U.S. embassy in,
227–228
Mortgages: home, 86
Mosaic, 498
Moscone, George, 386 (illus.), 387,
396
Moscow, *see* Soviet Union
Moses, Robert, 208, 283, 284
Mossadeq, Mohammed, 147, 148
Most-favored-nation status: hu-
man rights and, 332

Motherhood: women's movement
and, 307–308. *See also* Family;
Women
Mothers Against Drunk Driving
(MADD), 442
Motown, 293
Movies and movie industry: World
War II and, 33, 53; in 1950s,
74; Red Scare and, 74, 134; sex-
uality in, 104; teen rebellion
and, 107; nuclear energy and,
185, 341; depicting U.S. war
heroes, 476–480; Latinas and
Latinos in, 509
Moynihan, Daniel Patrick, 354;
report on poverty, 235, 353
Mozambique, 182
Muhammad, Elijah, 285
Mujahidin factions, 474
Multiculturalism: politics of, 314
Multinationals: in oil industry,
148, 149
Munich agreement, 18
Murphy, Frank, 38
Murrow, Edward R., 19, 20 (illus.),
57, 99; as television journalist,
91; McCarthy and, 140
Music: rhythm and blues (R&B),
105–106; rock 'n' roll,
105–106; jazz, 292; whites and
blacks in, 293
Muskie, Edmund, 365–366
Muslim Bosnians, 524
Muslims: in Lebanon, 152; funda-
mentalist, 474. *See also* Islam;
Middle East
MX missiles, 468
My Lai massacre, 263–264, 289

NAACP, *see* National Association
for the Advancement of Colored
People (NAACP)
Nader, Ralph, 90, 315, 342, 529
NAFTA, *see* North American Free
Trade Agreement (NAFTA)
Nagasaki: atomic bombing of, 42
(illus.), 47, 49
Napalm: in Vietnam, 249
NASA, *see* National Aeronautics
and Space Administration
(NASA)
NASDAQ, 501–505, 505; drop in,
506
NASDC, *see* New American Schools
Development Corporation
(NASDC)
Nasser, Gamal Abdel, 148–149,
151, 152, 239; United Arab Re-
public and, 152; Lebanon and,
153; death of, 339
National Aeronautics and Space
Administration (NASA), 159,
199–200
National Aeronautics and Space
Council: Johnson and, 210

National Association for the Ad-
vancement of Colored People
(NAACP), 114, 115, 194; in
New Deal, 15; civil rights move-
ment and, 282
National Association of Home
Builders, 86
National Association of Realtors, 86
National Defense Education Act
(NDEA), 109–110, 124, 159
National Endowment for the Arts
(NEA), 222
National Endowment for the Hu-
manities (NEH), 222
National Environmental Policy Act
(1970), 342
National Foundation for Infantile
Paralysis, 98
National Foundation for the Arts
and Humanities, 222
National Guard: Little Rock and,
118; at People's Park, 302; Kent
State killings and, 304, 304
(illus.); Vietnam War and, 323
National health insurance: Tru-
man and, 70; Red Scare and, 71
National Industrial Recovery Act
(NIRA), 8, 9
Nationalist China, 46, 79, 131,
146. *See also* China
National Labor Relations Act
(Wagner Act, 1935), 10, 16
National Liberation Front (NLF,
Vietcong), 246, 247, 249, 254,
256, 290, 322, 406–407; Tet
offensive and, 272. *See also*
Vietnam War
National Mobilization Committee
Against the War, 266
National Negro Congress, 15
National Organization for Women
(NOW), 305
National origin: immigration quo-
tas and, 223
National Origins Act (1924): Jews
and, 35–36
National Public Radio, 222
National Science Foundation, 28,
57, 159, 222
National security: military spend-
ing and, 57; Truman and,
80–81; Johnson and, 237;
advisers to Reagan, 467
National Security Act (1947), 64
National Security Council (NSC),
64; NSC-68 and, 80, 159; NSC-
162/3 and, 136; Kissinger and,
320; Iran-contra and, 483
National Student Association,
290
National System of Defense High-
ways, 90, 186
National Urban League, 15
National War Labor Board, 29
National Youth Administration, 13
Nation at Risk, A, 443

Native American Graves Repatriation Act, 456
Native American Rights Fund, 314
Native Americans: in New Deal, 12; women during World War II, 32; benefits withdrawn from, 121–122; civil rights of, 121–122; American Indian Movement and, 314
Native Son (Wright), 282
Nativism: in 1990s, 510–511
NATO (North Atlantic Treaty Organization), 67, 160, 239; Nixon and, 348; in Bosnia, 524
Nature Conservancy, 315
Navajo Power Plant, 201
Navajos: radioactivity and, 162
Nazi Germany, 17–18; atomic weapons and, 18; Soviet nonaggression pact with, 22; Holocaust and, 35–37; surrender of, 43. *See also* World War II
NDEA, *see* National Defense Education Act (NDEA)
NEA, *see* National Endowment for the Arts (NEA)
Negotiation Now!, 265
"Negroes": use of term, 199
Negro Family, The: The Case for National Action (Moynihan), 235, 353
NEH, *see* National Endowment for the Humanities (NEH)
Neoconservatives: in 1970s, 401
Netanyahu, Benjamin, 525
Netscape, 498
Neutrality: of Third World countries, 141
Neutrality acts (1935-1937), 17
Nevada: nuclear testing in, 162, 163
New Age movement, 313
New American Schools Development Corporation (NASDC), 446
New Deal, 1 (illus.), 6–17; benefits of, 14; end of, 39; Truman and, 68
New Democrats: 1992 election and, 460
New England: defense spending in, 58
New feminism, 311
New Frontier, 173, 192–193; women and, 305
New immigration: in 1990s, 507–511
New Left, 287–291, 300; after Kent State, 313
"New Look" strategy: of Eisenhower/Dulles, 137–138, 158, 166
New Mobilization, 302–303
New Right, 388, 400–406; gender issues and, 376; on sex and sexuality, 394; Reagan and, 428;

civil rights and, 440; education and, 444
News coverage: on television, 91; "spin" in, 267–270. *See also* Broadcast journalism
New South: Carter and, 408
Newspapers, 53; Pentagon Papers and, 325
Newton, Huey, 316
New World Order, 487–491
New York City: veterans in, 85–86; default by, 398
New York Labor Council: Vietnam War support by, 324
New York Stock Exchange, 225, 503 (illus.)
New York Times: Pentagon Papers and, 325
New York Times v. Sullivan, 231
Ngo family: in Vietnam, 247–248. *See also* Diem, Ngo Dinh
Nhu, Ngo Dinh, 247
Nicaragua, 475; CIA and, 154; Sandinistas and, 480–481
Nicholas, Terry, 516
Niebur, Reinhold, 69
Nike missiles, 58 (illus.)
Ninth Amendment, 233
NIRA, *see* National Industrial Recovery Act (NIRA)
Nitze, Paul, 78, 80
Nixon, E. D., 119
Nixon, Pat, 382 (illus.); China and, 335, 335 (illus.)
Nixon, Richard M., 71, 75 (illus.), 316, 372 (illus.); Chambers, Hiss, and, 74–76; 1952 election and, 94; 1956 election and, 123; McCarthy and, 129; on Truman, 133; Cold War and, 136; Martin Luther King, Jr., and, 143; Castro and, 155 (illus.); Soviet Union and, 160–161, 330–332, 348; 1960 election and, 170, 171–175; kitchen debate and, 226; Supreme Court and, 234; 1968 election and, 276–277, 278; space exploration and, 319; domestic issues and, 324; Pentagon Papers and, 325–326; 1972 election and, 326, 327–328, 365–370; enemies list of, 326; China and, 332–336, 335 (illus.), 348; Middle East and, 339–344; nuclear power and, 342; economy and, 346, 362–365; monetary crisis and, 346; foreign policy of, 347–349, 383; domestic policy and, 352–359; welfare system and, 352–359; on environmentalists, 355; Congress and, 357; civil rights and, 357–358; "southern strategy" of, 357–358; Burger Court and,

359–362; Watergate scandal and, 370–383; impeachment and, 381–382; resignation of, 382–383, 382 (illus.); historical assessment of, 384; childcare and, 392; pardon of, 406. *See also* Watergate scandal
NLF, *see* National Front for the Liberation of Vietnam (NLF); National Liberation Front (NLF)
Nobel Peace Prize: Kissinger, Le Duc Tho, and, 329
No-fault divorce laws, 388–389
Nonaggression pact: Soviet-Nazi (1939), 22
Nonviolent protests: by African Americans, 113; King and, 120
Noriega, Manuel, 269, 458–459, 491
Norman, Peter, 302
Normandy invasion, 23, 43
North (U.S.): African Americans in, 4
North, Oliver, 481–482, 482 (illus.)
North American Free Trade Agreement (NAFTA), 520
North Atlantic Treaty Organization (NATO), *see* NATO (North Atlantic Treaty Organization)
North Carolina National Bank, 224
North Korea, 130; *Pueblo* capture and, 271. *See also* Korean War
North Sea: oil production in, 149
North Vietnam, 245, 247, 290; in Vietnam War, 257–258; negotiations with, 271. *See also* Vietnam War
NOW, *see* National Organization for Women (NOW)
NSC, *see* National Security Council (NSC)
Nuclear arms race, *see* Arms race
Nuclear energy: fuel rod storage and, 343
Nuclear fallout, 164; shelters for, 185–188
Nuclear family, 392; in 1950s, 101; in 2000, 511
Nuclear Freeze Movement, 469
Nuclear fusion, 343
Nuclear plants, 340–341, 341 (illus.)
Nuclear power: as energy source, 340–343, 341 (illus.)
Nuclear Regulatory Commission (NRC), 342
Nuclear weapons: role of, 49; after World War II, 61; hydrogen bomb and, 78; in Cold War, 135; Atoms for Peace and, 161; testing of, 161, 162, 163–164, 165, 185; limited test ban treaty and, 191. *See also* Arms race; Atomic bomb; Atomic power; Weapons; specific weapons

Nunn, Sam, 460
Nuremberg: war criminal trials in, 61

O'Brien, Lawrence, 371–372
Obscenity: Court on, 231
Occupational Safety and Health Administration (OSHA), 356, 439
Occupation zones: in Germany, 46
O'Connor, Basil, 98
O'Connor, Sandra Day, 441
Office for Drug Abuse and Law Enforcement (ODALE), 359
Officeholders: black, 221
Office of Civil Defense, 187
Office of Civil Rights, 357, 361
Office of Economic Opportunity (OEO), 218, 219
Office of Homeland Security, 188
Office of Price Administration, 29
Office of Strategic Services (OSS), 467
Office of War Information (OWI), 31
Officers: in Vietnam War, 263
Oil and oil industry, 147–153, 340; after World War II, 61; in Iran, 147, 148; U.S. control of, 147; U.S. dependence on oil, 149 (illus.), 150; prices in, 151; Nasser and, 152–153; in Sunbelt, 224; elite compounds for employees, 229; Iran revolution and, 397, 418; OPEC and, 414 (illus.)
Oil embargo (1973), 345, 365
"Okie" migration: in Great Depression, 2–3, 3 (illus.)
Okinawa, 46
Oklahoma City bombing, 516
Older workers: in Great Depression, 5
Olympic Committee for Human Rights (OCHR), 301
Olympics: 1968 conflicts at, 301–302; Carter's withdrawal from, 418
O'Malley, Walter, 93
Omnibus Budget Reconciliation Act (1981), 430
One Flew Over the Cuckoo's Nest (Kesey), 202
O'Neill, Thomas P. ("Tip"), 344, 480
"One person, one vote," 233
On the Beach (Shute), 185
On Thermonuclear War (Kahn), 186
On the Road (Kerouac), 110, 292
OPEC, see Organization of Petroleum Exporting Countries (OPEC)
OPERATION ALERT, 185
Operation Mongoose, 179, 180, 188, 191
Operation Paperclip, 61

Operation Rolling Thunder, 253, 254
Operation Solarium, 135
Operation Wetback, 157
Oppenheimer, J. Robert, 78, 139
Oracle Corporation, 497 (illus.)
Oral contraceptives, 99–100
"Organization man": at Disneyland, 84
Organization Man, The (Whyte), 110
Organization of Petroleum Exporting Countries (OPEC), 149, 414 (illus.)
Organized crime: organized labor and, 96
Orwell, George, 270
Osborne, John, 406
OSHA, see Occupational Safety and Health Administration (OSHA)
Oswald, Lee Harvey, 203
Our Children Are Cheated (Fine), 445

Pacification program: in Vietnam War, 258
Pacific region: after World War II, 23; Truman and, 80
Pacifists: during Vietnam War, 261–262
Pahlavi, Mohammed Reza (Shah), 147, 148, 338–339
Pakistan: war with India, 334–335
Palestine: Jewish homeland in, 37
Palestine Liberation Organization (PLO), 339, 416, 493; Lebanon and, 471–472; peace agreement (1993) and, 526 (illus.)
Palestine National Authority (PNA), 525
Palestinians, 240, 344, 416, 472–473
Panama, 475; rioting in, 238; Noriega and, 269, 491; intervention in, 456
Panama Canal, 238; treaty over, 408
Panetta, Leon, 357, 361
Pardon: of Vietnam draft evaders, 261; of Nixon, 406
Paris: summit at, 161, 164; Kennedy trip to, 182; Vietnam peace talks in, 277–278; antiwar protests in, 291
Paris Peace Accords: Vietnam War and, 321, 326–330
Parks, Rosa, 119
Pataki, George, 515
Peace Corps, 181, 181 (illus.)
Peaceful coexistence policy: with Soviet Union, 139
Peacekeeping: by United Nations, 21, 23
Peace movement, see Antiwar movement

Peace talks: in Korean War, 138
Pearce, Diana, 389
Pearl Harbor: Japanese attack on, 22
Pell, Claiborne, 331
Pendergast, Tom, 44
Penicillin, 97
Pennsylvania v. Nelson, 122
Pensions: in Great Depression, 5; SSA and, 10; inflation and, 230. See also Retirement planning
Pentagon: antiwar march on, 290; 2001 terrorist attack on, 475
Pentagon Papers: Nixon and, 325–326
Pentecostals, 402
Penthouse magazine, 395
People of color: in Great Depression, 4; in suburbs, 85; housing for, 88, 111–112; women and, 391. See also specific groups
"People's capitalism," 96–100
People's Park: confrontation at, 302
People's Republic of China (PRC), see China
Peress, Irving, 140
Perestroika, 485
Perkins, Frances, 9, 13
Perot, H. Ross, 371; 1992 election and, 460; 1996 election and, 516–517
Persian Gulf region: oil industry in, 147
Persian Gulf War, see Gulf War (1991)
Person to Person (television program), 19
Pesticides, 96; environment and, 200–201
Petroleum, see Oil and oil industry
Peyton Place (Metalious), 104
Pharmaceutical companies: research expenditures by, 100
Philbrick, Herbert, 134
Philippines: defense agreement with, 143; Carter and, 416
Phillips, Kevin, 357–358
Phillips v. Martin Marietta, 362
Physicians, see Medicine
Pickens, T. Boone, 436, 504
Pierce, Samuel, 428
Pill, The, 99–100, 201. See also Birth control
Pincus, Gregory, 99
Pinochet, Augusto, 338
Planned Parenthood Federation of America, 99, 233
Planned Parenthood v. Casey, 457
Playboy magazine, 105, 201
Pledge of Allegiance: "Under God" added to, 101
Pleiku, 253
Plessy decision: overturning of, 114
PLO, see Palestine Liberation Organization (PLO)

Plumbers unit: Nixon and, 326
Pluralism: Democratic Party and, 367
Plutonium, 161
Poindexter, John, 467, 483, 485
Poland: Hitler and, 18; Soviets and, 25, 45; after World War II, 46; Solidarity in, 470–471; end of communism in, 488
Police action: Korean War as, 131
Polio: Roosevelt and, 8
Polio vaccine, 97–99
Political activism, *see* Activism
Political conventions: television coverage of, 54; 1968 Democratic Convention (Chicago), 275–276, 300–301; 1972 Democratic Convention (Miami), 367
Political machines: in Kansas City, 44
Political parties: 1960 election and, 171–172; realignment of, 363 (illus.). *See also* specific parties
Politics: during World War II, 39; in Cold War, 67–70; of moderation, 93–94; in 1960, 170–175; "spin" in news coverage and, 267–270; of multiculturalism, 314; of sexual scandal, 376–379; presidential (1970s), 406–413; of education, 444–447
Poll taxes, 113
Pollution: radioactive, 162; environment and, 355; of Love Canal, 413–414; George H. W. Bush and, 456. *See also* Environment and environmentalism
Pons, Stanley, 343
Ponzi scheme: Cornfeld and, 502
Popular culture: after World War II, 53–55; television and, 90–93; in 1950s, 104–108, 282
Popular vote: in 2000, 529–530
Population: geographic distribution of (1930-1970), 85; of suburbs, 85–86; baby boom and, 87; shift to West and Sunbelt, 93; non-European immigrants and, 417; of U.S. prisons, 477; in 1990s, 507–511; in 2000 census, 511; trends in, 511
Population Bomb, The (Ehrlich), 315, 355
"Population security" policy: in Vietnam War, 273
Pornography, 395
Port Huron Statement, 288, 290
Portugal: independence of colonies, 182
Postcolonial nations: Soviet-U.S. competition in, 56
Potsdam conference, 46

Potsdam Declaration, 47
Poverty: in Great Depression, 4; in 1950s, 110, 125; of Native Americans, 122; of African American, 170; Kennedy and, 170, 192; in Appalachia, 207 (illus.); in 1960s, 208–209; War on Poverty and, 215; legislation for, 218; government action and, 235; among women, 389; in 1980s, 436–437; feminization of, 437; in 1990s, 506–507. *See also* Great Society; Third World
Poverty line: in 1950s, 100
Powell, Colin, 467, 485, 487, 534
Powell, Lewis, 359, 360
Power (political), *see* Watergate scandal; specific individuals
Power Elite, The (Mills), 111
Powers, Francis Gary, 165, 165 (illus.)
POWs (prisoners of war): in Korean War, 138; in Vietnam War, 327
Pravda (newspaper), 241
PRC, *see* China
Preemption strategy: George W. Bush and, 533
Pregnancy rates: among teens, 102
Prescription drugs, *see* Drugs (prescription)
Presidency: politics in 1970s and, 406–413. *See also* specific presidents
Presidential Committee on Equal Opportunity: Johnson and, 210
Presidential debates: in 1960 election, 174; in 1976, 409; in 1980, 421
President's Committee on Civil Rights, 113
President's Science Advisory Committee (PSAC), 200–201
Presley, Elvis, 106–107, 293
Press: Vietnam War and, 289; women's movement ridiculed by, 311. *See also* Broadcast journalism; Media; Radio
Price(s), *see* Economy; Inflation; Stagflation
Price-Anderson Act (1957), 341
Price controls: during World War II, 29
Price support system: for farmers, 96
Primary elections: whites-only, 113
Prisoners: disenfranchisement of, 479
Prisoners of war, *see* POWs (prisoners of war)
Prison system, 478 (illus.); growth of, 477–480; costs of, 478, 479; population increase in, 511

Privacy rights, 233
Privatization: of schools, 446, 447
Productivity, 100; in 1990s, 505
Professionals: as immigrants, 224
Profiles in Courage (Kennedy), 172
Profits: during World War II, 27
Progesterone, 99–100
Progressive Party (1948), 69, 70
Progressives: Red Scare and, 56
Project Plowshare (1956), 341–342
Promise Keepers, 404
Proposition 13, 411–412
Proposition 187, 511
Prosperity: in 1980s, 431; in 1990s, 504
Prostitution: in Vietnam War, 259
Protest(s): against racial discrimination, 15; for civil rights, 113, 194; by antiwar movement, 265–271, 303–304; at 1968 Olympics, 301–302, 301 (illus.); in universities and colleges, 302; New Mobilization and, 302–303; by feminists, 304–313; by Mexican Americans, 314; by Native Americans, 314; counterrevolution against, 316. *See also* Activism; specific movements and protests
Protestant-Catholic-Jew (Herberg), 101
Protestantism: evangelical Christianity and, 401, 402–404
Prudhoe Bay, Alaska, 150
Psychedelic drugs, 293
PTL (Praise the Lord) club, 448
Public health: Medicare, Medicaid, and, 216
Public housing: Truman and, 70; racial discrimination ended in, 194; desegregation of, 236
Public Interest, The (magazine), 401
Public life: in 1990s, 499
Public relations: "spin" and, 267–268
Public television, 222
Pueblo (ship): capture of, 271
"Pumpkin papers," 75–76
Pusan, Korea, 132
Putin, Vladimir, 527

Qadaffi, Muammar, 473–474
al Qaeda, 474, 532, 533
Quakers, 261
Quemoy, 146, 174
Quiz-show scandal (1959), 92
Quotas: on immigrants, 77, 157, 223

Rabin, Yitzhak, 473, 525, 526 (illus.)
Race and racism: New Deal and, 15; during World War II, 31, 33–34;

Race and racism *(cont.)*
toward African Americans,
33–35; toward Mexicans, 35;
Jews, Holocaust, and, 35–37; defense spending and, 58; at Disneyland, 84; in postwar suburbs,
87; segregation and, 112–123;
international image of U.S. and,
141–143; in 1960s, 208; social
reform and, 219; Johnson on,
234–235; feminism and,
311–312; Burger Court and,
359–361; in industry, 399;
backlash in, 405; Reagan and,
441; education and, 445–446.
See also Desegregation; Segregation; specific groups
Race riots: during World War II,
34; in 1964, 235–236, 285; in
Watts, 236, 286
Racial discrimination, *see* Discrimination
Radiation Exposure Compensation
Act (1990), 164, 456
Radical feminists, 310–311
Radicalism: of Black Panthers,
287; of antiwar protesters,
289–291
Radio, 53; Roosevelt's fireside chats
and, 14; in World War II, 19;
evangelical, 404. *See also* Media
Radioactivity: residue from,
162; from weapons testing,
162–164; medical experiments
and, 163; compensation to vic-
tims of, 164, 456
Radio Free Europe, 156
Ramsey, Jon-Benet, 513
RAND Corporation, 186
Randolph, A. Philip, 33, 113
Rankin, John, 51, 72, 74
Ratification: of ERA, 358
Ray, James Earl, 275
Rayburn, Sam, 43
RCA, 521–524; in Mexico, 522
(illus.)
Reagan, Nancy, 426, 428
Reagan, Ronald, 212, 429 (illus.);
weapons and, 59; Red Scare
and, 74, 76; bomb shelters and,
187; as California governor,
236, 426–427; media under,
268–269; on campus activism,
288; student protests and, 302;
Right wing and, 316; new conservatism and, 401, 425–431;
evangelical Christianity and,
403, 448; Moral Majority and,
404; 1976 election and,
407–408, 427; on taxation,
412; on energy needs, 413;
hostage crisis and, 419; 1980
election and, 420–421,
427–428; presidency of, 425;
economy and, 428–431,
433–440; assassination attempt

against, 430; 1984 election
and, 431–432, 480; Iran-
contra scandal and, 433, 465,
480–484; S&Ls and, 440; civil
rights and, 440–442; society
and culture under, 442–454;
anti-drug campaign, 443; education and, 443–444; AIDS issues and, 452; Berlin Wall and,
463 (illus.); Soviet Union and,
464–465; foreign policy of,
465–495; arms race and,
466–467, 468–471; Latin
America and, 475–480; Latin
Noriega and, 491
Reaganomics, 430–431
Reagan Revolution, 431
Reapportionment, 233
Rebellions: by black soldiers,
34; after World War II, 62;
social, 110. *See also* Revolts;
Revolutions
Rebel Without a Cause (movie), 103,
107
Recession: in 1937-1938, 16; in
1980s, 413, 430–431; in
1990s, 459
Reconstruction Finance Corpora-
tion, 8
Record industry, 106
Recovery programs: in New Deal,
8–17
Redbaiting: in South, 96
Red China, *see* China
Red Chinese, 78–79
Red Cross, 33; segregation and, 34
Redistribution of wealth: in Great
society, 216
Reds: FBI and, 73
Red Scare, 56, 70–78; reversal of
restraints from, 122; McCarran
and, 134; unions during, 134.
See also McCarthyism
Reed, Ralph, 376
Reed v. Reed, 361–362
Reedy, George, 130
Reform(s): in 1930s and 1940s,
40; by Truman, 44; social,
218–219; of immigration, 223;
welfare, 354; in Soviet Union,
484–485; of healthcare, 515.
See also Great Society; specific
programs
Refugee Relief Act (1953), 157
Refugees, 224; Jews as, 36–37;
after World War II, 46; during
Cold War, 77; from Hungarian
uprising, 156–157; from East
Germany, 184; Palestinian,
240, 344, 472–473; in Vietnam
War, 258–259; Carter and,
416–417; policies toward, 454;
in Kosovo, 525
Regan, Donald, 485
Regulation: by federal government,
16; of obscenity, 231; criticisms

of, 438–439; reduction of, 439.
See also Supreme Court
Rehnquist, William, 234, 356,
359, 441, 447
Religion: in 1950s, 101; school
prayer and, 232; Eastern, 295;
abortion rights and, 362, 394;
New Right and, 400–406;
school vouchers and, 447; of
immigrants, 453. *See also* spe-
cific religions
Religious right, 448; George H. W.
Bush and, 456
Relocation camps: for Japanese
Americans, 38–39
Reno, Janet: Elian Gonzalez and,
513
Reproductive rights, 362, 388; in
Great Depression, 6; Carter and,
411; Court on, 457. *See also*
Abortion
Republican Party: after World War
II, 68; Red Scare and, 71; Mc-
Carthy and, 129; 1952 election
and, 135; in 1960s, 212–214;
Nixon's "southern strategy"
and, 357–358; 1976 election
and, 407–408; evangelical
Christianity and, 448; platform
in 1980 election, 449–450; in
1990 Congress, 457. *See also*
Elections; specific individuals
Republic of Korea, *see* South Korea
Republic of Vietnam, *see* South
Vietnam
Republics: former Soviet, 488
Research: during World War II, 28;
for defense purposes, 57–58
Reservations (Native American),
12, 121–122
Reserve Officers' Training Corps
(ROTC): Vietnam War and, 323
Resolution Trust Corporation, 440
Restrictive covenants: in housing,
111
Retailers: discount, 96
Retirement planning, 503
Reunification: of Germany, 488
Reuther, Walter, 69
Revenue sharing, 353
Revercomb, William, 157
Reverse discrimination, 440–441
Revolts: in Hungary (1956),
156–157. *See also* Rebellions
Revolutions: in Russia (1917), 17;
in Spain (1936), 17; in Iran
(1979), 150, 415; in Cuba
(1959), 155–156
Reykjavik, Iceland: Reagan-
Gorbachev meeting in, 485
Reynolds, William Bradford, 441
Rhee, Syngman, 130, 138
Rhodes, James, 304
Rhythm and blues (R&B),
105–106
Richards, Ann, 515

Richardson, Elliot, 380
Ridgway, Matthew, 133
Riesman, David, 110
Rights, *see* Civil liberties; Civil rights; specific rights
Right-to-work laws: in Sunbelt, 68
Right wing: Republican Party and, 212; in 1968, 300; reaction against 1960s activism by, 316. *See also* Conservatives and conservatism; New Right
Riley, Richard, 444
Riots: Zoot Suit, 35; after King's assassination, 275; at 1968 Democratic Convention, 300; at Stonewall Inn, 314. *See also* Race riots
Rivera, Geraldo, 21
Rivers, L. Mendel, 302
Roads and highways: upgrade of, 90; speed limit and, 449
Roberts, Granville (Oral), 402, 449
Roberts, Owen, 15
Robertson, Pat, 401, 403, 404, 448, 449
Robinson, Jackie, 34, 93
Robinson, JoAnn Gibson, 120
Robinson, Ruby Doris Smith, 284, 310
Rock, John, 99
"Rock Around the Clock," 106
Rockefeller, Nelson, 174, 213, 406, 408; fallout shelters and, 186, 187
Rockets, 61
Rock 'n' roll, 105–106; counterculture and, 292–293
Roe v. Wade, 362, 394, 407
Rogers, William P., 321, 336, 339
Rolfson, John, 299
Rolling Stone magazine, 296
Rolling Stones, 293
Roman Catholic Church, *see* Catholicism
Roosevelt, Eleanor, 13, 43, 69, 305; Mexican Americans and, 35
Roosevelt, Franklin D.: economy under, 3–6; New Deal and government under, 6–17; elections of, 7, 14, 15, 18–19, 39; personal background of, 7–8; appointees of, 13–14; southern whites and, 15; Supreme Court and, 15–16; foreign affairs and, 17–26; preparation for World War II and, 18; at Yalta, 25; Jewish refugees and, 36–37; Japanese Americans and, 37; death of, 39, 43–44; veterans and, 51; polio of, 97, 98; Reagan and, 426
Roosevelt, Kermit, 147
Rosenberg, Ethel and Julius, 76, 139
Rostker v. Goldberg, 393–394
Rostow, Walt Whitman, 237
Rothenberg, Randall, 270

Roth v. United States, 231
Rowan and Martin's Laugh-In, 298
Rubin, Jerry, 290, 300
Ruby, Jack, 203
Ruckelshaus, William, 380
Rumsfeld, Donald, 533
Rural areas: migration to urban areas from, 88
Rusk, Dean, 169, 176, 237, 241; Vietnam War and, 265
Russell, Richard, 244
Russia: Yeltsin and, 488–489, 527; Putin and, 527. *See also* Soviet Union
Russian Revolution (1917), 17
Rustbelt, 398, 399, 430
Rwanda: Clinton and, 524

Sadat, Anwar, 339–343, 416–417
Safety: OSHA and, 356
Sagebrush Rebellion, 415
Saigon: U.S. embassy in, 228; population during Vietnam War, 259; attack on U.S. embassy in, 272. *See also* South Vietnam; Vietnam; Vietnam War
St. Petersburg, *see* Leningrad
Salinger, J. D., 107
Salk, Jonas, 97, 98–99
SALT talks, 330–332, 407, 417–418; Reagan on, 469
Sanctuary Movement, 454
Sanders, Ed, 290
Sandinistas, 480–481, 482
S&Ls, *see* Savings and loan (S&L) debacle
SANE (Committee for a Sane Nuclear Policy), 185, 265
San Francisco: Beats in, 110; counterculture in, 294–295; homosexuality in, 387, 396
Sanger, Margaret, 99
Satellites: Sputnik I as, 109, 157; American, 159
Sato, Eisaku, 334
Saturday Night Massacre, 380
Saudi Arabia: in OPEC, 149; Gulf War and, 492
Save Our Children movement, 395–396, 396 (illus.)
Savings and loan (S&L) debacle, 439–440
Savio, Mario, 288
Scalia, Antonin, 441
Scandals: television coverage of, 21; in TV quiz shows, 92; in postwar America, 376–379; Agnew and, 380; among evangelical Christians, 404; Iran-contra, 433, 480–484. *See also* Watergate scandal
Schell, Jonathan, 188, 469
Schickel, Richard, 84
Schine, David, 140
Schlafly, Phyllis, 212
Schlesinger, Arthur, Jr., 69

Schneider, René, 337
School prayer, 232
Schools: baby boom and, 87; locating for homogeneous enrollment, 108; desegregation of, 113–116; segregation in, 193–194, 405–406; busing and, 360. *See also* Education; Universities and colleges
School vouchers, 446–447
Schwarzkopf, Norman H., 492
Schwerner, Michael, 283–284
Science: during World War II, 28; defense research in, 57–58; recruitment of former Nazis, 61; education in, 109–110, 159; in 1960s, 199–201
Science and Society (Commoner), 315
Scientific Research and Development (OSSRD), 28
Scopes, John, 232
Scotland: passenger plane bombing over, 473
Scowcroft, Brent, 487
Scranton, William, 213
Screen Writers Guild, 74
SDI, *see* Strategic Defense Initiative (SDI, Star Wars)
SDS, *see* Students for a Democratic Society (SDS)
Seaborg, Glenn, 342
Seadrift, Texas: anti-Vietnamese violence in, 400
Seale, Bobby, 300
Search-and-destroy operations: in Vietnam War, 256–258, 257 (illus.), 273
Searle, G. D., company, 99, 100
SEATO, *see* Southeast Asia Treaty Organization (SEATO)
SEC, *see* Securities and Exchange Commission (SEC)
Secondary schools, 108
Second World, 141
Second World War, *see* World War II
Securities and Exchange Commission (SEC), 12, 439
Security, *see* National security
Security Council (UN): Korean War and, 130–131; Iraq war and, 534
Seeger, Pete, 298
See It Now (TV program), 19, 91, 99; McCarthy and, 140
Segregation: Supreme Court and, 16; racial, 29; by gender, 31; during World War II, 33; of Mexicans, 35; of newspaper staffs, 53; after World War II, 69; polio vaccine trial and, 99; of African Americans, 112–123; in South, 171; civil rights movement and, 193–194; in interstate

Segregation *(cont.)*
transportation, 195; banning
of, 212; busing and, 360;
school, 405–406. *See also* Civil
rights; Civil rights movement;
Desegregation; Discrimination;
specific groups
Segretti, Donald, 366
Selective Service, 322; in Vietnam
War, 260–261. *See also* Draft
(military)
Selective Service Act (1947), 260
Selma, Alabama: voting-rights
demonstration in, 220; civil
rights marchers in, 285, 286
(illus.)
Selma-Montgomery march, 220
Senate: Lyndon Johnson in, 209
Senate Foreign Relations Commit-
tee: Vietnam War and, 252
Senate Internal Security Subcom-
mittee (SISS), 134
Senate Watergate Committee,
375–379
Sentencing: prison, 478–479
Separate-but-equal doctrine: in ed-
ucation, 114
Separation of church and state:
school vouchers and, 447
Separatism: black, 285
September 11, 2001: terrorist attacks of, 185, 229, 474, 499,
531–532, 531 (illus.)
Serbia: fighting in, 524–525
Serbs, 524
Service economy, 398–399
Service industry, 96
Servicemen's Readjustment Act
(1944), *see* GI Bill of Rights
Seuss, Dr. (Theodore Geisel), 97
700 Club (TV talk show), 403, 448
Sex and sexuality: anticommunists
and, 73; in 1950s, 102, 103;
popular culture and, 104–105;
women and, 201; in 1960s,
281; in rock music, 293; conservatives and, 387; sexual
revolution and, 394–395; in
1980s and 1990s, 450; end
of sexual revolution and, 451.
See also Homosexuals and
homosexuality
Sex and the Single Girl (Brown), 201
Sex discrimination: after World
War II, 52; Court and, 122–123
Sexism, 388; women's movement
and, 310–311
"Sex-plus" discrimination, 391
*Sexual Behavior in the Human Fe-
male* (Kinsey), 104
Sexual harassment: illegality of,
376; Clarence Thomas and,
377, 458; in industry, 399
Sexual scandals: politics of,
376–379; Clinton and, 378,
517–518

Shadow government: concept of,
185
Shah of Iran, *see* Pahlavi, Mo-
hammed Reza (shah)
Shapiro, Robert, 512 (illus.)
Sharon, Ariel, 526
Sheehan, Neil, 325
Shelley v. Kraemer, 113
Shelters: for women, 393
Shepard, Alan, 200
Shilts, Randy, 387
Shootings: at Columbine High
School, 499
Shopping centers: suburban, 85
Shoreham reactor, 342
Short, Jack, 43
Shriver, Sargent, 181, 218, 219
Shultz, George, 467, 485
Shute, Nevil, 185
Shuttle diplomacy, 344
Sick, Gary, 420
Sierra Club, 201, 315, 342
Sihanouk, Norodom, 323
Silent Spring (Carson), 200, 315
Silicon Valley, 498, 500–501; Ora-
cle Corporation in, 497 (illus.)
Simpson, Nicole Brown, 512
Simpson, O. J., 21, 499; trial of,
512–513, 512 (illus.)
Simpson-Rodino Act, 454
Sinai Field Mission, 229
Sinai Peninsula, 151, 239–240,
339, 343
Sino-Soviet alliance, 139
Sirhan, Sirhan, 275
Sirica, John J., 374–375, 380, 384
Sit-ins, 194; during World War II,
113; at Woolworth's, 121
Six-Day War (1967), 239–240,
339
$64,000 Question (TV program),
92
Smith, Al, 174
Smith, Gerald L. K., 15
Smith, Howard W., 305
Smith, Tommie, 301, 301 (illus.)
Smith, William French, 441
Smith Act (1940), 76–77, 122
Smith v. Allwright, 113
Smoking: lung cancer, heart dis-
ease, and, 216; warnings
against, 442
Smothers Brothers, 297–298
SNCC, *see* Student Non-Violent Co-
ordinating Committee (SNCC)
Soccer: immigrants in, 510
Socialism: Red Scare and, 71–72;
Third World and, 141
Social reform: Great Society and,
215–216; white distrust of,
236–237; in Latin America,
238
Social Security, 430; Truman and,
70; farm laborers excluded
from, 111; Medicare and, 216

Social Security Act (SSA, 1935), 5,
10, 16
Social Security Administration, 12
Social welfare: under Johnson,
218–219; Nixon and, 352–353
Society: in Great Depression, 2–6;
World War II and, 26–39,
50–53; in 1950s, 170–175;
gender roles in, 388–396; divisions in 1970s, 397–400; in
1980s, 442–454; in 1990s,
499. *See also* Great Society;
specific issues
Soldiers: black, 34; Japanese Americans as, 38; in Vietnam War,
260–264, 323; noncombat vs.
combat, 264. *See also* Military;
Veterans
Solidarity labor movement,
470–471
Somalia, 270, 520; peacekeeping
mission in, 21
Somoza, Anastasio, 480
Sorensen, Theodore, 201
Souter, David, 457–458
South (U.S.): African Americans in,
4; racial discrimination in New
Deal and, 15; World War II migration from, 29; defense spending in, 58; right-to-work laws
in, 68; labor in, 96; displaced
black workers in, 111; segregation in, 113–123, 360–361;
black migration from, 171;
1960 election and, 175; black
mayors in, 221; Nixon and,
276; party realignment in, 363
(illus.); industry in, 399
South America: immigration from,
223
Southeast Asia: in World War II,
25; foreign policy toward, 144;
Soviets and, 183; Vietnam War
and, 251 (illus.); immigrants
from, 400, 417. *See also* Vietnam War
Southeast Asia Treaty Organization (SEATO), 143, 246
Southern Christian Leadership
Conference (SCLC), 282
Southern Democrats, 71
Southern Manifesto, 115
"Southern strategy": of Nixon,
357–358
Southern Tenant Farmers' Union
(STFU), 9
South Korea: Korean War and, 67;
invasion of, 130; defense agree-
ment with, 143. *See also* Korean
War
South Pacific region: nuclear test-
ing in, 162
South Vietnam, 246; U.S. advisers
in, 247; coup in, 248; Lodge as
ambassador to, 248; Dinh in,
249; friendly fire in, 259 (illus.);

government of, 260; Nixon and, 322. *See also* Vietnam War

Southwest: Mexicans in, 4, 35; defense spending in, 58

Southwest Organizing Project, 315

Soviet Union: Roosevelt and, 17; World War II and, 18, 25–26, 45–46; Lend-Lease to, 22; Nazi nonaggression pact with, 22; Truman and, 45, 55; troop withdrawals by, 62; containment policy toward, 62–67, 135; Tito and, 63; Berlin and, 64–65; atomic bomb of, 78; Sputnik and, 109; Korean War and, 130–131; after Stalin's death, 138–139; peaceful coexistence with, 139; Third World and, 141; Geneva talks (1954) and, 145; oil and, 148; Cuba and, 155, 156, 180, 184–191, 475; Hungarian uprising and, 156–157; Eisenhower and, 159–161; détente and, 159–165, 330–332; Nixon and, 160–161, 321, 331, 348; U-2 spy plane incident and, 164–165; Kennedy and, 177–180, 182; Operation Mongoose and, 188; space race and, 199–200; Johnson and, 240–241; Czech uprising and, 241; Yom Kippur War and, 343; Carter and, 415; Afghanistan and, 418, 474; dissolution of, 456, 464, 490; Reagan and, 469, 484–487; former, 527. *See also* Cold War; Communism; Red Scare; Spies and spying

Space exploration, 199–200, 318 (illus.), 319; Sputnik and, 109; space race and, 157–159

Space race, 199–200

Spain: Fascist revolt in (1936), 17; defense agreement with, 143

Special Forces, *see* Green Berets

Special prosecutor: in Watergate scandal, 380

Spectator (periodical): Brock's articles in, 378–379

Spector, Arlen, 377

Speech: protection of, 231

Spending: during World War II, 27; military, 57–59; on environment, 355–356; domestic, 430

Spies and spying: Red Scare and, 72; FBI and, 73; Hiss case and, 75; Rosenbergs and, 76, 139; Fuchs and, 128; U-2 spy plane and, 158, 164–165

Spillaine, Mickey, 73

"Spin": in news reporting, 267–270

"Spirit of Camp David," 161

Split Level Trap, The (Gordon), 110

Spock, Benjamin, 87, 97, 290; antiwar activism of, 265

Sports: television coverage of, 92–93; desegregation in, 93; conflict in 1968, 301–302; franchises, 399; immigrants in, 510

Sports utility vehicles (SUVs), 150

Springer, Jerry, 21

Sputnik, 186; I, 109, 157; II, 157

Srebrenica, 524

SSA, *see* Social Security Act (SSA, 1935)

SSI, *see* Supplemental Security Income (SSI)

Stage Door Canteen (film), 33

Stagflation, 346, 363–364; in 1970s, 397

Stahl, Leslie, 433

Stalin, Joseph, 17, 23, 28; at Yalta, 25; World War II and, 45–46, 55–56; atomic bomb and, 46–47; United Nations and, 61; Korean War and, 132; death of, 138–139

Standard and Poor's, 505

Standardized testing, 445 (illus.), 446

Standard of living: after divorce, 388. *See also* Lifestyle

Stans, Maurice, 334

Starr, Kenneth: Clinton and, 517

Start-up companies: in 1990s, 505

Star Wars, *see* Strategic Defense Initiative (SDI, Star Wars)

State Department: Asian affairs and, 134; purging of, 139–140; NSC and, 320

States: HUAC-type committees in, 77; desegregation and, 115–116; prison costs and, 478

State-sponsored terrorism, 473

States' rights: over women, 122–123

States' Rights party, *see* Dixiecrat party

Status Seekers, The (Packard), 111

Stealth (B-2) bomber, 59

Steinem, Gloria, 311

Stem cell research, 506

Sterilizations: on women, 391

Stevens, John Paul, 447

Stevenson, Adlai, 103, 189 (illus.), 202–203; 1956 election and, 123

STFU, *see* Southern Tenant Farmers' Union (STFU)

Stimson, Henry, 22, 49

Stockman, David, 429–430, 468

Stock market: crash of 1929, 3; in 1960s, 225; collapse of (1987), 433, 504; in 1990s, 501–505; crash of 2000, 505. *See also* Bull market

Stokes, Carl, 314

Stone, I. F., 172

Stone, Oliver, 435

Stonewall riots, 314

"Straight" culture: in 1960s, 297

Strait of Tiran, 239

Strategic Air Command (film), 57

Strategic Arms Limitation Talks (SALT), *see* SALT talks

Strategic Defense Initiative (SDI, Star Wars), 59, 469

Strategic hamlets: in Vietnam, 246

Strauss, Lewis L., 340

Street crime, 358–359

"Stretch-out" practice: in factories, 10

Strict constructionism: contraception rights and, 233

Strider, Harold, 117

Strikes: in textile industry, 10; against RCA, 521, 522. *See also* Labor; Unions

Strip-mining, 201

Student Non-Violent Coordinating Committee (SNCC), 121, 194, 208, 219, 282, 283–284; split in, 285; women's position in, 310

Students: rights of, 231. *See also* Counterculture

Students for a Democratic Society (SDS), 288–291; Vietnam Summer and, 265; Weathermen faction of, 303

Sturgis, Frank, 372

Subculture: youth, 107–108, 282

Submarines: missiles launched from, 137

Suburbs: growth of, 83 (illus.), 85–87; conformity in, 86–87; discrimination in, 87, 88; employment and manufacturing in, 89; religion in, 101; criticisms of, 202; women's protests in, 305

Subversion: in schools, 445

Subversive Activity Control Board, 77

Subversive organizations: Red Scare and, 72; nullification of statutes against, 122

Suez Canal, 148–149, 339; Egyptian nationalization of, 151–152; Yom Kippur War and, 344

Sukarno (Indonesia): CIA operations against, 155

"Summer of Love" (1967), 294

Summit meetings: 1941–1945, 23; at Geneva (1955), 160; Eisenhower-Khrushchev, 161; Kennedy-Khrushchev, 182; Johnson-Kosygin, 240–241, 240 (illus.); Reagan-Gorbachev, 484–485, 484 (illus.)

Sunbelt, 399; World War II and, 29–30; right-to-work laws in,

Sunbelt, *(cont.)*
68; population shift to, 93;
economy in, 224–225
Sun Myung Moon, 377
Sununu, John, 456
Superpowers: United States as, 41,
465; in Cold War, 56
Supplemental Security Income
(SSI), 354
Supply-side economics, 428,
429–431
Supreme Court: Roosevelt and,
15–16; desegregation rulings
by, 113–116; Red Scare restraints and, 122; civil liberties
and, 230–234; under Burger,
359–362; Watergate scandal
and, 381–382; on gender discrimination, 391; Reagan appointments to, 441; conservative majority on, 442; on school
vouchers, 447; reproductive
rights and, 457; 2000 election
and, 530. *See also* specific
justices
Supremes, 293
Swaggart, Jimmy, 403–404,
448–449
*Swann v. Charlotte-Mecklenburg
Board of Education,* 360
"Swim-in": for civil rights, 113
Symbolic speech: protection of,
231
Symington, Stuart: on missile gap,
159
Synthetic Fuels Corporation, 413
Syria, 152, 343, 472; United Arab
Republic and, 152
Szilard, Leo, 187

Taft, Robert, 68, 69, 94, 212
Taft-Hartley Act (1947), 68, 70
Taiwan, 79, 131, 146; defense
agreement with, 143; Reagan
and, 465–466. *See also* China
Takeovers, 504
Taliban, 474, 532–533
Tape recordings: in Watergate
scandal, 379–380, 381, 384
Tarr, Curtis, 322
Taxation: Kennedy and, 192–193;
Proposition 13 and, 411–412;
revolt against, 412; Reagan and,
428–430; in 1980s, 432–433;
S&Ls and, 440; for education,
448; George H. W. Bush and,
456, 459; Clinton and, 514
Taylor, Maxwell, 253
Teach-ins: in Vietnam War, 265,
299
Teamsters Union, 96
Technology, 498; wartime spend-
ing on, 28; spending on, 58; in
1950s, 94; in 1960s, 199–201;

in Vietnam War, 256; in 1990s,
500–507
Teenagers: rock 'n' roll music and,
106–107; movies, literature,
and, 107–108; births to, 511
Teheran: coup in (1953), 147; attack on U.S. embassy, 229; Iran
hostage crisis and, 418–419
Tejano music, 509
Televangelists, 401, 403–404, 449
Television, 90–93; broadcast journalism and, 19–21; after World
War II, 53–55; programming
for, 91–93; African Americans
on, 92; quiz-show scandal and,
92; sports coverage on, 92–93;
anticommunist programs on,
134–135; Great Society and,
222; new "spin" on, 268–269;
news control on, 269–270;
youth market and, 297–298;
Vietnam War on, 298–299;
Reagan on, 431. *See also* Media;
Televangelists
Television debates, *see* Presidential
debates
Teller, Edward, 164, 187, 342,
469
Temporary Commission on Em-
ployee Loyalty, 72
Temptations (singing group), 293
Tenet, George, 533
Tennessee Valley Authority (TVA),
8, 12
Terkel, Studs, 43
Termination policy: for Native
Americans, 121–122
Terrorism, 473; on September 11,
2001, 185, 229, 474, 499,
531–532, 531 (illus.); by Mus-
lims, 474; war on, 532
Test ban: on nuclear weapons test-
ing, 164, 165
Testing: educational, 108
Tet offensive, 243 (illus.), 272–273
Texas: in Great Depression, 9;
Kennedy assassination in,
202–205
Textile industry: in Great Depres-
sion, 9–10; in Sunbelt, 68
Thatcher, Margaret, 485
Thermonuclear war, 186
Thieu, Nguyen Van, 321, 328,
407
Think tanks: on fallout shelters,
186
Third force: U.S. sponsorship of,
246
Third World, 56; Khrushchev in,
124; colonialism and independence in, 141–156; commu-
nism in, 143; military and
covert actions in, 144; Kennedy
and, 177; paramilitary operations in, 467

Thomas, Clarence, 458, 458
(illus.); sexual harassment
charges against, 377, 458
Thomas, J. Parnell, 74
Thompson, Florence, 2–3, 3
(illus.)
Thompson, Hunter S., 296
Three Mile Island: reactor mal-
function at, 341 (illus.), 342,
414
Threlkeld, Richard, 309
Thurmond, Strom, 69, 70
Tiananmen Square riot, 490
Tibbet, Paul, 47
Till, Emmett, 116–117
*Time Bind, The: When Work Becomes
Home and Home Becomes Work*
(Hochschild), 309–310
Tinian Island, 47
Tinker v. Des Moines School District,
231
Title IX: of Education Act (1972),
390, 444, 450
Title VII (Civil Rights Act of 1964),
305, 362, 388, 390
Tito, Joseph, 63
Tojo, Hideki, 22
Tokyo: in World War II, 46; war
criminal trials in, 61
Tonkin Gulf Resolution (1964),
252; repeal of, 324, 346
Torrijos, Omar, 491
Totalitarianism: after World War
II, 63
Tourism: auto, 90
Tower, John, 376, 457, 483
Tower Commission, 483
Townsend, Francis, 5, 15
Toxic wastes, 415
Trade: in Great Depression, 3–4;
most-favored-nation status and,
332; with Japan, 333–334;
349; with China, 336
Trade fairs: during Cold War, 226
Training programs, 353
Traitors, *see* McCarthyism; Red
Scare; Spies and spying
Tranquilizers: women and,
101–102
Transportation, Department of,
218
Travel: by car, 90
Treaties: Austrian occupation
ended by, 160
Treaty of Rome (1957), 135
Trial: of Democratic Convention
conspirators, 300–301
Triangulation policy: of Clinton,
516
Troops, *see* Armed forces
Trujillo, Rafael, 180, 238; CIA
operations against, 155
Truman, Harry S, 39, 60; assump-
tion of presidency, 43–44; So-
viet Union and, 45; communism

and, 67; Cold War and, 67–70, 80–81, 128; *vetoes by,* 68; civil rights and, 69; 1948 election and, 69–70; loyalty oath and, 72; China and, 79; NSC-68 and, 80–81; President's Committee on Civil Rights and, 113; Korean War and, 131–133; foreign aid under, 143; Vietnam and, 245; farewell address of, 495
Truman Doctrine, 63
Trumbo, Dalton, 74
Trump, Donald, 436
Tsongas, Paul, 459
Turkey: after World War II, 61; aid to, 63; IRBMs and, 188, 190, 191
TVA, *see* Tennessee Valley Authority (TVA)
Twenty-fifth Amendment, 380
Twenty-One (TV program), 92
Twenty-sixth Amendment, 369
Twining, Nathan, 145
Twinkie defense, 396
Tyack, David, 446

Ubico, Jorge, 153
Ugly American, The (Lederer and Burdick), 144
Undeclared War Against American Women, The (Faludi), 309
Underclass, 438
Underdeveloped nations, 141, 143
Underground weapons testing, 164
Undocumented migrants, 224; from Mexico, 157
Unemployed Councils, 9
Unemployment: in Great Depression, 3–4, 7; women and, 5; government programs for, 11; in New Deal, 14; after World War II, 67–68; of African Americans, 111, 171, 235; CETA training and, 218; in 1960s, 224; in Nixon years, 363; in 1970s, 398 (illus.); in 1980s, 412–413; Reagan and, 430. *See also* Employment
Unemployment insurance: SSA and, 10
Unfair trade practices: Japan and, 334
Unions: in Great Depression, 9–10; World War II and, 28–29, 51, 68; in 1950s, 96–100; during Red Scare, 134; in 1970s, 399
United Arab Republic, 152
United Automobile Workers (UAW): strike by, 51
United Electrical Workers (UEW): RCA and, 521–522
United Farm Workers, 314

United Fruit Company: in Guatemala, 153–154, 267, 268
United Kingdom, *see* England (Britain)
United Mine Workers, 9
United Nations: Somalia peace-keeping mission of, 21; charter of, 23; after World War II, 25; Soviets and, 61; Korean War and, 130–131; Belgian Congo and, 182; Cuban missile crisis and, 189 (illus.); Six-Day War and, 240; Gulf War and, 492; Iraq war and, 534
United Service Organizations (USO), 33
United States: after World War II, 25–26; as world leader, 49–50; in Caribbean and Central America, 178 (illus.); image of, 226
U.S. Chamber of Commerce: Red Scare and, 71–72
U.S. Information Agency (USIA), 19, 226
United States v. Nixon, 381–382
United States v. Seegar, 261–262
United Textile Workers of America, 9–10
Universities and colleges: growth after World War II, 52; NDEA and, 109–110; segregation in, 113–114; in 1960s, 281; student activism and, 288–291; protests in, 302. *See also* Higher education; specific schools
University of California, *see* Berkeley
University of California Board of Regents v. Bakke, 411
University of Mississippi: James Meredith and, 196–197
UNIX, 498
Unmarried couples, 392, 511
Unsafe at Any Speed (Nader), 315
Unwed mothers: in 1950s, 102
Uranium mining, 161–162
Urban Affairs Council, 353, 354
Urban areas: World War II migration to, 29; rural migration to, 88. *See also* Suburbs
Urban renewal, 171; in 1960s, 218
USIA, *see* U.S. Information Agency (USIA)
U-2 spy plane, 158, 160, 164–165, 182

VA, *see* Veterans Administration (VA)
Vaccine: for polio, 97–99
Vance, Cyrus, 417, 419
Vandenberg, Arthur, 63
Van Doren, Charles, 92

Vanik, Charles, 332
Varela, Maria, 310, 316
Venezuela, 180; in OPEC, 149
VENONA, 72
Veterans: after World War II, 50–53, 85–86; GI Bill and, 51–52; women and, 394
Veterans Administration (VA), 86; after World War II, 52
Vice presidency: Agnew's resignation and, 380
Vienna: summit conference in, 182–183
Vietcong, 290. *See also* National Liberation Front (NLF, Vietcong); Vietnam War
Vietminh, 80, 144, 245; in Dienbienphu, 145; Diem and, 246. *See also* Vietnam War
Vietnam, 80; Diem in, 145; U.S. and, 244, 245–252; partition of, 246; third force in, 246; immigrants from, 400; U.S. evacuation from, 407. *See also* Indochina; Vietnam War
Vietnamization policy, 321
Vietnam Summer (1967), 265, 290, 294
Vietnam Veterans Memorial, 329 (illus.)
Vietnam War, 59, 240–241; television coverage of, 19, 298–299; college students and, 110; background of, 144–146; social programs and, 218–219; inflation and, 225–230; Johnson and, 235; Tet Offensive during, 243 (illus.); Southeast Asia and, 251 (illus.); increased U.S. presence in, 252; Americanization of (1965), 252–255; 1966-1967, 255–260; military tactics in, 255–260; peasants during, 258–259; draft and soldiers during, 260–264; de-escalation of, 263; treatment of enemy during, 263; My Lai massacre during, 263–264; dissent over, 264–274; 1968 election and, 276; student protests against, 289; antiwar protests and, 289–291; television censorship and, 298; opposition to, 300; Nixon, Kissinger, and, 319–330; supporters of, 324; Pentagon Papers and, 325; escalation of, 326–327; end of, 328–329; Ford and, 406–407
Vigilantes: anti-black intimidation by, 283–284
Viguerie, Richard, 440
Vinson, Fred, 114
Violence: in labor strikes, 10; race riots and, 34, 236; in civil rights movement, 195, 197–198,

Violence *(cont.)*
208, 283–284; in families,
392–393; over immigration,
400
Violent crime, 479
VISA, 225
VISTA, *see* Volunteers in Service to
America (VISTA)
Volcker, Paul, 364, 412
Volkswagen Beetle, 296–297
Volunteers: women as, 33
Volunteers in Service to America
(VISTA), 219
Von Braun, Wernher, 61
V-1 rockets, 61
Voorhees, Jerry, 75
Voter Registration Act (1965), 285
Voting: in 1972 election, 367,
368–369; in 1976 election,
410
Voting rights: for African Ameri-
cans, 113, 219–221, 221 (illus.)
Voting Rights Act (1965),
220–221, 234, 440, 441
Voting-rights bill: Johnson and,
212
Vouchers: for schools, 446–447
V-2 rockets, 61, 158

Wages: World War II and, 29, 51;
for women, 390; in 1970s,
399–400; in 1980s, 435–436
Wages and hours provisions: of
Fair Labor Standards Act, 16
Wagner Act, *see* National Labor Re-
lations Act (Wagner Act, 1935)
Wag the Dog (movie), 267, 268
(illus.)
Walker, Daisy, 399
Wallace, George, 276–277, 278,
300, 366; 1972 election and,
408
Wallace, Henry A., 39, 69; on U.S.-
Soviet relations, 55; 1948 elec-
tion and, 69, 70
Wall Street: in 1980s, 435, 436,
503–504. *See also* Business;
Stock market
Wall Street (movie), 435
Walsh, Lawrence, 483
War(s) and warfare: military tac-
tics in Vietnam, 255–260; presi-
dential declaration of war and,
346–347. *See also* specific wars
War Department: atomic bomb
project of, 28
Warner, Jack, 74
War on Poverty, 215, 218; cut-
backs in, 237; Nixon and,
352–353, 354
War Powers Act (1973), 346, 347
War Refugee Board, 36–37
War Relocation Authority, 37

Warren, Earl, 114, 122, 232
(illus.), 359; Kennedy, John F.,
assassination and, 203–204;
Supreme Court, civil liberties,
and, 230–234; contraception,
privacy rights, and, 233
Warren Commission, 203–204
War Resisters League, 266
Warsaw Pact, 160; Hungary and,
156; dissolution of, 490
Warsaw talks: with China, 146
Wars of national liberation, 183
Washington, Booker T., 116
Washington, D.C., *see* March on
Washington
Washington Peace Center, 266
Washington Post, 53; Watergate
scandal and, 373, 384
Washington v. Davis, 359–360
Waste Makers, The (Packard), 111
Watergate Committee, 380
Watergate scandal, 320, 326, 345,
347, 370–384; trial of burglars
and, 374; tapes in, 379–380,
384
Watts, James, 428
Watts area (Los Angeles): race riot
in (1965), 236, 286
Wealth: distribution of, 8; during
World War II, 29; in 1950s,
100; redistribution of, 216; in-
come gap and, 436, 506–507,
507 (illus.); in 1990s, 506–507
Weapons: atomic bomb as, 18,
47–50; in World War II, 28;
defense industry and, 58–59;
nuclear, 137–138; in Vietnam
War, 249, 258; ABMs as, 331;
new technology for, 332; spend-
ing under Reagan, 468–471;
of mass destruction, 469, 533,
534. *See also* Arms control;
Nuclear weapons
Weathermen faction: of SDS, 303
Weather Underground, 303
Web browser: Mosaic as, 498;
Netscape as, 498
Webster, William, 485
*Webster v. Reproductive Services of
Missouri*, 457
Weinberg, Jack, 288, 289
Weinberger, Caspar, 467, 468, 485
Weir, Bob, 316
Welch, Joseph, 103, 129 (illus.);
Army-McCarthy hearings and,
140–141
Welfare programs: in New Deal, 7;
Nixon and, 352–359; in 1980s,
436–437; Clinton and reform
of, 516
Wenner, Jann, 296
"We Shall Overcome" (song), 199
West (U.S.): growth of, 29–31; de-
fense spending in, 58; popula-

tion shift to, 93; federal lands in,
415
West Bank, 240, 472, 473
Western Europe: Soviets and,
56–60; Marshall Plan and, 64;
military spending and, 135
Western Hemisphere: U.S. role in,
238; Reagan and, 475
West Germany, 65; in NATO, 65,
160; Bonn capital and, 183
Westmoreland, William, 254, 256,
259, 272 (illus.); on military
personnel policy, 263; on
Vietnam War status, 271
Weyrich, Paul, 376
Wheeler, Earl, 254
Wherry, Kenneth, 73
White, Byron, 196 (illus.), 230
White, Dan, 387, 396
White, Theodore, 205
White citizens' councils, 117
White-collar workers: in 1950s, 96
White flight: education and, 446
Whitehead, Don, 134–135
White Night Riot, The (San Fran-
cisco), 387
White primary, 113
Whites: women in Great Depres-
sion, 4–5; labor union control
by, 10; in New Deal, 14–15; in
suburbs, 87, 88; unwed moth-
ers and adoption services, 102;
record industry and, 106; rock
'n' roll music and, 106; Demo-
cratic Party and, 172; economic
gap with blacks, 235; backlash
by, 236
Whyte, William H., Jr., 110
WIC, *see* Women, Infants, and
Children (WIC) program
Wicker, Tom, 299
Wife beating, 393. *See also* Family;
Women
Wilderness areas: protecting, 201
Wild One, The (movie), 107
Wilkins, Roy, 116, 282
Wilson, Dagmar, 290
Wilson, Pete, 511
Wilson, Sloan, 110
WIN (Whip Inflation Now) pro-
gram, 406
Wise Men: Johnson and, 271, 274
Witch hunts: Court on, 122
Witness (Chambers), 73, 76
Wolfe, Tom, 296, 401
Women: in Great Depression, 4–5,
6; in cabinet, 13; in New Deal,
13–14; as welders, 31, 32 (il-
lus.); World War II and, 31–33,
50–51, 52–53; African Ameri-
can, 33; in aerospace workforce,
58; in 1950s, 101–104, 125;
sexual relations and, 105;
Supreme Court and, 122–123,

441; in work force, 171, 388; in 1960s, 282, 304–313; in antiwar movement, 289; education of, 306, 444; employment of, 306; in SNCC, 310; in military, 362, 393–394; politics of sexual scandal and, 376–379; burdens of divorce and, 388; nofault divorce and, 388; roles of, 388–396; poverty among, 389; of color, 391; sterilizations of, 391; crisis shelters for, 393; in Reagan cabinet, 428; as vicepresidential candidate, 432; Reagan administration and, 450. *See also* Feminists and feminism; Gender
Women, Infants, and Children (WIC) program, 437
Women's liberation movement, 305–313, 312 (illus.)
Women's Political Council, 119
Women's rights movement: new feminism and, 311
Women Strike for Peace, 266
Wonder, Stevie, 293
Wood, John S., 72
Woodward, Bob, 373, 373 (illus.), 374, 384
Woolworth's: Greensboro sit-in and, 121
Workers: in 1930s, 9–10; SSA benefits for, 10–11; women as, 31; in World War II, 33; displaced, 111; OSHA and, 356; in 1970s, 399; poverty among, 438. *See also* Older workers; Strikes; Work force
Work force: white women in, 4–5; of WPA, 11; after World War II, 50–51; women in, 52–53, 103, 171, 388, 450; unionization of, 96. *See also* Labor; Workers

Working class: Roosevelt and, 14; as soldiers in Vietnam War, 261
Works Progress Administration (WPA), 1 (illus.), 11, 11 (illus.)
Workweek: limits on, 16
World Bank: Soviets and, 60–61
WorldCom: fraud by, 533
World Trade Center (WTC): construction of, 227 (illus.); as symbol of U.S., 229; terrorist attacks on, 229; 1993 bombings of, 474; 2001 destruction of, 474, 499, 531–532, 531 (illus.)
World War II: German Blitzkrieg in, 18; radio during, 19; Japan and, 22; U.S. in, 22; Normandy invasion in, 23; Allied offensives in, 24 (illus.); home front during, 26–39; society and, 26–39, 50–53; Pacific War in, 26 (illus.); industry during, 28; women in, 32 (illus.); politics during, 39; consequences of, 41; GI Bill and, 43; Truman and, 44–48; atomic bombings in Japan and, 46–50; industrial powers after, 56; colonialism and independence after, 141–156. *See also* Cold War; specific groups; specific issues
World Wide Web, 498, 500
Wounded Knee: protest at, 314
WPA, *see* Works Progress Administration (WPA)
Wright, Jim, 457
Wright, Richard, 282
Writers: Beats as, 110, 292

X-ray lasers, *see* Strategic Defense Initiative (SDI, Star Wars)
Xuan Thuy, 324

Yalta meeting, 25, 45
Yalu River region: Korean War and, 132
Yarborough, Ralph, 202
Yates v. United States, 122
Yeltsin, Boris, 488–489, 490, 527
Yemen: United Arab Republic and, 152
Yippies (Youth International Party), 276, 300
Yom Kippur War (1973), 339, 343; oil prices during, 149
You Are There (television program), 19
Young, Andrew, 313
Young, Whitney, 282
Young Turks, 296–297
Youth movement: antiwar movement and, 289–291. *See also* Antiwar movement; Counterculture; Youth subculture
Youth subculture, 107–108; in 1960s, 282
Yugoslavia: Tito in, 63; humanitarian intervention in, 524–525
Yuppies, 436

Zablocki, Clement, 347
Zahedi, Fazollah, 147
Zhou Enlai, 145, 333, 334, 335
Ziegler, Ron, 370, 373
Zippo raids (Vietnam War), 257, 258, 266
Zones: in Berlin, 182–183
Zoot Suit riots, 35

Credits

Page 26: Map 1.2 from Carter Findley and John Rothney, *Twentieth-Century World*, Second Edition. Copyright © 1990 by Houghton Mifflin Company. Reprinted by permission. **Pages 30, 66, 95, and 142:** Map 1.3, Map 2.1, Figure 3.2, and Map 4.2 adapted from Mary Beth Norton et al., *A People and a Nation*, Sixth Edition. Copyright © 2001 by Houghton Mifflin Company. Reprinted by permission. **Pages 88, 178, and 438:** Figure 3.1, Map 5.1, and Figure 12.3 from Michael Schaller, Virginia Scharff, and Robert Schulzinger, *Coming of Age*. Copyright ©1998 by Houghton Mifflin Company. Reprinted with permission. **Page 112:** Map 3.1 reprinted from Figure 4.1 in *Dollars and Dreams: The Changing American Income Distribution*, by Frank Levy, © 1987 Russell Sage Foundation. Used with permission of the Russell Sage Foundation. **Page 221:** Map 6.2 reprinted by permission of Greenwood Publishing Group, Inc., Westport, Conn., from *Voter Mobilization and the Politics of Race: The South and Universal Suffrage, 1952-1984*, by Harold W. Stanley. Copyright © 1987 by Harold W. Stanley and published in 1987 by Praeger Publishers. **Page 224:** List from *Still the Golden Door*, by David Reimers. Reprinted by permission of Columbia University Press. **Page 437:** Figure 12.2 from *New York Times*, July 20, 1994. Copyright © 1994 by The New York Times Company. Reprinted by permission. **Page 489:** Map 13.1 from John P. McKay, Bennett D. Hill, and John Buckler, *A History of Western Society*, Seventh Edition. Copyright © 2003 by Houghton Mifflin Company. Reprinted with permission.